Alma Brodersen
The End of the Psalter

Beihefte zur Zeitschrift für die alttestamentliche Wissenschaft

Herausgegeben von
John Barton, Reinhard G. Kratz, Nathan MacDonald,
Carol A. Newsom und Markus Witte

Band 505

Alma Brodersen

The End of the Psalter

Psalms 146–150 in the Masoretic Text,
the Dead Sea Scrolls, and the Septuagint

DE GRUYTER

G

ISBN 978-3-11-053476-4
e-ISBN (PDF) 978-3-11-053609-6
e-ISBN (EPUB) 978-3-11-053495-5
ISSN 0934-2575

Library of Congress Cataloging-in-Publication Data
A CIP catalog record for this book has been applied for at the Library of Congress.

Bibliografic information published by the Deutsche Nationalbibliothek
The Deutsche Nationalbibliothek lists this publication in the Deutsche Nationalbibliografie;
detailed bibliografic data are available on the Internet at http://dnb.dnb.de.

© 2017 Walter de Gruyter GmbH, Berlin/Boston
Printing and binding: CPI books GmbH, Leck
♾ Printed on acid-free paper
Printed in Germany

www.degruyter.com

MIX
Papier aus verantwor-
tungsvollen Quellen
FSC
www.fsc.org   FSC® C083411

Preface

The end of the Psalter has fascinated me ever since I sang Psalms 146–150 with the Chapel Choir of St John's College, Oxford, and was asked by fellow singers to explain what those horses and legs in Psalm 147:10 or the loud cymbals in Psalm 150:5 meant. This monograph is a result of this fascination and presents a revised version of my doctoral thesis which was completed at the University of Oxford (Faculty of Theology and Religion and St John's College) in Hilary Term 2016. I am deeply grateful to my supervisor, Professor John Barton (University of Oxford), who encouraged and supported this project in every possible way. In and beyond Oxford, I was grateful to receive valuable advice from many researchers, especially Professor Susan Gillingham, Professor Friedhelm Hartenstein, Dr John Jarick, Professor Reinhard G. Kratz, Professor Will Kynes, Dr Friederike Neumann, Dr David Reimer, Dr Deborah Rooke, Professor Alison Salvesen, Professor Katherine Southwood, and Dr Judith Wolfe. I am also indebted to Dr Hilla Wait at the Bodleian Libraries, to the staff of the Faculty of Theology and Religion and of St John's College, Oxford, and to Dr Kylie Crabbe, Dipl.-Theol. Florentine Grünewald, Dr Birge-Dorothea Pelz, and Dr Laura Quick for their untiring and kind support.

My thanks go to the editors of "Beihefte zur Zeitschrift für die alttestamentliche Wissenschaft" (BZAW), Professor John Barton, Professor Reinhard G. Kratz, Professor Nathan MacDonald, Professor Carol A. Newsom, and Professor Markus Witte, for accepting this monograph for publication in the BZAW series. After the manuscript of this book had been submitted for publication, a monograph entitled "Schriftgelehrte Hymnen. Gestalt, Theologie und Intention der Psalmen 145 und 146–150" by Dr Friederike Neumann was published which comes to a different conclusion. In this book I was only able to include a short survey of the work, but I hope that the debate will continue. To Dr Eva Frantz, Johannes Parche, and Dr Sophie Wagenhofer at de Gruyter I am grateful for their prompt and professional support.

The research presented in this monograph was funded by the Rhodes Trust, Oxford. I am very grateful for my Oxford years as a Rhodes Scholar (Germany & St John's 2012), and for being a member of the Rhodes community which spans so many disciplines and continents. I am also indebted to the Agnes-Ament-Foundation, Munich, for its generous support.

Without the constant loving support of my parents Christiane and Kai, my siblings Isidor, Edna, and Rufus, and my partner Martin, this book would neither have been begun nor completed. I hope that my grandmother Gertraude would have enjoyed reading it.

May this book help to answer some questions about Psalms 146–150 to those reading and singing Psalms, and contribute new insights to the debate on the end of the Psalter.

University of Munich, December 2016
Alma Brodersen

Contents

I Introduction to Psalms 146–150

I.1 The End of the Psalter

The end of the Psalter seems to be a clear matter: Psalms 146–150 as one group form the end of the Psalter. The group is frequently called "Final Hallel"[1] or "Minor Hallel"[2] since it consists of Psalms containing praise.[3] Often, Psalms 146–150 are seen as a unit framing the Psalter together with Psalms 1–2.[4]

However, the unity of Psalms 146–150 is not obvious.[5] All of Psalms 146–150 contain praise, but in rather different ways, as a short rough summary shows:

---

[1] German original "Schlusshallel", cf. Ballhorn 2004b, 299 ("Schlußhallel"); Leuenberger 2004, 344 ("Schlußhallel"), 355; Zenger 2008b, 356 ("Schluss-Hallel"); Zenger and Hossfeld 2016, 440 ("Schlusshallel"); Zenger 2008c, 807 ("Schluss-Hallel", also "Kleines Hallel"/"Little Hallel").

[2] German original "Kleines Hallel", cf. Millard 1994, 145; Kratz 2004, 632–633; Zenger 2008c, 807 (also Final Hallel); Weber 2010, 200; Witte 2010, 416 (English translation Witte 2012, 529).

[3] "Hallel" from הלל/"praise" designates groups of Psalms containing praise in Jewish worship and in scholarly exegesis, cf. Millard 2010. The adjectives distinguish Psalms 146–150 from the "Egyptian Hallel" Ps 113–118, the "Great Hallel" Ps 136, and the "Daily Hallel" Ps 145–150. There is no Jewish tradition for the use of Ps 146–150 without Psalm 145 as a "Hallel" in worship, cf. Millard 2010. Thus, for Ps 146–150 "Hallel" is a scholarly term only, and though a worship-related term in origin used even by scholars who regard this Hallel as a literary work, cf. Zenger 1998a, esp. 35–48 (as criticised by Millard 2010, though Millard 1994, 34–35, 144–145, also uses Little Hallel for Psalms 146–150 as a literary end of the Psalter).

[4] Cf. Zenger 1997b, esp. 99, 104–105; Zenger 1998a, esp. 31, 35–40; Lange 1998, esp. 111; Miller 1998, 110; Scaiola 2010b, esp. 701–705; Weber 2010, 28–43, 200–212; Janowski 2012, 51. However, the numbers of two Psalms at the beginning and five at the end are unequal, and some scholars see Ps 1–2 and 149–150 only as a frame, cf. Barbiero 1999, 50–51; Loretz 2002, 355; Witte 2010, 417 (English translation Witte 2012, 530); or Ps 1 and 150 only, cf. Brueggemann 1991, 68.

[5] I first discussed this in my Master's thesis on "The Significance of Creation References for the Theology of Psalm 147" written in German at the University of Munich in 2011 and published as Brodersen 2013. Chapter V is partly based on Brodersen 2013, namely for V.1.2 p. 173 28–29; p. 173–177 30–35; p. 177 28–29, 35–36; p. 177–178 35–38; V.1.4 45–72; V.1.5 15, 42–43, 78; V.1.6 73–78; V.1.7 19–21, 38–42, 45; V.1.8 79–83; V.2 15–16, 19–22, 45–46, 48–49; V.3 22–26, with references to individual pages given in every other instance, but the chapter expands the material significantly, especially regarding DSS and LXX, while for MT it summarises and reevaluates results in English.

DOI 10.1515/9783110536096-001

Ps 146: *I* will praise YHWH,[6] he helps the weak.
Ps 147: Praise YHWH for the restoration of *Jerusalem* and his rule of nature!
Ps 148: *All nature and all people*, praise YHWH!
Ps 149: *Israel*, praise YHWH with music, *and take violent revenge!*
Ps 150: *All breath*, praise YHWH with music!

If despite their differences these Psalms are read as a single unit, this has major implications for their interpretation. For example, the Israel-specific violence of Ps 149 is often smoothed out by reading it in the context of the more universal surrounding Psalms.[7]

Why then are Psalms 146 – 150 seen as a unit? The view of Psalms 146 – 150 as a unit is based on *Psalter Exegesis*. Psalter Exegesis refers to the interpretation of Psalms in the context of the Psalter, i. e. the Hebrew Masoretic Book of Psalms. Psalter Exegesis in current research[8] is either oriented towards a synchronic reading of the Psalter as a canonical literary whole,[9] or towards a diachronic understanding of the redaction of the Psalter, reading Psalms not just as individual texts but also in the redactional context of the Psalter.[10]

---

6 The tetragrammaton YHWH is transliterated but not vocalised here since it may have been pronounced "Yahô" or "Yahû" rather than "Yahweh", cf. Römer 2015, 24 – 34, esp. 30 – 31.
7 See p. 93, 105 – 106.
8 For an overview of the history of reading the Psalter as a whole, with traditional liturgical and mainly 20th century literary approaches, cf. Gillingham 1994, 232 – 237; Gillingham 2008, esp. 210 – 213. For further historical examples cf. Zenger 1998a, 32 – 33.
9 Cf. e. g. Howard 1997 (esp. 23: "the focus of this study is on the Masoretic Text (MT) of the psalms. Thus, it is a synchronic study"); Mitchell 1997 (esp. 16: "my intention is to investigate the final form of the Masoretic Psalter"); Barbiero 1999 (esp. 20: synchronic approach only). Diachronic implications are sometimes recognised in synchronic Psalter Exegesis, but a synchronic focus on the "final form" of the Masoretic Psalter is still maintainted, c.f. e. g. McCann 1993 (esp. 7: "The purposeful placement of psalms within the collection seems to have given the final form of tbe whole Psalter a function and message greater than the sum of its parts."); De-Claissé-Walford 1997 (esp. vii-viii: "This study of the Hebrew Psalter approaches the text as a story within a canonical context. I began with the question, 'Why these 150 psalms and why in this order?' and found answers in the hermeneutical underpinnings-the footprints-of the text's shaping community. [...] The canonical approach to the text of the Hebrew Bible focuses questions about canon and authority away from questions about oral forms, authors, and redactors and toward the proper subject of study-the shaping community."); DeClaissé-Walford 2014 (esp. 365: "we might ask, why these 150 psalms and why in this particular order? What factors influenced the ancient Israelite community that shaped the book in its final form to order the psalms as it did?"); McCann 2014 (esp. 351: "I offer a reading of the Psalms that takes seriously the shape and shaping of the book.").
10 Cf. e. g. Wilson 1985; Hossfeld and Zenger 2008. Psalter Exegesis oriented towards a diachronic understanding also includes synchronic considerations, cf. Hossfeld and Steiner 2013,

Synchronic Psalter Exegesis reads individual Psalms only in the context of the whole Psalter, and then the end of the Psalter is indeed a clear matter: Psalms 146–150 are the last five Psalms in the Psalter, and are all framed by "Hallelujah", thus forming a clear unit at the end of the Psalter.[11] However, this clarity is based on a focus away from the ancient origins of the texts. While there are many ways of reading biblical texts,[12] it is a fact that they are ancient texts. In the tradition of historical-critical exegesis I regard the ancient origin as indispensable for understanding biblical texts,[13] and will therefore focus on diachronic approaches.

Diachronic Psalter Exegesis also necessarily has a synchronic dimension, and through asking about the diachronic development of the Psalter illuminates a complex history of individual Psalms and the possibility of later editing.[14] However, diachronic Psalter Exegesis explicitly stresses that Psalms as individual ancient texts have to be interpreted on their own before the additional interpretation within the Psalter.[15] As a prominent proponent of diachronic Psalter Exegesis, Erich Zenger, states: "Psalter Exegesis does not want to replace Psalms Exegesis, but builds on it and continues it".[16]

Thus, in diachronic Psalter Exegesis, Psalms 146–150 would have to be interpreted separately as individual Psalms before taking into account their place in the Psalter. But this is not the case in practice.[17] For the specific case of Psalms 146–150, Zenger, while recognising the individual profile of each Psalm,[18] mostly

---

esp. 284: "a synchronic exploration of the structure of the Psalter leads necessarily into a diachronic exploration. The diachronic and synchronic approaches are two parameters, which in a correlative way lead to the understanding of the growth of the final message(s) of the Psalter and of the final message itself."

11 Cf. e.g. DeClaissé-Walford 1997, 99–103; Mitchell 1997, 47; DeClaissé-Walford 2014, 374; McCann 2014, 361.

12 Cf. Oeming (2010).

13 On historical-critical exegesis cf. Seidl 1999, 1781; Steck 1999, 3–5.

14 Cf. Hossfeld 2015, 235–238, 246. See also fn. 10.

15 Cf. Zenger 2010a, 1–3.

16 Zenger 2010b, 61 (German original: "Die Psalterexegese will die Psalmenexegese nicht ersetzen, sondern baut auf ihr auf und führt sie weiter"). Cf. also Zenger 2010b, esp. 24–27, 61–62.

17 Cha 2006 starts by reading the individual Psalms but already including canonical considerations, e.g. p. 107 on Ps 150. Ahn 2008, 2–3, aims to read the individual Psalms 146–150 but with the focus already on their function in the (Masoretic) Psalter. More generally, the lack of Psalms Exegesis in diachronic Psalter Exegesis is criticised by Millard 1996; Steinberg 2006, 268–271.

18 Zenger 2008c, 807: "Es sind zwar fünf Einzelpsalmen mit je eigenem Textprofil, aber sie klingen in ihrer hymnischen Grundstimmung zusammen (es sind fünf imperativische Hymnen) und sind durch vielfältige Stichwortbezüge eng miteinander verwoben. Sie sind nicht durch Über-

conflates Psalms Exegesis (with its focus on individual Psalms and their authors[19]) and Psalter Exegesis (with its focus on the Psalter and its editors or redactors): He argues that these particular Psalms were largely *written* and not just compiled for the context of the end of the Psalter, namely that Psalms 146, 149, and 150 were authored entirely by the final redaction of the Psalter, as were Psalm 147:1–11 and Psalm 148:14[20] and the framing Hallelujahs.[21] Based on this argument of authors and redactors being identical for much more than half of Psalms 146–150, Zenger further argues that at least their redactional parts have to be read in the context of this group as their *original context* rather than as individual Psalms. For example, on Psalm 149 he states: "The Psalm must be read in the context of Ps 145.146–150 for which it was written."[22]

---

schriften voneinander abgegrenzt, sondern durch das jeweils an ihrem Anfang und an ihrem Schluss positionierte 'Hallelu-Ja' so zusammengebunden, dass sie – musikalisch gesprochen – eine fünfteilige Halleluja-Kantate bilden, deren Teile jeweils mit Halleluja beginnen und schließen." (English translation in Hossfeld and Zenger 2011, 605: "While these are five individual psalms, each with its own text profile, they harmonize in their hymnic base note (all five are imperative hymns) and are interwoven by numerous keyword references. They are not divided by superscriptions but are tied together by the 'Hallelu-Ya' placed at the beginning and end of each such that – in musical terms – they constitute a five-part Hallelujah cantata, each of whose parts begins and concludes with 'Hallelujah.'").

19 On the issue of female authors of Psalms cf. Eaton 2005, 8. On the use of male pronouns cf. Watson 2005, xvii.

20 Cf. Zenger 2008c, esp. 807–809: "Die Texte der Komposition Ps 146–150 sind weitgehend das Werk der Psalterschlussredaktion selbst (vgl. die Einzelauslegung). Auf ihre Hand gehen die drei Psalmen 146 149 150 zurück. In Ps 147 stammen von ihr die Verse 1–11, die sie dem ihr vorgegebenen 'Zionspsalm' Ps 147,12–20 vorgeschaltet hat, um so den engen Zusammenhang Ps 146–147 zu schaffen. In Ps 148 geht der Vers 14 auf sie zurück, der Ps 148 mit Ps 149 eng verbindet." (English translation in Hossfeld and Zenger 2011, 606: "The texts of the composition Psalms 146–150 are to a great extent the work of the redactors [literally: the redaction] of the Psalter's conclusion themselves (cf. the individual expositions). The three Psalms 146; 149; and 150 are traceable to their hands [literally: its hand (singular)]. In Psalm 147, vv. 1–11, which the redactors have placed in front of the existing 'psalm of Zion' (vv. 12–20) in order to create the close connection between Psalms 146 and 147, are due to them. Psalm 148:14, which closely links Psalm 148 to Psalm 149, goes back to the redactors [literally: it (the redaction)]."). It is unclear if according to Zenger the hand of the redaction refers to one or a group of redactor-authors, but either way the redaction is described as a unified entity.

21 Cf. Zenger 2008d, 66; Zenger 2010b, 61–64.

22 Zenger 2008j, 860–861 (German original: "Der Psalm muss im Zusammenhang von Ps 145.146–150 gelesen werden, für den er verfasst wurde"). Cf. similarly Zenger 2008g, 815 (Ps 146 redactional); Zenger 2008h, 827–828 (Ps 147:1–11 redactional); Zenger 2008i, 845–846 (Ps 148:14 redactional); Zenger 2008k, 875 (Ps 150 redactional).

Similar views are found in two different monographs on Books IV-V of the Psalter by Martin Leuenberger and Egbert Ballhorn.[23]

Leuenberger focusses on redaction history: Starting from a synchronic reading of the Masoretic Psalter he proceeds to the analysis of individual Psalms, but only includes the development of individual Psalms prior to their Masoretic form if connections with the editing of the Masoretic Psalter are likely.[24] Leuenberger concludes his analysis of Psalms 146–150 with the result that Ps 146, Ps 147:1–11, 20c, Ps 148 (except v. 14), and Ps 150 are redactional (i.e. written by the final redaction of the Psalter).[25] For example, Leuenberger writes on Ps 146: "Given the good embedding in its context it can then be concluded that in 146 we have an intertexually heavily receiving redactional Psalm, written for its context."[26] Thus, like Zenger, he argues for the identity of authors and redactors for more than half of the five final Psalms in the Masoretic Psalter, though, in contrast to Zenger's argument, he concludes that Ps 149 but *not* Ps 148 except for Ps 148:14 are redactional.

Ballhorn focusses on the synchronic canonical Psalter and the direction in which it is read, but also includes diachronic conclusions drawn from this reading.[27] Following his more synchronic analysis, the diachronic implication of Psalms 146–150 forming a purposeful end of the Psalter is less pronounced: "It thus remains to simply state that the Final Hallel makes up the end of the Psalter because no further Psalm or collection of Psalms stands after it."[28] Nevertheless, for Psalms 146–147, Ballhorn includes some considerations similar to Zenger's and Leuenberger's results,[29] for example that Ps 146–150 are late

---

23 Cf. Ballhorn 2004b; Leuenberger 2004.

24 Cf. Leuenberger 2004, 6–7.

25 Cf. Leuenberger 2004, 347 (Ps 146 redactional), 350 (Ps 147:1–11, 20c redactional), 352–353 (Ps 148 redactional except for v. 14), 356 (Ps 149 post-redactional, together with Ps 148:14), 360 (Ps 150 redactional), 364 (overview).

26 Leuenberger 2004, 347 (German original: "Angesichts der guten Kontexteinbettung läßt sich dann schließen, daß in 146 ein intertextuell stark rezipierender, für seinen Kontext verfaßter Redaktionspsalm vorliegt.").

27 Cf. Ballhorn 2004b, 18–19, 28–29, 32–33, 36–37, esp. the summary 36–37 ("Die Verfolgung der Leserichtung des Psalters [...] entspricht [...] auf diachroner Ebene auch weitgehend der Wachstumsrichtung des Buches."; my translation: "Following the reading direction of the Psalter [...] corresponds [...] on a diachronic level largely with the direction of the growth of the book.").

28 Ballhorn 2004b, 357 (German original: "So bleibt einfach zu konstatieren, daß das Schlußhallel deshalb den Schluß des Psalters darstellt, weil kein weiterer Psalm oder keine Psalmensammlung mehr danach zu stehen kommt.").

29 Cf. Ballhorn 2004b, 304, 306 (Ps 146 anthological, literary, late), 310–311 (Ps 147 composed for Final Hallel, with Ps 147:12–20 being older); 327–330 (esp. 329: Ps 149 late like Ps 146–150).

Psalms, or for Psalm 147 "that the Psalm in its current form is compiled for the Final Hallel".[30]

In all these cases, reading Psalms 146 – 150 as one unit leads to interpretations stressing common themes in these Psalms. For example, Zenger highlights the theme of God's kingship and finds eschatological aspects in Psalms 149 – 150; thus, Psalms 146 – 150 show a progression towards eschatology.[31] Leuenberger also emphasises God's kingship, but at the same time the lack of any eschatology except in Ps 149.[32] Ballhorn stresses God's kingship as the eschatological theocracy in a new world,[33] with praise concerning humans only,[34] God's congregation replacing a Davidic messiah, and theocratic rule as the only form of power.[35] Overall, these readings of the whole group of Psalms 146 – 150 put a strong emphasis on God's kingship and eschatology[36] at the end of the Psalter.

The view that Psalms 146 – 150 were at least partly written as a group is not uncontested. Erhard Gerstenberger argues that Psalms 146 – 150 are originally separate Psalms: "Recent studies in the composition of the Psalter [...] emphasize the relative compositional and theological unity of the Final Hallel (Psalms 146 – 150). Zenger is most outspoken in this endeavor. [...] According to Zenger, from the beginning the Final Hallel was meant to be read and meditated on as a uniform text, just as the canonical Psalter served as a reading book. In my opinion,

---

30 Ballhorn 2004b, 310 (German original: "daß der Psalm in seiner jetzigen Form für das Schlußhallel zusammengestellt ist").
31 Cf. Zenger 2008c; Zenger 2008g, 823; Zenger 2008h, 837; Zenger 2008i, 853; Zenger 2008j, 870 – 871; Zenger 2008k, 885.
32 Cf. Leuenberger 2004, 90 – 91, 348, 351, 353, 356 – 358, 360, 364.
33 Cf. Ballhorn 2004b, 355 – 356 , 307 – 308, 312 – 314, 316 – 320, 330, 340, 348, 355 – 356.
34 Cf. Ballhorn 2004b, 356.
35 Cf. Ballhorn 2004b, 359 – 360.
36 Eschatology is also stressed by Lange 1998, 119 – 120, 130, though on the level of the *compilation* of Ps 146 – 150 (see fn. 39); this is used as an argument for the late date of the Psalter by Zenger 2008b, 366; Zenger and Hossfeld 2016, 450. Against eschatology e. g. Koch 1994, 244, who states for MT but not LXX "daß es *im gesamten Psalter keinen einzigen eindeutigen eschatologischen Satz* gibt"/"that there is *not a single explicitly eschatological sentence in the entire Psalter*" (Koch's italics). Ballhorn 2004b, 308, 320, 327 – 329 mentions some eschatological motifs (308 fn. 803: fundamental change in the history of Israel and the nations, manifestation of the universal kingship of God; 320 fn. 840: universal incorporation of nations; 329: participation of Israel in the last judgement; 329 fn. 873: eschatology but not apocalypticism) but also notes (328 fn. 870) that the phenomenon of eschatology cannot be put into one unified system. Leuenberger 2004, 54 fn. 157, 87 – 91, mentions the motif of future and final actions of YHWH but distinguishes eschatology from theocracy, while Zenger 2008c, 808, stresses the connection with God's kingship. On God's kingship see p. 244, on eschatology see p. 53.

the uniformising tendencies of redactional work are vastly overrated in these reconstructions. Each individual text, as it stands now, is still counted as a hymn in its own right, showing a definite profile and a rootage in community service."[37] Gerstenberger argues that the Psalter is a collection rather than a book, and compares it to a basket of fruits rather than a mixed fruit jam.[38] Similarly, Armin Lange states: "The individual Psalms, at least concerning the Little Hallel, are likely to have been merely collected by the compilers of the final form of the proto-Masoretic Psalter, and hardly changed at all in their textual form. Its final redaction thus was more likely a final compilation."[39] Gerald Wilson notes "At the other end of the Psalter the final collection concludes with the exalted praise of the *final hallel* in Psalms 146–150",[40] and compares the Psalter to an oratorio with separate yet connected parts rather than a hymnbook.[41] But with regard to Ps 146–150 few other scholars explicitly adopt similar views of a collection rather than an original unit.[42] Most recently, such a view has been put forward by David Willgren[43] who on the basis of a comparison of MT, DSS, and LXX argues that "the actual basis for regarding Pss 146–150 as a unified collection is far less impressive than what might have been suspected. Ultimately, it

---

37 Gerstenberger 2001, 440–441.
38 Cf. Gerstenberger 1994, 12.
39 Lange 1998, 110–111 (German original: "Die einzelnen Psalmen dürften, zumindest was das Kleine Hallel betrifft, von den Kompilatoren der Endgestalt des protomasoretischen Psalters nur gesammelt und kaum in ihrer Textgestalt verändert worden sein. Bei seiner Endredaktion handelte es sich also wohl eher um eine Endkompilation."). Cf. also Lange 1998, 101–104.
40 Wilson 1993, 74.
41 Wilson 1993, 82.
42 Cf. Risse 1995, 227–243, esp. 241; Brütsch 2010, 221: "Eine einheitliche Rahmung des Psalters durch ein 'doppeltes Eingangstor' (1–2) plus eine fünf Psalmen umfassende 'Schlussdoxologie' wurde nicht bewusst geschaffen. Jeder dieser Psalmen ist unterschiedlich entstanden und an seinen Platz gelangt" (my translation: "A unified frame of the Psalter through a 'double portal' (1–2) plus a 'final doxology' consisting of five Psalms was not consciously created. Each of these Psalms originated and reached its place in different ways"). Cf. also on Ps 150 Reindl 1981b, 337; Whybray 1996, 81, 84 (referring to Reindl); Eaton 2005, 484 ("This colourful poem surely existed first in its own right as a psalm for festal worship, before it came to serve as the seal of praise for the joyful sequence 145–9, for the fifth division of the Psalter (107–50), and for the whole book."); Gillingham 2012, 388 ("Psalm 150 is similarly an *independent unit* [...] Because the calls to praise in Ps 150 create *correspondences with the Hallel before it*, it is easy to see why *it was added here*", my italics); on the Psalter more generally Gillingham 2014, 207 ("This is not to say the Levitical singers composed such psalms but rather that they sought to include them and set them in strategic places within the collections.").
43 Willgren 2016. Since Willgren's work was published after the manuscript of this monograph had already been submitted for publication, only a short overview of his view on Ps 146–150 can be provided here.

rests on the identification of keywords and shared themes, but if they are unsatisfactory tools, not only because many of Zenger's suggestions are quite common terms in the Hebrew Bible but more so in light of the artifactual diversity, not much remains of the foundation for a sequential reading of the five psalms."[44]

Still, the view of Psalms 146 – 150 as one unit which was at least partly written to form the end of the Psalter is found frequently in Psalms research. To quote a few more examples, Joachim Becker mentions "the possibility of a *serial production* of Psalms for the final form of the Psalter" in which Psalms 145 – 150 are likely to have been written by the same author.[45] Matthias Millard states: "The overall impression of the group, its relatively late date, and the lack of information about its use as a group in ancient worship allow the conclusion that not only individual Psalms at the end of the Psalter, but the Little Hallel as a whole was composed as the conclusion of the Psalter".[46] Reinhard Kratz notes that the Hallelujah in "Ps 145.146 – 150 (initially still without 149) dominates the texts – possibly even written only for this place in the Psalter – in form and content".[47] Dennis Tucker, who explicitly stresses the necessity of further re-

---

44 Willgren 2016, 277. Cf. also Willgren 2016, 135, 275 – 286, esp. 135 (comparison of MT, DSS, LXX), 276 (catchword connections in MT are weak for Ps 147), 280 – 281 (Hallelujahs secondary except in Ps 147:1 and Ps 150:6), 282 ("the presence of shared vocabulary and themes could still be appropriately interpreted as providing the basis for their juxtaposition, a juxtaposition suggested to have been intended to create a final doxology to the MT 'Book' of Psalms."), 286 ("the addition of (Hallelujahs to) Pss 145.146 – 150, together with the addition of several Hallelujahs to psalms throughout the 'Book' of Psalms, would have eventually lead to the conceptualizing of the collection as a ספר תהלים, a 'scroll of praises.'"). On the entire Psalter, Willgren 2016, 391 – 392, concludes: "Being an anthology of psalms, the 'Book' of Psalms does not tell a (linear) story, but rather spins an intricate web of multiple traditions that are preserved and put in dialogue with each other despite (or perhaps because of) the tension of perspective created by such a compilation. Like a garden of flowers, the 'Book' of Psalms does not primarily provide a literary context for individual psalms, but rather preserves a dynamic selection of psalms that had proven to stand the test of time".
45 Becker 1975, 115 (German original: "die Möglichkeit einer *Serienproduktion* von Psalmen für die Endgestalt des Psalters", Becker's italics). Leuenberger 2004, 347, 353, refers to Becker and Millard (see fn. 46) when arguing for a redactional origin of Psalm 146.
46 Millard 1994, 145 (German original: "Der Gesamteindruck der Gruppe, ihr relativ spätes Alter und die fehlenden Nachrichten über ihre Verwendung als Gruppe im antiken Gottesdienst lassen den Schluß zu, daß nicht nur einzelne Psalmen am Schluß des Psalters, sondern das kleine Hallel insgesamt als Abschluß des Psalters komponiert sind"). Millard also refers to Becker, see fn. 45.
47 Kratz 1996, 31 (German original: "Ps 145.146 – 150 (zunächst noch ohne 149) beherrscht es die – möglicherweise überhaupt nur für diesen Platz im Psalter verfaßten – Texte nach Form und Inhalt").

search on Psalms 146–150,[48] notes that "Pss 146–150 were likely part of the final composition of the Psalter".[49]

Most recently, this view has been presented in a monograph on Psalms 145.146–150 by Friederike Neumann[50] which concludes "that Ps 145 and the Psalms of the Minor Hallel were written for the Psalter which was available to them".[51] Neumann individually analyses Psalms 145–150[MT] in this order, followed by a discussion of these Psalms in the contexts of the Masoretic Psalter and the Dead Sea Scrolls.[52] 11QPs[a] (Qumran Psalms Scroll[a], 11Q5) is seen as depending on MT and deconstructing the Minor Hallel.[53] The monograph's German title "Schriftgelehrte Hymnen" (in English best paraphrased as "scribal hymns interpreting scripture") expresses the two main arguments of the monograph: Psalms 145–150 are hymns, and they interpret scripture.[54] Neumann argues that "Hymnus"/"hymn", beyond a cultic genre, is a group of texts praising God in theological reflexion.[55] "Schriftauslegung"/"interpretation of scripture" is used to refer to the interpretation of other, previously existing texts in "scripture" meaning the Old Testament, and used largely synonymously with "Intertextualität"/"intertextuality".[56] Authors and addressees of texts interpreting scrip-

---

48 Tucker 2014, 190: "While an extensive analysis of the final Hallel remains the task of a subsequent study, a brief review does reveal certain connections between the final book in the Psalter and the concluding Hallel."

49 Tucker 2014, 196.

50 Neumann 2016. Since Neumann's work was published after the manuscript of this monograph had already been submitted for publication, only a short overview can be provided here. In future research, a detailed comparison of the approaches and results in these two independent monographs on Psalms 146–150 – as well as Willgren 2016 (see fn. 43) – is desirable.

51 Neumann 2016, 429 (German original "dass Ps 145 und die Psalmen des kleinen Hallels für den ihnen vorliegenden Psalter verfasst worden sind").

52 Cf. Neumann 2016, VII-X, 25–26. There is no separate treatment of the LXX which appears, e.g., in footnotes to translations of MT, cf. Neumann 2016, 100–102.

53 Cf. Neumann 2016, 450–469, 483, esp. 461 ("dass die Gruppe des kleinen Hallels in 11Q5 dekomponiert ist"/"that the group of the Minor Hallel is deconstructed in 11Q5; referring to Jain 2014, 256–266), 468 ("11Q5 setzt den protomasoretischen Psalter in seiner Endgestalt voraus"/ "11Q5 presupposes the proto-masoretic Psalter in its final form").

54 Cf. Neumann 2016, 3–5.

55 Cf. Neumann 2016, 7–15, 22–23, 470–477.

56 Cf. Neumann 2016, 16–21, 23–34. "Intratextualität"/"intratextuality" (23) is used when further literary development ("Fortschreibung") occurs within one text; this may be connected with intertextuality. "Old Testament" is implicitly identified with HB (rather than e.g. LXX including apocrypha, cf. the index 503–513). Possible intertextual relations with texts outside HB are still sometimes discussed, e.g. 266 (Onomasticon of Amenope), 274, 344 (Qumran texts), but the main focus is on HB as "scripture" (cf. e.g. 472: "Die Psalmen leben aus der Schrift."/"The Psalms live out of scripture.").

ture are argued to belong the same circles, wherefore despite a lack of explicit intertextuality it is precisely in this intertextuality centered on interpretation of scripture that the texts have to be read.[57] Neumann's criteria for identifying "interpretation of scripture" in each individual case are "common lexemes, words and combinations of words in at least two texts, elsewhere called catchword connections"[58] in combination with either shared rare words, or a large number of references within the same text; the direction of a reference is then assessed based on the number of references within the same text, and on changes of content.[59] A detailed exegesis of each of Psalms 145 – 150[60] leads Neumann to the following conclusions: Psalms 145 – 150 appear too different to be written by the same author yet too similar to be entirely disconnected, and it is thus most likely that rather than having one common origin, this group of Psalms was successively enlarged in a process of literary development ("Fortschreibung"). According to Neumann's analysis, each of Psalms 145 – 150 in this order refers to the preceding but not the following Psalm,[61] while none of the Psalms explicitly mentions a concluding function for the Psalter.[62] The framing

---

57 Cf. Neumann 2016, 18: "Da für diese Schriftkultur und Verbreitung der Texte nur kleine, überschaubare Zirkel anzunehmen sind, war eine Fortschreibung und Weiterarbeit an den immer gleichen Texten gut möglich. Die Texte signalisieren in der Regel nicht selbst, dass sie Auslegungsliteratur sind. Es gibt keine expliziten Hinweise auf Intertextualität. Gleichwohl setzt aber das hohe Maß an Intertextualität, das über Stichwortverbindungen und direkte oder indirekte Zitate erreicht wird, ein solches Lesen voraus"/"Since for this scribal culture and distribution of texts only small, limited circles have to be assumed, literary development and further work on the ever same texts is very well possible. The texts themselves do not usually indicate that they are interpretative literature. There are no explicit indications of intertextuality. At the same time, the high measure of intertextuality which is achieved through catchword connections and direct and indirect quotations presupposes such a reading". Neumann 2016, 18, fn. 85 – 87, here refers to Edenburg 2010, 147 – 148 (see fn. 147); Schmid 2011a, 275 – 276; Schmid 2011b, 51, 54; Kratz 2013a, 124 – 125; Kratz 2013b, 141 – 142.
58 Neumann 2016, 24 (German original "gemeinsame Lexeme, Wörter und Wortverbindungen in mindestens zwei Texten, andernorts auch als Stichwortverbindung bezeichnet").
59 Cf. Neumann 2016, 24 – 25. See I.3.2 for intertextual criteria used here (especially including syntactical similarity).
60 A detailed comparison with the exegesis provided here would be desirable. For example, the argument that Ps 150:1 refers to "holiness" as a reason for praise rather than a sanctuary, see p. 44–47, is developed independently in Neumann 2016, 388 – 389, 394 – 398.
61 Cf. Neumann 2016, 430 – 431. See VII which concludes that Psalms 146 – 150 do not contain references to one another.
62 Cf. Neumann 2016, 432 (referring to Ballhorn 2004b, 357– 358): "Gleichwohl ist bei der Frage nach möglichen Abschlüssen des Psalters festzuhalten, dass keiner der Psalmen den Abschluss des Psalters auf der Metaebene benennt. [...] Die Psalmen des Hallels sind somit in erster Linie Schlusspsalmen, weil sie am Ende des Psalters stehen. Grundsätzlich wäre eine weitere Ergän-

Hallelujahs of Psalms 146–150 are argued to be original rather than secondary, although Neumann notes they were seen as secondary by LXX and 11QPs[a].[63] According to Neumann, Ps 145, Ps 146, Ps 147, Ps 148:1–5, 7–13, Ps 148:6, Ps 148:14 and Ps 149, and Ps 150 were written successively, each in dependance on the previous ones in this order,[64] around 200 BCE at the time of the final form of the Psalter,[65] as literary rather than cultic texts.[66]

The view of Psalms 146–150 as one unit at least partly written to form the end of the Psalter is based on three main reasons: *the context of Psalms 146– 150 in this order at the end of the Masoretic Psalter, the framing Hallelujahs of Psalms 146–150*, and *intertextual links between Psalms 146–150*.[67] However, all three of these reasons are highly problematic, as an introductory look at the sources of Psalms 146–150 and at their intertextual links will indicate now.

I.2 Sources

I.2.1 Masoretic Text, Dead Sea Scrolls, Septuagint

Before any analysis of Psalms 146–150, the basic question "What is the text of Psalms 146–150?" needs to be answered. This is easier said than done as for none of these Psalms – or indeed of any texts in the Hebrew Bible – any autographs are preserved. The only sources available are manuscripts written

---

zung von Texten möglich (vgl. LXX) und / oder eine Umstellung der Texte (vgl. 11Q5)."/"Nevertheless, regarding the question of possible conclusions of the Psalter it has to be said that none of the Psalms mentions the conclusion of the Psalter on a meta-level. [...] The Hallel Psalms therefore are final Psalms primarily because they have their place at the end of the Psalter. In principle, further additions of texts (cf. LXX) and / or different arrangements of the texts (cf. 11Q5) are possible."

63 Cf. Neumann 2016, 444–449, esp. 449 on LXX and 11QPs[a]: "Die Halleluja-Rahmung wird demnach durchgehend als sekundäres Element wahrgenommen."/"The Hallelujah-frame is thus consistently perceived as a secondary element.".

64 Cf. Neumann 2016, 284 (on Ps 148:6), 432–444. The Masoretic order of Psalms is important: For example, Ps 146 is argued to refer to Ps 145 not least because Ps 145 is its "Vorgängerpsalm"/ "preceding Psalm" (Neumann 2016, 114); in contrast, in 11QPs[a] Ps 146 precedes Ps 145, cf. Sanders 1965, 5.

65 Cf. Neumann 2016, 475.

66 Cf. Neumann 2016, 470–477.

67 Cf. Leuenberger 2004, 346 (plus genre and content); Zenger 2008c, 807–810 (plus genre), esp. 807 (see fn. 18); Neumann 2016, 22–26 (Masoretic order, intertextual links), 444–449 (Hallelujahs), 481–483 (Masoretic order, intertextual links).

much later than the texts themselves.[68] Scholarly printed editions are based on these later manuscripts. Even though the manuscripts preserve very similar texts, they differ from one another in many details. A choice of sources has to be made before any interpretation of any biblical text. While the old age of the manuscripts themselves does not in itself imply a closeness to the original text,[69] the oldest manuscripts are still the closest available sources and have to be taken into account. I will therefore introduce the oldest extant manuscripts of Psalms 146 – 150 and their modern editions, and explain my choice of sources.

Hebrew Masoretic Text (MT)

The Hebrew text of the Hebrew Bible (HB) found most commonly in both manuscripts and modern editions is called "Masoretic Text" (MT)[70] because of its transmission through Jewish scholars called "Masoretes" around the 10th century CE. This transmission included writing out all the consonants as well as adding vowel pointing, accents, division markers, and "Masorah" comments. "Masoretic Text" is an abstract summarising term for a text form preserved on numerous manuscripts with slight differences. The two oldest dated and (at least partly) complete manuscripts of HB, the Leningrad and Aleppo Codices, reflect MT, and form the basis for most scholarly editions of HB.[71]

The *Aleppo Codex*, written in the first half of the 10th century CE and the oldest formerly complete manuscript of the complete HB, was partly destroyed in the 1940s.[72] Its diplomatic edition in the Hebrew University Bible (HUB) Project[73] as yet contains no volume for the Psalms.

Codex L (Saint Petersburg B19ᴬ, also called Leningrad Codex, or Leningradensis) was written in 1008 – 1010 CE, much more than a thousand years after the texts it contains. It is the *oldest complete Hebrew manuscript* of HB which is preserved.[74] The widely used Biblia Hebraica Stuttgartensia (BHS)[75] and the

---

68 For Hebrew manuscripts cf. Würthwein 1988, 37 – 47; Wegner 2006, 140 – 161; for Greek manuscripts cf. Würthwein 1988, 82 – 86; Wegner 2006, 182 – 184. The Dead Sea Scrolls from the 3rd century BCE onwards are the oldest Hebrew sources for any text of the Hebrew Bible apart from two silver rolls with parts of Num 6:24 – 26 from the 7th or 6th century BCE, cf. Tov 2012, 111.
69 Cf. Tov 2012, 274.
70 On MT cf. Würthwein 1988, 13 – 53; Tov 2012, 24 – 26, 66.
71 On editions cf. Tov 2012, 344; Flint 2013, 21 – 22.
72 Cf. Würthwein 1988, 43 – 44, 176 – 177 (1st half of 10th century CE, damaged 1947); Tov 2012, 24 – 26, 44 (925 CE, damaged 1948). Ben-Zvi Institute 2007 is the most recent facsimile.
73 The first HUB volume, Goshen-Gottstein 1995, XX, mentions the Aleppo Codex as its basis.
74 On Codex L cf. Würthwein 1988, 44 – 45; Tov 2012, 45. It is named after the former name of Saint Petersburg (Russia) where it is kept, on this issue cf. Fischer 2009, 53 – 54. For its date cf.

new Biblia Hebraica Quinta (BHQ)[76] are diplomatic editions of the Codex L. So far, only BHS contains the Psalms; a BHQ volume for the Psalms has not yet been published. As BHS is the only current complete scholarly edition of the Leningrad Codex and used most widely,[77] it is used here as a basis for the exegesis of MT.[78] In MT, Psalms 146–150 stand at the end of the Book of Psalms.[79]

Hebrew Dead Sea Scrolls (DSS)

As for many texts in HB, the earliest manuscripts preserved at all for Psalms 146–150 are manuscripts found in the Judaean desert, the so-called Dead Sea Scrolls (DSS).[80] Parts of the consonantal texts of Psalms 146–150 are preserved in manuscripts found in *Qumran* from 1947 and in *Masada* from 1963 onwards.[81] *Terminus ante quem* for all Qumran manuscripts is 68 CE when Qumran was destroyed by the Roman army,[82] for Masada manuscripts, it is 73/74 CE when Masada was destroyed by the Roman army.[83] While the Dead Sea Scrolls are the old-

---

Würthwein 1988, 182, (1008 CE); Lebedev 1998, xxi–xxii (1010 CE); Tov 2012, 45 (1009 CE). Freedman 1998 is the most recent facsimile.

75 Elliger and Rudolph 1997, XII, mentions Codex L as its basis.

76 Schenker 2004 (first BHQ volume published), VII-IX, mentions Codex L as its basis.

77 According to Dotan 2001, x-xi, his edition sometimes deviates from Codex L. According to Flint 2013, 21–22, most English translations of HB are based on the BHS and BHQ editions. BHS also forms the basis of the Hebrew WTT text in *BibleWorks 9* 2013.

78 Variants in *other MT manuscripts* are in the BHS apparatus, as are fragments of manuscripts found in a *Genizah in Cairo*, cf. Elliger and Rudolph 1997, LXIX, on the Genizah in general cf. Würthwein 1988, 13–14, 42–43. The Genizah fragments show the consonantal text of MT, cf. Reif 2000, 100; Tov 2012, 33. Some fragments date from the 9th century CE, cf. Tov 2012, 32–33, or the 5th century CE, cf. Würthwein 1988, 42; Reif 2000, 105, onwards, and are thus older than Codex L, but most date from the 13th century CE onwards, cf. Goshen-Gottstein 1962, 38. Further research including the dates of the unedited fragments containing Psalms 146–150, cf. Jewish Manuscript Preservation Society 2013, is desirable.

79 In Codex L the end is made explicit by a note after Ps 150, cf. Elliger and Rudolph 1997, 1226; Freedman 1998, 804=fol. 396v:

סכום הפסוקים שלספר אלפים וחמש מאות ועש[רים] ושבעה פסוקים

"The sum of the verses for the book: two thousand and five hundred and twenty and seven verses."

80 The term "Dead Sea Scrolls" is used to refer either to manuscripts found at Qumran and other Judaean desert sites, e. g. by Lange 2003, 1873, or to refer to Qumran manuscripts only, e. g. by Vermès 2011, xiii. I employ "Dead Sea Scrolls" as referring to all Judaean desert manuscripts.

81 Cf. Würthwein 1988, 38–39. BHS is based on earlier editions, cf. Fischer 2009, 60–61.

82 Cf. Lange 2003, 1879.

83 Cf. Talmon 1999, 17, 24; Foerster 2002, 886.

est extant manuscripts, they are only preserved as fragments, and therefore the later complete Masoretic codices still serve as a basis to which the DSS fragments of biblical texts are compared.[84] As explained above, BHS serves as the point of comparison here.

The following table lists all DSS manuscripts containing Psalms 146 – 150.[85]

Table: Psalms 146 – 150 in the Dead Sea Scrolls

Ps 146 (parts of 2 verses out of 10):	**11QPs^a:**
Ps 146:9 – 10 (plus addition, fragmentary)	11QPs^a
Ps 147 (parts of 12 verses out of 20):	**4QPs^d, 11QPs^a, MasPs^b:**
Ps 147:1 – 4, 13 – 17, 20 (fragmentary)	4QPs^d
Ps 147:2, 18 – 20 (fragmentary)	11QPs^a
Ps 147:18 – 19 (fragmentary)	MasPs^b
Ps 148 (parts of 12 verses out of 14):	**11QPs^a:**
Ps 148:1 – 12 (fragmentary)	11QPs^a
Ps 149 (2 verses out of 9):	**11QPs^a:**
Ps 149:7 – 9 (complete)	11QPs^a
Ps 150 (all 6 verses):	**11QPs^a, MasPs^b:**
Ps 150:1 – 6 (complete)	11QPs^a
Ps 150:1 – 6 (fragmentary)	MasPs^b

Thus, the relevant manuscripts for Psalms 146 – 150 are 4QPs^d, 11QPs^a, and MasPs^b. Facsimiles and editions are used here.[86]

The *4QPs^d (Qumran Psalms Scroll^d, 4Q86)* fragments (which according to their late Hasmonaean script may date from the mid-first century BCE)[87] preserve parts of Psalms 106(?), 147, and 104 in this order.[88]

11QPs^a (Qumran Psalms Scroll^a, 11Q5) (which according to its early to late Herodian script may date from the first half-century CE)[89] contains various bib-

84 Cf. Tov 2012, 29 – 32.

85 Table based on Lange 2009, 557, with alterations especially for 4QPs^e (Qumran Psalms Scroll^e, 4Q87), see V.2.3, VI.2.2, VI.2.3. For an overview of all DSS Psalms manuscripts cf. Flint 2013.

86 The facsimiles and editions used here are for 4QPs^d Skehan, Ulrich, and Flint 2000a; for 11QPs^a Sanders 1965 and Sanders 1967; for MasPs^b Talmon 1999, 91 – 97. For 4QPs^d and MasPs^b also cf. for more detailed images Israel Antiquities Authority 2012. None of the Psalms scrolls is included in Israel Museum 1995 – 2016 yet. For the Psalms, neither the new "Biblia Qumranica" volume nor the new edition of 11QPs^a mentioned by Flint 2013, 20, 31, are published yet, but all the material collated there, namely MT, DSS, and LXX, is included here.

87 Cf. Skehan, Ulrich, and Flint 2000a, 64.

88 Cf. Skehan, Ulrich, and Flint 2000a, 63.

89 Cf. Sanders 1965, 9.

lical and non-biblical psalms, again in an order different from MT.[90] Parts of Psalms 146–150 are found in the order 105–*146–148*–120[91] and later 143–*149–150*-Hymn to the Creator,[92] then followed by five other texts and finally Ps 151 A, B.[93] Neither Ps 148 nor Ps 150 have an opening Hallelujah. It is debated whether the opening Hallelujah was left out in 11QPs[a] or whether 11QPs[a] is independent of MT.[94] There are additional passages in Ps 146 and Ps 149. Psalm 147 is found on Fragment E of 11QPs[a] in the order 104–*147*–105 (and with one word on Fragment F).

MasPs[b] (*Masada Psalms Scroll*[b], *Mas1f*) (probably written in the last half-century BCE)[95] contains fragments of every verse of Psalm 150 and two words probably belonging to Psalm 147.

Greek Septuagint (LXX)

The oldest complete Hebrew manuscripts of HB date from the 10th and 11th centuries CE.[96] However, its oldest complete manuscripts at all are not in Hebrew but in Greek: They contain the Greek translation of the Hebrew Bible called Sep-

---

90 Cf. Sanders 1965, 5–6.

91 Cf. Sanders 1965, 5–6, 23.

92 For details on 11QPs[a] Hymn to the Creator cf. Sanders 1965, 89–91.

93 On the two texts Ps 151 A, B in 11QPs[a] Column XXVIII corresponding with Ps 151[LXX] cf. Sanders 1965, 54–64. Ps 151[LXX] is probably a translation from Hebrew, cf. Sanders 1965, 59–64. However, the Greek text may be an independent literary edition of a previous now lost Hebrew original, thus Debel 2008, 472–473; Debel 2010, 178–179; whether in 11QPs[a] or LXX are closest to this lost Hebrew original is debated, cf. Salvesen 2003, 862. It is sometimes argued that Ps 151 A, B in 11QPs[a] shows Qumran-specific features, but this does not answer the question of a dependance of 11QPs[a] on the Masoretic Psalter, cf. Dimant 2012, 114. Rather, the existence of Ps 151 in two early sources may even point towards the independence of both 11QPs[a] and LXX on MT, cf. for 11QPs[a] and LXX Flint 1997, 210, 212, 226, 234–236; Flint 2000, 342; for LXX Debel 2010, 173–190, esp. 178–179.

94 Dahmen 2003, 227, due to the missing opening Hallelujahs on 11QPs[a] in Ps 147:1 (but may be due to damaged fragment); 148:1 (complete); 135:1 (complete), argues for a dependence of 11QPs[a] on MT. Similarly Ballhorn 2004b, 300–304, and Dahmen 2003, 118–119 (following Ballhorn's 2000 doctoral thesis published as Ballhorn 2004b), note that with regard to Ps 146–150 11QPs[a] leaves out the opening Hallelujah, LXX leaves out the final Hallelujah, and it is easiest to explain the changes in both 11QPs[a] and LXX as two independent changes based on MT. Similarly Willgren 2016, 187–195, argues that these changes in 11QPs[a] and LXX are secondary to MT, but for Qumran superscriptions other than Hallelujahs concludes that "the superscriptions never anticipated or related to anything other than the individual psalm itself." (191).

95 Cf. Talmon and Yadin 1999, 92.

96 See p. 12–13.

tuagint (LXX).[97] The oldest almost complete Septuagint manuscript, Codex Vaticanus (Vatican Vat. Gr. 1209, also called Codex B), was written in the 4th century CE, more than 600 years before Codex L.[98] The oldest LXX manuscripts even date from the 3rd century BCE onwards, with Psalms manuscripts from the 2nd century CE onwards,[99] although for Ps 145–150^{LXX} the oldest manuscripts are the codices Vaticanus and Sinaiticus, both dating from the *4th century CE*,[100] and making this the only absolute *terminus ante quem* for Ps 145–150^{LXX}.

The Septuagint is also closer to the origin of the Hebrew Bible than almost any manuscript preserved at all:[101] The Septuagint translation was probably made from the 3rd century BCE to the 1st or 2nd century CE.[102] Thus, it is the oldest extant translation of the Hebrew Bible.[103] The LXX-Psalter was probably finished in the 2nd century BCE.[104]

Regarding Septuagint editions,[105] Codex Vaticanus is the basis for the diplomatic edition of the Cambridge Septuagint which is incomplete with no Psalms volume.[106] Therefore, the non-diplomatic critical edition Göttingen Septuagint

---

97 For the origin of the name Septuagint and its abbreviation LXX cf. Ziegert and Kreuzer 2012. Tov 2012, 128–129, discusses the use of the term Septuagint for the present *collection* of sacred Greek writings and for the reconstructed original *translation* for which he prefers the term Old Greek (OG). I use the term for both, as the extant collection is the starting point in either case.
98 On Codex Vaticanus cf. Würthwein 1988, 84–85; Wegner 2006, 183; Fischer 2009, 142–144; Tov 2012, 133. For an overview of LXX manuscripts cf. Jobes and Silva 2000, 57–68; Siegert 2001, 96–98; Fischer 2009, 126–146; Wegner 2006, 182–184; Tov 2012, 132–133.
99 Cf. Siegert 2001, 96–97 in combination with Septuaginta-Unternehmen der Akademie der Wissenschaften zu Göttingen 2012; Rahlfs and Fraenkel 2004, 467, 489–497.
100 Cf. Rahlfs 1979, 10–11.
101 See fn. 68.
102 Cf. Siegert 2001, 34–43.
103 Other translations are probably younger: The Syriac Peshitta is dated to the 1st–2nd century CE, cf. Fischer 2009, 164–169, the Latin Vulgate to the 4th–5th century CE, cf. Fischer 2009, 169–175. The Aramaic Targumim may date from as early as the 4th–3rd century BCE, but are paraphrases rather than translations, cf. Fischer 2009, 157–164. Other translations mainly depend on LXX, cf. Fischer 2009, 175–184. Cf. similarly Tov 2012, 127, 147–154.
104 Cf. for overviews Bons 2009a, 752 (2nd half 2nd century BCE, place debated); Janowski 2003, 1774 (2nd century BCE, place debated), for detailed discussions Schaper 1995, 44–45 (2nd half of 2nd century BCE, Palestine); Siegert 2001, 41–43 (2nd century BCE, Judaea); Williams 2001, esp. 263, 276 (2nd century BCE, not necessarily Judaea); Gzella 2002, 49–52 (2nd century BCE but debated 3rd to 2nd century BCE, place debated). On the identity of LXX translators in general cf. Siegert 2001, 30–31, 74–75; for the LXX-Psalter Gzella 2002, 52–55.
105 For an overview cf. Wegner 2006, 185–187; Fischer 2009, 151–156; Tov 2012, 134–135.
106 Brooke, McLean, and Thackeray 1906–1940.

which does have a Psalms volume[107] is used here, and Rahlfs' complete Septuagint edition[108] where the Göttingen Septuagint is incomplete.

On this basis, the most striking differences to MT can be summarised as follows:

Psalm 147^{MT} is divided into two Psalms in LXX. Psalm 146^{LXX}(=147:1–11^{MT}) and Psalm 147^{LXX}(=147:12–20^{MT}). Psalms 145–148^{LXX}(=146–148^{MT}) have the superscription αλληλουια· Αγγαιου καὶ Ζαχαριου/"Hallelujah; of Haggai and Zechariah",[109] whereas Psalms 149–150^{LXX}(=149–150^{MT}) have the superscription αλληλουια/"Hallelujah". There is a final Hallelujah in none of Psalms 145–149^{LXX}(=146–149^{MT}) but only in Ps 150^{LXX}(=150^{MT}). There are additional cola in Ps 146:8^{LXX}(=147:8^{MT}) and 148:5^{LXX}. Ps 151^{LXX} – although designated as ἔξωθεν τοῦ ἀριθμοῦ/"outside the number" –,[110] follows Ps 150^{LXX}.

---

107 Rahlfs 1979. A new Psalms volume is in progress, cf. Septuaginta-Unternehmen der Akademie der Wissenschaften zu Göttingen 2013.

108 Rahlfs 1935 forms the basis for the Greek LXT text in *BibleWorks 9* 2013, and is almost entirely unchanged in the revised edition Rahlfs and Hanhart 2006, cf. Hanhart 2006.

109 The superscriptions assign the Psalms to Haggai and Zechariah, who are not found in extrabiblical sources and according to biblical sources (esp. Ezra 5:1; 6:14; Hag 1:1; Zech 1:1; in the Septuagint 2 Esdr 5:1; 6:14^{LXX}; Hag 1:1^{LXX}; Zech 1:1^{LXX}) were prophets in the time of the rebuilding of Jerusalem and its temple after the Babylonian exile around 520 BCE, cf. Frevel 2016, 307. The reason for these superscriptions may be common topics such as rebuilding Jerusalem and its temple in the books of Haggai and Zechariah and the biblical texts where both prophets are mentioned (Ezra 5:1; 6:14; in the Septuagint 2 Esdr 5:1, 6:14^{LXX}; 1 Esdr 6:1; 7:3^{LXX}), cf. Pietersma 2001, 113–118; Rösel 2001, 140; Ballhorn 2004b, 300–301; Zenger 2008c, 809, and possibly shared words with Hag and Zech, cf. Slomovic 1979, 363–364; Allen 2002, 389 (referring to Slomovic); Bauks 2011, 1877 (referring to Slomovic). It is debated whether the superscription is secondary to MT, thus Pietersma 2001, esp. 100, 113–118; Rösel 2001, 140, 145; Allen 2002, 389; Ballhorn 2004b, 300–301; Zenger 2008c, 809; Bauks 2011, 1877; Willgren 2016, 175, 190, 252; or the translation of a different original with LXX superscriptions being older than MT, thus Stichel 2007, esp. 171; Brütsch 2010, 200, 203–204 (for LXX superscriptions in general Bons 2009a, 750. Gauthier 2014, 249–256, discusses different arguments and concludes (256): "In the case of Αγγαιου καὶ Ζαχαριου it is very difficult to make a decision for or against originality". The superscriptions show text-critical variations within LXX, see e.g. IV.3.7, V.3.7, VI.3.7.

110 Ps 151:1^{LXX} in Rahlfs 1979, 339, with little Greek text-critical variation in this part of the superscription. However, Ulrich 2000, 324–325, argues that the designation is a secondary addition (noting that even Codex L only counts 149 Psalms). For a commentary on Ps 151^{LXX} cf. Bons 2011a. On Ps 151 in 11QPs^a see fn. 93, on Syriac traditions fn. 160.

I.2.2 Parallel Use of Sources

The manuscripts and editions chosen for Psalms 146 – 150 are important not simply because they are the oldest (or the oldest complete) manuscripts for Psalms 146 – 150 preserved at all, but also because they represent *text forms* found on numerous younger manuscripts. These text forms are the Masoretic Text, text forms preserved in the Dead Sea Scrolls, and the Septuagint.[111] A choice of editions has been explained for all text forms. However, no single source has been chosen. There are still different text forms.

An ongoing general debate about textual criticism of the Hebrew Bible[112] features two opposite models for the origin and solution of the problem of different text forms. Model A assumes that slightly different but equally original versions of a text in written form existed at the same time, Model B assumes that there was one original text in written form from which all other versions derived.[113] If Model A is adopted, each of the oldest extant manuscripts has to be read and interpreted in its own right, if Model B is adopted, one hypothetical original text has to be reconstructed and used as the basis for interpretation. In his textbook on textual criticism, Emanuel Tov stresses the necessity to adopt either Model A or B as a view on the original texts: "There seems to be no room for an intermediary position between these two views".[114]

While Model B is accepted by many scholars,[115] who consequently *merge* the different text forms to find one original text,[116] this is not a consensus.[117] For the

---

111 The term "text form" is used here for MT, different DSS, and LXX, similar to Ulrich 1996, 91, on the debate about different terms for "text forms", cf. Ulrich 1999, 32, 95. MT and LXX are usually regarded as two different text forms preserved on multiple manuscripts, but the affiliation of DSS is debated, cf. Debel 2010, 165 – 171. On the fundamental importance of MT, DSS, and LXX as the main sources for textual criticism (with the Samaritan Pentateuch) cf. Tov 2012, 17 – 19. Tov 2012, 158 – 161, argues that MT, LXX, and the Samaritan Pentateuch are just texts. However, they are preserved on many different manuscripts each containing a text of one of these three text forms.

112 For different perceived goals of textual criticism of HB cf. Wegner 2006, 31.

113 Cf. Tov 2012, 155 – 190: Influential scholars were Paul Kahle for Model A, Paul de Lagarde for Model B.

114 Cf. Tov 2012, 163. However, this position is revised in Tov 2014, esp. 381 – 383, see below, esp. fn. 124.

115 Model B is adopted by Würthwein 1988, 117 – 118; Wegner 2006, 36 – 37; Fischer 2009, 200 – 201; Tov 2012, 168 – 169, 263 – 268.

116 Cf. Würthwein 1988, 125 – 127; Steck 1999, 38 – 43; Wegner 2006, 130 – 134; Fischer 2009, 220 – 222; Tov 2012, 271 – 274.

117 Cf. Ulrich 1996, 98 – 99; van Seters 2006, 327; Debel 2011, 84 – 85, who all explicitly reject the concept of "the original text" for HB.

Septuagint on its own, Model B is more of a consensus as one translator or one team of translators can be assumed for every book of the Septuagint. Thus the translators' text can be assumed to be the original from which all other versions derived and which is to be reconstructed,[118] but the Septuagint is still only one text form.

I think that adopting an intermediary position is possible and necessary. Since due to the lack of manuscripts we simply cannot know whether Model A or B is correct,[119] we can only try to get as far back to the original ancient texts as we can, *but only as far as manuscripts are preserved*. Rather than going beyond the preserved manuscripts and their editions to construct a more original text as the basis of my exegesis, or simply choosing MT as the only basis, I read the text forms *separately*.[120] While this is close to Model A, in my approach not *every* extant manuscript is read and interpreted separately, but the *best representative manuscripts or editions* of what are usually regarded as *the oldest text forms*.[121] The manuscripts and editions chosen here as sources may contain errors or alterations,[122] and younger manuscripts or versions can be useful for explaining the texts on the oldest extant manuscripts. Thus, textual criticism remains important, and the critical apparatus in BHS for the Hebrew Text and the Göttingen Septuagint for the Greek Text is considered in the analysis of the individual Psalms (especially under the heading "Unity"). The critical apparatus is, however, used to reconstruct a text different from the chosen sources which is then taken as the basis for an exegesis.[123]

---

118 Cf. Jobes and Silva 2000, 124; Siegert 2001, 74–75, 107–118; Fischer 2009, 146–151; Tov 2012, 131.

119 This applies especially to the Hebrew text of HB. New Testament manuscripts preserved are much closer to the time of origin of the texts, and a more convincing case can be made for a single author and thus Model B. For a comparison of Old and New Testament textual criticism cf. Wegner 2006, 26–43.

120 Similarly Ulrich 1996, esp. 91, 99–105, takes MT, DSS, and LXX as the most important text forms, but only discusses DSS with the example of 11QPs[a].

121 See fn. 111.

122 A distinction between unintentional and intentional variants in order to find intentional literary variants is made both by scholars opposing one original text, cf. Ulrich 1996, 88; Debel 2011, 75–76, and scholars looking for one original text, cf. Würthwein 1988, 118–124; Fischer 2009, 205–218. This distinction can be made likely in each case but not proven.

123 A reconstructed text is found in "The Hebrew Bible: A Critical Edition" (HBCE) (formerly called "Oxford Hebrew Bible", cf. Fox 2015, xi, fn. 1). An edition of Proverbs (Fox 2015) has been published, an Psalms edition is planned (cf. Flint 2013, 21–31). Of the main and oldest sources for the HBCE text, namely MT, the Samaritan Pentateuch, DSS, and LXX (cf. Hendel 2008, 347), all relevant ones (MT, DSS, LXX) are taken into account here. HBCE aims to show multiple ancient editions where they can be reconstructed in parallel columns (cf. Hendel

This approach is confirmed by a more recent, different proposal by Tov: "I am not happy with the attempted reconstruction and perpetuation of an Urtext that in my view never existed. [...] I would like Bible scholars to be able to work simultaneously with MT, the LXX, SP [Samaritan Pentateuch], and some Qumran scrolls on an equal footing."[124]

The separate reading of text forms is especially important for the *Psalter* due to the question whether or not 11QPs[a] and LXX depend on MT: 11QPs[a] may depend on MT,[125] or may be independent.[126] The answer to this question has significant impact on the question of the original unity of Psalms 146 – 150. Scholars reading Ps 146 – 150 as one unit often argue that 11QPs[a] depends on MT.[127] At the same time, the deconstruction of the unit is used as one reason for this dependence.[128] Thus, there is circularity in an argument specifically referring to Ps 146 – 150. Since, in addition, the question of the overall dependence of 11QPs[a] on MT and related questions of the date of the completion of the Masoretic Psalter in the 2nd century BCE or 1st century CE are still debated,[129] for Ps 146 – 150 starting by reading 11QPs[a] separately is the best option available.[130]

For the Septuagint, at least for Psalms a Hebrew text similar to MT is usually assumed to predate its Septuagint translation.[131] However, even this is some-

---

2013, esp. 64, 67, 74 – 75, 95 – 96, 99; Hendel's series foreword in Fox 2015, ix), thus recognising the limits of deciding on one archetype only.

124 Tov 2014, 382 – 383.

125 Thus Goshen-Gottstein 1966, esp. 29; Talmon 1966, esp. 12; Skehan 1973, esp. 205; Dahmen 2003, esp. 311 – 315; Jain 2014, 278.

126 Thus Sanders 1967, esp. 13 – 14; Wilson 1983, esp. 388; Flint 1997, 198 – 201; Lange 2009, 434 – 436.

127 Thus Ballhorn 2004b, 336; Leuenberger 2004, 15, 20; Zenger 2008c, 810.

128 Thus Dahmen 2003, 309, 315; Leuenberger 2005, 200 – 203. Jain 2014 states "Das kleine Hallel Ps 146 – 150 ist aufgelöst"/"The Minor Hallel Ps 146 – 150 is dissolved" (256) *before* the conclusion that 11QPs[a] is based on the final redaction of the proto-Masoretic Psalter (278).

129 The proto-Masoretic Psalter is argued to have been completed in the 2nd century BCE e. g. by Lange 1998, 108; Zenger 2008b, 366; Janowski 2003, 1770; Jain 2014, 240; Zenger and Hossfeld 2016, 450 – 451. In contrast, Wilson 1990, esp. 136 – 137, 139, argues for a stabilisation of the entire Psalter only after the mid-1st century CE; Flint 2014, esp. 240 – 241, argues for 11QPs[a] and MT as independent parallel editions, and an early stabilisation of approximately Books I-III of the Psalter only. On the question of the editing of the Masoretic Psalter cf. Whybray 1996, 124 ("There is no evidence of the thorough and systematic changes that would have been necessary if the Psalter were to become the expression of a single theology. The stages by which it took its present shape lie mainly beyond our knowing."); on the instability of MT Yarchin 2015, esp. 789.

130 Cf. Ulrich 1996, 99 – 105, the addition mentioned there in 11QPs[a] is not in Psalm 146 but 145.

131 Cf. Gzella 2002, 62; Bons 2009a, 750 – 752.

times questioned,[132] for example due to Ps 151^{LXX}.[133] In addition to the issue of superscriptions,[134] it is also questioned if the LXX-Psalter is one unit[135] and even if so if the Psalms of the LXX-Psalter were translated in the Masoretic order.[136]

I.2.3 Impact on the End of the Psalter

For the end of the Psalter, the order and frame of Psalms 146–150 in the *Masoretic Text* allow for seeing them as a unit. However, Psalms 146–150 are preserved in the *Dead Sea Scrolls* in different orders. In their oldest extant manuscripts, out of Psalms 146–150 at least Ps 146, Ps 147, and Ps 148 are preserved as separate texts in contexts other than the Masoretic order. This calls into doubt the context of Psalms 146–150 in this order at the end of the Masoretic Psalter as a reason for their original coherence. The lack of opening Hallelujahs in Ps 148 and Ps 150 calls into doubt the framing Hallelujahs of Psalms 146–150 as a reason for their original coherence. Differences in the separate Psalms themselves such as the additions in Ps 146 and Ps 149 further stress the need for a more detailed analysis of DSS. The almost complete lack of final Hallelujahs, and the different grouping through superscriptions in the *Septuagint* calls into doubt the framing Hallelujahs of Psalms 146–150 as a reason for their original coherence. Psalms 146–147^{LXX} and Ps 151^{LXX} call into doubt the context of Psalms 146–150 in this order at the end of the Masoretic Psalter as a reason for their original coherence since in LXX six instead of five Psalms are the context, followed by another Psalm after the conclusion of Ps 150^{LXX}. Differences in the Psalms themselves such as the additions in Ps 146^{LXX} and Ps 148^{LXX} further stress the need for a more detailed analysis of LXX. Since there is no consensus on the relation of these text forms but the *differences between the text forms are noticeable*, it seems best to *read the three oldest text forms separately*.

---

132 Cf. Siegert 2001, 306–307, 311–312; Brütsch 2010, 101–115; Debel 2010, 173–190; Gauthier 2014, 20–21, 29.
133 See fn. 93, 110.
134 See fn. 109.
135 Thus Williams 2001, 260; Gzella 2002, 64. In contrast, a diachronic development is preferred by Siegert 2001, 311–312, and Ulrich 2000, 334, 336, argues that the LXX-Psalter was secondarily brought into conformity with MT.
136 Cf. Bons 2009a, 752.

I.3 Intertextuality

In addition to the Masoretic order and frame of Psalms 146 – 150, diachronic intertextual references are often given as a main reason for the argument that Psalms 146 – 150 are one originally coherent group. The first part of this reason is that *Psalms 146 – 150 are connected through intertextual references to one another*,[137] the second that *Psalms 146 – 150 are connected through shared reference texts*.[138] Psalms 146 – 150 are often seen to contain numerous intertextual references in an "anthological" style showing their late date and their literary composition for the end of the Psalter.[139] Whole lists of references are given to support this view.[140] However, these lists mostly include no indication of whether the texts share words, or phrases, or just topics, or how the direction of reference is established. Other commentators argue for similarities based on genre rather than references.[141] The intertextuality of Psalms 146 – 150 remains to be analysed.[142]

---

137 Cf. Leuenberger 2004, 346, 360 – 361 fn. 337; Zenger 2008c, esp. 807; Zenger 2008h, 827 (see fn. 18, 20).

138 Cf. Zenger 2008h, 827; Tucker 2014, 191 ("While an extensive analysis of the final Hallel remains the task of a subsequent study, a brief review does reveal certain connections between the final book in the Psalter and the concluding Hallel.").

139 Thus Ballhorn 2004b, 299 – 360, esp. 306; Leuenberger 2004, esp. 346 – 364; Weber 2010, 202 (referring to Ballhorn and Leuenberger).

140 Cf. e.g. for Ps 147 Leuenberger 2004, 348 – 351; Zenger 2008h, 827 – 828; for further examples see Brodersen 2013, 43 fn. 54.

141 Cf. e.g. Seybold 2010, 153 – 154, on Ps 147: "The reference to the close context of Ps 146 shows some parts (146:7 – 10) with similar motifs, but no actual quote of a verse. It has to be asked if this is what a substantial intertextual reference going beyond hymnic reminiscences looks like? [...] pointing out individual words [...] does not suffice to prove a close direct relation, let alone a dependence" (German original: "Der Rückgriff auf den 'Nahkontext' Ps 146 ergibt einige Stellen (146,7 – 10) mit ähnlichen Motiven, jedoch kein eigentliches Verszitat. Es stellt sich die Frage, ob so eine substantielle intertextuelle Beziehung aussieht, die über hymnische Anklänge hinausgeht? [...] genügen Hinweise auf einzelne Wörter [...] doch wohl nicht, um eine enge direkte Beziehung oder gar Abhängigkeit zu belegen". Even Leuenberger 2004, 349 – 350 fn. 290, writes that for Ps 147 "the most important correspondences with 148 can [...] be explained overall as coming from a common hymnic creation tradition" (German original: "können die wichtigsten Entsprechungen zu 148 [...] mehrheitlich aus gemeinsamer hymnischer Schöpfungstradition erklärt werden").

142 On the recent publication Neumann 2016 see I.1.

I.3.1 Diachronic Intertextuality

Intertextuality is a term to designate relations "between texts". In biblical studies, it is used in two main ways. The first, based on the postmodern origin of the term, is a reader-oriented, synchronic approach focussing on one text's relation to all other texts (be they written texts or abstract concepts) to which the modern reader has access. The second is an author-oriented, diachronic approach focussing on one texts's relation to the texts (usually written) to which the author had access.[143] Given the fact that the biblical texts are written texts (wherefore there must be at least one person, be it an author or compiler, who wrote them down) and ancient texts (wherefore ahistorical associations are not necessarily helpful for their explanations), I will focus on the author-oriented approach to intertextuality, and on *direct intertextual references* to written texts where an authorial intent is likely.[144] Since the development of MT is often unknown, absolute and relative dates have to be taken into account.

For the Septuagint, an analysis of intertextual references is important for three main reasons. Firstly, as for any text, inner-Greek intertextual references affect the interpretation of the LXX text on its own. Secondly, they affect the interpretation of the LXX text as compared to the MT: References in the LXX translation may be the same or different, different references may highlight peculiarities of the translation. Thirdly, they may in turn affect the interpretation of MT: Since the ancient LXX translators were close in time to MT, identical references may highlight the importance of such references in the Hebrew original whereas the lack of references in the translation puts a question mark on their importance in the original. This question mark is to be used with caution: For example, the text of LXX at the time of translation, its *Vorlage*, and the availability of LXX-translations of other biblical texts to the translator of one text are unknown. Furthermore, the translators may have failed to recognise intertextual references

---

143 For a literature survey cf. Miller 2011. Barton 2012, esp. 12, uses the terminology of a "hard" use of the term "intertextuality" as a post-structural theory about texts following the work of Julia Kristeva and her communist political opinions, and a "soft" use as a method for interpreting texts. Following Kynes 2012, 19 – 20, I take "intertextuality" in its "soft" meaning. Miller 2011, 305, proposes different terms for this "soft" meaning, but neither "inner-biblical allusion" nor "inner-biblical exegesis" cover references to extra-biblical texts (which are mentioned by Miller himself, 303), and both include the New Testament which is later and therefore not taken into account here. Carr 2012, esp. 524, argues for the term "influence" instead of intertextuality for diachronic intertextuality, but this term does not included the dimension of "text".
144 Only texts which can be dated to an earlier or overlapping time period are considered. While earlier traditions may be reflected in later texts, cf. Emanuel 2012, 72, this is less secure.

even though they were of importance in the original.[145] However, as an ancient witness LXX may still shed some light on the intertextuality of MT.

I.3.2 Criteria for Intertextual References

No standard criteria for the analysis of diachronic intertextual references exist, and given the unavoidable subjectivity of every interpreter there will always be different criteria, but there is a consensus that lexical resemblance is a necessary criterion.[146] The main purpose of this book is not to establish a theoretical framework for diachronic intertextuality and develop criteria,[147] but to apply them to explain Psalms 146 – 150 which so far lack an intertextual analysis based on *any* criteria. The analysis provided here for Ps 146 – 150 primarily aims at the use of criteria *at all*, and thus uses the best criteria currently available, in the awareness that they may well be refined in future research. The methods used for the two steps of identification and analyis of intertextual references are based on recent research by Will Kynes and David Emanuel on intertextual criteria for the Hebrew Bible.[148]

---

145 Cf. Dogniez 2005, 82–83, 95–96; Theocharous 2012, 5–8 (referring to Dogniez); Ngunga 2013, 38–47, esp. 40 (referring to Dogniez).

146 Cf. Miller 2011, 295–298.

147 Literary theory identifies "markers" for intertextual references without more detailed criteria, cf. e.g. Ben-Porat 1976, esp. 108 ("The marker is always identifiable as an element or pattern belonging to another independent text."). Sommer 1998, 6–31, also speaks about common topics, but the reuse of vocabulary is still central to intertextual connections, esp. 30–31. While the criteria of lexical and syntactical similarity are mostly seen as obvious, cf. e.g. Leonard 2008, esp. 245–246 ("To use an obvious example, a paragraph-long quotation, complete with citation, would naturally present a stronger claim for a textual connection than would a single, subtle wordplay offered without citation."), there is some empirical evidence in intratextual references, cf. for Job Kynes 2012, 46–49. Further research on empirical evidence of texts known to refer to each other is desirable, especially given debates about orality and textuality, on this cf. Edenburg 2010, esp. 144–146.

148 Out of a vast amount of literature, cf. for an overview Miller 2011, the most recent examples (which build on, e.g., Hays 1989, esp. 29–32; Carr 2012, esp. 524) are used here: Emanuel 2012, 17–20, and Kynes 2012, 37–60 (both based on earlier literature including Hays 1989, esp. 29–32). Out of the eight steps Kynes 2012 mentions, the first three are especially important: The first step gives criteria for the identification of references between two texts, the second and third step help to find out the direction of the reference. The following five steps may be important for further interpretation, but this depends on the outcome of the first three steps. The criteria used in Brodersen 2013, 43–44, based on Utzschneider 1989, 42–44, are refined here.

The first step is the synchronic identification of intertextual references. Texts both in HB and then other ancient Near Eastern (ANE) literature[149] are compared to the text which is to be interpreted. *Criteria* for the identification of intertextual references are lexical and syntactical similarity measured by the *number, order, and frequency of the shared words*. Specifically, an intertextual reference is likely if two texts share

- *[number of words]* a high number of words (excluding conjunctions and prepositions on their own, and specifically in LXX the very frequent conjunction or particle ὅτι/"for" for כִּי/"for", Greek relative pronouns or articles for the relative particle אֲשֶׁר, and Greek articles for the accusative marker אֶת on their own); the more words are shared the more likely is a reference, and/or
- *[order of words]* a number of words in syntactical similarity (i.e. in the same phrasing including word order and word forms); the more words are shared and the closer the syntactical similarity is the more likely is a reference, and/or
- *[frequency of words]* rare words (e.g. used only in the two texts compared and nowhere else in HB); the less frequent a word is the more likely is a reference.[150]

Other similarities are to be taken into account such as
- *[shared content]* a common topic, and/or
- *[shared form]* a common structure (e.g. genre, poetic devices).

If such other similarities occur without strong lexical resemblance, an intertextual reference is not usually likely, though the similar texts can still be helpful for the interpretation of the content. They can, however, not be used to date

---

149 While some of the ancient reference texts accessible to ancient authors may no longer be extant, it is still possible to at least use all extant texts for the explanation of the referring texts. When searching for reference texts, I start with other texts in *HB* and then proceed to *other ANE texts and non-textual sources*, since for the explanation of HB texts other HB texts are usually more important as they are written in the same language and in a similar tradition, and thus the progression is from limited and essential to potentially unlimited, less essential information for a historical-critical interpretation of the text. On this importance of HB above ANE texts cf. Kynes 2012, 42–46, esp. 45 (for Job HB "is its main contextual and intertextual background"). Given the same-language criterion, for the Greek Septuagint the Septuagint itself is the primary point of comparison, and references intended by the translator are examined.
150 The criterion of rare frequency is to be used with caution as it may be due to a lack of sources. For example, some words only occuring twice in HB are also found in the Hebrew Ben Sira discovered from 1896 CE (cf. Beentjes 1997, 1–2), e.g. מְנִים/"strings" in Sir 39:15, see p. 40–41 and p. 50, esp. fn. 197.

the text through direct authorial intent, and may only point towards a certain period of time sharing certain themes.

Similarities in language, form, and content may also point to a formula or a common third source instead of an intertextual reference between two texts, especially when there is

- *[formula]* a combination of words that could be formulaic language, genre-specific language, topic-specific language, or a common phrase, and/or
- *[multiple references]* close similarity to more than one passage which may point to interdependance of multiple texts but also to formulaic language, and/or
- *[no recurrence]* a lack of other connections to the same text.

The criteria for the identification of intertextual references cannot be applied mechanically, and cannot prove intertextual relations.[151] The evaluation provided here is based on the criteria with individual reasons given for every likely intertextual reference. Thus, the (mainly quantitative) criteria of number, order, and frequency of words are used to identify but not to define a reference, a (qualitative) evaluation is given in every case.[152] While the criteria used here are very strict, and could be criticised as being too strict since sometimes one frequent word or even a topic may also point to an intertextual reference, the use of strict criteria here aims to make a distinction between diachronic intertextual references and the more general use of common words or themes.[153] In addition to making such a distinction for Ps 146–150 *at all* rather than merely listing similar passages,[154] the novel comparison of intertextuality in the LXX[155] leads to new insights.

---

151 This is stressed by Miller 2011, 298. Cf. also Hays 1989, 29: "Precision in such judgment calls is unattainable, because exegesis is a modest imaginative craft, not an exact science; still, it is possible to specify certain rules of thumb".
152 Cf. Kynes 2012, 32.
153 This distinction is also stressed by Carr 2012, esp. 516, 524–525 (using the term "intertextuality" for the general and "influence" for the specific dimension, on this see fn. 143).
154 Risse 1995, 55–98, similarly distinguishes ""Intertextualität/"intertextuality" (analysed using Ben-Porat 1976) and "Wort- und Motivgeschichte"/"history of words and motifs", but similarity of motifs is included in criteria for intertextuality (Risse 1995, 64–65), thus leading to different results (e.g. Risse 1995, 93, on Job). On Neumann 2016 see I.1. See also fn. 148.
155 Similar criteria are used in LXX studies, cf. Ngunga 2013, esp. 49–50; van der Vorm-Croughs 2014, 299–204, esp. 302 (intertextuality within LXX named "anaphoric translation"). For Psalms cf. also Joosten 2012 (comparison with Pentateuch in MT and LXX, focus on rare words).

The second and third steps analyse the *direction of reference*, i.e. whether text one is earlier or later than text two, and whether text one refers to text two or vice versa.

In some cases it is possible to find *absolute dates* for a text, based on the primary evidence of explicit reference to historical events showing that the text is later than the events (though it remains unclear how much later the text is). Otherwise, secondary evidence for dating biblical texts such as inner-biblical parallels, the development of the language (e.g. early or late Hebrew words), and the development of (religious) topics has to be used. All secondary evidence depends on the dating of other texts.[156]

If step two is not possible because one or both of the texts cannot be dated or because the date ranges for the two texts overlap, step three is taken to find the *relative date* of the texts to each other.[157] Since intertextual references are an important source of information for dating of biblical texts, finding an absolute date in step two cannot be separated from finding a relative date in step three. Thus, even if step two is possible, step three is still necessary to strengthen the case for one direction above the other.

To answer the question "Which relative order of the texts makes better sense?", the internal and external coherence of both texts and their proclivity to allusions is examined according to the following criteria for relative dates:
- *[internal coherence]* the text in which the alluding text as a part of the text is less fitting is later (this assumes that parts of texts fit best in their original contexts),
- *[external coherence]* the text in which the alluding text as a reference to another text is more fitting later (this assumes that the reference to another text includes the context of this text),
- *[recurrence of allusions]* the text which shows more allusions in total is later.

I.3.3 Impact on the End of the Psalter

As I have demonstrated previously, Psalm 147 shows very few intertextual links with Psalms 146; 148–150, and none with Psalms 1–2, thus calling into doubt the argument that Psalms 146–150 are connected through intertextual references

---

156 Emanuel 2012, takes the development of language as a primary criterion. However, it depends on the dating of other texts. Kynes 2012, 49–50, 51, 53, stresses the general inconclusiveness of secondary evidence but also that inner-biblical allusions can make at least a relative date likely.
157 Cf. Kynes 2012, 51–54.

to one another, and opening up the question whether Psalms 146–150 are connected through shared reference texts.[158] Intertextuality also is of significance for the argument of a dependance of 11QPs[a] on MT: It is sometimes argued that 11QPs[a] shows weaker links between neighbouring Psalms than MT.[159]

I.4 Structure of this Study

An introductory look at the sources of Psalms 146–150 and their intertextual links has indicated that the main reasons for the argument of an original coherence of the end of the Psalter, namely *the context of Psalms 146–150 in this order at the end of the Masoretic Psalter*, the *framing Hallelujahs of Psalms 146–150*, and *intertextual links between Psalms 146–150*, are all highly problematic. Thus, a *hypothesis of a separate origin of each of Psalms 146–150* and their compilation for the end of the Masoretic Psalter but not other Psalters can be formulated. A closer separate analysis of each of Psalms 146–150 as well as a separate interpretation of each of their oldest text forms, MT, DSS, and LXX, is necessary to confirm this hypothesis. (Texts such as those at the end of 11QPs[a] or Ps 151[LXX] are not included in this book since it asks about the origin of Psalms 146–150 which stand at the end of the Masoretic Psalter rather than aiming to compare different "ends of Psalters".[160]) Therefore, a detailed historical-critical exegesis of each of the separate Psalms 146–150 in all of their separate oldest Hebrew and Greek sources, clarifying as far as possible the extent of direct intertextual references, and their relevance for the dating and interpretation of Psalms 146–150, is provided in the following five main chapters (II-VI).

In each chapter, MT as the only complete text in the original Hebrew is analysed first, then the fragmentary Hebrew DSS before LXX as a Greek translation. For DSS and LXX, despite their independent interpretation the focus is on relevant differences to MT since DSS are fragmentary, and for LXX the two aspects of interpretation on its own and comparison to MT cannot entirely be separated: the

---

158 Cf. Brodersen 2013, esp. 73–75.

159 Thus Leuenberger 2004, 15; Leuenberger 2005, 201. Intertextual links in 11QPs[a] are noted and discussed by Dahmen 2003, esp. 276–312; Jain 2014, 241–277, esp. 265.

160 Further research on different ends of Psalters is desirable. For example, both 11QPs[a] (cf. Kleer 1996, 282–286) and LXX but "outside the number" (cf. Schenker 2005, 27) stress David at the end. Syriac Psalters often end with Ps 151–155 (Syriac text: Baars 1972, 1–12; English translation: van Rooy 1999, 4–10) which partly also have 11QPs[a] equivalents, cf. Sanders 1967, 93–112. These different traditions may point towards the instability of any end of the Psalter before the 1st century CE, cf. Fabry 1986, 66. See also fn. 129.

finished translation is its own text in its own language, but still a translation of another text in another language. Differences between the translation and the original both highlight peculiarities of the translation and may reflect on its original. A repetition of explanations where DSS and LXX do not differ from MT would result in too much redundancy.

For each Psalm in each source, following a *translation* from the Hebrew or Greek (for LXX with the main differences to MT in *italics*)[161] and an *outline* (for LXX with the main differences to MT in **bold**),[162] an analysis focussing on its *form*, including *syntax*, *structure*, and *poetic devices*[163] (especially parallelism[164]) provides a framework for the interpretation of the content, and highlights features of the Psalm.[165] Following an analysis of *intertextuality*,[166] the main ques-

---

161 For MT, verses are numbered according to BHS, and additionally split into two half-verses at every athnaḥ, or at rviaᶜ gadol in Ps 146:10; 147:20; 149:9[MT] where there is no athnaḥ. For Ps 146:7–9; 147:8; 148:13–14[MT], to ease orientation within the respective Psalm and its secondary literature, tricolic verses are split into three cola (a, b, c) using rviaᶜ gadol (plus pazer in Ps 148:14[MT]). On the Masoretic disjunctive accents athnaḥ (ֽ, marking the middle of a verse), rviaᶜ gadol (ֺ, in poetic texts), and pazer (ֺ) cf. Joüon and Muraoka 2011, §15gh. For all Psalms, the framing "Hallelujahs", i.e. the imperative phrases הַלְלוּ־יָהּ/"Praise-Yah!", are put outside marked as H before the first and after the last verse due to the structure of Ps 146–150. For DSS sources, see p. 13–15, esp. fn. 86. For LXX, verses are numbered and split into half-verses according to the line breaks of Rahlfs 1979, 334–339, but the numbering of tricolic verses is kept in line with MT to ease comparison. The framing Hallelujahs or superscriptions are marked as H due to the structure of the Psalms.

162 The outline anticipates and summarises results especially regarding content and, set in italics, *syntax*, but is placed at the beginning to serve as a point of orientation.

163 Metre is not included since there is little consensus on Hebrew metre, cf. for an overview Hartenstein 2003a, 1763, for details Seybold 2003, esp. 102–127, and it does not contribute to the argument of this book. Further research on LXX metre is desirable, for Prov 9[LXX] cf. Louw 2007, esp. 199–206.

164 While there is a debate about parallelism in HB, the categories of *parallelismus membrorum* with *membra* referring to two parallel sentences forming two halves of one verse, and of synonymous (A=B, "which is the same as"), antithetic (A<>B, "but"), and synthetic (A+B "and also") parallelisms still provide a guideline while every text has to be analysed individually, cf. Hartenstein 2003a for an overview, Seybold 2007, for the debate and arguments for using the categories introduced by Robert Lowth, cf. Lowth 1753, esp. 82, 180. Further research on LXX parallelisms is desirable, cf. Bons 2007, esp. 117–119, 128–130.

165 On form cf. Schweizer 1977, 37.

166 Only references with some probability or a significant impact on previous interpretations are analysed. Shared words are listed in their order of occurrence in the reference text. For LXX, very frequent words shared in Greek *but not in Hebrew*, specifically κύριος/"Lord" for the name of God and αὐτός/"he" which often replaces Hebrew suffixes, are not listed unless they are of specific importance.

tions about *content* are answered.[167] The interpretation further includes an analysis of each Psalm's *genre*,[168] *date*,[169] and *unity*[170] before an *overall interpretation*. For the fragmentary DSS, interpretations are restricted to relevant differences to MT.

The analysis of the individual Psalms 146 – 150 is presented in reverse order compared to MT for two reasons: Firstly, Psalm 150 as the final Psalm of the Masoretic Psalter is of special importance for the end of the Psalter, and attracts an especially large number of contradicting interpretations and intertextual assumptions. It is thus treated extensively including the critical analysis of numerous commentaries in several modern languages to serve as an example for the analysis of the other Psalms. Secondly, the reverse order emphasises the importance of reading Psalms 146 – 150 individually rather than in a progressing order. While any random order of the five Psalms would also emphasise this point, the reverse order has the pragmatic advantage of ensuring that the discussion of each Psalm may still be found easily without referring to the table of contents.

---

167 Comparison to other biblical and non-biblical texts as well as non-textual sources cannot be exhaustive, but at least those sources most commonly found in scholarly literature which are most relevant are covered. Oral traditions may have existed but are inaccessible as such.
168 The genre "hymn" is most important for Ps 146 – 150. A minimal definition of "hymn" includes an introduction calling to praise and a main section, often introduced with ‫כִּ‬/"for", with God's actions for which praise is in order, cf. Hartenstein 2003b, 1764 – 1765. Hymn in this minimal definition does not necessarily point to a cultic setting. Further research on LXX genres is desirable.
169 While absolute dates are of importance already for analysing intertextual references, dates depend on the analyses of content and genre and are discussed after those.
170 Textual criticism and literary criticism are discussed as far as they are of relevance to the interpretation. For LXX, manuscript evidence is taken from Rahlfs 1979, 333 – 339, with a focus on Greek manuscripts rather than those in other languages.

II Psalm 150

II.1 Psalm 150^{MT}

II.1.1 Translation of Psalm 150^{MT}

1H	Praise-Yah!	הַלְלוּ יָהּ	1H
1a	Praise God for his holiness,	הַלְלוּ־אֵל בְּקָדְשׁוֹ	1a
1b	praise him for his mighty firmament!	הַלְלוּהוּ בִּרְקִיעַ עֻזּוֹ:	1b
2a	Praise him for his strong deeds,	הַלְלוּהוּ בִגְבוּרֹתָיו	2a
2b	praise him according to his abundant greatness!	הַלְלוּהוּ כְּרֹב גֻּדְלוֹ:	2b
3a	Praise him with a blast of a horn,	הַלְלוּהוּ בְּתֵקַע שׁוֹפָר	3a
3b	praise him with harp and lyre!	הַלְלוּהוּ בְּנֵבֶל וְכִנּוֹר:	3b
4a	Praise him with drum and dance,	הַלְלוּהוּ בְתֹף וּמָחוֹל	4a
4b	praise him with strings and pipe!	הַלְלוּהוּ בְּמִנִּים וְעוּגָב:	4b
5a	Praise him with cymbals of sound,	הַלְלוּהוּ בְצִלְצְלֵי־שָׁמַע	5a
5b	praise him with cymbals of noise!	הַלְלוּהוּ בְּצִלְצְלֵי תְרוּעָה:	5b
6	Let all the breath[1] praise Yah!	כֹּל הַנְּשָׁמָה תְּהַלֵּל יָהּ	6
6H	Praise-Yah!	הַלְלוּ־יָהּ:	6H

II.1.2 Form of Psalm 150^{MT}

Outline of Psalm 150^{MT}

1H	Framing *Imperative*	
1a–2b	Calls to Praise	Reasons: God's Qualities
	Imperatives + Object Suffixes	*Prepositional Phrases (3x בְּ, 1x כְּ) + Suffixes*
3a–5b	Calls to Praise	Means: Musical Instruments
	Imperatives + Object Suffixes	*Prepositional Phrases (6x בְּ)*
6	Calls to Praise	Subject: All Humans
	Subject + Jussive + Object	
6H	Framing *Imperative*	

Syntax of Psalm 150^{MT}

The only *verb* in Ps 150, הלל/"praise", is used 12 times in a piᶜel imperative plural masculine (twice in the frame, twice each in vv.1–5) and once in a piᶜel jussive

---

1 Less literal: "all that breathes".

DOI 10.1515/9783110536096-002

singular feminine (v.6).[2] The exclusive use of imperatives and jussives of הלל/
"praise" indicates that the main message of Ps 150 is a *call to praise*.

The *subject, i.e. who is to praise,* is not made explicit before v.6: Whereas in
the preceding verses the subject is an anonymous *"you"* (masculine plural, can
include feminine subjects),[3] in v.6 the subject is כֹּל הַנְּשָׁמָה/"*all the breath*" (construct כֹּל/"all of" followed by the feminine נְשָׁמָה/"breath", determined by the article). Thus, v.6 can be taken as a summary of the preceding verses, and "all the
breath" seems to be addressed by all the imperatives. The summarising character
of v.6 is confirmed by the reversed *word order* which stresses the subject rather
than the act of praising.[4]

The *object, i.e. who is to be praised,* is made explicit at the beginning and
end: It is יָהּ/"*Yah*" (vv.1, 6),[5] also known as אֵל/"*God*" (v.1, without article probably determined like a proper name given the uniqueness of God expressed in the
Psalm).[6] The suffixes of הַלְלוּהוּ/"praise him" in vv.1–5 refer to the object אֵל/
"God" in v.1. Not only the framing הַלְלוּ־יָהּ/"Praise-Yah!" in vv.1 and 6 makes it
clear that אֵל/"God" is the same as יָהּ/"Yah", but יָהּ/"Yah" is also the object of
the jussive in v.6. While God = Yah is central to every verse, he is not the subject
but the object of Ps 150.[7]

Every sentence in Ps 150 also has an *adverbial phrase*[8] except for v.6, again
an indication of its summarising nature. All adverbial phrases consist of one or
more nouns preceded by בְּ/"in" (except v.2b) or כְּ/"according to" (v.2b) (prepositions in Ps 150 are discussed in detail on p. 44–47). In vv.1–2, all nouns are determined by a suffix referring to אֵל/"God" in v.1,[9] but in vv.3–5 the nouns are
undetermined, thus referring to musical instruments in general.

Structure of Psalm 150^MT

The structure of Ps 150 is very regular: It begins and ends with הַלְלוּ־יָהּ/"Praise-
Yah!". Within this frame, all the asyndetic sentences except the summarising v.6

---

2 Due to the surrounding imperatives a jussive is more likely than an imperfect with a possible
future meaning "she will praise", cf. Gesenius and Kautzsch 1909, §107.

3 Cf. Gesenius and Kautzsch 1909, §122g.

4 Cf. Gesenius and Kautzsch 1909, §142f; Joüon and Muraoka 2011, §155k, nb. For Ps 150:6 similarly Human 2011, 4.

5 יָהּ/"Yah" is a short form of יהוה/"YHWH", cf. Gesenius 2013, s.v. יָהּ u. יָהּ-.

6 Cf. Gesenius and Kautzsch 1909, §125f.

7 Criticised theologically by Brueggemann 1988, 108. However, the reason for praise includes
God's strong deeds, see p. 44–47.

8 Cf. Gesenius and Kautzsch 1909, §100b; Joüon and Muraoka 2011, §102a.

9 Also noted by Seidel 1981, 89; Human 2011, 4.

start with the imperative הַלְלוּ/"praise!" followed by a prepositonal phrase. In vv.1–2 these prepositional phrases refer to God's qualities as reasons[10] for praise, in vv.3–5 to musical instruments as means of praise. In vv.1–2 the phrases alternate between one noun (vv.1a, 2a) and two nouns connected by a construct state (vv.1b, 2b), in vv.3–5 there are always two nouns, connected at the beginning and end of this group of verses by a construct state (vv.3a, 5ab) and in the middle by a waw copulativum (vv.3b, 4ab). The break between verses 2 and 3 is further stressed by כְּ/"according to" instead of בְּ/"in" in v.2b.[11] Furthermore, while בְּ is used in both vv.1–2 and 3–5, its meaning changes from "because of" to "with".[12]

Some commentators note that in vv.1–2 the nouns refer to places or abstract ideas connected with God, whereas in vv.3–5 the nouns refer to concrete instruments and actions, wherefore vv.3–5 are more dynamic than the static vv.1–2.[13] However, vv.1–2 also contain action[14] (e.g. גְּבוּרֹתָיו/"his strong deeds"), and action is not stressed in vv.3–5 as in the place of verbal forms there are two nouns (תֵּקַע/"blast", שֵׁמַע/"sound", see p. 48, 51). Either way, vv.1–2 are clearly separated from vv.3–5 through the suffixes referring to God. There is only one instrument in v.3a, and one instrument is repeated in v.5.[15] This frame points to a coherence of vv.3–5.

Thus, Ps 150 is structured into a Hallelujah-frame around three parts: vv.1–2 (why and how) – vv.3–5 (how) – v.6 (by whom God is to be praised). Within v.2, the change of preposition changes the question answered from "why" to "how".

A similar structure is recognised by many commentators.[16] Other structures are less likely.[17]

---

10 See p. 44–47.

11 Also noted by Zenger 1997b, 100; Mathys 2000, 339.

12 See p. 44–47, esp. fn. 140.

13 Cf. Schweizer 1977, 41; Zenger 2008k, 873 (referring to Schweizer).

14 Cf. Seidel 1981, 89.

15 Also noted by Seidel 1981, 89, 94; Ballhorn 2004b, 350; Zenger 2008k, 873–874.

16 Cf. Allen 1983, 323; Gerstenberger 2001, 458; Auffret 2002, 258-260 (referring to Auffret 1995, 284–287); with v.1 answering "where" Gunkel 1926, 622; Buttrick 1955, 760 (referring to Gunkel); Auffret 1995, 284; Weber 2003, 384 (why in v.2b only); Leuenberger 2004, 358; Cha 2006, 109–110; Zenger 2008k, 873–874, 876; Scaiola 2010a, 295; Weber 2010, 204; Human 2011, 4-8; with v.1 answering "who" Keck 1996, 1278.

17 Cf. Mowinckel 1957, 86–87 (vv.1–2, 3–4, 5–6), however, this is against the coherent content of vv.3–5, similarly criticised by Allen 1983, 323 (see fn. 16); Rodd 2007, 405 (ten imperatives only structure); Janowski 2012, 51–52 (vv.1–2, 3–4, 5, 6; temple imagery), however, see p. 52–54; leaving out verses Mathys 2000, 339 (vv.1, 2, 3–5); Strawn and LeMon 2007, 460–462 (vv.1, 3–5, 6).

Poetic Devices in Psalm 150[MT]

Ps 150:1–5 consists of *synthetic parallelisms:* vv.3–4 refer to different instruments in each half-verse. v.5 probably also refers to different kinds of instruments or maybe to different ways of playing them, and vv.1–2 most likely refer to different qualities giving reasons to praise God.[18] V.6 only comprises one sentence and is thus without parallelism, which again stresses the concluding character of v.6.

Ps 150 is often connected with *number symbolism*. Most commentators choose the number *ten* as significant[19] and regard it as a possible reference to ten words of creation (in Gen 1),[20] the ten commandments (in Ex 20/Deut 5),[21] or both,[22] or to completeness.[23] *Thirteen* is sometimes seen as a reference to the thirteen attributes of God.[24] Some see *twelve* as referring to the twelve tribes of Israel and the twelve months of the year.[25] Some also note occurrences of *seven* referring to completeness (seven instruments in vv.3–5[26]), or *four* referring to all the earth (four lines in vv.1–2[27]), and there are further suggestions.[28] Others see number symbolism as insignificant.[29]

While in HB four, seven, ten, and twelve do sometimes have symbolic meaning, thirteen is entirely insignificant, and number symbolism is of little significance in HB overall.[30] This general background combined with the fact that there are at least three different counts of the same word הלל/"praise" in

---

18 Ballhorn 2004b, 348, argues that all parallelisms in Ps 150 are synonymous. However, this is unlikely, see p. 46, 51.
19 Cf. Gunkel 1926, 622; Human 2011, 5.
20 Cf. Gillingham 2012, 389 (referring to Gen 1); Rodd 2007, 405 (referring to Mishna Abot 5.1).
21 Cf. Mathys 2000, 332 (explicit number ten in Deut 4:13; 10:4); Weber 2003, 385 (Ex 21:1–17; Deut 5:6–2 with Deut 4:13; 10:4).
22 Cf. Zenger 2008k, 875; Human 2011, 5 (Gen 1, Ex 20:1–17; Deut 4:13; 5:6–21; 10:4; "Torah character" of praise).
23 Cf. Weber 2003, 385; Zenger 2008k, 875.
24 Cf. Zenger 2008k, 875 (unlikely possibility, postbiblical Jewish interpretation of Ex 34:6–7); possibility mentioned but not adopted by Mathys 2000, 332 (referring to Feuer 1985, 1736); Gillingham 2012, 389 (referring to later Jewish tradition and specifically Cohen and Oratz 1992, referring to Kimḥi). For the medieval commentary of Kimḥi cf. the edition Kimḥi, Baker, and Nicholson 1973, 166–167, referring to Rosh Hashana 17b in the Talmud for which cf. the edition Simon 1983 (the thirteen attributes are based on Ex 34:6–7).
25 Cf. Zenger 2008k, 875; mentioned but not adopted by Mathys 2000, 332 (twelve tribes).
26 Cf. Zenger 2008k, 875; however, cymbals are only counted once, and dance is left out.
27 Cf. Zenger 2008k, 875.
28 Cf. Zenger 2008k, 875. However, as Zenger himself notes, little is known about number symbolism in biblical times, see fn. 30.
29 Cf. Hupfeld 1871, 461.
30 On number symbolism cf. Herrmann 2004, esp. 472–473; Boring 2009, esp. 296–299.

Ps 150, the sheer amount of different suggestions for counting and the meaning of numbers in Ps 150, and the lack of intertextual references to specific texts such as Ex 20/Deut 5 make it unlikely that Ps 150 refers to specific numbers. Indeed, most interpretations of number symbolism in Ps 150 rely on later Jewish writings.[31]

Neither alphabetic features,[32] assonances,[33] or vowel patterns[34] are nearly as dominant as the regular structure of Ps 150.

II.1.3 Intertextuality in Psalm 150[MT]

Importance

Some scholars merely list other HB passages when commenting on Ps 150.[35] Some claim that Ps 150 definitely depends on other texts such as Gen 1–2,[36] Deut 3:24,[37] 2 Sam 6:5,[38] Ps 98,[39] Ps 149,[40] or the entire group of Ps 146–150.[41] Others claim that Psalm 150 definitely does not depend on other texts such as 2 Sam 6:5,[42] or Ps 98,[43] and shows remarkable differences to Ps 146–149.[44] Since the assumption of a dependence of Ps 150 on other texts leads to further assumptions regarding date and content of the Psalm, for example that Ps 150 definitely dates from postexilic times,[45] that the origin of the Psalm is connected to the group Ps 146–150 and it must be read as a literary Psalm concluding the Psalter,[46] or that Ps 150 must be read after Ps 149 and its overall interpretation

---

31 Cf. Feuer 1985, 1736, for rabbinic sources. Mathys 2000, 332-333, stresses a difference in dignity between the Old Testament and its later interpretation.
32 Cf. Ceresko 2006. However, an alphabetic structure is hardly discernible.
33 Cf. Dahood 1970, 360; Allen 1983, 324; Human 2011, 4.
34 Cf. Seybold 1996, 547; Human 2011, 4. However, there are many other vowels.
35 Cf. Gerstenberger 2001, 459; Human 2011, 6.
36 Cf. Human 2011, 2, 8–9.
37 Cf. Ballhorn 2004b, 349.
38 Cf. Mathys 2000, 336, 343.
39 Cf. Zenger 2008k, 876.
40 Cf. Mathys 2000, 343; Ballhorn 2004b, 352.
41 Cf. Mathys 2000, 343; Zenger 2008c, 808–809; Zenger 2008k, 875.
42 Cf. Ballhorn 2004b, 352.
43 Cf. Ballhorn 2004b, 351.
44 Cf. Brueggemann 1991, 67; Scaiola 2010a, 295.
45 Cf. Human 2011, 9.
46 Cf. Zenger 2008c, 808–809; Zenger 2008k, 875.

must be eschatological,[47] a precise analysis of possible intertextual references is of fundamental importance for the interpretation of Ps 150.

Analysis

While commentators argue that Psalm 150 refers to *Genesis*,[48] especially Gen 1:6–20,[49] Gen 2:7, and Gen 7:22,[50] such arguments rest on two cases of one isolated shared word only, רָקִיעַ/"firmament" in Ps 150:1 which also appears multiple times in Gen 1:6–20, and נְשָׁמָה/"breath" in Ps 150:6 which also appears in Gen 2:7 and Gen 7:22. In all three cases, only one significant word is shared in the entire relevant chapter of Genesis. Since both words appear in various texts other than Genesis and Ps 150 (for example, רָקִיעַ/"firmament" multiple times in Ezek 1 in a non-creation context, and likewise נְשָׁמָה/"breath" in Josh 10–11), neither the number nor the order nor the frequency of shared words suffice to make a reference between Ps 150 and Genesis likely.[51]

While it is sometimes argued that Ps 150:4 refers to *Exodus 15:20*,[52] the only shared word is תֹּף/"drum". For "dance", in Ex 15:20 מְחֹלֹת/"dances" as the feminine plural of מְחֹלָה/"dance" is used, whereas Ps 150:4 uses the masculine singular noun מָחוֹל/"dance". Even if the two nouns for "dancing" are taken as essentially the same noun, neither the number nor the order nor the frequency of shared words suffice to make a reference from Ps 150 to Ex 15 likely.

Some commentators view Ps 150:2 as referring to *Deuteronomy 3:24* and therefore to the Exodus (even though Deut 3 in fact recounts conquests).[53] However, all of the three words which Ps 150:1–2 and Deut 3:24 have in common – אֵל/"god", גֹּדֶל/"greatness", and גְּבוּרֹת/"strong deeds" – are found in many other texts. Neither the number nor the order nor the frequency of shared words suffice to make a reference from Ps 150 to Deut 3 likely.[54]

---

47 Cf. Ballhorn 2004a, 16.
48 Cf. Zenger 1997a, 18; Ballhorn 2004a, 16; Human 2011, 2.
49 Cf. Human 2011, 9.
50 Cf. Human 2011, 9.
51 Cf. Seidel 1981, 93–94 (no reference to Gen 1 since רָקִיעַ/"firmament" in Gen is used only in a construct state with הַשָּׁמַיִם/"the heavens"). However, רָקִיעַ/"firmament" is first mentioned in Gen 1:6–7 with no form of שָׁמַיִם/"heavens" connected to it.
52 Cf. Mathys 2000, 335; Weber 2010, 208.
53 Cf. Zenger 2011 [1996], 61 (but Ps 150 also refers to all of history); Ballhorn 2004b, 349.
54 Similarly Zenger 2011 [1996], 61, despite assuming a reference to Deut 3:24 and the Exodus, notes: "Der Plural "Machterweise" und die Verwendung des Motivs in der Psalmensprache (vgl. Ps 20,7; 71,16; 106,2; 145,4.11.12) legen freilich nahe, nicht an einzelne Heilstaten, sondern an JHWHs gesamtes Geschichtshandeln zu denken."/"The plural form "strong deeds" and the

Without explicitly assuming a reference to *Joshua 6*, the horn in Ps 150 is often associated with priests,[55] and Josh 6 is a prime example for this association[56] (e.g. Josh 6:4). שׁוֹפָר/"horn" and תְּרוּעָה/"noise" (and the root תקע/"blow" used in a different form in Ps 150:3) all occur multiple times in Josh 6 (e.g. Josh 6:20). However, since only two words are shared (low number), their order differs (low syntactic similarity), and both are common words (high frequency), a reference is unlikely.

Some commentators argue for a reference to *2 Samuel 6:5*.[57] Shared are כֹּל/ "all", כִּנּוֹר/"lyre", נֵבֶל/"harp", תֹּף/"drum", and צֶלְצְלִים/"cymbals". Syntactical similarity is limited: In 2 Sam 6:5 כִּנּוֹר/"lyre, נֵבֶל/"harp", תֹּף/"drum", and צֶלְצְלִים/ "cymbals" are used with בְּ/"with". However, in Ps 150 the order of words is נֵבֶל/"harp", כִּנּוֹר/"lyre", תֹּף/"drum", צֶלְצְלִים/"cymbals", whereas in 2 Sam 6:5 the first two are reversed, and plural instead of singular forms are used. צֶלְצְלִים/"cymbals" is rare and used only in Ps 150 and 2 Sam 6:5.[58] In the same chapter, 2 Sam 6:14–15 have additional words in common with Ps 150, namely כֹּל /"all", עֹז/"might" (though used of David in 2 Sam 6:14 but of God's firmament in Ps 150:1), תְּרוּעָה/"noise", and שׁוֹפָר/"horn". For an overview, words shared with Ps 150 are <u>underlined</u> here:

2 Sam 6:5:

וְדָוִד ׀ וְכָל־בֵּית יִשְׂרָאֵל מְשַׂחֲקִים לִפְנֵי יְהוָה בְּכֹל עֲצֵי בְרוֹשִׁים וּבְכִנֹּרוֹת וּבִנְבָלִים וּבְתֻפִּים וּבִמְנַעַנְעִים וּבְצֶלְצֶלִים׃

"And David and <u>all</u> the house of Israel were being merry before YHWH with <u>all</u> wood of cypresses, with <u>lyres</u> and <u>with harps</u> and <u>with drums</u> and with rattles and <u>with cymbals</u>."

2 Sam 6:14–15:

וְדָוִד מְכַרְכֵּר בְּכָל־עֹז לִפְנֵי יְהוָה וְדָוִד חָגוּר אֵפוֹד בָּד׃ ¹⁵וְדָוִד וְכָל־בֵּית יִשְׂרָאֵל מַעֲלִים אֶת־אֲרוֹן יְהוָה בִּתְרוּעָה וּבְקוֹל שׁוֹפָר׃

"And David whirled with <u>all</u> <u>might</u> before YHWH, and David was girded with an ephod of white linen. ¹⁵And David and <u>all</u> the house of Israel were bringing up the ark of YHWH with <u>noise</u> and with the voice of the <u>horn</u>."

Ps 150 and 2 Sam 6 also share a topic (music made for YHWH). While the form is different (Ps 150 is a call to make music, 2 Sam 6 a narrative describing music

---

use of this motif in the language of the psalms (cf. Ps 20:7; 71:16; 106:2; 145:4, 11, 12) suggest to think not of individual deeds of salvation but of all of YHWH's action in history."

55 See p. 48–52.

56 Cf. Gunkel 1926, 622; Buttrick 1955, 760; Mathys 2000, 334; criticised by van der Ploeg 1974, 507.

57 Cf. Mathys 2000, 336; Zenger 2008k, 876; criticised by Ballhorn 2004b, 352.

58 Cf. Clines 2010, s.v. צֶלְצְלִים; Gesenius 2013, s.v. צֶלְצָלִים.

being made), there is strong lexical similarity including a rare word found only in these two texts, but little syntactical similarity, and another rare word מְנַעַנְעִים/ "rattles" only appears in 2 Sam 6:5 in HB and not in Ps 150. The shared words might be due to the common topic of music: Except for צֶלְצְלִים/"cymbals", all of the words are collocated at least in pairs in numerous other related texts (multiple references).[59] Furthermore, there is virtually no recurrence of intertextual references between 2 Sam and Ps 150. It is therefore unlikely that Ps 150 refers to 2 Sam 6:5 (thus restricting music to all of Israel outside the temple and connecting it with David) or that 2 Sam 6:5 refers to Ps 150 (thus including a hymn into its narrative about music made by all of Israel).

A reference to *1 Chronicles 15:16–28 and 2 Chronicles 5:12–14* is sometimes seen.[60] There are, however, much closer similarities between 1 Chr 15:28 and 2 Sam 6:14, and it is usually assumed that the author of 1+2 Chr knew some form of 1+2 Sam (and 1+2 Kings).[61] A reference between Ps 150 and 1 Chr 15:16–28 or 2 Chr 5:12–14 is unlikely: The only word shared between these texts that does not appear in 2 Sam 6 is the frequent הלל/"praise" (2 Chr 15:13), whereas the rare word צֶלְצְלִים/"cymbals" is not used in Chr.

Some commentators maintain that Ps 150 refers to *Psalms 1–2* at least implicitly since they see at least parts of Ps 146–150 and Ps 1–2 as written specifically to frame the book of Psalms,[62] or Psalms 1–2 and 146–150[63] or 149–150[64] as forming a frame for the Psalter. However, shared frequent words such as כֹּל/ "all" in Ps 150:6, Ps 1:3, Ps 2:12 and קֹדֶשׁ/"holiness" in Ps 150:1 and Ps 2:6 do not suffice to make a reference likely.[65]

Some commentators argue for a reference to *Psalm 96 and 98*,[66] or a reference from the group Ps 146–150 to a group including Ps 96 and 98, leading to eschatological interpretations,[67] while for Ps 98 sometimes only a weak reference is seen.[68] With Ps 96 only the frequent words כֹּל/"all", הלל/"praise", עַ/

59 See p. 48–52.
60 Cf. Zenger 2008k, 876.
61 Cf. Steins 2016, 321.
62 Cf. Zenger 1993a, 45; Zenger 1993b, 51; Zenger 1997b, 100, 104; Zenger 2008c, 808–809; Janowski 2012, 50–54 (following Zenger).
63 Cf. Janowski 2012, 50–54.
64 Cf. Ballhorn 2004b, 344.
65 Also noted by Weber 2010, 207, who nevertheless reads Ps 1 and 150 as a frame for the Psalter.
66 Cf. Zenger 2008k, 876.
67 For Ps 93–100 cf. Ballhorn 2004b, 359; for Ps 96; 98; 100 Zenger 2008c, 808; for YHWH-king-Psalms Vincent 1999, 69 (eschatology).
68 Cf. Ballhorn 2004b, 351.

"might", and קֹדֶשׁ/"holiness" are shared, with Ps 98 קֹדֶשׁ/"holiness", כֹּל/"all", כִּנּוֹר/"lyre", and שׁוֹפָר/"horn". Due to the lack of syntactical similarity a reference is unlikely.

A reference to *Psalm 103* is sometimes seen,[69] but only the frequent words כֹּל/"all" and קֹדֶשׁ/"holiness" are shared without syntactical similarity, wherefore a reference is unlikely.

Many commentators hold the view that there is a reference to *Psalm 145*,[70] and Ps 150 is sometimes taken to be written as a new end of the Psalter after Ps 145,[71] or it is argued that Ps 146–150 all refer to Ps 145,[72] or together grew out of Ps 145 as a new end of the Psalter.[73] However, with Ps 150 only כֹּל/"all", הלל/"praise", גְּבוּרָה/"strength" and קֹדֶשׁ/"holiness" (in Ps 145:21, like in Ps 150:1, probably "holiness" and not "sanctuary", as praising the holy name of YHWH is more likely than praising the name of his temple) are shared without syntactical similarity, wherefore a reference is unlikely.[74]

Similarities with *Psalm 146* are stressed by some commentators,[75] while others either do not mention Ps 146[76] or stress the differences.[77] Only הלל/"praise", אֵל/"god" and כֹּל/"all" are shared, and the main syntactical and structural similarity is the framing הַלְלוּ־יָהּ/"Praise-Yah!". Apart from this frame, a reference is unlikely.

Similarities with *Psalm 147* are stressed.[78] However, only the frequent words הלל/"praise", כֹּל/"all", כִּנּוֹר/"lyre", and גְּבוּרָה/"strength" are shared. Thus, apart from the shared frame הַלְלוּ־יָהּ/"Praise-Yah!", a reference is unlikely.

A reference to *Psalm 148* is seen by some commentators[79] and similarities are stressed,[80] while other commentators stress differences.[81] Frequently, Ps 148 is used to support the assumption that in Ps 150:1 heavenly beings are called to

---

69 Cf. Zenger 2008k, 876.
70 Cf. Risse 1995, 202, 212; Zenger 1997b, 99–100; Zenger 2008k, 876, 884; Scaiola 2010a, 282; Weber 2010, 209; Human 2011, 3, 8.
71 Cf. Weber 2010, 204.
72 Cf. Kratz 2004, 629; Kratz 2012, 233.
73 Cf. Janowski 2013, 370.
74 References to Ps 145 are also unlikely for Ps 147–149 but not Ps 146, see p. 238–239.
75 Cf. Human 2011, 2.
76 Cf. Zenger 2008k, 876.
77 Cf. Brueggemann 1988, 93; Weber 2010, 204.
78 Cf. Human 2011, 3.
79 Cf. Mathys 2000, 343 ("universalisierende Korrektur"/"universalising correction" of Ps 148); Zenger 2008k, 876; Human 2011, 3 (following Mathys).
80 Cf. Mathys 2000, 339 (Ps 148 "Zwillingsbruder"/"twin brother"); Weber 2003, 385.
81 Cf. Seidel 1981, 93.

praise YHWH,[82] and that Ps 150:6 includes in its call to praise humans and animals as well as heavenly beings,[83] but also to support the opposite statement that Ps 150 in contrast to Ps 148 focusses on humans.[84] However, only the frequent words הלל/"praise", and כֹּל/"all" are shared. Since the number of shared words is so small and both words are so frequent, even the syntactical similarity in the frequent use of הַלְלוּהוּ/"praise him!" does not suffice for a reference. Thus, apart from the shared frame הַלְלוּ־יָהּ/"Praise-Yah!", a reference is unlikely.

Many commentators argue for a reference to *Psalm 149*,[85] and similarities between Psalm 150 and Psalm 149 are often stressed,[86] leading to reading Ps 150 as following on from Ps 149, up to the assumption that kings and rulers are not included in the universal praise of Ps 150.[87] Shared are הלל/"praise", מָחוֹל/"dance", תֹּף/"drum", כִּנּוֹר/"lyre", אֵל/"god", and כֹּל/"all". There is limited syntactical similarity as in Ps 149:3 like in Ps 150:3 – 4 מָחוֹל/"dance", תֹּף/"drum", and כִּנּוֹר/"lyre" are in some way combined with בְּ/"with" and הלל/"praise", but the order of the words and the use of the preposition differs. Thus, apart from the shared frame הַלְלוּ־יָהּ/"Praise-Yah!", a reference is unlikely.

It is sometimes argued that Psalm 150 refers to *Isaiah 6*[88] or at least shares the idea of either a heavenly temple where heavenly beings worship YHWH[89] or (using the same text Isa 6!) an earthly temple.[90] However, since Isa 6 and Psalm 150 share no significant words, any reference between the texts is unlikely.

A reference to *Ezekiel 1 – 3; 10* is sometimes seen.[91] However, the only significant word these chapters have in common with Ps 150 is רָקִיעַ/"firmament", and as in the case of Gen 1 a reference is unlikely.

Commentators argue for a reference from *Ben Sira 39:15* to Psalm 150 (not vice versa), taking this as an indication that the final redaction of the Psalter is close to the time and place of Ben Sira,[92] and similarities are often stressed.[93]

---

82 Cf. Kraus 1978, 1149 – 1150; Allen 1983, 322 – 323.

83 Cf. Keck 1996, 1280; Weber 2003, 148; Human 2011, 8.

84 Thus despite the "twin brother" connection (see fn. 80) Mathys 2000, 339, 342.

85 Cf. Zenger 2011 [1996], 56; Mathys 2000, 343; Ballhorn 2004b, 339 (see fn. 87), 352; Zenger 2008j, 870; Zenger 2008k, 876; Weber 2010, 204.

86 Cf. Gunkel 1926, 623; Ballhorn 2004a, 16; Human 2011, 3; Gillingham 2012, 386.

87 Cf. Ballhorn 2004b, 339. However, neither kings nor rulers are mentioned in Ps 150 which refers to all humans, see p. 55 – 57.

88 Cf. Human 2011, 9.

89 Cf. Mathys 2000, 338; Hartenstein 2007, 118.

90 Cf. Seidel 1981, 93 – 94.

91 Cf. Seidel 1981, 99; Human 2011, 9.

92 Cf. Zenger 1999, 124-125.

93 Cf. Gunkel 1926, 623.

The extant Hebrew of Sir 39:15 shares נֵבֶל/"harp", מִנִּים/"strings" (rare word only used in these two texts and Ps 45:9) and תְּרוּעָה/"noise" with Ps 150.[94] However, the late rediscovery of the Hebrew text of Ben Sira[95] shows that the rare-word criterion has to be used with caution: Through its preservation in Ben Sira, מִנִּים/ "strings" can be proven to be less rare than its use in only two HB texts would suggest. There is no syntactical similarity between Ps 150 and Sir 39:15, and no recurrence of intertextual links, wherefore an intertextual reference cannot be established.

Results

References to Gen 2; 7; Ex 15; Deut 3; Josh 6; 2 Sam 6; 1 Chr 15:16 – 28; 2 Chr 5:12 – 14; Isa 6; Ezek 1– 3; 10; Ps 1– 2; 96; 98; 103; 145; Sir 39 are unlikely. Ps 146; 147; 148; 149 show no references except the framing Hallelujahs. Even if only the shortness of Ps 150 prevents the identification of intertextual references, interpretations cannot be based on the Psalm's intertextuality but have to take into account the general meaning of the words. This will now be done in the following.

II.1.4 Content of Psalm 150^{MT}

"Hallelujah" in Ps 150^{MT}

While in Codex L Ps 150 starts and ends with הַלְלוּיָהּ/"Praise-Yah!" (with maybe a tiny maqqef[96] at the end),[97] the BHS adds spaces, writing הַלְלוּ יָהּ/"Praise Yah!" at the beginning and הַלְלוּ־יָהּ/"Praise-Yah!" at the end.[98] All three forms (one word, two words, two words linked by a maqqef) consist of an imperative masculine plural pi'el of הלל/"praise" plus יָהּ/"Yah". Whether or not there is a difference between the three forms is not clear in Hebrew texts.[99] The spacing may indicate a difference between understanding the phrase as an imperative plus object

---

94 For the Hebrew text of Sir 39:15 cf. Beentjes 1997, 67, based on Schechter 1896, 5 – 6, and the facsimile of manuscript B IX recto Abegg and Parker [no year]c.
95 See p. 25 fn. 150.
96 Maqqef is a small line in MT closely connecting two words, cf. Joüon and Muraoka 2011, §13.
97 Cf. Freedman 1998, 804=fol. 396v.
98 Cf. Elliger and Rudolph 1997, 1226.
99 For example, Gesenius 2013, 278, according to BHS (cf. Gesenius 2013, VIII) lists Ps 106:1 as the only occurrence of הַלְלוּיָהּ without a space, whereas Clines 1995, 561, lists occurrences of הַלְלוּיָהּ, הַלְלוּ־יָהּ, and הַלְלוּ יָהּ together in one paragraph without distinguishing between the three. Both forms with and without a space are used in Qumran, cf. Bott 2011, 792.

"Praise Yah!"[100] or as a formula "Hallelujah",[101] but there is no clear distinction, and the content of a call to praise Yah is the same in both cases. The translation "Praise-Yah!" imitates the ambiguity of imperative and formula.

In the specific case of Ps 150:1[MT] both the lack of spaces in Codex L and the structure of the text suggest a focus on the formula "Hallelujah": Ps 150:1[MT] and Ps 150:6[MT] are complete sentences with further verbal form(s) of הלל/"praise". The two Hallelujahs frame the Psalm with a formulaic call to praise Yah, thus making clear both the theme (call to praise) and the object of the Psalm (Yah).

Some commentators claim that Ps 150 consists of calls to praise only with the proclamation of praise done by a temple orchestra,[102] or that the framing Hallelujahs function as the proclamation of praise,[103] or that the final Hallelujah functions as the proclamation of praise called for in all preceding verses.[104] However, the assumption of praise by instruments ignores v.6[105] as well as problems regarding a temple orchestra.[106] The framing Hallelujahs could function as a proclamation of praise as well as a call to praise, but the same could be said for the entire Psalm. The frame with an opening Hallelujah makes it unlikely that only the final Hallelujah functions as a proclamation of praise. Overall, the call to praise and the praise itself are one and the same, and comprise the entire Psalm.

"His mighty firmament", "His abundant greatness" in Ps 150:1–2[MT]

בִּרְקִיעַ עֻזּוֹ is translated as "in his mighty firmament" rather than "in the firmament of his might" for two reasons: Firstly, the genitive *nomen rectum* "might" expresses a quality of the *nomen regens* "firmament" (like an adjective).[107] Secondly, the suffix "his" does not affect the second of the two nouns forming a genitive group but it affects the entire genitive group.[108] In English, the ideas "firmament whose quality is might" plus "his" are best rendered as "his mighty firmament". While the suffix "his", i.e. God's, strictly extends to "firmament whose quality is might" and not just "might", someone who has a mighty firmament has to be mighty

---

100 E.g. Ps 147:1.
101 E.g. Ps 149:1.
102 Cf. Crüsemann 1969, 79 (Hallelujah as the reduction of an imperative hymn following Westermann 1968, 99 fn. 85, against Gunkel 1933, 37–38).
103 Cf. Mowinckel 1962a, 83; Seidel 1989, 166; Ballhorn 2004a, 16; Human 2011, 4–5.
104 Cf. Ballhorn 2004b, 346, 358.
105 Noted against Crüsemann, see fn. 102, by Allen 1983, 323.
106 See p. 82.
107 Cf. Gesenius and Kautzsch 1909 §128a, p; Joüon and Muraoka 2011, §129b, f.
108 Cf. Gesenius and Kautzsch 1909 §135; Joüon and Muràoka 2011, §140b.

himself, and thus the phrase implies the might of God when mentioning the might of his firmament.

The same applies to כְּרֹב גֻּדְלוֹ/"according to his abundant greatness": in English, the ideas "abundance of greatness" plus "his" are best rendered as "his abundant greatness".

Who is called to praise in Psalm 150:1–2^{MT}?

הלל/"praise" in HB is most often used in plural imperative or jussive forms calling a group, sometimes in the temple in Jerusalem, to praise the God of Israel. The verb appears most frequently in the book of Psalms or texts referring to cult.[109] Thus, the extensive use of הלל/"praise" may indicate that Ps 150 presupposes or at least alludes to some kind of worship of the God of Israel by some group of the people Israel, maybe in a cultic setting. However, הלל/"praise" even in plural imperative forms is not restricted to this use. It is also used to call all peoples to praise (Ps 117:1), animals and all creation (Ps 69:35; 148), and heavenly beings such as angels (Ps 148:2). While vv.1–2 with their plural imperatives must address a group, it cannot be determined which group this might be, since vv.1–2 refer to neither an earthly nor a heavenly temple but to God's qualities.[110] The answer can only be given in combination with vv.3–5, and the summarising v.6.[111]

Which God is to be praised in Psalm 150:1–2^{MT}?

The object of praise is אֵל/"god",[112] used without article like a proper name "God".[113] In Ps 150,[114] this word refers to YHWH, the God of Israel, since it follows the opening הַלְלוּ־יָהּ/"Praise-Yah!" which includes יָהּ/"Yah". This is confirmed in v.6 with יָהּ/"Yah" and the closing הַלְלוּ־יָהּ/"Praise-Yah!".

---

109 Cf. Westermann 1975; Ringgren 1977; Bott 2011.
110 See p. 44–47.
111 See p. 32–33, 55–57.
112 On the general use of אֵל/"god" cf. Cross 1973; Schmidt 1975; Burnett 2011.
113 See fn. 6.
114 See p. 31–32.

Where or why or how is God to be praised in Psalm 150:1–2ᴹᵀ?

It is debated if God is to be praised in a certain *place*, because of, in the circumstance of, or according to a certain *quality*, and whether the place or quality concerns the call to praise or God as the object of praise.

Some commentators see בְּקָדְשׁוֹ/"in his sanctuary" in v.1a as referring to God's *place*. This place may be a heavenly place where God is[115] or a heavenly place where those praising God are,[116] or – in contrast – a sanctuary on earth,[117] specifically the temple in Jerusalem[118] which may be connected to heaven.[119] Other commentators argue for both a heavenly and an earthly sanctuary.[120] The place can even be seen as a place in the world to come,[121] or those praising God themselves as a living sanctuary (instead of the place in which they are).[122] However, according to other commentators, בְּקָדְשׁוֹ refers to God's *quality*, namely the *reason* for praise "because of his holiness".[123] Finally, it is seen by some as *both* a place and a quality.[124]

Similarly, בִּרְקִיעַ עֻזּוֹ/"in his mighty firmament" in v.1b is seen by some commentators as a *place:* a heavenly place in general,[125] a heavenly place where God is,[126] a heavenly place where worshippers are,[127] or either a heavenly or earthly place.[128] However, others see it as a *quality* giving a *reason* for praise "because of his mighty firmament",[129] yet others as *both* a place and a quality.[130]

---

115 Cf. Feuer 1985, 1737; with the reason of a synonymous parallel v.1b referring to heaven Duhm 1922, 484; Dahood 1970, 359; Seybold 1996, 547.
116 Cf. van der Ploeg 1974, 508; Allen 1983, 322–23; with the reason of a synonymous parallel v.1b referring to heaven Mathys 2000, 337–38. However, v.6 as calling all humans to praise (see p. 55–57) makes this less likely: Heavenly beings are not included, and human worshippers could not be in a heavenly sanctuary or firmament (see fn. 127).
117 Cf. Seidel 1981, 93; Cha 2006, 103, 103 (due to a synthetic parallel v.1b referring to heaven); Human 2011, 5 (due to a synthetic parallel/merism v.1b referring to heaven).
118 Cf. with the reason of a synthetic parallel v.1b referring to heaven Zenger 2008k, 876–77. Jerusalem is also implied by Hupfeld 1871, 461; Gunkel 1926, 623; Buttrick 1955, 760; Hartenstein 2007, 118; Strawn and LeMon 2007, 458; Janowski 2012, 51.
119 Cf. Metzger 1970, 145 (due to a synonymous parallel v.1b referring to heaven).
120 Cf. Keck 1996, 1279; Weber 2003, 384; Rodd 2007, 405.
121 Cf. Ballhorn 2004a, 16–17; Ballhorn 2004b, 348 (due to a synonymous parallel v.1b referring to heaven, and an eschatological message of Ps 146–150).
122 Cf. Zenger 2011 [1996], 60 (due to the context of Ps 149).
123 Cf. Briggs 1906, 544–545.
124 Cf. Auffret 2002, 259.
125 Cf. Weber 2003, 384; Strawn and LeMon 2007, 458.
126 Cf. Hupfeld 1871, 461; Zenger 2011 [1996], 60; Gerstenberger 2001, 459.
127 Cf. Kraus 1978, 1149–50; Allen 1983, 323. However, this is unlikely, see fn. 116.
128 Cf. Seidel 1981, 93 (earthly if synonymous, heavenly if synthetic parallelism).

בִּגְבוּרֹתָיו/"in his strong deeds" in v.2a is sometimes seen as a *quality* of God giving a *proportion*[131] or a *reason*[132] for praise, whether the reason is God's action in history[133] or creation[134] or both.[135] It is rarely seen as a *place*.[136]

גֹּדֶל/"greatness" in v.2b may be God's *quality* of greatness in history[137] or nature,[138] and in *proportion* with this quality of greatness God is to be praised. Greatness thus is both an attribute of praise and of God who is to be praised. As a positive attribute it still implies a reason for praise.

The *general use of the words* in Ps 150:1–2 can only shed some light on this debate: בְּ can amongst others refer to a *place* "in", a *circumstantial quality* "in", a *causal quality* "because of", an *accompaniment* "accompanied by", or an *instrument* "with";[139] it rarely means "according to".[140] קֹדֶשׁ can refer to both a *place* "sanctuary" and a *quality* "holiness".[141] רָקִיעַ/"firmament" generally refers to a heavenly *place*.[142] עֹז is a general term for the *quality* "might".[143] Thus, for *v.1* the general use of the words does not make it clear whether the verse refers to *places* or *qualities*.

---

129 Cf. Briggs 1906, 544.
130 Cf. Auffret 2002, 259; Cha 2006, 103, 103.
131 Cf. Ballhorn 2004b, 347; however, בְּ is hardly ever used like כְּ, see fn. 140.
132 Cf. Mathys 2000, 329; Cha 2006, 104; Janowski 2012, 51.
133 Cf. Seidel 1981, 94; Ballhorn 2004a, 17.
134 Cf. Strawn and LeMon 2007, 458, 460.
135 Cf. Kraus 1978, 1150; van der Ploeg 1974, 509; Mathys 2000, 339; Human 2011, 5.
136 Cf. Schweizer (1977), 40, 44.
137 Cf. Seidel 1981, 94.
138 Cf. Loader 1991, 167.
139 Cf. Clines 1995, s.v. בְּ; Gesenius 2013, s.v. ־בְּ.
140 On the rare use of בְּ as "according to" cf. Jenni 1992, 350–351; Clines 1995, s.v. בְּ.
141 For the general use of קֹדֶשׁ cf. Müller 1976; Kornfeld and Ringgren 1989. קֹדֶשׁ even when collocated with הלל/"praise" and used in a temple context can refer both to the place "temple" as in Isa 62:9 and the "holiness" as in Isa 64:10 (the praise is in the temple whose destroyal is lamented but the temple is described as בֵּית קָדְשֵׁנוּ וְתִפְאַרְתֵּנוּ/"our holy and beautiful house", with קֹדֶשׁ as a quality "holiness"). In Ps 60:8=Ps 108:8 אֱלֹהִים דִּבֶּר בְּקָדְשׁוֹ "God has spoken in his holiness/sanctuary", קֹדֶשׁ could be "holiness" (thus KJV), or "sanctuary" (thus NRSV). The phrase בְּקָדְשׁוֹ appears apart from Ps 60:8; 108:8; 150:1 only in Am 4:2 נִשְׁבַּע אֲדֹנָי יְהוָה בְּקָדְשׁוֹ "the Lord YHWH has sworn in his holiness" ("holiness" both in KJV and NRSV) and Job 15:15 where the Qere is plural. Examples for the quality קֹדֶשׁ "holiness" in the Psalter are Ps 5:8 אֶשְׁתַּחֲוֶה אֶל־הֵיכַל־קָדְשְׁךָ "I will bow down towards your holy temple", Ps 29:2 הִשְׁתַּחֲווּ לַיהוָה בְּהַדְרַת־קֹדֶשׁ "worship YHWH in holy splendour", and Ps 145:21 (also see p. 39) וִיבָרֵךְ כָּל־בָּשָׂר שֵׁם קָדְשׁוֹ "and all flesh will bless his holy name". An example for the place קֹדֶשׁ "sanctuary" is Ps 74:3 כָּל־הֵרַע אוֹיֵב בַּקֹּדֶשׁ "an enemy has destroyed everything in the sanctuary".
142 Cf. Görg 1993.
143 Cf. van der Woude 1976; Wagner 1989.

In v.2, גְּבוּרָה/"strength" and its plural גְּבוּרֹת/"strong deeds" refer to the *quality* "might", and regarding God's strong deeds the term is not restricted to creation or history.[144] In its plural form in v.2, the word probably refers to a *causal* quality rather than a circumstantial quality since "strong deeds" are not a static circumstance. כְּ/"according to" can be used for a parallel, expressing comparison or similarity.[145] רֹב/"abundance" is a general word expressing a large quantity.[146] גֹּדֶל/"greatness" is a general mostly abstract term for a *quality*.[147] Thus, the general use of the words makes it likely that *v.2* refers to *qualities*.

The *context within Ps 150* illuminates vv.1–2 a little more.

In v.1, a *synonymous parallelism* is often used to argue for a heavenly sanctuary in v.1a,[148] and a *synthetic parallelism* for an earthly sanctuary.[149] In v.1, the two expressions בְּקָדְשׁוֹ/"for his holiness" and בִּרְקִיעַ עֻזּוֹ/"for his mighty firmament" are parallel to each other. If they refer to places, they could be in a synonymous or a synthetic parallelism (if synthetic, the two places are different but connected through the same preposition and through God who appears in both suffixes). If they refer to qualities, a synthetic parallelism is likely as the qualities cover different meanings. In v.2, the two expressions בִגְבוּרֹתָיו/"for his strong deeds" and כְּרֹב גֻּדְלוֹ/"according to his abundant greatness" are parallel to each other. Here, the parallelism is synthetic given the two different prepositions. Since like v.2 most parallelisms in Ps 150 are synthetic, this also is most likely for v.1.

In the *structure* of Ps 150,[150] בְּ in v.1 could refer to a place or quality, in v.2 it must refer to a quality (since the words in v.2 refer to qualities as confirmed by v.2b with כְּ/"according to"), and in vv.3–5 בְּ refers to means.[151] Since Ps 150 thus contains more than one meaning of בְּ, it can be debated whether v.1 and v.2 are closely connected and therefore בְּ in v.1 probably refers to qualities in both verses, or whether v.1 and v.2 are disconnected and the meaning of בְּ changes from "in" in v.1 to "for" in v.2. Even though unlike v.1, v.2 includes כְּ/"according to", all of the nouns in vv.1–2 (unlike in vv.3–6) through suffixes explicitly refer back to

---

144 For history cf. Kühlewein 1975, 401; for creation Kosmala 1973, 908; for both Reymond 2011, 570.
145 Cf. Seybold 1984; Clines 1998, s.v. כְּ; Gesenius 2013, s.v. ־כְּ.
146 Cf. Hartmann 1976; Fabry, Blum, and Ringgren 1993.
147 Cf. Bergman, Ringgren, and Mosis 1973, esp. 937–938; Jenni 1975, esp. 404; Beyerle 2011, esp. 579.
148 See fn. 115–116.
149 See fn. 117.
150 See p. 32–33.
151 See p. 47.

אֵל/"God" in v.1. Thus, the stronger argument seems to be that these two verses *vv.1–2 are connected, and both refer to qualities.*[152] קֹדֶשׁ then refers to a quality "holiness" rather than a place "sanctuary". The instruments in vv.3–5 are unlikely to refer to temple music,[153] and thus do not confirm a reference to the temple in v.1a. While רָקִיעַ/"firmament" still refers to a place, it can be regarded as the product of a quality of God which is a reason for praise, especially since it is connected not with a spatial term like הַשָּׁמַיִם/"heavens" but with עֻזּוֹ/"his might". Given the connection between v.1 and v.2, it is likely that all the qualities of God mentioned in vv.1–2 are *causal qualities* with בְּ meaning "for".

In conclusion, vv.1–2 call to praise God because of *qualities*. God is to be praised for his holiness, for his mighty firmament, and for his strong deeds in history and/or creation, in short: in accordance with his greatness. בְּ/"for" in vv.1–2a introduces reasons for praise. כְּ/"according to" is a link from reasons (vv.1–2a) over measure (v.2b) to means (vv.3–5).

The interpretation of v.1 as referring to places can, however, not be excluded: Given the complicated character of the argument for v.1 as referring to reasons, and its reference to the use of a small preposition, there might be intentional ambiguity between reasons and places.

Vv.1–2 express very general reasons for praise.[154] This might be intentional, to stress the universal aspect of praise in Ps 150. However, because the terms are such general ones, and cannot be filled by the context within Ps 150, they are often filled by commentators using the context of other Psalms, or other general ideas.

Why or how is God to be praised in Psalm 150:3–5^MT?

With musical instruments בְּ/"with" usually signifies a means.[155] Thus, the instruments in vv.3–5 show "how" (rather than "why") God is to be praised.[156]

---

152 Against Zenger 2008k, 873.
153 See p. 52–54.
154 Against the lack of reasons held by Brueggemann 1991, 67; Vincent 1999, 67.
155 Cf. Jenni 1992, 1118–119, 130–131. On the general use of בְּ see fn. 140.
156 It is unlikely that בְּ here means "accompanied with", thus Ballhorn 2004b, 346, since בְּ hardly ever is used like כְּ, see fn. 140, and the instruments in Ps 150 are not used solely for accompaniment, see p. 48–52.

What are the individual instruments in Psalm 150:3–5^{MT}?

Ps 150 contains a number of undetermined[157] words referring to musical instruments. Both the words and the instruments referred to are explained here.[158] For these explanations, all available information about music in HB and its ANE surroundings is taken into account: A precise period of origin of Psalm 150 cannot be specified,[159] even if it could be specified the Psalm could refer to earlier periods, and the scarcity of evidence makes it necessary to use all available ancient sources.

The blast of a horn is the first musical sound mentioned in Ps 150. The Hebrew root תקע is most often used meaning "to blow" with respect to a שׁוֹפָר/ "horn" or חֲצֹצְרָה/"trumpet".[160] תֶּקַע is extant in Ps 150:3 only as a hapax legomenon and is probably a noun "blowing" or "blast".[161] As a noun instead of an infinitive construct, the blowing remains abstract and no stress is put on the activity of blowing and those who blow the horn.[162]

שׁוֹפָר/"horn" refers to an instrument made from a goat's or ram's horn[163] which produces a limited number of tones and thus mainly serves as a signal instrument.[164] It is used in HB in a variety of contexts (such as war, the announcement of kingship, or worship), with the instrument most often serving as a signal,[165] and sometimes but not always played by priests.[166] In Ps 150 as well as in more than one other text, שׁוֹפָר/"horn" is collocated with תקע/"blow", נֵבֶל/ "harp", כִּנּוֹר/"lyre", or תְּרוּעָה/"noise".[167] In the structure of Ps 150, שׁוֹפָר/"horn" is the first instrument mentioned, and unlike all the other instruments has its own half-verse.[168] As it is used as a signal for beginning in other contexts, it may signify a beginning in Ps 150. Whether this is an imagined scene (in

---

157 See p. 31–32.

158 The English translations of instruments refer to the best modern equivalents available, for these cf. Oxford Music Online 2001–2014.

159 See II.1.6. Skulj 1998, 1118, focusses on music during the period of the first temple. However, little is known even about this, see p. 52–54.

160 Cf. Zobel 1995, esp. 755; Clines 2011b, s.v. תקע; Gesenius 2013, s.v. תקע.

161 Cf. Clines 2011b, s.v. [תֶּקַע]; Gesenius 2013, s.v. תֶּקַע* with a reference to Meyer 1992, §34 3. For similar "qitl" forms cf. Joüon and Muraoka 2011, §88 C h. Against Skulj 1998, 1127–1128, תקע is not used for the human voice.

162 Cf. Mathys 2000, 334. On the infinitive construct cf. Joüon and Muraoka 2011, §49.

163 Cf. Sendrey 1969, 343.

164 Cf. Sendrey 1969, 344; King and Stager 2001, 296.

165 Cf. Ringgren 1993b; Clines 2011b, s.v. שׁוֹפָר; Gesenius 2013, s.v. שׁוֹפָר.

166 E.g. Josh 6:8 (seven priests) vs. 2 Sam 20:1 (Sheba, the son of Bichri, an enemy of David) and Jer 6:1 (people of Benjamin).

167 Cf. Clines 2011b, s.v. שׁוֹפָר.

168 See p. 32–33, esp. fn. 15.

which the שׁוֹפָר/"horn" is blown before the other instruments) or just an opening to the enumeration of instruments (שׁוֹפָר/"horn" as the beginning) has to be left open.[169] Due to the lack of direct intertextual references from Ps 150 to any other texts[170] it cannot be determined whether in Ps 150 the horn is blown by priests only,[171] not always blown by priests,[172] or not blown by priests at all.[173]

נֵבֶל/"harp" probably refers to a harp-like stringed instrument played with the fingers of both hands.[174] In HB the instrument is used in various contexts (king's court, temple), sometimes but not always for accompanying singing,[175] and it is sometimes but not always played by Levites.[176] In Ps 150 as well as in more than one other text, נֵבֶל/"harp" is collocated with כִּנּוֹר/"lyre", or תֹּף/"drum".[177]

כִּנּוֹר/"lyre" probably refers to a lyre-like stringed instrument, sometimes played with a plectrum and as a solo instrument.[178] The כִּנּוֹר/"lyre" may have had fewer strings than a נֵבֶל/"harp",[179] but that כִּנּוֹר/"lyre" is a more popular instrument and נֵבֶל/"harp" a more professional one[180] cannot be shown.[181] In HB it is used in various mainly joyful contexts (feast with wine, temple),[182] sometimes but not always for accompanying singing,[183] and sometimes but not always

---

169 According to Ballhorn 2004b, 350-351, the שׁוֹפָר/"horn" announces the kingship of God as in Ps 98, but, as Ballhorn himself notes, there is no intertextual reference. Kraus 1978, 1150, sees it as indicating the beginning of singing praises.
170 See II.1.3.
171 See on Josh p. 37, on temple imagery p. 54.
172 Thus van der Ploeg 1974, 507.
173 Thus Ballhorn 2004b, 350 (Josh 6 is excluded as a source due to its legendary character).
174 Cf. Sendrey 1969, 278–289, esp. 288–289. Instead of harp it could also be a lyre, cf. Lawergren 1998, 56; Braun 1999, 45–46; King and Stager 2001, 291.
175 E.g. 1 Chr 25:6 (with singing) and Neh 12:27 (with singing) vs. 2 Chr 20:28 (no singing mentioned) and Isa 5:12 (no singing mentioned); for more examples (with singing) cf. Seybold 1986, 187.
176 E.g. Neh 12:27 (Levites) and 2 Chr 29:25 (Levites) vs. Isa 5:12 (godless people) and Isa 14:11 (Babylonians).
177 Cf. Clines 2011b, s.v. שׁוֹפָר.
178 Cf. Sendrey 1969, 266–278, esp. 268, 271–273, 278.
179 Cf. Sendrey 1969, 274 (maybe more strings), 286 (fewer); Braun 1999, 40; King and Stager 2001, 291.
180 Thus Zenger 2011 [1996], 62; but both נֵבֶל/"harp" and כִּנּוֹר/"lyre" are associated with Levites in Zenger 2008k, 879–880.
181 Cf. Braun 1999, 41, 44–45.
182 Cf. Görg and Botterweck 1984, esp. 215–216.
183 E.g. 1 Chr 25:6 (with singing) and Neh 12:27 (with singing) vs. 2 Chr 20:28 (no singing mentioned) and Isa 5:12 (no singing mentioned) as for נֵבֶל/"harp" (see fn. 175).

played by Levites.[184] In Ps 150 as well as in more than one other text, כִּנּוֹר/"lyre"
is collocated with תֹּף/"drum", עָגָב/"pipe", or נֵבֶל/"harp".[185]

Due to the lack of direct intertextual references it cannot be determined
whether in Ps 150 both נֵבֶל/"harp" and כִּנּוֹר/"lyre" are played by Levites only.[186]

תֹּף/"drum" refers to a small drum played with the hand (not a modern tambourine with added metal plates).[187] In HB it is used in various contexts (wel-
come after victory, feast, procession),[188] and often played by women though
also by men.[189] In Ps 150 as well as in more than one other text, תֹּף/"drum" is
collocated with with כִּנּוֹר/"lyre", נֵבֶל/"harp", or מָחוֹל/"dance".[190]

מָחוֹל/"dance" is used in HB mostly in poetic texts with women dancing as
well as men.[191] Dance in general (with the related מְחֹלָה/"dance") also appears
in HB in various contexts with women dancing as well as men.[192] In Ps 150 as
well as in more than one other text, מָחוֹל/"dance" is collocated with תֹּף/
"drum".[193] In the structure of Ps 150, מָחוֹל/"dance" is in the centre of all the instruments (there are four instruments before and after it).[194] Thus, in the centre
of all these instruments is something that is not an instrument at all, but a
human activity unaided by instruments.[195]

מִנִּים/"strings" (singular מֵן*/"string") probably is a collective term for instruments with strings.[196] It is used only in Ps 150:4, Ps 45:9 (king's court), and the
Hebrew Sir 39:15 (praise to God).[197]

עוּגָב/"pipe" may refer to a flute[198] or a serve as collective term for flute- and
pipe-like instruments.[199] It is used in HB only in Ps 150:4, Gen 4:21 (Jubal), Job

---

184 E.g. 2 Chr 29:25 (Levites) and Neh 12:27 (Levites) as for נֵבֶל/"harp" (see fn. 176) vs. Isa 5:12
(godless people) as for נֵבֶל/"harp" (see fn. 176) and Job 21:12 (wicked people).
185 Cf. Clines 1998, s.v. כִּנּוֹר.
186 See p. 54.
187 Cf. Sendrey 1969, 373.
188 Cf. Ottosson 1995, 727–728.
189 E.g. Ex 15:20 (women) vs. 1 Sam 10:5 (prophets). For more examples cf. Meyers 1991, 21–22.
190 Cf. Clines 2011b, s.v. תֹּף.
191 E.g. Jer 31:4 (woman figure) vs. Lam 5:15 (people). מָחוֹל/"dance" only appears in Ps 30:12;
149:3; 150:4; Jer 31:4, 13; Lam 5:15 (lemma search in BibleWorks 9 2013).
192 E.g. Ex 15:20 (women) vs. Ex 32:19 (people Israel). Cf. King and Stager 2001, 298–300.
193 Cf. Clines 2001, s.v. מָחוֹל I.
194 Noted by Auffret 1995, 286.
195 See p. 52–54.
196 Cf. Sendrey 1969, 272–273; Braun 1999, 57; Clines 2001, s.v. [מֵן] I; Gesenius 2013, s.v. מֵן*₁.
197 Cf. Clines 2001, s.v. [מֵן] I.
198 Cf. Braun 1999, 52–53.
199 Cf. Sendrey 1969, 309. According to Seidel 1981, 96, and (following Seidel) Mathys 2000,
335–336, Gen 4:21 suggests a string (!) instrument of professional itinerant musicians.

21:12 (feast), and Job 30:31 (feast turned into mourning). It is also used in 11QPs^a Ps 151:2.[200] In all of these texts, עוּגָב/"pipe" is collocated with כִּנּוֹר/"lyre".

צֶלְצְלִים/"cymbals" refers to bronze cymbals played with the hands, probably large instruments rather than small castanets (מְצִלְתַּיִם/"cymbals" seems to refer to the same instruments). Archaeological data from various parts of the ANE seems to suggest that there were two different sizes of cymbals, and that cymbals could be played in two different ways holding them horizontally or vertically.[201] In HB, it is used only in Ps 150:5 and in 2 Sam 6:5 (David and the ark).[202] In Ps 150:2, צֶלְצְלִים/"cymbals" appears twice in the construct state, once with שֶׁמַע/"sound" and once with תְּרוּעָה/"noise".

שמע means "to hear" in various contexts.[203] שֶׁמַע is a pausal form of שֶׁמַע, a noun "sound" which is extant as a hapax legomenon in Ps 150:5 only.[204]

תְּרוּעָה/"noise" is used in various contexts (noise of voices or musical instruments, in war, in joy, in praise to YHWH as king).[205]

Both nouns indicate that cymbals were loud, and תְּרוּעָה/"noise" is probably more specific and stronger than שֶׁמַע/"sound". Since the parallelisms in Ps 150 are usually synthetic, since all the instruments in the other verses are different ones, and given the archaeological data, Ps 150:5 may refer to two different kinds or sizes of cymbals (the first quieter and smaller, the second louder and bigger), but it could also refer to two different ways of playing cymbals (quieter and louder, maybe through vertical and horizontal playing), or both.[206] In any case, the focus seems to be on the increasing sound.

---

200 Cf. Sanders 1965, 55; Clines 2007, s.v. עוּגָב.

201 Cf. Sendrey 1969, 375–376 (the material might also be brass for smaller and bronze for larger instruments, but brass and bronze are used interchangeably), 378–380; Braun 1999, 42–44, 98–100. Unlike for vertical and horizontal playing, no evidence for rubbing and clashing is given.

202 Cf. Clines 2010, 127; Gesenius 2013, 1121. Other texts use מְצִלְתַּיִם/"cymbals", cf. Sendrey 1969, 375, 380; Braun 1999, 42–44.

203 Cf. Clines 2011b, s.v. שמע I; Gesenius 2013, s.v. שמע.

204 Cf. Clines 2011b, s.v. [שֶׁמַע]; Gesenius 2013, s.v. שֶׁמַע*₁ with a reference to Bauer and Leander 1922, §61 uʻ. For similar "qatl" forms cf. Joüon and Muraoka 2011, §88 C d; ֶ, unlike ֵ, becomes ֶ in pause, cf. Joüon and Muraoka 2011, §32 c; שֶׁמַע as a "qitl" form as listed in Joüon and Muraoka 2011, §88 C h, is less likely in Ps 150:5.

205 Cf. Ringgren 1993a; Clines 2011b, s.v. תְּרוּעָה; Gesenius 2013, s.v. תְּרוּעָה.

206 The view of different *kinds or sizes of cymbals* (higher smaller and lower bigger cymbals) is adopted by Hupfeld 1871, 462; Duhm 1922, 485; Kraus 1978, 1150; Braun 1999, 43 (also possibility of different ways of playing). The view of different *methods of playing cymbals* is adopted by Keel and Hallett 1978, 340; Zenger 2011 [1996], 63 (rubbing and clashing). The view of both *sizes and methods* of playing (with a vertical way of playing being louder) is adopted by Sendrey 1969, 378 (perhaps plus material brass and bronze); van der Ploeg 1974, 509. See fn. 201.

That Ps 150 refers to silence for hearing words such as sermons, readings and prayers after the first sounding of the cymbals of שֶׁמַע/"sound" and then loud rejoicing with the second sounding of the cymbals of תְּרוּעָה/"noise"[207] is unlikely since within Ps 150 what is to be heard are probably the cymbals mentioned in Ps 150 rather than words not mentioned anywhere in the Psalm.[208]

What is the ensemble of instruments in Psalm 150:3–5[MT]?

It is debated whether Ps 150 refers to *temple music* in the earthly temple in Jerusalem with temple worship and a temple orchestra,[209] the abstract idea of the Jerusalem temple and its music rather than the actual performance,[210] or whether it refers to a more universal and abstract idea of *music beyond the temple*,[211] such as a *full list of instruments*,[212] a general joyful *feast*,[213] or even *eschatological music*.[214] Some commentators also argue that instruments were played only to accompany singing, that musical praise was necessarily tied to words (which only humans can use), and that Ps 150 reflects this dominance of words only accompanied by instruments.[215]

Few facts are known about *temple music*. Jerusalem probably had a first temple (probably built in the 10th century BCE and destroyed in 587 BCE), and a second temple (built around 520 BCE, rebuilt by Herod around 1 BCE/1 CE and destroyed by Titus in 70 CE). There is no archaeological evidence for either of the temple buildings, but Herodian outer walls of the temple area remain today, and a large amount of literature, mainly in HB, on both temples.[216]

---

207 Cf. Seybold 1996, 547-548; Mathys 2000, 336–337 (following Seybold).
208 In addition, in 1 Chr 15:19 and 16:5 שמע/"hear" is used in hifʿil forms for the sounding of מְצִלְתַּיִם/"cymbals", cf. Feuer 1985, 1740.
209 Cf. Kraus 1978, 1149; Seybold 1996, 548; Weber 2003, 384-385; Rodd 2007, 405.
210 Cf. Mathys 2000, 330-331, 333–339.
211 Cf. Seidel 1981, 98.
212 Cf. Duhm 1922, 485; Zenger 2011 [1996], 61; however, there are more instruments in HB, cf. Braun 1999, 36–57.
213 Cf. Duhm 1922, 485; Schweizer 1977, 45.
214 Cf. Ballhorn 2004a, 17 (referring to Ps 149); Ballhorn 2004b, 351–353 (referring to Ps 146–150, esp. Ps 149).
215 Ballhorn 2004b, 351, 353 (exception of שׁוֹפָר/"horn" announcing rather than accompanying words), 355. However, since the Psalms are words it is not surprising to find music connected with words in the Psalter, and there is a lack of knowledge about temple music, see fn. 218.
216 For an overview on the sources and the history of the temple cf. Fritz 2002, 48–50; Bieberstein 2005; Roberts 2009; for details on archaeological data Bieberstein and Bloedhorn 1994.

Regarding *music and musical instruments* in ancient Israel and the ANE, there are many archaeological finds (artefacts such as figurines and pictures) and texts (mainly in HB). These sources show that there was music in everyday activites and in more or less formal religious practices, that music had both positive and negative connotations (such as worship versus drunken feasts), and that there were several instruments which could be played on their own, in ensembles, and together with singing.[217]

Biblical and non-biblical texts link worship in both the first and second temple with sung and instrumental music, and it is thus likely that there was music in temple worship. However, little is known about details of the rituals of worship in either of the two temples and about temple music, let alone a temple orchestra.[218]

Since Ps 150 does not refer to other texts and little is known about temple worship and music (in either Jerusalem temple), any claims that Ps 150 refers to temple music (whether abstract or concrete) or that it goes beyond temple music, while remaining possible, cannot be substantiated.

The list of musical instruments is not a full list of those in HB, and while music can be used in joyful feasts it is not limited to this use.[219]

Eschatological music is hard to grasp with no clear definition of eschatology (the term refers to imaginings beyond the end of one or all human beings or the world) and many different concepts of eschatology in HB.[220] While some texts in HB which could be described as eschatological contain references to music,[221] there are no intertextual references to such texts in Ps 150,[222] and in general, music in HB primarily refers to past or present activities rather than an imagined future.[223] Thus, it is unlikely that Ps 150 refers to eschatological music.

---

217 For an overview on music in and surrounding HB cf. Hübner 2002; Kammerer 2002; Burgh 2009, esp. 170–173. For an overview on musical instruments cf. Braun 1994; Braun 2009, for details Sendrey 1969, esp. 262–387 (with notes 575–590), and Braun 1999, esp. 36–57. For a list of verses in HB with musical instruments cf. Kolari 1947, 92–94. Further research on music in and surrounding HB is desirable.

218 For an overview of the lack of knowledge about temple music cf. Braun 1996, esp. 1522–1524; Reif 2009, esp. 903–905. Further research on biblical and non-biblical sources about worship and music in the first and second temples is desirable.

219 See fn. 217.

220 Cf. Filoramo 1999, 1542; Müller 1999, esp. 1547.

221 E.g. Isa 30:29; Zech 9:14.

222 See II.1.3.

223 See fn. 217.

It is also unlikely that Ps 150 refers to music accompanying singing only as in Ps 150 dancing is included which cannot easily be tied to words, and in other HB texts instrumental music is used for religious praise without singing.[224]

What is the order of instruments in Psalm 150:3–5[MT]?

A mainstream interpretation of the instruments in Ps 150 sees שׁוֹפָר/"horn" in v.3a as the instrument of priests, נֵבֶל/"harp" and כִּנּוֹר/"lyre" in v.3b as the instruments of Levites, and the instruments in vv.4–5 as those of laypeople, with תֹף/ "drum" and sometimes מָחוֹל/"dance" in v.4a as the instruments of lay women, and therefore Ps 150 as a call to priests, Levites, and the people in this order,[225] possibly reflecting the temple with its inner sanctuary, inner courtyard, and outer courtyard (and the world beyond).[226]

Indeed, at least Herod's temple certainly had different courtyards (for priests and Jewish men, Jewish women, and non-Jews).[227] However, none of the instruments in Ps 150 are clearly and solely connected with priests, Levites, or women, and it cannot be decided whether or not Ps 150 refers to temple music at all.[228] Thus, this interpretation, while still possible, is unlikely.[229]

The order of instruments in Ps 150 may be without any climax.[230] However, there is only one instrument, the signal-giving horn, at the beginning, two sets of cymbals at the end, and three pairs of musical terms in the middle. Dance is at the centre of this structure.[231] Thus, there could be a climax at dance in the middle, or at the increasing sound of cymbals at the end. If the latter is stressed, Psalm 150 ends with a crescendo.[232]

---

224 E.g. Num 10:10 (priests playing trumpets), 2 Chr 20:28 (harps, lyres, and trumpets on the way to the temple).

225 Cf. Duhm 1922, 484–85; Buttrick 1955, 762; Allen 1983, 323; Cha 2006, 105–106.

226 Cf. Seidel 1981, 97; Seidel 1989, 166-167; Weber 2003, 384-385; following Seidel 1981 Mathys 2000, 334–336; Hartenstein 2007, 119; following Hartenstein Zenger 2008k, 878–883; Human 2011, 6; Gillingham 2012, 389–390; Janowski 2012, 51–52.

227 Cf. Fritz 2002, 51–52; Roberts 2009, esp. 504–506: There were probably two courtyards in the first and second temple, in Herod's version three.

228 See p. 48–54.

229 Cf. van der Ploeg 1974, 507-508 (nevertheless assuming a progression from old and venerable to more popular instruments); Mathys 2000, 335 fn. 24 (still with temple imagery), see fn. 226; Human 2011, 6–7 (following van der Ploeg, nevertheless following Seidel 1981 and Hartenstein 2007 regarding temple imagery).

230 Cf. Schweizer 1977, 44.

231 See p. 32–33 and p. 48–52, esp. fn. 194.

232 Cf. van der Ploeg 1974, 509; Zenger 2008k, 881.

Who is called to praise in Psalm 150:3–5^{MT}?

Since musical instruments and dance in HB are used only by humans or human figures, vv.3–5 call humans to praise. While animal praise appears in HB, animals playing instruments or dancing do not, and neither do heavenly beings.[233]

The individual instruments are not restricted to specific groups,[234] or a temple orchestra,[235] and musical instruments in general are not limited to Israel.[236] Vv.3–5 thus call all to praise the God of Israel with musical instruments.

Who is called to praise in Psalm 150:6^{MT}?

כֹּל/"all" in its construct state can be translated as "entirety", "every", "whole".[237] נְשָׁמָה/"breath" is most often used for the breath and therefore the life of *humans* (prominently in Gen 2:7: God forms man out of earth and gives him breath). It can also refer to other living beings such as *animals* (prominently in Gen 7:22: all animals and humans die in the flood),[238] and the breath of *God* (e.g. Ps 18:16; Job 4:9; 37:10; Isa 30:33), but in HB it is *not* used for other heavenly beings. כֹּל/"all" in the construct state followed by נְשָׁמָה/"breath" most often refers to Israel's enemies whom God commands to be killed (Deut 20:16; Josh 10:40; 11:11, 14; 1 Kings 15:29). Whether or not this includes animals is debated,[239] but at least Josh 11:14 and 1 Kings 15:29 refer to humans only. While humans are a strong candidate, the question cannot be answered by the general use of words. The two main suggestions for an answer made by commentators are *humans* (an *anthropocentric* interpretation), or *all life* (a *universal* interpretation).[240]

Within the *anthropocentric interpretation*, some commentators see v.6 as addressed to *humans only*. Reasons given[241] include that נְשָׁמָה/"breath" generally

---

233 Result of checking passages with musical instruments listed in Kolari 1947, 92–94. The complete lack of animal music and dance (as opposed to general animal praise) in HB makes the argument for animal music and dance in Ps 150 in Strawn and LeMon 2007, esp. 472–473, 479, less convincing.

234 See p. 48–52.

235 Cf. Crüsemann 1969, 79, but unlikely, see p. 52–54.

236 E.g. Isa 14:11 (כִּנּוֹר/"lyre" in Babylon), Ezek 26:13 (נֶבֶל/"harp" in Tyre).

237 Cf. Sauer 1975; Ringgren 1984; Stadel 2013.

238 Cf. Lamberty-Zielinski 1986; Schneider 2013a.

239 Cf. Strawn and LeMon 2007, 455–456.

240 Those adopting the anthropocentric interpretation claim the majority of scholars adopts a universal interpretation, cf. Ballhorn 2004b, 354; Zenger 2008a, 570; and vice versa, cf. Strawn and LeMon 2007, 452. The survey here suggests that the universal interpretation is more widespread.

241 Without reasons Janowski 2012, 52; Scaiola 2010b, 710.

refers to humans,[242] that the context within Ps 150 with instruments in vv.3–5 refers to humans,[243] the interpretation of the context of Psalms 146–150,[244] and the general assumption that only humans have speech.[245] Others see v.6 as addressed to *humans first*, only then other living beings. Reasons given[246] include that within Ps 150 v.6 follows on from the mention of instruments in vv.3–5 and is therefore connected with humans[247] who stand in contrast with the lifeless musical instruments.[248]

That v.6 refers to Israel only[249] is seen as unlikely by commentators, with reasons including that unlike in Ps 146–149 Israel is not mentioned in Ps 150,[250] an interpretation in the context of the Psalms 146–150,[251] or the anthropology of Gen 2.[252] It is also unlikely that due to the interpretation of Ps 149 rulers are excluded from all humans in Ps 150,[253] or that נְשָׁמָה/"breath" refers to a human's soul.[254]

Within the *universal interpretation*, commentators see v.6 as addressed to *humans and animals*. Reasons given include that נְשָׁמָה/"breath" generally refers to both humans and animals,[255] iconographical evidence for animals playing musical instruments in the ANE combined with texts about animal praise in ANE and HB,[256] creation language in Ps 150,[257] and that the context of Psalms 146–150 includes animals, especially in Ps 148.[258] Other commentators similarly speak of *all living creatures* (on earth). Reasons given[259] include that נְשָׁמָה/"breath" generally

---

242 Cf. Ballhorn 2004a, 17; Ballhorn 2004b, 355 (Gen 7:22 as an exception).
243 Cf. Ballhorn 2004b, 355.
244 Cf. Ballhorn 2004b, 355.
245 Cf., referring to Koch 1991 on Gen 2:7, Zenger 2008a, 570–571; Zenger 2008k, 883–885.
246 Without reasons Hupfeld 1871, 462; Weber 2010, 209.
247 Cf. Cha 2006, 106–107.
248 Cf. Hupfeld 1871, 462.
249 Implied by Brueggemann 1988, 155.
250 Cf. Cha 2006, 107.
251 Cf. Ballhorn 2004b, 356.
252 Cf. Zenger 2008a, 571.
253 Cf. Ballhorn 2004a, 17.
254 Cf. Feuer 1985, 1740–1742.
255 Cf. van der Ploeg 1974, 509; Seidel 1981, 97, 99–100; Keck 1996, 1279; Strawn and LeMon 2007, 453–457.
256 Cf. Strawn and LeMon 2007, 462–479.
257 Cf. Strawn and LeMon 2007, 457–462.
258 Cf. van der Ploeg 1974, 509 (Ps 148:10–12); Weber 2003, 148; Strawn and LeMon 2007, 477 (Ps 146–150, especially Ps 148).
259 Without reasons Kraus 1978, 1150; Allen 1983, 323; Rodd 2007, 405; Scaiola 2010a, 295.

refers to both human (Gen 2:7) and human and animal life (Gen 7:22),[260] that in Ps 150 the lifeless instruments in vv.3–5 are complemented by living beings,[261] that the context of Ps 148 shows how even non-living beings are called to praise,[262] that only praise offered by all earthly creatures is appropriate for the greatness of God,[263] and the eschatological vision of a feast of creation in the hope that God will be all in all as expressed in the New Testament.[264] Even more universal is a view that includes not only humans and animals on earth, but *also heavenly beings and inanimate things*. Reasons given include that such beings are included in ANE images and texts,[265] and that Ps 148 includes all heavenly and earthly beings, even inanimate ones.[266]

In support of the *anthropocentric* view נְשָׁמָה/"breath" most often refers to humans, and musical instruments and dance in vv.3–5 are connected with humans. There is no intertextual reference to Psalm 148.[267] *Beyond Israel*, נְשָׁמָה/ "breath" refers to Israel's enemies, and a reference to the Jerusalem temple depends on an unlikely interpretation of v.1,[268] although it is still יָהּ/"Yah" the God of Israel who is to be praised in Ps 150:6 and the entire Psalm. In *conclusion*, the *anthropocentric* view is most likely. In vv.1–2, it is not clear who is addressed, but in vv.3–5 it is all human beings. While a more universal interpretation cannot be excluded, and again there may be some intentional ambiguity, vv.1–2, vv.3–5 and the summarising v.6 probably refer to *all humans*.

II.1.5 Genre of Psalm 150ᴹᵀ

Psalm 150 is often described as a hymn.[269] However, it mainly consists of calls to praise, with hardly any main section giving reasons for praise and without כִּי/

---

260 Cf. Keck 1996, 1279; Human 2011, 8.

261 Cf. Auffret 2002, 259.

262 Cf. Cha 2006, 107. However, this could also include heavenly beings and inanimate things.

263 Cf. Allen 1983, 324.

264 Cf. Zenger 2011 [1996], 64–65 (with a quote of but without a reference to 1 Corinthians 15:28, in contrast to the anthropocentric view in later publications, see fn. 245).

265 Cf. Keel and Hallett 1978, 59–60. Further research on the praise of heavenly and inanimate beings (similar to Strawn and LeMon 2007 on animal praise) is desirable.

266 Cf. Keck 1996, 1280; Mathys 2000, 342–344.

267 See p. 39–40.

268 See p. 44–47.

269 Ps 150 is described as a hymn by Gunkel 1933, 27, 32, 37, 42 (with Ps 150 being one of the hymns, like Ps 148 and the "Song of the Three", consisting exclusively of "erweiterten Einfüh-

"for" introducing such a section as typical for hymns.[270] Some commentators therefore argue for the sub-genre of a hymnic introit,[271] but give hardly any other examples for hymnic introits.[272] For this reason, others stress the uniqueness of the Psalm.[273] Yet others call it a litany,[274] but again without other examples for this proposed hymnic sub-genre. While in the broad sense of "song of praise" Ps 150 can be described as a hymn, its unique features are more important than its relation to a genre.

It is debated whether Ps 150 was written for a setting in life in the *temple cult*, or for the *literary context* of the end of the Psalter as meditation literature, or whether this cannot be decided. Within the *cultic* view, most scholars argue that the Psalm was written for temple cult,[275] possibly later used as a doxology.[276] Within the *literary* view, some scholars see Ps 150 as written with the group of Psalms 146–150,[277] sometimes as a doxology,[278] others focus on Ps 150 as an in-

---

rungen", 42; English translation Gunkel 1998, 19, 23, 25, 29: "expanded introductions", 29); Dahood 1970, 359; Kraus 1978, 1148–49; Brueggemann 1991, 79; Rodd 2007, 405.

270 See p. 30 fn. 168.

271 Cf. Westermann 1967, 69–77 (Ps 150 in the category of "beschreibende[r] Lobpsalm oder Hymnos", 69 – English translation: Westermann 1980, 81–96, "psalm of descriptive praise or hymn", 81 –, but refined with Ps 150 as "ein eigener Psalmtyp", 75 – "an independent type of psalm", 89 – entirely domininated by imperatives which developed out of the hymn as the call to praise grew); Mowinckel 1962a, 83 (introit, cultic setting according to Mowinckel 1962b, 302); Crüsemann 1969, 78–79 (hymnic imperative, only in Ps 134 and Ps 150 due to cultic settings, in Ps 150 the instruments are answering the call to praise); Allen 1983, 323 (calls to praise only like in Ps 134, cultic setting, Crüsemann 1969, 79 ignores Ps 150:6); Gerstenberger 2001, 458, 460 (response or introit to hymns, cultic setting); Zenger 2008k, 874 (hymnic call, literary setting).

272 Westermann 1967, 75, 77 – English translation: Westermann 1980, 89, 92 – mentions Ps 95A; 145; 148 as further examples, and compares PsSal 18:10–12^LXX and 1 Chr 29:10–12 which also rely solely on God's majesty for praise; Crüsemann 1969, 78–79, mentions Ps 134 as the only other example. Gunkel 1933, 42 (see fn. 269) categorizes Ps 150 with Ps 148 and the "Song of the Three".

273 Cf. Mathys 2000, 329-330.

274 Cf. Seybold 2001, 172 (anaphoric repetition of imperative, other examples Ps 29; 136).

275 Cf. Hupfeld 1871, 461; Dahood 1970, 359; Allen 1983, 323; Gerstenberger 2001, 458, 460.

276 Cf. Dahood 1970, 359; Allen 1983, 323.

277 Cf. Seidel 1981, 92–93; Mathys 2000, 343; Leuenberger 2004, 360; Hartenstein 2007, 118; Zenger 2008c, 808–809; Zenger 2008k, 875; with a question mark Seybold 1991, 22; Weber 2003, 385 (referring to Zenger and Leuenberger); Weber 2010, 202, 204 (referring to Zenger 2003, but stressing that the final Psalms are then also liturgical); Human 2011, 3–4, 8.

278 Cf. Mathys 2000, 333, 343; Leuenberger 2004, 360 (not a doxology itself due to differences to other doxologies but used like one); Human 2011, 3–4.

dependent Psalm written for the end of the Psalter as a doxology.[279] Some scholars combine *both* with the Psalm first written for the cult and then used as a literary doxology at the end of the Psalter.[280] Others argue the other way round that the Psalm was first meant to be read and then performed later.[281] Generally, the view as a doxology is sometimes rejected due to the lack of similarites with the four doxologies in the Psalter.[282] The question of a cultic or literary origin of Ps 150 has to be left open.

II.1.6 Date of Psalm 150^{MT}

Ps 150 is rarely seen as preexilic,[283] mostly as postexilic.[284] Within the postexilic view, suggestions for dates range from the time of Nehemiah before Chronicles (before 400–350 BCE),[285] over a postexilic date before Chronicles[286] (and Daniel)[287] (before 250 BCE), and over around the same time as Chronicles (300–250 BCE),[288] to the time after Ezra, Nehemiah, and Chronicles (350–250 BCE),[289] the time of the final redaction of the Psalter (3rd century or 200–150 BCE[290] or 300–250 BCE),[291] or some time in the 3rd century BCE (300–200 BCE).[292]

---

279 Cf. van der Ploeg 1974, 507-508 (but Ps 150 could also be the end of the group Ps 146–150).
280 Cf. Buttrick 1955, 759-760; Reindl 1981b, 337; Gillingham 2012, 387–388.
281 Cf. Weber 2010, 204, 208.
282 Cf. Seidel 1981, 92 (lack of similarities – no amen – to the doxologies in Ps 41:14; 72:18; 89:53; 106:48, Ps 146–150 as a literary imitation of doxologies for a literary fifth book of the Psalter).
283 Cf. Goldingay 2008, 747 (use of ram's horn rather than trumpet as in Chronicles, use of word for cymbals otherwise only used in 2 Sam 6:5, put at the end of mostly postexilic Psalms).
284 Cf. DeClaissé-Walford 1997, 99.
285 Cf. Seidel 1981, 99–100 (horn instead of trumpets, no reference to Gen 1 but to Ezek 1, more universal than Chr and therefore earlier, time of Nehemia before the Levites change temple music).
286 Cf. Gunkel 1926, 623 (postexilic division of Priests and Levites, presence of instruments not mentioned and thus rejected in Chr).
287 Cf. Buttrick 1955, 760 (postexilic division of Priests and Levites, absence of instruments mentioned in Chr and Dan, presence of instruments not mentioned and thus rejected in Chr).
288 Cf. Mathys 2000, 331 (orchestra an imagined one, שׁוֹפָר/"horn" used for dignity not because of age). Allen 1983, 323, similarly notes, against Gunkel (see fn. 286), that the use of instruments may have rhetorical reasons.
289 Cf. Human 2011, 9 (allusions to postexilic texts Gen, Eze, Isa, importance of Torah number symbolism and music in Ps 150 and in Ezr/Neh and Chr, more universal view than that in Chr).
290 Cf. Zenger 2008c, 808–9; Zenger 2008k, 875.

Reasons given for dates of Ps 150 include the instruments mentioned (horn instead of the later trumpet or lack of instruments mentioned in Chronicles and Daniel for an early date,[293] or the intentional literary use of older instruments for a late date[294]), and a more universal view of the use of music than that found in Chronicles (for both a date earlier than Chronicles[295] and the opposite[296]). However, little is known about the use of musical instruments.[297] Even if the trumpet is younger than the horn[298] it did not simply replace the horn: in texts like Ps 98:6 and 1 Chr 15:28 both are mentioned in the same scene. A lack of instruments mentioned in other texts is an *argumentum e silentio* which is hard to substantiate, especially in the absence of intertextual references to Chronicles. Thus Ps 150 cannot be dated on the basis of the musical instruments mentioned in it.

Other reasons are equally weak. They include the mention of קֹדֶשׁ/"holiness, sanctuary" as referring to the second temple (however, קֹדֶשׁ may not refer to a temple at all),[299] the postexilic division of priests and Levites (however, these groups are implied by instruments which are not necessarily connected with them),[300] intertextual references to postexilic texts (however, there are no intertextual references at all),[301] and number symbolism (however, this is unlikely).[302] It could also be argued that רָקִיעַ/"firmament" is used in exilic or postexilic texts only,[303] but this would presuppose that Ps 150 also is an exilic or postexilic text.

For Ps 150, the only absolute *terminus ante quem* is the oldest of the Dead Sea manuscripts of Ps 150, MasPs^b, which probably dates from the second half of the 1st century BCE and has to be older than 73/74 CE. However, the Septuagint translation of the Psalms was probably finished in the 2nd century BCE,[304] and Psalm 150 must predate its translation. Thus, *Psalm 150 is older than some*

---

291 Cf. Human 2011, 8.
292 Cf. van der Ploeg 1974, 508.
293 See fn. 284–286.
294 See fn. 288.
295 See fn. 285.
296 See fn. 289.
297 See p. 48–52.
298 Cf. Braun 1999, 38–39, 47–50 (main use of trumpet in second temple period, but contemporary with continued use of horn). Sendrey 1969, 332–342, even sees trumpets as early instruments used in Egypt as early as the 15th century BCE (332) and in Israel known to Moses (334) and used in the first and second temples (337).
299 See p. 44–47.
300 See p. 48–52, 54.
301 See II.1.3.
302 See p. 34–35.
303 Cf. Hartenstein 2001, 34, 44.
304 See p. 15–17, esp. fn. 104.

time in the 2nd century BCE. While a postexilic origin is likely given the scholarly consensus, an earlier origin cannot be excluded.

II.1.7 Unity of Psalm 150^MT

Ps 150^MT is one unit with regular syntax, structure, parallelisms, and content. While most commentators do not doubt the unity of Ps 150[305] excluding the Hallelujah frame, it is often argued that the framing Hallelujahs were not part of the original Psalm.[306] It is possible that the framing Hallelujahs are a later addition[307] since they are inconsistent in Hebrew manuscripts and versions: The opening Hallelujah is missing on a few Hebrew manuscripts and in the Syriac version, and the final Hallelujah is missing in various Septuagint manuscripts, the Coptic and Syriac versions and Jerome's Latin Psalterium.[308] However, the Hallelujahs could also have been there originally and left out later.[309]

II.1.8 Overall Interpretation of Psalm 150^MT

Psalm 150 is often read in conjunction with other Psalms to make its universal praise more specific: Ps 150 is sometimes seen as an answer to all other Psalms.[310] The closing function for the Psalter is often stressed with a general importance for the Psalter,[311] even if this is not the original context,[312] and seen as a

---

305 Seidel 1981, 89, based on a few manuscripts but against MT and DSS changes בְ in v.2b to כְּ; against this Mathys 2000, 339.

306 Cf. Loretz 1979, 412; Seidel 1981, 90; Leuenberger 2004, 360 (referring to Loretz); Cha 2006, 109.

307 Cf. on the Hallelujahs in general Lange 1998, 109–110 (comparison with DSS: opening Hallelujahs in Ps 148 and Ps 150 added by the final redaction of the protomasoretic Psalter). Zenger 2008d, esp. 66, argues that the Hallelujahs are secondary and written by the final redactors that wrote parts of Ps 146–150. Their provenance is seen as unclear by Gerstenberger 2001, 437–438 (integral liturgical cry more likely though scribal divider possible).

308 On DSS see II.2.

309 Zenger 2008d, 66, sees the framing Hallelujahs in Ps 146–150 as redactional, but since according to Zenger 2008k, 875, the same redactors wrote Ps 150, the Hallelujahs must be original in Ps 150. Ballhorn 2004b, 304, sees the Hallelujahs as integral at least to Ps 146 due to the use of הלל/"praise" within Psalms 146–150.

310 Cf. Gerstenberger 2001, 460 (even though Ps 150 not written for the end of the Psalter); Human 2011, 8; noted as unlikely by Brueggemann 1988, 92.

311 Cf. Zenger 2011 [1996], 56.

312 Cf. Allen 1983, 323–324; Gerstenberger 2001, 458.

frame with Ps 1.[313] However, it is also stressed that Ps 150 is not merely an end but an open end inviting more praise and even more Psalms.[314] These views depend on a view of the Psalter as a whole. Some commentators see Ps 150 as praise without reason with a sole *focus on God*,[315] but while the praise of God is at the centre of Psalm 150,[316] it does give reasons for praise if very general ones.[317] Due to the importance of הלל/"to praise", Ps 150 is sometimes connected with the Hebrew title of the book of Psalms, תְּהִלִּים/"praises".[318] The importance of *music* for the praise of God is stressed by some commentators,[319] while others emphasise the importance of God over music.[320] Psalm 150 includes both. Due to assumed references to Ps 93–98, or 146–150, some commentators view Ps 150 as referring to a *kingship of YHWH*, with the praise of Ps 150 as anticipating an *eschatological future*[321] or taking place in an eschatological future.[322] In this view, Ps 146–150 are sometimes seen as *criticising human rulers*.[323] However, overall Ps 150 is *universal* in its call to praise.[324]

Overall, Yah, the God (of Israel), is to be praised in any location as no place is specified. The reasons for praise are general ones: his holiness, his mighty firmament, his strong deeds and his abundant greatness which also and mainly gives a measure for the praise. He is to be praised greatly with musical instruments and dance by all humans. The lack of specific locations, specific reasons, and specific people emphasises the universal praise due to God.

---

313 Cf. Gerstenberger 2001, 458; Scaiola 2010b, 710.

314 Cf. Allen 1983, 324; Seybold 1996, 548; Human 2011, 3 (referring to Allen).

315 Cf. Schweizer 1977, 44; Brueggemann 1988, 92-93, 108, 155; Brueggemann 1991, 67; Brueggemann 1993, 37; Vincent 1999, 67.

316 See p. 31–32.

317 See p. 44–47.

318 Cf. Zenger 2008k, 875.

319 Cf. Keck 1996, 1279.

320 Cf. Kraus 1978, 1150.

321 Cf. Zenger 2011 [1996], 64–65 (see fn. 264); Zenger 1997a, 15; Zenger 2008c, 807; Zenger 2008k, 885.

322 Cf. Vincent 1999, 69; Ballhorn 2004b, 353, 356, 359; Strawn and LeMon 2007, 472.

323 Cf. Zenger 1997b, 99–104; Ballhorn 2004b, 354, 359.

324 Similarly Mathys 2000, 343–344; Cha 2006, 102–103; Human 2011, 3 (referring to Mathys).

II.2 Psalm 150^{DSS}

II.2.1 Psalm 150 in 11QPs^a

11QPs^a XXVI contains the complete text of Psalm 150 in its entirety: the part of the manuscript preserving Ps 150 is undamaged.[325] Psalm 150 is preceded by the end of Ps 149 (Ps 149:7–9) and followed by a "Hymn to the Creator". It is separated from both by large spaces at the beginning of the first and the end of the last line.

In Ps 150:1, the first הַלְלוּ־יָהּ/"Praise-Yah!" is missing. Thus, Ps 150 in 11QPs^a starts with הללו אל/"Praise God!". This is significant as this makes the frame of Ps 150 much less clear (while הלל/"praise" is in the opening and closing phrases, the end stands by itself whereas the beginning goes on with a prepositional phrase),[326] and it must be intentional as the manuscript is undamaged here.[327] בקודשו/"in his holiness" is spelled plene instead of defective בְּקָדְשׁוֹ, the same applies to עוזו/"his might" instead of עֻזּוֹ.

In Ps 150:2 there are more plene spellings: בגבורותיו/"his strong deeds" instead of בִגְבוּרֹתָיו, and כרוב גודלו/"according to his abundant his greatness" instead of כְּרֹב גֻּדְלוֹ.

In Psalm 150:3 11QPs^a reads בתקוע instead of בְּתֵקַע/"with a blast". This could be a qal infinitive construct of תקע/"blow" (which for example is used in Josh 6:4) and thus mean תְּקוֹעַ/"blowing" rather than being a hapax legomenon as a verbal noun "blast".[328] Thus, the blowing is less abstract and the activity of blowing and those who blow the horn are implied.[329]

In Ps 150:4 בתוף/"with a drum" is spelled lene instead of בְּתֹף.

Ps 150:5 is identical.

Ps 150:6 has a final plene spelling כול/"all" instead of כֹּל, and the plural הנשמות/"the breaths" instead of the singular הַנְּשָׁמָה/"the breath". Since the verb is still feminine singular, both possible subjects, the plural הנשמות/"the breaths" and the singular masculine כול/"all", lead to incongruencies.[330] A gen-

---

325 Cf. Sanders 1965, 47, Plate XVI; Sanders 1967, 84–85.
326 Against Dahmen 2003, 227.
327 On the debate whether this is independent of MT see p. 15 fn. 94.
328 Cf. Gesenius 2013, s.v. תְּקוֹעַ, s.v. תקע, s.v. תֵּקַע*.
329 See fn. 162.
330 Cf. Dahmen 2003, 227. Dahmen also notes that the plural is used in Isa 57:16 and Sir 9:13 only and thus suggests that the plural shows a late date in the development of the Hebrew language. However, Sir 9:13 actually contains a singular form, cf. Abegg and Parker [no year]b. Depending on the reconstruction of 4Q401 3,1 there may be another plural there (the only other

eralising plural[331] is the most likely solution, which leads to little change in meaning.

For the final words תהלליה הללויה/"let her praise Yah, Praise-Yah!", the editions[332] suggest that they are written without spaces before יה/"Yah", though on the facsimile there is a little space.[333] There are no spaces in Codex L (but a tiny maqqef), and the editions have spaces with maqqefs. Thus, contrary to what the editions suggest, there could actually be spaces in 11QPsᵃ and none in Codex L. This adds to the argument that the use of the phrase as an imperative plus object or a formula has to be decided in each case according to the context.[334] In 11QPsᵃ like in Codex L, the last sentence is complete without an extra imperative, and the final הללויה can be seen as a formulaic "Praise-Yah!". However, this is less secure than in Codex L since there is no opening formula.

Regarding *intertextuality*, Ps 149 is not preserved in its entirety in DSS,[335] the only preserved verses in 11QPsᵃ (Ps 149:7–9) share three words with Ps 150: כֹּל/"all", קֹדֶשׁ/"holiness" (which is not in Ps 149^MT), and the final הַלְלוּ־יָהּ/"Praise-Yah!". Given the fragmentary nature of Ps 149 in Qumran, it is not possible to say if Ps 149 – unlike Ps 150 – is framed by Hallelujahs in 11QPsᵃ, or to assess all shared words between Ps 149 and Ps 150.[336]

Since only two significant words are shared between Ps 150 and the Hebrew versions of *Ps 151* in 11QPsᵃ,[337] עוּגָב/"pipe" and כִּנּוֹר/"lyre", a reference is unlikely. Ps 150 is not placed next to the Hebrew versions of Ps 151 in 11QPsᵃ.[338]

In *summary*, in 11QPsᵃ Psalm 150 is preceded by the end of Psalm 149 but also followed by a non-biblical hymn. There is no opening Hallelujah. Two individual words in Ps 150:3 and 6 have slight changes. Most of the differences in

---

plural form in the Dead Sea Scrolls according to Schneider 2013b), cf. Newsom 1998, 200–201 with Plate XVII in Eshel et al. 1998.

331 Cf. Gesenius and Kautzsch 1909, §124a (collective notion of plural); Joüon and Muraoka 2011, §136j (plural of generalisation). A collective plural is also likely in Isa 57:16 (see fn. 330) since the verb and preceding subject of the verse are singular and the noun רוּחַ/"wind" is used collectively, cf. Gesenius and Kautzsch 1909, §123b; Joüon and Muraoka 2011, §135b.

332 See fn. 325.

333 Cf. Sanders 1965, 47, and Plate XVI.

334 See p. 41–42.

335 See p. 13–15.

336 Dahmen 2003, 302–305, argues that Ps 149 and Ps 150 are connected as one pair in MT (according to 302 fn. 174 following Zenger 1997a, 14–21; Zenger 1997b, 99–104; Ballhorn 2004b, 351–388, esp. 375–375) and also in 11QPsᵃ.

337 On Ps 151 in 11QPsᵃ cf. Sanders 1965, 54–64, esp. 55. See also p. 15 fn. 93.

338 Cf. Sanders 1965, 5.

Psalm 150 are simply variant spellings due to the addition of wav as consistent with the orthography of most of the entire scroll.[339]

II.2.2 Psalm 150 in MasPs^b

MasPs^b contains fragments of every verse of Ps 150 as preserved in MT, and the ends of two words which probably belong to Ps 147. All verses are fragments only. There is a blank space to the left of Ps 150 before the end of the parchment, and the bottom of the parchment is damaged.[340]

It is conjecturally assumed that in contrast to 11QPs^a MasPs^b ended with Ps 147–150 in the Masoretic order.[341] Reasons given for this are firstly the ends of two words assumed to belong to Ps 147:18–19,[342] secondly the blank space to the left of Ps 150,[343] and furthermore the textual affinity between the text of MasPs^b and MT in spelling,[344] words,[345] and text division (blank space before the beginning of every half-verse).[346] While the first reason may indicate a Masoretic order of Psalms, the second is less convincing: While there is a space on the left, the bottom of the parchment is not preserved at all. The claim that the "bottom part of the last column was evidently left blank, a clear indication that the text of the scroll indeed ended here, ruling out the possibility that another Psalm (Psalm 151) was yet to follow as in LXX and 11QPs^a"[347] is conjectural: There might have been more text! While MasPs^b may have contained the entire Masoretic Psalter, the reconstruction of Ps 147–150 for MasPs^b remains speculative and is based on the presupposed order of MT.[348]

There are further problems with spellings and words in comparison to MT: In Ps 150:1, the first הַלְלוּ־יָהּ/"Praise-Yah!" is missing, but as the manuscript is damaged it may just not be preserved.

---

339 Cf. Sanders 1965, 9; Sanders 1967, 15. For Ps 150, Human (2011), 9, argues that the textual closeness also implies a closeness in the date of Ps 150 ("between 350–250 BCE") to Qumran.
340 Cf. Talmon 1999, 17, 24, 91–97, for more details Talmon 1993, 322.
341 Cf. Talmon 1999, 94–97.
342 Cf. Talmon 1999, 92.
343 Cf. Talmon 1999, 91–92.
344 Cf. Talmon 1999, 93.
345 Cf. Talmon 1999, 94.
346 Cf. Talmon 1999, 94. Ballhorn 2004b, 348, sees this as stressing the parallelistic structure.
347 Talmon 1999, 96. Cf. also Talmon 1999, 95–96.
348 Thus also Jain 2014, 211–216, esp. 214 fn. 549 (against Talmon 1999, 96).

בקדשו/"in his holiness" is spelled defective as in L בְּקָדְשׁוֹ, as is עזו/"his might" as in L עֻזּוֹ. In these two spellings, MasPs[b] agrees with L against 11QPs[a].

In Ps 150:2 the spelling of בִגְבוּרֹתָיו/"in his strong deeds" is not preserved, but in כרב גדלו/"according to his abundant greatness" like in L כְּרֹב גֻּדְלוֹ, MasPs[b] again agrees with L against 11QPs[a] in its defective spelling.

However, in Ps 150:2 (twice), 4, and 5 (twice) הללהו/"praise him!" is spelled defectively instead of הַלְלוּהוּ, though there seems to be a plene spelling in the damaged Ps 150:1.[349] In these spellings, L and 11QPs[a] agree against MasPs[b].

In Ps 150:3, שפר/"horn" is spelled defectively instead of שׁוֹפָר, thus again L and 11QPs[a] agree against MasPs[b].[350] In the same verse, however, MasPs[b] reads בתקע like L בְּתֵקַע/"with a blast" against 11QPs[a] – although if 11QPs[a] does mean a qal infinitive construct of תקע/"blow" this could be spelt defective תְּקֹע[351] or plene תְּקוֹע, and thus MasPs[b] could, with a variant defective spelling, agree with 11QPs[a] rather than L.

In Ps 150:4, בתף/"with a drum" is spelled defectively בְּתֹף as in L against 11QPs[a], but עוּגָב/"pipe" plene in L, MasPs[b], and 11QPs[a] alike.[352]

In Ps 150:6 there is another defective spelling כל/"all" like כֹּל in L. Nothing can be said about an agreement with L against 11QPs[a] in הנשמה/"the breath" and the last two words of Ps 150:6 as only parts of a few consonants of this verse are preserved in MasPs[b]. The reconstructed singular תהלל/"let her praise" does not help as even if this reconstruction of parts of consonants is correct, it is identical with 11QPs[a] as well as MT.[353]

In Ps 150:6, the final Hallelujah is missing, but as the manuscript is damaged it may just not be preserved.

Overall, MasPs[b] seems to do the opposite of 11QPs[a] as far as spelling is concerned: Rather than having additional plene spellings, there are even more defective spellings than in L. However, there is still a plene spelling in Ps 150:4, and there are spelling variants where 11QPs[a] and L agree against MasPs[b]. This weakens the case for a close textual affinity between MasPs[b] and MT based on spelling, especially since the spelling is inconsistent within MT itself: עֻגָב/ "pipe" in Ps 150:4 is spelled defectively in Codex A but plene in Codex L.[354]

---

349 Cf. Talmon 1999, 93.

350 Cf. Talmon 1999, 93.

351 As in its only HB occurrence in Isa 18:3[MT]. Isa 18:3 is mentioned by Dahood 1970, 360 as confirming the reading in 11QPs[a] rather than MasPs[b].

352 Cf. Talmon 1999, 93.

353 Against Talmon 1999, 94.

354 Cf. Ben-Zvi Institute 2007, Ps 150; Freedman 1998, 804=fol. 396v. Also noted by Talmon 1999, 93.

Against MT both 11QPs^{a}[355] and MasPs^{b}[356] have the largest blank space between verses 3 and 4.[357] In addition, blank spaces before the beginning of every half-verse are found in MasPs^{b} and Codex A but not consistent in Codex L, and Codex L like both 11QPs^{a} and MasPs^{b} does not present the Psalm in columns.[358] This weakens the case for a close textual affinity between MasPs^{b} and MT based on text division.

Regarding *intertextuality*, small fragments of *Ps 147* in MasPs^{b} may be on the same fragment as Ps 150. This may point towards a composition where Ps 147 and Ps 150 are placed close to each other, but it does not suffice to assume the Masoretic order of all of Ps 147–150, let alone Ps 146. However, the close placing of Ps 147 and Ps 150 in MasPs^{b} stands in contrast to 11QPs^{a} E II-III with parts of Ps 147 between Ps 104 and 105,[359] and to 4QPs^{d} with parts of Ps 147 between Ps 106(?) and 104.[360]

---

355 Cf. Sanders 1965, Plate XVI.

356 The end of Ps 150:3 and beginning of Ps 150:4 are not preserved, but a blank space above v.4 can be seen in the facsimile, cf. Talmon 1999, 93.

357 Also noted by Talmon 1999, 94, who nevertheless argues for an affinity between MasPs^{b} and MT, and by Seybold 1996, 547, without further comments.

358 Against Talmon 1999, 94, BHS which includes spaces and columns does not reproduce the layout of Codex L, compare Elliger and Rudolph 1997, 1226, with Freedman 1998, 804=fol. 396v. Talmon sees 11QPs^{a} as a non-biblical compilation due to the lack of columns, but they are also lacking in both MasPs^{b} and Codex L (though present in Codex A, cf. Ben-Zvi Institute 2007).

359 Cf. Martínez, Tegchelaar, and van der Woude 1998, 33–36.

360 Cf. Skehan, Ulrich, and Flint 2000a, 63.

II.3 Psalm 150^{LXX}

II.3.1 Translation of Psalm 150^{LXX}

1H *Hallelujah!*	1H Αλληλουια.
1a Praise *the* God *in* his *holiness,*	1a Αἰνεῖτε τὸν θεὸν ἐν τοῖς ἁγίοις αὐτοῦ,
1b praise him *in* the firmament of his might;	1b αἰνεῖτε αὐτὸν ἐν στερεώματι δυνάμεως αὐτοῦ·
2a praise him *because of* his strong deeds,	2a αἰνεῖτε αὐτὸν ἐπὶ ταῖς δυναστείαις αὐτοῦ,
2b praise him according to the abundance of his greatness!	2b αἰνεῖτε αὐτὸν κατὰ τὸ πλῆθος τῆς μεγαλωσύνης αὐτοῦ.
3a Praise him with a *sound* of a *trumpet,*	3a αἰνεῖτε αὐτὸν ἐν ἤχῳ σάλπιγγος,
3b praise him with harp and lyre;	3b αἰνεῖτε αὐτὸν ἐν ψαλτηρίῳ καὶ κιθάρᾳ·
4a praise him with drum and dance,	4a αἰνεῖτε αὐτὸν ἐν τυμπάνῳ καὶ χορῷ,
4b praise him with strings and *instrument;*	4b αἰνεῖτε αὐτὸν ἐν χορδαῖς καὶ ὀργάνῳ·
5a praise him with *well-sounding* cymbals,	5a αἰνεῖτε αὐτὸν ἐν κυμβάλοις εὐήχοις,
5b praise him with cymbals of noise!	5b αἰνεῖτε αὐτὸν ἐν κυμβάλοις ἀλαλαγμοῦ.
6 Let every breath praise *the Lord!*	6 πᾶσα πνοὴ αἰνεσάτω τὸν κύριον.
6H *Hallelujah!*	6H αλληλουια.

II.3.2 Form of Psalm 150^{LXX}

Outline of Psalm 150^{LXX}

1H	Framing **Hallelujah**	
1a – 2b	Calls to Praise	**Circumstances** and Reasons
	Imperatives + Objects	*Prepositional Phrases (**2x ἐν, 1x ἐπί,** 1x κατά)+αὐτοῦ*
3a – 5b	Calls to Praise	Means: Musical instruments
	Imperatives + Objects	*Prepositional Phrases (6x ἐν)*
6	Calls to Praise	Subject: All humans
	*Subject + **Imperative** + Object*	
6H	Framing **Hallelujah**	

Syntax of Psalm 150^{LXX}

The exclusive use of imperative forms of αἰνέω/"praise" indicates that the main message of Ps 150^{LXX} is a *call to praise,* with one particularly emphatic imperative aorist in v.6.[361] The subject is an anonymous plural *"you"*,[362] in v.6 πᾶσα πνοή/

---

361 In New Testament Greek, the imperative aorist is used in prayers and probably expresses

"every breath". The summarising character of v.6 is confirmed by the order subject – verb – object, which stresses the subject rather than the act of praising (as
in MT).[363]

There are three instead of two different prepositions: ἐν/"in" (v.1a, 1b), ἐπί/
"because of" (v.2a), κατά/"according to" (v.2b). Thus, v.1 is connected to v.2
through the same possessive pronouns ἀυτοῦ/"his" only, not through the
same preposition (but with the addition of articles).

Structure of Psalm 150^LXX

Articles are placed before almost every noun in vv.1–2 and 6, but not in vv.3–5
(in Hebrew, the equivalent nouns are determined by virtue of being proper
names or by suffixes), but v.1b has no articles at all, which may point to a circumstance rather than a place of God.[364] With regard to vv.3–5, the lack of articles
stresses the general nature of the instruments mentioned and the coherence of
vv.3–5 (as in Hebrew). In v.6, the lack of an article before πνοή/"breath" (in Hebrew with article) stresses the unrestricted general nature of the subject called to
praise (all humans),[365] whereas the article preceding the object τὸν κύριον/"the
Lord" (in Hebrew a proper name) stresses the definite nature of the one to be
praised.

Ps 150^LXX consists of a Hallelujah-frame around three parts: vv.1–2 (v.1 how,
v.2 why and how)[366] – vv.3–5 (how) – v.6 (by whom God is to be praised).[367]

Poetic Devices in Psalm 150^LXX

There is no difference in *parallelism* to Ps 150^MT.[368] Due to the transliteration of
the framing Hallelujahs, there are *eleven* forms of αἰνέω/"praise" with *ten* second person plural imperatives (and one third person singular imperative in

---

the imperative's unconditional and absolute character, cf. Blass, Debrunner, and Rehkopf 1979,
§335, 337.
362 Greek verb forms do not distinguish genders, cf. Smyth and Messing 1956, §355, 382–383.
363 Cf. Blass, Debrunner, and Rehkopf 1979, §472.
364 See p. 75–78, esp. fn. 412.
365 See p. 83.
366 See p. 75–78.
367 A similar structure v.1 (where) – v.2 (why) – vv.3–5 (how) is recognised by Skulj 1998, 1127,
though v.6 is not mentioned and v.1 not treated in detail. Dafni 2006, 438, notes a structure
vv.1a–2a (where) – vv.2b–5b (how) – v.6a (who).
368 In the framework for LXX parallelisms provided by Bons 2007, esp. 117–119, 128–130, the
examples of Ps 146–150 confirm the closeness of LXX to MT. See p. 29 fn. 164.

v.6).[369] Regarding *number symbolism*, unlike in Hebrew the numbers *thirteen* and *twelve* do *not* even appear in the Septuagint. *Eleven* is an insignificant number in HB,[370] *ten* is the only number that could be seen as significant, but there are no indications for this. These observations make it less likely that thirteen and twelve and indeed any numbers were of central importance to the Hebrew text of Ps 150: It is possible that they were important and the translation failed to notice this, but given the small significance of number symbolism in HB in general, LXX probably confirms their lack of importance.

II.3.3 Intertextuality in Psalm 150^{LXX}

Importance
For Ps 150^{LXX} as for Ps 145–149^{LXX}, possible references have so far only preliminarily been listed without analysis.[371]

Analysis
While it is sometimes argued that Ps 150^{LXX} refers to creation in *Genesis 2:7^{LXX}*,[372] any references to Gen^{LXX} are unlikely as in MT: Apart from the frequent word θεός/"god", Ps 150^{LXX} shares with Gen 1:6–20^{LXX} στερέωμα/"firmament" which in LXX is used even more frequently than רָקִיעַ/"firmament" in MT, with Gen 2:7^{LXX} and 7:22^{LXX} as in MT only πνοή/"breath".

A reference to *Exodus 15:20^{LXX}* is unlikely as in MT since only τύμπανον/ "drum" and a plural of χορός/"dance" are shared. While χορός/"dance" is used to translate both מְחֹלָה/"dance" in Ex 15:20^{MT} and מָחוֹל/"dance" in Ps 150^{MT}, thus making the connection stronger than in MT, there are still only two shared significant words.

A reference to *Deuteronomy 3:24^{LXX}* is less likely than in MT: Only θεός/"god" is shared as in MT, in addition to MT δύναμις/"might", but the translations of גֹּדֶל/"greatness" (ἰσχύς/"power" and δύναμις/"might" instead of μεγαλωσύνη/ "greatness") and גְּבוּרֹת/"strong deeds" (ἰσχύς/"power" instead of δυναστεῖαι/ "strong deeds") differ.

---

369 See p. 68–69.
370 See p. 34–35, esp. fn. 30. Further research on LXX number symbolism is desirable.
371 Cf. Bons 2009b, 894–898; Kraus and Karrer 2009, XXII (explanatory note).
372 Cf. Dafni (2006), 438.

A reference to *Joshua 6^LXX* is less likely than in MT: While σάλπιγξ/"trumpet" for שׁוֹפָר/"horn" and ἀλαλαγμός/"noise" for תְּרוּעָה/"noise" are shared, σαλπίζω/ "trumpet" is used for תקע/"blow" instead of ἦχος/"sound" for תֵּקַע/"blast".

A reference to *2 Samuel 6:5^LXX* is less likely than in MT. כֹּל/"all" is missing, כִּנּוֹר/"lyre" is translated with κινύρα/"lyre-instrument" rather than κιθάρα/ "lyre", נֵבֶל/"harp" with νάβλα/"harp-instrument" rather than ψαλτήριον/ "harp", and צֶלְצְלִים/"cymbals" with αὐλός/"aulos". κύμβαλα/"cymbals" is shared but translates מְנַעַנְעִים/"rattles" rather than צֶלְצְלִים/"cymbals". Only תֹּף/"drum" is translated with τύμπανον/"drum". In addition to MT, ὄργανον/"instrument" is shared. In 2 Sam 6:14–15^LXX as in MT πᾶς/"all" for כֹּל/"all" and σάλπιγξ/"trumpet" for שׁוֹפָר/"horn" are shared, in addition to MT again ὄργανον/"instrument", but עֹז/"might" is missing, and תְּרוּעָה/"noise" is translated as κραυγή/"noise" rather than ἀλαλαγμός/"noise".

A reference to *1 Chronicles 15:16–28^LXX and 2 Chronicles 5:12–14^LXX* is unlikely as in MT. While all three texts share κύμβαλον/"cymbal", הלל/"praise" (2 Chr 15:13) is translated with ἐξομολογέομαι/"acknowledge" rather than αἰνέω/ "praise".

A reference to *Psalms 1–2^LXX* is unlikely as in MT. All additional shared words are very frequent, namely in Ps 1–2^LXX κύριος/"Lord", αὐτός/"he", and πᾶς/"all", in Ps 2^LXX plus ἅγιος/"holy".

A reference to *Psalm 95^LXX(=96^MT)* is less likely than in MT: Shared are πᾶς/ "all" for כֹּל/"all", αἰνετός/"praiseworthy" (a verbal adjective derived from αἰνέω/ "praise")[373] for a pu^cal participle of הלל/"praise", and ἅγιος/"holy" for קְדֶשׁ/"holiness" in line with MT, but ἁγιωσύνη/"sanctity" and τιμή/"honour" are used for עֹז/"might" instead of δύναμις/"might". A reference to *Psalm 97^LXX(=98^MT)* is unlikely as in MT: Shared are ἅγιος/"holy" for קֹדֶשׁ/"holiness", πᾶς/"all" for כֹּל/"all", κιθάρα/"lyre" for כִּנּוֹר/"lyre" in line with MT. σάλπιγξ/"trumpet" is used to translate שׁוֹפָר/"horn" but also חֲצֹצְרָה/"trumpet".

A reference to *Psalm 102^LXX(=103^MT)* is unlikely as in MT: Only πᾶς/"all" for כֹּל/"all" and ἅγιος/"holy" for קֹדֶשׁ/"holiness" are shared, in addition to MT δύναμις/"might" but for צָבָא/"host".

A reference to *Psalm 144^LXX(=145^MT)* is unlikely as in MT. In line with MT, πᾶς/ "all" for כֹּל/"all", αἰνέω/"praise" for הלל/"praise", αἰνετός/"praiseworthy" for הלל/"praise", and ἅγιος/"holy" for קֹדֶשׁ/"holiness" are shared, גְּבוּרָה/"strength" is translated with δυναστεία/"might" but also δύναμις/"might", and δύναμις/ "might" is shared but for גְּבוּרָה/"strength" and עֱזוּז/"fierceness" rather than עֹז/ "might". Shared in addition to MT are the frequent words μεγαλωσύνη/"great-

---

373 Cf. Liddell and Scott 1889, s.v. αἰνετός.

ness" for גְּדוּלָה/"greatness", πλῆθος/"abundance" for רַב/"abundant", and θεός/ "god".

A reference to *Psalm 145^{LXX}(=146^{MT})* is less likely than in MT. In line with MT, αἰνέω/"praise" for הלל/"praise", θεός/"god" for אֵל/"god", and πᾶς/"all" for כֹּל/ "all" (and one extra πᾶς/"all") are shared, but there is no Hallelujah-frame.

A reference to *Psalm 146 – 147^{LXX}(=147^{MT})* is less likely than in MT. In line with MT, with Ps 146^{LXX} αἰνέω/"praise" for הלל/"praise", πᾶς/"all" for כֹּל/"all", κιθάρα /"lyre" for כִּנּוֹר/"lyre", and δυναστεία/"might" for גְּבוּרָה/"strength" are shared, plus πλῆθος/"abundance" for מִסְפָּר/"number", with Ps 147^{LXX} only αἰνέω/ "praise" for הלל/"praise" and πᾶς/"all" for כֹּל/"all". There is no Hallelujah-frame.

A reference to *Psalm 148^{LXX}* is less likely than in MT. In line with MT, αἰνέω/ "praise" for הלל/"praise", and πᾶς/"all" for כֹּל/"all" are shared, and in addition to MT δύναμις/"might" for צָבָא/"host" (Ps 148:2^{LXX}). The syntactical similarity of the two frequent words αἰνεῖτε αὐτὸν/"praise him!" for הַלְלוּהוּ/"praise him!" does not suffice for a reference. There is no Hallelujah-frame.

A reference to *Psalm 149^{LXX}* is less likely than in MT. Shared are αἰνέω/ "praise" for הלל/"praise", χορός/"dance" for מָחוֹל/"dance", τύμπανον/"drum" for תֹּף/"drum", θεός/"god" for אֵל/"god", and πᾶς/"all" for כֹּל/"all" in line with MT. ψαλτήριον/"harp" is shared but for כִּנּוֹר/"lyre" instead of נֵבֶל/"harp". There is limited syntactical similarity as in line with MT χορός/"dance" for מָחוֹל/"dance" and τύμπανον/"drum" for תֹּף/"drum" are combined with ἐν/ "with" for בְּ/"with" and αἰνέω/"praise" for הלל/"praise", but the order of the words and the use of the preposition differs. There is no Hallelujah-frame.

While *Psalm 151^{LXX}* is used for the interpretation of Ps 150^{LXX},[374] only two significant words are shared, ὄργανον/"instrument" and ψαλτήριον/"harp". While ὄργανον/"instrument" is used for עוּגָב/"pipe" as in Ps 150^{LXX},[375] ψαλτήριον/ "harp" stands for כִּנּוֹר/"lyre" rather than נֵבֶל/"harp".

References to *Isaiah^{LXX}*, especially Second Isaiah^{LXX}, are sometimes seen with the consequence of an interpretation stressing the holiness of God and his people.[376] However, similar to MT no significant words are shared with Isa 6; 63:15^{LXX}.

A reference to *Ezekiel 1 – 3; 10^{LXX}* is unlikely as in MT since the only significant shared word is στερέωμα/"firmament" for רָקִיעַ/"firmament".

None of the words shared in Hebrew are translated with shared words in *Sirach 39:15^{LXX}* (which shows various differences from the Hebrew) and Ps 150^{LXX},

---

374 See fn. 444.
375 On a Hebrew original of Ps 151^{LXX} see p. 15 fn. 93.
376 Cf. Dafni 2006, 450 – 451.

and no significant words are shared at all (only αὐτός/"he" and μεγαλωσύνη/ "greatness").

Results

References are equally unlikely or even less likely than in MT. Equally unlikely are references to Gen 2; 7^{LXX}; Ex 15:20^{LXX}; 1 Chr 15:16–28^{LXX}; 2 Chr 5:12–14^{LXX}; Isa 6; 63^{LXX}; Ezek 1–3; 10^{LXX}; Ps 1–2^{LXX}; 97^{LXX}(=98^{MT}); 102^{LXX}(=103^{MT}); 144^{LXX} (=145^{MT}); even less likely references to Deut 3:24^{LXX}; Josh 6^{LXX}; 2 Sam 6^{LXX}; Ps 95^{LXX}(=96^{MT}); 145^{LXX}(=146^{MT}); 146–147^{LXX}(=147^{MT}); 148^{LXX}; 149^{LXX}; Sir 39:15^{LXX}. A reference to Ps 151^{LXX} is also unlikely. There is no connection through framing Hallelujahs with Ps 145–149^{LXX}.

II.3.4 Content of Psalm 150^{LXX}

"Hallelujah" in Psalm 150^{LXX}

To translate הַלְלוּ/"praise!" plus יָהּ/"Yah", the Septuagint usually uses the transcription αλληλουια/"Hallelujah",[377] but sometimes a translation with a verbal form of αἰνέω/"praise" plus an object: αἰνεῖτε τὸν κύριον/"praise the Lord".[378] In Ps 150^{LXX}, both at the beginning of v.1 and at the end of v.6 αλληλουια/"Hallelujah" is used. This stresses the formulaic and framing character. The frame is especially important to note since – unlike in MT – this is the only occurrence in the entire LXX where αλληλουια/"Hallelujah" is used not only at the beginning but also at the end of a Psalm.[379] While the aspects of formula and frame are in line with MT, the Greek αλληλουια/"Hallelujah" makes the theme (call to praise)

---

377 Cf. Westermann 1975, 502; Ringgren 1977, 434–435; Seiler 2011a, 1794–1795. Outside the Psalter the word is used in LXX only in Tob 13:18^{LXX} (in a praise context similar to a Psalm, with an eschatological vision of Jerusalem) and in 3 Mac 7:13^{LXX} (in a violent context with killing).

378 E.g. Ps 134:3^{LXX}; 146:1^{LXX} (following a superscription including αλληλουια/"Hallelujah").

379 Cf. Seiler 2011a, 1794–1795. This is also noted by Zenger 2008d, 67 (with the conclusion that LXX sees αλληλουια/"Hallelujah" as a name for a genre only and uses it in superscriptions, except in Ps 150 the genre is also a subscription), and Zenger 2008k, 885 (noting that the final αλληλουια is missing in some LXX-manuscripts). Dahmen 2003, 119, similarly notes that LXX usually sees αλληλουια/"Hallelujah" as a name for a genre only and therefore does not put it at the end of Psalms, and that Ps 150:6^{LXX} is an exception as shown in the 2000 thesis version of Ballhorn 2004b, 300–302. Ballhorn 2004b, 358, concludes that the unusual final Hallelujah in the Septuagint confirms that the final Hallelujah in Ps 150:6^{MT} serves as the implementation of the praise called for in Ps 150 – however, this is unlikely, see p. 41–42.

and the object of the Psalm (God) less clear: They can only be inferred from the formula rather than being obvious due to the verbal component of the Hebrew.

Genitive constructions in Psalm 150:1–2^{LXX}

ἐν στερεώματι δυνάμεως αὐτοῦ mirrors the Hebrew syntax in a construction where the genitive denotes a quality.[380] However, unlike in Hebrew the second genitive αὐτοῦ/"his" primarily depends on and extends to the first genitive δυνάμεως/"might",[381] shifting the emphasis to the might of God. In English, "firmament whose quality is *his* might" is rendered as "firmament of his might". As in Hebrew the suffix determines the entire genitive group, in New Testament and LXX Greek (unlike in Classical Greek) definite articles are often left out in genitive constructions.[382] Given this frequent omission, the definite article "the" is best added in English "the firmament of his might" since "a firmament of his might" is a possible (there is no indefinite article in Greek)[383] but unlikely meaning as multiple firmaments are not mentioned in LXX. The lack of article increases the ambiguity of the meaning of στερέωμα as "firmness".

The construction κατὰ τὸ πλῆθος τῆς μεγαλωσύνης αὐτοῦ is less unusual since in Classical Greek genitives can denote measure,[384] and πλῆθος is usually used with a following genitive.[385] Similar to v.1b, in τὸ πλῆθος τῆς μεγαλωσύνης αὐτοῦ in v.2b the emphasis is shifted to the greatness of God.[386]

Who is called to praise in Psalm 150:1–2^{LXX}?

The opening word αλληλουια/"Hallelujah" in the Septuagint is used as a word connected with the praise of God in the Psalms (mostly for individuals or groups of the people Israel, but also creation in Ps 148^{LXX}) and in texts calling Israelites

---

380 Cf. Smyth and Messing 1956, §1320–1321; Blass, Debrunner, and Rehkopf 1979, §165.
381 Cf. Blass, Debrunner, and Rehkopf 1979, §168.
382 Cf. Blass, Debrunner, and Rehkopf 1979, §259.
383 Cf. Smyth and Messing 1956, §1118.
384 Cf. Smyth and Messing 1956, §1325–1327.
385 Cf. Liddell, Scott, and Jones 1996, s.v. πλῆθος.
386 Brucker 2011e, 1883, states that πλῆθος is often used in an adjectival manner. Bons 2009b, 897, to the translation "gemäß der Fülle seiner Majestät"/"according to the abundance of his majesty" adds an alternate "gemäß seiner gewaltigen Majestät"/"because of his immense majesty". However, there is a stronger connection between τῆς μεγαλωσύνης/"of greatness" and αὐτοῦ/"his".

to praise outside the temple (Tob 13:18ᴸˣˣ; 3 Mac 7:13ᴸˣˣ).[387] Since vv.1–2 refer to neither an earthly nor a heavenly temple but circumstances and reasons for praise,[388] it cannot be determined who is called to praise in vv.1–2. The answer can only be given in combination with vv.3–5, and, most importantly, the summarising v.6.[389]

Which God is to be praised in Psalm 150:1–2ᴸˣˣ?

The object of praise is ὁ θεός/"the God". While the name of YHWH, the God of Israel, is hidden in the transcription αλληλουια/"Hallelujah" at the beginning and end, the identity of "the God" with the God of Israel is confirmed by ὁ κύριος/"the Lord" in v.6 which is a frequent translation of יהוה/"YHWH".[390] As in MT, it is the God of Israel who is to be praised.

Where or why or how is God to be praised in Psalm 150:1–2ᴸˣˣ?

It is debated whether in v.1a ἐν τοῖς ἁγίοις αὐτοῦ refers to a *place* such as the temple "in his holy place",[391] or to people as a place "in his holy ones",[392] or whether this has to be left open.[393] Additionally, ἐν τοῖς ἁγίοις αὐτοῦ may also refer to a *quality* of God "in his holiness".[394] ἐν στερεώματι δυνάμεως αὐτου/ "in the firmament of his might" in v.1b is seen as a *place*.[395] ἐπὶ ταῖς δυναστείαις

---

387 See p. 73–74. Dafni 2006, 438-439, maintains that the Greek reciprocal pronoun ἀλλήλων/ "one another" is mentioned in αλληλουια/"Hallelujah", wherefore Ps 150ᴸˣˣ emphasises both the variety and unity of all humans. However, no Greek texts confirming this mention in a transliteration from Hebrew are given by Dafni, and the reciprocal aspect of ἀλλήλων as "one another" rather than "all together" is ignored: Humans are not called to praise one another but to praise God in Ps 150ᴸˣˣ.
388 See p. 75–78.
389 See p. 69, 83.
390 Cf. Hatch et al. 1998, s.v. κύριος.
391 Cf. Bons 2003, 133; Bons 2009b, 897 (implied by the translation "in seinem Heiligtum"/"in his sanctuary", though with the alternative "unter seinen Heiligen"/"among his saints" as in Greek Orthodox lectionaries today).
392 Cf. Ps 67:36ᴸˣˣ (one manuscript of Ps 67ᴸˣˣ reads ἐν τοῖς ὁσίοις αὐτοῦ/"in his pious ones", cf. Rahlfs 1979, 192), and the Latin Ps 150:1 *in sanctis eius*/"in his holy ones". Cf. also Dafni 2006, 437–451, esp. 437 and 450, where both the saints and God are imagined in the same eschatological place. However, as shown in on p. 44–47, MT probably refers to a place rather than a quality.
393 Cf. Zenger 2008k, 885 (also leaving open if holy ones would be on earth or in heaven).
394 See fn. 402.
395 Cf. Dafni 2006, 438 (question "where"); Bons 2009b, 897 (translation "in"/"in").

αὐτοῦ/"because of his strong deeds" in v.2a is seen as a *quality* of God giving a *reason* for praise[396] (with the reason being God's action in history and creation),[397] or a *place*.[398] τὸ πλῆθος τῆς μεγαλωσύνης αὐτοῦ/"the abundance of his greatness" in v.2b is seen as God's *quality*.[399] Praise according to the greatness implies greatness as a reason for praise since praise is positive, and greatness is an attribute both of praise and of God who is to be praised (as in MT).

Regarding the *general use of words*, ἐν/"in" with dative can (amongst others including a time "in") refer to a *place* "in", *beings* as a *place* "among", a circumstantial *quality* "in", a causal *quality* "because of", an accompaniment "accompanied by", or an instrument "through" or "with".[400] ἅγιος/"holy" may refer to *places*, things, and *beings (human or heavenly)* with the *quality* "holy". The Greek plural dative τοῖς ἁγίοις in v.1a is the same for masculine (nominative: οἱ ἅγιοι/"the holy ones") and neuter (nominative: τὰ ἅγια/"the holy things").[401] The specific phrase ἐν τοῖς ἁγίοις in the Septuagint is used mostly for "in the sanctuary",[402] but it cannot be decided if the form here is masculine or neuter, and even if it is neuter, τὰ ἅγια in the Septuagint does not always mean "sanctuary".[403] The possibility of a masculine leads to a possible reference to *holy beings* (unlike in Hebrew). στερέωμα may refer to a *quality* "firmness" (unlike in Hebrew) or a heavenly *place* "firmament".[404] δύναμις is a general term for the *quality* "might", but may also refer to the *beings* of a human or heavenly "host" (Hebrew צָבָא) unlike in Hebrew.[405] Thus, from the general use of the words it cannot be decided if *v.1* refers to *places (sanctuary, firmament)*, *qualities*

---

396 Cf. Bons 2009b, 897 (translation "aufgrund"/"because of").
397 Cf. Dafni 2006, 438.
398 Cf. Dafni 2006, 438 (question "where").
399 Cf. Dafni 2006, 438 (question "how").
400 Cf. Lust, Eynikel, and Hauspie 2003, s.v. ἐν.
401 Cf. Lust, Eynikel, and Hauspie 2003, s.v. ἅγιος; on declined forms Smyth and Messing 1956, §229.
402 In almost every instance ἐν τοῖς ἁγίοις in LXX refers to "sanctuary": The full list from a search with *BibleWorks 9* 2013 (LXT) is Ex 29:30^{LXX}; Num 4:12^{LXX}; Ps 67:36^{LXX} (may also refer to people); 73:3^{LXX} (probably refers to Jerusalem temple); 150:1^{LXX} (discussed above); Isa 41:16^{LXX} (may also refer to people); Ezek 44:7–8, 11^{LXX}; 1 Mac 6:54^{LXX}. Against Dafni 2006, 447, every instance in the LXX-Psalter uses ἐν τοῖς ἁγίοις to designate God's sanctuary. Thus, that "the Hebrew form of Psalm 150 talks about the historic worship of God in his sanctuary, the LXX version reflects on the eschatological presence of God in the community of his saints" (Dafni 2006, 450) is unlikely for both MT (see p. 44–47) and LXX.
403 E.g., τὰ ἅγια refers to God's "holiness" in Ex 15:11^{LXX} (though ambiguous dative plural form) and to "holy things" in Deut 26:13^{LXX}.
404 Cf. Lust, Eynikel, and Hauspie 2003, s.v. στερέωμα.
405 Cf. Lust, Eynikel, and Hauspie 2003, s.v. δύναμις.

(holiness, firmness, might), or, in addition to Hebrew, *people* or other *beings (holy people or beings and heavenly beings)*.

As for v.2, ἐπί/"because of"[406] in v.2a refers to a causal *quality* "because of". δυναστεία/"strength" and the plural δυναστείαι/"strong deeds" can refer to any expression of the *quality* "might",[407] though given the plural in v.2a it is most probably a causal *quality* rather than a circumstantial quality since "strong deeds" are not a static circumstance. κατά has many meanings[408] and in the construction in v.2b refers to a corresponding *quality* "according to". πλῆθος is a general term expressing a large quantity "abundance",[409] and μεγαλωσύνη/"greatness" a general term for a quality.[410] Thus, the general use of the words makes it likely that v.2 refers to *qualities*, and the verse answers the question why and how God is to be praised. Compared to Hebrew, ἐπί points more towards a *quality* giving a *reason* for praise.[411]

The *context* within Ps 150 illuminates vv.1–2 further. In v.1b there are no *articles* at all unlike in v.1a and v.2ab. This lack of definite articles may point to στερέωμα as "firmness" rather than "firmament".[412] While (as in Hebrew) the *parallelism* in v.2 with different prepositions and most parallelisms in Ps 150^LXX are synthetic, and thus this is also a likely option for v.1, this still does not answer the question whether v.1 refers to places or qualities or beings (whether human or heavenly). In the *structure* of Ps 150^LXX, ἐν has at least two meanings: in v.1 it could refer to a place, a quality, or beings, in vv.3–5 it refers to means. *Unlike in Hebrew*, ἐν/"in" is not found in v.2, and thus vv.1–2 are not as strongly connected, even disconnected by the change of preposition. V.2 refers to qualities. Since ἐπί in v.2a probably refers to a quality and means "because of", this indicates that the different preposition ἐν in v.1 does *not* mean "because of". However, in v.1 it may still refer to a *place* "in" such as *sanctuary and firmament*, *beings in a surrounding place* "among" such as *holy people and heavenly beings*, or a circumstantial *quality* "in" such as *holiness and might*. Thus, the interpretation of v.1 has to rely more heavily than in Hebrew on the interpretation of v.6 as calling

---

406 Cf. Lust, Eynikel, and Hauspie 2003, s.v. ἐπί.
407 Cf. Lust, Eynikel, and Hauspie 2003, s.v. δυναστεία.
408 Cf. Lust, Eynikel, and Hauspie 2003, s.v. κατά.
409 Cf. Lust, Eynikel, and Hauspie 2003, s.v. πλῆθος.
410 Cf. Lust, Eynikel, and Hauspie 2003, s.v. μεγαλωσύνη.
411 Against Dafni 2006, 436, there is no reason to assume an original בְּרֹב/"in the abundance" instead of MT כְּרֹב/"according to the abundance". Indeed, כְּרֹב is more likely as the Greek preposition changes to κατά/"according to" and not back to ἐν/"in".
412 E.g. in Gen 1^LXX στερέωμα/"firmament" translating רָקִיעַ/"firmament" is (after its first mention without an article in Gen 1:6^LXX) always used with a definite article. στερέωμα/"firmness" translating other or no Hebrew words has no article, e.g. Ps 72:4^LXX; 1 Esdr 8:78^LXX.

all humans to praise God.[413] As in Hebrew, the places would have to be those where God is rather than where the worshippers called to praise in Ps 150 are since heavenly beings are not included in v.6. A synthetic parallelism in combination with the content of v.6 also makes the option of *places* of worshippers addressed by Ps 150 (earthly and heavenly place) even *less likely:* Human worshippers could be in the earthly sanctuary but not the heavenly firmament. In addition and unlike in Hebrew, the same logic applies to a *less likely* circumstantial reference to *people and other beings:* God could be among his heavenly host (v.1b) and/or heavenly saints (v.1a) and be praised by all humans, but if he was among his earthly saints (v.1a) these saints would not explicitly be included in the call to praise. Thus, *circumstantial qualities* are most likely. The change of preposition could then be due to a change from static circumstances in which God is when he is to be praised (holiness and might) to a dynamic reason (strong deeds). The only difference to MT would then be a change in the preposition with v.1 answering in what static circumstantial quality God is to be praised, giving "his holiness" and "the firmament of his might" as an answer.

Unlike in Hebrew στερέωμα may refer to a quality "firmness".[414] However, some ambiguity remains as στερέωμα may refer to a place "firmament" rather than a quality "power" and is here used to translate רְקִיעַ/"firmament" which in Hebrew is probably a place. In this case, the synthetic parallelism would have to include both a quality "holiness" and a place "firmament" as circumstances of God when he is to be praised, and the notion of God residing in a *heavenly place* would be stronger than in Hebrew due to the change of preposition.

While as in Hebrew much ambiguity remains, the change of preposition makes it likely that in v.1 God is to be praised *in* certain circumstances rather than *because of* certain qualities. Thus, unlike in Hebrew, v.1 answers "how" rather than "why" God is to be praised (at least primarily, as "how" may imply "why"): in his holiness and in the firmament of his might.

Why or how is God to be praised in Psalm 150:3–5^LXX?

As in Hebrew, ἐν/"with" with a musical instrument refers to a means,[415] and vv.3–5 answer the question how God is to be praised.

413 See p. 83.
414 See fn. 404, 412.
415 E.g. Zech 9:14^LXX (as in MT, see fn. 155).

What are the individual instruments in Psalm 150:3–5^LXX?

Both the Greek words referring to musical instruments and the instruments referred to are explained in the following, and compared to the Hebrew words and corresponding instruments. The Septuagint translation of the Psalms can be dated to 2nd century BCE, but a precise period and location of the origin of Psalm 150^LXX cannot be specified,[416] and even if it could be the Psalm could refer to earlier periods, and the scarcity of evidence makes it necessary to use all available ancient sources on ancient Greek music.[417]

ἦχος is a general abstract noun for "sound". Unlike in Hebrew, it is not necessarily connected with trumpets or any other instruments, and it is not a hapax legomenon.[418]

σάλπιγξ/"trumpet" refers to a long straight trumpet-like instrument made out of metal (bronze) which produces loud tones often used as signals, especially in war.[419] In the Septuagint, a σάλπιγξ/"trumpet" is sometimes but not always blown by priests,[420] and used to translate (among others) שׁוֹפָר/"horn" as well as חֲצֹצְרָה/"trumpet", while only the latter translation is correct as far as the instrument referred to (metal trumpet, not natural horn) is concerned.[421] Thus, instead of a horn as in Hebrew a trumpet is found in Ps 150^LXX.

ψαλτήριον/"harp" is a generic word for harp-like stringed instruments plucked with the fingers of both hands (though it may refer to any instrument with plucked strings).[422] The word may be specific to Hellenistic Greek.[423] In the Septuagint a ψαλτήριον/"harp" is sometimes but not always used for accompanying singing,[424] and sometimes but not always played by Levites.[425] As a

---

416 See II.3.6.
417 Against Skulj 1998, 1118, who argues for a focus on Greek music in the 3rd century BCE, but in fact mostly quotes, e.g. on p. 1120, Riemann 1967 which is a compact general lexicon on music and does not have this narrow focus. In general, literature on Greek music has a much broader focus than the 3rd and 2nd century BCE only, cf. e.g. Maas and Snyder 1989 (stringed instruments only, 28th century BCE to 4th century BCE); West 1992 (38: 8th to 4th centuries BCE); Anderson 1994 (5th century BCE); Pöhlmann 1995 (around 8th century BCE to 3rd century CE).
418 Cf. Lust, Eynikel, and Hauspie 2003, s.v. ἦχος (twice). It is used to translate various Hebrew words, cf. Hatch et al. 1998, s.v. ἦχος.
419 Cf. West 1992, 118–119.
420 E.g. Josh 6:8^LXX (seven priests) vs. Jer 6:1^LXX (people of Benjamin) as in MT; in 2 Sam 20:1^LXX a different translation is used.
421 Cf. Hatch et al. 1998, s.v. σάλπιγξ; Braun 1999, 38–40. Cf. also Skulj 1998, 1120.
422 Cf. West 1992, 60, 74 (used from the later 4th century BCE), 78; Skulj 1998, 1121–1122.
423 Cf. Maas and Snyder 1989, 184 (Hellenistic general term); West 1992, 74 (used as the ordinary word for harp from the later 4th century BCE).
424 E.g. 2 Esdr 22:27^LXX(=Neh 12:27^MT) (with singing) vs. Isa 5:12^LXX (no singing mentioned) as in MT; in 1 Chr 25:6^LXX and 2 Chr 20:28^LXX different translations are used.

word for a harp-like instrument, it corresponds to the instrument referred to by נֵבֶל/"harp", and thus the Greek translation here is close to the Hebrew. However, in the Septuagint it is used to translate (among others) both נֵבֶל/"harp" (more often)[426] and כִּנּוֹר/"lyre".[427]

κιθάρα/"lyre" refers to a lyre-like instrument with a wooden box and two arms and strings played with a plectrum, usually as an accompanying instrument to song.[428] In the Septuagint it sometimes but not always used for accompanying singing.[429] It is *never* played by Levites (unlike in MT).[430] As a word for a lyre-like instrument, it corresponds to the instrument referred to by כִּנּוֹר/"lyre",[431] and thus the Greek translation here is close to the Hebrew. However, in the Septuagint it is used to translate (among others) both כִּנּוֹר/"lyre" (more often)[432] and נֵבֶל/"harp".[433]

τύμπανον/"drum" probably refers to a small drum played with the hand which was mostly played by women.[434] In the Septuagint it is sometimes but not always played by women[435] (as in Hebrew).

χορός/"dance" generally refers to dancing, usually in a group, sometimes while singing, or a group dancing and/or singing.[436] In the Septuagint it is mostly used for dancing of an individual or a group,[437] with women dancing as well

---

425 E.g. Neh 12:27[LXX] (Levites) vs. Isa 5:12[LXX] (godless people) as in MT; in 2 Chr 29:25[LXX] and Isa 14:11[LXX] different translations are used.

426 Cf. Hatch et al. 1998, s.v. ψαλτήριον; Braun 1999, 45.

427 Cf. Braun 1999, 40.

428 Cf. West 1992, 49–56, 64–70; Anderson 1994, 176–177; Škulj 1998, 1122.

429 E.g. Neh 12:27[LXX] (with singing) vs. Isa 5:12[LXX] (no singing mentioned) as for ψαλτήριον/"harp", see fn. 424, as in MT; but in 1 Chr 25:6[LXX] and 2 Chr 20:28[LXX] different translations are used.

430 E.g. Isa 5:12[LXX] (godless people) and Job 21:12[LXX] (wicked people) as in MT; in 2 Chr 29:25[LXX] and Neh 12:27[LXX] different translations are used. Unlike ψαλτήριον/"harp", see fn. 425, κιθάρα/"lyre" does not even appear in Neh 12:27[LXX] (Levites) and is never connected with Λευίτης/"Levite" in LXX.

431 Also noted by Škulj 1998, 1122.

432 Cf. Braun 1999, 40.

433 Cf. Hatch et al. 1998, s.v. κιθάρα; Braun 1999, 45.

434 Cf. West 1992, 124; Anderson 1994, 185 (only women).

435 E.g. Ex 15:20[LXX] (women) vs. 1 Sam 10:5[LXX] (prophets).

436 Cf. West 1992, 13–38; Liddell, Scott, and Jones 1996, s.v. χορός.

437 Cf. Lust, Eynikel, and Hauspie 2003, s.v. χορός. An example for an individual dancing is Judg 11:34[LXX] (Jephta's daughter), for a group Ex 15:20[LXX] (Miriam and all women).

as men.[438] It is used to translate (among others) מָחוֹל/"dance" as well as מְחֹלָה/"dance".[439]

χορδαί/"strings" (singular χορδή/"string") probably is a collective term for instruments with strings (as in Hebrew).[440] It is a rare word in the Septuagint used only in Ps 150:4^{LXX} (for מִנִּים/"strings") and in Nah 3:8^{LXX} (where its relation to the Hebrew original is unclear),[441] but unlike in Hebrew not in Ps 44:9^{LXX}(=Ps 45:9^{MT}) and Sir 39:15^{LXX}.

ὄργανον/"instrument" is a general term for any instruments, including musical instruments.[442] In the Septuagint it is often used for musical instruments and to translate various Hebrew words.[443] It appears for עוּגָב/"pipe" in Ps 150:4^{LXX} and Ps 151:2^{LXX} but unlike in Hebrew not in Gen 4:21^{LXX}, Job 21:12^{LXX}, and Job 30:31^{LXX}. It cannot be said if it here refers to an aerophone or a chordophone or another instrument.[444] It may be used as a collective term.

κύμβαλα/"cymbals" probably refers to bronze cymbals played with the hands, and probably large instruments rather than small castanets.[445] Archaeological findings show different sizes of κύμβαλα/"cymbals" though (unlike for HB) there is *no* limit to two sizes,[446] and they do *not* show that cymbals could be played in two different ways, only vertically.[447] Cymbals were mostly played by women in Ancient Greek contexts,[448] but in the Septuagint they are also played by men.[449] In the Septuagint κύμβαλα/"cymbals" is used to translate (among others) both צֶלְצְלִים/"cymbals" and מְצִלְתַּיִם/"cymbals" and thus (unlike

---

438 E.g. Ex 15:20^{LXX} (women) and vs. Lam 5:15^{LXX} (people) and Ex 32:19^{LXX} (people Israel), as in MT; in Jer 38:4^{LXX}(=Jer 31:4^{MT}) (woman figure) συναγωγή/"gathering" is used for מָחוֹל/"dance".
439 Cf. Hatch et al. 1998, s.v. χορός.
440 Skulj 1998, 1124, doubts whether the translator knew the Hebrew meaning. However, the correct equivalent is used.
441 Cf. Hatch et al. 1998, s.v. χορδή; Lust, Eynikel, and Hauspie 2003, s.v. χορδή. Cf. Anderson 1994, 174 for a description of strings.
442 Cf. Liddell, Scott, and Jones 1996, s.v. ὄργανον.
443 Cf. Hatch et al. 1998, s.v. ὄργανον; Lust, Eynikel, and Hauspie 2003, s.v. ὄργανον.
444 Zenger 2008k, 885, argues for a chordophone due to Ps 151:2^{LXX}, but there is no reference to Ps 151^{LXX}, see p. 72. Skulj 1998, 1127, argues that the translator did not know the Hebrew meaning and used a general term.
445 Cf. Sendrey 1969, 379–380 (large loud instruments); but cf. also West 1992, 125 (maximum of 18 centimetres in diameter, smaller than modern concert cymbals).
446 Cf. Wegner 1963, 60–61; Anderson 1994, 185.
447 Cf. Wegner 1963, 60–61.
448 Cf. West 1992, 124; Anderson 1994, 185 (only women).
449 E.g. 2 Sam 6:5^{LXX} (David and all the house of Israel, Hebrew צֶלְצְלִים/"cymbals") and 2 Esdr 3:10^{LXX} (Levites, Hebrew מְצִלְתַּיִם/"cymbals").

in Hebrew) not a rare word,[450] but it is used for צֶלְצְלִים/"cymbals" only in Ps 150:5^{LXX}, whereas in 2 Sam 6:5^{LXX} αὐλός/"aulos" (usually translated as "flute", but in fact a reed instrument like modern oboes or clarinets)[451] is used instead: κύμβαλα/"cymbals" does appear in 2 Sam 6:5^{LXX} but for מְנַעַנְעִים/"rattles".[452]

εὔηχος/"well-sounding" is an adjective used in Ps 150:5^{LXX} but not as a hapax legomenon as it also appears in Job 30:7^{LXX} where its relation to the Hebrew original is unclear.[453] As usual in Greek, the quality is denoted by an adjective, contrary to ἀλαλαγμός/"noise".[454]

ἀλαλαγμός/"noise" is a noun used in various contexts. It is almost always used to translate תְּרוּעָה/"noise".[455] In ἐν κυμβάλοις ἀλαλαγμοῦ/"with cymbals of noise" the genitive denotes a quality.[456]

As in Hebrew, ἀλαλαγμός/"noise" seems to be stronger in volume than εὔηχος/"well-sounding", while unlike in Hebrew the latter points to the good quality of the sound. As in Hebrew the two mentions of cymbals in Ps 150:5^{LXX} could refer to two different kinds or sizes of cymbals (the first quieter and smaller, the second louder and bigger), or εὔηχος/"well-sounding" and ἀλαλαγμός/ "noise" may point to different ways of playing cymbals, but there is a lack of external evidence for both different sizes and playing methods. In any case, the focus is on the difference in sound,[457] and more so than in Hebrew due to the specification of εὔηχος/"well-sounding", not just ἀλαλαγμός/"noise".

What is the ensemble of instruments in Psalm 150:3–5^{LXX}?
As for MT, the ensemble of instruments in Ps 150^{LXX} is not a complete list of instruments in the Septuagint and cannot be specified due to a lack of knowledge about temple music and a lack of intertextual references.

---

450 Cf. Hatch et al. 1998, s.v. κύμβαλον.
451 Cf. West 1992, 81–85.
452 Cf. Sendrey 1969, 380 (assuming a mistranslation); Braun 1999, 43 (assuming an avoidance).
453 Cf. Lust, Eynikel, and Hauspie 2003, s.v. εὔηχος.
454 See fn. 380, 456.
455 Cf. Hatch et al. 1998, s.v. ἀλαλαγμός.
456 See fn. 380. Cf. Brucker 2011e, 1883.
457 Also noted by Zenger 2008k, 885 (unlike MT which refers to different ways of playing). However, the Hebrew also stresses sound, see p. 51–52.

What is the order of instruments in Psalm 150:3 – 5^{LXX}?
As for MT, the order of instruments does not reflect the order priests – Levites – laypeople (especially women) as no instrument is associated with priests or Levites or women only. The association of Levites with particular instruments is even weaker than in MT as in LXX Levites are never associated with κιθάρα/ "lyre".

In addition to MT, v.3 and v.5 are connected through the related words ἦχος/ "sound" and εὔηχος/"well-sounding",[458] stressing the frame of an opening sound of a trumpet and the final increasing sound of cymbals.

Who is called to praise in Psalm 150:3 – 5^{LXX}?
As in MT, Ps 150:3 – 5^{LXX} refers to all humans.

Who is called to praise in Psalm 150:6^{LXX}?
In the Septuagint, πνοή/"breath" can refer to the breath of humans (Gen 2:7^{LXX}), of all humans and animals (Gen 7:22^{LXX}), or God (Job 37:10^{LXX})[459] but (as in MT) not of other heavenly beings.[460] There is no contrast between humans and animals where only humans have πνοή/"breath",[461] and no intertextual reference to another text which could help to answer the question.[462] As in MT, the most likely explanation is that the summarising phrase refers to all humans since musical instruments and dance in Ps 150:3 – 5^{LXX} are connected with humans, and Ps 150:1^{LXX} refers to humans.

II.3.5 Genre of Psalm 150^{LXX}

The question whether Ps 150^{LXX} was made from and for a cultic or literary context can only be answered in general for the LXX-Psalter.

---

458 Also noted by Brucker 2011e, 1883.
459 Cf. Lust, Eynikel, and Hauspie 2003, s.v. πνοή.
460 πᾶς/"all" with πνοή/"breath" is used only in 1 Kings 15:29^{LXX} for Israel's human enemies.
461 Against Dafni 2006, 438.
462 Against Brucker 2011e, 1883 (phrase must be interpreted with Gen 7:22^{LXX} and Josh 10:40^{LXX}).

II.3.6 Date of Psalm 150^{LXX}

Ps 150^{LXX} does not include indications about its date or translators and its dating has to rely on general considerations about the 2nd century BCE LXX-Psalter.[463]

II.3.7 Unity of Psalm 150^{LXX}

Ps 150^{LXX} is one unit, but the opening and final Hallelujah are missing in some manuscripts, others add an extra Hallelujah at the beginning, and yet others add Αγγαιου καὶ Ζαχαριου/"of Haggai and Zechariah" as in Ps 145 – 148^{LXX}(=146 – 148^{MT}).

While some manuscripts add τῆς/"the" before δυνάμεως αὐτοῦ/"his might", this does not happen before στερεώματι/"firmament". This may confirm the unspecified character of στερέωμα/"firmament" in Ps 150:1^{LXX}.[464] Some manuscripts and versions use the plural ὀργάνοις/"instruments" instead of the singular ὀργάνῳ/"instrument" in Ps 150:4^{LXX}. This may confirm the collective character of ὄργανον/"instrument" in Ps 150:4^{LXX}.[465]

II.3.8 Overall Interpretation of Psalm 150^{LXX}

The God and Lord (specified by definite articles) is to be praised in any location as no place is specified, but (unlike in Hebrew) the circumstances of God as he is to be praised are specified: he is in his holiness and in his mighty firmament. The reasons for praise are general ones: his strong deeds and the abundance of his greatness which also and mainly gives a measure for the praise. He is to be praised greatly with musical instruments (with a trumpet instead of a horn, a general "instrument" instead of a pipe, and cymbals mainly differing in their sound) and dance by all humans (the connection with Levites and therefore the idea of temple music is even weaker than in MT). Ps 150^{LXX} is universal: The lack of specific locations (for worshippers, as unlike in Hebrew for God the firmament is his location), specific reasons, and specific people emphasises the universal praise due to God (the use of articles emphasises the specific character of God and

---

463 See p. 16, esp. fn. 104. Against Dafni 2006, 437 (after 70 CE).
464 See p. 75 – 78, esp. fn. 412.
465 See p. 75 – 78.

the unspecific character of his location and worshippers and the musical instruments).[466]

---

466 As in MT, there is no indication of an eschatological future. While the jussive תְּהַלֵּל/"let her praise" in Ps 150:6 (see fn. 2) could have been translated with a future form (as e.g. in Ps 149^{LXX}, see p. 115), LXX uses the imperative aorist αἰνεσάτω/"let him/her/it praise" (see fn. 361).

II.4 Comparison

For Ps 150, both DSS and LXX are very *close* to MT, with only minor differences.

The framing *Hallelujahs* are least consistent: *11QPs^a* has *no opening Hallelujah* (MasPs^b is too fragmentary), both the *opening and closing Hallelujah are transliterated* rather than translated in *LXX*, and LXX manuscripts show variations of the frame. This weakens the likelihood of an original connection of Psalms 146–150.

Regarding *order*, Ps 150 is preceded by Ps 149 in MT and LXX and 11QPs^a but followed by different texts in each (MT: no text, LXX: Ps 151^{LXX}, 11QPs^a: Hymn to the Creator). This weakens the likelihood of an original connection of Psalms 146–150. MasPs^b is too fragmentary to say anything about texts preceding and following Ps 150, though it does include fragments of Ps 147 close to Ps 150.

Regarding *intertextuality*, both DSS and LXX either confirm the lack of references in MT or even weaken the likelihood of references in MT.

In *summary*, the interpretation of Psalm 150 as an individual Psalm is confirmed by a complete lack of intertextual references in all three text forms: As shown in this chapter, contrary to previous interpretations Ps 150 lacks references not only to Psalms 146–149 but to any other texts at all. The lack of original connection of Psalms 146–150 is further confirmed by the variant contexts and frames of Psalm 150 in its three oldest text forms.

III Psalm 149

III.1 Psalm 149^{MT}

III.1.1 Translation of Psalm 149^{MT}

1H	Praise-Yah!	הַלְלוּ יָהּ׀	1H
1a	Sing to YHWH a new song,	שִׁירוּ לַיהוָה שִׁיר חָדָשׁ	1a
1b	his praise (is) in an assembly of faithful ones!	תְּהִלָּתוֹ בִּקְהַל חֲסִידִים׃	1b
2a	Let Israel be glad in its maker,	יִשְׂמַח יִשְׂרָאֵל בְּעֹשָׂיו	2a
2b	let the sons of Zion rejoice in their king.	בְּנֵי־צִיּוֹן יָגִילוּ בְמַלְכָּם׃	2b
3a	Let them praise his name with dance,	יְהַלְלוּ שְׁמוֹ בְמָחוֹל	3a
3b	with drum and lyre let them make music to him.	בְּתֹף וְכִנּוֹר יְזַמְּרוּ־לוֹ׃	3b
4a	For delighting is YHWH in his people,	כִּי־רוֹצֶה יְהוָה בְּעַמּוֹ	4a
4b	he adorns poor ones with help.	יְפָאֵר עֲנָוִים בִּישׁוּעָה׃	4b
5a	Let faithful ones exult in honour,	יַעְלְזוּ חֲסִידִים בְּכָבוֹד	5a
5b	let them shout for joy on their beds,	יְרַנְּנוּ עַל־מִשְׁכְּבוֹתָם׃	5b
6a	high praises of God in their throats,	רוֹמְמוֹת אֵל בִּגְרוֹנָם	6a
6b	and a sword of two mouths[1] in their hand,	וְחֶרֶב פִּיפִיּוֹת בְּיָדָם׃	6b
7a	to execute revenge on the nations,	לַעֲשׂוֹת נְקָמָה בַּגּוֹיִם	7a
7b	punishments [on][2] non-peoples,	תּוֹכֵחֹת בַּל־אֻמִּים׃	7b
8a	to bind their kings with chains,	לֶאְסֹר מַלְכֵיהֶם בְּזִקִּים	8a
8b	and their honoured ones with with fetters of iron,	וְנִכְבְּדֵיהֶם בְּכַבְלֵי בַרְזֶל׃	8b
9a	to execute on them a written judgement.	לַעֲשׂוֹת בָּהֶם׀ מִשְׁפָּט כָּתוּב	9a
9b	Splendour (is) he for all his faithful ones.	הָדָר הוּא לְכָל־חֲסִידָיו	9b
9H	Praise-Yah!	הַלְלוּ־יָהּ׃	9H

III.1.2 Form of Psalm 149^{MT}

Outline of Psalm 149^{MT}

1H	Framing *Imperative*	
Part I		
1	Calls to	Subject: Israel, Object/Reason: YHWH,
– 2	+ Reasons for <u>Praise</u> *Imperatives/Jussives/ Nominal clause*	Means: Music
3	Calls to *Imperatives*	Subject: Israel, Object: YHWH, Means: Music

---

1 Less literally: "a two-edged sword".
2 See p. 104–105.

DOI 10.1515/9783110536096-003

– 4	+ Reason for <u>Praise</u> *Participle/Imperfect*	Subject: YHWH, Object: Israel
<u>Part II</u>		
5 – 6	Calls to <u>Praise</u> *Jussives, Nominal clauses*	Subject: Israel, Object: YHWH, Means: Voice, Sword
7 – 9a	<u>Judgement</u> *Infinitives*	Subject: Israel, Object: Nations, Means: Violence
<u>Summary</u>		
9b	<u>Summary:</u> Reason for <u>Praise</u> + <u>Judgement</u> *Nominal clause*	Subject: [YHWH], Object: Israel
9H	Framing *Imperative*	

Syntax of Psalm 149[MT]

Imperatives in v.1a and the frame and *jussives*[3] in vv.2ab, 3ab, 5ab are both connected with the first theme of *praise*. V.4 has a *participle* רוֹצֶה/"delighting" (the
only other participle is v.2a בְּעֹשָׂיו/"in its maker")[4] followed by an *imperfect*
יְפָאֵר/"he adorns".[5] These forms found only once within Ps 149 are probably
due to the change in subject, and both are connected with the first theme of
praise. In vv.7a, 8a, 9, *infinitives* are connected with the second theme of *judgement*.

Several sentences have *no verb:* Vv.1b, 6ab, and 9b are (as v.4a with a participle) nominal clauses.[6] In v.7b and 8b (due to the parallels,[7] and וְ/"and" connecting v.8a and 8b), the missing verb can be supplied from the context as the same
verb as in the preceding half-verse.[8] While it would be possible to do the same in
v.1b with the same verb as in v.1a (שִׁירוּ/"sing!"),[9] a nominal clause is more probable in v. 1b given the nominal clauses in vv.4a, 6ab, and 9b: The nominal clauses
in vv.1b, 4a, 6ab, and 9b connect all parts of Ps 149, and the two themes of *praise*
and *judgement*.

---

3 Cf. Gesenius and Kautzsch 1909, §48, 109; Joüon and Muraoka 2011, §46, 114 g-l. See p. 32 fn. 2
4 See p. 99 – 100.
5 A jussive would have a shortened vowel יְפָאֵר/"let him adorn", cf. Gesenius and Kautzsch 1909,
§48; Joüon and Muraoka 2011, §46, 69 Paradigm 5.
6 Cf. Gesenius and Kautzsch 1909, §141; Joüon and Muraoka 2011, §154. A form of "to be" is inserted in English.
7 On v.7b see p. 104 – 105.
8 Cf. Gesenius and Kautzsch 1909, §147a.
9 Thus Zenger 2008j, 854, 870.

Subjects are the *people Israel* and *YHWH*, whereas the *nations never appear as a subject:* The anonymous "you"[10] in v.1a and the framing imperatives, "Israel" in v.2a synonymous with "sons of Zion" in v.2b, "they" in vv.3ab (referring back to "Israel" = "sons of Zion" in v.2), "faithful ones" in v.5a, and "they" in v.5b (referring back to "faithful ones" in v.5a) are connected through jussives and refer to the same subject, the *people Israel*. The final clauses[11] in vv.7a – 9a have no subject, but are connected with the subjects of the nominal clauses v.6a *"high praises of God"*, and v.6b *"a two-edged sword"*, which in turn are connected through *suffixes* with "faithful ones" in v.5a, again referring to the people Israel. In the nominal clause v.4a the subject is יהוה/*"YHWH"*, also included in the verb in v.4b ("he adorns"). In the other nominal clauses the subjects are v.1b *"his praise"*, and v.9b *"he"* [12] (both referring to YHWH).

The *word order*[13] in v.2b (subject – verb – object, forming a chiastic structure with v.2a) and v.3b (adverbial phrase – verb including subject – object, forming a chiastic structure with v.3a which has verb including subject – object – adverbial phrase) stands out and stresses the element of praise. In verbless sentences, the usual order subject-predicate is reversed in v.9b since personal pronouns as the subjects of nominal clauses tend to stand after the predicate which is stressed.[14]

Suffixes connect vv.1b, 3a, 4a, and 9b referring to *YHWH*, vv.2ab, 5ab, and 6ab referring to the *people Israel*, and vv.8a – 9a with v.7 referring to the *peoples*.

The preposition בְּ in various meanings "in/with/on" is found in almost every half-verse (vv.1b, 2ab, 3ab, 4ab, 5a, 6ab, 7a,[15] 8ab, 9a) except for three half-verses with לְ/"to, for" referring from the people Israel to YHWH (vv.1a, 3b) and then vice versa (v.9b), and one half-verse with עַל/"on" (v.5b).

In vv.5 – 9, the question of subordination of clauses leads to different interpretations of the content. If v.7 and v.8 are parallels without subordination, judgement is executed on the nations *and* their rulers. If, however, v.8 is subordinate to v.7, and v.8 specifies what is said in v.7, judgement is executed amongst the nations specifically on their rulers, in other words on the rulers of nations

---

10 See p. 32 fn. 3.

11 Cf. Joüon and Muraoka 2011, §168.

12 See fn. 14.

13 See p. 32 fn. 4.

14 Cf. Gesenius and Kautzsch 1909, §141 l-n; Joüon and Muraoka 2011, §154f, fa. On Ps 149:9b see p. 108.

15 On v.7b see p. 104 – 105.

only, not the nations themselves.[16] In Ps 149, parallels are more likely: Both v.7a and v.9a beginn with the infinitive לַעֲשׂוֹת/"to do" followed by "the nations" in v.7a and "they" in v.9a, each with בְּ/"on". Thus, v.7a mentioning nations and v.9a are parallel to each other and tied together. V.8 could still be subordinate to v.7, but this would be grammatically unique,[17] and since v.8 is enclosed by parallels and introduced by another infinitive it is probably parallel to v.7 and v.9a.

Structure of Psalm 149[MT]

The structure of Psalm 149[MT] is debated.[18] A two-fold structure (Hallelujah – vv.1–4 – vv.5–9 – Hallelujah) is seen by many commentators[19] due to calls to praise (including imperatives) in vv.1–3 and 5–6, two topics (praise with music, praise with violence), and vv.7–9 as final clauses connected with the main clause v.6 which in turn is connected with v.5, tying together vv.5–9.[20] Both Parts I and II consist of calls to praise (vv.1–3/vv.5–6) followed by reasons for praise (v.4/vv.7–9a), with כִּי/"for" in v.4a indicating a reason for praise, namely God's deeds for his people (Israel), and with לְ/"to" in vv.7a, 8a, 9a indicating the aim or consequence of praise for other peoples.[21] Thus, the structure of Parts I and II is similar. The pattern of בְּ/"in" which appears twice in most verses but only once in v.1, 5, and 9, also points to a two-fold structure.[22] Some commentators see v.5[23] or v.6[24] as a hinging verse between the two parts, but the syntactical connection of vv.5–9 is too strong.[25]

Other commentators argue for a three-fold structure (Hallelujah – vv.1–3 – vv.4–6 – vv.7–9 – Hallelujah)[26] due to the general view of regular structures

---

16 Thus Füglister 1999, 41–42; Lohfink 1990, 125 (referring to Füglister); Zenger 2008j, 856–857 (referring to Lohfink); Ballhorn 2004b, 339–340 (including v.9a in the subordination, referring to Arabic grammar).

17 The phenomenon is not mentioned in Gesenius and Kautzsch 1909; Joüon and Muraoka 2011. Ballhorn 2004b, 339, refers to Zech 9:9; 2 Kings 8:9. However, these verses feature nouns and וְ/"and" rather than infinitives and whole sentences.

18 For overviews cf. Ceresko 1986, 185; Prinsloo 1997, 396; Allen 2002, 396–398; Zenger 2008j, 857–859.

19 Cf. Gunkel 1926, 619; Seybold 1996, 544–545; Gerstenberger 2001, 452, 454–455 (though v.4 is separate on 452); Allen 2002, 396–398; Zenger 2008j, 854–855, 857–859, and see fn. 18.

20 Cf. Zenger 2008j, 857–859.

21 Cf. Zenger 2008j, 858. Similarly Allen 1983, 321.

22 Cf. Allen 2002, 398.

23 Cf. Ceresko 1986, 180, 185–187.

24 Cf. Prinsloo 1997, 399.

25 Zenger 2008j, 859, only criticises that Prinsloo 1997 underestimates the importance of v.4.

26 Cf. Loretz 2002, 358–362; further references in Zenger 2008j, 857–859.

of Psalms, and the tricolic structure of vv.7–9.[27] However, the syntactical connection of vv.5–9 is too strong,[28] vv.1–4 are connected as a call to praise followed by reasons for praise,[29] and the Psalm has to be read backwards to find a tricolic structure.[30]

A twofold structure is thus most likely, but one observation remains to be added: V.9a with the repetition of the infinitive לַעֲשׂוֹת/"to do" which first appears in v.7a connects vv.7a–9a.[31] V.9a thus serves as a summary of vv.7a–8b. V.9b as the final verbless sentence may serve as a summary of either the second part (vv.5a–9a)[32] or the whole Psalm. V.9b is the only verse which does not stand in a *parallelismus membrorum*,[33] and given its subject and topic (YHWH is splendour),[34] and its final mention of חֲסִידִים/"faithful ones" (also in v.1b in Part 1, in v.5a in Part II),[35] v.9b provides a summary of the entire Psalm.

Thus, the structure of Psalm 149 is Hallelujah – vv.1–4 (Part I: Calls to Praise and Reasons for Praise) – vv.5–9a (Part II: Call to Praise and Violence) – v.9b (Summary: Reason for Praise and Violence) – Hallelujah. This structure makes the sudden appearance of violence in v.6b surprising but also ties it in with the theme of praise.

Poetic Devices in Psalm 149^{MT}

Vv.1–8 show a *synonymous parallelism* in vv.2 and 7, and a *synthetic parallelism* in vv.1, 3, 4, and 5. In vv.6 and 8, the parallelism could be synonymous or synthetic depending on the interpretation of the content. The concluding character of v.9a (for vv.5–8) and of v.9b (for the entire Psalm)[36] is stressed by the absence of parallel structures.[37]

---

27 Cf. Loretz 2002, 358–362 (v.9b later addition), and see fn. 18.
28 Cf. Zenger 2008j, 857–859.
29 Cf. Zenger 2008j, 858. See III.1.5.
30 Thus explicitly Loretz 2002, 359.
31 Similarly Zenger 2008j, 857–857.
32 Cf. Seybold 1996, 545; Gerstenberger 2001, 454; Zenger 2008j, 859.
33 Loretz 2002, 358–359, without text-critical evidence sees v.9b as a later redactional addition for this and colometric reasons.
34 See p. 108.
35 Similarly Zenger 2008j, 858.
36 See p. 90–91.
37 See fn. 33.

Chiastic structures can be seen in v.1 and v.3[38] and thus in Part I only. A strong chiasm is found in v.3: v.3a *Let them praise (A)* his name *with dance (B)*, v.3b *with drum and lyre (B) let them make music (A)* to him.

Repetitions of words underline the structure and unity of Psalm 149. הלל/ "praise" occurs in the framing imperatives הַלְלוּ־יָהּ/"Praise-Yah!" and in the jussive in v.3a יְהַלְלוּ/"let them praise". יהוה/"YHWH" appears in v.1a and 4a as well as in the framing Hallelujahs. In Part II, אֵל/"God" is used in v.6a, and in the Summary he appears as הוּא/"he".[39] Thus, the mention of God connects all parts of the Psalm and the frame (Part I, Part II, Summary, Frame).

חֲסִידִים/"faithful ones" is repeated three times in vv.1b, 5a, and 9b.[40] Thus, the mention of faithful ones connects all parts of the Psalm, as does the use of one preposition, mostly בְּ/"in",[41] in every half-verse.

בְּכָבוֹד/"in honour" in v.5a has the same root כבד/"be heavy, be honoured" as וְנִכְבְּדֵיהֶם/"and their honoured ones" (a nifʿal participle) in v.8b. Neither of the two words is connected with God (unlike הָדָר/"splendour" in v.9b).[42] בְּכָבוֹד/"in honour" in v.5a refers to Israel and is connected with joy and active vengeance. In contrast, וְנִכְבְּדֵיהֶם/"and their honoured ones" refers to the peoples and is connected with the vengeance against them.[43] This word play on כבד/"be heavy, be honoured" occurs within Part II.

עשה/"do" appears in v.2a בְּעֹשָׂיו/"in its maker" calling Israel to praise YHWH and in vv.7a and 9a לַעֲשׂוֹת/"to do" in connection with Israel's execution of revenge and judgement. This word play connects Parts I-II and the ideas of YHWH making Israel and Israel executing revenge: Israel is able to do anything only because it was itself made by YHWH.[44]

מֶלֶךְ/"king" appears in v.2b בְמַלְכָּם/"in their king" referring to Israel's king YHWH who causes joy, and in v.8a מַלְכֵיהֶם/"their kings" referring to the kings of the peoples which are bound in chains. This word play contrasts YHWH as the king of Israel with the powerless kings of the peoples,[45] and connects Parts I-II.

---

38 Cf. Zenger 2008j, 858.
39 See p. 108.
40 See fn. 35.
41 See p. 88–90.
42 This makes it more likely that v.9b is a summary of the entire Psalm, against Allen 2002, 398, and Zenger 2008j, 859, who see v.9b with הָדָר/"splendour" together with v.5a with כָּבוֹד/"glory" as a frame for Part II, with a similar motif יְפָאֵר/"he adorns" in v.4b at the end of Part I.
43 Similarly Ceresko 1986, 190–193; Ballhorn 2004b, 326; Zenger 2008j, 857.
44 Similarly Ceresko 1986, 190–193; Ballhorn 2004b, 325.
45 Similarly Ceresko 1986, 190–193 (ironic repetition); Ballhorn 2004b, 325–326 (YHWH's kingship excluding all other kings, even a Davidic king).

III.1.3 Intertextuality in Psalm 149^MT

Importance

Intertextual references are of fundamental importance for the interpretation of Psalm 149 for three main reasons:

Firstly, the Psalm itself contains כָּתוּב/*"written"* in v.9a, which usually is a reference to written texts.[46]

Secondly, commentators often hold the view that there are intertextual references to Psalms 96 and 98 as well as Isaiah 40–66 and use these references to argue for an *eschatological, less violent* interpretation of Psalm 149.[47]

Thirdly, intertextual references to Psalms 146–148 and 150 are sometimes used to argue for reading the *group of Psalms 146–150* as a unit, thus reading Psalm 149 within this group as eschatological.[48] However, references from Psalm 149 to the same Psalms 146–150 are also used to argue for a later addition of Psalm 149 within Psalms 146–150, and thus for reading *Psalm 149 separately*.[49] In addition to such contradictory interpretations based on intertextuality within Psalms 146–150, a high number of intertextual references is sometimes seen from Psalm 149 to other texts.[50]

Analysis

Some commentators argue for references from Ps 149 to *Exodus 14–15*, either directly[51] or indirectly through Isaiah[52] or a "new song" motif.[53] Others explicitly maintain that there is no reference from Ps 149 to Ex 14–15.[54] Since Ps 149 and Exodus 14–15 only share frequent words, a direct reference is unlikely.

The argument that there are references to *Joshua* and *Judges*, mainly due to a sword of two mouths in Judg 3:16, leads to a violent interpretation of the judgement in Ps 149:6–9 as killing enemies.[55] Josh contains references to the written

---

46 See p. 106–107.
47 Cf. Allen 1983, 319; Ballhorn 2004b, 323–324.
48 Cf. Ballhorn 2004b, 323–324; Zenger 2008j, 860–861. See also fn. 61.
49 Cf. Leuenberger 2004, 356; against this Ballhorn 2004b, 338; Zenger 2008j, 861 (referring to Leuenberger).
50 Cf. Zenger 2008j, 860–861.
51 Cf. Zenger 2008j, 855, 861 (Ex 14–15 read eschatologically in Ps 149).
52 Cf. Ceresko 1986, 180–184.
53 Cf. Patterson 2007, 430–431 (via Ps 33); Weber 2009, 40, 42–43.
54 Cf., all explicitly against Ceresko 1986, see fn. 52, Gerstenberger 2001, 454; Ballhorn 2004b, 324; Leuenberger 2004, 354 fn. 308.
55 Cf. Ceresko 1986, 188–190.

"torah" law in which the participle כָּתוּב/"written" is shared with Ps 149:9 (e. g. Josh 1:8; 8:34). However, overall Ps 149 and Joshua and Judges only share frequent words (for plural forms of פֶּה/"mouth" see below on *Isaiah*), wherefore a reference is unlikely.

Some commentators argue for references to *Deuteronomy*, leading to the interpretation of Ps 149 as referring to actual violence.[56] Since only frequent words are shared, e. g. in Deut 32:41 חֶרֶב/"sword", מִשְׁפָּט/"judgement", and יָד/"hand", references are unlikely.

Some commentators hold that there are references to *Psalm 2*, which leads to eschatological interpretations.[57] Given an inner frame of the book of Psalms with Ps 2 and Ps 149, Ps 2 is even seen to be the written judgement mentioned in Ps 149, with Israel having a messianic role.[58] However, only גּוֹי/"nation", מֶלֶךְ/"king", יהוה/"YHWH", לְאֹם/"people",[59] צִיּוֹן/"Zion", בֵּן/"son", בַּרְזֶל/"iron", גִּיל/"rejoice", and כֹּל/"all" are shared without syntactical similarity. There are no references from Ps 149 to Ps 2, and the stress on their similarities due to their position in the final collection of the book of Psalms is secondary to the writing of the individual texts.[60]

Commentators argue for a reference to *Psalm 96* and *Psalm 98*, supporting an eschatological interpretation of Ps 149,[61] or for a reference from the group Ps 146–150 to a group of Psalms including Ps 96 and 98, again often with a stress on eschatology.[62] Ps 96 shares שִׁירוּ לַיהוָה שִׁיר חָדָשׁ/"sing to YHWH a new song",[63] and the words שִׁיר/"sing", יהוה/"YHWH", כֹּל/"all", שְׁמוֹ/"his name", וִישׁוּעָה/"help", גּוֹי/"nation", כָּבוֹד/"honour", עַם/"people" (though referring to other peoples in Ps 96:3, 5, to Israel in Ps 149:4), הלל/"praise", עשה/"to make", הָדָר/"splendour", the root מלך/"be king" (verb referring to YHWH in Ps 96:10, noun referring to non-Israelite kings in Ps 149:8), בַּל/"not" (for Ps 149:7 see p. 104–105), שׂמח/"be glad", גִּיל/"rejoice", עלז/"exult", רנן/"shout for joy". Ps 98 shares שִׁירוּ לַיהוָה שִׁיר חָדָשׁ/"sing to YHWH a new song", and the words עשה/"do", יהוה/"YHWH", יְשׁוּעָה/"help", גּוֹי/"nation", יִשְׂרָאֵל/"Israel", כֹּל/

---

56 Cf. Gerstenberger 2001, 455. This possibility is mentioned as unlikely by Allen 1983, 319; Ballhorn 2004b, 331 fn. 882.
57 Cf. Ballhorn 2004b, 343–344; Leuenberger 2004, 355–356; Zenger 2008j, 861.
58 Cf. van Grol 2011, 107–108.
59 See p. 104–105.
60 Cf. Gerstenberger 2001, 456. Claimed for Ps 106 and Ps 149 but not Ps 2 by Leuenberger 2004, 355 fn. 310 ("nur aufgrund der Positionierung überhaupt auffallender Rückbezug"/"reference noticeable only because of the position").
61 Cf. Allen 1983, 319–320; Ballhorn 2004b, 324; Zenger 2008j, 855, 860–861, 868–869.
62 See p. 38 fn. 67.
63 See p. 99.

"all", רנן/"shout for joy", זמר/"make music", כִּנּוֹר/"lyre", מֶלֶךְ/"king" (though referring to YHWH in Ps 98:6, to non-Israelite kings in Ps 149:8), עַם/"people" (though referring other peoples in Ps 98:9, to Israel in Ps 149:4). Given the differences in order and the high frequency of shared words, there is no reference to Ps 96 and 98, but a more general thematic similarity.

Similarities between Ps 149 and *Psalm 146* are often stressed as Ps 146 is a part of the group Ps 146–150.[64] However, Ps 149 and Ps 146 only share the frequent words הלל/"praise", יהוה/"YHWH", זמר/"make music", בֵּן/"son" (though in Ps 146 referring to the sons of man i.e. humans, in Ps 149 to the sons of Zion i.e. Israelites), אֵל/"god", עשׂה/"do", מִשְׁפָּט/"judgement", אסר/"bind", the root מלך/ "be king" (verb referring to YHWH in Ps 146:10, noun referring to non-Israelite kings in Ps 149:8), and צִיּוֹן/"Zion". Thus, apart from the shared frame הַלְלוּ־יָהּ/ "Praise-Yah!", a reference is unlikely.

References to *Psalm 147* are seen,[65] similarities are stressed,[66] and Ps 147 is also a part of the group Ps 146–150. However, Ps 149 and Ps 147 only share the frequent words זמר/"make music", תְּהִלָּה/"praise", יהוה/"YHWH", יִשְׂרָאֵל/"Israel", כֹּל/"all", שֵׁם/"name", עָנָו/"poor", כִּנּוֹר/lyre", בֵּן/"son" (referring to sons of ravens and sons of Zion in Ps 147, only sons of Zion in Ps 149), רצה/"delight", הלל/ "praise", צִיּוֹן/"Zion", and מִשְׁפָּט/"judgement". Thus, apart from the shared frame הַלְלוּ־יָהּ/"Praise-Yah!", a reference is unlikely.

Commentators often argue for references to *Psalm 148*, especially from Ps 149:1 to Ps 148:14,[67] and Ps 148 also is a part of the group Ps 146–150. However, other commentators stress the differences or explicitly maintain that there is no reference from Ps 149 to Ps 148.[68] Psalm 148:14 reads וַיָּרֶם קֶרֶן לְעַמּוֹ תְּהִלָּה לְכָל־חֲסִידָיו לִבְנֵי יִשְׂרָאֵל עַם־קְרֹבוֹ הַלְלוּ־יָהּ "And he will lift up a horn for his people, praise for all his faithful ones, the sons of Israel, his close people. Hallelujah." The underlined words רום/"lift up", עַם/"people", תְּהִלָּה/"praise", כֹּל/"all", חָסִיד/ "faithful", בֵּן/"son", and יִשְׂרָאֵל/"Israel", also appear in Ps 149, but there is little syntactical similarity (the combination לְכָל־חֲסִידָיו/"for all his faithful ones" appears only in Ps 149:9 and Ps 148:14, though without לְ/"for" also in Ps 31:24, and חֲסִידָיו/"his faithful ones" in other Psalms such as Ps 30:5), and none of the words are rare. The root רום/"lift up" is even used in Ps 149:6 as the rare

---

64 See fn. 48.
65 Cf. Zenger 2008j, 865 (on Ps 147).
66 Cf. Zenger 2008 h, 832, 836; Zenger 2008j, 869–870.
67 Cf. Seybold 1996, 544–545 (though stressing differences); Zenger 2003, 147–148; Ballhorn 2004b, 323, 338; Booij 2008, 104.
68 Cf. Allen 1983, 321.

noun רֹומָם/"high praise" which appears only here and in Ps 66:17,[69] but not in Ps 148, thus the only rare word is *not* shared between the Psalms. Other shared words between Ps 149 and Ps 148 are הלל/"praise", יהוה/"YHWH", שֵׁם/ "name", עשׂה/"do", and מֶלֶךְ/"king", without syntactical similarity. Thus, apart from the shared frame הַלְלוּ־יָה/"Praise-Yah!", a reference is unlikely. Neverthe-less, the combination לְכָל־חֲסִידָיו/"for all his faithful ones" appears only in Ps 149:9 and Ps 148:14, i.e. the last verses of Ps 149 and 148. In addition, תְּהִלָּה/"praise" and חֲסִידִים/"faithful ones" appear in the last verse of Ps 148 and, immediately following it in MT, the first verse of Ps 149. Therefore, Ps 148 and Ps 148 can be seen an example for the connection of Ps 146–150 in MT. Given the unlikelihood of an intertextual reference shown above, it seems un-likely that Ps 148 and Ps 149 had the same author or that the author of one Psalm knew and drew on the other.[70] Thus, an *original* connection is unlikely. However, there are two other possibilities: (1) the similarities might have been inserted into the Psalms by the compilers to serve as redactional connections (i.e. the original Psalms did not contain the connecting parts),[71] or (2) the two Psalms could have had two different authors but have been placed next to each other by the compilers because of their similarities especially regarding the end of Ps 148 and the beginning of Ps 149.[72] For possibility (1), there is no evidence in any source.[73] Thus, it is possible that the Psalms were altered by their compilers, but this possibility remains conjectural. Possibility (2) is more likely since the individual Psalms are extant in different sources in different or-ders.[74] However, neither Ps 148:14 nor Ps 149:1 are preserved in DSS,[75] making a complete comparison impossible.

As shown on p. 40 on Ps 149, references to Ps 149 from *Psalm 150* are unlikely.

---

69 Ps 66 otherwise only shares frequent words with Ps 149 and without syntactical similarity.
70 For example, the possibility that the author of Ps 149 drew on Ps 148 is seen by Seybold 1996, 544–545.
71 For example, Leuenberger 2004, 352–356; Zenger 2008c, 807–809; Zenger 2008i, 845–846; Zenger 2008j, 860–861, argue that both Ps 148:14 and the entire Ps 149 were written by the same redactors, i.e. that Ps 148 did not originally contain v. 14.
72 Thus for example Allen 1983, 321: "There is little warrant for regarding the psalm as a devel-opment of the last line of Ps 148 [...] However, the similarity provides apt reason for the present juxtaposition of the two psalms.".
73 For a more detailed discussion see IV.1.7, for references esp. p. 150 fn. 182–183.
74 See I.2.1.
75 See III.2, IV.2.

References seen to Isaiah, especially *Isaiah 40–66*, often lead to an eschatological interpretation of Ps 149 downplaying any actual violence,[76] but also to the opposite interpretation of actual violence.[77] While most passages in Isaiah only share frequent words[78] with Ps 149 without syntactical similarity, Isa 42:12 shows syntactical similarity with Ps 149:1 through שִׁירוּ לַיהוָה שִׁיר חָדָשׁ/"sing to YHWH a new song",[79] and Isa 41:15 shares the rare פִּיפִיּוֹת/"mouths" (following a construct בַּעַל "owner", with respect to מוֹרַג/"threshing sled"), a reduplicated plural of פֶּה/"mouth, edge",[80] with Ps 149 (in addition to the frequent word חָדָשׁ/"new"; other frequent words are shared with Isa 45:8–20). The plural פִּיפִיּוֹת/"mouths" is found only in these two texts, and other plural forms of פֶּה/"mouth" are also rare, appearing in HB only in Judg 3:16 (חֶרֶב וְלָהּ שְׁנֵי פֵיוֹת/ "a sword and for it two mouths") and Prov 5:4 (כְּחֶרֶב פִּיּוֹת/"like a sword of mouths"), but also in the Hebrew Sir 9:4.[81] A reference to Isa 41:15 is unlikely since only one rare word in different construct combinations is uniquely shared.[82]

The view of Ps 149 as referring to *Hosea* leads to a non-violent reading of the Psalm with words as a sword and beds as places of worship.[83] However, none of the verses mentioned as points of reference share enough words for any reference to be likely: Hos 5:9 shares the rare word תּוֹכֵחָה/"punishment" and the frequent word יִשְׂרָאֵל/"Israel" without syntactical similarity. Hos 6:5 only shares the frequent word מִשְׁפָּט/"judgement". In Hos 8:14, only יִשְׂרָאֵל/"Israel" and a participle of עשׂה/"do" are shared. In Hos 9:1, the frequent words שׂמח/"be glad", יִשְׂרָאֵל/ "Israel", גִּיל/"rejoice", עַם/"people", כֹּל/"all" are shared without syntactical similarity.

---

76 Cf. Allen 1983, 319–320; Ceresko 1986, 182–183; Gosse 1994, 262; Füglister 1999, 32–33, 38; Ballhorn 2004b, 323, 334; Zenger 2008j, 855, 861, 864–869.

77 Cf. van Grol 2011, 107.

78 Against Ceresko 1986, 182–183; Füglister 1999, 32–33, 38 (see fn. 76), a suffixed plural participle of עשׂה/"do" appears in Ps 149 and Isa 54:5 but also (as noted by Ceresko) in Job 35:10, and פאר/"adorn" even in its piʿel form is not unique to Isa, cf. Ezra 7:27.

79 See p. 99.

80 Cf. Gesenius and Kautzsch 1909, §96; Joüon and Muraoka 2011, §98e. When referring to weapons, פֶּה "mouth" means "edge", cf. Gesenius 2013, s.v. פֶּה.

81 However, Sir 9:4[LXX] translates ἐπιχείρημα/"attempt", not ῥομφαῖαι δίστομοι/"two-edged swords" as in Ps 149:6[LXX], Sir 21:3[LXX] has ῥομφαία δίστομος/"two-edged sword" (like Ps 149[LXX], Hebrew not extant, cf. Blachorsky [2014], 15. Sir 9:4; 21:4[21:3][LXX] are noted by Tournay 1985, 353.

82 Similarity in content, cf. Füglister 1999, 38; van Grol 2011, 107, is not exclusive to Isaiah.

83 Cf. Tournay 1985, esp. 354, 356–357; Gosse 1994, 261–262.

Results

References to Ex 14–15; Deut 7; Josh; Judg; Isa 40–66; Hos; Ps 2; 96; 98 are unlikely. Ps 146; 147; 148; and 150 show no references except the framing Hallelujahs.

III.1.4 Content of Psalm 149^MT

Who is called to praise in Psalm 149^MT?

חֲסִידִים/"faithful ones" does not refer to a special limited group within Israel only rather than the entire people Israel,[84] nor does עֲנָוִים/"poor ones",[85] but both are identified with the people Israel who are called to praise in the entire Psalm.[86]

It is debated whether the people Israel in Ps 149 are in an actual cultic assembly,[87] an actual cultic assembly but anticipating the ideal eschatological Israel,[88] all of Israel with both cultic and military connotations,[89] or no actual group at all but the perfect eschatological Israel.[90] None of the words used for the people Israel in Ps 149, קָהָל/"assembly" (v.1b),[91] חֲסִידִים/"faithful ones" (v.1b, 5a, 9b),[92] יִשְׂרָאֵל/"Israel" (v.2a),[93] בְּנֵי־צִיּוֹן/"sons of Zion" (v.2b),[94] עַמּוֹ/"his [YHWH's] people" (v.4a),[95] and עֲנָוִים/"poor ones" (v.4b),[96] support only one of those interpretations as they all appear in multiple contexts. However, all words are used in *cultic* but not military and eschatological contexts which hints towards a *cultic* setting.

---

84 Against Lohfink 1990, 121–122 (חֲסִידִים/"faithful ones" special group within Israel to be saved at eschaton); van Grol 2011, esp. 104–108, 112–113 (חֲסִידִים/"faithful ones" politically active group in 2nd century BC, connected to Maccabean revolt). Against van Grol 2011, 105, Ps 149 uses the suffixed חֲסִידָיו/"his holy ones" in v.9b like many other Psalms (e.g. Ps 30:5), and the word is not a proper name. See fn. 92.

85 Against Ballhorn 2004b, 333. All of Israel is called poor, not vice versa.

86 See p. 88–90.

87 Cf. Gerstenberger 2001, 452–454.

88 Cf. Allen 1983, 294, 318–321; Seybold 1996, 544–545.

89 Cf. Zenger 2008j, 855, 862, 863.

90 Cf. Füglister 1999, 33–37 (not Maccabees); Loretz 2002, 362 (referring to Füglister).

91 The word is usually used in general and cultic contexts, cf. Hossfeld, Kindl, and Fabry 1989, esp. 1218 for Psalms (cultic), 1219–1220 for Qumran (military, eschatological).

92 Usually used in cultic contexts, cf. Ringgren and Fabry 1982, esp. 85–88. See p. 98.

93 Cf. Zobel 1982, esp. 1010 (cultic).

94 בְּנֵי־צִיּוֹן/"sons of Zion" appears only here and in Lam 4:2, but there is no intertextual reference.

95 Cf. Lipiński 1989, esp. 188 (military), 192 (cultic).

96 Cf. Gerstenberger 1989, 259–270, esp. 264 (cultic), 269 (eschatological).

What is "a new song" in Psalm 149:1[MT]?

It is debated whether "a new song" points towards a special *cultic* form or situation of Ps 149,[97] such as its spontaneous composition,[98] or its *unique militant* character[99] or *eschatological* meaning.[100]

שִׁירוּ לַיהוָה שִׁיר חָדָשׁ/"sing to YHWH a new song" also appears in Ps 96:1, Ps 98:1, Ps 149:1, and Isa 42:10, with the phrase שִׁיר חָדָשׁ/"new song" additionally appearing in Ps 33:3, 40:4, and 144:9.[101]

Little is known about *cultic* situations.[102] While Israel as the executor of *militant* revenge with a sword is an idea unique to Ps 149, it is unclear whether other texts using שִׁיר חָדָשׁ/"new song" are similarly *unique*, as for example Ps 96 and Ps 98 are less unique and very similar to each other.[103] The phrase שִׁירוּ לַיהוָה שִׁיר חָדָשׁ/"sing to YHWH a new song" could be connected with *eschatological* visions (Ps 96 and Ps 98 refer to a coming judgement, though Isa 42:10 may refer to an actual end of the exile), but in Ps 33, Ps 40, and Ps 144 with שִׁיר חָדָשׁ/"new song", there is *no* obvious eschatological context.[104] There are no intertextual connections with eschatological texts, though "new song" hints towards *eschatological* content.

Why is God to be praised in Psalm 149:2[MT]?

בְּעֹשָׂיו/"in its maker" is a plural participle with a singular suffix (literally "in the ones making it"). Since the participle refers to the singular "YHWH" (v.1), who with respect to the "sons of Zion" is "their king" (v.2b), a singular form could be expected. The plural form may be due to a "plural of majesty" used to describe God (in analogy to the plural אֱלֹהִים/"God"),[105] or an "apparent plural" (in roots ending with הthe original יappears).[106] Since a "plural of majesty" is used more commonly,[107] and since Isa 54:5 contains with reference to YHWH two suffixed participles בֹעֲלַיִךְ עֹשַׂיִךְ/"your ruler(s), your maker(s)" where the "ap-

---

97 Cf. Gerstenberger 2001, 452.

98 Cf. Seybold 1996, 545.

99 Cf. Tomes 2007, esp. 237, 243–247 (Maccabean ideology).

100 Cf. Patterson 2007, 430; Zenger 2008j, 862; Weber 2009, esp. 39–40, 42–43 (referring to Witte 2002, 535–536, who defines שִׁיר חָדָשׁ/"new song" as eschatological).

101 See p. 94–95 on Psalm 96 and Psalm 98.

102 See p. 52–54.

103 Also noted by Tomes 2007, 247, see fn. 99.

104 Very few eschatological elements are mentioned by Witte 2002, esp. 536 fn. 61.

105 Cf. Joüon and Muraoka 2011, §136e.

106 Cf. Gesenius and Kautzsch 1909, §93ss, a, 124k; Joüon and Muraoka 2011, §94j, 96Ce.

107 Cf. Gesenius and Kautzsch 1909, §124 g-i; Joüon and Muraoka 2011, §136d.

parent plural" would only apply to the second one,[108] a "plural of majesty" is probable,[109] rendered with a singular form in English. The participle usually expresses a present constant activity,[110] and the suffix designates the object of the activity:[111] In Ps 149:2, YHWH is constantly making Israel. In English this is rendered with a possessive pronoun and a noun "its maker".

"Maker" is regarded as a reference to creation[112] and history (especially Exodus[113] and Exile[114]), "king" as a reference to God's justice and help for his people,[115] celebrations in the Jerusalem sanctuary,[116] or the promise of God's presence in Jerusalem.[117] Since there are no intertextual references, the interpretation depends on the choice of other texts with similar topics.

"He adorns" in Psalm 149:4b[MT]

The subject of both the participle and the imperfect in v.4 is יהוה/"YHWH". A participle usually expresses a present constant activity,[118] and is often continued by a finite verb.[119] In Ps 149:4, the participle refers to the present:[120] Imperatives are usually calling for immediate actions rather than actions in a more remote future,[121] whereas jussive forms are less clear in this respect.[122] Collocated with imperatives, the jussives[123] in Ps 149 call for immediate action in the present rather than actions in a more remote future: The imperative at the beginning of Ps 149 calls to immediate praise, and Ps 149:4 gives reasons for praise. While the imperfect יְפָאֵר/"he adorns" could in other contexts (or if the temporal ambiguity of

---

108 Cf. Gesenius and Kautzsch 1909, §124k fn. 1.

109 Thus also Allen 2002, 396. Zenger 2008j, 855, does not decide between a plural of majesty and an archaising form (possibly meaning the phenomenon in Gesenius and Kautzsch 1909, §124k).

110 Cf. Gesenius and Kautzsch 1909, §107d, 116a, n; Joüon and Muraoka 2011, §121c.

111 Cf. Gesenius and Kautzsch 1909, §116 g; Joüon and Muraoka 2011, §121k.

112 Cf. Zenger 2008j, 862.

113 Cf. Seybold 1996, 545; Zenger 2008j, 862.

114 Cf. Zenger 2008j, 862.

115 Cf. Zenger 2008j, 862–863.

116 Cf. Allen 1983, 318.

117 Cf. Seybold 1996, 545.

118 See fn. 110.

119 Cf. Gesenius and Kautzsch 1909, §116x; Joüon and Muraoka 2011, §121a-h.

120 Cf. Gesenius and Kautzsch 1909, §116d; Joüon and Muraoka 2011, §121c-d.

121 Cf. Joüon and Muraoka 2011, §114 m.

122 Cf. Gesenius and Kautzsch 1909, §109a; Joüon and Muraoka 2011, §114 g-l.

123 See p. 88–90.

jussive forms is stressed over the imperatives) refer to a future,[124] here following a participle it refers to the present,[125] describing a general activity of YHWH.[126]

What is "help" in Psalm 149:4^MT?

Depending on the overall interpretation of Ps 149, יְשׁוּעָה/"help"[127] can be seen as the anticipation of an eschatological military victory of the people Israel,[128] or as general help for them but by YHWH (such as past help in the Exodus or out of the Exile).[129] The term itself is *ambiguous*.

Whose "honour" is it in Psalm 149:5^MT?

כָּבוֹד/"honour" can refer to the honour of humans or of God.[130] In v.5a in Ps 149 it probably refers to the honour of God given to humans since all previous verses only mention God's achievements. בְּכָבוֹד/"in honour" could refer to the cause ("because of honour") or the mode ("in honour") of exulting,[131] and in v.5a probably alludes back to the cause in v.4[132] while mainly referring to the mode in parallel with v.5b.

What are the "beds" Psalm 149:5^MT?

עַל־מִשְׁכְּבוֹתָם/"on their beds" is hard to explain.[133] It only appears here, in Isa 57:2, Hos 7:14, and Mic 2:1, and the five main explanations suggested by commentators are as follows: The phrase could refer to (1) *literal beds* for rest at night, either (a) for daily as well as *nightly worship* similar to the use of the root שׁכב/"lie down" in Deut 6:7, and the idea of Ps 1:2 and Josh 1:8,[134] or (b) followed by a *dream*,

---

124 Cf. Gesenius and Kautzsch 1909, §107i-l; Joüon and Muraoka 2011, §113b.

125 Cf. Gesenius and Kautzsch 1909, §107 f-h; Joüon and Muraoka 2011, §113c-d.

126 Also noted by Allen 1983, 319 (with reference to Gesenius and Kautzsch 1909, §116x); Zenger 2008j, 865 (however, present seen as eschatological, cf. Zenger 2008j, 855).

127 Cf. Sawyer and Fabry 1982, esp. 1039–1040 (general help), 1042 (military victory), 1046 (Qumran: eschatological victory).

128 Cf. Gunkel 1926, 620.

129 Cf. Zenger 2008j, 855, 865.

130 Cf. Weinfeld 1984, esp. 26.

131 Cf. Zenger 2008j, 855–856, 866 (God's honour).

132 Cf. Allen 1983, 318.

133 For overviews cf. Booij 2008; Zenger 2008j, 855–856. For references to emendations without text-critical evidence cf. Allen 1983, 318; Zenger 2008j, 856.

134 Cf. Zenger 2008j, 867.

making Ps 149 more an imagination rather than reality, similar to the מִשְׁכָּב/
"bed" in Cant 3:1 (if Cant 3 is interpreted as a dream).[135] However, none of
these texts have intertextual links with Psalm 149. Thus, this interpretation is
possible but unlikely.

It could also refer to (2) beds as *private places* for meditation, for private as
opposed to public worship, similar to the use of מִשְׁכָּב/"bed" in Ps 4:5 (positive
worship on beds), Mic 2:1 (negative schemes developed on beds over night), and
Hos 7:14 (negative worship on beds).[136] Again, none of these texts have intertextual links with Psalm 149, but they do at least use the same noun.

This interpretation is rejected by scholars who associate Ps 149 with cult,[137]
who instead opt for the explanation of (3) *cultic prostration*,[138] i. e. lying down in
worship, specifically on *prayer mats or carpets*,[139] based on a cultic interpretation of Psalm 149. However, neither מִשְׁכָּב/"bed" nor שכב/"lie down" are connected with prostration anywhere in HB.[140]

Based on a military interpretation of Psalm 149, some think of (4) *campbeds*
for soldiers after battle.[141] However, מִשְׁכָּב/"bed" is not used in this context in
HB.

Another explanation is a reference to (5) *deathmats* in a grave, because
מִשְׁכָּב/"bed" is used in this sense in 2 Chr 16:14, Ezek 32:25, and Isa 57:2, with
the possibilities that (a) the praising ones could be *on deathmats* in graves or
(b) they could be above graves and thus *resurrected*, similar to the idea of Isa
26:19, Dan 12:2, or Sap 3:7–8[LXX].[142] However, (a) is unlikely since there is no
other indication of the praising ones being dead, and (b) is unlikely as מִשְׁכָּב/
"bed" or the root שכב/"lie down" is not used in any of the texts seen as referring
to resurrection, עַל usually means "on", and the same phrase in 2 Chr 16:14, Ezek
32:25, and Isa 57:2 does not imply a resurrection but lying on deathmats.

It seems most likely that the reference is to beds as *private places* for meditation, and thus for private meditation (in a *non-cultic and non-military* context),
since this meaning of עַל־מִשְׁכְּבוֹתָם/"on their beds" is supported by two other texts
(Hos 7:14, Mic 2:1). This interpretation still leads to difficulties as the Psalm then

---

135 Cf. Booij 2008, 107–108 (Cant 3 is also a dream).
136 Cf. Gerstenberger 2001, 454.
137 Cf. Allen 1983, 318.
138 Cf. Allen 1983, 318.
139 Cf. Tournay 1985, 356 (prostration in Lev 9:24; 1 Kings 18:39; Ps 95:6; 2 Chr 20:18; Sir 50:17).
140 Also noted by Allen 1983, 318.
141 For references cf. Booij 2008, 106; Zenger 2008j, 855.
142 Cf. Füglister 1999, 46–49; Loretz 2002, 364–366 (following Füglister). שכב/"lie down" does
not appear in Isa 26:19 (against Füglister).

seems to jump from public worship in vv.1–3 to private worship in v.5 (possibly including both v.5b and v.5a) and then back to public action in vv.6–9.[143]

What is "sword" Psalm 149:6^MT?

Following much praise, and high praises in throats in v.6a, in v.6b suddenly a sword is in hand,[144] and Ps 149 goes on to depict Israel taking violent revenge on rulers of other nations with a sword – a unique image in the Psalter, where usually revenge is God's prerogative, and rare in HB.[145] This uniquely violent picture with the sudden appearance of a sword has led to much debate.

The sword is seen as (1) an *actual sword*, either in (a) an actual *military* battle – similar to holy war themes such as those in Deut,[146] or Isa 41:15–16[147] – or (b) a *cultic* celebration of an eschatological victory – based on the cultic background and prophetic promises[148] – or (c) an *eschatological* vision of battle – based on similar prophetic promises,[149] or the general eschatological content and Maccabean date and position in the Psalter,[150] or similar ideas in non-canonical post-exilic texts[151] –, or (2) as a *song* in mouths with the power of a sword – based on similar ideas in prophetic promises and other texts in HB and the apocrypha[152] and on the position in the Psalter,[153] or on the meaning of "sword of two mouths" as "potency of speech"[154] (however, the sword is explicitly held in a *hand*).

The debate centres on the small conjunction ו/"and" at the beginning of v.6b which is seen as (1) referring to an actual sword a *waw coniunctivum* "and" – be-

---

143 The same difficulty would apply to nightly worship.

144 חֶרֶב/"sword" is singular (unlike the parallel plural רוֹמְמוֹת/"high praises" in v.6a) which may point to its metaphorical use, cf. Zenger 1997c, 187, but it may also be used collectively (cf. Gesenius and Kautzsch 1909, §123b) as the singular חֶרֶב/"sword" in Isa 2:4 where it appears in addition to the plural (while Ps 59:8 uses the plural חֲרָבוֹת/"swords" metaphorically). יָד/"hand" stands for a plural given its plural suffix, cf. Gesenius and Kautzsch 1909, §124s; the same applies to גְּרוֹן/"throat" in v.6a. On רוֹמְמָם/"high praise" see p. 95–96 on Ps 148, esp. fn. 69; on פִּיפִיּוֹת/"mouths" see p. 97 on Isaiah, esp. fn. 80.

145 Cf. Füglister 1999, 30, 37–46; Leuenberger 2010, 637–638.

146 Cf. Gerstenberger 2001, 454–455.

147 Cf. van Grol 2011, 107.

148 Cf. Allen 1983, 318, 321; Seybold 1996, 544–545 (secondary meaning, primary: songs).

149 Cf. Füglister 1999, 38, 49.

150 Cf. Leuenberger 2004, 357.

151 Cf. Ballhorn 2004b, 327–329, 339.

152 Cf. Zenger 2008j, 860 (2 Chr 20:15–24), 867–868.

153 Cf. Zenger 1997c, 184.

154 Cf. Berman 2002, 295.

cause of the parallelism of v.6,[155] and the general rarity and specific unlikeliness of occurrences of *waw adaequationis* and *explicativum*[156] – or (2) (a) a *waw adaequationis* "as" – based on similar ideas in other biblical and extracanonical texts[157] –, or (b) a *waw explicativum* "and this means" – based on content, position in the Psalter, and a Targum interpretation[158] –, or (c) a *waw coniunctivum* but introducing a metaphor – based on similar ideas in other HB texts.[159]

Grammatically, the conjunction is a simple *waw coniunctivum* due to the general rarity and specific unlikelihood of occurrences of *waw adaequationis* and *explicativum*.[160] Given the lack of intertextual references, the interpretation of v.6b as referring to an actual sword in battle, cult, or the eschaton, or as a methaphor for speech depends on the overall interpretation of Psalm 149. However, metaphors do not appear in the first half of Ps 149 which hints towards an *actual* sword.

"Non-peoples" in Psalm 149:7b[MT]

In Codex L and BHS, Ps 149:7 ends with בַּל־אֻמִּים/"non-peoples",[161] whereas other Hebrew manuscripts and editions,[162] e.g. the Aleppo Codex,[163] read בַּלְאֻמִּים/"on the peoples". Commentators often assume the latter reading without explanation,[164] and the issue also occuring in Ps 44:15; 57:10; and 108:4 is seldom discussed.[165]

בַּלְאֻמִּים/"on the peoples"[166] is an easier reading (*lectio facilior*): As in v.7a, v.7b has בְּ/"on" followed by the article (dagesh forte omitted as often before shva)[167] followed by the plural noun לְאֻמִּים/"peoples".[168] Thus, v.7b can be trans-

---

155 Cf. Prinsloo 1997, 405.

156 Cf. Vanoni 1991 (against Tournay, Zenger, and Lohfink, see fn. 157–158); Sautermeister 2000.

157 Cf. Tournay 1985; Lohfink 1990, 124–125; Seybold 1996, 544–546.

158 Cf. Zenger 1987, 53–54, criticised in Zenger 2008j, 856, 867 (see fn. 159).

159 Cf. Zenger 2008j, 867.

160 See fn. 156.

161 Cf. Freedman 1998, 804=fol. 396v; Elliger and Rudolph 1997, 1226.

162 Cf. Elliger and Rudolph 1997, 1125 (on Ps 44:15), 1226. Cf. also Barbiero and Pavan 2012, 598. For 11QPs^a see III.2.1.

163 Cf. Ben-Zvi Institute 2007, Ps 149:7.

164 Cf. Gerstenberger 2001, 452–457; Zenger 2008j, 854, 857; Seybold 1996, 544. Allen 2002, 92–93, 396 mentions the maqqef in Codex L and BHS without explanation.

165 Cf. the exception Barbiero and Pavan 2012.

166 Cf. Barbiero and Pavan 2012, 598 ("among the peoples").

167 Cf. Gesenius and Kautzsch 1909, §20 m; Joüon and Muraoka 2011, §18b (also mentioned by Barbiero and Pavan 2012, 598–599).

lated as "punishments on the peoples", in a clear parallel to v.7a "revenge on the nations".

בַּל־אֻמִּים/"non-peoples" seems to be the poetic particle בַּל/"not" followed by the plural noun אֻמִּים/"peoples",[169] united by a maqqef.[170] This reading is more difficult (*lectio difficilior*), with two grammatical problems: The particle בַּל/ "not" is not used with a noun anywhere else[171] – though the similar particle לֹא/"not" is used with nouns[172] –, and v.7b with the verb already omitted would also omit a preposition.[173] V.7b can be translated as "punishments non-peoples" or, assuming an omitted preposition, "punishments [on] non-peoples". In addition to the two grammatical problems, the parallel between v.7a and v.7b is weaker in words and content (in v.7a there are "nations" without any negative description, in v.7b "non-peoples").[174] However, the content of Ps 149 allows for a disqualification of peoples.[175] The idiosyncratic reading in Codex L and the difficulties in grammar and parallelism stress this disqualification of peoples in Codex L.[176]

Who is subject to what "revenge" in Psalm 149:7–8^{MT}?

The nature of the revenge and punishments described in Ps 149:7–8 also lead to debate. Some commentators argue for (1) a reference to defeating and destroying all nations and their rulers in battle – similar to Deut 7:23–24 –,[177] others argue,

---

168 לְאֹם/"people" is frequent, cf. Gesenius 2013, 589–590, s.v. לְאֹם.

169 אֻמָּה*/"people" is rare but does appear e.g. in Ps 117:1, cf. Gesenius 2013, 71, s.v. אֻמָּה*.

170 On the maqqef's uniting function making a phonetic explanation less likely cf. Barbiero and Pavan 2012, 601.

171 Cf. Barbiero and Pavan 2012, 599. The particle usually negates an entire sentence, cf. Joüon and Muraoka 2011, §160a, m.

172 Cf. Joüon and Muraoka 2011, §160a. Barbiero and Pavan 2012, 602–603, argue for implicit references to Deut 32:21; Hos 1:9; 2:1, 25 where לֹא/"not" is used in connection with peoples; due to the lack of other shared words between these passages and Psalm 149 this cannot be substantiated.

173 Cf. Barbiero and Pavan 2012, 599.

174 Deut 32:21 includes two negative descriptions, against Barbiero and Pavan 2012, 603.

175 Against Barbiero and Pavan 2012, 600 (positive interpretation of נכה as "to correct", context of Ps 146–150 leads to positive view of peoples in Ps 149). A negative view of non-Israelites may be possible in Ps 44; 57; 108 (against Barbiero and Pavan 2012, 600) since at least Ps 44 and 108 do not have a positive view of peoples, but this would need further investigation. In Ps 148:11, לְאֻמִּים/"peoples" are called to praise (noted by Barbiero and Pavan 2012, 600) contrary to Ps 149.

176 Cf. Barbiero and Pavan 2012, 604–605.

177 Cf. Allen 1983, 318.

less violently, (2) that only the kings and rulers are bound[178] and the nations are freed from them and, if at all, then bound in an execution of justice to lead them to worship YHWH – because of similar themes in Isa 24:21–23 and Isa 45:14,[179] or (3) even more restricted that just the kings and rulers are bound and nothing happens to the nations – because v.8 is seen as a restriction of the punishment in v.7, and Ps 150 calls all humans to praise.[180] The last two interpretations presuppose the interpretation of the sword as metaphorical rather than actual[181] (a sword would not be needed for binding), and see connections with Ps 2.[182] The first is unlikely as v.7 and 8 are in a parallel without a hint of restriction, and Ps 150 is a separate poem.

נְקָמָה/"revenge" only appears in contexts including violence and death;[183] the word does not appear anywhere in Isaiah. The rare word תּוֹכֵחָה/"punishment" only appears in similarly negative contexts (in Hos 5:9 and 2 Kings 19:3=Isa 37:3). The rare word זֵק/"chain" is used to bind godly people (Job 36:8) but also Israel's enemies (Nah 3:10; with aim of their worship of YHWH Isa 45:15). The rare כֶּבֶל/"fetter" is used only here and in Ps 105:18 (to bind Joseph).

The *entirely negative connotations* of נְקָמָה/"revenge" and תּוֹכֵחָה/"punishment", and the parallel structure of v.7 and v.8 without a hint of restriction (which would also be unusual in HB) make it unlikely that the nations in v.7 are treated better than the rulers in v.8. While it is possible that both nations and rulers are bound and led to worship YHWH rather than killed, this is not made clear within Ps 149, and there are no intertextual references to texts containing the theme of either killing other nations or binding them in order for them to worship YHWH. It is thus improbable that revenge and punishment are restricted to rulers rather than the entire nations, and there is a hint towards *actual* violence.

What is "written" in Psalm 149:9[MT]?

Psalm 149:9 uniquely in HB refers to a מִשְׁפָּט כָּתוּב/"written judgement". Since כתב/"write" and in particular its participle כָּתוּב/"written" in v.9a usually refer to written texts,[184] numerous texts containing this written judgement have

---

178 Cf. Ballhorn 2004b, 340.
179 Cf. Füglister 1999, 43; Zenger 2008j, 868–869.
180 Cf. Ballhorn 2004b, 339–340.
181 Cf. Ballhorn 2004b, 325; Zenger 2008j, 867 (see fn. 159).
182 See p. 94 on Psalm 2.
183 Cf. Lipiński 1986.
184 Cf. Haag 1984; Metzenthin 2013.

been suggested by commentators, (1) leading to the judgement referring to *actually* killing enemies (a) texts in the *Torah* such as Deut 20:13, 16–18, because this seems "more logical (and less eschatological)"[185], (b) texts in *Joshua and Judges* because of similar words such as the two-edged sword in Judg 3:16, and general similarity in the theme of Israel fighting against other kings and nations,[186] (2) leading to an *eschatological* interpretation of the judgement *prophetic texts* because of similar words like the plural "mouths" in Isa 41:14–16, and general similarity in the theme of Israel itself taking revenge,[187] (3) leading to a *messianic* interpretation of Ps 149, *Psalm 2* because of the composition of the Book of Psalms, and the similar theme of war against nations,[188] (4) some *unknown text* which may be lost,[189] (5) leading to an *eschatological* interpretation, a *heavenly book* containing God's notes for future judgement because of similar ideas in texts like Isa 4:3; 56:6, Mal 3:16, and Dan 12:1,[190] or (6) *no text at all but the general idea* of YHWH's justice and judgement because of the use of כָּתוּב/"written" in Qumran texts with reference to general ideas rather than specific texts.[191]

Given the lack of intertextual references in Ps 149, references to (1) Deut-Judg, (2) prophetic books or (3) Psalm 2 are unlikely, and nothing is known about (4) other texts. While a reference to the idea of (5) a heavenly book for future judgement, leading to an *eschatological* interpretation of Ps 149, is possible, there is no clear reference to this idea in Ps 149, and (6) a *general* reference to God's justice depends on the view of God's justice in HB and thus is tied in with the overall interpretation of Ps 149.

---

185 Gerstenberger 2001, 455. Cf. also Ballhorn 2004b, 331 fn. 882 (Deut 32:14 in medieval Jewish commentaries).

186 Cf. Ceresko 1986, 188–190.

187 Cf. Seybold 1996, 545 (Ezek 25:13–14; Zech 9:13ff); Füglister 1999, 38–40 (Isa 41:14–16, also Mic 4:13; Ob 17; Ezek 25:13–14; Zech 9:13–15); van Grol 2011, 107–108 (Isa 60:12; Isa 35:4, but concluding that Ps 2 is more important, see fn. 188). Cf. also Ballhorn 2004b, 331 fn. 882 (Ezek 25:14 in medieval Jewish commentaries).

188 Cf. van Grol 2011, 107–108. See p. 94 on Ps 2.

189 Cf. Schreiner 1963, 208; Allen 1983, 319 (referring to Schreiner).

190 Cf. Haag 1984, 394–395; Metzenthin 2013, 459 (referring to Haag).

191 Cf. Niebuhr 1994, esp. 46–53 (Qumran texts); Ballhorn 2004b, 330–331 (referring to Niebuhr); Zenger 2008j, 869 (without reasons).

"Splendour is he" in Psalm 149:9b^MT

It is debated whether the personal pronoun הוּא/"he" in v.9b is "he" (referring to
YHWH)[192] or "it" (referring to the activities of faithful ones).[193] Grammatically,
both are possible as הוּא/"he" can be used as a demonstrative pronoun referring
to a known person or thing.[194] However, the most usual expression of a neuter
demonstrative pronoun is the feminine זֹאת/"this",[195] and it is not clear to
which activities "it" could refer.[196] These two reasons make the second interpretation less likely. Furthermore, in Ps 149:9b the masculine suffix in חֲסִידָיו/"his
faithful ones" refers back to YHWH in v.4 (as implied by חֲסִידִים/"faithful ones"
in v.1b close to יהוה/"YHWH" in v.1a, and the חֲסִידִים/"faithful ones" in v.5a
and אֵל/"God" in v.6a, and confirmed by the concluding imperative הַלְלוּ־יָהּ/
"Praise-Yah!"). Thus, הוּא/"he" refers to YHWH. YHWH is known as he is mentioned previously in Ps 149, and thus the subject of the nominal clause, preceded
by the emphasised predicate הָדָר/"splendour".[197] Thus, v.9b can be translated
into English as "Splendour is he for all his faithful ones."

III.1.5 Genre of Psalm 149^MT

Ps 149 fits the main criteria for "hymn" with its imperatives calling to praise and
כִּי/"for" in v.4 giving reasons for praise, and is thus seen as a hymn by commentators.[198] However, infinitives stating an aim of praise as in Ps 149:5–9 are unusual in hymns.[199] The Psalm's setting is seen as (1) a song of victory in a military
context,[200] (2) a non-eschatological cultic hymn,[201] (3) an eschatological cultic

---

192 Thus Prinsloo 1997, 404 (suffix in v.9b); Zenger 2008j, 857 (suffix in v.9b), 869 (הָדָר/"glory"
attribute of God and king).

193 Thus with reference to vv.5–9 Gerstenberger 2001, 455, and NRSV "This is glory for all his
faithful ones", with reference to vv.7a–9a Duhm 1922, 484 (reference to judgement) and Zenger
2008j, 869 (referring to Duhm and Gunkel, but not following this interpretation, see fn. 192); the
reference of "it" may also be left unclear, cf. Gunkel 1926, 622.

194 Cf. Gesenius and Kautzsch 1909, §136a-b: the masculine pronoun הוּא/"he" can be used like
a neuter. There is no neuter in Hebrew, cf. Gesenius and Kautzsch 1909, §80a.

195 Cf. Joüon and Muraoka 2011, §143a-b, 152a-b.

196 See fn. 193.

197 See fn. 14.

198 Cf. Ceresko 1986, 178; and see fn. 199–203.

199 Cf. Crüsemann 1969, 79–80 fn. 3; Allen 1983, 319 (referring to Crüsemann); Gerstenberger
2001, 454.

200 Cf. Duhm 1922, 482–484, referring to Maccabean wars, cf. the summary in Zenger 2008j,
859; for further literature cf. Prinsloo 1997, 396–398.

201 Cf. Allen 1983, 320; Prinsloo 1997, 406–407; Gerstenberger 2001, 454–457.

hymn as part of a cultic play,[202] (4) a literary eschatological hymn written as a poem only,[203] depending on the overall interpretation of the Psalm.

III.1.6 Date of Psalm 149[MT]

Psalm 149 is rarely seen as preexilic,[204] usually dated into the postexilic period because of the unity of hymn and instruction,[205] intertextual references to other postexilic texts in HB,[206] thematical similarity with other postexilic texts in HB with eschatological content,[207] and thematical similarity with other postexilic texts outside HB[208]. Within the postexilic view, it is debated whether Psalm 149 was written together with the context of Psalms 146–150 (because of intertextual links with Ps 146–148; 150)[209] or later than this context but still for insertion into it (because of intertextual links but thematic dissimilarity given the militant-eschatological character of Ps 149).[210] However, intertextual references to Ps 146–148; 150 cannot be shown at all.[211] It is also debated whether[212] or not[213] the Psalm can be dated to Maccabean times (i.e. early 2nd century BCE). Reasons for setting the Psalm in Maccabean times are the identification of Hasidim with Maccabean fighters[214] (which is unlikely),[215] intertextual links to Ps 2

---

202 Cf. Gunkel 1926, 620; Seybold 1996, 544; Lange 1998, 118–119.
203 Cf. Füglister 1999, 49; Zenger 2008j, 860.
204 Cf. Weiser 1966, 581 (preexilic date just as possible as a Maccabean date due to general themes); Dahood 1970, 356–357 (referring to Weiser, preexilic due to reference to Deuteronomy); Ceresko 1986, 177, 194 (date open but Ps 149 referring to premonarchic ideas of kingship where only YHWH is king); Kraus 1978, 1146 (very early or postexilic date due to cultic setting).
205 Cf. Gerstenberger 2001, 456.
206 Cf. Seybold 1996, 545 (Dan 7:12; Sap 3:5^{LXX}). See fn. 78.
207 Cf. Füglister 1999, 38.
208 Cf. Leuenberger 2010, 638–642 (Hen(aeth); 2 Mac 15:15–16^{LXX}); Ballhorn 2004b, 327–330, esp. 329 (Hen(aeth) and others); in contrast, Zenger 2008j, 866 (also mentioning Hen(aeth), 1QM) stresses the unique focus on praise of Ps 149.
209 Cf. Zenger 2008j, 860–861 in combination with Zenger 2008c, 808–809 (with editing of Psalter either in antiseleucid period 200–150 BCE or 3rd century BCE).
210 Cf. Leuenberger 2004, 356. However, this does not explain why Ps 149 was added before 150, and why the universal perspective was left at the end.
211 See III.1.3.
212 Cf. Ballhorn 2004b, 329–330; Zenger (see fn. 209).
213 Cf. Allen 1983, 320 (without reasons); Lange 1998, 108 (Psalm too general, 11QPs^a stresses non-identification of Hasidim with Maccabean fighters). On 11QPs^a see III.2.1.
214 Cf. Duhm 1922, 482–484; Tomes 2007, 244, 247 (written by Hasidim); van Grol 2011, 104 (200–175 BCE, written by Hasidim)

and Ps 146–148; 150 (which are unlikely), and the general militant-eschatological character also shown in other texts from similar times[216] (which is more likely, but would need further research on thematic links). Overall, the Psalm is not specific enough to point to a specific date.

III.1.7 Unity of Psalm 149[MT]

Ps 149 is one unit.[217] The final Hallelujah is missing only in the versions of the Septuagint as well as the Syriac version and Jerome's Latin Psalterium.

III.1.8 Overall Interpretation of Psalm 149[MT]

There are three main possibilities for an overall interpretation of Psalm 149 with its combination of praise and judgement:[218] (1) the judgement is actual violence, whether in a military context or acted in a cultic setting with praise, (2) the judgement is eschatological violence, whether in a cultic song or a literary poem with praise, (3) the judgement is not violent at all but also praise in a literary poem.

However, with a lack of intertextuality, neither the general meaning of words nor texts with similar themes unanimously point in one direction: The subjects called to praise indicate a *cultic* content and setting, the "new song" an *eschatological* content, "help" is *ambiguous*, "beds" point towards a *non-cultic, non-military private* setting, "sword" and "revenge" to a *military* content, "written" to an *eschatological* or *general* content. Thus, Ps 149 proves elusive for a definite overall interpretation, and it is understandable that the Psalm is often read in conjunction with other Psalms to make it more specific. However, for Ps 149 read on its own, a violent interpretation cannot be excluded. In any case, Ps 149 centres on Israel.

Overall, YHWH, the God (of Israel), is to be praised in an assembly of faithful ones. The reasons for praise are his creation, kingship, delight in and help for his people. He is to be praised with musical instruments and dance but also on beds

---

215 See p. 98.
216 Cf. Leuenberger 2004, 356 fn. 313; Leuenberger 2010.
217 For literary criticism without text-critical evidence cf. Loretz 2002, 359 (v.9b addition due to colometry); Kraus 1978, 1147 (v.9 addition due to difficulty of its interpretation). For further examples cf. Leuenberger 2004, 355–356. For v.7 see p. 104–105.
218 Cf. Sautermeister 2000, 65–69.

by Israel. Israel itself is also to take violent revenge on nations and their rulers with sword, chains, and fetters, as in a written judgement. Israel's splendour is YHWH.

III.2 Psalm 149^{DSS}

III.2.1 Psalm 149 in 11QPs^a

11QPs^a Column XXVI contains the complete text of Psalm 149:7–9, followed by Ps 150 in its entirety, and preceded in Column XXV by preserved parts of Ps 142 and 143.[219] It is separated from the following Ps 150 by a large space at the beginning of the first line of Ps 150. The beginning of Ps 149 is not preserved.

There is an *additional passage in Psalm 149:9:* Between חסידיו/"his faithful" and the end of the Psalm with the closing הללו יה/"Praise Yah!", לבני ישראל עם קודשו/"for the sons of Israel, his holy people" is added. While the phrase literally means "the people of his holiness", it should be translated as "his holy people".[220] The suffixes for "his" in both "his saints" and "his holy people" refer back to הוא/"he" in the same verse which in turn refers to YHWH. While הוא/"he" in MT probably refers to *YHWH*,[221] this is *even more likely in 11QPs^a* due to the extra suffix in עם קודשו/"his holy people".

11QPs^a explains "his faithful" with a double apposition. Thus, it makes it clear that they, "the sons of Israel", and "his holy people" are one and the same.[222]

Whether these people are all Israel or only a part of Israel such as a Qumran-specific group cannot be decided as חסידיו/"his faithful", בני ישראל/"sons of Israel" and עם קודשו/"his holy people" are used in both senses in HB and Qumran literature.[223] חסידיו/"his faithful" in HB is sometimes seen to refer to a specific group,[224] but this is unlikely both in HB in general and in Ps 149 in particular.[225] In Qumran, חסידיו/"his faithful" is sometimes seen as a group compiling 11QPs^a and sympathising with a group of (pre-)Maccabean "faithful",[226] but again the term is used more generally in other Qumran literature.[227]

---

219 Cf. Sanders 1965, 46–79, Plate XV-XVI; Sanders 1967, 84–85.

220 See p. 42–43.

221 See p. 108.

222 Cf. Dahmen 2003, 224. Appositions further explain the first noun, cf. Gesenius and Kautzsch 1909, §131a, expressing identity, cf. Joüon and Muraoka 2011, §131a. The subject thus is Israel as in MT, see p. 98.

223 Cf. Dahmen 2003, 224–226.

224 Cf. Dahmen 2003, 224–225 (pre-Maccabean group, referring to Zenger 1998a, 46); see fn. 84 (Maccabean group).

225 See p. 98.

226 Cf. Ringgren and Fabry 1982, 87 (Maccabean); Dahmen 2003, 225 (pre-Maccabean).

בני ישראל/"sons of Israel" in HB is a general term for all Israel. In Qumran it can refer to a specific group[228] but is also used in its general sense.[229]

The last phrase עם קודשו/"his holy people" does not appear in HB (though in Isa 63:18 עַם־קָדְשֶׁךָ/"your holy people" is used with reference to Israel and the destroyed temple, and in the Aramaic Dan 7:27 עַם קַדִּישֵׁי עֶלְיוֹנִין/"the people of the holy ones of the Most High" in an eschatological vision), and it is often though not exclusively[230] used in a restrictive sense in Qumran literature for fighters (in the War Scroll 1QM=1Q33) and for the Qumran community itself.[231] This leads to two contradicting interpretations: Either, the addition makes the entire Psalm Qumran-specific as Israel is restricted to a specific group,[232] or it does the opposite by making it clear that all of Israel and not just a specific group is meant.[233]

Given the general terms for Israel used in both Ps 149 as in MT and in the addition which does not use any exclusively specific terms, and the fact that the two appositions use even more general terms than חסידיו/"his faithful", thus identifying the possibly smaller with the larger group rather than vice versa, it is most likely that the addition does not restrict the people Israel to one specific group. However, it does stress Israel over other nations, making Ps 149 even *more Israel-specific*.

Other than this addition, there are few differences in Ps 149 in 11QPs[a] as compared to Codex L: All other differences are *orthographic variations* in defective and plene spellings.

In Ps 149:7, בַּגּוֹיִם/"on the nations" is spelled plene בגויים, and תּוֹכֵחֹת/"punishments" plene תוכחות. בלאומים is written together and could be pointed בְּלְאָמִים/"on the peoples" (consisting of the preposition בְּ/"on", the definite article, and the plural of לְאֹם/"people") instead of Codex L בַּל־אָמִּים/"non-peoples".

In Ps 149:8, לאסור/"to bind" is spelled plene instead of לֶאְסֹר, and ונכבדיהמה/"and their glorified ones" with an extra ה at the 3rd masculine plural suffix[234] instead of וְנִכְבְּדֵיהֶם.

---

227 Cf. Dahmen 2003, 225; Schlenke 2011, 1033; similarly on Ps 148 Ballhorn 2004b, 322. In addition to non-biblical texts, cf. Abegg et al. 2003, 272, חָסִיד/"faithful" is also used in 11QPs[a] in Ps 132; 145, cf. Abegg et al. 2010, 260.

228 Cf. Dahmen 2003, 226.

229 Cf. Zobel 1982, 1012; Dahmen 2003, 226; Fabry 2013, esp. 296, 298.

230 Cf. Kornfeld and Ringgren 1989, 1203 (Temple Scroll).

231 Cf. Kornfeld and Ringgren 1989, 1203–1204; Dahmen 2003, 226.

232 Cf. Dahmen 2003, 226, 304.

233 Cf. Lange 1998, 108 (11QPs[a] could thus be post-Maccabean and independent of MT-Psalter).

234 This is common in Qumran literature, cf. Sanders 1965, 13; Joüon and Muraoka 2011, §94i.

In Ps 149:9, plene spellings are כול/"all" for כָּל־, and there is the additional passage discussed above.

Ps 149:9 has a final הללו יה/"Praise Yah!" (with a small space; in BHS with a maqqef as in Codex L).[235]

Regarding *intertextuality*, Ps 148 is of special importance because Ps 148:14[MT] contains the phrase לִבְנֵי יִשְׂרָאֵל עַם־קְרֹבוֹ/"for the sons of Israel, the people close to him", with the only difference being עַם קודשו/"his holy people" in Ps 149:9 in 11QPs[a] instead of עַם־קְרֹבוֹ/"the people close to him". Some commentators argue that the addition in Ps 149:9 refers to Ps 148:14.[236] However, Ps 148:14 is not preserved in 11QPs[a] and thus cannot be compared to Ps 149:9 in 11QPs[a], and Ps 148 does not precede Ps 149 in 11QPs[a].[237] As in MT, there is little similarity between Ps 148 and Ps 149, while the exact verse Ps 148:14 is found in the Hebrew Sir 51:12o (sic).[238] A reference is unlikely.

Ps 149 is not preserved in its entirety in any Dead Sea Manuscript,[239] the only preserved verses in 11QPs[a] (Ps 149:7–9) share three words with *Ps 150:* כֹּל/"all", קֹדֶשׁ/"holiness" (which is not in Ps 149[MT]), and the final הַלְלוּ־יָהּ/"Praise-Yah!". Given the fragmentary nature of Ps 149 in Qumran, it is not possible to say if Ps 149 – unlike Ps 150 – is framed by Hallelujahs in 11QPs[a], or to assess all shared words between Ps 149 and Ps 150.[240]

In *summary*, in 11QPs[a] Ps 149 is followed by Ps 150 but probably preceded by the end of Ps 143 (of which the beginning is preserved). The opening of Ps 149 is not preserved, but the final Hallelujah is. There is an additional passage in Psalm 149:9 stressing Israel, and בלאומים/"on the peoples" in Psalm 149:7. Most of the differences are simply variant spellings due to the addition of wav as consistent with the orthography of most of the entire scroll.[241]

---

235 Cf. Elliger and Rudolph 1997, 1226; Freedman 1998, 804=fol. 396v. See also II.2.1.

236 Cf. Sanders 1965, 47 (comparing Ps 148:14; also mentioning one manuscript (no. 40) in Kennicott 1780, 437 reading חסידיו לבני ישראל עם קרובו/"his faithful, for the sons of Israel, his close people"); Seybold 1996, 545; Dahmen 2003, 224; Ballhorn 2004b, 336 (addition taken from Ps 148:14; thus 11QPs[a] depends on MT-Psalter); Leuenberger 2004, 14 (addition since tricolic structure is unique in Ps 149; taken from Ps 148:14; thus 11QPs[a] depends on MT-Psalter).

237 Cf. Sanders 1965, 5, 23.

238 Cf. Abegg and Parker [no year]d. Cf. Skehan 1973, 203 (Sir 51:12o from 2nd century CE). See p. 141–142.

239 See p. 13–15.

240 Dahmen 2003, 302–305, argues that Ps 149–150 are connected as one pair in MT (according to 302 fn. 174 following Zenger 1997a, 14–21; Zenger 1997b, 99–104; Ballhorn 2004b, 351–388, esp. 375–375) and also in 11QPs[a].

241 See p. 65 fn. 339.

III.3 Psalm 149^LXX

III.3.1 Translation of Psalm 149^LXX

1H	Hallelujah!		1H	Αλληλουια.
1a	Sing to the Lord a new song,		1a	Ἄσατε τῷ κυρίῳ ᾆσμα καινόν,
1b	his praise (is) in an assembly of faithful ones!		1b	ἡ αἴνεσις αὐτοῦ ἐν ἐκκλησίᾳ ὁσίων.
2a	*Let* Israel be glad in the one *having made it,*		2a	εὐφρανθήτω Ισραηλ ἐπὶ τῷ ποιήσαντι αὐτόν,
2b	*and* let the sons of Zion rejoice in their king;		2b	καὶ υἱοὶ Σιων ἀγαλλιάσθωσαν ἐπὶ τῷ βασιλεῖ αὐτῶν·
3a	*let* them praise his name with dance,		3a	αἰνεσάτωσαν τὸ ὄνομα αὐτοῦ ἐν χορῷ,
3b	with drum and harp *let* them *sing praise for* him,		3b	ἐν τυμπάνῳ καὶ ψαλτηρίῳ ψαλάτωσαν αὐτῷ,
4a	for the Lord *delights* in his people,		4a	ὅτι εὐδοκεῖ κύριος ἐν λαῷ αὐτοῦ
4b	*and* he *will* lift up poor ones *in safety.*		4b	καὶ ὑψώσει πραεῖς ἐν σωτηρίᾳ.
5a	Faithful ones *will* exult in glory,		5a	καυχήσονται ὅσιοι ἐν δόξῃ
5b	*and* they *will rejoice* on their beds;		5b	καὶ ἀγαλλιάσονται ἐπὶ τῶν κοιτῶν αὐτῶν·
6a	*the* high praises of God in their throat,		6a	αἱ ὑψώσεις τοῦ θεοῦ ἐν τῷ λάρυγγι αὐτῶν,
6b	and two-edged swords in their hands		6b	καὶ ῥομφαῖαι δίστομοι ἐν ταῖς χερσὶν αὐτῶν
7a	to execute revenge on the nations,		7a	τοῦ ποιῆσαι ἐκδίκησιν ἐν τοῖς ἔθνεσιν,
7b	rebukes *on the* peoples,		7b	ἐλεγμοὺς ἐν τοῖς λαοῖς,
8a	to bind their kings with chains		8a	τοῦ δῆσαι τοὺς βασιλεῖς αὐτῶν ἐν πέδαις
8b	and their glorious ones with iron *handcuffs,*		8b	καὶ τοὺς ἐνδόξους αὐτῶν ἐν χειροπέδαις σιδηραῖς,
9a	to execute on them an *inscribed* judgement;		9a	τοῦ ποιῆσαι ἐν αὐτοῖς κρίμα ἔγγραπτον·
9b	*glory is this* for all his faithful ones.		9b	δόξα αὕτη ἐστὶν πᾶσι τοῖς ὁσίοις αὐτοῦ.
9H	–			

III.3.2 Form of Psalm 149^LXX

Outline of Psalm 149^LXX

1H	**Opening** *Imperative*	
Part I		
1	**Calls to**	Subject: Israel, Object/**Reason:** Lord,
–2	**+ Reasons for Praise**	Means: Music
	Imperatives/Nominal clause	
3	**Calls to**	Subject: Israel, Object: Lord,
	Imperatives	Means: Music
–4	**+ Reason for** Praise	Subject: Lord, Object: Israel
	Present/Future	

Part II

5–6	Calls to <u>Praise</u>	Subject: Israel, Object: Lord,
	Future, Nominal clauses	Means: Voice, Swords
7–9	<u>Judgement</u>	Subject: Israel, Object: Nations,
	Aorist Infinitives, ***Present***	Means: Violence
9H	–	

Syntax of Psalm 149^{LXX}

Imperatives appear in v.1a, unlike in MT not in a frame, but in vv.2ab, 3ab for Hebrew jussives. All imperatives except v.2b (present imperative)[242] are aorist imperatives.[243] However, the jussive forms in vv.5ab are translated with *future forms*. Thus, unlike in MT, all imperatives *but also future forms* are connected with the first theme of *praise*.

V.4 has a *present* and a *future* form which unlike in MT are not unique in Ps 149: Present forms also appear in v.9b, and two future forms in v.5. However, v.4 shows the *first* appearance of these forms, as in MT probably due to the change in subject, and both forms in v.4 are connected with the first theme of *praise*.

V.5 unlike in MT also has *future forms*, connected with the second theme of judgement through the following *infinitives* in vv.7a, 8a, and 9a which are aorist infinitives with a genitive article, thus describing a specific aim.[244] As in MT, all *infinitives* are connected with the second theme of *judgement*, as are the *future forms* in v.5, though this future is described as a *present* glory in v.9b. Since *future forms* only appear in *v.4b and v.5ab*, the two themes of *praise and judgement are more strongly connected* than in MT, and v.4b mentions a future action, possibly the action in vv.5–9, as a reason for praise.

Unlike MT, v.4a and 9b contain present verb forms, as in MT vv.1b and 6ab are nominal clauses,[245] whereas in v.7b and 8b (due to the parallels connecting

---

242 -σθωσαν as in v.2b ἀγαλλιάσθωσαν/"let them rejoice" sometimes appears instead of the usual imperative middle present third person plural ending –σθων, cf. Smyth and Messing 1956, §466.

243 Present imperatives tend to be more general, aorist imperatives more specific (and used in prayers), but the difference is minimal, cf. Blass, Debrunner, and Rehkopf 1979, §335, 337.

244 Present infinitives tend to be more general, aorist infinitives more specific, cf. Blass, Debrunner, and Rehkopf 1979, §338. On the genitive infinitive cf. Conybeare and St. Stock 1995; Blass, Debrunner, and Rehkopf 1979, §400.

245 Ellipsis of indicative present or optative forms of εἶναι/"to be" is frequent, but ellipsis of future forms also exists, cf. Blass, Debrunner, and Rehkopf 1979, §127–128. A form of "to be" is inserted in English.

καί/"and" in v.8a and 8b) the verb is the one in the preceding half-verse.[246] Unlike in Hebrew, it is not possible to assume the same verb as in v.1a (ᾄσατε/ "sing!" for שִׁירוּ/"sing!") for v.1b since ἡ αἴνεσις αὐτοῦ/"his praise" is a nominative, not an accusative. Thus, *v.1b has to be a nominal clause* (as likely in Hebrew).[247] Unlike in MT, nominal clauses appear in Part I (v.1b) and Part II (v.6a and 6b) only, not in v.9b, but as in MT they connect *praise* and *judgement*.

As in MT, *subjects* are the *people Israel* and *YHWH*, but unlike in MT *the final subject in v.9b is not God but* αὕτη/"this",[248] with the predicate δόξα/"glory" stressed through its position at the beginning. Since δόξα/"glory" also appears in v.5a, v.9b refers to the content of vv.5–9a.

As usual in Hebrew-influenced Greek the *word order*[249] is verb – subject – object, but as in MT this order is reversed in v.2b (forming a chiastic structure with v.2a) and in v.3b (forming a chiastic structure with v.3a), stressing the element of praise. In verbless sentences, the order subject – predicate is found in v.1b, v.6a and 6b as in MT even though the usual Greek word order would be predicate – subject, thus putting extra stress on the subjects. V.9b is not a nominal clause unlike in Hebrew, but the subject αὕτη/"this" is still stressed by being placed before the verb.

Genitive pronouns translate Hebrew suffixes, in v.9b referring to "he", i.e. God, since the genitive αὐτοῦ/"his" is masculine or neuter and cannot refer to the feminine subject δόξα/"glory".

Unlike in Hebrew the *preposition* ἐν/"in" for בְּ/"in" is found in most half-verses of Psalm 149 (vv.1b, 3a, 3b, 4a, 4b, 5a, 6a, 6b, 7a, 8a, 8b, 9a) but not in v.2a-b where, as in v.5b for עַל/"on", ἐπί/"on, because of" with a genitive[250] is used. ἐπί/"because of" with datives in v.2 points towards *reasons of praise* already being mentioned in v.2 in a *more explicit* manner than in MT. Unlike in Hebrew, no preposition is needed for לְ/"to" since datives (vv.1a, 9b) and accusatives (v.3b) are used. Thus, unlike in MT, the prepositionless vv.1a and 9b both have dative forms, forming a frame even without Hallelujahs.

---

246 In v.7 an asyndetic construction is used (as in MT), cf. Blass, Debrunner, and Rehkopf 1979, §460.

247 Cf. Brucker 2011d, 1882; in contrast to Zenger 2008j, 870.

248 αὕτη/"this" could be used adjectively as an attribute to δόξα/"glory" ("this glory is") or substantively as a subject with δόξα/"glory" as a predicate ("glory is this"), as noted by Zenger 2008j, 870, cf. Smyth and Messing 1956, § 1238–1239, 1252. Given that in MT "glory" is the predicate (see p. 108), αὕτη/"this" as a substantive and subject is most likely.

249 Cf. Blass, Debrunner, and Rehkopf 1979, §472.

250 Cf. Lust, Eynikel, and Hauspie 2003, s.v. ἐπί.

As in MT, the syntax of vv.5–9 is parallel rather than subordinate: Both v.7a and v.9a begin with the infinitive τοῦ ποιῆσαι/"to do" followed by "the nations" in v.7a and "they" in v.9a, with ἐν/"on". V.8 is enclosed by the parallel vv.7a and 9a, and introduced by another infinitive. A subordination is grammatically unlikely.[251]

Structure of Psalm 149^{LXX}

Psalm 149^{LXX} can be divided into two parts without the framing Hallelujahs: vv.1–4 and vv.5–9. This two-fold structure is indicated by calls to praise (imperatives) in both vv.1–3 (but unlike in MT not in vv.5–6), and by the facts that the Psalm seems to cover two topics (praise with music and praise with violence), and that vv.7–9 are infinitives in a final sense which have to be connected with a main clause which in Psalm 149^{LXX} is at least v.6 which in turn is connected with v.5, thus tying together vv.5–9.

Unlike in MT *v.4 has a stronger connection with vv.5–9 through future forms* starting in v.4b followed by further future forms in v.5ab. As in MT, the appearance of violence in v.6b is surprising, but also tied in with the theme of praise.

As in MT, v.9a with the repetition of the infinitive τοῦ ποιῆσαι/"to do" which first appears in v.7a connects vv.7a–9a, and v.9a serves as a summary of vv.7a–8b. V.9b may serve as a summary of either the second part (vv.5a–9a) or the whole Psalm. As in MT, v.9b is the only verse which does not stand in a *parallelismus membrorum*, and includes the final mention of ὅσιοι/"faithful ones" for חֲסִידִים/"faithful ones" (which also appear in v.1b in Part I and in v.5a in Part II), but unlike in MT *v.9b is a summary of vv.5–9* (see p. 116–118).

Thus, unlike in MT the structure of Psalm 149 is twofold: Hallelujah – vv.1–4 (Part I), vv. 5–9 (Part II). The two parts are connected but through *future forms* rather than a summary.

Poetic Devices in Psalm 149^{LXX}

The *parallelisms* in v.2b, v.4b, and v.5b are syndetic (instead of asyndetic as in Hebrew), but the difference in meaning is minimal.[252]

Unlike in MT, v.3b has a word play ψαλτηρίῳ ψαλάτωσαν/"with a harp let them play".[253]

---

251 Cf. Smyth and Messing 1956, §2189.
252 Cf. Blass, Debrunner, and Rehkopf 1979, §458, 462. See p. 69 fn. 368.
253 Cf. Brucker 2011d, 1882.

Unlike in MT, v.4b and v.6a are connected through the related words ὑψώσει/ "he will lift up" and ὕψωσις/"high praise".[254] In combination with the two future forms in v.5, this supports an eschatological reading of v.4b as well as v.6a, where in v.5 the future answer of Israel (lifting up praises and swords) to God's future action (lifting up Israel) is described.

As in MT, v.5a with ἐν δόξῃ/"in glory" for בְּכָבוֹד/"in honour" is connected with v.8b through τοὺς ἐνδόξους αὐτῶν/"their glorified ones" for וְנִכְבְּדֵיהֶם/ "and their honoured ones", but in addition to MT there is δόξα/"honour" for הָדָר/"splendour" in v.9a. This word play contrasts God's and Israel's glory with those glorified by the nations.[255]

As in MT, ποιέω/"do" connects vv.2a, 7a, and 9a; βασιλεύς/"king" v.2b and v.8a. Unlike MT, the other repeated verb is one of praise, but not αἰνέω/"praise" for הלל/"praise", but ἀγαλλιάομαι/"rejoice" which connects the sons of Zion in v.2b with ἀγαλλιάσθωσαν/"let them rejoice" with the faithful ones through ἀγαλλιάσονται/"they will rejoice" in v.5b.

III.3.3 Intertextuality in Psalm 149^{LXX}

Importance
A distinct connection of Psalms 149^{LXX} and 150^{LXX} as the closing pair of Psalms in the Psalter with the same superscription is sometimes seen to strengthen the reference to Psalms 1^{LXX} and 2^{LXX} as the opening pair.[256] However, possible references have so far only been listed.[257]

Analysis
Ps 149^{LXX} and *Exodus 14–15^{LXX}* only share frequent words, wherefore a reference is unlikely as in MT.

Since with *Deuteronomy^{LXX}* only frequent words are shared, for example κρίμα/"judgement" for מִשְׁפָּט/"judgement" and χείρ/"hand" for יָד/"hand" in Deut 32:41^{LXX} (not even ῥομφαία/"sword" for חֶרֶב/"sword" because Deut 32:41^{LXX} uses μάχαιρα/"sword"), references are less likely than in MT.

---

254 Also noted by Zenger 2008j, 870.
255 See p. 101.
256 Cf. Zenger 2008c, 809.
257 See p. 70 fn. 371.

For *Joshua^LXX* and *Judges^LXX* a reference is less likely than in MT, since for
כָּתוּב/"written" verses referring to the written law in those books (e. g. Josh
1:8^LXX; 9:2e^LXX=8:34^MT) use forms of γράφω/"write" rather than the hapax legomenon ἔγγραπτος/"inscribed".

Ps 149^LXX and *Psalm 2^LXX* share ἔθνος/"nation" for גּוֹי/"nation", βασιλεύς/
"king" for מֶלֶךְ/"king", κύριος/"Lord" for יהוה/"YHWH", λαός/"people" for לְאֹם/
"people",²⁵⁸ Σιων/"Zion" for צִיּוֹן/"Zion", υἱός/"son" for בֵּן/"son", the adjective
σιδηροῦς/"iron" for the noun בַּרְזֶל/"iron", ἀγαλλιάομαι/"rejoice" for גִיל/"rejoice",
and πᾶς/"all" for כֹּל/"all" without syntactical similarity, and references are unlikely as in MT.

A reference to *Psalm 95^LXX(=96^MT)* and *Psalm 97^LXX(=98^MT)* is less likely than
in MT: Ps 149^LXX and Ps 95^LXX(=96^MT) share the phrase ᾄσατε τῷ κυρίῳ ᾆσμα
καινόν/"sing to the Lord a new song" for שִׁירוּ לַיהוָה שִׁיר חָדָשׁ/"sing to YHWH a
new song", and the words ᾄδω/"sing" for שִׁיר/"sing", κύριος/"Lord" for יהוה/
"YHWH", πᾶς/"all" for כֹּל/"all", τὸ ὄνομα αὐτοῦ/"his name" for שְׁמוֹ/"his
name", ἔθνος/"nation" for גּוֹי/"nation", δόξα/"honour" for כָּבוֹד/"honour",
λαός/"people" for עַם/"people" (though referring to other peoples in Ps 95:3,
7^LXX and translated with ἔθνος/"nation" in Ps 95:5^LXX, but to Israel in Ps 149:4^LXX),
αἰνετός/"praiseworthy" for הלל/"praise", ποιέω/"do" for עשׂה/"do", βασιλεύω/
"be king" for מלך/"be king" (though as in MT as a verb βασιλεύω/"be king" referring to YHWH in Ps 95:10^LXX, but as a noun βασιλεύς/"king" referring to non-
Israelite kings in Ps 149:8^LXX), and εὐφραίνω/"be glad" for שׂמח/"be glad". However, יְשׁוּעָה/"help" is translated as σωτήριον/"help" rather than σωτηρία/"help",
θεός/"god" is used for אֱלֹהִים/"gods" in Ps 95:4–5^LXX referring to other gods,
whereas in Ps 149:6^LXX θεός/"god" for אֵל/"god" refers to YHWH, ὡραιότης/
"beauty" is used for הָדָר/"splendour" instead of δόξα/"honour" (also for כָּבוֹד/
"honour"), χαίρω/"be joyful" for עָלוּ/"exult" instead of καυχάομαι/"exult",
ἀγαλλιάομαι/"rejoice" for גִיל/"rejoice" but also for רנן/"shout for joy", and
while οὐ/"not" is used for בַּל/"not" in Ps 95^LXX, it does not appear in Ps 149:7^LXX.
There are more differences in shared words than in MT, and the shared phrase is
the only syntactical similarity. Ps 149^LXX and Ps 97^LXX(=98^MT) also share the
phrase ᾄσατε τῷ κυρίῳ ᾆσμα καινόν/"sing to the Lord a new song" for שִׁירוּ
לַיהוָה שִׁיר חָדָשׁ/"sing to YHWH a new song", as well as the words ποιέω/"do"
for עשׂה/"do", κύριος/"Lord" for יהוה/"YHWH", ἔθνος/"nation" for גּוֹי/"nation",
Ισραηλ/"Israel" for יִשְׂרָאֵל/"Israel", πᾶς/"all" for כֹּל/"all", ψάλλω/"sing praise"
for זמר/"make music", βασιλεύς/"king" for מֶלֶךְ/"king" (though referring to
YHWH in Ps 97:6^LXX, to non-Israelite kings in Ps 149:8^LXX), and λαός/"people"

---

258 See p. 104–105.

for עַם/"people" (though referring to other peoples in Ps 97^LXX, to Israel in
Ps 149:4^LXX). However, יְשׁוּעָה/"help" is translated as σωτήριον/"help" in
Ps 97:2, 3^LXX (as in Ps 95:2^LXX) rather than σωτηρία/"help", ἀγαλλιάομαι/"rejoice"
is shared but for רנן/"shout for joy" rather than גיל/"rejoice", and כִּנּוֹר/"lyre" is
translated as κιθάρα/"lyre" rather than ψαλτήριον/"harp". In addition to MT,
θεός/"god" and χείρ/"hand" (though referring to faithful in Ps 149^LXX, to rivers
in Ps 97^LXX) are shared. There are more differences in shared words than in
MT, and the shared phrase is the only syntactical similarity.

Ps 149^LXX and *Psalm 145^LXX(=146^MT)* share αἰνέω/"praise" for הלל/"praise",
κύριος/"Lord" for יהוה/"YHWH", ψάλλω/"sing praise" for זמר/"make music",
υἱός/"son" for בֵּן/"son" (though in Ps 146 referring to the sons of man i.e. humans, in Ps 149 to the sons of Zion i.e. Israelites), θεός/"god" for אֵל/"god"
(also for אֱלֹהִים/"god"), ποιέω/"do" for עשׂה/"do", κρίμα/"judgement" for מִשְׁפָּט
/"judgement", βασιλεύω/"be king" for the root מלך/"be king" (though as in
MT as a verb βασιλεύω/"be king" referring to YHWH in Ps 145:10^LXX, but as a
noun βασιλεύς/"king" referring to non-Israelite kings in Ps 149:8^LXX), and
Σιων/"Zion" for צִיּוֹן/"Zion". In addition to MT, σωτηρία/"help" is shared but
for תְּשׁוּעָה/"help" rather than יְשׁוּעָה/"help". אסר/"bind" is translated with
πεδάω/"bind" rather than δέω/"bind". Since in addition to these differences
the only syntactical and structural similarity in MT, the Hallelujah-frame, is
missing, references are less likely than in MT.

Ps 149^LXX and *Psalm 146^LXX(=147:1–11^MT)* share αἴνεσις/"praise" for תְּהִלָּה/
"praise", κύριος/"Lord" for יהוה/"YHWH", Ισραηλ/"Israel" for יִשְׂרָאֵל/"Israel",
πᾶς/"all" for כֹּל/"all", ὄνομα/"name" for שֵׁם/"name", πραΰς/"poor" for עָנָו/
"poor", υἱός/"son" for בֵּן/"son" (referring to sons of ravens in Ps 146^LXX, but
sons of Zion in Ps 149^LXX), and εὐδοκέω/"delight" for רצה/"delight". The translation of זמר/"make music" is ψάλλω/"sing praise" in Ps 146:7^LXX but ψαλμός/
"song of praise" in Ps 146:1^LXX. θεός/"god" is shared for אֱלֹהִים/"god" rather
than אֵל/"god". כִּנּוֹר/"lyre" is translated as κιθάρα/"lyre" instead of ψαλτήριον/
"harp". Since fewer words are shared, and there is no Hallelujah-frame, references are less likely than in MT.

Ps 149^LXX and *Psalm 147^LXX(=147:12–20^MT)* share κύριος/"Lord" for יהוה/
"YHWH", αἰνέω/"praise" for הלל/"praise", Σιων "Zion" for צִיּוֹן/"Zion", υἱός/
"son" for בֵּן/"son" (referring to sons of Zion in both), κρίμα/"judgement" for
מִשְׁפָּט/"judgement", and Ισραηλ/"Israel" for יִשְׂרָאֵל/"Israel". θεός/"god" is shared
but for אֱלֹהִים/"god" rather than אֵל/"god". Since there is no Hallelujah-frame, references are less likely than in MT.

Ps 149^LXX and *Psalm 148^LXX* share fewer words than in MT, especially in
Ps 148:14^LXX: While six words are shared (ὑψόω/"lift up" for the root רום/"lift
up", λαός/"people" for עַם/"people", πᾶς/"all" for כֹּל/"all", ὅσιος/"faithful"

for חָסִיד/"faithful", υἱός/"son" for בֵּן/"son", and Ισραηλ/"Israel" for יִשְׂרָאֵל/"Isra-el"), תְּהִלָּה/"praise" is translated with ὕμνος/"chant" rather than αἴνεσις/"praise". There is little syntactical similarity (the combination of πᾶσι τοῖς ὁσίοις αὐτοῦ/"for all his faithful ones" for לְכָל־חֲסִידָיו/"for all his faithful ones" appears only in Ps 149:9ᴸˣˣ and Ps 148:14ᴸˣˣ as in MT, but a nominative of the same phrase, πάντες οἱ ὅσιοι αὐτοῦ/"all his faithful ones" is also found in Ps 30:24ᴸˣˣ as in Ps 31:24ᴹᵀ, οἱ ὅσιοι αὐτοῦ/"his faithful ones" in other Psalms such as Ps 29:5ᴸˣˣ). The hapax legomenon ὕψωσις/"high praise" for the rare noun רוֹמְמ/"high praise" does not appear in Ps 148ᴸˣˣ,²⁵⁹ thus the only rare word is *not* shared, whereas the shared form ὑψώσει/"he will lift up"²⁶⁰ is not unique to Ps 148ᴸˣˣ and 149ᴸˣˣ. Otherwise, αἰνέω/"praise" for הלל/"praise", κύριος/"Lord" for יהוה/"YHWH", ὄνομα/"name" for שֵׁם/"name", ποιέω/"do" for עשׂה/"do", and βασιλεύς/"king" for מֶלֶךְ/"king" are shared without syntactical similarity. Since there is no Hallelujah-frame, references are less likely than in MT.

As shown on p. 72 on Ps 149ᴸˣˣ, references to Ps 149ᴸˣˣ from *Psalm 150ᴸˣˣ* are less likely than in MT.

References to Isaiahᴸˣˣ, especially *Isaiah 40 – 66ᴸˣˣ*, are less likely than in MT since no rare word is shared and a shared phrase is translated differently:²⁶¹ In Isa 41:15ᴸˣˣ the rare פִּיפִיּוֹת/"mouths" is translated with the hapax legomenon πριστηροειδής/"saw-shaped" instead of δίστομος/"two-edged". As in MT, frequent words (such as καινός/"new" and, in addition to MT, ποιέω/"do") are shared without syntactical similarity. In Isa 42:12ᴸˣˣ, שִׁירוּ לַיהוָה שִׁיר חָדָשׁ/"sing to YHWH a new song" is translated as ὑμνήσατε τῷ κυρίῳ ὕμνον καινόν/"Chant to the Lord a new chant" rather than ᾄσατε τῷ κυρίῳ ᾆσμα καινόν/"sing to the Lord a new song".

References to *Hoseaᴸˣˣ* are less likely than in MT: In Hos 5:9ᴸˣˣ the rare תּוֹכֵחָה/"punishment" is translated with ἔλεγχος/"rebuke" rather than ἐλεγμός/"rebuke", and only Ισραηλ/"Israel" for יִשְׂרָאֵל/"Israel" is shared. In Hos 6:5ᴸˣˣ, κρίμα/"judgement" for מִשְׁפָּט/"judgement" is the only shared word. In Hos 7:14ᴸˣˣ עַל־מִשְׁכְּבוֹתָם/"on their beds" is translated as ἐν ταῖς κοίταις αὐτῶν/"in their beds" with a different preposition than ἐπὶ τῶν κοιτῶν αὐτῶν/"on their beds". In Hos 8:14ᴸˣˣ, only Ισραηλ/"Israel" for יִשְׂרָאֵל/"Israel" and ποιέω/"do"

---

259 It also does not appear in Psalm 65ᴸˣˣ(=66ᴹᵀ) where ὑψόω/"lift up" is used, making a reference between Ps 149ᴸˣˣ and Psalm 65ᴸˣˣ less likely than in MT, see p. 96 fn. 69.
260 Seen as an additional connection by Zenger 2008j, 870.
261 Even פאר/"adorn", see fn. 78, is translated in Ps 149ᴸˣˣ with the much more frequent ὑψόω/"lift up", in Isa 55:5; 60:7ᴸˣˣ; 2 Esdr 7:27ᴸˣˣ with δοξάζω/"honour". In Isa 60:9ᴸˣˣ the adjective ἔνδοξος/"honoured" is used which also appears in Ps 149ᴸˣˣ but as a translation of נִכְבְּדֵיהֶם/"their honoured ones" rather than a form of פאר/"adorn".

for עשה/"do" are shared. In Hos 9:1^LXX, χαίρω/"be glad" is used for שמח/"be glad" instead of εὐφραίνω/"cheer", εὐφραίνω/"cheer" for גיל/"rejoice" instead of ἀγαλλιάομαι/"rejoice"; and only ישְׂרָאֵל/"Israel", עַם/"people", and כֹּל/"all" are translated as Ισραηλ/"Israel", λαός/"people", and πᾶς/"all" like in Ps 149^LXX.

Results

It is unlikely that Ps 149^LXX contains intertextual references. References to Deu^LXX; Josh^LXX and Judg^LXX; Isa 40–66^LXX; Hos^LXX; Ps 95^LXX(=96^MT); 97^LXX(=98^MT); 145–147^LXX(=146–147^MT); 148^LXX; and 150^LXX are less likely than in MT. To Ex 14–15^LXX and Ps 2^LXX, references are equally unlikely as in MT. References to Ps 145–150^LXX are less likely than in MT even in addition to the lack of framing Hallelujahs.

III.3.4 Content of Psalm 149^LXX

Who is called to praise in Psalm 149^LXX?

The only two occurrences of αλληλουια/"Hallelujah"[262] in LXX outside the Psalter in are in 3 Mac 7:13^XX in the context of a violent battle, and in Tob 13:18 in a praise context with an eschatological vision of Jerusalem.

As in MT, the words used for the people Israel ἐκκλησία/"assembly" (v.1b),[263] ὅσιοι/"faithful ones" (v.1b, 5a, 9b),[264] Ισραηλ/"Israel" (v.2a), υἱοὶ Σιων/"sons of Zion" (v.2b),[265] λαὸς αὐτοῦ/"his people" (v.4a),[266] and πραεῖς/"poor ones" (v.4b),[267] all appear in multiple contexts. ἐκκλησία ὁσίων/"assembly of faithful ones" for קְהַל חֲסִידִים/"assembly of faithful ones" is even less likely to point to one specific group than in MT: It stands in contrast to συναγωγὴ Ασιδαίων/"company of Hasideans" in 1 Mac 2:42^LXX or to the name Ασιδαῖοι/"Hasideans" in 1

---

262 See p. 73–74.

263 Cf. Hossfeld, Kindl, and Fabry 1989, esp. 1221–1222 (in the Psalms, ἐκκλησία/"assembly" is always used for קְהַל/"assembly"); Lust, Eynikel, and Hauspie 2003, s.v. ἐκκλησία.

264 Cf. Ringgren and Fabry 1982, esp. 87: ὅσιοι/"faithful ones" is used as usual in LXX, not Ἀσιδαῖοι/"Hasideans" as for the limited group in 1 Mac 2:42; 7:13^LXX; 2 Mac 14:6^LXX.

265 As in MT, υἱοὶ Σιων/"sons of Zion" appears only here and in Lam 4:2^LXX, cf. Brucker 2011d, 1882, but there is no intertextual reference.

266 Cf. Lust, Eynikel, and Hauspie 2003, s.v. λαός.

267 Cf. Lust, Eynikel, and Hauspie 2003, s.v. πραΰς.

Mac 7:13^{LXX} and 2 Mac 14:6^{LXX}.[268] A *cultic* content and setting may be hinted at, and the subject is Israel, *not a group of Hasideans*.

What is "a new song" in Psalm 149:1^{LXX}?

שִׁירוּ לַיהוָה שִׁיר חָדָשׁ/"sing to YHWH a new song" is translated as ᾄσατε τῷ κυρίῳ ᾆσμα καινόν/"sing to the Lord a new song" in Ps 95:1^{LXX}(=96:1^{MT}) and in Ps 97:1^{LXX} (=98:1^{MT}) as in Ps 149:1^{LXX}, but in Isa 42:12^{LXX} as ὑμνήσατε τῷ κυρίῳ ὕμνον καινόν/ "chant to the Lord a new chant". ᾆσμα καινόν/"new song" for שִׁיר חָדָשׁ/"new song" appears also in Ps 32:3^{LXX}(=33:3^{MT}); 39:4^{LXX}(=40:4^{MT}), while Ps 143:9^{LXX} (=144:9^{MT}) uses ᾠδὴ καινή/"new ode".[269] Thus, in LXX ᾄσατε τῷ κυρίῳ ᾆσμα καινόν/"sing to the Lord a new song" appears in eschatological contexts in Ps 95:1^{LXX}(=96:1^{MT}) and in Ps 97:1^{LXX}(=98:1^{MT}), and may point towards *eschatological* content in Ps 149:1^{LXX}, but ᾆσμα καινόν/"new song" is used without obvious eschatological connotations in Ps 32^{LXX}(=33^{MT}) and Ps 39^{LXX}(=40^{MT}). As in MT, there are no intertextual connections with eschatological texts.

Why is God to be praised in Psalm 149:2^{LXX}?

The singular ἐπὶ τῷ ποιήσαντι αὐτόν/"in the one having made it"[270] corresponds to the Hebrew plural of majesty. Since aorist participles can refer to actions both before and simultaneously with the main verb, though the former is more common,[271] as in Hebrew it is unclear whether the reference here is to first creation or continual preservation, though the *past creation* is more likely.[272]

What is "safety" in Psalm 149:4^{LXX}?

σωτηρία/"safety" usually refers to help and safety but can also refer to military victory,[273] and the future ὑψώσει/"he will lift up" in v.4b makes it unlikely that the reference is to past victories or past help, but rather to *future* help which may be *eschatological*. σωτηρία as "safety" is also supported by ἐν/"in" for בְּ/"in".

---

268 Against van Grol 2011, 99, 113.
269 ὕμνος καινός/"new chant" also appears in Jdt 16:13^{LXX} (context final judgement) and PsSal 3:1^{LXX} (context eternity). According to Witte 2002, 536, all these phrases (and also ψαλμὸς καινὸς/ "new song" in PsSal 15:3^{LXX}, context final judgement) introduce an eschatological song of praise.
270 Same phrase in Isa 17:7^{LXX}, cf. Brucker 2011d, 1882, but without an intertextual reference.
271 Cf. Blass, Debrunner, and Rehkopf 1979, §339; Smyth and Messing 1956, §1872.
272 Zenger 2008j, 870, sees the aorist as a reference to the first creation only.
273 Cf. Bons 2009b, 897 (Ps 149:4^{LXX} a), 767 (Ps 17:51^{LXX} a).

Whose "glory" is it in Psalm 149:5^{LXX}?

כְּבוֹד/"honour" is translated as δόξα/"glory" in v.5a, and unlike in MT the same word δόξα/"glory" is also used in v.9a, where – again unlike in MT – the word refers to the content of Ps 149 as glory rather than God as glory. It is thus likely to refer to the glory of humans rather than God. As in Hebrew this glory could be a cause or mode of exulting, with the parallel in v.5b making a mode likely, but unlike in Hebrew more likely referring forward to the following verses with human actions rather than back to God's actions. Unlike in Hebrew, the related ἔνδοξος/"glorified" in v.8b between the two uses of δόξα/"glory" marks a contrast between Israel's glory and the powerless glory of rulers of other nations.[274]

What are "beds" Psalm 149:5^{LXX}?

עַל־מִשְׁכְּבוֹתָם/"on their beds" is uniquely translated as ἐπὶ τῶν κοιτῶν αὐτῶν/"on their beds" in Ps 149:5^{LXX}; but Ps 4:5^{LXX} uses the similar phrase ἐπὶ ταῖς κοίταις ὑμῶν/"on your beds", and Hos 7:14^{LXX} and Mic 2:1^{LXX} use ἐν ταῖς κοίταις αὐτῶν/"in their beds".

As in MT, it is unlikely that the beds are (1) *literal beds*, either (a) for *nightly worship* or (b) a *dream*, since neither (a) Deut 6:7^{LXX} (with κοιτάζω/"lie down") nor Ps 1:2^{LXX}, nor (b) Cant 3:1^{LXX} (just κοίτη/"bed" is shared) have intertextual links with Psalm 149^{LXX}. As in MT, (2) beds as *private places* for meditation are likely: While again there are no intertextual links, the same word κοίτη/"bed" for מִשְׁכָּב/"bed" is used in Ps 4:5^{LXX}, Mic 2:1^{LXX}, and Hos 7:14^{LXX}. As in MT, (3) *cultic prostration* is unlikely as κοίτη/"bed" or κοιτάζω/"lie down" are not used in such contexts in LXX. As in MT, (4) *campbeds* are unlikely as κοίτη/"bed" is not used in military contexts in LXX. Unlike in MT, (5) *deathmats* can be ruled out since κοίτη/"bed" does not appear in 2 Chr 16:14^{LXX} (κλίνη/"couch"), Ezek 32:25^{LXX} (different text), or Isa 57:2^{LXX} (ταφή/"burial"). As in MT, no dead people are mentioned in Ps 149^{LXX}, and κοίτη/"bed" or κοιτάζω/"lie down" are not used in resurrection contexts.[275] The use of ἐπί/"on, above" with genitive in Ps 149:5^{LXX} is unique compared to texts with similar themes: Hos 7:14^{LXX} and Mic 2:1^{LXX} use ἐν/"in" rather than ἐπί/"on, above", Ps 4:5^{LXX} ἐπί/"on" with dative. However, since ἐπί/"on, above" with genitive may still mean "on" rather than "above",[276] there is no indication of death or resurrection.

---

274 Cf. Zenger 2008j, 870; Brucker 2011d, 1883.
275 Cf. Lust, Eynikel, and Hauspie 2003, s.v. κοίτη, s.v. κοιτάζω.
276 Cf. Lust, Eynikel, and Hauspie 2003, s.v. ἐπί.

Even more likely than in MT, the beds are *private places* for meditation, since this meaning is supported by other texts (Ps 4:5^[LXX]; Hos 7:14^[LXX]; Mic 2:1^[LXX]). As in MT, the Psalm then jumps from public worship in vv.1–3 to private worship in v.5 (possibly including both v.5b and v.5a) and back to public action in vv.6–9.

What are "swords" in Psalm 149:6^[LXX]?

וְחֶרֶב פִּיפִיּוֹת בְּיָדָם/"and a sword of two mouths in their hand" is translated with plural forms καὶ ῥομφαῖαι δίστομοι ἐν ταῖς χερσὶν αὐτῶν/"and two-edged swords in their hands". The image of multiple swords for multiple hands makes the interpretation as *actual* swords more likely than in MT, especially given that while ὑψώσεις/"high praises" (hapax legomenon both in MT and LXX)[277] in v.6a are also plural, λάρυγξ/"throat" is not.[278] וְ/"and" is translated as καί/"and", making the interpretation of a waw copulativum likely as in MT. As in MT, given the lack of intertextual references, the interpretation of v.6b as referring to actual swords in battle,[279] cult, or the eschaton, or as a methaphor depends on the overall interpretation of Ps 149^[LXX].

Who is subject to what "revenge" in Psalm 149:7–8^[LXX]?

ἐκδίκησις/"revenge" for נְקָמָה/"revenge" appears in different violent contexts in the Septuagint;[280] unlike in MT twice in Isaiah (with aim of worship of YHWH Isa 59:17^[LXX]; but also with death Isa 66:17^[LXX]). ἐλεγμός/"rebuke" for תּוֹכֵחָה/"punishment" is found in more positive contexts than in MT.[281] πέδη/"chain" for זִק/ "chain" and χειροπέδη/"handcuff" for כֶּבֶל/"fetter" (used in Job 36:8^[LXX]; Nah 3:10^[LXX]; Isa 45:15^[LXX] and others for זִק/"chain") are used more frequently than in MT.[282]

---

277 Cf. Brucker 2011d, 1883.

278 While as in Hebrew this singular could be distributive, cf. Blass, Debrunner, and Rehkopf 1979, §140, it highlights the plural in v.6b.

279 As e. g. 2 Mac 15:27^[LXX], cf. Brucker 2011d, 1883.

280 Cf. Lust, Eynikel, and Hauspie 2003, s.v. ἐκδίκησις; lemma search on ἐκδίκησις in Bible-Works 9 2013. Zenger 2008j, 870, sees it as the restitution of justice only.

281 Cf. Lust, Eynikel, and Hauspie 2003, s.v. ἐλεγμός; lemma search on ἐλεγμός in BibleWorks 9 2013. Zenger 2008j, 870 notes the connotation of God's pedagogy as in MT. However, the word is more negative in Hebrew.

282 Cf. Lust, Eynikel, and Hauspie 2003, s.v. πέδη, s.v. χειροπέδη.

While the Greek words for *revenge and rebuke are not as entirely negative* as in MT, and hint towards a less real interpretation of the Psalm, the parallel structure of v.7 and v.8 without any restriction is the same as in MT.

What is "written" in Psalm 149:9^LXX?

Psalm 149:9^LXX uniquely refers to a κρίμα ἔγγραπτον/"inscribed judgement" for מִשְׁפָּט כָּתוּב/"written judgement", using the adjective hapax legomenon ἔγγραπτος/"inscribed" for כָּתוּב/"written" (in LXX otherwise mostly translated with forms of γράφω/"write", especially γεγραμμένος/"written" and γέγραπται/"it is written").[283] Given the lack of intertextual references in Ps 149^LXX, references to (1) Gen-Judg^LXX, (2) prophetic books or (2) Psalm 2^LXX are unlikely. Nothing is known about (4) other texts as in MT, and the hapax legomenon ἔγγραπτος/"inscribed" makes a reference to a written text even less likely than in MT. While a reference to the idea of (5) a heavenly book for future judgement such as in Dan 12:1^LXX,[284] leading to an eschatological interpretation of Ps 149^LXX, is possible, there is no clear reference to this idea in Ps 149^LXX, and (6) a general reference to God's justice depends on the overall view of God's justice. The Septuagint stresses the *uniqueness* of Ps 149^LXX with a hapax legomenon even more than in MT, and Dan 12:1^LXX hints towards an *eschatological* interpretation.

III.3.5 Genre of Psalm 149^LXX

Unlike in MT, due to the future forms *eschatological* interpretations of the Psalm's setting in life, whether cultic or literary, are more likely than non-eschatological cultic or military interpretations.

III.3.6 Date of Psalm 149^LXX

Ps 149^LXX does not use the term Ασιδαῖοι/"Hasideans",[285] making an identification with Maccabean fighters less likely than in MT, but does not contain further information about its date. This has to rely on the 2nd century BCE LXX-Psalter.[286]

---

283 Form search on כָּתוּב in *BibleWorks 9* 2013.
284 Dan 12:1^LXX though not Dan 12:1^Theodotion uniquely uses ἐγγεγραμμένος/"inscribed" of ἐγγράφω/"inscribe" for כָּתוּב/"written".
285 See p. 123–124.
286 See p. 16, esp. fn. 104.

III.3.7 Unity of Psalm 149^{LXX}

Ps 149^{LXX} is one unit, with no final Hallelujah in any manuscript. Some manuscripts add an extra opening Hallelujah, others add Αγγαιου καὶ Ζαχαριου/"of Haggai and Zechariah" as in Ps 145–148^{LXX}(=146–148^{MT}). Some manuscripts with ἔσται/"will be" instead of ἐστίν/"is" in v.9[287] confirm the importance of future forms in Ps 149^{LXX}.

III.3.8 Overall Interpretation of Psalm 149^{LXX}

As in MT, there is a lack of intertextual references, and neither the general meaning of words nor similar themes point unanimously into one direction for interpreting Ps 149^{LXX} as cultic, military, or eschatological: The subjects called to praise indicate a *cultic* content and setting (even more clearly than in MT the subjects are the people Israel, *not a specific group of Hasideans*), the "new song" suggests an *eschatological* content (*more strongly* than in MT), Israel's creation is set in the *past*, "help" is *ambiguous* (but unlike in MT connected with a *future* form and thus possibly *eschatological*), "beds" point towards a *non-cultic, non-military private* setting (*more strongly* than in MT), "swords" to a *military* content (*more strongly* than in MT), "revenge" to a *military* content (though *less strongly* than in MT), "written" to an *eschatological* content (*more strongly* than in MT, but also with a stress on the *uniqueness* of Ps 149). Thus, as in MT Ps 149^{LXX} seems elusive for a definite overall interpretation. Unlike in MT, *future forms* point towards an *eschatological* understanding of the Psalm with future revenge as a reason for present and future praise and present glory. In combination with *hints towards an eschatological understanding in the individual words*, this makes it more likely that Ps 149^{LXX} is understood *with reference to the future and thus eschatologically.* A *verbal sentence at the end* summarising mainly judgement rather than judgement and praise in the entire Psalm leads to an end with a stress on Israel as a subject rather than YHWH.

Overall, YHWH, the God (of Israel), is to be praised in an assembly of faithful ones. The reasons for praise are his *past* creation, his present kingship, delight in and *future* help for his people. He is to be praised with musical instruments and dance but also *in the future* on beds by Israel. Israel itself is also (also *in the fu-*

---

[287] Also in Greek Orthodox lectionaries today, cf. Bons 2009b, 897; Kraus and Karrer 2009, XXII.

ture) to take violent revenge on nations and their rulers with swords, chains, and fetters, as in an inscribed judgement. *This* is their *present glory*.

III.4 Comparison

Both DSS and LXX are very *close* to MT, though DSS stresses Israel through an *additional passage*, LXX stresses the future and Israel as a subject.

There are opening *Hallelujahs* in MT and LXX (not preserved in DSS) and closing Hallelujahs in MT and DSS, but not LXX. In the LXX, the *lack of a Hallelujah-frame* (LXX only has an opening Hallelujah,[288] transliterated rather than translated, and some LXX manuscripts show variations of the frame), and the connection only to Ps 150^{LXX} but not Ps 148^{LXX} though a common superscription weakens the likelihood of an original connection of Psalms 146–150.

Regarding *order*, Ps 149 is followed by Ps 150 in all text forms but preceded by Ps 148 in MT and LXX but not 11QPs^a where it is preceded by Ps 142–143.

Regarding *intertextuality*, both DSS and LXX either confirm the lack of references in MT or (in LXX) even weaken the likelihood of references in MT.

---

288 The final Hallelujah is missing as always in LXX except for Ps 150^{LXX}, see p. 73–74, esp. p. 73 fn. 379.

IV Psalm 148

IV.1 Psalm 148^MT

IV.1.1 Translation of Psalm 148^MT

1H	Praise-Yah!	הַלְלוּ יָהּ ׀	1H
1a	Praise YHWH from the heaven,	הַלְלוּ אֶת־יְהוָה מִן־הַשָּׁמַיִם	1a
1b	praise him in the heights.	הַלְלוּהוּ בַּמְּרוֹמִים׃	1b
2a	Praise him, all his angels,	הַלְלוּהוּ כָל־מַלְאָכָיו	2a
2b	praise him, all his host.	הַלְלוּהוּ כָּל־צְבָאָו׃	2b
3a	Praise him, sun and moon,	הַלְלוּהוּ שֶׁמֶשׁ וְיָרֵחַ	3a
3b	praise him, all stars of light.	הַלְלוּהוּ כָּל־כּוֹכְבֵי אוֹר׃	3b
4a	Praise him, the heaven of the heaven,	הַלְלוּהוּ שְׁמֵי הַשָּׁמָיִם	4a
4b	and the water which (is) above the heaven.	וְהַמַּיִם אֲשֶׁר ׀ מֵעַל הַשָּׁמָיִם׃	4b
5a	Let them praise the name of YHWH,	יְהַלְלוּ אֶת־שֵׁם יְהוָה	5a
5b	for he himself commanded and they were created.	כִּי הוּא צִוָּה וְנִבְרָאוּ׃	5b
6a	And he has established them for ever for eternity,	וַיַּעֲמִידֵם לָעַד לְעוֹלָם	6a
6b	a decree he gave and it will not pass.	חָק־נָתַן וְלֹא יַעֲבוֹר׃	6b
7a	Praise YHWH from the earth,	הַלְלוּ אֶת־יְהוָה מִן־הָאָרֶץ	7a
7b	sea monsters and all floods,	תַּנִּינִים וְכָל־תְּהֹמוֹת׃	7b
8a	fire and hail, snow and fog,	אֵשׁ וּבָרָד שֶׁלֶג וְקִיטוֹר	8a
8b	wind of storm doing his word,	רוּחַ סְעָרָה עֹשָׂה דְבָרוֹ׃	8b
9a	the mountains and all hills,	הֶהָרִים וְכָל־גְּבָעוֹת	9a
9b	tree of fruit and all cedars,	עֵץ פְּרִי וְכָל־אֲרָזִים׃	9b
10a	the wild animal and all cattle,	הַחַיָּה וְכָל־בְּהֵמָה	10a
10b	creeping animal and bird of wing,[1]	רֶמֶשׂ וְצִפּוֹר כָּנָף׃	10b
11a	kings of earth and all nations,	מַלְכֵי־אֶרֶץ וְכָל־לְאֻמִּים	11a
11b	rulers and all judges of earth,	שָׂרִים וְכָל־שֹׁפְטֵי אָרֶץ׃	11b
12a	young men and also young women,	בַּחוּרִים וְגַם־בְּתוּלוֹת	12a
12b	old people with young people.	זְקֵנִים עִם־נְעָרִים׃	12b
13a	Let them praise the name of YHWH,	יְהַלְלוּ אֶת־שֵׁם יְהוָה	13a
13b	for exalted (is) his name alone,	כִּי־נִשְׂגָּב שְׁמוֹ לְבַדּוֹ	13b
13c	his majesty above earth and heaven.	הוֹדוֹ עַל־אֶרֶץ וְשָׁמָיִם׃	13c
14a	And he has lifted up a horn for his people,	וַיָּרֶם קֶרֶן ׀ לְעַמּוֹ	14a
14b	praise for all his faithful ones,	תְּהִלָּה לְכָל־חֲסִידָיו	14b
14c	for the sons of Israel, the people near to him.	לִבְנֵי יִשְׂרָאֵל עַם־קְרֹבוֹ	14c
14H	Praise-Yah!	הַלְלוּ־יָהּ׃	14H

---

1 Less literally: "winged bird".

DOI 10.1515/9783110536096-004

IV.1.2 Form of Psalm 148^{MT}

Outline of Psalm 148^{MT}

1H	Framing *Imperative*	
Part I		
1–4	Calls to Praise Imperatives (7)	Subject: Heavenly Beings, Object: YHWH
5–6	Summarising Call to *Jussive (1)*	Subject: Heavenly Beings, Object: YHWH
	+ Reasons for Praise *Perfect, Waw-Imperfect*	Subject: YHWH, Object: Heavenly Beings
Part II		
7–12	Calls to Praise *Imperative (1)*	Subject: Earthly Beings, Object: YHWH
13–14	Summarising Call to *Jussive (1)*	Subject: Earthly Beings, Object: YHWH
	+ Reasons for Praise *Participle, Waw-Imperfect*	Subject: YHWH, Object: Earthly Beings (including Israel)
14H	Framing *Imperative*	

Syntax of Psalm 148^{MT}

Ps 148 is dominated by הלל/"*praise*" in *imperatives* v.1ab, 2ab, 3ab, 4a, and 7a (with the object אֶת־יהוה/"YHWH" in v.1a and 7a, suffixes referring back to v.1a in vv.1b–4a) and the framing imperatives הַלְלוּ־יָהּ/"Praise-Yah!", and *jussives* in vv.5a, 13a.[2] הלל/"praise" is the only verb appearing more than once, 10 times plus 2 times in the frame. While it appears much more frequently in Part I (8 times) than in Part II (2 times), it connects both parts in addition to the frame.

V.5b first contains other verbs, *perfect* forms of צוה/"command" and ברא/ "create" followed by a *waw-imperfect* of עמד/"establish" in v.6a, a *perfect* of נתן/"give" and an *imperfect* (possibly representing a *perfect*)[3] of עבד/"pass" in v.6b, and one further *waw-imperfect* of רום/"lift up" in v.14a. The use of *waw-im-*

---

2 Also noted by Ballhorn 2004b, 315.

3 As it is separated from the verb by לא/"not", ו/"and" could either be a *waw copulativum* introducing an imperfect, or a *waw consecutivum* introducing a perfect replaced by an imperfect, and thus express an unfinished or finished action, cf. Gesenius and Kautzsch 1909, §47 fn. 1, 49b fn. 1.

perfect connects v.6 and v.14,[4] although in v.6 the waw-imperfect follows perfect forms in v.5 (thus likely referring to past events), and in v.14 a nominal sentence with a participle (thus likely referring to ongoing events).[5] There are three *participles* (of עשׂה/"do" in v.8b, of שׁפט/"judge" in v.11b, though this probably stands for a noun,[6] and of שׂגב/"exalt" in v.13b).

Some sentences have *no verb*. V.4b has a relative nominal clause introduced by אֲשֶׁר/"which" referring to הַמַּיִם/"the waters". The participle of שׂגב/"exalt" in v.13b forms the stressed predicate for the subject שְׁמוֹ/"his name" in a nominal sentence.[7] V.13c could either be an independent nominal sentence with the subject הוֹדוֹ/"his majesty",[8] or this subject could depend on the predicate נִשְׂגָּב/"exalted" in v.13b.[9] Similarly, v.14b could be an independent nominal sentence with the subject תְּהִלָּה/"praise",[10] or praise could be an object of וַיָּרֶם/"and he has lifted up" in v.14a. Neither v.13c nor v.14b are independent sentences: v.13c is an addition compared to the parallel v.5b and depends on v.13b. V.14b is framed by v.14a which does and v.14c which does not form an independent sentence, while both v.14a and v.14c are connected through עַם/"people", and v.14a and v.14b are form parallels with an object followed by לְ/"for", followed by a double apposition in v.14c.

Even more important than calls to praise are the *subjects:* Nouns dominate the entire Psalm. Heavenly and earthly beings (including kings and rulers of all nations unlike in Ps 149) are the subjects of vv.1–5a, 7a–13a. In all other verses, namely vv.5b–6b and vv.13b–14c, the dominating subject is YHWH (הוּא/"he" in v.5b referring back to יהוה/"YHWH" in v.5a, suffixes in v.13bc and the subject and suffixes in v.14abc referring back to יהוה/"YHWH" in v.13a).

---

4 Ballhorn 2004b, 320, sees the waw-imperfect as bringing past and future aspects to both verses. However, this depends on a future view of v.14 which in turn depends on an eschatological interpretation of the Psalm, cf. Ballhorn 2004b, 318–321. Within Ps 148, waw-imperfects are unlikely to refer to future events, cf. Gesenius and Kautzsch 1909, §111a, n-w. A jussive in v.14, cf. Hillers 1978, 327, is unlikely given the parallel in v.6 (and the vocalisation, see fn. 252). Future and jussive meanings in v.14 are also seen as unlikely by Ruppert 1986, 276; Zenger 2008i, 839.
5 Cf. Gesenius and Kautzsch 1909, §111a, n-w.
6 Cf. Gesenius 2013, s.v. שׁפט.
7 Cf. Joüon and Muraoka 2011, §154a, d, f.
8 See p. 88 fn. 6.
9 See p. 88 fn. 8.
10 Cf. Hupfeld 1871, 456 (תְּהִלָּה/"praise" in the Psalms must mean praise of God and thus has to be a subject); Zenger 2008i, 839–840 (תְּהִלָּה/"praise" Israel's praise of God in Ps 146–150).

In v.5b the subject הוּא/"he" (referring to YHWH) and in v.6b the object חֹק/ "decree" are stressed before the verb.[11] In verbless sentences, the usual *word order* is reversed in v.13bc where נִשְׂגָּב/"exalted" is stressed.[12]

Suffixes referring to *YHWH* connect vv.1–4 (יהוה/"YHWH" in v.1a, verbal suffixes in vv.1b–4a, nominal suffixes in v.2ab) and also appear in vv.8b, 13bc, 14abc (nominal suffixes; לְבַדּוֹ/"only" in v.13b refers to YHWH's name and thus to YHWH), thus connecting v.7 with v.8, and v.13 with v.14. The only suffix not referring to YHWH is וַיַּעֲמִידֵם/"and he has established them" in v.6a where YHWH is subject. Thus, despite the number of subjects in Ps 148, the suffixes stress YHWH's importance.

Two repetitions of *prepositions* stand out: מִן/"from" appears in v.1a and v.7a, and לְ/"for" twice within v.6a and three times within v.14. Only the last two subjects of the calls to praise in v.12b are connected with עִם/"with", marking the end of the list (this end is also announced by גַּם/"also" in the preceding v.12a).

Structure of Psalm 148[MT]

Ps 148 shows a twofold structure. Both v.1 and v.7 start with הַלְלוּ אֶת־יְהוָה מִן־/ "praise YHWH from" (followed by הַשָּׁמַיִם/"the heaven" in v.1a and הָאָרֶץ/"the earth" in v.7a), and both v.5 and v.13 start with יְהַלְלוּ אֶת־שֵׁם יְהוָה כִּי/"let them praise the name of YHWH, for". Vv.1b–4b and vv.7b–12b list subjects of the calls to praise, with vv.1b–4a repeating the call to praise whereas vv.7b–12b depend on v.7a. The sentences introduced by כִּי/"for" are one line in v.5b but two in v.13bc, and are followed by a waw-imperfect introducing two lines in v.6ab but three lines in v.14abc. In both cases, כִּי/"for" introduces reasons for praise.[13] Thus, the twofold structure is vv.1–6 (heaven) and vv.7–14 (earth), with the first part showing anaphoric imperatives, and the second part being longer than the first one both in the number of subjects and the concluding summary.[14] Thus, while vv.13–14 primarily summarise vv.7–12, they also serve as a summary for the subjects called to praise earlier in the Psalm. The twofold structure is supported by the four occurrences of יהוה/"YHWH" in vv.1a, 5a, 7a, and 13a, with two occurrences each at the beginning and end of each part.[15] The entire Psalm is framed with הַלְלוּ־יָהּ/"Praise-Yah!".

---

11 See p. 32 fn. 4.
12 See p. 89 fn. 14.
13 Cf. Kuntz 1999, esp. 162–170, 179–183.
14 Cf. Prinsloo 1992, 47–48, 60–61; Krüger 2001, 77; Allen 2002, 390–391, 393; Ballhorn 2004b, 317–318; Zenger 2008i, 841.
15 Cf. Prinsloo 1992, 48.

However, some commentators take v.14 (or parts of v.14, or vv.13–14) as a separate part though still with two main parts, vv.1–6 (Part I) and vv.7–13 (Part II),[16] and sometimes even see v.14 as a secondary addition.[17] Other divisions into three[18] or seven[19] strophes depend on content only and are syntactically unlikely.

Poetic Devices in Psalm 148^MT

Most parallelisms in the bicola of Ps 148[20] are *synthetic parallelisms* (vv.2–12), with one *synonymous parallelism* (v.1). While there is a clear parallelism between v.1ab, with subjects appearing in vv.2–4, there is no equivalent in v.7ab as subjects appear immediately in vv.7b–12. In addition to the parallel bicola, there are two tricola in v.13 and v.14. While both contain *synthetic* elements, v.14bc also contains *synonymous* elements with designations of Israel. Thus, both the beginning (v.1) and the end (v.14) show synonymous structures, whereas the middle is dominated by synthetic structures.

Some commentators connect Ps 148 with *number symbolism*. For example, they note *ten* calls to praise with הלל/"praise" (*eight* imperatives and *two* jussives, with *seven* of the eight imperatives in Part I[21]), with the number *ten* signifying completeness (as in the ten words of creation on Gen 1 and the ten commandments in Ex 20=Deut 5).[22] Including the framing imperatives some see *twelve* calls to praise also signifying completeness (as in the twelve tribes of Israel and the twelve months of the year),[23] and *ten* occurrences of כל/"all", again signifying completeness.[24] Some commentators see *seven* strophes of two verses

---

16 Cf. Hupfeld 1871, 451, 456 (vv.13–14 separate; Part II vv.7–12 only); Gunkel 1926, 617–618 (v.14bc separate); Hillers 1978, 327–328 (v.14 separate); Ballhorn 2004b, 315–318 (v.14 separate). Prinsloo 1992, 60–61, lists more examples. See fn. 181.

17 Cf. Duhm 1922, 480–483 (vv.13–14 separate, v.14ac secondary; Part II vv.7–12 only); Gerstenberger 2001, 447–451 (v.14bc or all of v.14 separate and secondary); Leuenberger 2004, 351–353 (v.14 separate and secondary); Zenger 2008i, 840–845, outline 846 (v.14 separate and secondary; due to the new topic of Israel, and the verbal sentence v.14a following a nominal sentence v.13c). See fn. 182.

18 Cf. Dahood 1970, 352–354 (content: heaven, nether world, earth); Spieckermann 1989, 58 (content: heaven, earth, kingdoms).

19 Cf. Ruppert 1986, 278–288 (content: 3 heavenly, 4 earthly strophes).

20 On v.1 and v.2 see p. 142–144. Against Zięba 2009, 111, the contrast heaven (v.1) – earth (v.7) is a feature of the Psalms' structure, see p. 134, not a *parallelismus membrorum* within one verse.

21 Importance of seven questioned by Prinsloo 1992, 56–57.

22 Cf. Ruppert 1986, 279–280; Zenger 2008i, 841–842.

23 Cf. Zenger 2008i, 841–842.

24 Cf. Prinsloo 1992, 48, 50; Zenger 2008i, 842.

each in the Psalm (signifying seven days of creation as in Gen 1) with *three* strophes for heaven and *four* for earth, with the number *three* signifying the holiness of heaven and YHWH (as e.g. the threefold "holy" in Isa 6:2), and the number *four* signifying the completeness of the earth (as e.g. all four corners of the earth in Jer 49:36),[25] but this division of Psalm 148 into seven strophes is criticised by others.[26] There are *seven* subjects called to praise in the heavenly part,[27] and *twenty-three* in the earthly part.[28] Thus, there are *thirty*, i.e. *ten* times *three*, subjects called to praise in the Psalm, signifying the completeness and order of creation called to praise,[29] a completeness reached only by the combination of heaven and earth.[30] Other numbers are mentioned without further interpretation.[31]

While in HB three, four, seven, ten, and twelve do sometimes appear to have symbolic meaning, twenty-three and thirty are entirely insignificant, and number symbolism is of little significance in HB in general.[32] This general background in combination with different numbers of the same word הלל/"praise" in Ps 148, different divisions into strophes, the unlikely suggestion of the significance of twenty-three and thirty, and the lack of intertextual references to specific texts such as Ex 20/Deut 5 (ten commandments), make it unlikely that Ps 148 refers to specific numbers.

Among *other poetic devices* noted by commentators,[33] v.11 shows a chiastic structure with construct forms followed by אֶרֶץ/"earth" at the beginning and end.[34] A larger chiastic structure is found in the first and last occurrences of the words heaven and earth in Ps 148: heaven (v.1a) – earth (v.7a) and earth – heaven (v.13c),[35] though since the word heaven occurs five and the word earth

---

25 Cf. Ruppert 1986, 279–280 (last strophe vv.13–14a); Zenger 2008i, 841–842 (last strophe v.13).

26 Cf. Prinsloo 1992, 61.

27 Cf. Gerstenberger 2001, 449; Zenger 2008i, 842. See fn. 21.

28 Cf. Ruppert 1986, 279–280; Gerstenberger 2001, 449.

29 Cf. Ruppert 1986, 279–280; Zenger 2008i, 842.

30 Cf. Ruppert 1986, 280.

31 Cf. Prinsloo 1992, 48: e.g. heaven occurs *four* times in vv.1–6, and earth *four* times in the Psalm. However, heaven also occurs in v.13 and thus *five* times. Cf. also Gerstenberger 2001, 449.

32 See p. 34 fn. 30.

33 For extensive lists cf. Prinsloo 1992; Allen 2002, 392; Zięba 2009.

34 Cf. Prinsloo 1992, 51; Zięba 2009, 12.

35 Cf. Allen 2002, 392; Zenger 2008i, 840 (v.13c marks the end of the two main parts).

four times throughout the Psalm this does not have to be a sign that v.13c is the
end of the main parts of the Psalm.[36]

The repetition of שֵׁם/"name" connects v.13a and v.13b (with v.5a); the repetition of עַם/"people" v.14a and v.14c.

Several commentators note merisms (expression of a totality by naming
some of its members)[37] in Psalm 148, namely heaven and earth for all of creation,[38] and a merismic list with pairs of earthly creatures for all of earthly creation.[39]

IV.1.3 Intertextuality in Psalm 148ᴹᵀ

Importance
In addition to the general background of ANE lists and hymns,[40] Psalm 148 is
sometimes seen as using other texts,[41] with its interpretation and date dependent
on Ps 146–150.[42] Ps 148:14 in particular is seen in connection with Ps 149.[43] Commentators also argue for various other intertextual references with significant influence on the interpretation of Ps 148 as shown in the following analysis.

Analysis
Many commentators argue, more[44] or less[45] strongly, for a reference from Ps 148
to *Genesis 1*, leading to interpretations of Ps 148 in the light of the worldview of
Gen 1 where heaven and earth are a merism for the entire cosmos,[46] where creation is the central message,[47] where creation is connected with God's word,[48]

---

36 A chiastic pattern of articulate to large non-articulate subjects for heavenly beings, and vice
versa for earthly beings, is broken by sea monsters, cf. Allen 2002, 392. See p. 145–147.
37 On merisms cf. Watson 1984, 321–324.
38 Cf. Zenger 2008i, 841, 846–847.
39 Cf. Prinsloo 1992, 50; Zenger 2008i, 841, 849–850; Zięba 2009, 12–13.
40 See IV.1.5.
41 Cf. Duhm 1922, 482; Ruppert 1986, 295; Prinsloo 1992, 56.
42 See IV.1.6, esp. fn. 175.
43 See p. 141 on Ps 149.
44 Cf. Mathys 2000, 342 (direct citation); Zenger 2008i, 852 (strongly inspired by Gen 1).
45 Cf. Ruppert 1986, 293 (very close); Prinsloo 1992, 55–56 (borrowing either way or common
source); Allen 2002, 393 ("partial influence"); Leuenberger 2004, 351 (referring to Ruppert).
46 Cf. Zenger 2008i, 847.
47 Cf. Seybold 1996, 543; Zenger 2008i, 848 (referring to Seybold).
48 Cf. Ruppert 1986, 293; Prinsloo 1992, 55.

and where the waters above the heavens are those above the firmament.[49] The order of creation in Gen 1 is sometimes seen to reflect the order in Ps 148.[50] However, the lack of literary similarity is also noted by commentators.[51] Ps 148 and Gen 1:1–2:4a share nineteen words, namely ברא/"create", שָׁמַיִם/"heaven", אֶרֶץ/ "earth", תְּהוֹם/"flood", רוּחַ/"wind", מַיִם/"water", אוֹר/"light", עשׂה/"do", עֵץ/ "tree", פְּרִי/"fruit", כּוֹכָב/"star", נתן/"give", תַּנִּין/"sea monster", כֹּל/"all", כָּנָף/ "wing", בְּהֵמָה/"cattle", רֶמֶשׂ/"creeping animal", חַיָּה/"wild animal", and צָבָא/ "host". However, none of these words are rare, and there is little syntactical similarity: only עֵץ פְּרִי/"tree of fruit" is unique to Ps 148:9 and Gen 1:11 (but in Gen 1:11 it is explained further as עֵץ פְּרִי עֹשֶׂה פְּרִי/"tree of fruit making fruit", in Gen 1:12 as עֵץ עֹשֶׂה־פְּרִי/"tree making fruit", in Gen 1:29 as הָעֵץ אֲשֶׁר־בּוֹ זֶרַע זֹרֵעַ זֶרַע פְּרִי־עֵץ/"the tree on which is fruit of tree producing seed"). While the plural תַּנִּינִם/"sea monsters" is rare (it appears in Gen 1:21; Ps 74:13; 148:7 with reference to sea monsters, and also in Ex 7:12 and Deut 32:33 probably with reference to serpents), there is a singular rather than a plural of תְּהוֹם/"flood" in Gen 1, and the rare word קִיטוֹר/"fog" does not appear in Gen 1 either (only in Gen 19:28; Ps 119:83; 148:8). While the theme of creation is shared, the lack of syntactical similarity makes references between Ps 148 and Gen 1 unlikely. There is one syntactical similarity with Gen 2:4b: אֶרֶץ וְשָׁמַיִם/"earth and heaven" appears only here and in Ps 148:13. References to Gen 2 are not assumed by commentators, but the similarity is noted in the context of Gen 1 (sometimes as if it was supporting references to Gen 1:1–2:4a).[52] Ps 148 and Gen 2:4b–25 share the frequent words עשׂה/"do", יהוה/"YHWH", אֶרֶץ/"earth", שָׁמַיִם/"heaven", כֹּל/"all", לֹא/"not", עֵץ /"tree", שֵׁם/"name", הוּא/"he", צוה/"command", לְבַדּוֹ/"only", חַיָּה/ "wild animal", and בְּהֵמָה/"cattle" without syntactical similarity, wherefore no reference is likely.

Some commentators argue that Ps 148:14 refers to *Deuteronomy 4:7*, thus including an allusion to Israel's Torah.[53] While Deut 4:7 only shares קָרֹב/"near" with Ps 148:14 (and the frequent words יהוה/"YHWH" and כֹּל/"all" with the entire Psalm 148), the context of Deut 4:1–18 shares twenty-two words (more than Gen 1!) with Psalm 148, namely יִשְׂרָאֵל/"Israel", חֹק/"decree", עשׂה/"do, יהוה/ "YHWH", אֶרֶץ/"earth", נתן/"give", לֹא/"not", צוה/"command", דָּבָר/"word", כֹּל/ "all", עַם/"people", קָרֹב/"near", בֵּן/"son", עמד/"pass", אֵשׁ/"fire", הַר/"mountain",

---

49 Cf. Hupfeld 1871, 453; Zenger 2008i, 849.
50 Cf. Hupfeld 1871, 451–452, 455; Duhm 1922, 481; Ballhorn 2004b, 315; Zenger 2008i, 842, 847–850; Giere 2009, 36.
51 Cf. Hillers 1978, 328 (different order of creation elements); Giere 2009, 36.
52 Cf. Gunkel 1926, 619; Prinsloo 1992, 55; Ballhorn 2004b, 315; Zenger 2008i, 850.
53 Cf. Ballhorn 2004b, 321; Zenger 2008i, 851.

שָׁמַיִם/"heaven", בְּהֵמָה/"cattle", צִפּוֹר/"bird", כָּנָף/"wing", רמש/"creep", and מַיִם/ "water". There is syntactical similarity in צִפּוֹר כָּנָף/"bird of wing" used only in Deut 4:17 and Ps 148:10, but the similarities overall do not suffice to make an intertextual reference likely.

Similarities with *Psalm 2* lead to interpretations of Ps 148 within the frame of Ps 1–2 and 146–150,[54] and Ps 148 is even seen as a redactional Psalm written for this frame.[55] However, only the frequent words לְאֹם/"people", מֶלֶךְ/"king", אֶרֶץ/ "earth" (also in מַלְכֵי־אֶרֶץ/"kings of earth")[56], יהוה/"YHWH", שָׁמַיִם/"heaven", הַר/ "mountain, חֹק/"decree", בֵּן/"son", נתן/"give", שפט/"judge", and כֹּל/"all", are shared with very little syntactical similarity, wherefore a reference is unlikely.

Some commentators argue for references to *Psalm 33*,[57] in particular from Ps 148:5–6 to Ps 33:5–6.[58] Ps 33 shares יהוה/"YHWH", תְּהִלָּה/"praise", דְּבָר/ "word", כֹּל/"all", אֶרֶץ/"earth", שָׁמַיִם/"heaven", עשה/"do", רוּחַ/"wind", צָבָא/ "host", מַיִם/"water", נתן/"give", תְּהוֹם/"flood", הוּא/"he", צוה/"command" (in הוּא צִוָּה/"he himself commanded"), עָם/"people", עוֹלָם/"eternity", בֵּן/"son", מֶלֶךְ/ "king", לֹא/"not", and שֵׁם/"name" with Ps 148, but there is insufficient syntactical similarity to make a reference likely.

It is sometimes argued that Ps 148 refers to *Psalm 96*[59] and has close affinities with *Psalm 96 and Psalm 98*,[60] leading to interpretations on the background of YHWH-king-Psalms[61] (despite the fact that YHWH's kingship is not mentioned in Ps 148).[62] Ps 96 shares יהוה/"YHWH", כֹּל/"all", אֶרֶץ/"earth", שֵׁם/"name", עַם/ "people", הלל/"praise", הוּא/"he", שָׁמַיִם/"heaven", עשה/"do", הוֹד/"majesty", עֵץ/ "tree", and שפט/"judge", Ps 98 shares יהוה/"YHWH", עשה/"do", יִשְׂרָאֵל/"Israel", כֹּל/"all", אֶרֶץ/"earth", מֶלֶךְ/"king", הַר/"mountain", שפט/"judge", and עַם/ "people", but without syntactical similarity, wherefore a reference is unlikely.

Commentators argue that the author of Ps 148 knew and drew on *Psalm 103*,[63] *Psalm 104*,[64] or both *Psalm 103 and Psalm 104*,[65] with consequences including

---

54 Cf. Ballhorn 2004b, 320; Leuenberger 2004, 351.

55 Cf. Leuenberger 2004, 353.

56 Against Ballhorn 2004b, 320, this phrase does not only appear in Ps 2:2, Ps 148:11, and Lam 4:12, but also in Ezek 27:33, with כָּל־/"all" prefixed in Ps 138:4 and twice in Jer 25:20.

57 Cf. Vosberg 1975, 19, 21; Zenger 2008i, 853.

58 Cf. Duhm 1922, 481; Allen 2002, 389; Leuenberger 2004, 351.

59 Cf. Zenger 2008i, 850.

60 Cf. Ruppert 1986, 284–285; Ballhorn 2004b, 316; Watson 2005, 209; Zenger 2008i, 842.

61 Cf. Ballhorn 2004b, 316; Leuenberger 2004, 353; Zenger 2008i, 842.

62 Cf. Ballhorn 2004b, 316.

63 Cf. Duhm 1922, 482.

64 Cf. Vosberg 1975, 111.

that the writing of Ps 148 was inspired by Ps 103:20 – 22[66] but emphasises all of Israel,[67] or that Ps 148:6b is a compressed interpretation of Ps 104:6b – 9 with a border set for waters.[68] Ps 103 shares יהוה/"YHWH", כֹּל/"all", שֵׁם/"name", עשׂה/ "do", בֵּן/"son" and יִשְׂרָאֵל/"Israel" (including the frequent לִבְנֵי יִשְׂרָאֵל/"for the sons of Israel"), לֹא/"not", עוֹלָם/"eternity", שָׁמַיִם/"heaven", אֶרֶץ/"earth", הוּא/ "he", רוּחַ/"wind", עבר/"pass", מַלְאָךְ/"angel" (מַלְאָכָיו/"his angels"), דָּבָר/"word" (with a participle of עשׂה/"do" followed by דְבָרוֹ/"his word" as in Ps 148:8 but also in Joel 2:11), and צָבָא/"host" (כָּל־צְבָאָיו/"all his hosts" as in the Qere of Ps 148:2; כֹּל/"all" followed by צָבָא/"host" with a masculine singular suffix is found only in these two verses). There is little syntactical similarity, and the calls to praise in Ps 103:20 – 22 use the imperative בָּרֲכוּ/"bless!" instead of הַלְלוּ/"praise!". Thus, a reference is unlikely. Ps 104 shares יהוה/"YHWH", הוֹד/ "majesty", אוֹר/"light", שָׁמַיִם/"heaven", מַיִם/"water", כָּנָף/"wing", רוּחַ/"wind", עשׂה/"do", מַלְאָךְ/"angel", אֵשׁ/"fire", אֶרֶץ/"earth", עוֹלָם/"eternity", עַד/"ever", תְּהוֹם/"flood", הַר/"mountain", עמד/"stand", עבר/"pass", כֹּל/"all", חַיָּה/"wild animal", נתן/"give", פְּרִי/"fruit", בְּהֵמָה/"cattle", עֵץ/"tree", אֶרֶז/"cedar", צִפּוֹר/"bird", יָרֵחַ/"moon", שֶׁמֶשׁ/"sun", רֶמֶשׂ/"creeping animal", ברא/"create", and הלל/ "praise" (including הַלְלוּ־יָהּ/"Praise-Yah!"). However, even though much creation vocabulary is shared, due to the lack of syntactical similarity a reference is unlikely.

Similarities with *Psalm 146* are stressed as Ps 146 is a part of the group Ps 146 – 150,[69] leading to a postexilic date and the reading of "horn" in Ps 148:14 as having military significance.[70] However, Ps 148 and Ps 146 only share the frequent words הלל/"praise", יהוה/"YHWH", בֵּן/"son", רוּחַ/"wind", עשׂה/"do", שָׁמַיִם/ "heaven", אֶרֶץ/"earth", כֹּל/"all", עוֹלָם/"eternity", and נתן/"give". Thus, apart from the shared frame הַלְלוּ־יָהּ/"Praise-Yah!", a reference is unlikely.

Similarities with *Psalm 147* are stressed as Ps 147 is a part of the group Ps 146 – 150,[71] with the consequence of interpreting Ps 148:14 as possibly referring to the exile,[72] or on the contrary the consequence of seeing parts of Ps 148:14 as a later addition since this verse is most similar to Ps 147, while other similar-

65 Cf. Ruppert 1986, 283, 294 – 295; Prinsloo 1992, 56; Leuenberger 2004, 353; Zenger 2008i, 842, 847, 850.

66 Cf. Duhm 1922, 482; Ruppert 1986, 294 – 295.

67 Cf. Ruppert 1986, 294.

68 Cf. Vosberg 1975, 111.

69 Cf. Leuenberger 2004, 351.

70 Cf. Schmutzer and Gauthier 2009, 162.

71 Cf. Leuenberger 2004, 349 – 351; Zenger 2008i, 836, 845, 849, 852.

72 Cf. Hupfeld 1871, 451; Zenger 2008i, 840.

ities can be explained through the theme of creation within a hymn.[73] Ps 147 and Ps 148 only share the frequent words תְּהִלָּה/"praise", יהוה/"YHWH", יִשְׂרָאֵל/"Israel", כּוֹכָב/"star", כֹּל/"all", שֵׁם/"name", אֶרֶץ/"earth", שָׁמַיִם/"heaven", הַר/"mountain", נתן/"give", בְּהֵמָה/"cattle", בֵּן/"son", לֹא/"not", הלל/"praise", דָּבָר/"word", שֶׁלֶג/"snow", עמד/"stand", רוּחַ/"wind", מַיִם/"water", and עשׂה/"do" without syntactical similarity. Thus, apart from the shared frame הַלְלוּ־יָהּ/"Praise-Yah!", a reference is unlikely.[74]

Ps 148:14 is often seen to refer to *Psalm 149* so strongly that v.14 is argued to have been written by the redaction authoring Ps 149.[75] However, as shown on p. 95–96 on Ps 148, references between Ps 148 and Ps 149 are unlikely.

As shown on p. 39–40 on Ps 148, references to Ps 148 from *Psalm 150* are unlikely.

The argument that Ps 148 contains references to *Isaiah* (Isa 12:4),[76] specifically Second Isaiah (42:11, 44:23, 49:13, 55:12),[77] leads to eschatological interpretations of Ps 148,[78] whereas the opposite argument of a lack of references leads to the rejection of an eschatological interpretation.[79] Isa 12:4 and Ps 148 share the phrase כִּי נִשְׂגָּב שְׁמוֹ/"for exalted is his name" (Ps 148:13) as well as the individual frequent words הוּא/"he", יהוה/"YHWH", שֵׁם/"name", and עַם/"people". There is no further syntactical similarity in the context of Isa 12, and a reference is unlikely. Isa 42:11 only shares the single frequent word הַר/"mountain" with Ps 148. Isa 44:23 shares the frequent words שָׁמַיִם/"heaven", עשׂה/"do", יהוה/"YHWH", אֶרֶץ/"earth", הַר/"mountain", כֹּל/"all", עֵץ/"tree", and יִשְׂרָאֵל/"Israel", Isa 49:13 שָׁמַיִם/"heaven", אֶרֶץ/"earth", הַר/"mountain", יהוה/"YHWH", and עַם/"people", Isa 55:12 הַר/"mountain", גִּבְעָה/"hill", and עֵץ/"tree" without syntactical similarity. Thus, while there is thematical similarity (such as nature rejoicing),[80] an intertextual reference from Ps 148 to Isa is unlikely.

The entire verse Ps 148:14 וַיָּרֶם קֶרֶן לְעַמּוֹ תְּהִלָּה לְכָל־חֲסִידָיו לִבְנֵי יִשְׂרָאֵל עַם־קְרֹבוֹ הַלְלוּ־יָהּ/"And he has lifted up a horn for his people, praise for all his faithful ones, for the sons of Israel, the people near to him. Praise-Yah!" also appears

---

73 Cf. Leuenberger 2004, 350–351, 362–363.

74 Cf. Brodersen 2013, 67, 74.

75 Cf. Leuenberger 2004, 352–353; Zenger 2008i, 840, 845, 852.

76 Cf. Zenger 2008i, 842, 845, 850 (First and Second Isaiah, esp. Isa 12:4; 44:23; 49:13).

77 Cf. Ruppert 1986, 284–285 (Second Isaiah, esp. Isa 42:11; 43[44]:23; 44:23; 49:13; 55:12).

78 Cf. Ballhorn 2004b, 316 (Second Isaiah).

79 Cf. Hupfeld 1871, 451.

80 Thematical similarity can also be found e.g. in Ps 19, cf. Gerstenberger 2001, 448 (nature praising); Zenger 2008i, 848 (heavens and order).

in the Hebrew *Ben Sira 51:12o*.[81] It is sometimes argued that Sir 51:12o quotes Ps 148:14,[82] with consequences for the date of the Psalter[83] and the connection of Ps 148:14 with Ps 149.[84] Since Sir is seen to refer to Ps 148 rather than vice versa, there is no intertextual reference from Ps 148 (or Ps 148[LXX], as the verse does not appear in Greek Sir at all), and Sir is relevant for the date but not the content of Ps 148.[85]

Results

References to Gen 1–2; Deu; Isa; Ps 2; 33; 96; 98; 103; and 104 are unlikely. Ps 146; 147; 149; and 150 show no references except the framing Hallelujahs. There is a reverse reference from Sir 51:12o (sic) to Ps 148:14.

IV.1.4 Content of Psalm 148[MT]

Who is called to praise in Psalm 148:1–4[MT]?

שָׁמַיִם/"heaven" only appears in a plural of extension[86] and usually refers to heaven in contrast to the earth.[87] מָרוֹם/"height" can refer to a height on earth or to heaven's height,[88] and in v.1 is most probably a synonymous parallel to heaven,[89] with its plural form signifying extension.[90]

V.4 calls to praise שְׁמֵי הַשָּׁמָיִם/"the heaven of the heaven", and הַמַּיִם אֲשֶׁר מֵעַל הַשָּׁמָיִם/"the water which (is) above the heaven".[91] Both subjects are invisible

---

81 Cf. Abegg and Parker [no year]d. Sir is usually dated to the 2nd century BCE, cf. Marböck 2016, 412–414. Sir 51:12a-o does not appear in Greek or Syriac, only in the Genizah manuscript, and the passage may not be authentic, cf. Di Lella 1966, 101–105 (not by Ben Sira, but still 2nd century BCE).

82 Cf. Ballhorn 2004b, 321 fn. 847; Zenger 2008b, 366; Zenger and Hossfeld 2016, 450.

83 Cf. Zenger 2008b, 366; Jain 2014, 238–239; Zenger and Hossfeld 2016, 450. However, against Zenger a redactional origin of Ps 148:14 is unlikely, see IV.1.7.

84 Cf. MacKenzie 1970, 223.

85 See IV.1.6. Sir 43 is also seen as an imitation of Ps 148, cf. Allen 2002, 393. Further research on the relation of Sir and Ps is desirable.

86 For the plural (not dual) of שָׁמַיִם/"heaven" and מַיִם/"water" cf. Gesenius and Kautzsch 1909, §88d, for the plural of extension §124ab.

87 Cf. Bartelmus 1995, 204–205 (plurale tantum), 210–214 (mostly tripartite world: heaven – earth – underworld), 230 (on LXX: later concept of multiple heavens).

88 Cf. Gesenius 2013, s.v. מָרוֹם.

89 Cf. Bartelmus 1995, 208–209; Gerstenberger 2001, 448.

90 Cf. Gesenius and Kautzsch 1909, §124b.

91 See fn. 86.

heavenly regions, and again may be personified in order to praise.[92] Ps 148 may imagine the heaven to consist of multiple, layered parts or "heavens",[93] possibly three: the visible heaven with the heavenly bodies mentioned in v.3, the waters above it, the highest heaven[94] above it (though this could also be a summary of vv.2–3 instead of an extra layer). The water above the heaven could also be above the highest heaven.[95] Ps 148 shows no clear number or order of possible "heaven(s)" except that "water" is above.[96] The translation of "heaven" and "water" with a singular form is chosen here due to the usual plural of extension,[97] and the parallel of "heaven" in v.1 and the singular "earth" in v.7.

In v.1, combined with the call to praise YHWH, this place "heaven" could be where the ones praising YHWH are, or where YHWH is. Given the parallel in v.7 מִן־הָאָרֶץ/"from the earth", and the subjects of vv.1–4 and 7–12, it is likely that the place is that of the ones praising YHWH.[98] This is also supported by מִן/"from" which may indicate the place of origin of a sound.[99]

מַלְאָךְ/"messenger" can refer to human or divine messengers, and in the celestial context in v.2 is refers to divine messengers, namely heavenly beings which could be called "angels".[100] צָבָא/"host" can refer to a human army, stars, or heavenly angels, and here in the context of angels refers to a host of heavenly beings.[101] These subjects are seen by commentators to represent lesser deities submitting themselves under YHWH,[102] or articulate heavenly beings, YHWH's servants, praising him in his celestial court.[103] Since Ps 148 shows no sign of other deities, heavenly beings seems to be more likely here. Some commentators see the heavenly host and the angels as a one group only in a synonymous par-

---

92 Cf. Allen 2002, 393 (but may also praise by fulfilling their role in YHWH's cosmic order).
93 Cf. Hupfeld 1871, 453 (similar to 2 Cor 12:2; Gen 1); Duhm 1922, 481 (similar to 2 Cor 12:2; Gen 1); Gunkel 1926, 618 (three or seven heavens; Gen 1 for water;); Gerstenberger 2001, 448 (similar to later Jewish, Hellenistic, and Gnostic writings); Zenger 2008i, 847–848 (similar to Neh 9:6; Gen 1; YHWH above or outside all heavens, and heavens full of servants of YHWH).
94 שְׁמֵי הַשָּׁמַיִם/"the heavens of heavens" is probably a superlative, cf. Gesenius and Kautzsch 1909, §133i. Hupfeld 1871, 453 (see fn. 93), nevertheless states it may consist of multiple heavens.
95 Cf. Watson 2005, 209.
96 On water above the heaven cf. Bartelmus 1995, 212–214.
97 See fn. 86.
98 Cf. Allen 2002, 393; Zenger 2008i, 847. Against Vosberg 1975, 111.
99 Cf. Allen 2002, 389.
100 Cf. Hupfeld 1871, 452 (angels); Freedman and Willoughby 1984, 888–889, 901–903.
101 Cf. Ringgren 1989, 872–874. In Deut 4:19 the "host" is "sun", "moon", and "stars", but they are separate in Ps 148.
102 Cf. Gerstenberger 2001, 448; Cho 2007, 282, 289.
103 Cf. Prinsloo 1992, 57, 61 (synonymous parallelism in v.2) (see fn. 104); Allen 2002, 393; Zenger 2008i, 846.

allelism,[104] others see them as two separate groups of heavenly beings.[105] Since all other subjects stand in synthetic parallelisms, it seems likely that this is the case here.

V.3 calls to praise שֶׁמֶשׁ/"sun", יָרֵחַ/"moon", and כָּל־כּוֹכְבֵי אוֹר/"all stars of light". They are visible heavenly bodies,[106] and may stand for all of the visible heaven.[107] According to v.6, they explicitly are YHWH's creation, and thus while they may be personified, they are not deified.[108]

In vv.1–4, the list of heavenly beings seems to follow the order of a general designation of heavenly spheres in v.1 with (1) animate articulate invisible heavenly beings in v.2, (2) inanimate inarticulate visible heavenly bodies in v.3, and (3) inanimate inarticulate invisible heavenly spheres in v.4.[109]

The Ketib[110] צבאו/"his host" which could be vocalised as צְבָאוֹ/"his host" is a singular form, but in its Qere reading it is a plural צְבָאָיו/"his hosts". The usual plural of צָבָא/"host" is צְבָאוֹת/"hosts",[111] thus a plural form with a third person singular masculine suffix would be צְבָאֹתָיו/"his hosts". The Qere plural is thus seen as an unlikely reading by some commentators,[112] while other commentators support the plural reading as it also appears in Ps 103:21 and many manuscripts and versions.[113] The difference in meaning is marginal, and here the Ketib singular reading of Codex L is given preference.

What are the reasons for praise in Psalm 148:5–6[MT]?

Vv.5–6 summarise the call to praise[114] for the subjects mentioned in vv.1–4 and gives reasons for their praise, namely their creation by YHWH (emphasised as the subject through the pronoun הוּא/"he") and their indestructible order given

---

104 Cf. Prinsloo 1992, 57, 61.
105 Cf. Gerstenberger 2001, 448; Zenger 2008i, 847.
106 Cf. Zenger 2008i, 847–848.
107 Against Gerstenberger 2001, 448, the triad cannot signify "the totality of heaven" as other heavenly spheres are mentioned in Ps 148.
108 Cf. Prinsloo 1992, 57 (personified as YHWH's servants, not deified); Zenger 2008i, 847–848 (no living beings, in YHWH's service, not deified).
109 Similarly Allen 2002, 393; Zenger 2008i, 846–848. Against Gerstenberger 2001, 448.
110 On Ketib and Qere cf. Fischer 2009, 29–30; Tov 2012, 54–59.
111 Cf. Gesenius 2013, s.v. צָבָא.
112 Cf. Duhm 1922, 480; Gunkel 1926, 618.
113 Cf. Allen 2002, 389; Brucker 2011c, 1881.
114 The object in v.5a as in v.13a is אֶת־שֵׁם יְהוָה/"the name of YHWH" rather than יהוה/"YHWH" as in v.1a and v.7a, but they are used synonymously, even though in v.13b YHWH's name is also used like an attribute, parallel to YHWH's majesty.

by YHWH.[115] Some commentators stress that just the order, not the creation is thought as permanent[116] so as not to exclude a new eschatological creation, but there is no indication of this thought within Ps 148 (especially v.5b, which stresses the idea of eternity[117]), pointing towards its non-eschatological interpretation.[118]

While עבר/"pass" may mean "to transgress",[119] and חק/"decree" may mean "boundary",[120] leading to emendations with a plural or passive form of עבר/ "transgress",[121] the first two meanings are most likely in Psalm 148: "decree" is the subject of "will not pass" (in the sense of "pass away" as in Esth 1:19; 9:27), and thus the entire heavenly order mentioned in vv.1–4 and summarised in vv.5–6 is in view.[122]

Who is called to praise in Psalm 148:7–12^MT?

The call to praise YHWH from the earth starts with calling sea monsters and floods to praise. This already indicates that by "earth" the Psalm does not mean "dry land" but the entire earth in contrast to heaven, and thus shows a bipartite view of the cosmos.[123]

תַּנִּין/"sea monster" here refers to sea monsters within creation rather than as chaos powers,[124] just as תְּהוֹם/"flood" refers to sea waters but without a reference

---

115 Cf. Hupfeld 1871, 453–454; Gerstenberger 2001, 448–449; Zenger 2008i, 848.

116 Cf. Zenger 2008i, 848.

117 Hillers 1978, 325–326, translates עַד as "ordinance" to eliminate the redundancy, but this meaning relies on languages other than Hebrew, and the Hebrew phrase used in Ps 148:5 has a parallel in Ps 111:3–9, cf. Allen 2002, 389.

118 Cf. Duhm 1922, 481.

119 Cf. Gesenius 2013, s.v. עבר₁.

120 Cf. Gesenius 2013, s.v. חק.

121 Cf. Duhm 1922, 481 (plural). See fn. 122.

122 Cf. Hupfeld 1871, 454 (though with a connotation of border and transgressing); Hillers 1978, 326; Prinsloo 1992, 60; Allen 2002, 389; Ballhorn 2004b, 318 (חק/"decree" alluding to the Torah due to Ps 147:19); Zenger 2008i, 839, 848 (חק/"decree" alluding to the Torah due to Psalms 146; 147; 149; possibly also צוה/"command" alluding to the Torah); Brucker 2011c, 1882. Watson 2005 mentions both all heavenly elements (211) and only the waters above the heavens (222) as the receiver of a "boundary", but the latter is unlikely as vv.5–6 summarise the subjects of vv.1–4. Vosberg 1975, 111, argues for a boundary due to a reference to Ps 104.

123 Cf. Tsumura 1988, 264–266, esp. 265.

124 Cf. Niehr 1995 (תַּנִּין/"sea monster" is sometimes but not always associated with pre-creation chaos), esp. 718; Brüning 1998, 225; Watson 2005, 210.

to chaos. Whether this is in constrast to chaos motifs[125] or independent of them cannot be decided, but either way the order of the current creation is stressed.

While v.7b calls to praise waters on the earth, v.8 mentions weather phenomena coming from above the earth.[126]

אֵשׁ/"fire" here in the context of בָּרָד/"hail" and שֶׁלֶג/"snow" and רוּחַ סְעָרָה/ "wind of storm" is used figuratively for lightning.[127] קִיטוֹר/"fog" is a rare word referring to "smoke" in its two other occurrences in Gen 19:28 and Ps 119:83.[128] In Ps 148:8a, it may be translated as "fog" given the weather phenomena mentioned in the verse,[129] just as "fire" is used figuratively for lightning. Alternatively, both "fire" and "smoke" could be used literally, and chiastically frame cold phenomena with hot phenomena not of weather, but general life on earth,[130] but in Ps 148 weather phenomena are most likely. The next weather phenomenon, רוּחַ סְעָרָה/"wind of storm", is classified as "doing his word".[131]

הַר/"mountain" and גִּבְעָה/"hill" can be seen as a merismic word pair[132] for steep and flat and thus all risings of the ground. The same applies to עֵץ פְּרִי/ "tree of fruit" and אֶרֶז/"cedar" for all trees or even all plants, חַיָּה/"wild animal" and בְּהֵמָה/"cattle" ("domestic animal") as well as רֶמֶשׂ/"creeping animal" and צִפּוֹר כָּנָף/"bird of wing" for all animals on and above the earth.[133]

Equally, מַלְכֵי־אֶרֶץ/"kings of earth" and לְאֹם/"nation" as well as שַׂר/"ruler" and שֹׁפְטֵי אֶרֶץ/"judges of earth" could represent peoples and rulers outside Israel. בָּחוּר/"young man" and בְּתוּלָה/"young woman", זָקֵן/"old" and נַעַר/"young" could refer to all humans of all genders and ages without and within Israel. V.12 shows no restriction to worshippers in Jerusalem,[134] but rather underlines the lack of restrictions in the calls to praise.[135] A specific period in time is also not indicated.[136]

---

125 Cf. Zenger 2008i, 849.
126 Cf. Zenger 2008i, 849.
127 Cf. Hupfeld 1871, 455; Bergman, Krecher, and Hamp 1973, esp. 459; Allen 2002, 389, 394.
128 Due to the LXX translation κρύσταλλος/"ice-crystal" (see p. 166), a similar Hebrew word such as קֶרַח/"ice" is sometimes assumed, cf. Duhm 1922, 481, but there is no text-critical evidence for this emendation, cf. Allen 2002, 389.
129 Cf. Gunkel 1926, 619 (based on Aramaic); Allen 2002, 389.
130 Cf. Hupfeld 1871, 455. For smoke, there is no indication of a theophany, thus Hillers 1978, 326, or a volcano, thus Clements 1993, 12.
131 For a similar idea in Ps 147 see p. 195–196.
132 See p. 137.
133 Cf. Zenger 2008i, 849–850.
134 Against Allen 2002, 394.
135 Cf. Ruppert 1986, 282 (leaving out v.14bc).
136 Cf. Gerstenberger 2001, 450 (stereotypical language, no exilic-postexilic functionaries).

Vv.7b – 12 contain at least two subjects per half-verse except in v.8b where "wind of storm doing his word" stands alone, stressing the wind as God's servant.

In vv.7b – 12, all the subjects in one colon are either singular (vv.8ab, 10ab) or plural (vv.7b, 9a, 11ab, 12ab) with the exception of v.9b. Articles occur at the beginning of v.9a and v.10a only, stressing the changes to geographical features and plants (v.9), and to animals and humans (vv.10 – 12).

The order of subjects in vv.7 – 12 is seen by commentators to be mythical chaotic powers – superhuman forces of nature – humans,[137] sea – atmosphere – land,[138] or water below and above the earth – plants and animals on the earth – humans on the earth.[139] Non-human nature is further refined as metereological phenomena (v.8), geographical phenomena (v.9a), trees (v.9b), animals (v.10).[140] In v.7, sea monsters and floods are probably chaotic powers rather than sea creatures. Thus, the order sea (v.7b) – atmosphere (v.8) – land with trees and animals (vv.9 – 10) – humans (vv.11 – 12) is likely. The order of vv.11 – 12 can be further refined as foreign politics (v.11a) – domestic politics (v.11b) – genders (v.12a) – ages (v.12b).[141] This seems to be a descending order of hierarchy, and humans, while mentioned last, are unlikely to be seen as the climax of creation,[142] possibly stressing the humility of humankind in the praise of God.

What are the reasons for praise in Ps 148:13 – 14^MT?

The summarising v.13 calls to praise all subjects mentioned in vv.7 – 12, for two reasons: the exaltation of YHWH over both earth and heaven (v.13),[143] and the exaltation of Israel through YHWH (v.14).[144]

The metaphor "lift up the horn of" usually refers to God's intervention to empower either those faithful to him or their enemies,[145] and in Psalm 148 God's people are in view. However, it is debated whether v.14a refers to Israel's

---

137 Cf. Gerstenberger 2001, 449.

138 Cf. Allen 2002, 394.

139 Cf. Zenger 2008i, 846.

140 Cf. Gerstenberger 2001, 449; Zenger 2008i, 849 – 850.

141 Cf. Zenger 2008i, 850.

142 Cf. Gerstenberger 2001, 449. Against Allen 2002, 394.

143 Cf. Zenger 2008i, 850.

144 Cf. Ballhorn 2004b, 322 (all of Israel).

145 Cf. e.g. Ps 89:18 (God's people), 25 (king); 1 Sam 2:1 (Hannah), 10 (anointed). Ballhorn 2004b, 318 – 319 focusses on messianic aspects only (Ps 89:25; 2 Sam 2:10), while concluding that the meaning is more general. For an overview of horn metaphors in HB and ANE cf. Zenger 2008i, 851 – 852; for raising a horn Schmutzer and Gauthier 2009, 163 – 172; Riede 2010, 210 – 213.

general empowerment,[146] postexilic restoration,[147] eschatological constitution,[148] or special status as God's people[149].

Even if a nominal sentence in v.14b is unlikely,[150] it is debated whether תְּהִלָּה/"praise" in v.14b is another object of וַיָּרֶם/"and he has lifted up" in v.14a (thus meaning "and he has lifted up a horn ..., (and also) praise"),[151] or an apposition to the first object קֶרֶן/"horn" in v.14a (thus meaning "and he has lifted up a horn ..., (namely) praise"),[152] or whether this cannot be decided.[153] תְּהִלָּה/"praise" can also mean "glory",[154] and this possibility is entertained both for the object (with the result of Israel having glory from YHWH)[155] and the apposition (with the result of both praise and glory being from YHWH rather than humans,[156] or the result of the lifted horn being the power to praise including praise on behalf of all creation[157]). Given the syntax of v.14,[158] תְּהִלָּה/"praise" in v.14b is an object, and like קֶרֶן/"horn" in v.14a refers to YHWH's general empowerment of Israel, and vv.13–14 (like the parallel vv.5–6) introduce reasons for praise.[159]

IV.1.5 Genre of Psalm 148^MT

Ps 148 fits the main criteria for the genre "hymn" with its imperatives calling to praise and כִּי/"for" in vv.5b and 13b giving reasons for praise, and is thus seen as

---

146 Cf. Hupfeld 1871, 451, 456; Gunkel 1926, 618.
147 Cf. Allen 2002, 394–395 (Ps 147); Zenger 2008i, 851–852 (redactional character of Ps 148:14, context of Psalms 146–147); Schmutzer and Gauthier 2009, esp. 162, 182–183 (context of postexilic Psalms 146–150).
148 Cf. Ballhorn 2004b, 316, 319–321 (neither heavenly beings nor foreign nations actually praise God with words, and the Psalm shows universalism), 322 (all of Israel rather than a particular group).
149 Cf. Zenger 2008i, 851–852 (Israel's special mention within Ps 148).
150 See p. 133. Against Zenger 2008i, 840, 851–852 (power as reason for praise).
151 Cf. Prinsloo 1992, 61–62.
152 Cf. Schmutzer and Gauthier 2009, 172–177, esp. 172–173.
153 Cf. Ballhorn 2004b, 318–321.
154 Cf. Gesenius 2013, s.v. תְּהִלָּה.
155 Cf. Zenger 2008i, 839 (but rejected since תְּהִלָּה means "praise" in the Final Hallel).
156 Cf. Ballhorn 2004b, 321, esp. fn. 846.
157 Cf. Zenger 2008i, 839–840 (but rejected since v.13 suggests vv.13–14 as containing reasons for rather than methods of praise).
158 See p. 133.
159 See p. 134–135.

a hymn by many commentators,[160] even though some note that the reasons for praise are less prominent than the calls to praise.[161]

Based on the list of subjects called to praise, some commentators argue for a familiarity of the author of Psalm 148 with a genre of lists,[162] more specifically, an ANE wisdom genre of lists, sometimes called Onomastica, and represented for example by the 11th century Egyptian Onomasticon of Anemope, and within HB in Job 38, Sir 43, Psalm 148, and in LXX in the "Song of the Three" in Dan 3:52–90^LXX.[163] Others see a direct influence as unlikely due to a lack of similarities.[164] Some see an influence of ANE hymns calling lists of beings to praise.[165] This is also seen with reservations due to a lack of similarities.[166] Some commentators argue for both the genres of lists and hymns as sources of inspiration for Psalm 148.[167] While both lists and hymns may form a background, neither can be ascertained.

Ps 148 is usually seen as having a cultic setting,[168] rarely a literary one.[169] There are no indications in the Psalm itself.

IV.1.6 Date of Psalm 148^MT

Psalm 148 is usually seen as postexilic due to its form of an extended call to praise,[170] language,[171] content,[172] redactional origin,[173] or juxtaposition with

---

160 Cf. Gunkel 1926, 617–618; Prinsloo 1992, 53–55; Gerstenberger 2001, 451; Allen 2002, 390; Ballhorn 2004b, 315; Zenger 2008i, 841.

161 Cf. Ruppert 1986, 281, 289–292; Ballhorn 2004b, 314–315; Allen 2002, 390.

162 Cf. Rad 1960 (English translation: Rad 1984); Gerstenberger 2001, 451; Allen 2002, 392; Zenger 2008i, 842–843.

163 Cf. Rad 1960, esp. 295, (English translation: Rad 1984, esp. 285–286) (plus Onomasticon of Amenope); Gerstenberger 2001, 449–450 (plus other HB examples). See p. 164–165 on Dan 3:52–90^LXX.

164 Cf. Hillers 1978, 329–331; Ruppert 1986, 292–293; Prinsloo 1992, 53–55, 61; Mathys 2000, 340. Krüger 2001, esp. 82, 87 sees Ps 148 as an expansion of an ANE "heaven and earth" formula.

165 Cf. Zenger 2008i, 843–844 (e. g. Egyptian hymn to Amun-Re 2nd millennium BCE); Hillers 1978, 331–334 (examples from 13th century BCE onwards).

166 Cf. Ruppert 1986, 282–292.

167 Cf. Gerstenberger 2001, 451; Allen 2002, 392; Zenger 2008i, 842–844.

168 Cf. Duhm 1922, 482; Gunkel 1926, 617–618; Vosberg 1975, 58; Prinsloo 1992, 54–55 (but literary use also possible); Gerstenberger 2001, 451–452; Allen 2002, 393; Zenger 2008i, 841–845 (v.14 literary addition).

169 Cf. Leuenberger 2004, 350–351, 353.

170 Cf. Leuenberger 2004, 350–351, 353; Watson 2005, 208–209.

Ps 147[174] or all of Psalms 146–150.[175] The Psalm is not specific enough to point to a date,[176] but must have been written before its translation into Greek and thus before the 2nd century BCE,[177] which may also align with its quote in Sir 51:12o.[178]

IV.1.7 Unity of Psalm 148[MT]

Ps 148[MT] is one unit.[179] Although only in the Septuagint and Peshitta the final Hallelujah is missing, the *framing Hallelujahs* are seen by some commentators as secondary additions to Psalm 148,[180] while others stress their integral connection with the Psalm which only uses הלל/"praise" for expressing praise.[181]

Despite a lack of any text-critical evidence, the entire *v.14* or parts of it are sometimes excluded from the unit of Psalm 148 and seen as a secondary addition or original superscription of Psalm 149,[182] while other commentators stress the unity of Psalm 148 including v.14.[183]

---

171 Cf. Hillers 1978, 328–329 (various examples, early 4th century BCE); Gerstenberger 2001, 448 (late use of plural "heights" as synonym for "heaven" in Job and Ps 148 only).
172 Cf. Vosberg 1975, 58, 112 (creation and history, but no chaos); Watson 2005, 208–209 (no chaos, personification of astral bodies), 213; Sollamo 2006 (creation accounts with combination of angels and natural phenomena).
173 Cf. Leuenberger 2004, 350–351, 353.
174 Cf. Allen 2002, 394–395 (both originally and redactionally postexilic).
175 Cf. Schmutzer and Gauthier 2009, 162.
176 Cf. Prinsloo 1992, 54–55.
177 See p. 16, esp. fn. 104.
178 See p. 141–142 on Sir 51:12o, esp. fn. 81.
179 Thus also Prinsloo 1992, 42, 60; against emendations e.g. Hillers 1978, 326–327.
180 Cf. Duhm 1922, 480; MacKenzie 1970, 222–223 (two stages: first one Hallelujah between each of Ps 146–150, then two); Hillers 1978, 324–325; Ruppert 1986, 275; Gerstenberger 2001, 447 (closing Hallelujah secondary).
181 Cf. Ballhorn 2004b, 315, 317 (eschatological connotation of הלל/"praise" in Final Hallel).
182 Cf. Duhm 1922, 482–483 (v.14ac should be following Ps 149:6); MacKenzie 1970, esp. 222–223 (v.14bc originally a superscription for Ps 149); Ruppert 1986, 277–278 (v.13c+14a as a final bicolon and v.14b+c as a secondary subscription); Spieckermann 1989, 57–58 (entire v.14, also v.13b and vv.4–6 secondary additions); Gerstenberger 2001, 447–451 (at least v.14bc, possibly entire v.14); Leuenberger 2004, 352, 356 (entire v.14 secondary addition, simultaneous with Ps 149); Zenger 2008i, 840–845 (entire v.14). See fn. 17.
183 Cf. Gunkel 1926, 617–618 (v.14bc subscription but original part of the Psalm); Hillers 1978, 328; Prinsloo 1992, 51–53; Allen 2002, 390–391; Ballhorn 2004b, 316, 318, 321 (quote of entire v.14 in Sir 51:12o as evidence for its unity); Schmutzer and Gauthier 2009, 172–177. See fn. 16.

IV.1.8 Overall Interpretation of Psalm 148^{MT}

Ps 148 calls to YHWH's praise all beings in heaven (because of their creation and ordering through YHWH) and on earth (because of YHWH's exaltation and Israel's exaltation through him). Psalm 148 eludes precise definitions,[184] and expresses a universal idea of praise without giving a specific time, but the final reason for praise is Israel-specific.

---

184 Against Allen 2002, 395 (just Israel insufficient for proper praise, thus nature included); Ballhorn 2004b, 316 (YHWH's kingship defining topic of Ps 148 though never explicitly mentioned, eschatological praise); Zenger 2008i, 842 (reasons: ordered creation and Israel's role in history), 853 (comprehensive praise of all creation will lead to the perfect aim of creation); Tucker 2014, 192, 194–195 (YHWH's kingship at centre of Ps 148, human power simply a part of his creation).

IV.2 Psalm 148^{DSS}

IV.2.1 Psalm 148 in 11QPs^a

11QPs^a Column II contains parts of Psalm 146 followed by parts of the first 12 of 14 verses of Psalm 148. Psalm 148 is separated from Ps 146 by a new line with a large space in the previous line. The parchment is broken off at the left side and the bottom, the last two verses of Psalm 148 (including the Israel-specific v.14) are not preserved. Psalm 148 may conjecturally have been followed by Ps 120;[185] Column III starts with Psalm 121.[186]

In Ps 148 in 11QPs^a, the opening Hallelujah is missing,[187] the final Hallelujah is not preserved.

In v.1a, the accusative marker אֶת־ is missing, and instead of מִן־הַשָּׁמַיִם/"from the heaven" משמים/"from heaven" is found (meaning that the article of הַשָּׁמַיִם/ "the heaven" is missing).[188] Thus, v.1a differs from v.7a where אֶת־ is not missing ("earth" and its possible article are not preserved).[189]

In v.2b, צבא/"host" is broken off after the aleph, thus it cannot be seen whether the Qere or Ketib reading of MT is found here.[190]

In v.4b, לשמים/"with respect to (the) heaven"[191] is found instead of הַשָּׁמַיִם/ "the heaven".[192]

---

185 Cf. Sanders 1965, 23.

186 Cf. Sanders 1965, 23–24, Plate IV.

187 On the debate whether this is independent of MT see p. 15 fn. 94.

188 Cf. Gesenius and Kautzsch 1909, §102ab.

189 It is not possible to tell whether this reading is more original than MT. Dahood 1970, 352, concludes that v.7a^{MT/DSS} is more original than v.1a^{DSS} due to the number of syllables. The view of MT as the original is also adopted by Dahmen 2003, 129–130, who, however, also notes that the presence or omission of the accusative marker את may be insignificant given the variation within 11QPs^a itself in v.1 and v.7. On the contrary, Hillers 1978, 325, concludes that v.1a^{DSS} is more original than v.1a^{MT} as the former is more poetic and the latter more prosaic, though אֲשֶׁר/"which" in v.4b is also prosaic.

190 See p. 144.

191 Whether or not there is an article cannot be determined from the consonants only, cf. Gesenius and Kautzsch 1909, §35n.

192 Dahmen 2003, 130, explains ל as either a dittography with the final consonant of the preceding word, or an intentional stronger reference to Gen 1:7. However, Gen 1:7 uses רְקִיעַ/"firmament" rather than שָׁמַיִם/"heaven" with ל/"for", and a reference is unlikely, see p. 137–138 on Gen 1.

V.5a has an imperative plural הללו/"praise!" instead of the jussive יהללו/"let them praise". Since the beginning of v.13 is not preserved, it cannot be seen whether this happens twice in Ps 148^{DSS}.[193]

Other than these minor differences, there is some *orthographic* variation: In v.1a and 7a, YHWH is written in palaeo-Hebrew. In all preserved occurrences (vv.2ab, 3b, 9a, 10a, 11a), כָּל־/"all" is spelt plene as כול as within the entire scroll.[194] Other plene spellings as in the rest of the scroll[195] include in v.7b תהומות/"floods" for תְּהֹמוֹת, in v.8b עושה/"doing" for עֹשָׂה, and in v.11a לאומים/"peoples" for לְאֻמִים.

Regarding *intertextuality*, as shown in III.2.1 there is no reference to or from *Ps 149*. The order of Psalms in which Ps 148 does not preceed Ps 149 makes it less likely that there is a reference between the Qumran addition to Ps 149^{DSS} and Ps 148:14,[196] but Ps 148:14^{DSS} is not preserved and cannot be compared to Ps 149^{DSS}.

In *summary*, in 11QPs^a Psalm 148 follows Ps 146 and may have preceded Ps 120 (not preserved) and the preserved Ps 121. There is no opening Hallelujah, the end of Ps 148 is not preserved. There are small differences in wording and orthography.

---

193 Dahmen 2003, 130, maintains that there are imperatives only, secondary to MT.
194 Cf. Sanders 1965, 11.
195 Cf. Sanders 1965, 9.
196 Against MacKenzie 1970, 223–224.

IV.3 Psalm 148^{LXX}

IV.3.1 Translation of Psalm 148^{LXX}

1H	Hallelujah; of Haggai and Zechariah.	1H	Αλληλουια· Αγγαιου καὶ Ζαχαριου.
1a	Praise the Lord from the heavens,	1a	Αἰνεῖτε τὸν κύριον ἐκ τῶν οὐρανῶν,
1b	praise him in the *highest ones!*	1b	αἰνεῖτε αὐτὸν ἐν τοῖς ὑψίστοις.
2a	Praise him, all his angels;	2a	αἰνεῖτε αὐτόν, πάντες οἱ ἄγγελοι αὐτοῦ·
2b	praise him, all his hosts.	2b	αἰνεῖτε αὐτόν, πᾶσαι αἱ δυνάμεις αὐτοῦ.
3a	Praise him, sun and moon;	3a	αἰνεῖτε αὐτόν, ἥλιος καὶ σελήνη·
3b	praise him, all *the* stars *and the* light.	3b	αἰνεῖτε αὐτόν, πάντα τὰ ἄστρα καὶ τὸ φῶς.
4a	Praise him, the heavens of the heavens	4a	αἰνεῖτε αὐτόν, οἱ οὐρανοὶ τῶν οὐρανῶν
4b	and the water above the heavens.	4b	καὶ τὸ ὕδωρ τὸ ὑπεράνω τῶν οὐρανῶν.
5a	Let them praise the name of the Lord,	5a	αἰνεσάτωσαν τὸ ὄνομα κυρίου,
5b	*for he himself spoke, and they were made,*	5b	ὅτι αὐτὸς εἶπεν, καὶ ἐγενήθησαν.
5c	he himself commanded, and they were created.	5c	αὐτὸς ἐνετείλατο, καὶ ἐκτίσθησαν.
6a	And he has established them for *the* eternity *and* for *the eternity of the eternity;*	6a	ἔστησεν αὐτὰ εἰς τὸν αἰῶνα καὶ εἰς τὸν αἰῶνα τοῦ αἰῶνος·
6b	an ordinance he *put* and it *will* not pass.	6b	πρόσταγμα ἔθετο, καὶ οὐ παρελεύσεται.
7a	Praise the Lord from the earth,	7a	αἰνεῖτε τὸν κύριον ἐκ τῆς γῆς,
7b	sea monsters and all deeps;	7b	δράκοντες καὶ πᾶσαι ἄβυσσοι·
8a	fire, hail, snow, *ice-crystal,*	8a	πῦρ, χάλαζα, χιών, κρύσταλλος,
8b	wind of storm, the ones doing his word;	8b	πνεῦμα καταιγίδος, τὰ ποιοῦντα τὸν λόγον αὐτοῦ·
9a	the mountains and all *the* hills,	9a	τὰ ὄρη καὶ πάντες οἱ βουνοί,
9b	*fruit-bearing* trees and all cedars;	9b	ξύλα καρποφόρα καὶ πᾶσαι κέδροι·
10a	the wild animals and all *the* domestic animals,	10a	τὰ θηρία καὶ πάντα τὰ κτήνη,
10b	creeping ones and *winged* birds;	10b	ἑρπετὰ καὶ πετεινὰ πτερωτά·
11a	kings of *the* earth and all peoples,	11a	βασιλεῖς τῆς γῆς καὶ πάντες λαοί,
11b	rulers and all judges of earth;	11b	ἄρχοντες καὶ πάντες κριταὶ γῆς·
12a	young men and young women,	12a	νεανίσκοι καὶ παρθένοι,
12b	old ones with *younger* ones.	12b	πρεσβῦται μετὰ νεωτέρων·
13a	Let them praise the name of the Lord,	13a	αἰνεσάτωσαν τὸ ὄνομα κυρίου,
13b	for *lifted up* is his name *alone;*	13b	ὅτι ὑψώθη τὸ ὄνομα αὐτοῦ μόνου·
13c	his majesty *is* above earth and heaven.	13c	ἡ ἐξομολόγησις αὐτοῦ ἐπὶ γῆς καὶ οὐρανοῦ.
14a	And he *will* lift up a horn *of* his people;	14a	καὶ ὑψώσει κέρας λαοῦ αὐτοῦ·
14b	a *chant is* for all his faithful ones,	14b	ὕμνος πᾶσι τοῖς ὁσίοις αὐτοῦ,
14c	for the sons of Israel, a people *coming near* to him.	14c	τοῖς υἱοῖς Ισραηλ, λαῷ ἐγγίζοντι αὐτῷ.
14H	–		

IV.3.2 Form of Psalm 148^{LXX}

Outline of Psalm 148^{LXX}

1H	**Hallelujah of Haggai and Zechariah**	
Part I		
1–4	Calls to Praise *2nd Person Imperatives (7)*	Subject: Heavenly Beings, Object: Lord
5–6	Summarising Call to *3rd Person Imperative (1)*	Subject: Heavenly Beings, Object: Lord
	+ **Reasons** for Praise *Aorists, **Future***	Subject: Lord, Object: Heavenly Beings
Part II		
7–12	Calls to Praise *2nd Person Imperative (1)*	Subject: Earthly Beings, Object: Lord
13–14	Summarising Call to *3rd Person Imperative (1)*	Subject: Earthly Beings, Object: Lord
	+ Reasons for Praise	Subject: Lord, Object: Earthly Beings (including Israel)
	*Aorist, **Future, Nominal Sentences***	
14H	–	

Syntax of Psalm 148^{LXX}

As in MT the Psalm is dominated by imperatives of αἰνέω/"praise". Hebrew jussives are translated with aorist imperatives (v.5a, 13a).[197] *Unlike in MT,* imperatives are not found in the frame. Thus, αἰνέω/"praise" appears only 10 times. Unlike in MT, another verb is used more than once: ὑψόω/"lift up" connects v.13a and v.14a.[198]

As in MT, v.5 contains the first forms of other verbs, though v.5b is an addition with *aorist* forms of λέγω/"speak" and γίνομαι/"become". V.5c (as v.5b in MT) contains *aorist* forms for Hebrew *perfect* forms followed by another *aorist* for a *waw-imperfect* in v.6a, and another *aorist* for a *perfect* form and a *future* form for a Hebrew *imperfect* (possibly representing a *perfect*) form in v.6b. The participle in v.13b is translated with an *aorist* passive 3rd person singular form. There is another *future* form for a *waw-imperfect* in v.14a. Thus, as in

---

197 See p. 116 fn. 243.
198 See p. 158.

MT, the use of *future* forms (though not only for *waw-imperfect* forms) connects
v.6 and v.14. This connection seems stronger than in MT since *all* other verb forms
are *aorist* forms, making the two *future* forms in v.6b and v.14a stand out.

Unlike in Hebrew, there is one *participle* (a present participle of ποιέω/"do"
in v.8b; the participle of שֹׁפֵט/"judge" in v.11b is translated with the noun κριτής/
"judge", and the participle of שֹׂגָב/"exalt" in v.13b with an aorist of ὑψόω/"lift
up") plus another present participle (not there in Hebrew) of ἐγγίζω/"be near"
for the adjective קָרֹב/"near" in v.14c.

As in Hebrew, some sentences have *no verb*, but unlike in Hebrew the relative nominal clause in v.4b is represented by a simple attributive in Greek,[199] and
v.13b is a verbal sentence, while also unlike in Hebrew v.13c must be a nominal
sentence since ἡ ἐξομολόγησις αὐτοῦ/"his majesty" is a nominative just as
ὕμνος/"chant" in v.14b.[200] Vv.14a and 14c are connected through λαός/"people",
v.14bc more strongly through dative forms in a triple apposition.

As in Hebrew, subjects are important, nominative nouns dominate Psalm
148[LXX], and heavenly and earthly beings are the subjects of vv.1–5a, 7a–13a.
In almost all other verses, namely vv.5b–6b and vv.13b–14a, the dominating
subject is YHWH, while unlike in Hebrew v.14bc has the subject ὕμνος/"chant".

As in MT, the subject αὐτός/"he himself" is stressed before the verb in v.5c
and the added v.5b, just as πρόσταγμα/"ordinance" in v.6b.[201] In verbless sentences, the usual Hebrew though unusual Greek order subject – predicate is followed with stressed subjects (unlike in Hebrew, v.13bc is a verbal sentence).

Pronouns (for Hebrew *suffixes)* referring to the κύριος/"Lord" for YHWH connect vv.1–4 (κύριος/"Lord" in v.1a, pronouns in vv.1b–4a) and also appear in
vv.8b, 13bc, 14abc as in Hebrew, and in addition to Hebrew as stressed subjects
in v.5bc. As in Hebrew, the only pronoun not referring to YHWH is αὐτά/"them"
in v.6a where YHWH is subject. Thus, as in Hebrew, despite the number of subjects in Ps 148, the pronouns stress YHWH's importance.

As in Hebrew, repetitions of the *prepositions* ἐκ/"from" for מִן/"from" in vv.1a,
7a, and εἰς/"in" twice for לְ/"for" in v.6a stand out, but v.14 uses one genitive and
two dative forms for the three occurrences of לְ/"for". As in Hebrew, only the last
two subjects in v.12b are connected with μετά/"with" for עִם/"with", marking the
end of the list (though unlike in MT without an additional stress in v.12a).

---

199 Cf. Smyth and Messing 1956, §1154, 1156, 1158.
200 See p. 116 fn. 245. Bons 2009b, 897, assumes the ellipsis of an optative or present in
Ps 148:13c[LXX].
201 See p. 117 fn. 249.

Structure of Psalm 148^{LXX}

As in MT, Psalm 148^{LXX} shows a twofold structure: Both v.1 and v.7 start with αἰνεῖτε τὸν κύριον ἐκ/"praise the Lord from", and both v.5 and v.13 start with αἰνε-
σάτωσαν τὸ ὄνομα κυρίου ὅτι/"let them praise the name of the Lord, for".
Vv.1b–4b and vv.7b–12b list subjects of the calls to praise, with vv.1b–4b repeating the call to praise whereas vv.7b–12b depend on v.7a.

Unlike in MT, tricola appear not only in v.13 and v.14 but also in v.5 through
the addition of v.5b. Unlike in MT *v.14bc forms a separate nominal sentence*. However, given that there is another nominal sentence in *v.13c* preceded by a verbal
sentence with ὑψόω/"lift up", and that v.6b and v.14a are connected through *future forms*, as in MT vv.13–14 are connected and primarily summarise vv.7–12
while also serving as a summary for the subjects called praise earlier in the
Psalm.[202]

The two sentences introduced by ὅτι/"for" are *two* lines in v.5bc (unlike in
MT due to the additional v.5b) and two in v.13bc (as in MT). In v. 6ab, this is followed by an aorist form introducing two lines, but in v.14a by καί/"and" and a
future form introducing one line, with the two lines of v.14bc forming a separate
nominal sentence. In both cases ὅτι/"for" introduces reasons for praise as in MT.
While as in MT the number of subjects called to praise is greater in Part I, unlike
in MT the number of reasons given is almost the same in Part I (four cola) and
Part II (five cola).[203] As in MT, four occurrences of κύριος/"Lord" in vv.1a, 5a, 7a,
and 13a underline the twofold structure.

Poetic Devices in Psalm 148^{LXX}

Parallelisms are as in MT[204] with the exception of v.5, which through the *addition*
is a tricolon of which the second and third colon form a *synonymous* parallel (as
in Ps 32:9^{LXX}, thus confirming a reference to Ps 32^{LXX}).[205]

Regarding *number symbolism*, unlike in Hebrew due to the translation of the
framing Hallelujahs, there are *ten* but not twelve forms of αἰνέω/"praise". As in
MT, there are ten occurrences of πᾶς/"all", but *eight* rather than seven subjects
are called to praise in the heavenly part due to the separate "light" in v.3b, and
twenty-three in the earthly part. Thus, *thirty-one* subjects are called to praise in
Psalm 148^{LXX}. Unlike in Hebrew, the numbers *twelve* and *thirty* do not even ap-

---

202 Against Zenger 2008i, 852–853, who sees v.13c as the summary of the entire Ps 148^{LXX}.
203 Hillers 1978, 325, without Hebrew text-critical evidence sees v.5b^{LXX} as original also in Hebrew, but this is unlikely, cf. Allen 2002, 391.
204 See p. 69 fn. 368.
205 See p. 160–161 on Ps 32^{LXX}(=33^{MT}).

pear in the Septuagint, *seven* does not appear as in MT, and additional intertextual references are unrelated to number symbolism. The importance of number symbolism for the interpretation of Ps 148^{LXX} is even less likely than in MT.

Unlike in MT, v.13b and v.14a are connected through the repetition of ὑψόω/ "lift up", a verb also related to the adjective ὕψιστος/"highest" in v.1b.[206]

Unlike in MT, the lasting order of creation is stressed in v.6a by the threefold repetition of αἰών/"eternity" in the phrase εἰς τὸν αἰῶνα καὶ εἰς τὸν αἰῶνα τοῦ αἰῶνος/"for the eternity and for the eternity of the eternity" for לְעַד לְעוֹלָם/"for ever for eternity".

As in MT, v.11 shows a chiastic structure with genitives of γῆ/"earth" at the beginning and end, but unlike in MT there is an article (τῆς γῆς/"of the earth") in v.11a and no article (γῆς/"of earth") in v.11b which weakens the chiasm.

As in MT, a larger chiastic structure is found in the first and last occurrences of the words heaven and earth in Ps 148: heavens (v.1a) – earth (v.7a) and earth – heaven (v.13c). Unlike in MT, a plural οἱ οὐρανοί/"the heavens" is used everywhere except in v.13c where a singular οὐρανός/"heaven" is found. However, as in MT, since the word heaven occurs five and the word earth four times throughout the Psalm, this does not have to be a sign that v.13c is the end of the Psalm's main parts.

As in MT, the repetition of ὄνομα/"name" connects v.13a and v.13b (with v.5a); the repetition of λαός/"people" v.14a and v.14c, but unlike in MT λαός/ "people" is also used in v.11a for לְאֹם/"nation".

IV.3.3 Intertextuality in Psalm 148^{LXX}

Importance
Texts similar to Ps 148^{LXX} have been merely listed so far.[207]

Analysis
A stronger intertextual connection to *Genesis 1^{LXX}* is sometimes seen due to the additional conjunction in v.3b (making light and stars two separate entities as in Gen 1:3 – 5, 16 – 18^{LXX}), the waters above the heavens in v.4b, and the additional reference to creation by speaking in v.5b.[208] However, the order of light and stars

---

206 Cf. Bons 2009b, 897. See p. 155.
207 See p. 70 fn. 371.
208 Cf. Giere 2009, 101.

is reversed, hardly any words are shared with Gen 1:6 – 8^LXX, and αὐτὸς εἶπεν καὶ ἐγενήθησαν/"he himself spoke and they were made" is shared with Ps 32:9^LXX rather than Gen 1^LXX. As in MT, Gen 1:1 – 2:4a^LXX shares ποιέω/"do" for ברא/"create" (but also for עשׂה/"do"), οὐρανός/"heaven" for שָׁמַיִם/"heaven", γῆ/"earth" for אֶרֶץ/"earth", ἄβυσσος/"deep" for תְּהוֹם/"flood", πνεῦμα/"wind" for רוּחַ/"wind", ὕδωρ/"water" for מַיִם/"water", φῶς/"light" for אוֹר/"light", ξύλον/"tree" for עֵץ/"tree", τίθημι/"put" for נתן/"give" (though also δίδωμι/"give"), πᾶς/"all" for כֹּל/"all", πτερωτός/"winged" for כָּנָף/"wing", and ἑρπετόν/"creeping animal" for רֶמֶשׂ/"creeping animal" (but also for שֶׁרֶץ/"swarming animal" and רמשׂ/"creep"), θηρίον/"wild animal" for חַיָּה/"wild animal", κτῆνος/"domestic animal" for בְּהֵמָה/"cattle" (though also τετράπους/"four-footed animal"). However, פְּרִי/"fruit" in combination with ξύλον/"tree" for עֵץ/"tree" is translated as κάρπιμος/"fruitful" (only in Gen 1:11 – 12^LXX) rather than καρποφόρος/"fruit-bearing" (only in Jer 2:21^LXX; Ps 106:34^LXX; 148:9^LXX), כּוֹכָב/"star" as ἀστήρ/"star" instead of ἄστρον /"star", תַּנִּין/"sea monster" as κῆτος/"sea monster" instead of δράκων/"sea dragon", and צָבָא/"host" as κόσμος/"world" instead of δύναμις/"might". In addition to MT, λέγω/"speak", γίνομαι/"become", and πετεινός/"bird" for עוֹף/"bird" (followed by πτερωτός/"winged" for כָּנָף/"wing" in both Gen 1:21^LXX and Ps 148:10^LXX) are shared. Unlike in MT, the syntactical similarity of עֵץ פְּרִי/"tree of fruit" does not exist, תַּנִּינִם/"sea monsters" is translated with a different word, and κρύσταλλος/"crystal" for the rare קִיטוֹר/"fog" is less rare. As in MT, ἄβυσσος/"deep" in Gen 1:2^LXX is singular rather than a plural. Overall, a reference is less likely than in MT. This conclusion also applies to Gen 2:4b – 25^LXX: The syntactical similarity of Gen 2:4b אֶרֶץ וְשָׁמַיִם/"earth and heaven" does not appear in Gen 2:4b^LXX τὸν οὐρανὸν καὶ τὴν γῆν/"the heaven and the earth". As in MT, shared with Gen 2:4b – 25^LXX are ποιέω/"do" for עשׂה/"do", κύριος/"Lord" for יהוה/"YHWH" (but also ὁ θεός/"the God"), οὐρανός/"heaven" for שָׁמַיִם/"heaven", γῆ/"earth" for אֶרֶץ/"earth", πᾶς/"all" for כֹּל/"all", οὐ/"not" for לא/"not", ξύλον/"tree" for עֵץ/"tree", ὄνομα/"name" for שֵׁם/"name", ἐντέλλομαι/"command" for צוה/"command", μόνος/"alone" for לְבַדּוֹ/"only", θηρίον/"wild animal" for חַיָּה/"wild animal", and κτῆνος/"domestic animal" for בְּהֵמָה/"cattle". Unlike in MT, οὗτος/"this" is used for הוּא/"he", and in addition to MT, γίνομαι/"become", τίθημι/"put", λέγω/"speak", and πετεινός/"bird" are shared. Overall, a reference is unlikely.

Deuteronomy 4:7^LXX only shares ἐγγίζω/"come near" for קָרֹב/"near" with Ps 148:14^LXX (and κύριος/"Lord" for יהוה/"YHWH" and πᾶς/"all" for כֹּל/"all" with the entire Psalm 148^LXX), the context of Deut 4:1 – 18 shares Ισραηλ/"Israel" for יִשְׂרָאֵל/"Israel", ποιέω/"do" for עשׂה/"do", κύριος/"Lord" for יהוה/"YHWH", γῆ/"earth" for אֶרֶץ/"earth", οὐ/"not" for לא/"not", ἐντέλλομαι/"command" for צוה/"command", λόγος/"word" for דָּבָר/"word" (though also ῥῆμα/"saying"), πᾶς/"all" for כֹּל/"all", λαός/"people" for עַם/"people" (though also ἔθνος/"nation"), ἐγγίζω/"come near" for קָרֵב/"near", υἱός/"son" for בֵּן/"son", πῦρ/"fire" for אֵשׁ/"fire", ὄρος/"mountain" for הַר/"mountain", οὐρανός/"heaven" for שָׁמַיִם /"heaven", κτῆνος/"domestic animal" for בְּהֵמָה/"cattle", πτερωτός/"winged" for כָּנָף/"wing", ἑρπετόν/"creeping animal" for רמשׂ/"creep", and ὕδωρ/"water" for מַיִם/"water". In addition to MT, λέγω/"speak" is shared, and ἵστημι/ "stand", but for עמד/"pass" translated as παρέρχομαι/"pass" in Ps 148:6[LXX], δικαίωμα/"decree" for חֹק/"decree" instead of πρόσταγμα/"ordinance", δίδωμι/ "give" for נתן/"give" instead of τίθημι/"put", and ὄρνεον/"bird" for צִפּוֹר/"bird" instead of πετεινός/"bird". Overall, a reference is less likely than in MT.

Psalm 2[LXX] and Ps 148[LXX] share λαός/"people" for לְאֹם/"people", γῆ/"earth" for אֶרֶץ/"earth", βασιλεύς/"king" for מֶלֶךְ/"king" (also βασιλεῖς τῆς γῆς/"kings of the earth" for מַלְכֵי־אֶרֶץ/"kings of earth"), κύριος/"Lord" for יהוה/"YHWH", οὐρανός/"heaven" for שָׁמַיִם/"heaven", ὄρος/"mountain" for הַר/"mountain", πρόσταγμα/"ordinance" for חֹק/"decree", υἱός/"son" for בֵּן/"son", and πᾶς/ "all" for כֹּל/"all". נתן/"give" is translated with δίδωμι/"give", שׁפט/"judge" with κρίνω /"judge". In addition to MT, ἄρχων/"ruler" and λέγω/"speak" are shared. As in MT, there is little syntactical similarity, wherefore a reference is unlikely.

Regarding Psalm 32[LXX](=33[MT]), it is often argued that Ps 148:5bc[LXX] quotes Psalm 32:9[LXX209] in the addition αὐτὸς εἶπεν καὶ ἐγενήθησαν/"he himself spoke and they were made", a word-by-word parallel with Ps 32:9[LXX] ὅτι αὐτὸς εἶπεν καὶ ἐγενήθησαν αὐτὸς ἐνετείλατο καὶ ἐκτίσθησαν/"for he himself spoke and they were made, he himself commanded and they were created". As in MT, Ps 148[LXX] also shares with Ps 32[LXX] κύριος/"Lord" for יהוה/"YHWH", λόγος/ "word" for דָּבָר/"word", πᾶς/"all" for כֹּל/"all", γῆ/"earth" for אֶרֶץ/"earth", οὐρανός/"heaven" for שָׁמַיִם/"heaven", πνεῦμα/"wind" for רוּחַ/"wind", δύναμις/ "might" for צָבָא/"host", ὕδωρ/"water" for מַיִם/"water", τίθημι/"put" for נתן/ "give", ἄβυσσος/"deep" for תְּהוֹם/"flood", αὐτός/"he" for הוּא/"he", ἐντέλλω/ "command" for צוה/"command" (αὐτὸς ἐνετείλατο/"he commanded"), λαός/ "people" for עַם/"people", αἰών/"eternity" for עוֹלָם/"eternity", υἱός/"son" for בֵּן /"son", βασιλεύς/"king" for מֶלֶךְ/"king", οὐ/"not" for לֹא/"not", and ὄνομα/ "name" for שֵׁם/"name". תְּהִלָּה/"praise" is translated as αἴνεσις/"praise" instead of ὕμνος/"chant", עשׂה/"do" as στερεόω/"make firm" instead of ποιέω/"do", עמד/"stand" as κτίζω/"create" (but also as μένω/"remain") instead of ἵστημι/ "establish".[210] κτίζω/"create" is shared but for עמד/"stand" rather than ברא/"cre-

---

209 Cf. Allen 2002, 389; Zenger 2008i, 853; Brucker 2011c, 1882.
210 These differences may point towards a limitation of the method for intertextual analysis used here: even if there is an intertextual reference, not necessarily all *individual* Hebrew

ate". In addition to MT, ἄρχων/"ruler" (in the additional καὶ ἀθετεῖ βουλὰς ἀρχόντων/"and he brings to nothing counsels of rulers" in Ps 32:10^LXX), μόνος/ "alone", δύναμις/"might", and γίνομαι/"become" are shared. Unlike in MT, the major syntactical similarity between Ps 148:5bc^LXX and Ps 32:9^LXX makes it likely that Ps 148^LXX refers to Ps 32^LXX or vice versa. Since Ps 148:5b^LXX is an addition as compared to Ps 148^MT whereas the same phrase in Ps 32:9^LXX also appears in Ps 33^MT, Ps 148^LXX probably refers to Ps 32^LXX. Additional support to Ps 148:5bc^LXX referring to Ps 32:9^LXX rather than the other way round comes from the additional synonymous parallel: Ps 148^LXX is dominated by synthetic parallels,[211] while Ps 32^LXX contains many synonymous parallels. Ps 32^LXX stresses God's majesty and sole responsibility for the creation and preservation of heaven, earth, and all humans.[212] The creation reference to Ps 32^LXX thus emphasizes this aspect within Ps 148^LXX. While unlike Ps 148^LXX Ps 32^LXX is addressed to God's chosen people (Ps 32:12^LXX), this Israel-specific aspect is not taken up in Ps 148^LXX. Rather, the *universal aspect of creation* is stressed.

Regarding *Psalms 95; 97^LXX(=96; 98^MT)*, Ps 95^LXX shares κύριος/"Lord" for יהוה/"YHWH", πᾶς/"all" for כל/"all", γῆ/"earth" for אֶרֶץ/"earth", ὄνομα/ "name" for שֵׁם/"name", λαός/"people" for עַם/"people" (though also ἔθνος/ "nation"), οὐρανός/"heaven" for שָׁמַיִם/"heaven", ποιέω/"do" for עשׂה/"do", ἐξομολόγησις/"majesty" for הוֹד/"majesty", and ξύλον/"tree" for עֵץ/"tree". הלל/ "praise" is translated as αἰνετός/"praiseworthy", שׁפט/"judge" as κρίνω/ "judge", הוּא/"he" is not translated. In addition to MT, only λέγω/"speak", and οὐ/"not" for בַּל/"not" instead of לא/"not" are shared. As in MT, there is no syntactical similarity, wherefore a reference is unlikely. Ps 97^LXX shares κύριος/ "Lord" for יהוה/"YHWH", ποιέω/"do" for עשׂה/"do", Ισραηλ/"Israel" for יִשְׂרָאֵל/ "Israel", πᾶς/"all" for כל/"all", γῆ/"earth" for אֶרֶץ/"earth", βασιλεύς/"king" for מֶלֶךְ/"king", ὄρος/"mountain" for הַר/"mountain", and λαός/"people" for עַם /"people". שׁפט/"judge" is translated as κρίνω/"judge". As in MT, there is no syntactical similarity, wherefore a reference is unlikely.

Regarding *Psalms 102; 103^LXX(=103; 104^MT)*, Ps 102^LXX shares κύριος/"Lord" for יהוה/"YHWH", πᾶς/"all" for כל/"all", ὄνομα/"name" for שֵׁם/"name", ποιέω/ "do" for עשׂה/"do", υἱός/"son" for בֵּן/"son", and Ισραηλ/"Israel" for יִשְׂרָאֵל/"Israel" (including τοῖς υἱοῖς Ισραηλ/"for the sons of Israel" for לִבְנֵי יִשְׂרָאֵל/"for the sons of Israel"), οὐ/"not" for לא/"not", αἰών/"eternity" for עוֹלָם/"eternity", οὐρανός/"heaven" for שָׁמַיִם/"heaven", γῆ/"earth" for אֶרֶץ/"earth", αὐτός/"he"

---

words in the surrounding text are translated with the same Greek words. However, where there is syntactical similarity, the same Greek equivalents are prominent.

211 See p. 157.
212 Cf. Bons 2005, 63; Bons 2011b, 1588.

for הוּא/"he", πνεῦμα/"wind" for רוּחַ/"wind", ἄγγελος/"angel" for מַלְאָךְ/"angel" (through πάντες οἱ ἄγγελοι αὐτοῦ/"all his angels" for מַלְאָכָיו/"his angels" even more similar than in MT to Ps 148:2^{LXX} – but also to Ps 96:7^{LXX}), λόγος/"word" for דָּבָר/"word" (with a participle of ποιέω/"do" for עשׂה/"do" followed by דְּבָרוֹ/"his word" as in Ps 148:8, unlike in MT only in these to verses and not in Joel 2:11^{LXX}), and δύναμις/"might" for צָבָא/"host" (πᾶσαι αἱ δυνάμεις αὐτοῦ/"all his hosts" as in Ps 148:2^{LXX}, only in these two verses). עבר/"pass" is translated as διέρχομαι/"pass through" instead of παρέρχομαι/"pass". However, as in MT the calls to praise in Ps 102:20 – 22^{LXX} use εὐλογεῖτε/"bless!" for בָּרְכוּ/"bless!" instead of αἰνεῖτε/"praise!" for הַלְלוּ/"praise!".[213] Ps 103^{LXX} shares κύριος/"Lord" for יהוה/"YHWH", ἐξομολόγησις/"majesty" for הוֹד/"majesty", φῶς/"light" for אוֹר/"light", οὐρανός/"heaven" for שָׁמַיִם/"heaven", ὕδωρ/"water" for מַיִם/"water", πνεῦμα/"wind" for רוּחַ/"wind" (though also ἄνεμος/"wind"), ποιέω/"do" for עשׂה/"do", ἄγγελος/"angel" for מַלְאָךְ/"angel", πῦρ/"fire" for אֵשׁ/"fire", γῆ/"earth" for אֶרֶץ/"earth", αἰών/"eternity" for עוֹלָם/"eternity" and עַד/"ever", ἄβυσσος/"deep" for תְּהוֹם/"flood", ὄρος/"mountain" for הַר/"mountain", ἵστημι/"stand" for עמד/"stand", παρέρχομαι/"pass" for עבר/"pass", πᾶς/"all" for כֹּל/"all", θηρίον/"wild animal" for חַיָּה/"wild animal" (but also ζῷον/"living thing"), κτῆνος/"domestic animal" for בְּהֵמָה/"cattle", ξύλον/"tree" for עֵץ/"tree", κέδρος/"cedar" for אֶרֶז/"cedar", σελήνη/"moon" for יָרֵחַ/"moon", ἥλιος/"sun" for שֶׁמֶשׁ/"sun", ἑρπετόν/"creeping animal" for רֶמֶשׂ/"creeping animal", and κτίζω/"create" for ברא/"create". In addition to MT, τίθημι/"put" is shared but for שׂים/"put" instead of נתן/"give", οὐ/"not" for בַּל/"not" instead of לֹא/"not", πετεινόν/"bird" for עוֹף/"bird" instead of צִפּוֹר/"bird"; צִפּוֹר/"bird" is translated with στρουθίον/"sparrow", δράκων/"dragon" is used for לִוְיָתָן/"Leviathan" instead of תַּנִּין/"sea monster". γίνομαι/"become" is also shared. כָּנָף/"wing" is translated as πτέρυξ/"wing" instead of πτερωτός/"winged", נתן/"give" as δίδωμι/"give" instead of τίθημι/"put", פְּרִי/"fruit" as καρπός/"fruit" instead of the rare καρποφόρος/"fruitful", and הלל/"praise" is translated as εὐλογέω/"bless" (הַלְלוּ־יָהּ/"Praise-Yah!" is missing). Due to the lack of syntactical similarity a reference is unlikely.

Psalm 145^{LXX}(=146^{MT}) shares αἰνέω/"praise" for הלל/"praise", κύριος/"Lord" for יהוה/"YHWH", υἱός/"son" for בֵּן/"son", πνεῦμα/"wind" for רוּחַ/"wind", ποιέω/"do" for עשׂה/"do", οὐρανός/"heaven" for שָׁמַיִם/"heaven", γῆ/"earth" for אֶרֶץ/"earth", πᾶς/"all" for כֹּל/"all", and αἰών/"eternity" for עוֹלָם/"eternity". In addition to MT, ἄρχων/"ruler" and οὐ/"not" are shared. הוּא/"he" is translated

---

213 εὐλογεῖτε/"bless!" is also used in the "Song of the Three", see p. 164–165 on Dan 3:52–90^{LXX}.

as ἐκεῖνος/"that", נתן/"give" as δίδωμι/"give". Since there is no Hallelujah-frame (the superscription is shared with Ps 148ᴸˣˣ but also with Ps 146ᴸˣˣ and Ps 147ᴸˣˣ), a reference is unlikely.

For *Psalms 146–147ᴸˣˣ(=147ᴹᵀ)*, Ps 148ᴸˣˣ is seen to contain an additional reference to both Ps 146ᴸˣˣ and Ps 147ᴸˣˣ: ἐξομολόγησις/"majesty" in Ps 148:13ᴸˣˣ and Ps 146:6ᴸˣˣ,[214] and κρύσταλλος/"crystal" in Ps 148:8ᴸˣˣ and Ps 147:6ᴸˣˣ.[215]

Ps 146ᴸˣˣ and Ps 148ᴸˣˣ share κύριος/"Lord" for יהוה/"YHWH", Ισραηλ/"Israel" for יִשְׂרָאֵל/"Israel", ἄστρον/"star" for כּוֹכָב/"star", πᾶς/"all" for כֹּל/"all", ὄνομα/"name" for שֵׁם/"name", γῆ/"earth" for אֶרֶץ/"earth", οὐρανός/"heaven" for שָׁמַיִם/"heaven", ὄρος/"mountain" for הַר/"mountain", κτῆνος/"domestic animal" for בְּהֵמָה/"cattle", υἱός/"son" for בֵּן/"son", and οὐ/"not" for לֹא/"not". תְּהִלָּה/"praise" is translated as αἴνεσις/"praise" instead of ὕμνος/"chant", נתן/ "give" as δίδωμι/"give". In addition to MT, ἐξομολόγησις/"majesty" is shared for תּוֹדָה/"thanksgiving" instead of הוֹד/"majesty" as in Ps 148:13ᴸˣˣ. There is no Hallelujah-frame. Ps 147ᴸˣˣ and Ps 148ᴸˣˣ share κύριος/"Lord" for יהוה/ "YHWH", αἰνέω/"praise" for הלל/"praise", υἱός/"son" for בֵּן/"son", γῆ/"earth" for אֶרֶץ/"earth", λόγος/"word" for דָּבָר/"word", χιών/"snow" for שֶׁלֶג/"snow", πνεῦμα/"wind" for רוּחַ/"wind", ὕδωρ/"water" for מַיִם/"water", Ισραηλ/"Israel" for יִשְׂרָאֵל/"Israel", οὐ/"not" for לֹא/"not", ποιέω/"do" for עשׂה/"do", and πᾶς/ "all" for כֹּל/"all". נתן/"give" is translated as δίδωμι/"give", עמד/"stand" as ὑφίστημι/"stand". In addition to MT, τίθημι/"put" for שׂים/"put" and κρύσταλλος/"crystal" for קֶרַח/"frost" instead of קִיטוֹר/"fog" are shared.[216] There is no Hallelujah-frame. The superscription is also shared with Ps 145ᴸˣˣ. Thus, a reference from Ps 148ᴸˣˣ to Ps 146ᴸˣˣ or Ps 147ᴸˣˣ is unlikely.

Intertextual links with *Psalm 149ᴸˣˣ* (see p. 121–122 on Ps 148ᴸˣˣ) and *Ps 150ᴸˣˣ* (see p. 72 on Ps 148ᴸˣˣ) are less likely than in MT.

Isaiah 12:4ᴸˣˣ and Ps 148ᴸˣˣ as in MT share ὅτι ὑψώθη τὸ ὄνομα αὐτοῦ/"for lifted up is his name" for כִּי נִשְׂגָּב שְׁמוֹ/"for exalted is his name" as well as κύριος/ "Lord" for יהוה/"YHWH", and ὄνομα/"name" for שֵׁם/"name", but ἔθνος/"nation" is used instead of λαός/"people" for עַם/"people" (and ἐκεῖνος/"that" is used for הוּא/"he"). In addition to MT, λέγω/"speak" is shared. As in MT, there is no further syntactical similarity in the context Isa 12ᴸˣˣ, and a reference is unlikely. As in MT, Isa 42:11ᴸˣˣ only shares ὄρος/"mountain" for הַר/"mountain". Isa 44:23ᴸˣˣ shares οὐρανός/"heaven" for שָׁמַיִם/"heaven", ποιέω/"do" for עשׂה/

---

214 Cf. Zenger 2008i, 852–853.

215 Cf. Zenger 2008i, 853; Brucker 2011c, 1882.

216 While in the Psalter κρύσταλλος/"crystal" appears only in these two Psalms in a weather context as "ice-crystal", cf. Brucker 2011c, 1882, it is also used in Job 6:16; 38:29 in similar contexts.

"do", γῆ/"earth" for אֶרֶץ/"earth", ὄρος/"mountain" for הַר/"mountain", πᾶς/"all" for כֹּל/"all", ξύλον/"tree" for עֵץ/"tree", and Ισραηλ/"Israel"for יִשְׂרָאֵל/"Israel". In addition to MT, βουνός/"hill" is shared, but unlike in MT, ἐλεέω/"have pity" is used for עשׂה/"do" instead of ποιέω/"do", and θεός/"god" for יהוה/"YHWH" instead of κύριος/"Lord". Isa 49:13^{LXX} shares οὐρανός/"heaven" for שָׁמַיִם/"heaven", γῆ/"earth" for אֶרֶץ/"earth", and ὄρος/"mountain" for הַר/"mountain". In addition to MT, βουνός/"hill" is shared, but θεός/"god" is used for יהוה/"YHWH" instead of κύριος/"Lord". Isa 55:12^{LXX} shares ὄρος/"mountain" for הַר/"mountain", βουνός/"hill" for גִּבְעָה/"hill", πᾶς/"all" for כֹּל/"all", ξύλον/"tree" for עֵץ/"tree". As in MT, there is little syntactical similarity, and a reference is unlikely.

The Greek "Song of the Three" (also known as "Benedicite") in *Daniel 3:52–90^{LXX}* is often seen as based on Ps 148,[217] but also as independent,[218] though possibly of the same period as Ps 148.[219] Since Dan 3^{LXX} is seen to refer to Ps 148 rather than vice versa, there is no intertextual reference from Ps 148, and references from Dan 3:52–90^{LXX} to Ps 148^{LXX} are also unlikely since there are various differences. In detail, Ps 148^{LXX} and Dan 3:52–90^{LXX} share the frequent words κύριος/"Lord", αἰών/"eternity", ὄνομα/"name", πᾶς/"all", ἄβυσσος/"deep", ἄγγελος/"angel" (plural ἄγγελοι/"angels" followed by a genitive referring to God), οὐρανός/"heaven" (plural οὐρανοί/"heavens"), ὕδωρ/water (the phrase ὕδατα πάντα τὰ ἐπάνω τοῦ οὐρανοῦ/"all the waters over the heaven" has no close similarity with Ps 148:4^{LXX} τὸ ὕδωρ τὸ ὑπεράνω τῶν οὐρανῶν), δύναμις/"might" (πᾶσαι αἱ δυνάμεις/"all his hosts" followed by a genitive referring to God, but Ps 102:21^{LXX} with the genitive αὐτοῦ/"his" rather than κυρίου/"Lord's" in Dan 3:61^{LXX} is closer to Ps 148:2^{LXX}), ἥλιος καὶ σελήνη/"sun and moon" (combination unique to these two texts), ἄστρον/"star" (ἄστρα/"stars"), πνεῦμα/"wind", πῦρ/ "fire", χιών/"snow", φῶς/"light", γῆ/"earth", ὄρη καὶ βουνοί/"mountains and hills" (similar to τὰ ὄρη καὶ πάντες οἱ βουνοί/"the mountains and all the hills" in Ps 148:9^{LXX}), πετεινός/"bird", θηρίον/"wild animal" (θηρία/"wild animals"), but τετράποδα/"four-footed animals" instead of τὰ κτήνη/"the domestic animals" as in Ps 148:10^{LXX}), υἱός/"son" (but of all humans, not Israel), Ιοραηλ/ "Israel", and ὅσιος/"faithful". There is syntactical similarity in repeated imperatives calling to praise (but with εὐλογεῖτε/"bless" rather than αἰνεῖτε/"praise"), a third person imperative in Dan 3:74^{LXX}, and thematical similarity with lists of beings – first heavenly, then earthly (but most weather phenomena are in the

---

217 Cf. Gunkel 1926, 618; Ruppert 1986, 281–282 (younger than Ps 148 but based mainly on Ps 136), 295–296 (possible relation to Hebrew original of Benedicite); Allen 2002, 393; Sollamo 2006, 285 (with a short comparison).
218 Cf. Kuhl 1930, 97–98 (based on poetry).
219 Cf. Rad 1960, 279 (English translation: Rad 1984, 286) (based on similarity).

heavenly rather than the earthly part) – called to praise. The similarities do not suffice to make an intertextual reference likely, though the texts may be related in genre.[220]

Results

References to Gen 1^LXX; Deu^LXX; Ps 149^LXX; 150^LXX are less likely than in MT, references to Isa^LXX; Ps 2^LXX; 95^LXX; 97^LXX; 102^LXX; 103^LXX; 145^LXX; 146^LXX; 147^LXX equally unlikely. A reference to the "Song of the Three" in Dan 3:52–90^LXX is unlikely. Unlike in MT, there is a word-by-word reference to Ps 32^LXX leading to a stress on the *universal aspect of creation*.

IV.3.4 Content of Psalm 148^LXX

Who is called to praise in Psalm 148:1–2^LXX?

Unlike in Hebrew, οὐρανός/"heaven" can be used in both a singular form (v.13c) and plural forms (v.1a, v.4a twice, v.4b). The plural form of "heavens" may point towards the thought of multiple heavens,[221] but since in Ps 148^LXX the singular form appears as a summary of the plural forms, it is more likely that only one heaven is in view, though possibly with layers as in the Hebrew Psalm: ὕδωρ/ "water" in v.4b may be such a layer. In v.1b, the adjective ὕψιστος/"highest" is used in a neuter plural form signifying the highest places as a synonym for the heavenly sphere[222] (as in Hebrew).

As in Hebrew, ἄγγελοι/"angels" (which can refer to human or divine messengers)[223] and δυνάμεις/"hosts" (which can refer to general powers, or human or divine hosts)[224] are two groups of heavenly beings called to praise in v.2.

Unlike in Hebrew, instead of כָּל־כּוֹכְבֵי אוֹר/"all stars of light" πάντα τὰ ἄστρα καὶ τὸ φῶς/"all the stars and the light" are called to praise, adding another subject, and both subjects are stressed by additional articles. The light may be that of sun, moon, and stars,[225] thus providing a summary of the other three subjects, but it is listed as a separate and possibly more general subject.[226]

---

220 See IV.3.5.
221 See p. 142 fn. 87.
222 Cf. Bons 2009b, 896.
223 Cf. Lust, Eynikel, and Hauspie 2003, s.v. ἄγγελος.
224 Cf. Lust, Eynikel, and Hauspie 2003, s.v. δύναμις; Dines 2007, 20.
225 Thus with a question mark Zenger 2008i, 853.

The plural αἱ δυνάμεις αὐτοῦ/"his hosts" in v.2b may follow the Qere reading in MT,[227] or the same plural in Ps 102:21^{LXX}(=103:21^{MT}).[228] In any case, the plural form stands in parallel to οἱ ἄγγελοι αὐτοῦ/"his angels" in v.2a, and stresses the number of beings praising.

What are the reasons for praise in Psalm 148:5 – 6^{LXX}?

The additional v.5b (taken out of Ps 32:9^{LXX})[229] stresses that all the subjects mentioned in vv.2 – 4 were created by God's word and command only. God is also emphasised as the subject by the repeated use of the pronoun αὐτός/"he".[230] As in MT, the indestructible order of creation οὐ παρελεύσεται/"will not pass",[231] here explicitly in the future, but as in MT there is no indication of eschatological intent, and rather the lasting order is stressed, as confirmed by the long phrase εἰς τὸν αἰῶνα καὶ εἰς τὸν αἰῶνα τοῦ αἰῶνος/"for the eternity and for the eternity of the eternity".[232] For נתן/"give" τίθημι/"put" is used in combination with πρόσταγμα/"ordinance", this is rarer than a combination with δίδωμι/"give", but also appears in Gen 47:26, and stresses the lasting order being in place.

Who is called to praise in Psalm 148:7 – 12^{LXX}?

While δράκων/"dragon" can refer to serpents as well as sea monsters,[233] in v.7 with ἄβυσσος/"deep, flood, sea"[234] it probably refers to sea monsters as in MT.

Even more likely than in MT, πῦρ/"fire" in v.8 refers to lightning as קיטור/ "fog" is translated with κρύσταλλος/"ice-crystal" rather than a word for "smoke".

---

226 Without text-critical evidence, Hillers 1978, 325 (Allen 2002, 389, follows Hillers) suggests the development of the LXX reading through scribal variation.
227 Cf. Brucker 2011c, 1881.
228 However, see p. 161–162 on Ps 102; 103^{LXX}(=103; 104^{MT}).
229 See p. 160–161 on Ps 32^{LXX}(=33^{MT}).
230 Cf. Bons 2009b, 896.
231 Like עבר/"pass", παρέρχομαι/"pass" may mean "to transgress", cf. Lust, Eynikel, and Hauspie 2003, s.v. παρέρχομαι; Zenger 2008i, 853, but the singular future form in LXX confirms that emendations in MT are unnecessary, cf. Brucker 2011c, 1882, and see p. 144–145.
232 See p. 158. While the extended phrase occurs only in the LXX-Psalter, cf. Zenger 2008i, 853, the shorter εἰς τὸν αἰῶνα τοῦ αἰῶνος/"for the eternity of the eternity" is used in Ps 110:8^{LXX} for the same Hebrew phrase לְעַד לְעוֹלָם/"for ever for eternity", and thus the extra stress on eternity is probably more than just a formula.
233 Cf. Lust, Eynikel, and Hauspie 2003, s.v. δράκων.
234 Cf. Lust, Eynikel, and Hauspie 2003, s.v. ἄβυσσος.

Unlike in MT, τὰ ποιοῦντα τὸν λόγον αὐτοῦ/"the ones doing his word" is plural, thus referring to all of the subjects of v.8 rather than just the storm.[235] This is confirmed by the lack of conjunctions καί/"and" between the subjects of v.8.

In v.9b, the Hebrew noun following a construct noun פְּרִי/"fruit" is translated with the rare adjective καρποφόρος/"fruit-bearing",[236] similarly in v.10b כָּנָף/ "wing" with πτερωτός/"winged".

The last subject μετὰ νεωτέρων/"with younger ones" in v.12b is a comparative adjective[237] unlike in MT, but this comparative is a usual translation for נַעַר/ "young".[238]

As in MT but with slight changes in the distribution, in vv.7b–12, all the subjects in one colon are either singular (vv.8a) or plural (vv.7b, 9ab, 10ab, 11ab, 12ab) with the exception of v.8b. As in MT, there are articles at the beginning of v.9ab and v.10ab only,[239] stressing the changes to geographical features and plants (v.9), and to animals and humans (vv.10–12).

What are the reasons for praise in Psalm 148:13–14^LXX?

The aorist passive ὑψώθη/"lifted up is" in v.13b expresses a general statement.[240]

ἐξομολόγησις used for הוֹד/"majesty" in v.13c can mean "praise" or "thanksgiving"[241] but also "majesty" as in MT,[242] and given the connected verses 13 and 14 as reasons for praise[243] in Ps 148^LXX it means "majesty".

In τὸ ὄνομα αὐτοῦ μόνου/"his name alone", more literally "the name of him alone", "alone" refers to "him",[244] thus placing more stress on God than MT.

---

235 Cf. Zenger 2008i, 853; Brucker 2011c, 1881–1882.

236 See p. 158–159 on Gen 1.

237 Cf. Lust, Eynikel, and Hauspie 2003, s.v. νέος. Some manuscripts also read πρεσβύτεροι/ "older ones" in v.12a, cf. Rahlfs 1979, 337, but more likely than such an interpretation by early Christian authorities, thus Bons 2009b, 897, is the assimilation to the colon's second subject.

238 Cf. Hatch et al. 1998, 942, Appendix 2 (Greek Ecclesiasticus [=Sir]) 185.

239 On the article in the middle of v.11a see p. 158.

240 Cf. Blass, Debrunner, and Rehkopf 1979, §333 (gnomic aorist). Thus Bons 2009b, 897; Brucker 2011c, 1882 (referring to Blass, Debrunner, and Rehkopf 1979, §333,1b fn. 5).

241 Cf. Lust, Eynikel, and Hauspie 2003, s.v. ἐξομολόγησις. A translation as "praise" is adopted by Zenger 2008i, 852–853; Bons 2009b, 897.

242 Cf. Ps 95:6^LXX; 103:1^LXX; 110:3^LXX where ἐξομολόγησις/"majesty" as a translation of הוֹד/"majesty" appears in the context of attributes of God and is unlikely to mean "praise".

243 See p. 157.

244 Cf. Bons 2009b, 897.

Since v.14bc is a nominal sentence rather than another object of the verb in v.14a,[245] it could be an explanation or consequence of v.14a[246] ("Israel will be lifted up, thus there will be a chant"), or a subscription to the entire Psalm[247] ("A chant"). The repetition of ὑψόω/"lift up" in v.13a and v.14a makes the former option of v.14bc expressing the *consequence* of praise more likely. However, ὕμνος/"chant" in v.14b refers to sung praise rather than general praise more explicitly than in MT where the more general תְּהִלָּה/"praise" is used.

Unlike in MT, לְ/"for" is translated in v.14a with the *genitive* forms λαοῦ αὐτοῦ/"of his people", but with dative forms in v.14bc. This stresses the connection between the raising of the horn and the people.[248] The dative forms could express a possessive aspect,[249] but beneficiaries[250] are more likely given the switch from genitive to dative.

The waw-imperfect וַיָּרֶם/"and he has lifted up" in v.14a is translated with the future καὶ ὑψώσει/"and he will lift up".[251] This future form is in parallel with the future παρελεύσεται/"it will pass" in v.6b, but while v.6b gives a future reason for praise pertaining to all entities mentioned in vv.1–4, v.14a introduces a new reason: Unlike MT, LXX stresses Israel's *future* rather than past exaltation.[252] Unlike in MT, due to the future form it is unlikely that v.14a refers to Israel's post-

---

245 See p. 157.

246 Thus Zenger 2008i, 853; Schmutzer and Gauthier 2009, 178–179.

247 Thus as an alternative Bons 2009b, 897.

248 Cf. Schmutzer and Gauthier 2009, 179–180.

249 Cf. Blass, Debrunner, and Rehkopf 1979, §189; thus Schmutzer and Gauthier 2009, 180.

250 Cf. Blass, Debrunner, and Rehkopf 1979, §188.

251 The Peshitta also has the equivalent to a future form, cf. Elliger and Rudolph 1997, 1225; Brucker 2011c, 1882; as does the Vulgate, cf. Schmutzer and Gauthier 2009, 180, esp. fn. 86 (also discussing other variants). Schmutzer and Gauthier 2009, 167, take into account all instances of ὑψόω/"lift up" for רום/"lift up" combined with κέρας/"horn" for קֶרֶן/"horn" except Ps 74:6[LXX] where רום/"lift up" is translated with ἐπαίρω/"raise".

252 Without text-critical evidence, commentators assume the influence of a different Hebrew vocalisation, cf. Hillers 1978, 327 (see fn. 4, criticised by Zenger 2008i, 839); Ruppert 1986, 276; Zenger 2008i, 839; Schmutzer and Gauthier 2009, 180–181, possibly a shortened hif'il imperfect וַיָּרֶם/"and he will lift up", possibly with the influence of 1 Sam 2:10 where the phrase with a hif'il jussive וְיָרֵם קֶרֶן מְשִׁיחוֹ/"and he will lift up the horn of his anointed" is translated with καὶ ὑψώσει κέρας χριστοῦ αὐτοῦ/"and he will lift up a horn of his anointed". וַיָּרֶם could be a shortened hif'il imperfect, cf. Gesenius and Kautzsch 1909, §72aa, or a hif'il jussive, cf. Joüon and Muraoka 2011, §80 g, but there is no Hebrew manuscript with this vocalisation. The statistics for consecutive verb forms in Schmutzer and Gauthier 2009, 167–168, esp. fn. 32, show that future forms are used more rarely than aorists. Thus, the future form here is probably not just a mechanic translation.

exilic restoration[253] (at least from a postexilic perspective).[254] However, given the future form in v.6b which is unlikely to be eschatological, v.14a may also not point towards an eschatological future but rather, as MT, to Israel's general empowerment as a reason for praise,[255] with the consequence of a chant for Israel.

IV.3.5 Genre of Psalm 148^{LXX}

As in MT, Ps 148^{LXX} fits the criteria for a hymn. ὕμνος/"chant" in v.14b refers to sung praise rather than general praise more explicitly than in MT.[256] The closest LXX parallel is the "Song of the Three" in Dan 3:52–90^{LXX}, which is both a hymn and a literary poem as it appears as a hymn within a written narrative.[257] A cultic or literary setting depends on the setting of the LXX-Psalter as a whole.

IV.3.6 Date of Psalm 148^{LXX}

An intertextual reference to Psalm 32^{LXX} leads to a relative date within the LXX-Psalter but no absolute date.[258] An intertextual relation to Dan 3:52–90^{LXX} is unlikely.[259] The dating of Ps 148^{LXX} thus has to rely on the 2nd century BCE LXX-Psalter.[260]

IV.3.7 Unity of Psalm 148^{LXX}

Ps 148^{LXX} is one unit, with no final Hallelujah in any manuscript. Some manuscripts add an extra opening Hallelujah, others miss out Αγγαιου καὶ Ζαχαριου/"of Haggai and Zechariah" as in Ps 149–150^{LXX},[261] yet others miss out Αγγαιου καὶ/"of Haggai and" but not Ζαχαριου/"of Zechariah".

---

253 Cf. Zenger 2008i, 853.

254 Against Schmutzer and Gauthier 2009, 180–181. See fn. 252.

255 Against Ruppert 1986, 276 (eschatological future, messianic aspect due to 1 Sam 2:10).

256 See p. 167–169.

257 Cf. Neef 2011, 3022–3023.

258 Ps 33^{MT} is dated into postexilic times mostly relying on content, cf. Zenger 1993c, 206; Watson 2005, 226. Ps 32^{LXX} does not contain information about its date.

259 See p. 164–165 on Dan 3:52–90^{LXX}.

260 See p. 16, esp. fn. 104.

261 See p. 17 fn. 109.

IV.3.8 Overall Interpretation of Psalm 148[LXX]

Ps 148 calls to YHWH's praise all beings in heaven (because of their *universal creation and ordering through YHWH*) and on earth (because of YHWH's exaltation and Israel's *future* exaltation through him, without indications of eschatology, *with the consequence of a song for Israel*). A word-by-word reference to Ps 32[LXX] stresses the *universal aspect of creation.*

IV.4 Comparison

Both DSS and LXX are very *close* to MT, though LXX stresses universalism and future.

There is an opening *Hallelujah* in MT, no opening Hallelujah in DSS, and a different opening superscription in LXX, and a closing Hallelujah in MT (not preserved in DSS), but not LXX. Ps 148^{LXX} is connected only with Ps $145-147^{LXX}$ ($=146-147^{MT}$) through its superscription.

Regarding *order*, Ps 148 is followed by Ps 149 and preceded by Ps 147 in MT and LXX (though Ps 147 is split), but not 11QPs^a where it is conjecturally followed by Ps 120 and preceded by Ps 146. This weakens the likelihood of an original connection of Psalms 146–150.

Regarding *intertextuality*, both MT and DSS show a lack of references. LXX mostly either confirms the lack of references in MT or even weakens the likelihood of references in MT, but shows *an additional verse with a word-by-word reference to Ps 32^{LXX}* not found in MT or DSS.

V Psalm 147

V.1 Psalm 147[MT]

V.1.1 Translation of Psalm 147[MT]

1H	Praise-Yah!	הַֽלְלוּ יָ֨הּ ׀	1H
1a	Yea, good [is it] to make music to our God,	כִּי־ט֭וֹב זַמְּרָ֣ה אֱלֹהֵ֑ינוּ	1a
1b	yea, pleasant, appropriate [is] praise.	כִּֽי־נָ֝עִ֗ים נָאוָ֥ה תְהִלָּֽה׃	1b
2a	The one building Jerusalem [is] YHWH,	בּוֹנֵ֣ה יְרוּשָׁלִַ֣ם יְהוָ֑ה	2a
2b	the scattered ones of Israel he gathers.	נִדְחֵ֖י יִשְׂרָאֵ֣ל יְכַנֵּֽס׃	2b
3a	The one healing broken ones of heart	הָ֭רֹפֵא לִשְׁב֣וּרֵי לֵ֑ב	3a
3b	and binding up their pains.	וּ֝מְחַבֵּ֗שׁ לְעַצְּבוֹתָֽם׃	3b
4a	Counting the number of the stars,	מוֹנֶ֣ה מִ֭סְפָּר לַכּוֹכָבִ֑ים	4a
4b	for all of them names he calls.	לְ֝כֻלָּ֗ם שֵׁמ֥וֹת יִקְרָֽא׃	4b
5a	Great [is] our Lord and much of power	גָּד֣וֹל אֲדוֹנֵ֣ינוּ וְרַב־כֹּ֑חַ	5a
5b	for his understanding there is no number.	לִ֝תְבוּנָת֗וֹ אֵ֣ין מִסְפָּֽר׃	5b
6a	Lifting up poor ones [is] YHWH,	מְעוֹדֵ֣ד עֲנָוִ֣ים יְהוָ֑ה	6a
6b	making low wicked ones unto earth.	מַשְׁפִּ֖יל רְשָׁעִ֣ים עֲדֵי־אָֽרֶץ׃	6b
7a	Answer YHWH with thanksgiving,	עֱנ֣וּ לַיהוָ֣ה בְּתוֹדָ֑ה	7a
7b	make music for our God with a lyre!	זַמְּר֖וּ לֵאלֹהֵ֣ינוּ בְכִנּֽוֹר׃	7b
8a	The one covering heavens with clouds,	הַֽמְכַסֶּ֬ה שָׁמַ֨יִם ׀ בְּעָבִ֗ים	8a
8b	the one fixing for the earth rain,	הַמֵּכִ֣ין לָאָ֣רֶץ מָטָ֑ר	8b
8c	the one making grow mountains [with] grass.	הַמַּצְמִ֖יחַ הָרִ֣ים חָצִֽיר׃	8c
9a	Giving for an animal its[1] food,	נוֹתֵ֣ן לִבְהֵמָ֣ה לַחְמָ֑הּ	9a
9b	for sons of ravens who call.	לִבְנֵ֥י עֹ֝רֵ֗ב אֲשֶׁ֣ר יִקְרָֽאוּ׃	9b
10a	Not in the strength of the horse does he take pleasure	לֹ֤א בִגְבוּרַ֣ת הַסּ֣וּס יֶחְפָּ֑ץ	10a
10b	not in the lower legs of the man does he delight.	לֹֽא־בְשׁוֹקֵ֖י הָאִ֣ישׁ יִרְצֶֽה׃	10b
11a	Delighting [is] YHWH in the ones fearing him,	רוֹצֶ֣ה יְ֭הוָה אֶת־יְרֵאָ֑יו	11a
11b	the ones waiting for his kindness.	אֶת־הַֽמְיַחֲלִ֥ים לְחַסְדּֽוֹ׃	11b
12a	Glorify, Jerusalem, YHWH,	שַׁבְּחִ֣י יְ֭רוּשָׁלִַם אֶת־יְהוָ֑ה	12a
12b	praise your God, Zion!	הַֽלְלִ֖י אֱלֹהַ֣יִךְ צִיּֽוֹן׃	12b
13a	For he has strengthened the bars of your gates,	כִּֽי־חִ֭זַּק בְּרִיחֵ֣י שְׁעָרָ֑יִךְ	13a
13b	he has blessed your sons in your midst.	בֵּרַ֖ךְ בָּנַ֣יִךְ בְּקִרְבֵּֽךְ׃	13b
14a	The one putting [in] your territory peace,	הַשָּֽׂם־גְּבוּלֵ֥ךְ שָׁל֑וֹם	14a
14b	[with] fat of wheat he satisfies you.	חֵ֥לֶב חִ֝טִּ֗ים יַשְׂבִּיעֵֽךְ׃	14b
15a	The one sending his saying [to the] earth,	הַשֹּׁלֵ֣חַ אִמְרָת֣וֹ אָ֑רֶץ	15a
15b	to speed[2] runs his word.	עַד־מְ֝הֵרָ֗ה יָר֥וּץ דְּבָרֽוֹ׃	15b
16a	The one giving snow like the wool,	הַנֹּתֵ֣ן שֶׁ֣לֶג כַּצָּ֑מֶר	16a
16b	hoarfrost like the ash he scatters.	כְּ֝פ֗וֹר כָּאֵ֥פֶר יְפַזֵּֽר׃	16b
17a	Throwing his ice like pieces,	מַשְׁלִ֣יךְ קַֽרְח֣וֹ כְפִתִּ֑ים	17a

1 Correction of Brodersen 2013, 27: "its food" referring to "animal".

2 Less literally: "fast".

DOI 10.1515/9783110536096-005

17b	before his cold – who stands?	לִפְנֵי קָרָתוֹ מִי יַעֲמֹד:	17b
18a	He sends his word and melts them,	יִשְׁלַח דְּבָרוֹ וְיַמְסֵם	18a
18b	he lets blow his wind, waters drip.	יַשֵּׁב רוּחוֹ יִזְּלוּ־מָיִם:	18b
19a	Declaring his word for Jacob,	מַגִּיד דְּבָרָו לְיַעֲקֹב	19a
19b	his decrees and his judgements for Israel.	חֻקָּיו וּמִשְׁפָּטָיו לְיִשְׂרָאֵל:	19b
20a	Not he has done so for every nation,	לֹא עָשָׂה כֵן לְכָל־גּוֹי	20a
20b	and judgements – not have they known them.	וּמִשְׁפָּטִים בַּל־יְדָעוּם	20b
20H	Praise-Yah!	הַלְלוּ־יָהּ:	20H

V.1.2 Form of Psalm 147^{MT}

Outline of Psalm 147^{MT}

Part I		
1H – 1	Call to Praise YHWH, the *Imperative*	
2 – 3	God of Israel	Jerusalem and Israel
4 – 5	Creator	Rule over Stars, Power, Understanding
6	God of Israel	*Antithesis:* For Poor, Against Wicked
Part II		
7	Call to Praise YHWH, the *Imperative*	
8 – 9	Creator	Care for Rain and Animals
10 – 11	God of Israel	*Antithesis:* Against Warriors, For Pious
Part III		
12	Call to Praise YHWH, the *Imperative*	
13 – 14	God of Israel	Care for Jerusalem
15 – 18	Creator	His Word and Weather
19 – 20	God of Israel	*Antithesis:* Law for Israel, Not every Nation
20H	Call to Praise YHWH *Imperative*	

Syntax of Psalm 147^{MT}

Imperatives of הלל/"praise" structure Psalm 147: It is *framed* by the imperatives
הַלְלוּ־יָהּ/"Praise-Yah!". Like the opening imperative, an imperative of הלל/"praise"
in v.12b stands close to כִּי/"for" (vv.1, 13) and יְרוּשָׁלַם/"Jerusalem" (vv.2, 12), indicating a division into two parts, vv.1–11 (Parts I+II) and 12–20 (Part III). However, in v.12b הלל/"praise" only appears following another imperative in a second
person singular feminine and without יָהּ/"Yah", and thus stands out less than

the framing imperatives. *Imperatives* appear only in vv.1, 7, and 12. This suggests a division into three parts, vv.1–6 (Part I) – vv.7–11 (Part II) – vv.12–20 (Part III).

All three parts are dominated by *participles:* 12 of 20 verses begin with a masculine singular active participle referring to YHWH. These participles are predicates of nominal clauses whose subject is YHWH, and they are emphasised through their place at the beginning of the sentence.[3] Thus, rather than the name of YHWH, his *actions* are in view. The active participles denote *general actions:*[4] The subject, YHWH, is continously taking the action described.[5] The *subject* YHWH is mentioned in vv.2a, 6a, and 11a only. In the other verses with participles (vv.3ab, 4a, 6b, 8abc, 9a, 14a, 15a, 16a, 17a, 19a), a personal pronoun referring to YHWH is omitted.[6] The participles opening vv.3a, 8abc, 14a, 15a, and 16a are preceded by *articles*. The content of the Psalm makes it unlikely that these articles merely have a determining function:[7] This would mean that in v.16 YHWH is *the* (only) one giving snow, but in the following v.17 (any) *one* throwing ice. It is more likely that all nominal clauses with YHWH as their subject express his uniqueness. This is further confirmed as the first nominal clause about YHWH in v.2 is an identifying clause: The participle בּוֹנֵה/"building" opening v.2a is a construct form followed by the object of the action[8] "Jerusalem" which in turn determines the participle:[9] YHWH is *the one* building Jerusalem, not *someone* building it. Regardless of whether this participle בֹּנֵה/"building" is seen as a noun "builder",[10] the predicate of the nominal clause in v.2a is determined, and YHWH is described as unique. This leads to the expectation that the following nominal clauses in which the predicate is stressed at the beginning also show YHWH's uniqueness. It is also unlikely that the articles mark the beginning of a new part of the Psalm:[11] The parts of vv.8, 14, 15, and 16 would then be rather short. Furthermore, v.14 which continues the content of v.13 would be separated from the preceding verse.[12] V.15 which is connected with vv.18 and 19 through דְּבָר/"word" would be separated from them through the article in v.16.

---

3 Cf. Gesenius and Kautzsch 1909, §116m, n, q, 141 l, m, n.
4 See p. 100 fn. 110.
5 For v.2a cf. Sedlmeier 1996, 78–79 (whether noun or participle of building is used). The continuous action fits with Westermann's describing hymn, but see fn. 175.
6 Cf. Gesenius and Kautzsch 1909, §116s.
7 Cf. Gesenius and Kautzsch 1909, §126d.
8 Cf. Gesenius and Kautzsch 1909, §116g.
9 Cf. Gesenius and Kautzsch 1909, §127.
10 Thus Sedlmeier 1996, 21–22, 45–80; Gerstenberger 2001, 442. Participle only in Gesenius 2013, s.v. בנה.
11 Thus Kratz 1992, 20 fn. 62. For a discussion cf. Sedlmeier 1996, 41–42 fn. 83.
12 Acknowledged in Kratz 1992, 20 fn. 62.

The call to praise in v.7 would be a part of Part I, vv.8–10 would lack a call to praise as they do not fit with v.12 in their content.

The articles preceding the participles are likely to function like demonstrative pronouns referring back to someone or something already mentioned:[13] YHWH in vv.1–2, 7, and 12. If the articles are thus read as *referring back* to the previously mentioned YHWH, the following structure appears: The three calls to praise all contain YHWH (abbreviated as יָהּ/"Yah" in v.1 and in its full form יהוה/"YHWH" in vv.7 and 12). In all three parts, these calls to praise YHWH are then followed by a row of participles. In every part, articles precede the participles referring back to YHWH. The verbal sentences v.2b and v.14 are bridged by the demonstrative function of the articles. In Parts II+III, the first three participles have an article.[14] Thus the *articles* clarify *whom* the participles describe, while the action stressed by the opening position of the *participles* explains *why* he is to be praised. Thus, the calls to praise introduce the three parts of the Psalm, the opening participles refer to these calls using articles. In terms of content, the article in v.3 thus stresses YHWH as the God of Israel, v.8 as creator, vv.14–15 as the God of Israel and v.16 as creator. This emphasises praise for the God of Israel in Part I, for the creator in Part II, and for the God of Israel who also is the creator in Part III. The articles in vv.14, 15, and 16 *identify the God of Israel with the creator.*[15]

In addition to imperatives and participles, the Psalm uses *imperfect* forms. In almost all cases where a participle and an imperfect are in the same verse (vv.2, 4, 9, 14, 15, 16, 17), the participle is placed at the beginning as the predicate of the first half-verse, the imperfect form is placed at the end as the predicate of the second half-verse. The subject YHWH is mentioned explicitly only in the first of these verses (v.2), where it is placed in the centre of the verse between the two predicates, but implicitly present in the other verses describing his actions. This constant structure in all three parts of the Psalm suggests that the imperfect forms do not have different meanings in every part but, since they are collocated with participles, are to be understood in the same *general* meaning: The actions mentioned by the imperfect forms have repeatedly been done in the past, occur repeatedly in the present, and are to be expected in the future.[16] In English, this notion is translated with present forms. This interpretation is confirmed by vv.4–5 which are connected through the repetition of מִסְפָּר/"number" and which contain a timeless participle, an imperfect form, and a timeless adjective

---

13 Cf. Gesenius and Kautzsch 1909, §126b, 138i.
14 Cf. Allen 1983, 307–308.
15 See p. 183–185 on Isa and V.1.6.
16 Cf. Gesenius and Kautzsch 1909, §107d, e, g, i.

followed by אֵין/"there is not". The content of the Psalm also confirms the general interpretation of imperfect forms and participles: For example, the weather phenomena in vv.16–17 where YHWH gives snow (participle), scatters hoarfrost (imperfect), throws ice (participle) and no one can stand before his frost (imperfect) are general phenomena. The four imperfect forms in v.18 add further general statements to the imperfect form in v.17. V.18 only contains imperfect forms. This can be explained as emphasising an order: The thawing in v.18 follows the freezing in vv.16–17 and occurs at a later point within the common general phenomenon.[17]

In these general statements, v.2b is also to be understood as a general statement: YHWH has gathered the scattered ones of Israel in the past, does so in the present, and is expected to do so in the future, in short, he generally gathers Israel's scattered ones.[18] This has consequences for the date of the Psalm: A gathering must have happened at least once in the past, but the imperfect form does not stress a singular past event but the general action. Similarly, the law in v.19 is constantly declared to Israel.[19] The calls to praise are also to be understood generally: YHWH is to be praised not just for a single past, present, or future event.

Perfect forms appear only in Part III, in vv.13 and 20, probably referring to past events which have consequences for the present.[20] This falls in line with the calls to praise: YHWH is to be praised for past actions from which the ones called to praise still benefit. While perfect forms can denote a future that is thought of as secure,[21] there is no indication of such anticipating praise in Ps 147.

The (partly implicit) subject of the Psalm is almost always YHWH, suggesting a *theocentric* view. Verses where YHWH is not the subject are the calls to praise in vv.1, 7, 12, and 20, the relative clause about "sons of ravens" in v.9b, v.15b with the subject "his word", v.17b with "who", v.18b with "waters" and v.20b where "nations" are the implicit subject. However, in the calls to praise YHWH is always mentioned, and "his word" is connected to him through the suffix and does not act on its own (it only "runs" in v.15b).[22] The subjects "ravens", "who", "water", and "nations" also depend on YHWH: Without him, the ravens do not have food, no one can stand before his cold, no waters flow without him

---

17 Cf. Bartelmus (1994), 201, 204–205.
18 Thus Sedlmeier 1996, 36–39, 52–64.
19 Cf. Ballhorn 2004b, 313 fn. 819 (revelatio continua).
20 Cf. Gesenius and Kautzsch 1909, §106g.
21 Cf. Gesenius and Kautzsch 1909, §106m.
22 See p. 195–197.

and he does not reveal his law to nations. This confirms the *theocentric* view of the Psalm.

Structure of Psalm 147^MT

The structure of Ps 147^MT is: Hallelujah – vv.1–6 (Part I) – vv.7–10 (Part II) – vv.12–20 (Part III) – Hallelujah. All parts start with calls to praise including הלל/"praise".[23] The two main motifs, *YHWH as the God of Israel* and *YHWH as creator* (as a *constant ruler over nature* rather than just a past creator), appear in all parts. The order "Call to Praise – God of Israel – Creator – God of Israel" in Parts I+III frames Part II in which the reason for the call to praise is the two- rather than threefold "Call to Praise – Creator – God of Israel".[24]

Poetic Devices in Psalm 147^MT

All verses except v.8 are bicola showing a *parallelismus membrorum*. The calls to praise vv.7 and 12 consist of *synonymous* parallels, identifing YHWH and "our God" (v.7), Jerusalem and Zion, and YHWH and Zion's and thus Jerusalem's God. The identifications "YHWH = our God = Jerusalem's God = Zion's God" make it more likely that "we" can be identified with "Jerusalem = Zion" than that two different addressees are called to praise the same God.[25] The synonymous parallel in v.19 identifies "Jacob" and "Israel". In the midst of the other *synthetic bicola*, v.8 is a *synthetic tricolon*. Its three constituents clouds, rain, and grass form an order where rain is at the centre:[26] YHWH first gives clouds, then rain, then grass. Even more central than the rain or the order clouds – rain – grass is YHWH who causes each of these elements, a theocentric view also found in vv.16–18.[27]

V.6 shows the only *antithetical* parallel within one verse (lifting up – bowing down, poor ones – wicked ones). However, there are two antithetical statements in two verses each, with the second verse in each case beginning with לא/"not" in a verbal sentence: Vv.10–11 (connected through the root רצה/"delight": not

---

23 For similar structures cf. Gunkel 1926, 615; Gerstenberger 2001, 442; Leuenberger 2004, 348; Zenger 2008h, 828–830. Similarly Lohfink 1990, 116–119 (two-fold structure since כִּי/"for" only appears twice, but also Ps 147:1–11 originally separate and two-fold Psalm, thus in fact threefold division).
24 Similarly Allen 1983, 308.
25 On the addressees see p. 188–190.
26 Cf. Seybold 2003, 100.
27 See p. 173–177.

warriors, pious ones) and vv.19–20 (connected through מִשְׁפָּט/"judgement": Israel, not every nation). Thus, every one of Parts I, II, and III is introduced with a call to praise in a synonymous parallelism and concluded by an antithetical statement.

In addition to הלל/"praise" (vv.1, 12, 20) close to כִּי/"for" (vv.1, 13) and יְרוּשָׁלַם/ "Jerusalem" (vv.2, 12),[28] other *word repetitions* connect the different parts. The first two calls to praise are connected through זמר/"make music" (vv.1, 7), the first and third through הלל/"praise" (vv.1, 12), all three through forms of יהוה/ "YHWH" and אֱלֹהִים/"God" (vv.1, 7, 12). Parts I, II, and III are connected by יהוה/"YHWH" (vv.1, 2, 6, 7, 11, 12, 20, abbreviated in vv.1, 20). The name of God connects the transitional verses 6 and 7 as well as 11 and 12 and thus together with the frame of vv.1–2 and v.20 holds the entire Psalm together. אֶרֶץ/"earth" also connects all three parts (vv.6, 8, 15). קרא/"call" (vv.4, 9) connects Parts I +II, connecting Parts I+III are יְרוּשָׁלַם/"Jerusalem" (vv.2, 12; in v.12 with synonym צִיּוֹן/"Zion"), עַד/"to" (vv.6, 15), יִשְׂרָאֵל/"Israel" (vv.2, 19; in v.19 with synonym יַעֲקֹב/"Jacob"), and כֹּל/"all" (vv.4, 20). The additional synonyms צִיּוֹן/"Zion" and יַעֲקֹב/"Jacob" lead to a greater emphasis on Israel in Part III than in Part I, but the topic explicitly appears in both parts. Parts II+III are connected through נֹתֵן/"giving" (vv.9, 16), בֵּן/"son" (vv.9, 13), and לֹא/"not" (vv.10 twice, 20). Within Part I, מִסְפָּר/"number" is used twice (vv.4–5), within Part II רצה/"delight" (vv.10–11), within Part III דָּבָר/"word" is used three times (vv.15, 18, 19) and שלח/"send" (vv.15, 18) and מִשְׁפָּט/"judgement" (vv.19–20) twice. Thus, in all three parts neighbouring verses are connected through the repetition of a word.[29]

Alliterations also appear in all three parts, e.g. in v.4 with two neighbouring words starting with מ and two with לכ, in v.8 with three cola beginning with המ each, v.9 with three neighbouring words beginning with ל, in v.13b two words beginning with ב, and in v.14b with ה, in v.15a with א. *Assonances* appear in Parts I +III: בֹּנֵה/"building" in v.2 sounds similar to מוֹנֶה/"counting" in v.4, שלח/"send" in vv.15 and 18 similar to שלך/"throw" in v.17.[30]

---

28 See p. 173–174.
29 Cf. Allen 1983, 308.
30 For further poetic devices cf. Allen 1983, 308; Weber 2003, 375–376; Zenger 2008h, 834.

V.1.3 Intertextuality in Psalm 147^MT

Importance

Some commentators argue for a high number of intertextual references in Ps 147:1–11 and a low number in Ps 147:12–20, leading to the interpretation of Ps 147:12–20 as an earlier separate text and Ps 147:1–11 as a later redactional addition[31] written for the literary context of the Psalter and specifically Psalms 146–147.[32] Others see the entire Psalm as containing various references to other texts in HB, with the consequence of a late date of Ps 147.[33] Ps 147 like Ps 145 and Ps 146 is also seen as referring to Ps 104 and other texts and containing references to one another, leading to their interpretation as late texts based on other texts in HB and possibly written for the literary context of the Psalter.[34] Yet others argue that shared words without actual quotations do not suffice to confirm intertextual references, and that there is much uncertainty regarding intertextual references in Ps 147.[35] My previous research shows that Ps 147 does contain intertextual references, but not to its neighbouring Psalms, thus suggesting an origin independent of Psalms 146–150.[36]

Analysis

Commentators often argue for a reference from Ps 147 to *Deuteronomy 4*, especially Deut 4:8,[37] with consequences including the interpretation of God's word as the Torah given to Israel only,[38] and a late date of Ps 147.[39] Deut 4:8 in syntactical similarity shares the combination of the plural words חֻקִּים וּמִשְׁפָּטִים/"decrees and judgements" with Ps 147:19 (there with suffixes referring to YHWH). Within

---

31 Cf. Zenger 2008h, 827–828.

32 Cf. Zenger 2008c, 808–809.

33 Cf. Allen 1983, 308–309.

34 Cf. Kratz 1992, 13, 36, 38.

35 Cf. Seybold 2010, 153–154, 158–159, 161–163. See V.1.7.

36 See Brodersen 2013, 73–75. The criteria used for assessing intertextual references in Brodersen 2013, 43–44, are refined here to include the importance of syntactical similarity, see I.3.2, esp. p. 24 fn. 148. Thus, some results differ (against Brodersen 2013, 54, 64–65, 71, 73–74, references to Ps 51 and 81 are unlikely, other differences are noted in each case), but the main result of Ps 147 referring to texts other than its neighbouring Psalms remains the same.

37 Cf. Risse 1995, 69–74 (Deut 4, esp. Deut 4:8); Sedlmeier 1996, 331–335, 339–340, 344–345 (Deut 4). For further literature see Brodersen 2013, 71–72.

38 Cf. Lohfink 1990, 119; Sedlmeier 1996, 352–355; Ballhorn 2004b, 313–314; Zenger 2008h, 835–836.

39 Cf. Zenger 2008h, 828 (Ps 147:12–20 earlier part).

Deut 4, this combination of the two plural nouns with וְ/"and" also occurs in
Deut 4:5, 14, 45. It is also prominent in Deut 5:1 (before the Ten Commandments)
and in Deut 6:1 (before the Shema Israel), and within HB it appears most frequently in Deuteronomy.[40] The reference to "decrees and judgements" in Deuteronomy 4[41] can be interpreted as a larger reference to the Torah in the general
sense of YHWH's law for Israel.[42] Deut 4:8 also shares the frequent words מִי/
"who", גּוֹי/"nation", גָּדוֹל/"great", כֹּל/"all", נָתַן/"giving" (same form) and פָּנִים/
"face" with Ps 147, and the wider context of Deut 4:1–8 includes the shared
words יִשְׂרָאֵל/"Israel", יהוה/"YHWH", אֱלֹהִים/"god", דָּבָר/"word" (as a synonym
to decrees and judgements), קֶרֶב/"midst", and קרא/"call". While the combination
of words is not unique to Ps 147 and Deut 4, it is likely that Ps 147 refers to Deut 4
since the combination most prominent in Deut probably refers to a law including
Deut,[43] and while Ps 147 could refer to other parts of Deut, Deut 4 fits the content
of Ps 147:19–20 best: Israel is the only nation to whom the Torah is given. While
the absolute date of Deut 4 is debated,[44] it may be earlier than the postexilic
Ps 147,[45] and the relative date also points towards a reference from Ps 147 to
Deut 4 rather than the other way round, since Ps 147 in terms of internal coherence contains a much more compressed reference to law than Deut, and in terms
of external coherence praise referring to the Torah is more likely than the Torah
referring to praise, as supported by the recurrence of references in Ps 147 and the
likely absolute dates.

Some commentators argue for references to *Job 38*, especially to Job 38:41
where young ravens cry.[46] However, others argue for general thematic similarities
only.[47] Job 38:41 shares the infrequent word עֹרֵב/"raven"[48] with Ps 147 in a similar
motif (young ravens crying for food, in Job: to God); מִי/"who" and כּוּן/"make
fast" are also shared. There is no syntactical similarity, and different words

40 Cf. Ringgren 1982, 152–153.
41 According to Braulik 1986, 41, 47–49, the two terms refer to the laws in Deut 5–28*; according to Christensen 2001, 79, in Deut 5–26; to the Torah according to Bultmann 2007, 139.
42 See fn. 38. The term "Torah" is here used in the general sense of YHWH's commandments for
Israel, not in the specific sense of the Pentateuch, for both cf. Watts 2009.
43 See fn. 41.
44 For the development of Deut from the 7th to 4th century BCE cf. Braulik 1986, 9–14; Bultmann
2007, 136–137. Deut 4 is at least partly exilic according to Bultmann 2007, 136–137, 139; partly
postexilic but also referring to the time of Solomon according to Braulik 1986, 39.
45 See V.1.6.
46 Cf. Risse 1995, 93–95; Lohfink 1990, 117; Seybold 2010, 158; Zenger 2008h, 833. For further
literature see Brodersen 2013, 55, 60, 66–67.
47 Cf. Gunkel 1926, 616; Sedlmeier 1996, 267 fn. 91, 270, 275.
48 Cf. Gesenius 2013, s.v. עֹרֵב.

are used for the same motif, e.g. עֵיד/"provision" instead of לֶחֶם/"food", יֶלֶד/
"child" instead of בֵּן/"son" for young ravens, and שׁוֵע/"cry" instead of קרא/
"cry". While other words are shared between Job 38 and Ps 147, including the
rare word כְּפוֹר/"hoarfrost" which only appears in Ps 147:16, Job 38:29, and
Ex 16:14, there is no syntactical similarity, wherefore a reference is unlikely.⁴⁹

Commentators often argue for a reference to *Psalm 33*,⁵⁰ especially a summary of Ps 33:16–19 in Ps 147:10–11,⁵¹ with consequences including the interpretation of Ps 147:10 as referring to war horses and warriors,⁵² and a late date of
Ps 147,⁵³ while others see limited if any influence.⁵⁴ In addition to the shared frequent words דָּבָר/"word", כֹּל/"all", מִשְׁפָּט/"judgement", אֶרֶץ/"earth", שָׁמַיִם/"heav-
en", עשׂה/"do", רוּחַ/"wind", כנס/"gather",⁵⁵ מַיִם/"water", נתן/"give", עמד/"stand",
גּוֹי/"nation", לֵב/"heart", אֱלֹהִים/"god", בֵּן/"son", אַיִן/"there is not", לֹא/"not", and
שֵׁם/"name", Ps 147:1 and Ps 33:1 share נָאוָה תְהִלָּה/"appropriate [is] praise" (only
in these two texts in HB) in syntactical similarity. Ps 147:7 and Ps 33:2 show some
syntactical similarity in the shared forms לַיהוָה/"to YHWH", בְּכִנּוֹר/"with a lyre",
and זַמְּרוּ/"make music!". רַב־כֹּחַ/"much of power" is shared in Ps 147:5 and
Ps 33:16 in syntactical similarity (though in Ps 33:16 this phrase is vocalised
with a noun רֹב/"multitude" as רָב־כֹּחַ/"multitude of power" as in Job 23:6;
30:18). Most importantly, in Ps 147:10–11 and Ps 33:16–18, יְרֵאָיו/"the ones fearing
him" is followed immediately by מְיַחֲלִים לְחַסְדּוֹ/"the ones waiting for his kindness" (phrase unique to Ps 147:11 and Ps 33:18) and preceded by words including
גִּבּוֹר/"warrior" (derived from גבר/"be strong" as גְּבוּרָה/"strength" in Ps 147:10),⁵⁶
הַסּוּס/"the horse", and יהוה/"YHWH". Given these recurrent syntactical similarities, an intertextual reference is likely. While both Psalms are probably postexilic,⁵⁷ more precise absolute dates are unknown for both. The direction of the reference has to be taken from relative dates. In terms of internal and external
coherence, it is likely that Ps 147 refers to Ps 33 rather than the other way
round since Ps 147:1 shows a more compressed syntax than Ps 33:1 (which has
an indirect object לַיְשָׁרִים/"for upright ones" to complement נָאוָה/"appropriate"),

49 Against Brodersen 2013, 55, 60, 66–67, 73.
50 Cf. Risse 1995, 85–88; Sedlmeier 1996, 29 fn. 43, 43, 221, 261 fn. 75. For further literature see
Brodersen 2013, 49–50, 53, 55–56, 57, 62–63, 67–69.
51 Cf. Lohfink 1990, 119; Kratz 1992, 14.
52 Cf. Hupfeld 1871, 447.
53 Cf. Sedlmeier 1996, 221–222, 233–234 (following Hossfeld and Zenger 1993); Zenger 2008h,
828 (possible common origin of Ps 33 and Ps 147:1–11).
54 Cf. Seybold 2010, 153–154, 159.
55 כנס/"gather", described as a rare word in Brodersen 2013, 53, is not unique to the two texts.
56 Cf. Gesenius 2013, s.v. גְּבוּר , s.v. גְּבוּרָה , s.v. גבר.
57 For Ps 33 cf. Zenger 1993c, 206 (postexilic); Rodd 2007, 377 (debated); for Ps 147 see V.1.6.

the attribute of power in Ps 147:5 is more likely to be transferred from a warrior to YHWH, and Ps 147:10 – 11 seem like a compressed summary of Ps 33:16 – 18. Ps 147 also has references to other texts.[58] Thus, the intertextual references from Ps 147 to Ps 33 lead to the likely translation of נָאוָה/"appropriate" in Ps 147:1 as in Ps 33:1 as an adjective, the stress of YHWH's power as opposed to military (rather than any other) power in Ps 147:10 – 11 as in Ps 33:16 – 18. רוּחַ/"wind" alludes to YHWH's breath in Ps 147:18 as in Ps 33:6, דְּבָר/"word" to the continual order of creation in Ps 147 as in Ps 33.[59]

Commentators hold the view that Ps 147 refers to *Psalm 104*,[60] with consequences including a late date of Ps 147,[61] or a stress of the separation of food for animals and humans in Ps 147.[62] Ps 104 and Ps 147 share ברך/"bless", יהוה/ "YHWH", אֱלֹהִים/"god", שָׁמַיִם/"heaven", מַיִם/"water", שׂים/"put", עָב/"cloud", רוּחַ/"wind", עשה/"do", אֶרֶץ/"earth", בַּל/"not", כסה/"cover", הַר/"mountain", עמד/"stand", גְּבוּל/"border", שלח/"send", כֹּל/"all", שבר/"break", נתן/"give", שבע/"be satisfied", בְּהֵמָה/"animal", לֶחֶם/"food", פָּנִים/"face", ידע/"know", גָּדוֹל/ "great", טוֹב/"good", זמר/"make music", and רָשָׁע/"wicked" (plural). Ps 147:5 and Ps 104:25 share אֵין מִסְפָּר/"there is no number" (though this phrase is not unique to these two texts), and Ps 147:8 and Ps 104:14 both collocate a hif'il participle of צמח/"grow" with חָצִיר/"grass" (uniquely, but in different word orders). The Psalms also share a final הַלְלוּ־יָהּ/"Praise-Yah!". However, the syntactical similarities do not suffice for a clear reference to Ps 104, it can only be assumed.

References to *Psalm 135* are seen by some commentators, while others see the similarities as based on the same genre only.[63] Ps 135 and Ps 147 share the frequent words הלל/"praise", שֵׁם/"name", יהוה/"YHWH", עמד/"stand", אֱלֹהִים/ "god", ידע/"know", יַעֲקֹב/"Jacob", יִשְׂרָאֵל/"Israel", גָּדוֹל/"great", אֲדֹנֵינוּ/"our Lord" (same form), כֹּל/"all", חפץ/"take pleasure", עשה/"do", שָׁמַיִם/"heaven", אֶרֶץ/ "earth", מָטָר/"rain", רוּחַ/"wind", בְּהֵמָה/"animal", שלח/"send", גּוֹי/"nation", רַב/ "much", נתן/"give", לֹא/"not", אֵין/"there is not", ברך/"bless", ירא/"fear", צִיּוֹן/ "Zion", and יְרוּשָׁלַם/"Jerusalem". Ps 135:3 and Ps 147:1 share the phrases הַלְלוּ־יָהּ כִּי־טוֹב/"Praise-Yah! For good" (the combination כִּי־טוֹב/"for good" is frequent in HB) and כִּי נָעִים/"for pleasant" (also in Prov 22:18) as well as the words יהוה/

---

58 See p. 185 – 186.

59 See p. 195 – 197.

60 Cf. Duhm 1922, 476 – 480; Gunkel 1926, 616; Risse 1995, 88 – 90; Sedlmeier 1996, 43, 268 – 270. For further literature see Brodersen 2013, 56, 60.

61 Cf. Zenger 2008h, 828 (Ps 146 and Ps 147:1 – 11 may have the same origin).

62 Cf. Kratz 1992, 14 – 15; Zenger 2008h, 832 – 833.

63 Cf. Risse 1995, 86 – 87 (fn. 4) (same genre only); Sedlmeier 1996, 258 (reference). For further literature see Brodersen 2013, 50 esp. fn. 78, 56, 63.

"YHWH" and זמר/"make music" (though in Ps 135:3 the adjective refers to YHWH rather than his praise).[64] The Psalms also share an opening and a final הַלְלוּ־יָהּ/ "Praise-Yah!". The syntactical similarities do not suffice for a clear reference to Ps 135, it can only be assumed.

Some commentators argue for a reference from *Psalm 146* to Psalm 147.[65] Others argue for a reference in the opposite direction from Ps 147 to Ps 146,[66] to the extent that Ps 146 and Ps 147 are called "twin Psalms".[67] Some even maintain that Ps 146 and Ps 147:1–11 were written by the same people,[68] while others merely stress their common reference texts.[69] Most notably, Ps 146 and Ps 147 share the rare verb עוד/"surround" in its only two poʿlel forms "to lift up", though the verb does appear in other forms in HB,[70] and the phrase אֱלֹהַיִךְ צִיּוֹן/ "your God, Zion" which is unique to the two Psalms within HB, though a similar phrase with these two forms occurs in Isa 52:7.[71] The Psalms also share the frequent words זמר/"make music", אֱלֹהִים/"god", יהוה/"YHWH" (including in the collocation אֶת־יְהוָה/"YHWH"), כֹּל/"all", אַיִן/"there is not", רָשָׁע/"wicked" (plural), אֶרֶץ/"earth", שָׁמַיִם/"heaven", נתן/"give" (singular participle נֹתֵן/"giving"), לֶחֶם/ "food", בֵּן/"son", הלל/"to praise" (including the female הַלְלִי/"praise!" appearing only in Ps 146:1 and 147:12), רוּחַ/"wind", יַעֲקֹב/"Jacob", מִשְׁפָּט/"judgement", and עשׂה/"do". There is little syntactical similarity, wherefore, apart from the shared frame הַלְלוּ־יָהּ/"Praise-Yah!", a reference is unlikely.

Intertextual links with *Psalm 148* (see p. 140–141 on Ps 147), *Psalm 149* (see p. 95 on Ps 147), and *Psalm 150* (see p. 39 on Ps 147) are unlikely.

Ps 147 is often argued to refer to to *Isaiah*, especially Isa 11:12; 40:7, 26–28; 54:12; 55:10–11; 56:8; 61:1, and thus primarily to Second (Isa 40–55) but also Third Isaiah (Isa 56–66).[72] Consequences include a stress on monotheism and

---

64 Also see p. 188–189.

65 Cf. Reindl 1981a, 124; Lohfink 1990, 113–114 (consequence of identification of poor ones and Israel in Ps 146); Sedlmeier 1996, 22 (referring to Lohfink), 243 fn. 16, 284 (Ps 147:12–20 as a later addition could be contemporary with Ps 146); Leuenberger 2004, 348–350 (especially the later Ps 147:1–11). For further literature see Brodersen 2013, 58, 63–64.

66 Cf. Kselman 1988, 597, 589; Kratz 1992, 19; Ballhorn 2004b, 310–314.

67 The German original "Zwillingspsalmen" was coined by Zimmerli 1972, and is applied to Ps 146–147 by Ballhorn 2004b, 311, 314. This is criticised by Scaiola 2010b, 706, who nevertheless argues for a close connection.

68 Cf. Zenger 2008g, esp. 822, also 813–815, 821; Zenger 2008h, 827–828.

69 Cf. Kratz 1992, 16.

70 Cf. Gesenius 2013, s.v. עוד₁.

71 Noted by Reindl 1981a, 124.

72 Cf. Hupfeld 1871, 444; Duhm 1922, 476–480; Gunkel 1926, 615–616; Lohfink 1990, 119; Risse 1995, 75–84; Sedlmeier 1996, 185–191, 196–201, 216, 251–257, 270, 272, 277, 312–314, 343. For

the end of the exile,[73] but due to Isa 61:1 also inner-Israelite tensions between "poor" and "wicked",[74] prophecies fulfilled and thus not eschatological any more[75] or with an eschatological outlook being secondary in the context of the Final Hallel[76] or on the contrary an eschatological assumption in both Isaiah and Ps 147,[77] and a postexilic date of Ps 147.[78] Other commentators see few explicit references and more common topics.[79] Most importantly, in Isa 40, Isa 40:26 – 28 shows syntactical similarity in לְכֻלָּם/"for all of them" and יִקְרָא/"he calls" combined with מִסְפָּר/"number" and שֵׁם/"name" and followed by רֹב/"muchness" and כֹּחַ/"power" in the same verse Isa 40:26 as in Ps 147:4–5. Isa 40:26 also shares the frequent words מִי/"who", אִישׁ/"man", לֹא/"not" with Ps 147. Isa 40:27 contains the shared words יַעֲקֹב/"Jacob" and יִשְׂרָאֵל/"Israel", יהוה/ "YHWH", אֱלֹהִים/"god", and מִשְׁפָּט/"judgement". Given the syntactical similarity, a reference is likely. Since Ps 147 is postexilic[80] while Isa 40 is probably exilic,[81] the absolute date points into the direction of a reference from Ps 147 to Isa 40, but since the dating of Ps 147 partly depends on this reference, relative dates have to be taken into account. In terms of internal and external coherence, it is also likely that Ps 147 refers to Isa 40 rather than the other way round: In Isa 40:27 Israel is lamenting God's absence, whereas in Ps 147 it is praising his presence. In terms of internal coherence Ps 147:4–5 contains a more compressed image than Isa 40:26–28, and while in terms of external coherence praise can be turned into lament,[82] Ps 147 may praise the fulfillment of a past promise, which given the recurrence of references in Ps 147 and the likely absolute dates is more likely. The reference to Isa 40:26–28 stresses God's power and creation, his power to care for Israel, and the fulfillment of his promises.[83] There are further possible references to Isa 40: Isa 40:7 shares the rare word נֹשֵׁב/

---

further passages and literature see Brodersen 2013, 52–54, 56–58, 60–61, 65, 67, 69, 71, 73–74. Against Brodersen 2013, Isa 9:7; 11:4; 26:5; 30:26; 44:23, 26, 28; 49:13; 60:17, are unlikely to be reference texts since there is no syntactical similarity. The same applies to Isa 11:12; 54:12; 55:10–11; 56:8; 61:1 as discussed below. On the terms Second and Third Isaiah cf. Coggins 2007, 433.

73 Cf. Zenger 2008h, 828, 830–831, 835.
74 Cf. Zenger 2008h, 832.
75 Cf. Kratz 1992, 20 fn. 62.
76 Cf. Zenger 2008h, 835.
77 Cf. Duhm 1922, 477.
78 Cf. Kratz 1992, 21.
79 Cf. Gerstenberger 2001, 443, 445.
80 See V.1.6.
81 Cf. Coggins 2007, 433; Berges 2008, 43–45.
82 Cf. Kynes 2012 (Job referring to Psalms), aspect missing in Brodersen 2013, 56–57.
83 See p. 191.

"blow" (only in these two texts and in Gen 15:11) which only in these two texts is combined with YHWH and his רוּחַ/"wind". The verse also shares the frequent words חָצִיר/"grass", יהוה/"YHWH", דָּבָר/"word" and אֱלֹהִים/"god" with Ps 147. Given the rare combination of words, a reference is likely, and given the arguments mentioned for Isa 40:26–28, Ps 147 is more likely to refer to Isa 40:7 than the other way round. Outside Isa 40, Isa 54:12 shares the frequent words גְּבוּל/"territory" (same form גְּבוּלֵךְ/"your territory", used only in these two texts, in both with reference to Jerusalem), שַׁעַר/"gate" (same form שְׁעָרַיִךְ/"your gates" with reference to Jerusalem, though this is not unique to the two texts, see e. g. Ps 122:2), כֹּל/"all", and חֵפֶץ/"pleasure" (of the root חפץ/"take pleasure") with Ps 147. However, there is little syntactical similarity, with only one form of a frequent word uniquely shared, wherefore a reference is unlikely. Isa 55:10–11 share שֶׁלֶג/"snow", שָׁמַיִם/"heaven", לֹא/"not", אֶרֶץ/"earth", צמח/"grow", נתן/"give", לֶחֶם/"food", כֵּן/"thus", דָּבָר/"word", עשה/"do", חפץ/"take pleasure",שלח/"send". However, גֶּשֶׁם/"rain" is used rather than מָטָר/"rain", and there is no syntactical similarity, wherefore a reference is unlikely. Isa 61:1 shares the frequent words רוּחַ/"wind", אָדֹן/"Lord", יהוה/"YHWH", עָנִי/"poor",שלח/"send", חבש/"bind", שבר/"break", לֵב/"heart" (in a similar construct form נִשְׁבְּרֵי־לֵב/"broken ones of heart"; the collocation of a participle of שבר/"break" in construct with לֵב/"heart" also appears in Ps 34:19 and 51:19, of which Ps 34:19 has the same form as Isa 61:1), and קרא/"call" with Ps 147. There is limited syntactical similarity with Ps 147, and a reference is unlikely. The phrase נִדְחֵי יִשְׂרָאֵל/"the scattered ones of Israel" is shared with Ps 147:2 with only two other texts in HB: Isa 11:12 shares נִדְחֵי יִשְׂרָאֵל/"the scattered ones of Israel" and the frequent words גּוֹי/"nation" and אֶרֶץ/"earth" with Ps 147. Isa 56:8 shares the same phrase נִדְחֵי יִשְׂרָאֵל/"the scattered ones of Israel" and the frequent words אָדֹן/"Lord" and יהוה/"YHWH" with Ps 147. A reference to both Isa 11:12 and Isa 56:8 is unlikely since there is little syntactical similarity and the phrase is shared by three rather than just two texts.

Results

References to Job 38 are unlikely. Ps 146; 148; 149; 150 show no references except the framing Hallelujahs. However, there are references to Deut 4; Isa 40 (namely 40:7, 26–28); and Ps 33. References to Ps 104 and 135 are possible but remain unclear. The references to Deut 4; Isa 40; and Ps 33 insert a reference to the *Torah*, and to the *fulfillment of prophecies*, and strengthen the aspects of *universal creation combined with help for Israel and the powerless*. The references may also point to a *postexilic* date of Ps 147 after the 6th century BCE based on the assumption of such a postexilic date of Isa 40 (dates for Deut 4 and Ps 33 are debated). They further confirm the unity of Ps 147^MT as they are found in both Ps 147:1–11 (Ps 33, Isa 40) and Ps 147:12–20 (Ps 33, Isa 40, and Deut 4).

No references are likely to Ps 1–2 or (except for the framing Hallelujahs) *Ps 146–150,* and *in contrast to Ps 148–150, Ps 147 does show other references, including references to Psalm 33 which is not a neighbouring Psalm in MT,* thus weakening the case for an original connection of Ps 146–150. In its inclusion of references it is *similar to Ps 146* (see p. 240), but Ps 104 is the only reference text possibly shared between the two Psalms, and unlike in Ps 146 there is no reference to Ps 145. Since there are also no references between Ps 146 and Ps 147, they may be of a similar time and genre but too different to be twin Psalms.

V.1.4 Content of Psalm 147^MT

Beginning of Psalm 147:1^MT
The beginning of Psalm 147 raises several syntactical questions:

(a) Is הַלְלוּ יָהּ a superscription "Hallelujah!" or a part of the first sentence "Praise Yah!"?
(b) Is (thus) כִּי a causal conjunction "for" or an affirmative particle "yea"?[84]
(c) How is the form זַמְּרָה/"to make music" to be parsed?
(d) To which words do the adjectives טוֹב/"good", נָעִים/"pleasant", and נָאוָה/"appropriate" refer?

Regarding (a): If הַלְלוּ יָהּ is a *superscription* "Hallelujah!" only, the Psalm begins with a *statement without a call to praise:* Praise is good. This interpretation is supported by the context within the Psalter: הַלְלוּ־יָהּ/"Praise-Yah!" does not only frame Ps 147 but also all of the final five Psalms 146–150.[85] In all other Psalms within Psalms 146–150, the opening Hallelujah is followed by another imperative starting a sentence which calls to praise; thus the opening Hallelujah can be understood as a superscription.

However, given the different contexts in which Ps 147 can be proven to have been written in the oldest preserved manuscripts,[86] it is unlikely that Ps 147:1 "never opened an independent Psalm"[87] and thus the reading as an imperative

---

84 Cf. Gesenius 2013, s.v. כִּי.
85 Thus Allen 1983, 305 (all Hallelujahs redactional).
86 See V.2, esp. V.2.2.
87 Zenger 2008h, 825 (Ps 147:1–11 written for Final Hallel).

can simply be ignored based on a hypothesis about its origin. Ps 147 may also have started with הַלְלוּ־יָהּ/"Praise-Yah!" and because of this beginning later been integrated with Psalms 146–150.[88]

The context within Ps 147 also makes it likely that it is opened with an imperative: הלל/"praise" followed by כִּי/"for/yea" does not only appear in v.1 but also in v.12 where הלל/"praise" is unambiguously used in an imperative form. The imperatives in v.1, 7, and 12 structure the Psalm, while v.1 together with v.20 also frames it. If הַלְלוּ־יָהּ/"Praise-Yah!" is read as a superscription, כִּי/"yea" in v.1 has to be read deictically and vv.1–6 are detached in terms of content ("Praise is good. YHWH takes action.") until v.7 where a call to praise is found. This is possible, but unlikely. The connection of a call to praise with הלל/"praise" in an imperative form followed by כִּי/"for" introducing reasons for praise is marked in vv.12–13 by feminine singular forms in both verses. Without an imperative in v.1, v.7 would have to release the tension of the pending vv.1–6 as well as introducing vv.8–11. Without the context of Psalms 146–150, this assumption seems unnecessarily complicated. Thus, Ps 147:1 does not begin with a superscription "Hallelujah" but the *imperative* "Praise Yah!".[89]

Regarding (b): Following this imperative, does כִּי introduce a statement "yea, praise is good" or a reason for the call to praise "for praise is good"?

Within Ps 147, כִּי is used also in v.13, where it is followed immediately by perfect forms describing YHWH's actions giving reasons for praise. Thus, in v.13 כִּי is best translated as "for" as the causal conjunction typical for the genre of hymns.[90] In contrast, v.1 contains כִּי twice within the same verse that also contains the call to praise itself. Thus, it does not give reasons for the call to praise, but underlines the call to praise itself through the statement that praise is good. Such a statement is not unique to Ps 147. A similar statement about praise can be found in Ps 92:1–4.[91] There, it is followed by כִּי/"for" in Ps 92:5 introducing YHWH's actions as reasons for praise.

Overall, in Ps 147:1 כִּי is best translated as an affirmative "yea". Reasons for the affirmed call to praise are then given from v.2 onwards.[92]

---

88 Thus Sedlmeier 1996, 62–63. Ballhorn 2004b, 310, argues that the imperative is part of Ps 147 wherefore the Psalm may have been written for the Final Hallel.

89 Similarly with liturgical assumptions Gerstenberger 2001, 442; Ballhorn 2004b, 310. Cf. also Gunkel 1926, 615, with the assumption that a hymn cannot start with כִּי/"for", but see on (b).

90 See V.1.5.

91 Cf. Risse 1995, 98–107, esp. 104–105.

92 The view of a twofold use of כִּי within Ps 147 is also adopted by Kuntz 1999, 162, 165, 169–170 (emphatic interjection v.1, causal conjunction v.13); despite reading a superscription by Allen 1983, 305; Zenger 2008h, 825, 830.

Regarding (c): The form זִמְרָה/"to make music" is a piʿel infinitive feminine construct which otherwise is found only in Lev 26:18 and Ezek 16:52.[93] The infinitive here is used as a noun and subject.[94] It is unlikely that זַמְּרָה is an augmented imperative piʿel singular masculine[95] "do make music!" since this form is not found anywhere else, and would lead to a tension between the singular form and the plural forms הַלְלוּ־יָהּ/"Praise-Yah!" and אֱלֹהֵינוּ/"our God".[96]

Regarding (d): טוֹב/"good" refers to זִמְרָה/"to make music".[97] In nominal clauses, preceding adjectives often remain uninflected,[98] wherefore the adjective is masculine while the reference word is feminine.

נָעִים/"pleasant" could also refer to זִמְרָה/"to make music" for the following reasons: כִּי with an adjective can form a complete nominal clause (see e. g. Gen 1 repeatedly כִּי טוֹב/"that it was good"). With נָעִים/"pleasant" such a clause is found in Ps 135:5 and Prov 22:18. In addition, the repetition of כִּי/"yea" with a following adjective in Ps 147:1 makes it likely that both adjectives refer to the same word, זִמְרָה/"to make music". Ps 147:1 could then be translated as "Praise Yah! Yea, good [is it] to make music to our God; yea, pleasant [is it]; appropriate [is] praise." However, it is more likely that נָעִים/"pleasant" like נָאוָה/"appropriate" refers to תְהִלָּה/"praise", given the synonymous parallelism of v.1ab (which is split by an atnaḥ). נָעִים/"pleasant" is masculine despite its reference to the feminine noun תְהִלָּה/"praise" because as above it is preceding its noun in a nominal clause. If the reference word of multiple adjectives is feminine, it is possible that only the adjective placed closest to the reference word is also feminine,[99] which in Ps 147:1 (as in Ps 33:1) applies to נָאוָה/"appropriate". In addition to the parallel in Ps 33:1, the fact that the form נָאוָה/"appropriate" can be verified in HB as a feminine adjective only[100] speaks against the interpretation of נָאוָה/ "to beautify" as an otherwise unknown infinitive piʿel.[101] Even with such an infinitive, the half-verses would not be entirely parallel: אֱלֹהֵינוּ/"our God" is an accusative object of זמר/"make music",[102] while תְהִלָּה/"praise" would have to be

---

93 Cf. Gesenius and Kautzsch 1909, §52p.

94 Cf. Gesenius and Kautzsch 1909, §114a.

95 Cf. Gesenius and Kautzsch 1909, §48i; Joüon and Muraoka 2011, §48d.

96 Cf. Hupfeld 1871, 443–444.

97 Hupfeld 1871, 443, states that טוֹב/"good" in the Psalter is used only for God, but while this is correct e. g. for Ps 106:1; 135:3, it is not for Ps 92:2; 133:1.

98 Cf. Gesenius and Kautzsch 1909, §145r.

99 Cf. Gesenius and Kautzsch 1909, §145t.

100 Cf. Gesenius 2013, s.v. נאה, s.v. נָאוֶה.

101 Infinitive piʿel assumed by Risse 1995, 20–22; Sedlmeier 1996, 21 (to beautify praise); Zenger 2008h, 825–826. Against this van der Ploeg 1974, 492.

102 Cf. Gesenius 2013, s.v. זמר₂.

read as an adverbial accusative with the object taken over from the previous half-verse: "Yea, good [is it] to make music to our God; yea, pleasant [is it] to beautify [him] [with] praise."

Overall, all adjectives in v.1 refer to the praise of God (as e.g. Ps 81:3; 92:2) and not to God himself (as e.g. Ps 106:1; 135:3). Thus, following the call to praise Ps 147:1 merely states that praise is good without giving reasons.[103] It can therefore be expected that reasons are provided in the following verses.

Who is called to praise in Psalm 147:1–2^{MT}?

Who is called to praise by the plural imperative הַלְלוּ־יָהּ/"Praise-Yah!"; and to whom does to plural suffix of אֱלֹהֵינוּ/"our God" refer? Ps 147:1 does not provide any hints except that the Psalmist is a part of the group called to praise, and that "Yah" is identified with "our God". A first person plural suffix is found not only in v.1 but also in vv.5 and 7. In v.12, Jerusalem is identified with Zion and called to praise. In v.20 another call to praise in a plural form is found. The synonymous parallelisms in v.7 and v.12 identify "YHWH = our God = Jerusalem's God = Zion's God",[104] which also implies the identification of "we" with "Jerusalem = Zion". The personified city of Jerusalem in v.12 is thus used as a metonymy for its inhabitants which are mentioned in v.13 as its "sons". Thus, called to praise are the "sons of Jerusalem" which again can be identified with "we".[105] In the entire Psalm, reasons for praise exist for all those people who benefit from YHWH's actions: "we", i.e. the ones referring to "our God" (vv.1, 5, 7), Jerusalem = Zion (vv.2, 12–13) and its sons (v.13), Israel = Jacob (vv.2, 19), broken ones (v.3), poor ones (v.6), and pious ones (v.11). The structure of the Psalm makes it likely that all these words refer to one and the same group of people which is called to praise. "We" and "Jerusalem = Zion" are to be found immediately within the calls to praise in vv.1, 7, and 12. "Jacob = Israel" is stressed in the antithesis preceding the call to praise in v.20. The broken ones are connected with YHWH in vv.1–2 through the article at the beginning of v.3. The name of God YHWH connects the poor ones in v.6 and the pious ones in v.11 with the calls to praise in the following verse in both cases. The poor ones in v.6 additionally follow "we" in "our God" in v.5. The first (v.2) and last

---

103 For postbiblical traditions explaining the value of praise cf. Risse 1995, 104–107; Risse 1999a.
104 See p. 177–178.
105 See p. 193–194.

(v.19) beneficiaries are both "Israel". All these observations suggest that the different beneficiaries all designate the *people Israel*.[106]

What are the reasons for praise in Psalm 147:2 – 3^MT?

Among the reasons of praise expected after v.1, the first one is the building of Jerusalem. Jerusalem in v.2a probably refers to the city: While בנה/"build" can be used for human communities, it usually refers to buildings.[107] However, the following v.2b connects the gathering of the scattered community of Israel and the building of Jerusalem. Both actions benefit the people Israel.

Vv.2 – 3 paint a picture of YHWH as a builder, shepherd, doctor, and comforter. With YHWH as its *builder* (the same image is used in Ps 51:20), Jerusalem is under his protection as in ANE traditions.[108] Like a *shepherd* he gathers the scattered community of Israel,[109] an image also found in Isa 40:11, Jer 31 and Ezek 34. V.3 connects two images: רפא/"heal" and חבש/"bind" are not used for external wounds but for internal pain, namely שְׁבוּרֵי לֵב/"broken ones of heart" (where "heart" can stand for the entire existence of a human being)[110] and עַצֶּבֶת/"pain, grief". This connects the images of a *doctor* and a *comforter*, looking after both external and internal wounds. Ps 147 does not include information about the origin of these wounds. Given the references to Isaiah,[111] the destruction of Jerusalem and the Babylonian exile may be the cause of these wounds (described at length in Lamentations).[112] However, the general statements in Ps 147[113] make it likely that the four images are not restricted to postexilic healing but serve the general praise of YHWH's actions for Israel.[114]

---

106 Thus Risse 1995, 102–104. For further literature see Brodersen 2013, 52 fn. 79. Ballhorn 2004b, 310–314, specifies Israel still affected by the exile. However, the Psalm contains general statements, see p. 173–177, V.1.6.
107 Cf. Gesenius 2013, s.v. בנה. Against Sedlmeier 1996, 348 (Israel); Ballhorn 2004b, 314 (referring to Sedlmeier), the mention of gates in v.13 marks the image of an actual city.
108 Cf. Keel 1996, 105–107; Zenger 2008h, 830.
109 Cf. Zenger 2008h, 830.
110 Cf. Fabry 1984.
111 See p. 183–185 on Isa.
112 Cf. Gerstenberger 2001, 443.
113 See p. 173–177.
114 Thus Ballhorn 2004b, 314; Zenger 2008h, 830–831. Gunkel 1926, 615 argues for a future rebuilding and a date at which Jerusalem is still in ruins after the Babylonian destruction, in contrast Allen 1983, 305, argues for a "later standpoint" praising YHWH as a past rebuilder.

What are the reasons for praise in Psalm 147:4–5^{MT}?

V.4 states that YHWH generally counts and calls the stars, not just once at their creation. Whether he even created them is no concern of Ps 147. Nowhere in HB does YHWH win power over the stars after their creation. Rather, passages like Ps 8:4, Ps 148:3, 5, and most importantly Psalm 147's reference text Isa 40:26, 28 explicitly mention YHWH's creation of the stars. Therefore, Ps 147 probably refers to this creation: Because YHWH created the stars, he has lasting power over them and can generally count and call them. According to Gen 15:5, no human being can count or name the stars. YHWH, in contrast, commands the stars like an army.[115] The reference to Isa 40:26–28 also implies that if YHWH can count all the stars, he can easily count all the scattered members of Israel.[116] Calling them with names shows that YHWH is the creator and owner of the stars.[117] In the ANE, stars were worshipped as gods,[118] but in Ps 147 is seems obvious that stars are no gods, polemic against stars as gods is unnecessary.[119] In אֲדוֹנֵינוּ/"our Lord", this powerful commander of the stars is emphatically identified with the God of Israel.

What are the reasons for praise in Psalm 147:6^{MT}?

YHWH supports the poor ones.[120] Within Ps 147, they can be identified with the people Israel: v.6 stands between "our Lord" in v.5 and "our God" in v.7 and is connected to the latter through יהוה/"YHWH" who both in content and colon stands on the side of the poor. There is no hint that the wicked ones are to be found within the people Israel, but rather in vv.19–20 the antithesis of Israel and other nations is included. Thus, the wicked ones are probably external enemies.[121]

---

115 Cf. Hupfeld 1871, 444.
116 Cf. Hupfeld 1871, 444.
117 In Isa 43:1, God calls his people Israel by their name. On such statements of ownership cf. Berges 2008, 154–155; against this Hupfeld 1871, 445.
118 Cf. Zenger 2008h, 831–832 (Marduk's power over stars in Enuma Elish).
119 Thus Risse 1995, 77–78; Gerstenberger 2001, 443.
120 On poor ones generally cf. Lohfink 1990, 115–120.
121 Cf., though all also mentioning the possibility of inner-Israelite enemies, Risse 1995, 166–167; Sedlmeier 1996, 235–237; Zenger 2008h, 832.

Who is called to praise in Psalm 147:7^{MT}?

Like the first call to praise in v.1, v.7 is addressed to the people Israel. With עֱנוּ/ "answer" and תּוֹדָה/"thanksgiving", the second call to praise focusses on a call to be thankful for the following actions.[122] While כִּנּוֹר/"lyre" is sometimes seen to refer to cult,[123] it is also used in various other contexts.[124]

What are the reasons for praise in Psalm 147:8–9^{MT}?

While clouds in the sky, rain for the earth, and mountains with grass appear in a natural order, vv.8–9 do not emphasise this order but the dependence of every part of it on YHWH:[125] He gives clouds, he gives rain, he gives grass, and he gives animals their food. Thus, the verses are theocentric: Nature is entirely dependent on YHWH, YHWH always is the subject. כסה/"cover" can also mean "to clothe", but the context does not imply a personification of the heaven. A double accusative[126] at the end of v.8 depends on the hifʿil הַמַּצְמִיחַ/"the one making grow": YHWH lets mountains grow with grass.

Without asking for anything in return, YHWH gives food even to young ravens, who (unlike in Ps 146^{LXX}, and in Job 38:41) do not call "him" but simply "call"[127] or (since they are ravens) "caw", and who according to Lev 11:15 and Deut 14:14 are unclean animals.[128] Humans and human labour are not mentioned in Ps 147 (unlike in Ps 146^{LXX} and in Ps 104:14).[129] Thus, the collective term בְּהֵמָה/ "animal" is more likely to refer to animals generally than specifically domestic animals.[130] Ravens are described using words also related to humans: לֶחֶם/ "food, bread" is used for animal food, קרא/"call" for the cawing of ravens, and בֵּן/"son" for nestlings.[131] The last word is used in v.13 for the sons of Jerusa-

---

122 Cf. Risse 1995, 100–101; Zenger 2008h, 832.

123 Thus Risse 1995, 99 (second temple cult); Brodersen 2013, 59, 78 (following Risse).

124 See p. 48–52.

125 Cf. Sedlmeier 1996, 262, 269.

126 Cf. Gesenius and Kautzsch 1909, §117cc.

127 The crying could also refer to the food "for which they cry" parallel to v.9a, thus Brucker 2011a, 1880. Both options are possible, cf. Gesenius and Kautzsch 1909, §138, but the relative particle is more likely to refer to the subject, i.e. the ravens, than to an omitted object.

128 Cf. Zenger 2008h, 833.

129 Cf. Zenger 2008h, 833.

130 Cf. Gesenius 2013, s.v. בְּהֵמָה. This is different in Ps 148:10 where wild and domestic animals are contrasted, see p. 146.

131 Cf. Risse 1995, 152–153; Risse 1999b, 388; Zenger 2008h, 833 (referring to Risse 1999b).

lem, i.e. Israel, pointing towards the image of ravens as also alluding to Israel.[132] קרא/"call" also connects the ravens with YHWH: At the end of v.4, YHWH יִקְרָא/ "calls", at the end of v.9 the ravens (which may allude to Israel) יִקְרָאוּ/"call". It is unlikely that Ps 147 here refers to God calling his creatures and his creatures calling him since the ravens do not call him but just call, and the creation of animals does not feature in Ps 147. It is more likely that God who himself calls and is always successful in his calling will also hear even the aimless calling of ravens (and humans). All of nature depends on YHWH rather than different individual gods for different natural elements.[133] YHWH is the only existing God.

A double accusative[134] at the end of v.8 depends on the hifʿil הַמַּצְמִיחַ/"the one making grow": YHWH lets mountains grow with grass.

What are the reasons for praise in Psalm 147:10 – 11^MT?
The image of a war horse is also found in Job 39:15 – 24 (using סוּס/"horse" and גְּבוּרָה/"strength" in Job 39:19). שׁוֹק/"lower leg" is a rare word in HB.[135] Its use in Cant 5:15 and Isa 47:7 as well as ANE images make it likely that the word refers specifically to lower legs rather than just legs.[136] Strong lower legs point to the strength of a *warrior* as emphasised in the reference text Ps 33:16 (they may also point to a warrior's speed as in Am 2:14 – 16).[137] However, as shown in vv.4 – 5, YHWH's strength is matchless. Horses, horsemen, war chariots and warriors frequently appear in HB as YHWH's inferior opponents, e.g. in Ex 15:1, Ps 20:8 – 9, Isa 31:1 – 3, Ezek 39:20, and Zech 9:10.

Who is called to praise in Psalm 147:12^MT?
Jerusalem, in the third call to praise identified with Zion, is mentioned as the first beneficiary of YHWH's actions in v.2a followed by Israel in v.2b. These

---

132 An allusion to the poor only, thus Lohfink 1990, 118, is unlikely for Ps 147: קרא/"call" stands for the crying of a עָנִי/"poor" in Deut 25:15 only, there explicitly with אֶל־יְהוָה/"to YHWH".
133 Cf. Keck 1996, 1268.
134 Cf. Gesenius and Kautzsch 1909, §117cc.
135 Cf. Gesenius 2013, s.v. שׁוֹק.
136 For an image cf. e.g. Keel 1996, 219. Assyrian palace decorations show numerous war horses and warriors with strong lower legs (the rest of their legs is covered by garments), cf. e.g. Collins 2008, esp. 40 – 41, 114 – 115. Further research on such images is desirable.
137 The view of military imagery is adopted by Hupfeld 1871, 447; Gunkel 1926, 616; Zenger 2008h, 833 – 834. Gerstenberger 2001, 444, sees sexual as well as military overtones; Scaiola 2010b, 708, also assumes a sexual reference. However, the reference text Ps 33 marks military imagery only.

two beneficiaries are repeated in Part III: Jerusalem is addressed in v.12, Israel is mentioned in v.19. The personification of Jerusalem or Zion is frequently found in Isaiah, e. g. in the whole chapters of Isa 54 and 66. Imperatives addressed to Jerusalem = Zion appear in Isa 40:9 and Isa 52:1.[138] "Our God" as well as "Jerusalem's = Zion's God" is YHWH, and the personified city of Jerusalem stands as a metonymy for the people Israel addressed in the previous calls to praise.[139]

What are the reasons for praise in Psalm 147:13 – 14^MT^?

The address of Jerusalem in v.12 is continued in vv.13 – 14 with reasons for praise introduced by כִּי/"for": Jerusalem is provided by YHWH with protection and blessing (in perfect forms), and peace and finest food (in participles and imperfect forms).[140] There is no indication of this being a future promise.[141] "Your territory" in v.14a is an accusativus loci,[142] the hif'il form in v.14b is combined with a double accusative.[143] In Ps 122, Jerusalem is addressed and wished שָׁלוֹם/"peace" as the city in which all of Israel gathers to praise YHWH. The fastening of bars requires the existence of city walls and gates. Since the gates are the most vulnerable part of a city's defences, their barring is especially important for safety.[144] Gates and their bars are built by humans in Neh 3. In Ps 147, Jerusalem is under the protection of YHWH himself.[145] The image of Jerusalem as a mother also appears in Isa 54 and Isa 66:10 – 14,[146] "your sons" are the people Israel (multiple times in Isa 49; 51; 54; 60; 62). In Ps 149:2, Israel and Zion's sons are explicitly identified with each other.[147] Ps 147 also points towards the identification of Jerusalem's sons with the people Israel.

---

138 Cf. Risse 1995, 103–104.
139 In Zeph 3:14 Jerusalem, Zion, and Israel are equated. Gerstenberger 2001, 444–445, points out that Jerusalem is still addressed ("your") rather than speaking ("my") in vv.13–14.
140 Cf. Risse 1995, 118–124. On verbal forms see p. 173–177.
141 Against Zenger 2008h, 835.
142 Cf. Gesenius and Kautzsch 1909, §118d.
143 Cf. Gesenius and Kautzsch 1909, §117cc.
144 Cf. Risse 1995, 118–120.
145 Cf. Keel 1996, 105–107.
146 Cf. Zenger 2008h, 834–835.
147 See p. 89.

What are the reasons for praise in Psalm 147:15–18^MT?

In vv.15 and 18, YHWH sends דְּבָרוֹ/"his word" which in v.15 is identified with אִמְרָתוֹ/"his saying"[148] and in v.18 with רוּחוֹ/"his wind/breath" to the earth. אֶרֶץ/"earth" in v.15a is an *accusativus loci*.[149] The noun מְהֵרָה/"speed" in עַד־מְהֵרָה/"to speed" in v.15b is always used adverbially,[150] thus the expression means "fast". The word is personified but does not act on its own: In accordance with the theocentric view of vv.8–9, the word is entirely dependent on YHWH. Through its suffixes, it is always designated as belonging to YHWH, and it is sent by YHWH. YHWH is the subject of all actions in vv.16–17.[151] The word is the subject of v.15b only, where it runs very fast like an *envoy* who inevitably and with superhuman speed executes the command of his superior.[152] In contrast to ANE parallels, the word does not have any power of its own.[153] The reference to Ps 33 suggests a further aspect of the word: The word is the *order of creation*, which in Ps 147 has to be upheld constantly by YHWH. A similar idea is found in Ps 104:29–30 where YHWH can give his רוּחַ/"breath" to all living beings but also take it from them. The interpretation of the word as thunder[154] is unlikely: Even though there is no reference to Isa 55:10–11,[155] in the Psalms thunder is usually connected with קוֹל/"voice" rather than דָּבָר/"word", e. g. in Ps 18:4; 29:3; 77:19; 104:7. The reference to Ps 33 where in Ps 33:6 the דְּבָר/ "word" of YHWH is used synonymously to the רוּחַ פִּיו/"breath of his mouth" also suggests that YHWH's רוּחַ/"breath" in v.18 which also is used as a synonym for his דְּבָר/"word" is not simply a warm thawing wind,[156] but YHWH's breath when speaking, without excluding an allusion to warm thawing wind.[157] In Ps 33, YHWH's word is right (Ps 33:4) and his counsel is lasting (Ps 33:11), and דְּבָר/"word" could refer to both the lasting order of creation and a command

---

148 Cf. Gesenius 2013, s.v. אִמְרָה*. In Ps 119 this word is used for the Torah, cf. Ballhorn 2004b, 313 fn. 818.

149 Cf. Gesenius and Kautzsch 1909, §118d.

150 Cf. Gesenius 2013, s.v. מְהֵרָה.

151 Cf. Sedlmeier 1996, 321.

152 Cf. for the image of an envoy Hupfeld 1871, 448; Gunkel 1926, 616; Sedlmeier 1996, 323, 351–352 (Ps 147 theocentric, the word is personified but not hypostatised).

153 Even in Isa 55:10–11 the word only enacts YHWH's power, not its own. A beginning of the later hypostatisation of the word in the New Testament in John 1 is noted by Kraus 1978, 1138; Allen 1983, 306.

154 Thus Dahood 1970, 348.

155 Against Brodersen 2013, 69, see p. 183–185 on Isa.

156 The view of a thawing wind is adopted by Hupfeld 1871, 449; Gunkel 1926, 616; Risse 1995, 162; Zenger 2008h, 835.

157 Cf. Kraus 1978, 1138–1139; Allen 1983, 306.

which is inevitably executed.[158] Both possibilities fit Ps 147 well as it contains both the order of creation and the sending of the word to reliably execute the thawing of ice. However, Ps 147:19–20 add another dimension to the word: it is God's Torah for Israel.[159]

Snow and hoarfrost are compared in a vivid image to white fluffy wool and light grey powdery ashes.[160] In Ex 16:14 the heavenly food Manna is compared to כְּפוֹר/"hoarfrost".[161] The thrown pieces of ice are probably hail as in the weather phenomena in Job 38 and Ps 148. However, בָּרָד/"hail" is not used in Ps 147, but פַּת/"piece" which usually refers to pieces of bread.[162] Like Job 38, Sir 43 also paints a vivid picture of YHWH as the ruler of all weather phenomena. "Who stands?" is a rhetorical question as in Ps 76:8 and Ps 130:3: No one can stand before YHWH.[163] Thus, in spite of the associations with bread and the wheat in v.14, weather phenomena are not only beneficial for humans but also pose a threat.

The wintry weather phenomena in vv.16–19 are sometimes interpreted as an image for the Babylonian exile which YHWH ends as he ends winter with warm spring breezes.[164] However, even in Job 38:22 where snow and hail are kept for a day of battle, it is unclear for or against whom they are to be used.[165] In Hag 2:17 YHWH uses hail to punish his people, in Sir 39:35 evil ones, but in most other passages where *hail* appears in HB YHWH uses it as a weapon *for the benefit of rather than against Israel*, e. g. in Ex 9:22–26 and Josh 10:11.[166] Since the hailstones in Ps 147 are melted (the suffix at the end of v.18a refers to פְּתִים/"pieces" in v.17a since there is no other preceding plural form), the focus of the image cannot be hail as a weapon against Israel's enemies as this weapon would then be made ineffective by YHWH, which is unlikely to lead to Israel's praise. The associations of hoarfrost and hail with bread also point against the image of winter as a punishment.[167]

Thus, Ps 147 does not paint the picture "winter = exile, spring = end of exile",[168] but describes YHWH's general influence on nature and the regular

---

158 Cf. Zenger 1993c, 209.
159 Cf. Gerstenberger 2001, 445. See p. 197.
160 Cf. Allen 1983, 306; Risse 1995, 157–159.
161 Cf. Risse 1995, 158.
162 Cf. Risse 1995, 160.
163 Cf. Risse 1995, 161; Sedlmeier 1996, 322.
164 Cf. Risse 1995, 163; Sedlmeier 1996, 321–322.
165 Cf. Groß 1986, 133; Clines 2011a, 1108–1109.
166 Cf. Briggs 1906, 536.
167 Against Zenger 2008h, 835.
168 Cf. Zenger 2003, 145 fn. 15.

order of the weather phenomena caused by him. This is supported by the imperfect forms in v.18 which stress the regular order.[169]

What are the reasons for praise in Psalm 147:19 – 20ᴹᵀ?

The synonymously used names יִשְׂרָאֵל/"Israel" and יַעֲקֹב/"Jacob" appear frequently within one verse in Isa 40 – 49 (first in Isa 40:27).[170] Both names refer to the people Israel. To these people, YHWH declares his word which in vv.15 – 17 functioned as an order and envoy for nature. דְּבָרוֹ/"his word" is identified in v.19 with חֻקָּיו וּמִשְׁפָּטָיו/"his decrees and his jugements" which according to Deut 4 are the Torah. The Torah is declared to Israel only among all nations as underlined by the antithesis in v.20. לֹא/"not" in collocation with כֹּל/"all" means "none at all":[171] For no nation at all does YHWH act as he does for Israel. The repetition of מִשְׁפָּט/"judgement" in v.20 suggests that the judgements are YHWH's. Thus, the verse does not imply that the nations have no judgements or laws at all, but that they do not know the judgements which all of nature follows and which have been declared to Israel: YHWH's word.[172] Israel alone knows the connection between the order of nature and YHWH's law.[173] The nations do not know it, but in Ps 147 (unlike e. g. Isa 49:6) Israel is not asked to tell the nations about YHWH's word.[174]

בַּל/"not" and לֹא/"not" can be used synonymously within the same verse, e. g. Prov 10:30; 12:3. In Ps 147, בַּל/"not" could be used in v.20b since the nations are the subject there, whereas לֹא/"not" in vv.10ab and 20a is connected with the subject YHWH.

---

169 See p. 173 – 177.

170 Cf. Berges 2008, 157. See p. 183 – 185 on Isa.

171 Cf. Gesenius and Kautzsch 1909, §152b.

172 Thus Hupfeld 1871, 450; Gunkel 1926, 616 – 617; similarly Ballhorn 2004b, 313 – 314 (focus on uniqueness of Israel rather than disqualification of nations). While "judgements" have a suffix referring to YHWH in v.19 and none in v.20, the repetition of the word suggests that the judgements are still YHWH's, but some commentators see the nations in v.20 as further away from YHWH's laws, cf. Sedlmeier 1996, 26; Dahmen 2003, 120 (referring to Sedlmeier).

173 Cf. Kraus 1978, 1139.

174 Against Zenger 2008h, 836.

V.1.5 Genre of Psalm 147^{MT}

Ps 147 fits into the genre of hymn:[175] Following imperatives calling to praise in vv.1, 7, and 12, it contains reasons for praise. The Psalm is characterised by participles which are typical for the genre of hymn but also contains other verb forms,[176] and closes with another call to praise. In v.1, the Psalm uses תְּהִלָּה/ "praise", as if designating itself as a hymn.[177] Given the three calls to praise it can be described as a threefold hymn.[178] A special feature of Ps 147 is the twofold use of כִּי/"yea, for": Only in v.13 it is used to introduce the reasons for praise as typical in hymns, while in v.1 appearing twice within a call to praise as an affirmative particle.[179]

Ps 147 calls the people Israel to praise their God YHWH. These people Israel could be an actual *cultic assembly* in the Jerusalem temple, with the Psalm having a *cultic setting in life*.[180] However, given that the temple is not mentioned in the Psalm, the Psalm could also refer to members of Israel which in principle could gather in the temple but can also praise YHWH on their own or in groups in different places, in meditation or recitation.[181] The Psalm would then address individuals or groups of *readers*, with a *setting in literature*.[182] However, the mention of praise with a lyre in v.7 makes it unlikely that the Psalm was composed for silent meditation only, and the plural calls to praise make it unlikely that the Psalm is addressed to an individual only.

While the intertextual references make it likely that the Psalm was composed as a written poem rather than noted down following oral tradition, they do not

---

175 See p. 30 fn. 168. Westermann 1983, 91–97, refines the genre of Ps 147 as a describing rather than reporting hymn, but Ps 147 has aspects of both these sub-genres since it describes YHWH's general greatness *and* reports actions.

176 Cf. Crüsemann 1969, 131–134 (late form mixing imperatival and participial hymns); Allen 1983, 307 (referring to Crüsemann).

177 Thus Seybold 1996, 539. Gerstenberger 2001, 443, argues for the genre of thanksgiving song for vv.7–11 due to תּוֹדָה/"thanksgiving" in v.7. However, the elements of thanksgiving songs mentioned in Hartenstein 2003b, 1766 (address of YHWH in the 2nd person, account of past help) are not prominent in Ps 147, and its unity (see V.1.7) makes more than one genre unlikely. Overall, Gerstenberger 2001, 445–446, designates the Psalm as a communal hymn, with a cultic setting. Zenger 2008h, 832, also notes תּוֹדָה as originally a technical term "song of thanksgiving" but here not as a reference to cultic use but to the general attitude of thankfulness.

178 Thus Seybold 1996, 538. See p. 177.

179 See p. 187.

180 Thus Gunkel 1926, 615; Allen 1983, 309; Sedlmeier 1996, 62 (first possibility); Gerstenberger 2001, 445–446.

181 Thus Sedlmeier 1996, 62 (second possibility); Zenger 1998b, 100–102.

182 Thus Zenger 1998b, 99–102 (German original: "Sitz in der Literatur").

make a cultic or literary setting in life more or less likely: Such references to other texts in HB could be used in a cultic setting as well as in a more private reading. The addressees of the Psalm can be imagined as "the cultic assembly, whether assembled in reality or in the imagination of the Psalmist only"[183] in Jerusalem, the city mentioned explicitly in Ps 147.[184]

V.1.6 Date of Psalm 147[MT]

Intertextual references to Deut 4, Isa 40, and Ps 33[185] lead to a relative date of Ps 147: Ps 147 is more likely to refer to the three texts than the other way round,[186] and it is more probable that Ps 147 refers to all three texts from entirely different parts of HB (and possibly different periods of time) than that these different texts all refer to Ps 147. Given that there are word-by-word references, the author of Ps 147 may have used the reference texts in some kind of scriptural meditation where biblical texts are the primary point of reference rather than extratextual events.[187] In terms of a *relative date*, Ps 147 has to be *younger than at least Deut 4, Isa 40, and Ps 33* (and possibly Ps 104 and Ps 135). A further study of the reference texts in their contexts (which, however, may differ diachronically) and their similarities and differences compared to Ps 147 is desirable (for example, like Second Isaiah, Ps 147 connects God's actions for Israel with his actions as a creator).[188] However, the reference of Ps 147 to such different texts makes it likely that its own message is more important than each individual reference text.[189]

The intertextual references may also point to a *postexilic* date of Ps 147 after the 6th century BCE based on the assumption of such a postexilic date of Isa 40[190] (dates for Deut 4[191] and Ps 33[192] are debated but may be postexilic; this also ap-

---

183 Risse 1995, 103 (German original: "die – in der Wirklichkeit oder nur in der Vorstellung des Psalmisten – versammelte Kultgemeinde").
184 Against Zenger 1999, 124–128 (imagined assembly for Ps 1–2 and Ps 146–150).
185 See p. 185–186.
186 See p. 179–185 on Deut 4, Isa, Ps 33.
187 Thus Sedlmeier 1996, 222.
188 Thus Gunkel 1926, 615. See also fn. 196.
189 See V.1.8.
190 Cf. Coggins 2007, 433, 465–44; Berges 2008, 94–98, 128–129.
191 See fn. 44.
192 See fn. 57.

plies to the possible reference texts Ps 104[193] and Ps 135[194]). Thus, the conquest of Babylon by the Persian king Cyrus II *539 BCE* is the *terminus post quem* for Ps 147. Since some reference texts may be much later (e. g. 4th century BCE for Ps 33 and Ps 135), Ps 147 may also be much later than the *4th century BCE*.

The *content* of Ps 147 also points towards a postexilic origin: The building of Jerusalem and the gathering of the scattered ones of Israel (v.2) are described as general actions and thus have already happened in the past, the same is true for the fastening of the bars of the gates of Jerusalem as well as for blessing, peace, and food for the city (vv.13 – 14).[195] The connection of YHWH's deeds for Israel and his actions as a creator may also be a postexilic phenomenon.[196]

Late Hebrew language also points to a late date of Ps 147, especially the aramaisms כנס/"gather" (v.2) and שבח/"glorify" (v.12), and the introduction of a direct object with ל/"for" (v.3).[197]

A *terminus ante quem* is the Septuagint translation of the Psalter which was probably completed in the *2nd century BCE.*[198]

The time of origin of Ps 147 is after its reference texts and before its Septuagint translation, thus in the *Hellenistic period of the 3rd to 2nd centuries BCE.* A Hellenistic origin may also be confirmed by similarities with Ben Sira (especially Sir 39; 43; 51).[199]

The Septuagint[200] attributes both Ps 146[LXX] and Ps 147[LXX] to Haggai and Zechariah, possibly in accordance with the content of Ps 146:2[LXX](=147:2[MT]) and Ps 147:2 – 3[LXX](=147:13 – 14[MT]) and thus places them in the time immediately fol-

---

193 Cf. Rodd 2007, 394 – 395 (debated, basis Gen 1 possible); Hossfeld 2008b, 88 – 89 (exilic-postexilic stages).

194 Cf. Rodd 2007, 401 (postexilic); Zenger 2008 f, 664 (4th century BCE).

195 See p. 173 – 177, 190, 194.

196 Thus Vosberg 1975, 58 – 59; Schmidt 2011, 241. See also fn. 188.

197 Thus Buttrick 1955, 750. Aramaisms are discussed in detail in VI.1.6. כנס/"gather" appears in late texts, cf. Gesenius 2013, s.v. כנס, and extrabiblical DSS, cf. Clines 1998, s.v. כנס, and stands in linguistic opposition with קבץ/"gather", cf. e. g. Isa 56:8. It is found in Aramaic, cf. Jastrow 1903, s.v. כְּנַס; Kaufman [no year], s.v. kns. שבח/"glorify" appears in late texts, cf. Gesenius 2013, s.v. שבח, and extrabiblical Qumran texts, cf. Clines 2011b, s.v. שבח, and stands in linguistic opposition with הלל/"praise" or other words as in Ps 147:1,7,12. It is found in Jastrow 1903, s.v. שְׁבַח; Kaufman [no year], s.v. šbḥ. For ל as an accusative marker in Aramaic cf. Gesenius 2013, Aramaic Part, s.v. –ל; Kaufman [no year], s.v. l_; this is in linguistic opposition with את as an accusative marker, though this use of ל is also found in biblical texts, cf. Clines 1998, s.v. ל (without DSS references for this use, but in general there are 6000 occurrences of ל in DSS, cf. Clines 1998, 60).

198 See p. 16, esp. fn. 104.

199 Thus Zenger 1999, 124 – 125. Further research on these similarities with Sir is desirable.

200 See V.3.

lowing the exile around 520 BCE, but given the intertextual references this is unlikely.

Given all these reasons, most commentators adopt the view of a postexilic origin of Ps 147,[201] usually with the general designation "postexilic"[202]. More specific dates range from the early postexilic 6th century BCE[203] over the time of Nehemia after the building of the city walls in the 5th century BCE[204] (however, no extrabiblical sources exist for Nehemiah and Ezra),[205] at the earliest after Ezra 379 BCE,[206] until the 3rd or even 2nd century BCE before 150 BCE with the tensions in Seleucid times, possibly in the same milieu as a Jerusalem wisdom school,[207] or the 2nd century BCE under John Hyrcanus or the 1st century under Salome Alexandra.[208]

A very late date is unlikely as Ps 147 seems to refer to the end of the exile and the building of Jerusalem, though this presupposes that the Psalm refers to these events in the 6th century BCE rather than later, similar events.[209] However, the reference text Isa 40 is connected with the Babylonian rather than any other exile. Ps 147 seems to refer to texts rather than events, with its general statements only containing a general reference to the Babylonian exile.[210] There is no indication that Ps 147 was written for the context of the Final Hallel.[211]

V.1.7 Unity of Psalm 147^MT

While syntax, structure, and content[212] make it likely that Psalm 147 is one unit, with framing Hallelujahs on all Hebrew manuscripts, some arguments for different original parts have to be considered.[213]

---

201 An exception is Weiser 1966, 577, who dates Ps 147 much earlier (after 721 BCE), but this rests on the unlikely assumption that Ps 147 does not refer to any other texts at all.
202 Thus Allen 1983, 309; Lohfink 1990, 119–120; Sedlmeier 1996, 221–223, 235–237, 335–336. For further literature see Brodersen 2013, 76–77.
203 Thus, due to Jerusalem being still in ruins, Gunkel 1926, 615; Gerstenberger 2001, 443–446.
204 Thus Vosberg 1975, 20–21.
205 On Nehemiah and Ezra in the history of Israel cf. Frevel 2016, 304–317.
206 Thus Buttrick 1955, 750–751.
207 Thus Zenger 1999, 124–128; Zenger 2003, 141; Zenger 2008c, 809; Zenger 2008h, 827–282.
208 Thus Duhm 1922, 478–479.
209 Briggs 1906, 534–535, argues for a reference to Syrian oppression and dates the Psalm to the late Maccabean period.
210 Thus Hupfeld 1871, 442–443.
211 Against Kratz 1992, 21 (possibility); Zenger 2008c, 809 (Ps 147:1–11 only).
212 See V.1.2, V.1.4.

Most importantly, the Septuagint contains two separate Psalms 146^{LXX} and 147^{LXX} where Ps 146^{LXX} equals Ps $147{:}1{-}11^{MT}$ (Parts I+II) and Ps 147^{LXX} equals Ps $147{:}12{-}20^{MT}$ (Part III). Hebrew manuscripts, in contrast, do not show a split of Psalm 147. In Codex L v.12 is not set on a new line, and the space between v.11 and v.12 is the same as between other verses.[214] The Septuagint shows differences to the Hebrew division of Psalms in more than one place in the Psalter: Ps 116^{MT} is split into Ps $114{-}115^{LXX}$, whereas Ps $9{-}10^{MT}$ are combined in Ps 9^{LXX} and Ps $114{-}115^{MT}$ in Ps 113^{LXX}.[215] Thus, the split of Ps 147 can be explained following the preceding alterations as a means to arrive at the number of 150 Psalms. Ps 151^{LXX} is explicitly excluded from the number of Psalms, making it likely that the number of 150 Psalms is important in the Septuagint. Given the differences in the LXX-Psalter in several places, it is more likely that the Septuagint split up a coherent Psalm 147 than that the Hebrew text connected two independent Psalms.[216]

Commentaries often include other arguments for Ps 147 consisting of originally separate parts, but none of these arguments prove to be strong.

That *perfect forms* appear in Part III only (vv.13 and 20), and a *tricolon* in Part II only (v.8), does not suffice to separate these parts given the numerous connecting features in syntax and structure. The perfect forms point to the completed building of Jerusalem in Part III, but it may equally be completed in Part I:[217] V.2 contains a general statement[218] which does not allow for finding "a diverging historical background"[219] in it.

The *syntactical features in v.1* can be explained without multi-layered redaction-critical hypotheses.[220]

The collocation of plural imperatives (vv.1, 7) and *singular imperatives* (v.12) can be explained given the content of Jerusalem which, after having been mentioned in v.2, is personified and called to praise in v.12 as a metonymy for Isra-

---

213 Conjectures are not included here, cf. e.g. on v.17 Allen 1983, 306; Risse 1995, 23–24; criticism by Zenger 2008h, 826.

214 Cf. Freedman 1998, 804=fol. 396v.

215 Cf. Bons 2009a, 750.

216 Thus Ballhorn 2004b, 38–43, 311, esp. 40 (number 150 inconsistent in different traditions). Duhm 1922, 478, assumes a split in Hebrew which LXX took over; Lohfink 1990, 115, assumes a split in Hebrew lost at the time of and thus secondary in LXX.

217 Against Leuenberger 2004, 349–350.

218 See p. 173–177.

219 Thus Leuenberger 2004, 349 (German original: "einen divergenten historischen Hintergrund"). Leuenberger argues that Part III was written before I+II without explaining why an older perspective was added later, and in imperfect rather than perfect forms.

220 See p. 186–189. Against Leuenberger 2004, 349–350; Zenger 2008h, 825–826.

el.[221] V.20 is concluded by another plural imperative (the framing הַלְלוּ־יָהּ/"Praise-Yah!"), which clarifies that with Jerusalem = Zion in v.12 and Jacob = Israel in v.19 one and the same group of people are addressed, namely the people Israel. The perspective of "us" thus is found in Part III as well as in the other two parts.[222] Thus, the address of Jerusalem in v.12 is not the beginning of a new Psalm but a different expression of the same call to praise.[223]

Alliterations and *assonances* appear in at least Parts I+III.[224]

Regarding *terms for God*, the three calls to praise at the beginning of each part in vv.1, 7, and 12, all contain forms of יהוה/"YHWH" and אֱלֹהִים/"God", and the last verse of each part (vv.6, 11, 20) contains יהוה/"YHWH". This points towards the coherence of all parts.[225] In Part I, יהוה/"YHWH" which in v.1 is the object is additionally mentioned as the subject of v.2, and v.5 contains the additional term אֲדוֹנֵינוּ/"our Lord".

The content of Parts I+II and Part III is not identical, otherwise Part III would form a superfluous repetition of Parts I+II. Thus, Part II mentions rain, Part III snow, ice, and water,[226] and YHWH's word only appears in Part III. However, the content also connects all three parts: They all contain a call to praise for YHWH as the God of Israel and the creator. In all parts, YHWH is the subject of almost all sentences.[227] That Parts I+II focus on YHWH's care for individuals whereas Part III focusses on his general care for the entire people[228] is unlikely since there are plural forms in vv.2, 3, 6, and 11, and YHWH's care benefits all of the people Israel.[229]

Intertextual references are found in both Parts I+II (Ps 33, Isa 40) and Part III (Ps 33, Isa 40, and Deut 4), underlining the unity of the Psalm.[230]

Some commentators either confirm the unity of Ps 147[231] or take it for granted.[232] Others argue for a composition out of two[233] or three[234] original parts, de-

---

221 See p. 189–190, 193–194.

222 Against Zenger 2008h, 826 ("Wir-Perspektive"/"we-perspective").

223 Against Leuenberger 2004, 349–350; Zenger 2008h, 826–829.

224 See p. 177–178. Against Leuenberger 2004, 349–350.

225 Against Lohfink 1990, 116.

226 Thus Weber 2003, 375.

227 See p. 173–177. Against Leuenberger 2004, 349–350.

228 Thus Lohfink 1990, 117–119; Leuenberger 2004, 349–350; Zenger 2008h, 826–829.

229 See p. 189–190.

230 Against Leuenberger 2004, 349–350; Zenger 2008h, 826–829.

231 Thus Allen 1983, 307–308; Gerstenberger 2001, 444.

232 Thus Hupfeld 1871, 441–450; Gunkel 1926, 614–617; Crüsemann 1969, 131–134.

233 Cf. Lohfink 1990, 115–120; Risse 1995, 191–193; Sedlmeier 1996, 27–29; Leuenberger 2004, 349–350; Zenger 2008h, 826–829.

bating whether Parts I+II or Part III is the younger addition.[235] The arguments against the unity of Ps 147 are based mainly on content and less strong than arguments for its unity based on syntax and structure as well as content. Thus, Ps 147 is probably a unit with one common origin and author.

There are two individual questions with text-critical evidence within MT: Firstly, in v.1, some Hebrew manuscripts read the imperative זַמְּרוּ/"make music!" instead of the infinitive זַמְּרָה/"to make music".[236] Thus the adjectives in the nominal clauses refer to YHWH,[237] and the atnaḥ has to be assumed after נָעִים/"pleasant". The reference to YHWH then leads to the interpretation of כִּי/"for" as a causal conjunction: "Praise Yah, for [he is] good; make music to our God, for [he is] pleasant; appropriate [is] praise." Thus, the statement can be paraphrased as "Praise YHWH, because *YHWH* is good" rather than, as in Codex L, "Praise YHWH, yes, *praise* is good", with reasons following implicitly from v.2. Codex L is here taken as the basis for exegesis.

Secondly, in v.19, the Ketib דְּבָרוֹ/"his word" is written like the Qere plural דְּבָרָיו/"his words" in many Hebrew manuscripts, manuscripts from the Cairo Genizah, and in Aramaic Targums, while Greek and Syriac translations read a singular.[238] The singular refers to the *previously* mentioned דְּבָרוֹ/"his word" in vv.15 and 18, whereas the plural refers to the decrees and judgements mentioned *later* in vv.19 and 20.[239] In the latter case, these later words of God are distinguished from the word in the creation context of vv.15–18. While the connection between v.15 and v.19 through דְּבָר/"word" remains, the connection in content is weaker. The Ketib of Codex L is here taken as the basis for exegesis.

V.1.8 Overall Interpretation of Psalm 147[MT]

In a coherent hymn, YHWH, the God of Israel = Jacob and Jerusalem = Zion, and the creator, is to be praised by the people Israel in an actual cultic or an imag-

---

234 Cf. Duhm 1922, 476–480 (though possibly by the same author). Seybold 2010, 155–156, 159, assumes thematic fragments (creation, salvation, Zion) as the original parts, criticised by Ballhorn 2004b, 310 fn. 810.

235 Parts I+II are argued to be older by Lohfink 1990, 115–120; Risse 1995, 191–193; Sedlmeier 1996, 27–29. Ballhorn 2004b, 311, follows Lohfink, Risse, and Sedlmeier, but stresses the secondary unity of the Psalm. Part III is argued to be older by Leuenberger 2004, 349–350; Zenger 2008h, 826–829.

236 Cf. Elliger and Rudolph 1997, 1224.

237 Abbreviated to יָהּ/"Yah", see p. 32 fn. 5.

238 Cf. Elliger and Rudolph 1997, 1225.

239 Therefore the Ketiv is preferred by Hupfeld 1871, 449; Allen 1983, 306; Zenger 2008h, 826.

ined assembly. The reasons for praise are YHWH's general actions for Israel and in nature (described with imperfect forms and participles) as well as past actions for Israel which have consequences for the present (described by perfect forms). YHWH is almost always the subject of the Psalm and its centre. Intertextual references, language and content place Ps 147 in postexilic times, and probably the 3rd to 2nd century BCE. Jerusalem is mentioned in the Psalm but it is unclear if it is the place of the Psalm's origin.

V.2 Psalm 147ᴰˢˢ

V.2.1 Psalm 147 in 11QPsᵃ

11QPsᵃ contains in Fragment E Column II parts of Ps 147:1–2 and in Column III parts of Ps 147:18–20, with Ps 147 placed between Ps 104 and Ps 105.[240] Fragment F contains parts of one word, [לעצבונ]יהם/"[for their] toils", which may belong to Ps 147:3 as a variant from MT which reads לְעַצְּבוֹתָם/"for their pains".[241]

Neither the opening nor the final *Hallelujah* of Ps 147 are preserved. (There is a final Hallelujah preserved for Ps 104.) In reconstructions, the opening Hallelujah of Ps 147 is unlikely to have existed on Fragment E due to the insufficient length of the line for vv.1–2.[242] The closing Hallelujah may have existed.[243]

The preserved words in 11QPsᵃ are identical with MT in Codex L with two exceptions.[244] The first exception is the variant in Ps 147:3 on fragment F mentioned already: It contains the form [לעצבונ]יהם/"[for their] toils" of עִצָּבוֹן/"toil"[245] instead of the MT form (also found in 4QPsᵈ)[246] לְעַצְּבוֹתָם/"for their pains" of עַצֶּבֶת/"pain, grief"[247]. The two words have a common root, עצב/"grieve, hurt",[248] and no great difference in meaning. In 11QPsᵃ F the aspect of the outer *toil* is stressed, in MT the inner *pain*.[249] However, the combination of the images of healing and comforting[250] applies to both variants.

---

240 Cf. Martínez, Tegchelaar, and van der Woude 1998, 33–36. The order Ps 118–104–147–105 can be seen in Fragment E alone. Given that the end of Ps 105 is preserved in 11QPsᵃ Column I, a likely reconstructed order of Psalms is Ps 104–147–105–146–148 – etc, thus Seybold 2010, 162 (Hallelujah-Psalms); Ballhorn 2004b, 302 (Hallelujah-Psalms); Jain 2014, 161–162, regardless of theories about the beginning of 11QPsᵃ as a whole, on these cf. Jain 2014, 168–177 (reconstructions impossible).

241 Cf. Martínez, Tegchelaar, and van der Woude 1998, 36. According to Dahmen 2003, 119, the fit with Ps 147:3 is better than with any other Psalms in MT or 11QPsᵃ.

242 Thus Dahmen 2003, 118–119, referring to Martínez, Tegchelaar, and van der Woude 1998, 34 (Hallelujah on a separate line possible but would be unique in 11QPsᵃ). On the debate whether this is independent of MT see p. 15 fn. 94.

243 Reconstructed in Martínez, Tegchelaar, and van der Woude 1998, 34.

244 Cf. Freedman 1998, 803=fol. 396r, 804=fol. 396v.

245 Cf. Gesenius 2013, s.v. עִצָּבוֹן; Clines 2007, s.v. עִצָּבוֹן.

246 Cf. Skehan, Ulrich, and Flint 2000a, 66.

247 Cf. Gesenius 2013, s.v. עַצֶּבֶת; Clines 2007, s.v. [עַצֶּבֶת] I.

248 Cf. Gesenius 2013, s.v. עצב₂; Clines 2007, s.v. עצבI.

249 Similarly Dahmen 2003, 119 (toil leads to positive results).

250 See p. 190.

The second exception is הודיעם/"he has made them know" (hif'il perfect 3rd person singular with suffix) in Ps 147:20[251] instead of the MT יְדָעוּם/"they have known them" (qal 3rd person plural with suffix). Thus, in 11QPs^a (similarly in Greek, Syriac, and Aramaic versions)[252] YHWH is the implicit *subject* of the singular הודיעם/"he has made them know" in both halves of Ps 147:20, not just the first half, whereas "they" are the *object*. This is in line with the preceding verses where YHWH is always the implicit subject. In the same verse Ps 147:20, ו/"and" is missing before משפטים/"judgements", making the verse asyndetic like v.19 and thus tying them closer together.[253] There is no indication of a restriction of "Israel" and "Jacob" to a Qumran group rather than all of Israel.[254]

Regarding *intertextuality*, while עִצָּבוֹן/"toil"[255] in 11QPs^a F in Ps 147:3 appears in HB only in *Gen 3:16–17 and Gen 5:29* designating a consequence of the disobedience of the first humans, no reference to these verses is likely due to a lack of lexical and syntactical similarity.[256] While the form הוֹדִיעָם/"he has made them know" in 11QPs^a E in Ps 147:20 appears in HB only in *Ezek 20:4*, no intertextual reference to this verse is likely. Since the preserved words in 11QPs^a are identical with MT with two exceptions not causing changes in intertextual references, references in MT may be confirmed by 11QPs^a, though the fragmentary state of the text does not allow for certainty here. However, the unclear reference to *Ps 104* may be strengthened by its neighbouring position preceding Ps 147.[257]

In *summary*, 11QPs^a puts Ps 147 between Ps 104 and 105, stresses outer toil and YHWH as the only subject, strengthens the reference to the creation Psalm 104, and does not have any preserved Hallelujahs.

---

251 Cf. Martínez, Tegchelaar, and van der Woude 1998, 34.

252 Cf. Elliger and Rudolph 1997, 1225.

253 Cf. Dahmen 2003, 120 (asyndesis instead of syndesis and vice versa common in 11QPs^a).

254 Against Dahmen 2003, 120 (addition in Ps 146), 287–288 (context in 11QPs^a, 1QH^a 12:10, consequence of proleptic praise in Ps 147). The additions in Ps 146 and Ps 149 also show no Qumran-specific restrictions, see III.2.1, VI.2.1. There is no reference to 1QH^a 12:10, for the text cf. Schuller and Newsom 2012, 38.

255 Cf. Gesenius 2013, s.v. עִצָּבוֹן; Clines 2007, s.v. עִצָּבוֹן.

256 Against Dahmen 2003, 119 (closeness to Hodayot, variant secondary to MT).

257 Thus Dahmen 2003, 286–287 (shared words, creation theme).

V.2.2 Psalm 147 in 4QPs^d

The 4QPs^d fragments preserve parts of Psalms 106(?), 147, and 104 in this order, with parts of Ps 147:1–4 in Column I and of Ps 147:13–17, 20 in Column II. The opening Hallelujah is partly preserved with יה/"Yah", the final Hallelujah is fully preserved.[258]

4QPs^d I reads in v.1a like MT הללו]יה כי טוב זמרה אלהינו/"Praise-Yah! Yea, good [is it] to make music to our God", but in v.1b:

נא]וה זמרה] | [אל]ה[י]נו נאוה נעים תהלה/"[it is] appropriate to make music | to our God; appropriate, pleasant [is] praise." V.1 in 4QPs^d therefore can be translated as: "Praise-Yah! Yea, good [is it] to make music to our God; appropriate *[is it] to make music to our God; appropriate,* pleasant [is] praise." It is likely that 4QPs^d has a different reading compared to MT due to the scribal mistake of a dittography: the passage in MT זַמְּרָה אֱלֹהֵינוּ כִּי־נָעִים נָאוָה/"to make music to our God; yea pleasant, appropriate" is repeated.[259] However, even when taking out the dittography 4QPs^d I still shows a text different to MT: the second כִּי/"yea" is missing (which in MT comes after the atnaḥ), and the order of the adjectives נָעִים/"pleasant" and נָאוָה/"appropriate" is reversed.[260] Thus, leaving out the possible dittography, v.1 in 4QPs^d could be translated as "Praise-Yah! Yea, good [is it] to make music to our God; appropriate, pleasant [is] praise." The main message of this verse regardless of these differences is, as in MT: Praise YHWH, yea, *singing praise* is good. However, given that with or without the dittography the second כִּי/"yea" is missing, and the first כי/"yea" is immediately preceded by הללו יה/"Praise-Yah" on the same line,[261] 4QPs^d may read הללו יה/ "Praise Yah!" as an *imperative* rather than a superscription, followed by כי/ "for" introducing the goodness of singing as a reason for praise.[262] Even if a superscription is read, 4QPs^d proves that Ps 147 could be understood outside the context of the Final Hallel.[263]

---

258 Cf. Skehan, Ulrich, and Flint 2000a, 63–64, 66–68. On Ps 106 (rather than Ps 146) see VI.2.2.

259 Cf. Skehan, Ulrich, and Flint 2000a, 66. In 11QPs^a E II only הלל[ת] at the end of the verse is preserved, the reconstruction may be as MT but with the Hallelujah on a separate line, cf. Martínez, Tegchelaar, and van der Woude 1998, 33–34. However, this is problematic, see V.2.1, esp. p. 206 fn. 242.

260 In 4QPs^d either both adjectives are uninflected, or as in MT only the adjective closer to the noun is uninflected since נאוה/"appropriate" can be pointed as a masculine נָאוֶה or as in MT as a feminine נָאוָה, see p. 188–189.

261 In contrast to Freedman 1998, 803=fol. 396r.

262 See p. 186–187.

263 Against Zenger, see fn. 87.

The addition of ו/"and" before חלב/"fat" in v.14 in 4QPs^d II does not significantly change the meaning of this verse.

Regarding *intertextuality*, since there are only minor differences to MT in the preserved parts, the intertextual references in MT may be confirmed by 4QPs^d, but the fragmentary state of the text does not allow for certainty here. There is less syntactical similarity with Ps 33 since v.1 ends with נעים תהלה/"pleasant [is] praise" rather than נאוה תהלה/"appropriate [is] a praise", but given the dittography in v.1 this may be coincidental. The unclear reference to *Ps 104* may be strengthened by its neighbouring position following Ps 147.

In *summary*, in 4QPs^d *Psalm 147* stands between 106(?) and 104, and has both an opening and a final Hallelujah.

V.2.3 Psalm 147 in 4QPs^e?

4QPs^e in analogy to 11QPs^a is sometimes thought to (conjecturally) have contained Psalms 118–104–147–105 in this order, thus setting Psalm 147 in yet another context between 104 and 105.[264] However, the analogy with 11QPs^a is doubtful as there are limited parallels between the two manuscripts and 4QPs^e is too fragmentary to be reconstructed.[265] Materially, Psalm 147 is not preserved in 4QPs^e at all,[266] and the manuscript cannot be used for an exegesis of Ps 147.

V.2.4 Psalm 147 in MasPs^b

MasPs^b contains five consonants which probably belong to Ps 147: חו[רו]/"his wind" is found in Ps 147:18 and ק[ח]יו/"his decrees" in Ps 147:19.[267] These five consonants are the same as in Ps 147:18–19^MT in Codex L.[268] Neither the opening nor the final Hallelujah are preserved.

It is conjecturally assumed that in contrast to 11QPs^a MasPs^b ended with Ps 147–150 in the Masoretic order,[269] but this is problematic.[270]

---

264 Thus Flint 1997, 160–164, esp. 161; Skehan, Ulrich, and Flint 2000b, 76, 81–82.
265 Thus Dahmen 2003, 52–59, esp. 53; Leuenberger 2004, 17; Jain 2014, 94–104.
266 Cf. Skehan, Ulrich, and Flint 2000b, Plate XI.
267 Cf. Talmon 1999, 92–97.
268 Cf. Freedman 1998, 804=fol. 396v.
269 Cf. Talmon 1999, 94–97.
270 See II.2.2.

Regarding *intertextuality*, since the five preserved consonants are identical with MT, intertextual references in MT, especially from Ps 147:18 to *Ps 33:6*[271] and from Ps 147:19 to *Deut 4*,[272] may be confirmed by MasPs^b, though the fragmentary state of the text does not allow for certainty here.

In *summary*, MasPs^b puts Ps 147 close to Ps 150, shows no differences to MT in the few preserved letters in either content or intertextuality, and does not have any preserved Hallelujahs.

---

271 See p. 181–182 on Ps 33.
272 See p. 179–180 on Deut 4.

V.3 Psalms 146 – 147^{LXX}

Psalm 147^{MT} equals two Psalms in LXX: Ps 146^{LXX}(=Ps 147:1– 11^{MT}) and Ps 147^{LXX} (=Ps 147:12– 20^{MT}). LXX probably split up Ps 147^{MT}.[273]

V.3.1 Translation of Psalms 146 – 147^{LXX}

	Ps 146^{LXX}		Ps 146^{LXX}
1H	Hallelujah; of Haggai and Zechariah.	1H	Αλληλουια· Αγγαιου καὶ Ζαχαριου.
1a	Praise the Lord, for something good [is] a psalm;	1a	Αἰνεῖτε τὸν κύριον, ὅτι ἀγαθὸν ψαλμός·
1b	for our God sweet may be praise.	1b	τῷ θεῷ ἡμῶν ἡδυνθείη αἴνεσις.
2a	Building Jerusalem [is] the Lord	2a	οἰκοδομῶν Ιερουσαλημ ὁ κύριος
2b	and the dispersions of Israel he will gather,	2b	καὶ τὰς διασπορὰς τοῦ Ισραηλ ἐπισυνάξει,
3a	the one healing the wounded ones in heart	3a	ὁ ἰώμενος τοὺς συντετριμμένους τὴν καρδίαν
3b	and binding up their wounds,	3b	καὶ δεσμεύων τὰ συντρίμματα αὐτῶν,
4a	the one counting multitudes of stars,	4a	ὁ ἀριθμῶν πλήθη ἄστρων,
4b	and for all them names calling.	4b	καὶ πᾶσιν αὐτοῖς ὀνόματα καλῶν.
5a	Great [is] our Lord, and great [is] his power,	5a	μέγας ὁ κύριος ἡμῶν, καὶ μεγάλη ἡ ἰσχὺς αὐτοῦ,
5b	and of his understanding there is no number.	5b	καὶ τῆς συνέσεως αὐτοῦ οὐκ ἔστιν ἀριθμός.
6a	Lifting up humble ones [is] the Lord,	6a	ἀναλαμβάνων πραεῖς ὁ κύριος,
6b	but making low sinners unto the earth.	6b	ταπεινῶν δὲ ἁμαρτωλοὺς ἕως τῆς γῆς.
7a	Begin for the Lord with thanksgiving,	7a	ἐξάρξατε τῷ κυρίῳ ἐν ἐξομολογήσει,
7b	sing praise for our God with a lyre;	7b	ψάλατε τῷ θεῷ ἡμῶν ἐν κιθάρᾳ,
8a	for the one covering the heaven with clouds,	8a	τῷ περιβάλλοντι τὸν οὐρανὸν ἐν νεφέλαις,
8b	for the one preparing for the earth rain,	8b	τῷ ἑτοιμάζοντι τῇ γῇ ὑετόν,
8c	for the one making grow on mountains grass and herb for the use of the humans,	8c	τῷ ἐξανατέλλοντι ἐν ὄρεσι χόρτον καὶ χλόην τῇ δουλείᾳ τῶν ἀνθρώπων,
9a	for a giving one for the domestic animals their food,	9a	διδόντι τοῖς κτήνεσι τροφὴν αὐτῶν
9b	and for the nestlings of the ravens the ones calling him.	9b	καὶ τοῖς νεοσσοῖς τῶν κοράκων τοῖς ἐπικαλουμένοις αὐτόν.
10a	Not in the strength of the horse will he take pleasure	10a	οὐκ ἐν τῇ δυναστείᾳ τοῦ ἵππου θελήσει
10b	and not in the lower legs of the man does he delight;	10b	οὐδὲ ἐν ταῖς κνήμαις τοῦ ἀνδρὸς εὐδοκεῖ·

[273] See V.1.7.

11a Lord delights in the ones fearing him

11b *and* the ones *hoping* for his kindness.

11a εὐδοκεῖ κύριος ἐν τοῖς φοβουμένοις αὐτὸν

11b καὶ ἐν τοῖς ἐλπίζουσιν ἐπὶ τὸ ἔλεος αὐτοῦ.

Ps 147^{LXX}

1H *Hallelujah; of Haggai and Zechariah.*

1a Glorify, Jerusalem, the Lord,

1b praise your God, Zion,

2a for he has strengthened the bars of your gates,

2b he has blessed your sons in *you;*

3a the one putting [in] your *borders* peace,

3b *and* [with] fat of wheat satisfy*ing* you;

4a the one sending his saying *for the* earth,

4b to speed *will* run his word,

5a *of* the one giving snow like *wool,*

5b *of* the one *mist* like ash scatter*ing,*

6a *of* the one throwing his ice like pieces,

6b *in the face of* his cold – who *will* stand?

7a He *will* send his word and he *will* melt them;

7b he *will* blow his wind, *and* waters *will flow.*

8a Declaring his word for Jacob,

8b his decrees and his judgements for Israel.

9a Not he has done so for every nation,

9b and *his* judgements *he has* not *revealed to* them.

9H –

Ps 147^{LXX}

1H Αλληλουια· Αγγαιου καὶ Ζαχαριου.

1a Ἐπαίνει, Ιερουσαλημ, τὸν κύριον,

1b αἴνει τὸν θεόν σου, Σιων,

2a ὅτι ἐνίσχυσεν τοὺς μοχλοὺς τῶν πυλῶν σου,

2b εὐλόγησεν τοὺς υἱούς σου ἐν σοί·

3a ὁ τιθεὶς τὰ ὅριά σου εἰρήνην

3b καὶ στέαρ πυροῦ ἐμπιπλῶν σε·

4a ὁ ἀποστέλλων τὸ λόγιον αὐτοῦ τῇ γῇ,

4b ἕως τάχους δραμεῖται ὁ λόγος αὐτοῦ

5a τοῦ διδόντος χιόνα ὡσεὶ ἔριον,

5b ὀμίχλην ὡσεὶ σποδὸν πάσσοντος,

6a βάλλοντος κρύσταλλον αὐτοῦ ὡσεὶ ψωμούς,

6b κατὰ πρόσωπον ψύχους αὐτοῦ τίς ὑποστήσεται;

7a ἀποστελεῖ τὸν λόγον αὐτοῦ καὶ τήξει αὐτά·

7b πνεύσει τὸ πνεῦμα αὐτοῦ, καὶ ῥυήσεται ὕδατα.

8a ἀπαγγέλλων τὸν λόγον αὐτοῦ τῷ Ιακωβ,

8b δικαιώματα καὶ κρίματα αὐτοῦ τῷ Ισραηλ.

9a οὐκ ἐποίησεν οὕτως παντὶ ἔθνει

9b καὶ τὰ κρίματα αὐτοῦ οὐκ ἐδήλωσεν αὐτοῖς.

V.3.2 Form of Psalms 146 – 147^{LXX}

Outlines of Psalms 146 – 147^{LXX}

Psalm 146^{LXX}

Part I

1H   **Hallelujah of Haggai and Zechariah**

1   Call to Praise the Lord, the *Imperative*

2 – 3	God of Israel	Jerusalem and Israel
	Future, Present Participles	
4 – 5	Creator	Rule over Stars, Power, Understanding
6	God of Israel	*Antithesis:* For Poor, Against Wicked
	Present Participles	
Part II		
7	Call to Praise the Lord, the	
	Imperative	
8 – 9	Creator	Care for Rain and Animals
10 – 11	God of Israel	*Antithesis:* Against Warriors, For Pious
	Future, Present	

Psalm 147^{LXX}

1H	**Hallelujah of Haggai and Zechariah**	
1	Call to Praise the Lord, the	
	Imperative	
2 – 3	God of Israel	Care for Jerusalem
	Aorist	
4 – 7	Creator	His Word and Weather
	Future	
8 – 9	God of Israel	*Antithesis:* Law for Israel, Not Every Nation
	Aorist	
9H	–	

Syntax of Psalms 146 – 147^{LXX}

Both Ps 146^{LXX} and Ps 147^{LXX} beginn with the *superscription* αλληλουια· Αγγαιου καὶ Ζαχαριου/"Hallelujah; of Haggai and Zechariah" and have no Hallelujah at the end. In Ps 146^{LXX} unlike in Ps 147^{LXX}, הַלְלוּ־יָהּ/"Praise-Yah!" is translated with αἰνέω/"praise" als well as being transcribed as αλληλουια/"Hallelujah". αἰνέω/"praise" is found in Ps 147:2^{LXX} only. Present *imperatives* in Ps 146:1^{LXX} and 147:1^{LXX} stress the beginning of each Psalm; there are aorist imperatives in Ps 146:7^{LXX}.[274]

Present participles referring to God are at the beginning of verses as in MT except in Ps 146:11^{LXX} which repeats the present εὐδοκεῖ/"he delights" as in Ps 146:10^{LXX}. Unlike in MT, Ps 146^{LXX} shows *nominative* participles in its *first* part (Ps 146:2 – 6^{LXX}), then *dative* participles (Ps 146:8 – 9^{LXX}) *depending on the*

---

274 See p. 116, fn. 243.

call to praise in Ps 146:7^{LXX}. Ps 147^{LXX} shows *nominative* participles in Ps 147:3 – 4^{LXX} and Ps 147:8^{LXX} with *genitive* partiples in the *middle* in Ps 147:5 – 6^{LXX} *depending on* λóγος/"*word*" in Ps 147:8^{LXX}. Thus, Ps 146^{LXX} stresses the importance of the call to praise, Ps 147^{LXX} the importance of the word. Present participles may refer to past or present or future, but even then they stress a continuous action.[275]

The *participles* are connected with *articles*[276] as in MT with an extra article at the beginning of Ps 146:4^{LXX}.

The imperfect forms in MT are most often translated with *future* forms (Ps 146:2b, 10a^{LXX}; Ps 147:4b, 6b, 7ab^{LXX}), otherwise with participles (Ps 146:4b, 9b^{LXX}; Ps 147:3b, 5b^{LXX}) and once with a present form (Ps 146:10b^{LXX}) immediately following a future form. In *Ps 146^{LXX}*, future forms appear at the gathering of Israel (Ps 146:2^{LXX}) and, though connected with three following present forms, God's lack of delight in war horses (Ps 146:10^{LXX}), thus contrasting Israel with war forces, and hinting towards a *future promise for Israel*. In *Ps 147^{LXX}*, the *future forms concern the word* (v.4b) and the weather phenomena connected with it (vv.6b – 7b). Rather than general repeated actions only, different time spheres appear in LXX, including different future spheres in both Psalms.

Perfect forms are translated with *aorist* forms and only appear in *Ps 147^{LXX}* (Ps 147:2ab, 9ab^{LXX}), framing the future forms in the middle of the Psalm.

As in MT, God is the subject of both Psalms, with the *theocentric view strengthened* by the participle used for the nestlings of ravens in Ps 146:9b^{LXX}, the addition of καί/"and" in Ps 147:7b making the flowing of waters a direct consequence of his actions, and most explicitly in Ps 147:9b^{LXX} where the nations are not the subject but the object of this action.

Structure of Psalms 146 – 147^{LXX}

Ps 146^{LXX} equals Parts I-II of Ps 147^{MT}, Ps 147^{LXX} Part III. In both, *future forms* set new accents: In Ps 146^{LXX}, the aspect of "God of Israel" is connected with future forms, but creation is not, the opposite applies to Ps 147^{LXX}. Both Psalms have the same superscription but no closing Hallelujah. The additional καί/"and" in vv.2 – 5, 9 – 10 connects the two cola each.[277]

---

275 Cf. Smyth and Messing 1956, §1872; Blass, Debrunner, and Rehkopf 1979, §318, 339.
276 The articles here are particular rather than generic, cf. Smyth and Messing 1956, §2050, 2052. On their fluctuation cf. Smyth and Messing 1956, §1124, 1126, 2050, 2052; Blass, Debrunner, and Rehkopf 1979, §273. Further research on LXX articles is desirable.
277 Cf. Zenger 2008h, 837; Brucker 2011a, 1879 – 1881; Brucker 2011b, 1881.

Poetic Devices in Psalms 146 – 147^{LXX}

Parallelisms and tricola (even though Ps 146:8^{LXX} is extended) are as in MT.[278]
Word repetitions are explained in V.3.4.

V.3.3 Intertextuality in Psalms 146 – 147^{LXX}

Importance

Texts similar to Ps 146 – 147^{LXX} have been merely listed so far.[279]

Analysis

In *Deuteronomy 4^{LXX}*, Deut 4:8^{LXX} in syntactical similarity shares δικαιώματα καὶ κρίματα/"decrees and judgements" with Ps 147:8^{LXX}, and ἔθνος/"nation", πᾶς/ "all", and δίδωμι/"give" with Ps 147^{LXX}; with Ps 146^{LXX} μέγας/"great", εἰμί/ "be", πᾶς/"all", and δίδωμι/"give". Deut 4:1–8^{LXX} shares Ισραηλ/"Israel", κύριος/"Lord", and θεός/"god" with Ps 147^{LXX}, but not the translations of דָּבָר/ "word" and קֶרֶב/"midst"; with Ps 146^{LXX} ἐπικαλέω/"call". The combination of δικαιώματα/"decrees" and κρίματα/"judgements" with καὶ/"and" is also promi-nent in Deut 5:1^{LXX} and in Deut 6:1^{LXX}, in addition to MT it is repeated in Deut 6:4^{LXX}.[280] Absolute dates[281] as well as internal and external coherence like in MT[282] point towards a reference from Ps^{LXX} to Deut^{LXX}. Ps 147^{LXX} but not Ps 146^{LXX} is likely to refer to Deut 4^{LXX}.

Job 38:41^{LXX} shares δέ/"but", ἑτοιμάζω/"prepare", κόραξ/"raven", νεοσσός/ "nestling", and κύριος/"Lord" with Ps 146^{LXX}, but βορά/"food" is used instead of τροφή/"food" and κράζω/"cry" instead of ἐπικαλέω/"call"; with Ps 147^{LXX} it only shares τίς/"who" and κύριος/"Lord". References are unlikely as in MT, even though the motif of ravens calling *to God* is shared.[283]

Regarding *Psalm 32^{LXX}(=33^{MT})*, Ps 146:7^{LXX} and Ps 32:2^{LXX} show some syntac-tical similarity in τῷ κυρίῳ/"to the Lord" for לַיהוָה/"to YHWH", ἐν κιθάρᾳ/"with a lyre" for בְּכִנּוֹר/"with a lyre", and ψάλατε/"sing praise!" (also in Ps 32:3^{LXX}) for זַמְּרוּ/"make music!", but נָאוָה תְהִלָּה/"appropriate [is] praise" is translated as πρέ-πει αἴνεσις/"praise fits" instead of ἡδυνθείη αἴνεσις/"praise may be sweet", and

278 See p. 69 fn. 386.
279 See p. 70 fn. 371.
280 Cf. Rahlfs and Hanhart 2006, 627.
281 See fn. 327.
282 See V.1.3.
283 In answer to Brodersen 2013, 23 fn. 24, there is no influence of Job 38:41^{LXX} on Ps 149:9^{LXX}.

רַב־כֹּחַ/"much of power" with πολύς/"much" and δύναμις/"might" rather than μέγας/"great" and ἰσχύς/"power". There is close syntactical similarity in Ps 146:10–11^LXX and Ps 32:16–18^LXX where τοῖς φοβουμένοις αὐτὸν and τοὺς φοβουμένους αὐτὸν/"the ones fearing him" for יְרֵאָיו/"the ones fearing him" is followed immediately by τοῖς ἐλπίζουσιν ἐπὶ τὸ ἔλεος αὐτοῦ and τοὺς ἐλπίζοντας ἐπὶ τὸ ἔλεος αὐτοῦ/"the ones hoping for his kindness" for מְיַחֲלִים לְחַסְדּוֹ/"the ones waiting for his kindness" and preceded by ἵππος/"horse" for סוּס/"horse" and κύριος/"Lord" for יהוה/"YHWH" (though גִּבּוֹר "warrior" is translated as γίγας/"giant" unrelated to δυναστεία/"strength"). Shared in Ps 32^LXX are also πᾶς/"all" for כֹּל/"all", γῆ/"earth" for אֶרֶץ/"earth", οὐρανός/"heaven" for שָׁמַיִם/"heaven", καρδία/"heart" for לֵב/"heart", θεός/"god" for אֱלֹהִים/"god", υἱός/"son" for בֵּן/"son", οὐ/"not" for אֵין/"there is not" and לֹא/"not", ἰσχύς/"power" for כֹּחַ/"power", and ὄνομα/"name" for שֵׁם/"name". In addition to MT, δέ/"but", εἰμί/"be", πλῆθος/"multitude" but for רֹב/"multitude" rather than רַב/"much", and ἐλπίζω/"hope" but for בטח/"trust" are shared. There is less syntactical similarity than in MT. Ps 147^LXX shares with Ps 32^LXX κύριος/"Lord" for יהוה/"YHWH", λόγος/"word" for דָּבָר/"word", πᾶς/"all" for כֹּל/"all", γῆ/"earth" for אֶרֶץ/"earth", πνεῦμα/"wind" for רוּחַ/"wind", ὕδωρ/"water" for מַיִם/"water", ἔθνος/"nation" for גּוֹי/"nation", θεός/"god" for אֱלֹהִים/"god", υἱός/"son" for בֵּן/"son", and οὐ/"not" for אֵין/"there is not" and לֹא/"not". In addition to MT, τίθημι/"put" is shared but for נתן/"give". מִשְׁפָּט/"judgement" is translated as κρίσις/"judgement" rather than κρίμα/"judgement". There is no syntactical similarity. Thus, while a reference to Ps 32^LXX is possible for Ps 146^LXX,[284] it is unlikely for Ps 147^LXX. The references in Ps 146^LXX lead to the stress of YHWH's power as opposed to military power.

Psalm 103^LXX(=104^MT) and Ps 146^LXX share κύριος/"Lord" for יהוה/"YHWH", θεός/"god" for אֱלֹהִים/"god", οὐρανός/"heaven" for שָׁמַיִם/"heaven", γῆ/"earth" for אֶרֶץ/"earth", οὐ/"not" for בַּל/"not", ὄρος/"mountain" for הַר/"mountain", πᾶς/"all" for כֹּל/"all", δίδωμι/"give" for נתן/"give", κτῆνος/"domestic animal" for בְּהֵמָה/"animal", μέγας/"great" for גָּדוֹל/"great", ψάλλω/"sing praise" for זמר/"make music", and ἁμαρτωλός/"sinner" for רָשָׁע/"wicked" (plural). In addition to MT, ἐξομολόγησις/"honour", καρδία/"heart", τροφή/"food", and ἡδυνθείη/"it may be sweet" are shared, but not the translations for other shared words in MT. With syntactical similarity, Ps 146:5^LXX and Ps 103:25^LXX share οὐκ ἔστιν ἀριθμός/"there is no number" for אֵין מִסְפָּר/"there is no number" (but the phrase is not unique to these two texts), and Ps 146:8^LXX and Ps 103:14^LXX collocate a participle of ἐξανατέλλω/"cause to grow" for the hif'il of צמח/"grow" with

---

284 On the direction of reference see V.1.3.

χόρτος/"grass" for חָצִיר/"grass" (uniquely, but in different word orders). There is no final Hallelujah in either Psalm in LXX. While fewer words are shared than in MT, there is an entire sentence shared in addition to MT making a reference more likely in LXX: καὶ χλόην τῇ δουλείᾳ τῶν ἀνθρώπων/"and herb for the use of the humans" appears in Ps 146:8^{LXX} but not in Ps 147:8^{MT}, and the same phrase forms the end of the aforementioned Ps 103:14^{LXX}. It is debated whether this verse is added in LXX, or whether at the time of translation it was part of the Hebrew text. Since there is no evidence for the sentence's existence in Hebrew, the former is more likely.[285] Thus, a reference to Ps 103^{LXX} (in this direction since the addition is in Ps 146^{LXX}) is much stronger than in MT. Given the universal creation content of Ps 103^{LXX}, this stresses the aspect of creation in Ps 146^{LXX}. Ps 103^{LXX} and Ps 147^{LXX} share εὐλογέω/"bless" for ברך/"bless", κύριος/"Lord" for יהוה/ "YHWH", θεός/"god" for אֱלֹהִים/"god", ὕδωρ/"water" for מַיִם/"water", τίθημι/ "put" for שׂים/"put", πνεῦμα/"wind" for רוּחַ/"wind" (but also ἄνεμος/"wind"), ποιέω/"do" for עָשָׂה/"do", γῆ/"earth" for אֶרֶץ/"earth", οὐ/"not" for בַּל/"not", ὅριον/"border" for גְּבוּל/"border", πᾶς/"all" for כֹּל/"all", δίδωμι /"give" for נתן/ "give", and πρόσωπον/"face" for פָּנִים/"face", but not the translations for other shared words in MT. There are no syntactical similarities, and in contrast to Ps 146^{LXX} there is no reference to Ps 103^{LXX} at all, thus showing a lack of interest in universal creation in Ps 147^{LXX}.

Psalm 134^{LXX}(=135^{MT}) and Ps 146^{LXX} share αἰνέω/"praise" for הלל/"praise", ὄνομα/"name" for שֵׁם/"name", κύριος/"Lord" for יהוה/"YHWH", θεός/"god" for אֱלֹהִים/"god", Ισραηλ/"Israel" for יִשְׂרָאֵל/"Israel", μέγας/"great" for גָּדוֹל/ "great", ὁ κύριος ἡμῶν/"our Lord" for אֲדֹנֵינוּ/"our Lord" (same form), πᾶς/"all" for כֹּל/"all", θέλω/"take pleasure" for חפץ/"take pleasure", οὐρανός/"heaven" for שָׁמַיִם/"heaven", γῆ/"earth" for אֶרֶץ/"earth", ὑετός/"rain" for מָטָר/"rain", κτῆνος/"domestic animal" for בְּהֵמָה/"animal", δίδωμι/"give" for נתן/"give", οὐ/"not" for לֹא/"not", φοβέομαι/"fear" for ירא/"fear", and Ιερουσαλημ/"Jerusalem" for יְרוּשָׁלַ͏ִם/"Jerusalem". Forms of οὐδέ/"not" and εἰμί/"be" are used for אֵין/ "there is not". In addition to MT, νεφέλη/"cloud" and ἄνθρωπος/"human" are shared, but not translations for other shared words in MT. Ps 134:3^{LXX} and Ps 146:1^{LXX} share the phrase αἰνεῖτε τὸν κύριον ὅτι ἀγαθός/v/"praise the Lord, for he/it (is) good" for הַלְלוּ־יָהּ כִּי־טוֹב/"Praise-Yah! For good" (in Ps 134:3^{LXX} the adjective refers to God rather than his praise), but כִּי נָעִים/"for pleasant" is translated as ὅτι καλόν/"is beautiful" rather than using ἡδύνω/"be sweet", though κύριος/"Lord" for יהוה/"YHWH" is still shared as well as ψάλλω/"sing praise" and ψαλμός/"song of praise" for זמר/"make music". Fewer shared words and phrases make a reference less likely. Ps 134^{LXX} and Ps 147^{LXX} share αἰνέω/"praise" for הלל/"praise", κύριος/"Lord" for יהוה/"YHWH", θεός/"god" for אֱלֹהִים/"god", Ιακωβ/"Jacob" for יַעֲקֹב/"Jacob", Ισραηλ/"Israel" for יִשְׂרָאֵל/"Israel", πᾶς/"all" for כֹּל/"all", ποιέω/"do" for עשׂה/"do", γῆ/"earth" for אֶרֶץ/"earth", ἔθνος/"nation" for גוֹי/"nation", δίδωμι/"give" for נתן/"give", οὐ/"not" for לֹא/"not", πνεῦμα/"wind" for רוּחַ/"wind", εὐλογέω/"bless" for ברך/"bless", Σιων/"Zion" for צִיוֹן/"Zion", and Ιερουσαλημ/"Jerusalem" for יְרוּשָׁלַם/"Jerusalem", but not the translations for other shared words in MT (partly since they do not appear in this half of Ps 147^{MT}, partly because they are translated differently). Fewer shared words and phrases make a reference less likely. The Psalms also all share an opening αλληλουια/"Hallelujah" though not the entire superscription of Ps 146–147^{LXX}; there are no final Hallelujahs. Overall, a reference to Ps 134^{LXX} is less likely than in MT for Ps 146^{LXX}, and unlikely for Ps 147^{LXX}.

In *Psalm 145^{LXX}(=146^{MT})* and Ps 146^{LXX}, ἀναλαμβάνω/"lift up" is used for the pol^{c}el עוד/"lift up", but the verb is much more frequent in LXX.[286] ὁ θεός σου Σιων/"your God, Zion" for אֱלֹהַיִךְ צִיוֹן/"your God, Zion" is uniquely shared between Ps 145^{LXX} (nominative) and Ps 147^{LXX} (accusative), though as in MT there is a similar phrase in Isa 52:7^{LXX}. Ps 145^{LXX} and Ps 146^{LXX} share ψάλλω/"sing praise" for זמר/"make music" (but also ψαλμός/"song of praise"), θεός/"god" for אֱלֹהִים/"god", κύριος/"Lord" for יהוה/"YHWH" (but also for אָדוֹן/"Lord"), πᾶς/"all" for כֹּל/"all", οὐκ ἔστιν/"there is not" for אַיִן/"there is not", ἁμαρτωλός/"sinner" for רָשָׁע/"wicked" (plural), γῆ/"earth" for אֶרֶץ/"earth", οὐρανός/"heaven" for שָׁמַיִם/"heaven", δίδωμι/"give" for נתן/"give" (singular participle), and τροφή/"food" for לֶחֶם/"food". בֶּן/"son" is translated with νεοσσός/ "young bird" instead of υἱός/"son". In addition to MT, ἕως/"until" and οὐ/"not" are shared. In the addition in Ps 146:8^{LXX}, ἄνθρωπος/"human" is shared. With Ps 147^{LXX}, Ps 145^{LXX} shares κύριος/"Lord" for יהוה/"YHWH" (including τὸν κύριον/"the Lord" for אֶת־יְהוָה/"YHWH"), αἰνέω/"praise" for הלל/"praise" (including αἴνει/"praise" for הַלְלִי/"praise!" appearing only in these two texts), υἱός/"son" for בֶּן/"son", γῆ/"earth" for אֶרֶץ/"earth", δίδωμι/"give" for נתן/ "give" (singular participle), πνεῦμα/"wind" for רוּחַ/"wind", Ιακωβ/"Jacob" for יַעֲקֹב/"Jacob", κρίμα/"judgement" for מִשְׁפָּט/"judgement", ποιέω/"do" for עשׂה/ "do", and πᾶς/"all" for כֹּל/"all". In addition to MT, ἕως/"until" and οὐ/"not" are shared. There is no Hallelujah-frame in either Psalm. Thus, in the LXX the main syntactical and structural similarity is missing, and while Psalms 145–147^{LXX} (and Ps 148^{LXX}) are connected by their superscriptions, an intertextual reference is unlikely.

---

286 Cf. Lust, Eynikel, and Hauspie 2003, s.v. ἀναλαμβάνω: 97 occurrences.

Psalm 146^LXX and Psalm 147^LXX share the frequent words αἰνέω/"praise", κύριος/"Lord", θεός/"god", Ιερουσαλημ/"Jerusalem", Ισραηλ/"Israel", πᾶς/ "all", οὐ/"not", ἕως/"until", γῆ/"earth", and δίδωμι/"give" (participle referring to God). Apart from the superscription, there is no reference between the two LXX-Psalms.

Intertextual links with *Ps 148^LXX* (see p. 163 on Ps 146 – 147^LXX), *Ps 149^LXX* (see p. 121 on Ps 146 – 147^LXX), and *Ps 150^LXX* (see p. 72 on Ps 146 – 147^LXX) are unlikely.

Isaiah 40:26 – 28^LXX shares πᾶς/"all", ἀριθμός/"number", ὄνομα/"name", καλέω/"call", ἰσχύς/"power" (with πᾶς/"all", ὄνομα/"name", and καλέω/ "call" following each other in this order in the same sentence), Ισραηλ/"Israel", θεός/"god", οὐ/"not", γῆ/"earth" and εἰμί/"be" with Ps 146^LXX; with Ps 147^LXX τίς/"who", πᾶς/"all", Ιακωβ/"Jacob", Ισραηλ/"Israel", θεός/"god", οὐ/"not", and γῆ/"earth". There are fewer shared words and less syntactical similarity, thus a reference is less likely than in MT, but remains possible, and then stresses God's power and creation and the fulfillment of his promises in Ps 146^LXX, and God's care for Israel in Ps 147^LXX. It is debated whether the LXX-Psalter depends on LXX-Isaiah or the other way round.[287] As shown for MT,[288] in this case the internal and external coherence points towards a reference from Ps 146 – 147^LXX to Isa 40:26 – 28^LXX. However, since there is less similarity in LXX than in MT, no strong case can be made on the basis of this example for a dependence of Ps^LXX on Isa^LXX. Since the second half of Isa 40:7^MT is missing in Isa 40:7^LXX,[289] Isa 40:7^LXX only shares the frequent word χόρτος/"grass" with Ps 146^LXX; with Ps 147^LXX there are no shared words. A reference is less likely than in MT. Isa 55:10 – 11^LXX share ὑετός/"rain" (for נֶשֶׁג/"rain" rather than מָטָר/"rain"), οὐρανός/"heaven", οὐ/"not", ἕως/"until", γῆ/"earth", δίδωμι/"give", εἰμί/"be", and θέλω/"take pleasure" with Ps 146^LXX; with Ps 147^LXX χιών/"snow", οὐ/ "not", ἕως/"until", γῆ/"earth", δίδωμι/"give", and οὕτως/"thus". As in MT a reference is unlikely. Isa 61:1^LXX shares κύριος/"Lord", ἰάομαι/"heal", συντρίβω/ "break" and καρδία/"heart" (τοὺς συντετριμμένους τῇ καρδίᾳ/"the broken ones for heart" similar to Ps 146:3^LXX τοὺς συντετριμμένους τὴν καρδίαν/"the broken ones in heart") with Ps 146^LXX; with Ps 147^LXX πνεῦμα/"wind", κύριος/ "Lord", and ἀποστέλλω/"send". There is some syntactical similarity with

---

287 Cf. Williams 2001, esp. 263 – 268, 275 – 276 (Isa^LXX depends on Ps^LXX); van der Meer 2010, esp. 162 – 167, 199 – 200 (Ps^LXX depends on Isa^LXX). For Ps 145 – 150^LXX overall, Ps 146 – 147^LXX show the only possible reference to Isa^LXX. Otherwise, the end of the LXX-Psalter does not show references to Isa^LXX nor the other way round (see II.3.3, III.3.3, IV.3.3, VI.3.3), which may even point towards their independence. Further research on this question is desirable.
288 See V.1.3.
289 Cf. Ziegler 1939, 267; Rahlfs and Hanhart 2006, 619.

Ps 146^{LXX}, but as in MT the collocation of a participle of συντρίβω/"break" with καρδία/"heart" also appears in other texts (Ps 33:19^{LXX} has the same phrase as Ps 146:3^{LXX}, Ps 50:19^{LXX}, Isa 57:15^{LXX}, and Isa 61:1^{LXX} have similar phrases), and a reference is unlikely. For Isa 11:12 and 56:8^{LXX} (נִדְחֵי יִשְׂרָאֵל/"the scattered ones of Israel" is uniquely translated as τοὺς ἀπολομένους Ισραηλ/"the destroyed ones of Israel" in Isa 11:12^{LXX} and as τοὺς διεσπαρμένους Ισραηλ/"the dispersed ones of Israel" in Isa 56:8^{LXX}, but Ps 146:2^{LXX} reads τὰς διασπορὰς τοῦ Ισραηλ/ "the dispersions of Israel"), as well as Isa 54:12^{LXX}, there is no syntactical similarity to either of Psalms 146–147^{LXX}, and a reference is less likely than in MT.

Results

For Ps 146–147^{LXX}, *some unlikely references are at least as unlikely in LXX* as in MT: Job 38^{LXX}. Ps 145^{LXX}(=146^{MT}) and 148^{LXX} show no reference except for the common superscription; there is no reference at all to Ps 149^{LXX} and 150^{LXX}.[290]

For Isa 40^{LXX} for both Psalms a *reference is less likely* than in MT. If present, it falls in line with the result of Ps 146^{LXX} stressing universal and Ps 147^{LXX} Israel-specific aspects. The reference to power and help in Ps 32^{LXX}(=33^{MT}) is *weaker than in MT* and applies to *Ps 146^{LXX} only*. The reference to Ps 134^{LXX}(=135^{MT}) is unclear as in MT though *less likely* in LXX, and if at all appears in Ps 146^{LXX} only.

Psalms 146–147^{LXX} show significant differences in their intertextuality both compared with MT and with each other. Firstly, a reference to Ps 103^{LXX} (=104^{MT}) which can only be assumed in MT is *clearly present* in *Ps 146^{LXX}*, but *not Ps 147^{LXX}*. Thus, the aspect of *universal creation* is stressed in Ps 146^{LXX} more than in MT and unlike in Ps 147^{LXX}. Secondly, the reference to Deut 4^{LXX} is as *likely as in MT* but for *Ps 147^{LXX} only*. Thus, the aspect of Israel's unique knowledge of God's law is stressed as in MT and unlike in *Ps 146^{LXX}*.

Through intertextuality Ps 146^{LXX} stresses the universal aspect of creation in contrast to Ps 147^{LXX} which stresses the Israel-specific aspect of the Torah. The two Psalms are not connected through references with each other.

No references at all are likely to Ps 1–2^{LXX} and Ps 145–150^{LXX}, not even framing Hallelujahs, and as in MT in contrast to Ps 148–150^{LXX} Ps 146–147^{LXX} do show other references, thus weakening the coherence of Ps 145–150^{LXX}. In its inclusion of references Ps 146–147^{LXX} are *similar to Ps 145^{LXX}*, but as in MT Ps 103^{LXX} (=104^{MT}) is the only reference text shared, and unlike in Ps 145^{LXX} there is no reference to Ps 144^{LXX}.

---

290 In answer to Brodersen 2013, 23 fn. 40, there is also no intertextual reference to 2 Mac 2:18^{LXX} due to a lack of shared words and syntactical similarity.

V.3.4 Content of Psalms 146 – 147^{LXX}

Beginning of Psalm 146:1^{LXX}

Following the superscription including αλληλουια/"Hallelujah", Ps 146^{LXX} begins with αἰνεῖτε τὸν κύριον/"praise the Lord".[291] It is debated whether LXX represents a different Hebrew original with two Hallelujahs,[292] translates the Hallelujah twice in a secondary, easier reading,[293] or translates the final Hebrew Hallelujah of Ps 146:10^{MT} as well as the opening Hallelujah of Ps 147^{MT}.[294] The last option would be unique in Ps 145 – 150^{LXX},[295] and it is most likely (though of course the exact Hebrew original of the LXX translation is unknown) that LXX translates the Hallelujah twice, thus making explicit its double function as a superscription and an imperative.

Compared to MT, the imperative following the superscription is a part of the first sentence, ὅτι/"for" is used only once as a causal conjunction, the unusual infinitive pi^{c}el is translated as a noun ψαλμός/"song of praise", and the adjectives refer to words for praise: ἀγαθόν/"good" is a neuter form forming the predicate for the general[296] ψαλμός/"song of praise", ἡδύνω/"be pleasing" for נָעִים/"pleasant" has αἴνεσις/"praise" as its subject, נָאוָה/"appropriate" is not translated.[297]

Who is called to praise in Psalm 146:1^{LXX}?

Ps 146:1a^{LXX} makes explicit with an imperative followed by ὅτι/"for" that the goodness of praise is a reason for praise. The recipient of praise, "our God", is found in v.1b instead of v.1a as in MT, stressing as a reason that praise is good *for God* as the recipient, not just generally. V.1b omits כִּי/"for" and נָאוָה/"appropriate" and translates the adjective נָעִים/"pleasant" with a verb.[298]

As in MT, a plural group of which the speaker is a member is called to praise "our God". Within Ps 146^{LXX}, a first person plural genitive pronoun is also found in vv.5 and 7. Those benefitting from God's actions are "we" (vv.1, 5, 7), Jerusalem

---

291 See p. 73 fn. 378.
292 Thus Allen 2002, 381 – 382 (but gloss also possible).
293 Thus Ballhorn 2004b, 310; similarly Allen 2002, 381 – 382 (gloss, but different original also possible).
294 Thus Allen 1983, 305; Zenger 2008h, 837.
295 As corrected in Allen 2002, 381 – 382.
296 Cf. Blass, Debrunner, and Rehkopf 1979, §131.
297 Cf. Zenger 2008h, 837; Brucker 2011a, 1879.
298 Cf. Zenger 2008h, 837; Brucker 2011a, 1879.

(v.2), Israel (v.2), wounded ones (v.3), humble ones (v.6), and pious ones (v.11). The repetition of κύριος/"Lord" (vv.1, 2, 5, 6, 7, 11) and θεός ἡμῶν/"our God" (vv.1, 7) connects these beneficiaries. While Jerusalem and Israel are only mentioned once, at the beginning, they are likely to designate "we" as the *people Israel, with a focus on their wounds, humility, and piety.*

What are the reasons for praise in Psalm 146:2–3^LXX?

Ps 146:2 contains a future form ἐπισυνάξει/"he will gather",[299] thus expressing a *future gathering of Israel* rather than a general one. Unlike in MT, the unique plural of διασπορά/"dispersion" can refer to real communities living in "diasporas", not just the abstract notion of being scattered.[300]

The additional καί/"and" in v.2 connects the two cola as in v.3.[301] Thus, the general[302] building of Jerusalem is connected with the future gathering of Israel.

The same root is used in Ps 146:3^LXX for συντετριμμένους/"wounded ones" and τὰ συντρίμματα/"wounds", connecting broken hearts and outer wounds, and thus placing an emphasis on inner rather than outer wounds, where God is needed as a comforter more than as a doctor. However, δεσμεύω/"bind" still keeps the image of outer wounds.[303] References to Isaiah[304] and thus the Babylonian exile are weaker in LXX than in MT. Instead, general and future actions are in view.

What are the reasons for praise in Psalm 146:4–5^LXX?

The article at the beginning of Ps 146:4^LXX connects v.4 with v.3, thus also connecting creation and healing. The additional καί/"and" in v.4 and v.5 connects the two cola of each as in vv.2–3.[305] מִסְפָּר/"number" is translated with the verb ἀριθμέω/"number, count" and then the noun ἀριθμός/"number" (Ps 146:4–5^LXX), but these stand at the beginning and end of the two verses like a frame.[306] Ps 146:5^LXX stresses God's greatness through the double use of μέγας/"great", and power as the subject of v.5a, though it is still dependent

---

299 Form used only here and in 2 Mac 2:18^LXX, but see fn. 290.
300 Thus Harl 1994, 286–287; Lust, Eynikel, and Hauspie 2003, s.v. διασπορά.
301 Cf. Zenger 2008h, 837.
302 See p. 213–214.
303 Cf. Lust, Eynikel, and Hauspie 2003, s.v. δεσμεύω.
304 See p. 219–220 on Isa.
305 Cf. Zenger 2008h, 837.
306 Cf. Brucker 2011a, 1880 (inclusio).

on God with the pronoun αὐτοῦ/"his", and connected through μέγας/"great".[307]
References to Isaiah are weaker in LXX, but God's power is clear.

What are the reasons for praise in Psalm 146:6^{LXX}?
As in MT, the humble ones are Israel, and the sinners non-Israelites, since in addition to MT, the repetition of κύριος/"Lord" connects vv.5, 6, and 7 and thus v.6 with "we" in vv.5 and 7. However, the Greek words stress a religious rather than physical aspect: πραΰς/"humble" is used mostly of persons in a religious context,[308] and ἁμαρτωλός/"sinner", while sometimes referring to physical enemies, can also be used in religious contexts.[309]

Who is called to praise in Psalm 146:7^{LXX}?
As in MT, Ps 146:7^{LXX} is addressed to the people Israel, calling them to be thankful. κίθαρα/"lyre" is even less specific for temple music than in MT.[310]

What are the reasons for praise in Psalm 146:8 – 9^{LXX}?
While as in MT vv.8 – 9 refer to creation, the dative participles depend on the call to praise for "our God" in v.7, further stressing the Psalm's theocentric view. Unlike in MT humans are found within these creation references through the addition of καὶ χλόην τῇ δουλείᾳ τῶν ἀνθρώπων/"and herb for the use of the humans" in v.8c.[311] As in MT, περιβάλλω/"cover" can mean "to clothe", but the context does not imply a personification of the heaven.[312] Mountains are not the direct object as in MT but God lets grass grow *on* mountains.[313] κτῆνος/"domestic animal" more explicitly than בְּהֵמָה/"animal" points to cattle,[314] thus hinting towards human labour as the additional sentence in v.8; the plural form makes the collective aspect in MT explicit. While the reference to Ps 103^{LXX}

---

307 Brucker 2011a, 1879, suggests that LXX may have read v.5b as a nominal sentence, "his" may be additional or due to the original Hebrew.
308 Cf. Lust, Eynikel, and Hauspie 2003, s.v. πραΰς.
309 Cf. Lust, Eynikel, and Hauspie 2003, s.v. ἁμαρτωλός.
310 See p. 80.
311 However, against Brucker 2011a, 1880, the aspect of care for humans is present in Ps 146:2, 3, 6, 10 – 11^{LXX}, not just 147:3 – 4^{LXX}.
312 Against Brucker 2011a, 1880.
313 Cf. Brucker 2011a, 1880.
314 Cf. Lust, Eynikel, and Hauspie 2003, s.v. κτῆνος.

(=104^{MT}) stresses the universality of creation, the reference back to v.7 stresses the subordination under one specific God, who shows universality as ravens in v.9 call *to him*, rather than just calling aimlessly as in MT.[315] The ravens' inequality with God is underlined through different translations for קרא/"call" as καλέω/"call" v.4 and ἐπικαλέω/"call upon" v.8. Unlike in MT, the ravens' food is τροφή/"food" without an allusion to "bread" of humans.[316] The additional καί/"and" in v.9 connects its two cola as in vv.2–5.[317]

What are the reasons for praise in Psalm 146:10–11^{LXX}?

Ps 146:10–11^{LXX} contains another future form θελήσει/"he will take pleasure", though this is followed by two present forms εὐδοκεῖ/"he delights". The connection between Ps 146:10–11^{LXX} is closer through the repetition of the same form εὐδοκεῖ/"he delights".[318] As in MT, the infrequent word κνήμη/"lower leg" refers to the lower leg.[319] οὐδὲ/"and not" in v.10 and the additional καί/"and" in v.11 connect the two cola of each as in vv.2–5, 9.[320] The reference text Ps 32^{LXX} (=33^{MT}) underlines war strength.

Thus, as in Hebrew, a general statement is in the foreground though including a stronger future aspect: God does not like strength in war but fear of himself, and this will especially be true for the future.

This is the final statement of Ps 146^{LXX}. Unlike in MT, the choosing of Israel does not appear as a reason for the God of Israel being the creator and ruler of nature who also cares for his people. Israel is mentioned in Ps 146:2^{LXX}, but the Psalm does not close with Israel as a chosen nation but with God's delight in those fearing him. The creation references are subordinate to God's goodness and his praise. God's greatness and rule of nature mainly functions as a reason to fear and praise him.

Who is called to praise in Psalm 147:1^{LXX}(=147:12^{MT})?

In Ps 147:1^{LXX}, Jerusalem is identified with Zion and called to praise. Those benefitting from God's actions are Jerusalem = Zion (vv.1–2) and its sons (v.2), and

---

315 Cf. Brucker 2011a, 1880.
316 Cf. Brucker 2011a, 1880.
317 Cf. Zenger 2008h, 837.
318 Cf. Brucker 2011a, 1880 (anadiplosis).
319 Cf. Lust, Eynikel, and Hauspie 2003, s.v. κνήμη; Bons 2009b, 895.
320 Cf. Zenger 2008h, 837.

Israel = Jacob (v.8). As in MT, Jerusalem is a metonymy for the people Israel. Thus, much more than in Ps 146^{LXX} the *people Israel as a nation* are in view.

What are the reasons for praise in Psalm 147:2 – 3^{LXX}(=147:13 – 14^{MT})?

As in MT, the reasons for the call to praise, introduced by ὅτι/"for", are God's protection and blessing (in aorist forms), and peace and finest food (with present participles). The singular גְּבוּלֵךְ/"your territory" is translated as a plural τὰ ὅριά σου/"your borders" (as in MT without a preposition as an accusative of space[321]), as in MT referring to an enclosed territory.[322]

What are the reasons for praise in Psalm 147:4 – 7^{LXX}(=147:15 – 18^{MT})?

Hebrew imperfect forms are translated with future forms where they are connected with God's word (vv.4b, 7), otherwise with participles (vv.4a, 5, 6a). The future form in v.6b is connected with creation but introduces the next future form which refers to the word. The genitive participles in vv.5 – 8 referring to creation depend on ὁ λόγος αὐτοῦ/"his word" in v.4b. Thus, creation is subordinate to the importance of the word, while serving to stress the power of the one sending the word. The word will, in the future, melt ice and let waters flow. The same word is (in a present participle) announced to Israel. There is no indication of a metaphoric use of future weather in Ps 147^{LXX}, it seems to refer to general weather phenomena. The dative τῇ γῇ/"for the earth" translates the Hebrew *accusativus loci*, thus likely representing a locative dative.[323]

πνεύσει τὸ πνεῦμα/"he will blow his wind" in Ps 147:7^{LXX} uses related words, literally "he will blow his blowing" if as in MT God is the subject (while τὸ πνεῦμα αὐτοῦ/"his wind" could be nominative or accusative, it is less likely that it is nominative and thus means "his wind will blow" since as in MT God is the subject of the preceding cola).[324]

כְּפוֹר/"hoarfrost" is translated as ὁμίχλη/"mist".[325] The accusative neuter plural αὐτά/"them" in v.7a refers to snow, mist, and ice mentioned in vv.5 – 6.[326]

---

321 Cf. Smyth and Messing 1956, §1580 – 1581; Blass, Debrunner, and Rehkopf 1979, §161.
322 Cf. Bons 2009b, 896.
323 Cf. Smyth and Messing 1956, §1530; Blass, Debrunner, and Rehkopf 1979, §199.
324 Cf. Bons 2009b, 896; Brucker 2011b, 1881.
325 Cf. Brucker 2011b, 1881 (translator did not know the rare Hebrew word).
326 The neuter plural may be a *constructio ad sensum* for more than one collective noun, cf. Blass, Debrunner, and Rehkopf 1979, §134, 282. Similarly Brucker 2011b, 1881.

What are the reasons for praise in Psalm 147:8 – 9^{LXX}(=147:19 – 20^{MT})?

Ps 147^{LXX} ends with the statement that God has not made his laws known to any nations except Israel, with unlike in MT God as the subject, and the laws explicitly being "his" unlike in MT.

Unlike in Ps 146^{LXX}, *Israel is the main concern of Ps 147^{LXX}*. The importance of creation is subordinate to that of God's word which he gives to Israel alone.

V.3.5 Genre of Psalms 146 – 147^{LXX}

Within Ps 146^{LXX}, תְּהִלָּה/"praise" in v.1b is translated as the general αἴνεσις/ "praise", but, pointing to a sung hymn, ψαλμός/"song of praise" is also used in v.1a as in superscriptions of other Psalms (e. g. Ps 99^{LXX}=100^{MT}).[327] However, the strong reference to Ps 103^{LXX} (=104^{MT}) in Ps 146^{LXX} also shows a literary connection, as does the reference to Deut 4 in Ps 147^{LXX}. A cultic or literary setting depends on the setting of the LXX-Psalter as a whole.

V.3.6 Date of Psalms 146 – 147^{LXX}

The intertextual references within LXX but outside the Psalter to *Deut 4^{LXX}* (and possibly Isa^{LXX}) point towards dating Ps 146 – 147^{LXX} *after the 3rd century BCE* (and possibly the 2nd century BCE),[328] in line with general considerations about a 2nd century BCE LXX-Psalter.[329] Thus, Ps 146 – 147^{LXX} are likely to have their time of origin after the 4th (because of MT), after the 3rd (because of Deu^{LXX}), *in the 2nd century BCE* (because of the LXX-Psalter).

V.3.7 Unity of Psalms 146 – 147^{LXX}

Ps 146^{LXX} and Ps 147^{LXX} are two separate texts, but each in itself one unit.

---

327 In Ps 99^{LXX}(=100^{MT}), the superscription also contains תּוֹדָה/"thanksgiving", translated as in Ps 146:7^{LXX} as ἐξομολόγησις/"thanksgiving". However, see fn. 177.
328 Cf. Siegert 2001, 42– 43 (Deut^{LXX} 3rd, Isa^{LXX} 2nd century BCE). However, manuscripts of Deut 4^{LXX} (or Isa^{LXX}) are not preserved from any time BCE, cf. Siegert 2001, 96 – 98 in combination with with Septuaginta-Unternehmen der Akademie der Wissenschaften zu Göttingen 2012. On Isa^{LXX} see also fn. 287.
329 See p. 16, esp. fn. 104.

For both Psalms some manuscripts miss out Αγγαιου καὶ Ζαχαριου/"of Haggai and Zechariah" as in Ps 149 – 150^{LXX}.[330] There are no final Hallelujahs for either LXX-Psalm.

In Ps 146:1^{LXX}, some manuscripts read the masculine ἀγαθός/"good" (in a nominative or accusative form), thus referring to God's goodness rather than the goodness of praise. καί/"and" is missing in some manuscripts in v.2a, and added in v.9b. In v.5, some manuscripts read αἴνεσις/"praise" instead of σύνεσις/"understanding", thus taking the focus away from the reasons for praise to praise itself. In v.6, the article before γῆ/"earth" is missing in some manuscripts as in MT. The additional sentence in v.8 strengthening the reference to Ps 103^{LXX} is missing in Codex Alexandrinus only. Whether within LXX this points to the later addition of the sentence or its later omission due to the duplication with Ps 103^{LXX} cannot be decided.[331] Some manuscripts change the tenses of εὐδοκεῖ/"he delights" in vv.10 – 11 to first future then aorist forms.

V.3.8 Overall Interpretation of Psalms 146 – 147^{LXX}

Ps 146^{LXX} and Ps 147^{LXX} form two separate, theocentric hymns, with the same superscription as Ps 145 – 147^{LXX}.

In Ps 146^{LXX}, the God of Israel and ruler of nature is to be praised by the people Israel with an emphasis on their *general piety*. The reasons for praise are God's general and *future actions for Israel* as well as general actions in creation. An intertextual reference to Ps 103^{LXX} strengthens the aspect of *universal creation*.

In Ps 147^{LXX}, the God of Israel = Jacob and Jerusalem = Zion and creator and ruler of nature through his word is to be praised by the people Israel with an emphasis on their status as the *only chosen people*. The reasons for praise are God's past and present actions for Israel and *future actions in creation*. An intertextual reference to Deut 4^{LXX} strengthens the aspect of *Israel's election*.

---

330 See p. 17 fn. 109.
331 It may be a secondary addition, thus Allen 1983, 306 (similar to Ps 148:5^{LXX}); Zenger 2008h, 826; Brucker 2011a, 1880; or either this or a different original, thus Bons 2009b, 895. In Ps 148:5^{LXX}, the addition is present in all manuscripts, cf. Rahlfs 1979, 337. The example of Ps 148^{LXX} and the lack of a different Hebrew original point to an addition in LXX.

V.4 Comparison

Both DSS (4QPs^d, 11QPs^a, and MasPs^b; 4QPs^e does not contain Ps 147) and (apart from the split of Ps 146–147^{LXX}) LXX are very *close* to MT, but also show significant differences. LXX adds a future perspective in both Psalms.

The framing *Hallelujahs* are inconsistent: both the opening and closing Hallelujah are preserved in 4QPs^d but not preserved in the other DSS, while LXX has no closing Hallelujahs at all and adds a superscription to each Psalm, the first of which thus both transliterates and translates the opening Hallelujah. This weakens the likelihood of an original connection of Psalms 146–150.

Regarding *order*, DSS show several different contexts for Ps 147 (Ps 104–147–105 in 11QPs^a, 106(?)-147–104 in 4QPs^d, and similar to MT close to Ps 150 only in MasPs^b), and LXX splits Ps 147 into two Psalms 146^{LXX} and Ps 147^{LXX}. This weakens the likelihood of an original connection of Psalms 146–150.[332]

Regarding *intertextuality*, LXX strengthens a reference to Ps 103^{LXX}(=104^{MT}) through an addition. This reference may be confirmed by DSS through collocation (Ps 104–147 in 11QPs^a, 147–104 in 4QPs^d).[333] LXX also separates the additional reference to creation in Ps 103^{LXX}(=104^{MT}) in Ps 146^{LXX} from the reference to Israel's election in Deut 4^{LXX} in Ps 147^{LXX}. Otherwise, the likelihood of references in MT is mostly weakened by LXX. There are no references to Ps 146–150^{MT} in either DSS or LXX.

DSS and LXX show two similarities against MT: the stronger reference to Ps 104, and God as a subject in the final colon of Ps 147 (preserved in 11QPs^a but not 4QPs^d), though the laws are "his" only in LXX.[334]

---

332 Seybold 2010, 162, concludes that MT and LXX may be later than DSS. This is contrary to Skehan, see fn. 333, and Dahmen, see fn. 334.
333 Also noted by Skehan 1973, 201–202, 205 (concluding that MT is earlier than 11QPs^a); Flint 1997, 165.
334 Dahmen 2003, 120, also notes this second similarity with its variation and concludes that 11QPs^a and LXX are independent recipients of MT. Against Dahmen, the aorist form in the final colon of Ps 147^{LXX} may represent a perfect form as in 11QPs^a since perfect forms are translated with aorists at the beginning of Ps 147^{LXX}, see p. 213–214.

VI Psalm 146

VI.1 Psalm 146^{MT}

VI.1.1 Translation of Psalm 146^{MT}

1H	Praise-Yah!	הַלְלוּ־יָהּ	1H
1	Praise, my soul, YHWH!	הַלְלִי נַפְשִׁי אֶת־יְהוָה:	1
2a	Let me praise YHWH during my life,	אֲהַלְלָה יְהוָה בְּחַיָּי	2a
2b	let me make music to my God during my continu-ance.	אֲזַמְּרָה לֵאלֹהַי בְּעוֹדִי:	2b
3a	Do not trust in rulers,	אַל־תִּבְטְחוּ בִנְדִיבִים	3a
3b	in a son of man who has no saving.	בְּבֶן־אָדָם‍׀ שֶׁאֵין לוֹ תְשׁוּעָה:	3b
4a	His breath goes out, he returns to his ground,	תֵּצֵא רוּחוֹ יָשֻׁב לְאַדְמָתוֹ	4a
4b	on that day have perished his thoughts.	בַּיּוֹם הַהוּא אָבְדוּ עֶשְׁתֹּנֹתָיו:	4b
5a	Happy (is) the one whose helper is the God of Jacob,	אַשְׁרֵי שֶׁאֵל יַעֲקֹב בְּעֶזְרוֹ	5a
5b	whose hope (is) on YHWH his God,	שִׂבְרוֹ עַל־יְהוָה אֱלֹהָיו:	5b
6a	making heaven and earth, the sea, and all which (is) in them,	עֹשֶׂה‍׀ שָׁמַיִם וָאָרֶץ אֶת־הַיָּם וְאֶת־כָּל־אֲשֶׁר־בָּם	6a
6b	the one preserving truthfulness for eternity,	הַשֹּׁמֵר אֱמֶת לְעוֹלָם:	6b
7a	making judgement for the oppressed ones,	עֹשֶׂה מִשְׁפָּט‍׀ לָעֲשׁוּקִים	7a
7b	giving bread for the hungry,	נֹתֵן לֶחֶם לָרְעֵבִים	7b
7c	YHWH freeing the bound ones.	יְהוָה מַתִּיר אֲסוּרִים:	7c
8a	YHWH opening blind ones,	יְהוָה‍׀ פֹּקֵחַ עִוְרִים	8a
8b	YHWH raising up bowed down ones,	יְהוָה זֹקֵף כְּפוּפִים	8b
8c	YHWH loving righteous ones,	יְהוָה אֹהֵב צַדִּיקִים:	8c
9a	YHWH preserving strangers;	יְהוָה‍׀ שֹׁמֵר אֶת־גֵּרִים	9a
9b	orphan and widow he restores,	יָתוֹם וְאַלְמָנָה יְעוֹדֵד	9b
9c	and a path of wicked ones he makes crooked.	וְדֶרֶךְ רְשָׁעִים יְעַוֵּת:	9c
10a	YHWH is king for eternity,	יִמְלֹךְ יְהוָה‍׀ לְעוֹלָם	10a
10b	your God, Zion, for generation and generation.	אֱלֹהַיִךְ צִיּוֹן לְדֹר וָדֹר	10b
10H	Praise-Yah!	הַלְלוּ־יָהּ:	10H

DOI 10.1515/9783110536096-006

VI.1.2 Form of Psalm 146^{MT}

Outline of Psalm 146^{MT}

1H	Framing *Imperative*	
Introduction		
1–2	Calls to Praise	Subject: Psalmist, Object: YHWH
	Imperatives/Cohortatives	
Part I		
3–4	Exhortation	Subject: Group, Object: Human Rulers
	Jussive/Imperfect, Perfect	
Part II		
5	Beatitude	Subject: Individual, Object: YHWH
	Nominal Sentence	
6–9	Reasons	Subject: YHWH, Object: Creation, Powerless
	Participles (referring to v.5)	
Conclusion		
10	Summary	Subjects: YHWH, Zion
	Imperfect	
10H	Framing *Imperative*	

Syntax of Psalm 146^{MT}

הלל/"praise" is used twice in the frame, and twice in the rest of the Psalm, stressing the aspect of praise. The only other verbs used twice are עשה/"make" and שמר/"preserve", both used in two singular participles referring to YHWH, the first one of each in the context of creation in v.6, and then in the context of help in v.7 and 9. Thus, *creation and help are connected.*[1] The first part of Ps 146 (vv.1–4) is dominated by *imperatives* (with cohortatives and a jussive)[2] (vv.1, 2a, 2b, 3a), with two *imperfect* forms (v.4a)[3] and one *perfect* form (v.4b). Thus, the call to praise is stressed in the first part. The second part (vv.5–10) is dominated by *participles* (vv.6ab, 7abc, 8abc, 9a), with three *imperfect* forms at the end (vv.9bc, 10).[4] Thus, the reasons for praise, namely YHWH's general[5]

---

1 Cf. Ballhorn 2004b, 305–306.

2 These are equivalents of imperatives, cf. Gesenius and Kautzsch 1909, §46, 48, 108–110.

3 The imperfect forms here probably refer to repeated present events, cf. Gesenius and Kautzsch 1909, §107, and are best translated into English by a present tense.

4 The last imperfect in v.10 is sometimes seen as a jussive due to the word order, cf. Zenger 2008g, 812 (contrast to Ex 15:18); Ballhorn 2004b, 308 (contrast to YHWH-king-Psalms to which Ps 146 refers, but in an eschatological light), but there is no specific word order for jussive forms, cf. Gesenius and Kautzsch 1909, §109, and, in contrast to v.9, v.10 shows the normal word

actions, are stressed in the second part. This second part, dominated by participles which do not appear in the first part, is longer than the first one, thus stressing YHWH's power over those of human rulers.[6] While the two participles in v.7ab have direct objects and indirect objects with לְ/"for", the participles in vv.7c–a only have direct objects. Only the participle in v.6b is preceded by an article, which may point to its introductory place regarding the following participles,[7] though it may also point to its concluding place regarding the preceding participle, or connect the preceding and following participles. The last seems most likely since the immediately surrounding participles both are עֹשֶׂה/"making".

The *subjects* are the Psalmist (i.e. the author's individual persona) in vv.1–2, a group of unknown addressees in v.3a warned about human rulers in vv.3–4 (their breath and thoughts are subjects in v.4), an unknown single addressee whose God is YHWH in v.5, YHWH in vv.6–9, and both God as a subject and Zion as an addressee in v.10. As also stressed by *suffixes* to אֱלֹהִים/"god" (first person singular "my" in v.2b, third person singular "his" in v.5b, second person singular "your" in v.10)[8] and the occurrence of God first as an object and then as a subject, there are many subjects praising, but only one subject is the reason for their praise: YHWH.

Objects in Ps 146 are YHWH or אֱלֹהִים/"god" as the object of praise in vv.1–2, 5, and 10, human rulers in vv.3–4, creation and powerless humans in vv.6–9b, and the indirect object of wicked ones in v.9c (their *path*), whereas v.10 has no direct objects but repeats the *adverbial phrase*[9] לְעוֹלָם/"for eternity" as in v.6b, and strengthens it with the synonymous לְדֹר וָדֹר/"for generation and generation". While v.6b summarises the creation aspect, v.10 summarises both this and the help aspect as reasons for the praise of YHWH. The accusative

---

order. Another reason for a jussive is seeing v.10 as an acclamation, cf. Michel 1956, 68, but it may also be a statement. In contrast, Reindl 1981a, 131, esp. fn. 54, gives examples of participles continued by imperfect forms.

5 The participle עֹשֶׂה/"making" is seen to refer to a general action of upholding creation ("creatio continuata") rather than a past action of creation ("creatio prima"; on these terms cf. Janowski 2004), cf. Ballhorn 2004b, 305; Zenger 2008g, 818–819. Since participles usually refer to general actions, see p. 100 fn. 110, this is possible, though the use of the same phrase עֹשֶׂה שָׁמַיִם וָאָרֶץ/"making heaven and earth" in other Psalms, see fn. 48, may – despite the repetition of the participle in Ps 146:6–7 – point towards a formula with past connotations, cf. Ps 115:15 where it is followed by a perfect form. For the imperfect forms see fn. 3.

6 Cf. Ballhorn 2004b, 305.

7 Cf. Reindl 1981a, 129–130; Ballhorn 2004b, 305–306 fn. 769 (referring to Reindl).

8 Cf. Allen 2002, 380.

9 See p. 32 fn. 8.

marker אֶת (with maqqef אֶת־)[10] stresses the objects of YHWH in v.1 (but not
v.2a), the sea and all creation in v.6a, and strangers in v.9a.

The *word order*[11] is reversed in vv.7c – 9c where the subject YHWH (vv.7c – 9a)
and the objects orphan, widow, and path of wicked ones are stressed (vv.9bc).[12]

Structure of Psalm 146[MT]

The structure of Ps 146[MT] is: Hallelujah – introduction vv.1–2 (with "my God") –
main body vv.3–9 (Part I: vv.3–4 exhortation, Part II: v.5 beatitude "his God",
vv.6–9 participles with v.6 creation and vv.7–9 help) – conclusion v.10 (with
"your God") – Hallelujah.[13] Vv.1–2 and v.10 as the frame both contain a vocative
and a suffixed form of אֱלֹהִים/"god" in chiastic orders.[14] The second part of the
main body is longer than the first part,[15] with vv.7–9 consisting of tricola rather
than bicola,[16] stressing the central importance of this second part which describes YHWH's power, giving reasons for the beatitude in v.5, and indirectly
for the call to praise in the introduction followed by the exhortation. V.5 forms
the centre of the Psalm, preceded by its negative contrast in vv.3–4 and followed
by reasons in vv.6–9.[17]

Other commentators also see a Hallelujah-frame, introduction vv.1–2, and
conclusion v.10, but divide the main body into two strophes of an equal number
of lines (4 each, thus vv.3–6a, 6b–9) with v.6b starting a new sentence with a
participle with article,[18] which is less likely since it could also conclude a sentence,[19] or into three chiastic parts (vv.3–4 wisdom, vv.5–8b creation and
help, vv.8c–10 wisdom),[20] which is less likely since it splits up the row of participles and is driven by categories of content (wisdom) coming from outside
the Psalm.[21]

---

10 Cf. Gesenius and Kautzsch 1909, §117.
11 See p. 32 fn. 4.
12 Cf. Reindl 1981a, 119–121 (like a litany and its double ending).
13 Cf. Lohfink 1990, 109–110; Gerstenberger 2001, 437; Ballhorn 2004b, 305 (referring to Lohfink); Zenger 2008g, 813–814, 816.
14 Cf. Kselman 1988, 592.
15 Cf. Lohfink 1990, 110; Ballhorn 2004b, 305.
16 Cf. Hupfeld 1871, 438 (plus v.6 as a tricolon).
17 Cf. Gunkel 1926, 613 (with v.6b starting a new sentence); Lohfink 1990, 110.
18 Cf. Allen 2002, 375–377 (also discussing other divisions). See fn. 7.
19 See p. 232.
20 Cf. Kselman 1988, 591.
21 Cf. Lohfink 1990, 109.

Poetic Devices in Psalm 146^{MT}

Between the framing Hallelujahs Ps 146 consists of monocola (v.1), bicola (vv.2, 3, 4, 5, 6, 10), and tricola (v.7, 8, 9). V.1 stands out as the only monocolon, serving as a general introduction. While most verses show *synthetic parallels* (bicola: vv.3, 4, 6, tricola: vv.7, 8, 9), the introduction, centre, and conclusion are stressed by *synonymous parallels* (vv.2, 5, 10).[22]

Among the many poetic devices noted by commentators,[23] the Psalm is sometimes seen as an *alphabetic* acrostic because the number of its cola corresponds to the number of letters in the Hebrew alphabet.[24] However, this depends on the number of cola assumed for Ps 146 (22 if v.6ab are counted as 2 cola, 23 if they are counted as 3, but 24 or 25 if the Hallelujah-frame is included), and ignores the fact that (contrary to e. g. Ps 119; 145) there are no alphabetic features in Psalm 146 at all, and any alphabetic connotations rest solely on the number of cola.[25]

The *repetition* of the relative particle[26] שֶׁ in v.3b and v.5a contrasts the inability of human rulers with the power of YHWH.[27] While the contrast between צַדִּיקִים/"righteous ones" in v.8c and רְשָׁעִים/"wicked ones" in v.9c is sometimes seen to form an *envelope* around v.9ab,[28] this rests on the semantic assumption that these contrasting words have to be connected,[29] but in Ps 146, צַדִּיקִים/"righteous ones" stands in a whole list of those looked after by YHWH whereas רְשָׁעִים/"wicked ones" stands on its own as the contrasting end of this whole list.[30] An *enveloping ABA structure* can be found in (A) vv.3 – 4 warning about the futility of human rulers and (A) v.9c describing how YHWH deals with the path of רְשָׁעִים/

---

22 This division into bicola and tricola is seen differently by commentators, see fn. 18, and cf. Kselman 1988, 593 (new tricolon starting in v.6c). In any division, the fivefold repetition of YHWH in vv.7c – 9a shows that neither mere bicola nor mere tricola can describe Ps 146. In any case, introduction, centre, and conclusion are highlighted through synonymous parallels.

23 Cf. Kselman 1988, 592–596.

24 Cf. Bickell 1883, 272 (as many cola as letters in the alphabet, like Ps 147); Gunkel 1926, 139, 612 (23 cola, counting v.6a as two); Kselman 1988, 591 (22 or 23 cola). The number of letters in the Hebrew alphabet is 22 (or 23 if שׂ and שׁ are counted as two letters), cf. Gesenius and Kautzsch 1909, §5b; Joüon and Muraoka 2011, §5c.

25 Cf. Reindl 1981a, 125–126.

26 On relative particles cf. Joüon and Muraoka 2011, §38, 145; Gesenius and Kautzsch 1909, §36, 138. Where relative pronouns cannot be used in English, their function is expressed by a colon in VI.1.

27 Cf. Kselman 1988, 593.

28 Cf. Kselman 1988, 594–595.

29 However, רְשָׁעִים/"wicked ones" appear without צַדִּיקִים/"righteous ones" e. g. in Ps 3:8; 12:9, the other way round e. g. in Ps 33:1; 52:8.

30 Cf. Ballhorn 2004b, 306–307.

"wicked ones", with (B) vv.5–9b describing his actions for the powerless in the middle. The repetition of לְעוֹלָם/"for eternity" in v.6b and v.10a envelops YHWH's actions. V.5 shows a *chiastic structure* with help and hope encircled by YHWH.

VI.1.3 Intertextuality in Psalm 146^MT

Importance

Psalm 146 is often described as an anthological[31] Psalm containing references to whole lists of other texts in HB,[32] written by a wise creative author,[33] or a late Psalm[34] written for the literary context of the end of the Psalter by its final redactors,[35] and universalising[36] or eschatologising[37] its reference texts. However, other commentators note that the similarities to other texts are common topics and forms of hymns,[38] that there are virtually no word-by-word references to any other text, that therefore the weight of references should not be overestimated, and readers have to fill in their own associations.[39]

Analysis

Commentators argue that Ps 146:4 refers to *Genesis* 3:19, Ps 146:6 to Gen 1 and Gen 9.[40] Gen 3:19 shares אֲדָמָה/"ground" and שׁוב/"return" with Ps 146:4 (also לֶחֶם/"food"; and in Gen 3:17 אָדָם/"human"). With reference to human mortality[41] the two words only appear in these two passages, but there is no syntactical similarity, and a common topic is more likely. Similarly, rather than a direct refer-

---

31 Cf. Reindl 1981a, 123–125 (referring to Deißler); Kselman 1988, 589; Ballhorn 2004b, 304, 306 (referring to Deißler), 308; Zenger 2008g, 815. Deißler 1955, 23 fn. 37, refers to A. Robert for the term, as does Kselman 1988, 589 fn. 8. The Greek word ἀνθολόγος means "flower-gathering", cf. Liddell, Scott, and Jones 1996, s.v. ἀνθολόγος.

32 Cf. Duhm 1922, 476 (Ps 146 a collection of quotations), and the lists in Reindl 1981a, 123–125; Malchow 1977, 1166; Kselman 1988, 589; Lohfink 1990, 111–114; Leuenberger 2004, 346–347; Zenger 2008g, 814–815.

33 Cf. Reindl 1981a, 123–125, 134–135.

34 Cf. Malchow 1977, 1166; Kselman 1988, 589 (postexilic); Lohfink 1990, 111–114.

35 Cf. Leuenberger 2004, 348; Zenger 2008g, 815.

36 Cf. Zenger 2008g, 819.

37 Cf. Ballhorn 2004b, 308.

38 Cf. Gunkel 1926, 612.

39 Cf. Mathys 1994, 269–270 (referring to Gunkel, see fn. 38).

40 Cf. Reindl 1981a, 123 (Gen 3:19), 128; Kselman 1988, 589 (Gen 3:19); Lohfink 1990, 111 (Gen 3:19; 9:12, 16); Zenger 2008g, 814, 817–819 (Gen 1:1–3; 3:19; 9:1–17).

41 In contrast to, e.g., the reference to returning to a land in Gen 28:15; Jer 16:15.

ence to Gen 1 which only shares frequent words with Ps 146, a formulaic reference to creation[42] and an indirect reference through Ex 20:11 (see below on Exodus) is likely. Gen 9 only shares frequent words with Ps 146, wherefore intertextual references are unlikely.

While some commentators hold that there is a reference from Ps 146:10 to *Exodus* 15:18 (Red Sea: Moses' Song),[43] others see the two verses as independent interpretations of a formula.[44] Ps 146:6 is often seen as quoting Ex 20:11 (Sabbath Commandment).[45] Ex 15:18 shares יְהוָה/"YHWH", יִמְלֹךְ/"he will be king" (same form) and לְעוֹלָם/"for eternity" (same combination) with Ps 146:10. The combination of these three words is unique to the two texts only through the imperfect form.[46] A common topic (YHWH's kingship) seems more likely.[47] Ex 20:11 shares the underlined words עָשָׂה יְהוָה אֶת־הַשָּׁמַיִם וְאֶת־הָאָרֶץ אֶת־הַיָּם וְאֶת־כָּל־אֲשֶׁר־בָּם/"YHWH made the heaven and the earth and the sea and all which (is) in them" with Ps 146 (and also יוֹם/"day"). Only the phrase אֶת־הַיָּם וְאֶת־כָּל־אֲשֶׁר־בָּם/"the sea and all which (is) in them" in Ps 146:6 is syntactically identical and shared only in these two texts, thus making a reference likely, while the beginning of Ps 146:6 with the frequent phrase עֹשֶׂה שָׁמַיִם וָאָרֶץ/"making heaven and earth" could be a formula.[48] Ex 20:11 refers to the seven days of creation in Gen 1:1–2:4a.[49] Thus, Ps 146 indirectly also refers to this creation account. Ex 20:11 is usually dated to the 6th to 5th century BCE,[50] as is Gen 1:1–2:4a,[51] but neither is certain.[52] A date of Ps 146 mainly rests on the date of its reference

---

42 Cf. Zenger 2008g, 818.

43 Cf. Gunkel 1926, 614; Reindl 1981a, 124; Kselman 1988, 589; Zenger 2008g, 815.

44 Cf. Ballhorn 2004b, 308; Leuenberger 2004, 27.

45 Cf. Reindl 1981a, 124 (addition in Ps 146:6 from Ex 20:11); Kselman 1988, 589; Ballhorn 2004b, 306 (v.6aβ quotes Ex 20:11); Zenger 2008g, 814.

46 See e.g. 1 Chr 28:4 (King David as subject; infinitive); Mic 4:7 (God as subject; waw-perfect) where all three words appear.

47 Ballhorn 2004b, 307–308, argues for an eschatologising reference from Ps 146 to Ps 93–99, but a common topic (see e.g. Ps 10; 29; 47) is more likely.

48 It appears in Ps 115:15; 121:2; 124:8; 134:3; 146:6, but everywhere except in Ps 146:6 with the construct state עֹשֵׂה/"making" instead of the absolute עֹשֶׂה/"making", cf. Reindl 1981a, 118–119. This may be due to the list of participles in the absolute state in Ps 146. See p. 231 fn. 5 Ex 20:11 uses the perfect form עָשָׂה "made".

49 Cf. Houston 2007, 81. Amongst other words, Gen 2:1–3 and Ex 20:11 uniquely share בַּיּוֹם הַשְּׁבִיעִי/"on the seventh day" with ברך/"bless", קדשׁ/"be holy", and the root שׁבת/"rest". Since Ex 20:11 only contains a part of the story of Gen 1:1–2:4a, it is more likely to refer to Gen than vice versa.

50 Cf. Houston 2007, 68 (P, "priestly author"), 81.

51 Cf. Whybray 2007, 41–42.

52 Cf. Davies 2007, 16; Whybray 2007, 39–43.

texts.[53] Thus, relative dates have to be considered: The shared phrase with Ex 20:11 is in Ps 146:6 preceded by another frequent phrase (internal coherence: Ps 146 less coherent). The Ten Commandments in Ex 20 are important for references within HB generally (external coherence: Ps 146 more likely to allude).[54] Although both Ex 20:11 and Ps 146 contain references (recurrence equal), Ps 146:7 probably refers to Ex 20:11 and thus to the Sabbath commandment rather than vice versa. Thus, Ps 146 contains a reference to the Sabbath commandment in Ex 20:11, and, indirectly, to the creation account in Gen 1:1–2:4a.

While some commentators argue for a reference from Ps 146:9 to *Deuteronomy* 10:18,[55] others see a similar topic but no direct intertextual link.[56] Deut 10:18 reads עֹשֶׂה מִשְׁפַּט יָתוֹם וְאַלְמָנָה וְאֹהֵב גֵּר לָתֶת לוֹ לֶחֶם וְשִׂמְלָה / "making judgement (for) orphan and widow, and loving stranger to give him food and clothing" and thus shares the underlined words plus the preposition לְ/"for" with the entire Psalm 146; the only word not shared is שִׂמְלָה/"clothing". Syntactical similarities are יָתוֹם וְאַלְמָנָה/"orphan and widow" (not unique to these two texts[57]), עֹשֶׂה מִשְׁפַּט/"making judgement" (only in these two passages used of God,[58] but referring to oppressed ones in Ps 146:7). The combination of יָתוֹם/"orphan", אַלְמָנָה/ "widow", and גֵּר/"stranger" is not unique to the two texts.[59] Since no rare words or rare combinations of words are shared,[60] and there is limited syntactical similarity, a direct intertextual reference is less likely than a common topic (protection for stranger, orphan and widow; a topic prominent in but not unique to Deuteronomy[61]).

Commentators sometimes hold the view that Ps 146 refers to *Psalm 1*,[62] with consequences including a stronger disqualification of human rulers and a uni-

53 See VI.1.6.

54 Cf. Otto 1999, esp. 628.

55 Cf. the lists in Reindl 1981a, 124; Kselman 1988, 589; Lohfink 1990, 113; Zenger 2008g, 814.

56 Cf. Ballhorn 2004b, 306. Kselman 1988, 593–594; Lohfink 1990, 113; Zenger 2008g, 821, mention the frequent appearance of the topic but still argue for an intertextual reference to Deut 10:18, see fn. 72.

57 Cf. Deut 10:18; 27:19; Ps 146:9; Jer 7:6; 22:3; Ezek 22:7.

58 Cf. Deut 10:18 (God); 2 Sam 8:15 (King David); 1 Chr 18:14 (King David); Ps 146:7 (God); Jer 5:1 (any person).

59 Cf. Deut 10:18; 14:29; 16:11, 14; 24:17, 19–21; 26:12–13; 27:19; Ps 94:6; 146:9; Jer 7:6; 22:3; Ezek 22:7; Zech 7:10; Mal 3:5.

60 Neither the participle אֹהֵב/"loving" nor the combination of נתן/"give" and לֶחֶם/"food" (cf. Kselman 1988, 594 fn. 27) are unusual.

61 See fn. 57. See also p. 243–244.

62 Cf. the lists in Kselman 1988, 589; Zenger 2008g, 814–815.

fied redactional origin of Ps 146,[63] or an eschatological interpretation of Ps 146,[64] or a secondary addition in Ps 146:8b, 9b on the basis of Ps 1:6.[65] The reference is sometimes seen as present but weak[66] due to differences.[67] Shared are אַשְׁרֵי/ "blessed", רָשָׁע/"wicked" and דֶּרֶךְ/"path" (דֶּרֶךְ רְשָׁעִים/"path of wicked ones"), יהוה/"YHWH", נתן/"give", כֹּל/"all", עשׂה/"make", רוּחַ/"wind", מִשְׁפָּט/"judgement", צַדִּיק/"righteous" (צַדִּיקִים/"righteous ones"), and אבד/"perish". The strongest syntactical similarity is in the phrase דֶּרֶךְ רְשָׁעִים/"path of wicked ones", but this phrase is not unique to the two Psalms,[68] wherefore an intertextual reference is unlikely.

Ps 146 is often thought to refer to *Psalm 103 and Psalm 104*,[69] with consequences including a late date of Ps 146[70] and the interpretation of Ps 146 on the background of YHWH's universal kingship[71] and highlighting the universalism of its praise.[72] Ps 103 shares נַפְשִׁי אֶת־יְהוָה/"my soul YHWH" (preceded by an imperative singular of ברך/"bless" in Ps 103 but הלל/"praise" in Ps 146) in Ps 103:1, 2, 22 and Ps 146:1, and the words אֱלֹהִים/"god" (first person singular suffix), כֹּל/"all", אַל/"not", חַיִּים/"life", עשׂה/"do" (including עֹשֶׂה/"doing"), יהוה/ "YHWH", מִשְׁפָּט/"judgement", עשׁק/"oppress" (עֲשׁוּקִים/"oppressed ones"), דֶּרֶךְ/ "path", בֵּן/"son", עוֹלָם/"eternity" (including לְעוֹלָם/"for eternity"), שָׁמַיִם/"heaven", אֶרֶץ/"earth", הוּא/"he", יוֹם/"day", רוּחַ/"wind", אַיִן/"there is not", עוֹד/"continuance", and שׁמר/"preserve". Ps 104 shares the phrases נַפְשִׁי אֶת־יְהוָה/"my soul YHWH" (preceded by an imperative singular of ברך/"bless" in Ps 104 but הלל/ "praise" in Ps 146) in Ps 104:1, 35 and Ps 146:1, and יְהוָה בְּחַיָּי אֲזַמְּרָה לֵאלֹהַי בְּעוֹדִי/"YHWH during my life, let me make music to my God during my continuance" in Ps 104:33 and Ps 146:2 (preceded by a cohortative singular of שׁיר/"sing" in Ps 104 but of הלל/"praise" in Ps 146). Both Psalms close with הַלְלוּ־יָהּ/"PraiseYah!", but Ps 104 does not open with this phrase. They also share יהוה/"YHWH", אֱלֹהִים/"god" (first person singular suffix), שָׁמַיִם/"heaven", רוּחַ/"wind", עוֹלָם/

---

63 Cf. Zenger 2008g, 815, 817, 821 (referring to Lohfink, see fn. 64). Zenger also argues for a reference to Ps 2 due to the frame Ps 1–2; 146–150, but Ps 2 shows no syntactical similarity.
64 Cf. Lohfink 1990, 111–112; Ballhorn 2004b, 309 (referring to Lohfink).
65 Cf. Levin 1993, esp. 363, also 370–371, 379.
66 Cf. Leuenberger 2004, 346–347, esp. fn. 272.
67 Cf. Reindl 1981a, 120, 124.
68 See Prov 4:19; 12:26; Jer 12:1.
69 Cf. the lists in Reindl 1981a, 123–124; Kselman 1988, 589; Lohfink 1990, 112 (Ps 103 only); Leuenberger 2004, 347–348; Zenger 2008g, 814–815.
70 Cf. the lists in Hupfeld 1871, 438–440; Duhm 1922, 475; Malchow 1977, 1166; Reindl 1981a, 123–124; Kselman 1988, 589; Leuenberger 2004, 346; Zenger 2008g, 814.
71 Cf. Leuenberger 2004, 347–348; Zenger 2008g, 815, 817, 819–820.
72 Cf. Ballhorn 2004b, 304.

"eternity" (including לְעוֹלָם/"for eternity"), אֶרֶץ/"earth", כֹּל/"all", נתן/"give", שׁוב/
"return", אָדָם/"human", יצא/"go out", לֶחֶם/"food", אֵל/"god", יָם/"sea", אַיִן/"there
is not", אֲדָמָה/"ground", חַיִּים/"life", רָשָׁע/"wicked" (רְשָׁעִים/"wicked ones"), and
עוֹד/"continuance". Since Ps 146 shares full phrases with Ps 103–104 (which
show an even closer connection with shared phrases in between them)[73]
found nowhere else in HB in addition to more frequent individual words, with
recurrent connections (e.g. parts of Ps 104:1 and Ps 104:33 are both shared
with Ps 146) and shared content (praise for creation) and form (hymn), while a
formula cannot be excluded a reference is likely. Ps 103 and Ps 104 cannot be
dated with any certainty.[74] The direction of the reference has to rely on relative
criteria. All three Psalms contain singular and plural adhortations, the shared
phrases fit the internal coherence equally well, and all three Psalms combine different aspects of praise and may allude to other texts.[75] Thus, external coherence
or the recurrence of allusions cannot define the direction of reference. However,
it is more likely that Ps 146 changes both ברך/"bless" and שׁיר/"sing" to הלל/
"praise" than that both Ps 103 and 104 choose one of the two former verbs instead of הלל/"praise".[76] This indicates that Ps 146 refers to Ps 103–104 rather
than vice versa. In the shared phrases, the reference to Ps 103–104 stresses
the aspect of lifelong individual praise in Ps 146. Ps 103 is superscribed with
לְדָוִד/"About David", but this superscription is not found in Ps 104 or Ps 146,
making the individual more universal. All Psalms stress the sovereignty of God
and mortality of humans. Ps 146 combines God's help for Israel and for the powerless from Ps 103 and God's universal creation from Ps 104.

Some commentators hold the view that there are references to *Psalm 145*,[77]
with the consequences of interpreting Ps 146 as a redactional sequel to Ps 145
with David as its speaker,[78] the non-identification of righteous ones and Israel
in Ps 146,[79] the unlikelihood of Ps 145 as a conclusion of the Psalter or its fifth
book,[80] or a late date of Ps 146.[81] Ps 145 and Ps 146 share זקף/"raise up" (rare
word appearing in Ps 145:14; 146:8 only, and in the same form זֹקֵף/"raising

---

73 Cf. for the connected Ps 103–104 Hossfeld 2008b, 87–88.
74 Cf. Rodd 2007, 349–395 for Ps 103–104. See VI.1.6 for Ps 146.
75 Cf. e.g. for Ps 103 Hossfeld 2008a, 55–56 (Ex), for Ps 104 Hossfeld 2008b, 87–88 (Ps 103).
76 Also noted by Ballhorn 2004b, 304.
77 Cf. Lohfink 1990, 113.
78 Cf. Leuenberger 2004, 346–348; Zenger 2008g, esp. 813, 821–822, also 814–815, 820.
79 Cf. Leuenberger 2004, 348 (against Lohfink 1990, 112–114). However, Lohfink primarily has
the poor rather than the righteous in sight, see p. 183 fn. 65.
80 Cf. Ballhorn 2004b, 304–305.
81 Cf. Hupfeld 1871, 438; Malchow 1977, 1166; Reindl 1981a, 124; Kselman 1988, 589.

up") and כפף/"bow down" (rare word appearing only in Ps 57:7; 145:14; 146:8; Isa 58:5; Mic 6:6, only in Ps 145:14; 146:8 in the form כְּפוּפִים/"bowed down ones"). In both Ps 145:14 and Ps 146:8, YHWH is the subject, זֹקֵף/"raising up" the verb and כְּפוּפִים/"bowed down ones" the object, in Ps 145:14 וְזוֹקֵף לְכָל־הַכְּפוּפִים/"and raising up for all the bowed down ones", in Ps 146:8 יְהוָה זֹקֵף כְּפוּפִים/"YHWH raising up bowed down ones". The two Psalms also share אֱלֹהִים/"god" (first person singular suffix), עוֹלָם/"eternity" (לְעוֹלָם/"for eternity"), יוֹם/"day", הלל/"praise" (including אֲהַלְלָה/"let me praise"), יהוה/"YHWH", אֵין/"there is not", דּוֹר/"generation" (doubled, including דּוֹר וָדוֹר/"generation and generation"), בֵּן/"son" and אָדָם/"human" (construct unit), נתן/"give" (נֹתֵן/"giving"), צַדִּיק/"righteous", דֶּרֶךְ/"path", שמר/"preserve" (שֹׁמֵר/"preserving"), אהב/"love", and רָשָׁע/"wicked" (plural).[82] Given the two shared rare words in syntactical and thematical similarity, other shared words and forms, and shared form (hymn) and content (praise for YHWH's majesty and mercy), a reference between Ps 145 and Ps 146 is likely. Since both Ps 145 and Ps 146 are probably postexilic but cannot be dated more precisely with any certainty,[83] the direction of the reference has to rely on relative criteria. Since the shared rare words fit the internal coherence of both Psalms equally well, and since they both combine different aspects of praise and may allude to other texts,[84] external coherence or the recurrence of allusions cannot define the direction of reference either. Thus, the direction of the reference remains unclear.

Intertextual links with *Psalm 147* are unlikely (see p. 183 on Ps 146). While similarities with *Psalm 148* are often stressed by commentators due to the surrounding group of Psalms 145.146–150,[85] intertextual references are unlikely (see p. 140 on Ps 146).[86] For the same reason, similarities with *Psalm 149* are often stressed, but references are unlikely (see p. 95 on Ps 146), and the same applies to *Psalm 150* (see p. 39 on Ps 146).

Commentators frequently argue for references to *Isaiah*,[87] especially from Ps 146:7–8 to Isa 42:7; 49:9, with consequences including a postexilic date of

---

82 חי/"living" is also shared. The plural of חַי/"living" is חַיִּים/"life", the distinction between the two forms is not always clear, cf. Gesenius 2013, s.v. חַי (includes חַיִּים); Clines 1996, s.v. חַי and s.v. חַיִּים, but here Ps 145:16 refers to a "living being", as confirmed by LXX, see fn. 242.

83 Cf. Hossfeld 2008c, 796, on Ps 145. On the date of Ps 146 see VI.1.6.

84 Cf. for Ps 145 Rodd 2007, 404; Hossfeld 2008a, 804–805.

85 Cf. for Ps 148–150 Zenger 2008g, 815 (Ps 145–150); for Ps 149 also Kselman 1988, 598 (Ps 146–150).

86 This also applies to Ps 146 in 11QPs^a, see VI.2.1.

87 Cf. the lists in Reindl 1981a, 123–124; Kselman 1988, 589; Lohfink 1990, 112–113; Zenger 2008g, 814–815.

Ps 146 and the transfer of exilic promises about a servant to YHWH himself.[88] Other commentators just argue for a common topic,[89] sometimes explicitly excluding a direct reference.[90] Isa 42:7 shares פקח/"open", עִוֵּר/"blind",[91] and the root אסר/"bind" with Ps 146:7–8 (and יצא/"go out" with Ps 146:4) without syntactical similarity. Isa 49:9 only shares אסר/"bind" (qal passive plural participle)[92] with Ps 146:7–8 (and with other verses of Ps 146 the frequent words יצא/ "go out", דֶּרֶךְ/"path", and כֹּל/"all"). While there are thematical similarities, there is little lexical and syntactical similarity, wherefore references to Isaiah are unlikely.

Results

References to Gen; Ex 15; Deu; Isa; Ps 1 are unlikely. Ps 147; 148; 149; 150 show no references except the framing Hallelujahs.

However, there are references to Ex 20:11 (and Gen 1:1–2:4a indirectly); Ps 103–104; and Ps 145. These references insert a reference to the *Sabbath Commandment*, and strengthen the aspects of *universal creation combined with help for Israel and the powerless*. The references may also point to a *postexilic* date of Ps 146 after the 6th century BCE based on the assumption of such a postexilic date of Ex 20:11 (and Gen 1:1–2:4a), supported but with unclear direction by a reference to or from a postexilic Ps 145, while Ps 103–104 are too difficult to date.

In contrast to Ps 148–150 Ps 146 does show other references, including references to Psalms 103–104 which are not neighbouring Psalms in MT, and Psalm 145 which is neighbouring but not part of Psalms 146–150, thus weakening the case for an original connection of Ps 146–150.

VI.1.4 Content of Psalm 146[MT]

Who is called to praise in Psalm 146[MT]?

While vv.1–2 are self-exhortations of the Psalmist as an individual, both the opening Hallelujah as a plural imperative and the following plural jussive in v.3 show that while the individual is called to praise, there is a group of other addressees of the call to praise YHWH, i.e. the God of Israel who is to be praised

---

88 Cf. Lohfink 1990, 112; Zenger 2008g, 815, 820.
89 Cf. Leuenberger 2004, 346 fn. 272.
90 Cf. Gerstenberger 2001, 440.
91 The collocation of these two words is rare but also appears in Isa 35:5.
92 This form also appears in e.g. Job 36:8.

by the people Israel. The address to Zion in v.10 makes it likely that this group is a cultic assembly (though whether this is real or imagined for literary purposes remains open).[93] Within Psalm 146, the group may be equated with צַדִּיקִים/"right-eous ones" in v.8 since they are the only group with positive connotations that allow for voluntary group membership,[94] though given the position of צַדִּיקִים/ "righteous ones" in a row of other nouns the group may identify with all of them, and given the mention of גֵּרִים/"strangers", the group may also identify with none of them. It is thus unclear if the addressees of Ps 146 identify with some or all of the concepts in vv.7–9, or whether these concepts are mere reasons for their praise.

The individual aims to praise YHWH בְּחַיָּי/"during my life" and בְּעוֹדִי/"during my continuance". Since it is combined with nouns of time, בְּ/"in" means "during",[95] thus indicating lifelong praise,[96] while it remains possible but less likely that it means "through" (praising throughout and through using all of his life)[97] or "because of" (praise for his life and existence).

Who is warned against in Psalm 146:3–4^MT?

While the parallelism in v.3 is synthetic[98] with the second colon adding information, there is a synonymous element: Given the asyndetic repetition of בְּ/"in" in v.3 and the content of vv.3–4, it is likely that the plural נְדִיבִים/"rulers"[99] and the singular בֶּן־אָדָם/"son of man" who is further characterised in v.4 are one and the same people, thus reducing rulers to mortal humans,[100] with the singular being used collectively[101] for all of humankind. These human rulers may be equated with רְשָׁעִים/"wicked ones" in v.9,[102] though this connection is looser than the

---

93 Cf. Gerstenberger 2001, 438 (community of listeners) 440 (congregation in or away from but oriented towards Jerusalem); Allen 2002, 378 (congregation assembled for worship), 379 (connection with temple); Ballhorn 2004b, 305 (at least fictional congregation), 308 fn. 804 (identification of addressees of Ps 146 and Zion, against Reindl 1981a, 133).

94 Thus Ballhorn 2004b, 308–309. See p. 260, esp. fn. 229.

95 Cf. Jenni 1992, 300, 316; Clines 1995, s.v. בְּ.

96 Thus Allen 2002, 378.

97 Thus Zenger 2008g, 812, 817, 823.

98 See p. 233–234.

99 נָדִיב can be used as a noun "ruler" or an adjective "noble one", cf. Gesenius 2013, s.v. נָדִיב, here a noun is more likely.

100 Thus Allen 2002, 378; Ballhorn 2004b, 308–309; Zenger 2008g, 812, 818.

101 While בֶּן־אָדָם/"human" usually refers to an individual, it may be used collectively, cf. Haag 1973, 683, and stresses human mortality, cf. Haag 1973, 685.

102 See p. 233–234.

one within v.4,[103] especially since vv.3–4 stress the mortality and thus ultimate failure of human rulers, whereas the path of the wicked in v.9 is "made crooked" rather than destroyed. נְדִיבִים/"noble ones" can be used to describe rulers within Israel as well as those of other nations,[104] and while it is sometimes argued that Psalm 146 refers to leaders in Hellenistic times, whether within[105] or foreign to Israel,[106] this cannot be substantiated.[107] לְ/"for" stresses that the lack of saving applies to humans directly (rather than indirectly to trusting "in" them).[108]

The mortality of any human rulers (in Ps 146 where human life is described in v.4a, רוּחַ/"wind" is used for "breath", denoting vitality)[109] is contrasted with the lasting kingship of YHWH in v.10.[110]

What are human and godly actions in Psalm 146:5–9[MT]?

The beatitude in v.5 introduced by אַשְׁרֵי/"happy" (literally "happinesses of", a plural construct of אֶשֶׁר/"happiness")[111] does not praise someone who does anything by himself (contrary to, e.g., Isa 56:2), but someone merely trusting in YHWH (similar to e.g. Prov 28:14). The beatitude may have educational purposes to show model behaviour[112] or ask for loyalty.[113]

In v.5, YHWH is also called אֵל יַעֲקֹב/"God of Jacob", using אֵל/"god" rather than אֱלֹהִים/"god", but these words can often be used interchangeably.[114] While the phrase אֵל יַעֲקֹב/"God of Jacob" is unique to Ps 146:5, the phrase אֱלֹהֵי יַעֲקֹב/ "God of Jacob" is used especially in the Psalter in contexts of God's power and help.[115] עֹזֵר/"helper" is the predicate of the relative clause in v.5a with בְּ/

---

103 Cf. Ballhorn 2004b, 308–309.
104 Cf. Conrad 1986, 242–244; Ballhorn 2004b, 308–309.
105 Cf. Ballhorn 2004b, 308–309 (if the Psalm is Maccabean, the rulers are Israel's own); without a reference to vv.3–4 Gerstenberger 2001, 439 (general impression of internal social conflict, thus wicked in v.9 within Israel).
106 Cf. Lange 1998, 115–116 (Ps 146 in itself is general in its statement against rulers, but Seleucid rulers are likely due to the connection with Ps 147 and the date of the final redaction of the Psalter).
107 Cf. Zenger 2008g, 817–818.
108 Cf. Reindl 1981a, 118.
109 Cf. Gesenius 2013, s.v. רוּחַ. Cf. Allen 2002, 378 (breath); Zenger 2008g, 812 (either, for vitality).
110 See p. 244–245.
111 Cf. Gesenius 2013, s.v. אֶשֶׁר*.
112 Thus Gerstenberger 2001, 438.
113 Thus Zenger 2008g, 818.
114 Cf. Ringgren 1973, 291.
115 Cf. Zenger 2008g, 818.

"in" as *beth essentiae* (untranslated in English),[116] thus the preposition here denotes YHWH's quality, while chiastically שֵׂבֶר/"hope" is the subject of v.5b with a suffix referring back to the anonymous subject. Thus, a causal relationship could be hinted at in the chiasm: YHWH is a helper, and (therefore) the happy one's hope is in him.

The threefold creation formula with heaven, earth, and sea in v.6 forms the first reason for the trustworthiness and praise of YHWH.[117]

In v.8, פקח/"open" is used with עִוְרִים/"blind ones" as an object, this is probably an abbreviation for "eyes of blind ones" as found with פקח/"open" in Isa 35:5 (עֵינֵי עִוְרִים/"eyes of blind ones") and Isa 42:7 (עֵינַיִם עִוְרוֹת/"eyes of blind ones").[118] כְּפוּפִים/"bowed down ones" refers to general oppression.[119]

Care for the powerless is the duty of kings in ANE contexts,[120] but in HB it can be the duty of God (e.g. Deut 10:18)[121] and every Israelite (e.g. Deut 24:17–21, Jer 7:6) as well as rulers (Ezek 22:7) and kings (Jer 22:3).[122]

The identity of those in YHWH's care (oppressed, hungry, bound, blind, bowed down, righteous, stranger, orphan, widow) includes both Israel (due to the connection with v.5 on which all verbs in vv.6–9 depend, and the mention of Zion in v.10),[123] and non-Israelites (given the inclusion of גֵּר/"stranger", though the word denotes a non-Israelite living in an Israelite community[124]).

---

116 Cf. Gesenius and Kautzsch 1909, §119i; Jenni 1992, 79–89, esp. 83; Clines 1995, s.v. בְּ; Joüon and Muraoka 2011, §133c (virtually no change in meaning through the preposition). The view of a *beth essentiae* is adopted by Allen 2002, 375; Leuenberger 2004, 346; Zenger 2008g, 812.

117 See fn. 5 for "creatio prima" and "continuata". Gerstenberger 2001, 438, sees the creation of the sea as a "very late theological statement" since no chaos powers are mentioned, but this depends on the history of the chaos motif, and the opposite could be the case, cf. Watson 2005, esp. 221 (assuming a late date of Ps 146), 242, 295 (connection of chaos and creation is if any then a late motif in the Psalter).

118 See p. 239–240 on Isa. Cf. Gunkel 1926, 613.

119 Against Zenger 2008g, 820–821, neither the general use of the word nor the context within Ps 146 (blind ones and righteous ones) make it likely that the verb specifically refers to forced labour or imprisonment, especially given the similarities with Ps 145, see p. 238–239 on Ps 145.

120 An example for an ANE king's duty to care for widow and oppressed can be found in the Ugaritic Kirta Epic, cf. Dietrich, Loretz, and Sanmartín 1995, 46 (text); Pardee 2003, 342 (English translation). That Ps 146 transfers an ANE king's duties to YHWH is assumed by Malchow 1977, 1168–1170; Lohfink 1990, 114; Ballhorn 2004b, 306; Zenger 2008g, 821.

121 See p. 236 on Deut.

122 For a king's duties of care in HB, e.g. in Ps 72, cf. Malchow 1977, 1168–1170.

123 Cf. Lohfink 1990, 112–114 (Israel only); Allen 2002, 379 (Israel only).

124 Cf. Kellermann 1973.

The order of those in YHWH's care is unclear,[125] and whether the wicked are within or without Israel and whether they are to be equated with the rulers in vv.3–4 also remains unclear.[126]

What are kingship and Zion in Psalm 146:10[MT]?

Some commentators interpret the imperfect[127] יִמְלֹךְ/"he is king" as eschatological,[128] but given the mention of creation in v.6,[129] the participles and imperfect forms in vv.7–9,[130] and the adverbial phrases in v.10 referring to long periods of time, YHWH's rule as king has to be true not just for the future but also the past and present. The concept of YHWH's kingship[131] (or rule as king)[132] in v.10 in contrast to human rulers in vv.3–4 points towards theocracy as a central thought of Ps 146.[133] The mortality of any human rulers is contrasted with the lasting kingship of YHWH in v.10, thus showing a strong rejection of human rulers.[134]

---

125 Different orders are suggested by Gerstenberger 2001, 440 (socially powerless: oppressed – hungry – bound; physically powerless: blind – bowed down; righteous; socially powerless: stranger – orphan – widow), but hungry and righteous are difficult to explain in this order; Zenger 2008g, 819 (life: oppressed – hungry; political liberation: bound – blind – bowed down; empowerment: righteous – stranger – orphan – widow), but oppressed, blind, and righteous are difficult to explain in this order. Kselman 1988, 594, merely equates oppressed ones with stranger – orphan – widow.

126 See p. 241–242, esp. fn. 106.

127 See fn. 4.

128 Thus Ballhorn 2004b, 308, esp. fn. 803 (due to the context of Ps 146–150, with a definition of eschatology from Haag 1995, 867).

129 Cf. Zenger 2008g, 813 (Ps 146 not eschatological).

130 Cf. Leuenberger 2004, 346, esp. fn. 270 (Ps 146 not eschatological), against Mathys 1994, 270 (translating v.10 with a future form, 267), who, although mentioning eschatological associations, warns against a strictly eschatological interpretation due to the complexity of the motif of YHWH's kingship according to Camponovo 1984, 97–98, 437. Eschatological kingship in Ps 146–150 is also seen by Janowski 2001, 1593.

131 On the complexity of the motif of God's kingship cf. Camponovo 1984, 437–446; Janowski 2001; Kratz 2004, 623–624; Neumann 2016, 31–33, 87–92.

132 Cf. Michel 1956, 56 (imperfect forms of מלך/"be king" are better translated as "to rule as king"). However, being king and ruling as a king are inseparable.

133 Cf. Ballhorn 2004b, 308–309; Leuenberger 2004, 347–348.

134 Cf. Zenger 2008g, 817–818. Cf. also Malchow 1977, 1167–1170 (Ps 146 shows late ideology against earlier Judaean kingship ideology and against ANE immortality beliefs for kings); Ballhorn 2004b, 305, 308–309 (such a statement would be impossible during the rule of a king). However, it is possible that the Psalm is criticising current kings rather than assuming the absence of a king.

The mention of Zion points towards the addressees of the Psalm as a worshipping community.[135]

VI.1.5 Genre of Psalm 146^{MT}

Ps 146 shows the main features of a *hymn:* an introduction calling to praise and a main section giving reasons for praise. While sung by an individual, and thus sometimes classified as an *individual hymn*,[136] it seems to have a communal background given the addressees,[137] leading commentators to see it as a *communal hymn*[138] or an individual hymn but with elements of a *thanksgiving song.*[139] Since Ps 146 lacks the two main features of a thanksgiving song – (1) sung by an individual for an audience: address to YHWH in the 2nd person, (2) report about saving, with YHWH in the 3rd person[140] – but contains general reasons for praise, the classification as a thanksgiving song is unlikely while elements of this remain.[141]

Within the reasons for praise, Ps 146 unusually has an *exhortation* in vv.3 – 4 providing a negative foil for reasons for praise, and a *beatitude* in v.5 followed by vv.6 – 9 to give positive reasons.[142] Exhortation and beatitude are linked to wisdom literature in the ANE and HB[143] and to educational settings.[144] Due to these particular elements,[145] Ps 146 is described as a *hymn* but with *wisdom* elements (exhortation in vv.3 – 4, beatitude in v.5),[146] leading to a late date of

---

135 See p. 240 – 241, esp. fn. 93. Zenger 2008g, 813, sees the mention of Zion as due to the context of Ps 147 and the origin of Ps 146 in this context, but this is unlikely, see p. 240.
136 Cf. Gunkel 1926, 612 (with unusual elements of exhortation and beatitude).
137 See p. 240 – 241.
138 Cf. Gerstenberger 2001, 440 – 441.
139 Cf. Allen 2002, 375 – 376 (referring to Crüsemann 1969, 299; background of thanksgiving song may have led to the inclusion of wisdom features).
140 See p. 198 fn. 177.
141 Cf. Reindl 1981a, 126 – 127.
142 Cf. Allen 2002, 375 – 376.
143 Cf. Reindl 1981a, 128 – 129 (the specific exhortation אַל־תִּבְטְחוּ/"do not trust" is not found in wisdom but prophetic literature, namely Jer 7:4; 9:3; Mic 7:5, thus the author of Ps 146 is not limited to wisdom references); Zenger 2008g, 818 (exhortation).
144 Cf. Gerstenberger 2001, 438.
145 Alphabetic features are also mentioned as a wisdom element, cf. Kselman 1988, 590 – 591, but their presence is unlikely, see p. 233.
146 Cf. Zenger 2008g, 813 (exhortation and beatitude), 818 (exhortation).

Ps 146,[147] or even as a *didactic Psalm*.[148] However, the elements are also linked with thanksgiving songs[149] and Zion theology.[150]

Given the broad concept of wisdom spanning different periods of time and literary devices,[151] and the appearance of exhortations and beatitudes outside wisdom literature,[152] it cannot be decided whether there is wisdom influence.

It is debated whether Ps 146 was written for the temple cult,[153] or a literary context,[154] possibly specifically the end of the Psalter (setting in life: literature for meditation),[155] or wise religious instruction.[156] This depends on theories about the end of the Psalter as a whole. Overall, it cannot be decided whether Psalm 146 was written for a cultic or literary context, but it is unlikely that it was written for the group of Psalms 146–150.

VI.1.6 Date of Psalm 146^MT

Ps 146 is most often seen as *postexilic*, with reasons including (1) *Late Biblical Hebrew (LBH) language*, particularly *aramaisms*,[157] (2) *intertextual references*,[158]

---

147 Cf. Zenger 2008g, 815.
148 Cf. Reindl 1981a, 133–135 (form: individual hymn, but intent: didactic Psalm, no direct wisdom influence; author: ideal wise but also deeply religious teacher as described in Sir 8:24–39^LXX).
149 Cf. Reindl 1981a, 128–129.
150 Cf. Allen 2002, 378.
151 Cf. DeClaissé-Walford 2009, esp. 863; Dell 2009, esp. 869, 873.
152 For exhortations see fn. 143 (in addition to the passages mentioned by Reindl, אַל־תִּבְטְחוּ/ "do not trust" only appears in Ps 62:11); for beatitudes see e.g. Deut 33:29 and Isa 30:18, and cf. Frenschkowski 2004, 1184–1185.
153 Cf. Allen 2002, 376 (Zion content); Gerstenberger 2001, 440–441 (against Zenger 1997a).
154 Cf. Duhm 1922, 476 ("Eine Sammlung von Zitaten wie der vorhergehende Psalm; wie zum Auswendiglernen zusammengestellt."/"A collection of quotations like the preceding Psalm [145]; compiled as if for learning by heart.").
155 Cf. Becker 1975, 115 (Ps 145–150); Millard 1994, 145 (Little Hallel Ps 146–150, referring to Becker); Leuenberger 2004, 347, 353 (Little Hallel Ps 146–150, referring to Becker, Millard, and Zenger, e.g. Zenger 1997a, 18 fn. 49; Zenger 1997b, 100; Zenger 1998a, 39); Zenger 2008g, 813.
156 Cf. Reindl 1981a, 132 (even if individual parts are liturgical formulas, the Psalm may not be liturgical), 133 (Zion may not be identical with the addressees). See fn. 148 for Reindl's conclusions.
157 Cf. Hupfeld 1871, 439; Duhm 1922, 475; Gunkel 1926, 613; Malchow 1977, 1166; Reindl 1981a, 118; Kselman 1988, 589 (זקף/"raise up"); Karasszon 1992, 123–124 (עוֹד/"continuance" as a noun in the young Ps 103:5; 104:33; 139:18 and in Gen 48:15 only; שֶׁ/"which" may be a sign for late language; רוּחַ/"breath" in this meaning postexilic); Allen 2002, 376; Watson 2005, 219–220 (the aramaisms עֶשְׁתֹּנָה/"thought", שָׂבָר/"hope", and זקף/"raise up" otherwise only occur in

especially an assumed quote in 1 Mac 2:63^{LXX},[159] (3) *wisdom influence*[160] or more specifically the mixture of hymn and wisdom elements[161] or a late genre,[162] self-exhortation to praise,[163] (4) without direct intertextual references parallels with other late compositions,[164] and late dates of texts with similar *themes*,[165] in particular the criticism of kings,[166] the lack of chaos in creation,[167] and the mention of oppression,[168] (5) the Hallelujah-frame, and a connection with the final editing of the *Psalter*,[169] and (6) the Septuagint superscription.[170]

(1) language and (2) intertextual references are the most substantial arguments for a postexilic origin: While there are fewer intertextual references than previously assumed (and none to 1 Mac 2:63^{LXX}), the likely references do point to a postexilic origin.[171] This is supported by Late Biblical Hebrew (LBH) language (vv.3+5 שֶׁ/"which")[172] including aramaisms (v.4 עֶשְׁתֹּנֹת/"thought" only

---

late texts, plus late language vv.3, 5 שֶׁ/"which", v.5 עַל/"in" instead of אֶל/"in"), Zenger 2008g, 815, 818. However, against Karasszon the use of עוֹד/"continuance" as a noun is more common and not restricted to late texts, cf. Gesenius 2013, s.v. עוֹד; for שֶׁ/"which" see fn. 172; and a semantic development of רוּחַ/"breath" is doubtful, cf. Tengström 1993, esp. 398–399; against Watson see fn. 172–175, while עַל/"in" instead of אֶל/"in" could indeed be LBH, cf. Hornkohl 2013.

158 Cf. Malchow 1977, 1166; Kselman 1988, 589; Allen 2002, 376.

159 Cf. Zenger 2008g, 822 (Ps 146 and thus final redaction of the Psalter before 1 Mac and thus before 100 BCE). However, the assumed quote is unlikely, see p. 264 on 1 Mac 2:63^{LXX}.

160 Cf. Malchow 1977, 1166–1167; Gerstenberger 2001, 438 ("The educational effort may be one indicator pointing to an early Jewish congregational background."), 446 ("early Jewish" refers to "communities in the Persian and Hellenistic ages"); Watson 2005, 220 fn. 27 (referring to Kselman 1988).

161 Cf. Karasszon 1992, 124–125; Zenger 2008g, 815.

162 Cf. Allen 2002, 376.

163 Cf. Karasszon 1992, 126 (a self-exhortation to praise cannot be explained in cultic surroundings, thus the setting in life has to be private). However, thanksgiving songs combine both, see p. 245.

164 Cf. Watson 2005, 220.

165 Cf. Watson 2005, 220 (Ps 96; 98; 148).

166 Cf. Malchow 1977, 1168; Ballhorn 2004b, 309.

167 See p. 243, esp. fn. 117.

168 Cf. Hupfeld 1871, 438.

169 Cf. Watson 2005, 219.

170 Cf. Reindl 1981a, 117 (late date, or assigning the Psalm to the reading of these two prophets); Malchow 1977, 1167 (late date though the "ascription is probably not literally true").

171 See p. 240.

172 On phases of Biblical Hebrew cf. Hornkohl 2013; Hurvitz 2013: Dating *poetic* texts such as Ps 146 on the basis of linguistic features is problematic, and even if LBH can be assumed for Ps 146 this does not lead to any more precise date than some time after the 6th century BCE. שֶׁ/"which" *is not an aramaism, but LBH*: It is used mostly in late documents, e.g. Eccl and Qumran, cf. Clines 2011b, s.v. -שֶׁ. שֶׁ אֲשֶׁרֵי/"happy who" appears in Ps 137:8, 9 (exilic due to content)

here and Sir 3:24;[173] v.5 שֵׂבֶר/"hope" only here and Ps 119:116;[174] v.8 זקף/"raise up" only here and Ps 145:14[175]). For any more specific date, the Psalm's content is too general.[176]

The views of (3) wisdom influence and (4) similar themes depend on assumptions about the development of these,[177] (5) the view of the final editing of the Psalter depends on an original connection of Psalms 146–150, (6) and as for the Septuagint superscription, its provenance is unknown.[178]

The only absolute *terminus ante quem* is 11QPs^a[179] which probably dates from the first half of the 1st *century CE*, definitely before 68 CE.[180] However, the LXX-Psalter was probably finished in the 2nd century BCE, and Psalm 146 must pre-

---

and Ps 146:5 only. All three criteria for LBH in Hurvitz 2013 – late biblical distribution, linguistic opposition with אֲשֶׁר (appears in Ps 146:6a, but Watson 2005, 220, explains this as a formula), extrabiblical corroboration in Qumran – apply, cf. Clines 2011b, s.v. -שֶׁ, and שֶׁ is listed as LBH in Hurvitz 2013 though as early northern dialect in Hornkohl 2013. It is not listed in Kaufman [no year]; Jastrow 1903 lists it as Biblical Hebrew (Aramaic relative particle is דִּי/"which"). Ps 145^LXX uses relative pronouns for שֶׁ and an article for אֲשֶׁר, but אֲשֶׁר is elsewhere translated with relative pronouns, e. g. Ps 1:1^LXX, and שֶׁ with articles, e. g. Ps 136:8 – 9^LXX(=137:8 – 9^MT).

173 עֶשְׁתֹּנָת/"thought" *is an aramaism and LBH*: It is preserved only in these two places, cf. Clines 2007, s.v. [עֶשְׁתּוֹן], though Sir 3:24 reads a masculine plural construct form, cf. Gesenius 2013, s.v. עשתון, while Ps 146:6 has a feminine form, cf. Gesenius 2013, s.v. עֶשְׁתֹּנָה. The word is similar to עַשְׁתּוּת/"thought", hapax legomenon in Job 12:5, cf. Hupfeld 1871, 439; Gesenius 2013, s.v. עַשְׁתּוּת. The verb עשׁת_II/"bear in mind" occurs more often in Hebrew, cf. Gesenius 2013, s.v. עשׁת_2; Clines 2007, s.v. עשׁת_II. In Aramaic, both the verb and the plural noun ʿštwnyn/"thoughts" appear in Kaufman [no year], עֶשְׁתּוֹנָא/"plan" in Jastrow 1903.

174 שֵׂבֶר/"hope" *is an aramaism and LBH*: It is preserved only in these two places (Ps 119 may be seen as late and dated to the 4th century BCE, cf. Zenger 2008e, 357–358), cf. Clines 2011b, s.v. [שֵׂבֶר].The verb שׂבר/"hope" is more common in Hebrew, cf. Clines 2011b, s.v. שׂבר. In Aramaic, סְבַר/"hope" is listed in Jastrow 1903, sbr/"hope" in Kaufman [no year].

175 זקף/"raise up" *is an aramaism and LBH*: It occurs in these two places but also various Qumran texts, cf. Clines 1996, s.v. זקף. In Aramaic, it is found in Jastrow 1903; Kaufman [no year].

176 Cf. Zenger 2008g, 817; despite postexilic dating Hupfeld 1871, 438; Gunkel 1926, 613; Allen 2002, 376, 379 ("Such was the experience of the community of Israel from generation to generation."). In contrast to this, the Psalm is sometimes dated more specifically to *pre-Hellenistic* times, cf. Karasszon 1992, 126; or to *Seleucid* times where noble and priestly milieus acted against their Hellenistic rulers, cf. Lange 1998, 115–116 (against the general nature of Ps 146 due to the context of the Final Hallel, and the quote in 1 Mac 2:63^LXX). However, both are unlikely, see p. 240 and p. 264 on 1 Mac 2:63^LXX. It is also dated to *Persian* times, cf. Gerstenberger 2001, 441; or to *Maccabean* times, cf. Ballhorn 2004b, 309 (due to the general criticism rulers including Davidic rulers). See also fn. 172.

177 For wisdom see VI.1.5.

178 See p. 17 fn. 109.

179 See VI.2.1.

180 See p. 13 – 15.

date its translation.[181] In addition, the intertextual reference from 4QMessAp to Ps 146 points to a date of Ps 146 before the 2nd half of the 2nd century BCE.[182] Thus, *Psalm 146 is older than some time in the 2nd century BCE*. Given the intertextual references, a *terminus post quem* is the 6th to 5th century BCE based on the assumption of a postexilic date of Ex 20:11. Due to the lack of strong arguments for various suggestions of postexilic periods of time, a more precise date for Ps 146 than *some time between the 6th and 2nd century BCE* cannot be determined.

VI.1.7 Unity of Psalm 146^{MT}

Ps 146^{MT} is one unit,[183] with no text-critical evidence for emendations.[184] While some commentators argue that the framing Hallelujahs are an integral part of Psalm 146,[185] they are inconsistent in Hebrew manuscripts and versions: The opening Hallelujah is missing on a few Hebrew manuscripts, and the final Hallelujah is missing in the Septuagint and Peshitta.

---

181 See p. 16, esp. fn. 104.
182 See fn. 208.
183 Cf. Allen 2002, 376–377; Leuenberger 2004, 347 (criticising emendations).
184 Against Reindl 1981a, 120–121, 131 (v.9b secondary, thus also Reindl 1981b, 346–350); Levin 1993, 363 (vv.8c, 9c secondary), both criticised by Zenger 2008g, 815–816 (assuming Ps 146 was written in one piece for the end of the Psalter, also criticising other emendations). V.8c is often moved to be placed before v.9c following Bickell (his translation of Ps 146 is found in Bickell 1883, 272–273, with v.8c moved before v.9c without any commentary, also v.7bc is reversed to 7cb), cf. Duhm 1922, 476 (referring to Bickell); Gunkel 1926, 613 (referring to Bickell and Duhm); this emendation is criticised as lacking text-critical evidence by Reindl 1981a, 119–120; Kselman 1988, 589, 594–595; Ballhorn 2004b, 306–307; Leuenberger 2004, 347; Zenger 2008g, 812. See p. 233–234, esp. fn. 30. Emendations on the basis of 1 Mac 2:63^{LXX}, cf. Duhm 1922, 475 (referring to Bickell), are also unlikely, see p. 264 on 1 Mac 2:63^{LXX}.
185 Cf. Gerstenberger 2001, 437–438, 440 (either liturgical or literary unit, based on Ps 147:1); with הלל/"praise" as typical for Final Hallel central in Ps 146, e.g. in quoting Ps 104, cf. Ballhorn 2004b, 304; Zenger 2008g, 816. Zenger 2008d, 66, sees the framing Hallelujahs in Ps 146–150 as redactional, but since according to Zenger 2008c, 808–809, the same redactors wrote Ps 146; 149; and 150 (as well as Ps 147:1–11 and 148:14), the Hallelujahs must be original in Ps 146; 149; 150, even if according to Zenger 2008g, 816, in Ps 146 they are outside the Psalm proper. See p. 61 fn. 309.

VI.1.8 Overall Interpretation of Psalm 146[MT]

YHWH, the God of Jacob and Zion, is to be praised both by an individual with a group of listeners and by a group. The reasons for praise are YHWH's creation, his help for powerless people, and his lasting kingship in contrast to the mortality of human rulers. There is no indication of a specific time or place for praise within the Psalm. However, intertextual references and language place Psalm 146 in postexilic times.

VI.2 Psalm 146^{DSS}

VI.2.1 Psalm 146 in 11QPs^a

11QPs^a II contains parts of Psalm 146:9, an *additional passage* not contained in the Masoretic Text of Psalm 146, and parts of Psalm 146:10. Psalm 146 is followed (in a new line) by the first 12 of 14 verses of Psalm 148, and probably preceded by Ps 105 of which parts are preserved in the preceding Column I.[186]

The additional[187] passage between ודרך/"and a path" in Psalm 146:9, a lacuna, and ימלוך/"he is king"[188] in Ps 146:10 is:

מ𐤉𐤄𐤅𐤄 [189] כול הארץ ממנ[...]

בהודעו לכול מעשעיו ברא[...]

גבורותיו

"From YHWH all the earth from [...] ¦ in his making himself known[190] with respect to all of his works[191] he created[192] [...] ¦ his strengths[193]".

---

186 Cf. Sanders 1965, 22–23, Plate IV. The bottom of Columns I-II is missing, but given the number of missing lines, cf. Jain 2014, 165, it is possible that the last verse of Ps 105 (Ps 105:45) of which parts are preserved in Column I was followed by the beginning of Ps 146, as assumed by Sanders 1965, 22; Flint 1997, 190; Dahmen 2003, 71; Jain 2014, 252.

187 The passage is usually seen as secondary to MT, see fn. 195. Since this depends on theories about the dependance of 11QPs^a on MT which cannot be proven, see I.2.2, "additional" is used here in a comparative rather than temporal sense.

188 MT reads the defective ימלך/"he is king".

189 יהוה/"YHWH" in palaeo-Hebrew script 𐤉𐤄𐤅𐤄/"YHWH", cf. Sanders 1965, 6 (explanation), 23 (text), Plate IV (facsimile).

190 This form could be a suffixed infinitive construct nif'al of ידע/"know", thus בְּהִוָּדְעוֹ/"in his making himself known", cf. Dahmen 2003, 127–128 (explicitly assuming a nif'al, and ל/"to" as referring to his works as the living recipients of this revelation), or "in his being known", cf. Sanders 1967, 37 (implicitly assuming a nif'al, and ל/"through" as his works as the means of this knowledge); Lange 1998, 109 (implicitly assuming a nif'al, and ל/"by" as his works as the recipients of this knowledge). A hif'il is less likely, cf. Dahmen 2003, 127–128, since there is usually (though not always due to possible defective spelling, cf. Gesenius and Kautzsch 1909, §9g) a י after the second consonant of the root, cf. Gesenius and Kautzsch 1909, §53a. בְּ/ "in" combined with in an infinitive construct could be temporal "when" or causal "because", cf. Jenni 1992, 316–327 (temporal), 349–350, 354–355 (temporal or causal); Dahmen 2003, 127–128, esp. 128 fn. 140 (referring to Jenni). The fragmentary text does not allow for a decision, and the general translation "in" is used here.

191 These works could be the recipients or means of knowledge, see fn. 190.

192 For the translation of ברא as "to create" cf. Sanders 1967, 33; Lange 1998, 109. Dahmen 2003, 127–128, also assumes ברא/"to create". Contrary to this, Skehan 1973, 205, assumes [...]ברא to be the beginning of [ותו]ברא as a suffixed hif'il infinitive construct of ראה/"see"

It includes an *additional reference to YHWH's creation and power.*[194] The addition also leads to an envelopment of YHWH's help for the powerless in vv.7–9 with his creation in v.6 and the addition between v.9 and v.10.[195] There is no indication of an eschatological reference.[196]

Regarding the *origin* of the passage, on the basis of Ps 146 it has been suggested to compare *Psalm 33:8* for the first line of the passage, and perhaps *Ps 145:10–12* for the following lines.[197] Psalm 33:8[MT] reads יִירְאוּ מֵיהוָה כָּל־הָאָרֶץ מִמֶּנּוּ יָגוּרוּ כָּל־יֹשְׁבֵי תֵבֵל/"Let them fear YHWH all the earth, let them dread him all the inhabitants of the world", sharing the underlined consonants with the first line as the only parallel for this phrase in HB. However, Ps 33 only shares two of the words in the second and third line with the passage (the frequent words כֹּל/"all" and מַעֲשֶׂה/"work"), and without any further syntactical similarity. Regarding Ps 145:10–12, there is no such close resemblance with the entire Ps 146 (כֹּל/"all", מַעֲשֶׂה/"work", גְּבוּרָה/"power", and ידע/"know" are shared without syntactical similarity). There are no close similarities to these texts in HB, and intertextual references from the additional passage are unlikely. Since the passage is not found in HB, it may have been influenced by texts outside it, but this remains speculative.

---

with בְּ but missing an ה ("as occurs sporadically at Qumran" without examples), and translates it as "when he shows", leading to an eschatological interpretation of the passage. However, a missing ה in a hif'il infinitive is rare, cf. Gesenius and Kautzsch 1909, §53q, and there is no intertextual reference to 1QH[a] on which Skehan bases the eschatological view, see VI.2.1.

193 גְּבוּרֹתָיו is a hapax legomenon in HB in the Qere of Job 26:14.

194 Importance of creation in 11QPs[a] additions is stressed by Dahmen 2003, 127–128, 287, 289.

195 Cf. Lange 1998, 110 (YHWH's kingship is related to his creation rather than help, thus the addition must be secondary as it destroys the scope of the Psalm; referring to Sanders 1967, 19); Dahmen 2003, 128 (also assuming other references to Ps 33, contrary to Lange the addition enhances the scope of the Psalm but is still secondary given the unanimous text-critical support for MT). However, the enveloping structure does not prove a secondary nature of the addition, and a reference to Ps 33 is unlikely, see VI.2.1.

196 See fn. 192.

197 Cf. Sanders 1965, 23 (comparison only); Sanders 1967, 19 (direct reference, for 145 according to "Monsignor Skehan"); Skehan 1973, 204–205 (direct reference, eschatological); Lange 1998, 109–110 (direct reference; referring to Sanders 1967); Dahmen 2003, 127–128 (influence of Ps 33 likely, but not of Ps 145; referring to Sanders 1965 and Sanders 1967 and Lange); Leuenberger 2004, 15, esp. fn. 37 (direct references; referring to Sanders 1965 and Skehan; regarding Ps 145 with the consequence of 11QPs[a] depending on the MT order of Ps 145–146). For possible influences of wisdom or other reconstructions for lines 2–3 cf. Dahmen 2003, 128, however, this remains speculative. Goshen-Gottstein 1966, 31, suggests that due to the addition the text could not be Ps 146 at all, but a new composition. However, the similarities with Ps 146:9–10 are too strong, even though the beginning of the Psalm is not preserved to further substantiate this.

Regarding *intertextuality* besides possible sources for the additional passage, Ps 146 in 11QPs^a is sometimes thought to show close connections with the Psalms surrounding it (Ps 118 – 104 – 147 – 105 – 146 – 148),[198] but on the contrary such connections are also denied.[199] Since according to the results of this study connections with neighbouring Psalms are usually overrated (with regard to Ps 118, 105, 147, and 148 no intertextual references are likely for Ps 146^{MT}; for example, many shared words could be listed for Ps 105^{MT}, with the additional word ידע/ "know" and the neighbouring position for 11QPs^a, but there is no syntactical similarity in either text form), the focus here is on additional references, and the passages where a reference is likely in MT: Ex 20:11 (and Gen 1:1 – 2:4a indirectly), Ps 103 – 104, and Ps 145.

Since Ps 146:6 is not preserved in 11QPs^a little can be said about a reference to *Ex 20:11* (and thus Gen 1:1 – 2:4a, although the ברא/"create" in the additional passage in Ps 146 in 11QPs^a also appears in Gen 1:1 – 2:4a; no additional words are shared with Ex 20:11).

Regarding *Ps 103 – 104*, none of the shared phrases are preserved in Ps 146^{11QPsa}. While the additional creation passage in Ps 146^{11QPsa} shares the additional words ידע/"know" and מַעֲשֶׂה/"work" with Ps 103^{MT}, and with Ps 104^{MT} ידע/ "know", מַעֲשֶׂה/"work", and ברא/"create", and while Ps 103:1 (or Ps 104:1) was probably placed closer to Ps 146 in 11QPs^a than in MT,[200] there is no additional syntactical similarity to Ps 103^{MT} or Ps 104^{MT}.

Regarding *Ps 145*, the shared rare words in Ps 146:8 are not preserved in Ps 146^{11QPsa}, and the additional creation passage in Ps 146^{11QPsa} shares the additional words מַעֲשֶׂה/"work", גְבוּרָה/"strength", and ידע/"know" with Ps 145, without additional syntactical similarity.

Ps 148 is in a neighbouring position and has the additional shared word ברא/ "create" in 11QPs^a,[201] but no syntactical similarity.

Commentators sometimes argue for references to or from other *Qumran texts*, namely a reference from the addition in Ps 146 to 1QH^a (Hodayot^a),[202]

---

198 Cf. Dahmen 2003, 286 – 287; Jain 2014, 264 – 268.
199 Cf. Leuenberger 2004, 15 (strong connections in MT but not 11QPs^a with the consequence that 11QPs^a depends on MT).
200 Cf. Sanders 1965, 5, 20.
201 Cf. Dahmen 2003, 286 – 287 (addition in Ps 146 could be there to provide a link to Ps 148), 289 (possible influence of the following Ps 148 on the addition in Ps 146).
202 Cf. Skehan 1973, 205 (interpretation of the additional passage in Ps 146 in the light of heavenly praise in 1QH xi:3 – 14); but no intertextual reference is likely to 1QH^a col. 19:6 – 17, for this passage cf. Schuller and Newsom 2012, 4 (conversion of column and line numbers), 58 – 61 (text and translation); García Martínez and Tigchelaar 1999, 188 – 189 (text and translation).

and a reference from 4QMessAp (Messianic Apocalypse, 4Q521) to Ps 146:7–8.[203] Only the second one is likely: 4QMessAp, Fragment 2 II line 8 reads, referring to אדני/"Lord"[204] in line 5, [מתיר אסורים פוקח עורים זוקף כ[פופים/"freeing the bound ones, opening blind ones, raising up bowed down ones", and in close syntactical similarity shares the underlined words with Ps 146:7c–8b which reads:

יהוה מַתִּיר אֲסוּרִים יְהוָה פֹּקֵחַ עִוְרִים יְהוָה זֹקֵף כְּפוּפִים/"YHWH freeing the bound ones, YHWH opening blind ones, YHWH raising up bowed down ones".

Further shared words with syntactical similarity between Ps 146 and 4QMessAp are כָּל־אֲשֶׁר־בָּם/"all which (is) in them" in collocation with שָׁמַיִם/"heaven" and אֶרֶץ/"earth" (Fragment 2,II,2) and with יַמִּים/"seas" (and close to אֶרֶץ/"earth") (Fragments 7+5,II,1–3).[205] There are further shared words, especially רְעֵבִים/"hungry ones" (Fragment 2,II,12),[206] and a reference is likely. However, it is usually argued that 4QMessAp refers to Ps 146,[207] which seems most likely since in terms of absolute dates it is probably younger than Ps 146,[208] and in terms of relative dates also seems to refer to other texts (such as Isaiah; external coherence and recurrence of allusions). Thus, while Ps 146 is of relevance for the interpretation of 4QMessAp, apart from questions of dating this is not the case vice versa.

In *summary*, in 11QPs[a] Psalm 146 is followed by Ps 148 and probably preceded by Ps 105. The opening of Ps 146 is not preserved, but there is a final Hallelujah. An additional passage following Psalm 146:9 and preceding Ps 146:10 refers to YHWH's creation and power. There are no intertextual references from Ps 146 to other texts.

VI.2.2 Psalm 146 in 4QPs[d]?

The 4QPs[d] fragments preserve parts of Psalms 147 and 104[209] preceded by the end of another Psalm. Remaining of this preceding Psalm are the letters ויה pre-

---

203 Cf. Puech 1997, 264–265; Puech 1998, 36; Brooke 1998, 45–46; for the text and translation of 4QMessAp cf. García Martínez and Tigchelaar 1999, 1044–1047 (based on Puech 1998, 1–38).
204 On this replacement of the tetragrammaton cf. Puech 1998, 36–38.
205 Cf. Brooke 1998, 45 fn. 34.
206 Cf. Brooke 1998, 45–46.
207 See fn. 203.
208 For the date of Ps 146 see VI.1.6, of 4QMessAp Puech 1998, 3–5 (manuscript 100–80 BCE based on palaeography; radiocarbon dating 93 BCE – 80 CE), 36–38 (content 2nd half of the 2nd century BCE).
209 Cf. Skehan, Ulrich, and Flint 2000a.

ceded by the damaged לל and the rest of a letter going below the line.[210] Thus, the last word can be reconstructed as הללויה/"Praise-Yah!".[211] The letter going below the line is probably a final consonant, i.e. ן, ך, ף, or ץ.[212] The Psalm of which these fragments form the end is identified either as Ps 106:48 or Ps 146:10.[213] Since Ps 106:48 is the only Psalm where the final Hallelujah is preceded by a final consonant, namely ן in אָמֵן/"Amen", this is seen as the most likely explanation for the fragment.[214] However, it could also be the end of a text not contained in MT. Either way, it is unlikely that the fragment contains the end of Ps 146:10 where the final Hallelujah is preceded by לְדֹר וָדֹר/"for generation and generation". Overall, *4QPs^d* is unlikely to contain the end of Ps 146 and *cannot be used as a textual basis for Ps 146*.

VI.2.3 Psalm 146 in 4QPs^e?

The 4QPs^e fragments (which according to their late Herodian script may date from the mid-first century CE like 11QPs^a)[215] preserve parts of twenty Psalms, possibly including *Psalm 146:1* following the end of Ps 105 (Ps 105:45) on Fragment 18 II.[216] However, the only word preserved after the end of fragments of Ps 105 is הללויה/"Praise-Yah!" (without a space between הללו and יה – as in the Masoretic Codices at the beginning of Ps 146[217]). This could be the beginning of Ps 106 (as in the Masoretic and Septuagint order), any of Ps 146–150, various other Psalms, or in fact the end of Ps 105 as הללויה is not preserved in its last damaged line on this fragment (this last option is less likely as the manuscript seems to have been written in prose format and new Psalms mostly begin on a new line[218]). Compared to 11QPs^a, it even is unlikely to be the beginning of Ps 146 given that

---

210 Cf. Skehan, Ulrich, and Flint 2000a, 66, Plate X. See also Israel Antiquities Authority 2012.
211 Cf. Skehan, Ulrich, and Flint 2000a, 66.
212 Cf. Lange 2009, 380–381 (Ps 106:48?), not mentioning ף. For final forms of consonants cf. Gesenius and Kautzsch 1909, §5b, ם does not go below the line.
213 For Ps 106:48? cf. Flint 1997, 165, esp. fn. 52; Skehan, Ulrich, and Flint 2000a, 63, 66; Jain 2014, 90–94. For Ps 146:10? cf. Fabry 1998, 140 (against Skehan/Ulrich/Flint). Both possibilities are retained by Leuenberger 2004, 16–17 (referring to Skehan/Ulrich/Flint and Fabry). Dahmen 2003, 347, 352, 375, does not mention 4QPs^d in connection with Ps 106 or 146.
214 Cf. Skehan, Ulrich, and Flint 2000a, 66.
215 Cf. Skehan, Ulrich, and Flint 2000b, 74.
216 Cf. Skehan, Ulrich, and Flint 2000b, 73, 82.
217 Cf. Ben-Zvi Institute 2007, Ps 146; Freedman 1998, 803=fol. 396r.
218 Cf. Skehan, Ulrich, and Flint 2000b, 74.

the opening Hallelujahs are not always present in 11QPs[a].[219] However, it is *assumed* by some scholars to be the beginning of Ps 146 *because of the order in 11QPs[a]*,[220] a position criticised by others who stress similarities with the *order of MT*,[221] but the fragmentary state of 4QPs[e] does not allow for a reconstruction in either way.[222] Overall, 4QPs[e] may or may not contain the beginning of Ps 146 and *cannot be used as a textual basis for Ps 146*.

---

219 There are no opening Hallelujahs in the preserved beginnings of Ps 135:1; 148:1; 150:1, cf. Dahmen 2003, 55, 58, 118. Cf. also Jain 2014, 253.

220 Skehan, Ulrich, and Flint 2000b, 82, "see the introduction", probably referring to 74 where 4QPs[e] "appears to be textually affiliated with the Psalter represented by 11QPs[a] (and 11QPs[b])" and 76: "Accordingly, this edition presents Psalms in the order of 11QPs[a], not that of [MT]." Cf. also Flint 1997, 160–161 (Ps 146:1?), 259 (Ps 146:1?); Lange 2009, 381–383 (Ps 146:1?).

221 Against Flint (see fn. 220): Fabry 1998, 142 (Ps 109:1?), 156; Dahmen 2003, 52–59, esp. 55, 127; Leuenberger 2004, 17 (Ps 106:1 more likely; referring to Fabry and Dahmen).

222 Cf. Jain 2014, 94–104 (95, 97: assuming Ps 106:1), against Flint, see fn. 220.

VI.3 Psalm 145^{LXX}

VI.3.1 Translation of Psalm 145^{LXX}

1H	*Hallelujah; of Haggai and Zechariah.*	1H	Αλληλουια· Αγγαιου καὶ Ζαχαριου.
1	Praise, my soul, the Lord!	1	Αἴνει, ἡ ψυχή μου, τὸν κύριον.
2a	I *will* praise Lord during my life,	2a	αἰνέσω κύριον ἐν ζωῇ μου,
2b	I *will* make music to my God *as long as I exist.*	2b	ψαλῶ τῷ θεῷ μου, ἕως ὑπάρχω.
3a	Do not trust in rulers,	3a	μὴ πεποίθατε ἐπ' ἄρχοντας
3b	*and* in sons of men for whom there is no saving.	3b	καὶ ἐφ' υἱοὺς ἀνθρώπων οἷς οὐκ ἔστιν σωτηρία.
4a	His breath *will* go out, *and* he *will* return to his ground;	4a	ἐξελεύσεται τὸ πνεῦμα αὐτοῦ, καὶ ἐπιστρέψει εἰς τὴν γῆν αὐτοῦ·
4b	on that day *will* perish *all their* thoughts.	4b	ἐν ἐκείνῃ τῇ ἡμέρᾳ ἀπολοῦνται πάντες οἱ διαλογισμοὶ αὐτῶν.
5a	Happy of whom the God of Jacob (is) a helper,	5a	μακάριος οὗ ὁ θεὸς Ιακωβ βοηθός,
5b	his hope (is) on Lord his God,	5b	ἡ ἐλπὶς αὐτοῦ ἐπὶ κύριον τὸν θεὸν αὐτοῦ
6a	*the* one *having made the* heaven and *the* earth, the sea, and all which (is) in them,	6a	τὸν ποιήσαντα τὸν οὐρανὸν καὶ τὴν γῆν, τὴν θάλασσαν καὶ πάντα τὰ ἐν αὐτοῖς,
6b	the one preserving truthfulness for *the* eternity,	6b	τὸν φυλάσσοντα ἀλήθειαν εἰς τὸν αἰῶνα,
7a	making judgement for the oppressed ones;	7a	ποιοῦντα κρίμα τοῖς ἀδικουμένοις,
7b	giving bread for the hungry ones;	7b	διδόντα τροφὴν τοῖς πεινῶσιν·
7c	Lord frees bound ones,	7c	κύριος λύει πεπεδημένους,
8a	Lord restores *broken* ones,	8a	κύριος ἀνορθοῖ κατερραγμένους,
8b	Lord *makes wise* blind ones,	8b	κύριος σοφοῖ τυφλούς,
8c	Lord loves righteous ones,	8c	κύριος ἀγαπᾷ δικαίους·
9a	Lord preserves *the* strangers,	9a	κύριος φυλάσσει τοὺς προσηλύτους,
9b	orphan and widow he *will lift up*	9b	ὀρφανὸν καὶ χήραν ἀναλήμψεται
9c	and a path of sinners he *will destroy.*	9c	καὶ ὁδὸν ἁμαρτωλῶν ἀφανιεῖ.
10a	Lord *will* be king for *the* eternity,	10a	βασιλεύσει κύριος εἰς τὸν αἰῶνα,
10b	your God, Zion, for generation and generation.	10b	ὁ θεός σου, Σιων, εἰς γενεὰν καὶ γενεάν.
10H	–		

VI.3.2 Form of Psalm 145^LXX

Outline of Psalm 145^LXX

1H	**Hallelujah of Haggai and Zechariah**	
Introduction		
1–2	Calls to Praise	Subject: Psalmist, Object: Lord
	*Imperatives/**Future Forms***	
Part I		
3–4	Exhortation	Subject: Group, Object: Human Rulers
	Imperative/Future Form	
Part II		
5	Beatitude	Subject: Individual, Object: Lord
	Nominal Sentence	
6–9	Reasons	Subject: Lord, Object: Creation, Powerless
	Participles (referring to v.5), ***Present Forms,*** *Future Forms*	
Conclusion		
10	Summary	Subjects: Lord, Zion
	Future Form	
10H	–	

Syntax of Psalm 145^LXX

αλληλουια/"Hallelujah" is transcribed at the beginning (with the addition of Αγγαιου καὶ Ζαχαριου/"of Haggai and Zechariah") and left out at the end. Otherwise, as in Hebrew, αἰνέω/"praise" for הלל/"praise", ποιέω/"make" for עשה/"make", and φυλάσσω/"preserve" for שמר/"preserve" are the only verbs used twice in the Psalm, connecting creation and help. However, in LXX there is an *aorist participle* of ποιέω/"make", *present participles* of φυλάσσω/"preserve" and then ποιέω/"make", and a *present form* of φυλάσσω/"preserve".

Since aorist participles can refer to actions both before and simultaneously with the main verb, though the former is more common,[223] as in Hebrew it is unclear whether the reference here is to first creation or continual preservation, though the former, i.e. *past creation*, is more likely.[224] Present participles may

---

223 See p. 124 fn. 271.
224 Zenger 2008g, 823, sees the aorist as a reference to first creation only.

refer to past or present or future, though present is most common,[225] as confirmed by the present form for the second occurrence of φυλάσσω/"preserve". Thus, a progression from *past creation to present preservation* is likely, especially given the two different participles of ποιέω/"make".

The first part of Ps 145^{LXX} (vv.1–4) unlike in Hebrew is dominated by *future forms* (vv.2a, 2b, 4a, 4b) rather than *imperatives* (vv.1, 3a). Thus, LXX stresses *future* praise. The second part (vv.5–10) is dominated by *present* forms (vv.7c, 8abc, 9a) and *participles* (vv.6ab, 7ab) with three *future* forms (vv.9bc, 10a) at the end. Thus, the reasons for praise are mostly general *but also future* actions, and *future forms* at the end link both parts, making it likely that v.10 is a summary for the entire Psalm. Unlike in MT, both participles in v.6 have an article, thus linking v.6 closer to the subject in v.5, while also maintaining a link to the following two participles. This underlines the link in both directions as in MT.

θεός/"god" appears twice in v.5 (for both אֵל/"god" and אֱלֹהִים/"god"), making the link between the God that is praised and the God of Jacob more explicit, and putting θεός/"god" twice in the centre of the Psalm, once as a subject and once as an object.

In vv.7c–9a where the subject κύριος/"Lord" is in a stressed position at the beginning of each sentence as in MT, the noun appears without an *article* as in MT.[226] The same applies to vv.2a, 5b, and 10, whereas there is an article in v.1 to translate the accusative marker אֵת. The translation of אֵת with an article which is not present in Hebrew is also found in Ps 145:9a^{LXX}: τοὺς προσηλύτους/"the strangers" for אֶת־גֵּרִים/"strangers". The addition of an article in εἰς τὸν αἰῶνα/ "for the eternity" for לְעוֹלָם/"for eternity" is common in the LXX-Psalter.[227]

Structure of Psalm 145^{LXX}

The structure of Ps 145^{LXX} is as in Ps 146^{MT}, but with the centre of v.5 stressed by the double occurrence of θεός/"god", and *future forms* in the introduction, both parts of the main body, and the conclusion. On the order of v.8ab see p. 266.

---

225 See p. 124 fn. 271.
226 The lack of an article is especially common in lists and when translating יהוה/"YHWH" without the accusative marker אֵת, cf. Blass, Debrunner, and Rehkopf 1979, §252, 254.
227 See e.g. Ps 135^{LXX}; similarly Ps 148:6^{LXX}.

Poetic Devices in Psalm 145^{LXX}

Parallelisms and tricola are the same as in MT.[228] There is an additional connection between ἀδικουμένοι/"oppressed ones" in v.7a and δίκαιοι/"righteous ones" in v.8c since both words are related to δίκη/"law". This supports the concept of MT where "righteous ones" are included in the list of those God cares for and who are called to praise (rather than being a separate group).[229]

VI.3.3 Intertextuality in Psalm 145^{LXX}

Importance

Texts similar to Ps 145^{LXX} have been merely listed so far.[230]

Analysis

A reference to *Genesis* 3:19^{LXX} is less likely than in MT: Only γῆ/"earth" is shared for אֲדָמָה/"ground", whereas שׁוּב/"return" is translated as ἀποστρέφω/"turn back" rather than ἐπιστρέφω/"return" (also, לֶחֶם/"food" is translated as ἄρτος/"bread" rather than τροφή/"food"; and Gen 3:17^{LXX} transliterates Αδαμ/ "Adam" rather than translating ἄνθρωπος/"human"). Gen 9^{LXX} only shares frequent words, and as in MT there are no references to Gen^{LXX}.

A reference to *Exodus* 15:18^{LXX} is less likely: κύριος/"Lord" for יְהוָה/"YHWH", βασιλεύω/"be king", and αἰών/"eternity" are shared, but there is no syntactical similarity, and the imperfect form is translated with the present participle βασιλεύων/"being king" rather than the future form βασιλεύσει/"he will be king".[231] As in MT, Ex 20:11^{LXX} shares the underlined words ἐποίησεν κύριος τὸν οὐρανὸν καὶ τὴν γῆν καὶ τὴν θάλασσαν καὶ πάντα τὰ ἐν αὐτοῖς/"the Lord made the heaven and the earth and the sea and all that is in them" with Ps 145^{LXX} (and also ἡμέρα/"day"). As in MT, τὴν θάλασσαν καὶ πάντα τὰ ἐν αὐτοῖς/"the sea and all that is in them" is syntactically identical and appears only in these two texts, and unlike in MT τὸν οὐρανὸν καὶ τὴν γῆν καὶ τὴν θάλασσαν καὶ πάντα τὰ ἐν αὐτοῖς/"the heaven and the earth and the sea and all that is in them" is also

---

228 See p. 69 fn. 368.
229 See p. 233–234 and p. 241, esp. fn. 94.
230 See p. 70 fn. 371.
231 The phrase βασιλεύσει κύριος εἰς τὸν αἰῶνα/"the Lord will be king for the eternity" is shared with Ps 9:37^{LXX}(=10:16^{MT}). A reference to Ps 9^{LXX} is unlikely due to a lack of other similarities, but the shared phrase makes a reference to Ex 15:18^{LXX} which uses a different phrase even less likely.

shared save for καί/"and". While as in MT a participle of ποιέω/"make" with τὸν οὐρανὸν καὶ τὴν γῆν/"the heaven and the earth" could be a formula,[232] a reference is more likely.[233] Both absolute[234] and relative[235] dates point towards a reference from Ps 145^{LXX} to Ex 20:11^{LXX}. The indirect reference to Gen 1^{LXX} is also stronger: while Gen 1:1^{MT} and Gen 2:4^{MT} use ברא/"create" rather than עשׂה/"make" as Ex 20:11^{MT} and Ps 146:7^{MT}, the same Greek verb ποιέω/"make" is used in all cases in LXX.

Deuteronomy 10:18^{LXX} shares fewer words with Psalm 145^{LXX}: As in Hebrew, ἱμάτιον/"clothing" is not shared, but מִשְׁפָּט/"judgement" is translated with κρίσις/"justice" instead of κρίμα/"judgement", and לֶחֶם/"food" is translated with ἄρτος/"bread" instead of τροφή/"food". While unlike in MT (through the addition of the first occurrence of the stranger in Deut 10:18^{LXX}) the order of stranger, orphan, and widow is shared, there is less syntactical similarity (dative vs. accusative), and the collocation of the three words is not unique to the two texts.[236] A reference to Deut 10:18^{LXX} is less likely than in MT, and a common topic (prominent in Deu^{LXX}) is more likely.[237]

Psalm 1^{LXX} and Ps 145^{LXX} share μακάριος/"blessed" for אַשְׁרֵי/"blessed", ἁμαρτωλός/"sinner" for רָשָׁע/"wicked" (but also for חַטָּא/"sinner", for רָשָׁע/"wicked" also ἀσεβής/"ungodly") and ὁδός/"path" for דֶּרֶךְ/"path" (but without syntactical similarity since דֶּרֶךְ רְשָׁעִים/"path of wicked ones" is translated as ὁδὸς ἀσεβῶν/"path of ungodly ones"), κύριος/"Lord" for יהוה/"YHWH", δίδωμι/"give" for נתן/"give", πᾶς/"all" for כֹּל/"all", ποιέω/"make" for עשׂה/"make", δίκαιος/"righteous" for צַדִּיק/"righteous" (plural), and ἀπόλλυμι/"perish" for אבד/"perish". However, in Ps 1^{LXX} רוּחַ/"wind" is translated as ἄνεμος/"wind", and מִשְׁפָּט/"judgement" as κρίσις/"justice". In addition to MT, οὐ/"not", ἡμέρα/"day", and γῆ/"earth" are shared. Since the shared phrase "path of wicked ones" is missing, a reference is less likely than in MT.[238]

Regarding *Psalm 102; 103^{LXX}(=103; 104^{MT})*, Ps 102^{LXX} shares the phrase ἡ ψυχή μου τὸν κύριον/"my soul the Lord" for נַפְשִׁי אֶת־יְהוָה/"my soul YHWH" (preceded by an imperative singular of εὐλογέω/"bless" for ברך/"bless" rather than

---

232 In "having made heaven and earth" (with aorist participles except in Ps 133:3^{LXX} with a present participle "making") articles are always added in the LXX-Psalter, see Ps 113:23; 120:2; 123:8; 133:3; 145:6^{LXX}, for MT see p. 235 fn. 48. Cf. Bauks 2011, 1878 referring to Seiler 2011b, 1822.
233 Gauthier 2014, 278–279, also argues for a stronger reference.
234 See fn. 272.
235 See VI.1.3.
236 Cf. e.g. Deut 24:17; 27:19^{LXX} as mentioned by Bons 2009b, 895.
237 Gauthier 2014, 282, does not decide between a reference and a common topic.
238 Thus also Gauthier 2014, 298.

αἰνέω/"praise" for הלל/"praise") in Ps 102:1, 2, 22^{LXX} with Ps 145^{LXX}, and the words θεός/"god" for אֱלֹהִים/"god" (followed by μου/"my" for the suffix), πᾶς/"all" for כֹּל/"all", μή/"not" for אַל/"not", ζωή/"life" for חַיִּים/"life", ποιέω/"make" for עָשָׂה/"make" (including ποιῶν/"making" for עֹשֶׂה/"making"), κύριος/"Lord" for יהוה/"YHWH", κρίμα/"judgement" for מִשְׁפָּט/"judgement", ἀδικέω/"oppress" for עָשַׁק/"oppress" (ἀδικουμένοις/"oppressed ones" for עֲשׁוּקִים/"oppressed ones"), ὁδός/"path" for דֶּרֶךְ/"path", υἱός/"son" for בֵּן/"son", αἰών/"eternity" for עוֹלָם/"eternity" (including εἰς τὸν αἰῶνα/"for the eternity" for לְעוֹלָם/"for eternity"), οὐρανός/"heaven" for שָׁמַיִם/"heaven", γῆ/"earth" for אֶרֶץ/"earth", αὐτός/ "he" for הוּא/"he", ἡμέρα/"day" for יוֹם/"day", πνεῦμα/"wind" for רוּחַ/"wind", and φυλάσσω/"preserve" for שֹׁמֵר/"preserve". אַיִן/"there is not" is translated with ὑπάρχω/"exist" (shared but for עוֹד/"continuance"), עוֹד/"continuance" with ἔτι/"still".[239] In addition to MT, οὐ/"not", εἰμί/"be", and ἄνθρωπος/ "human" are shared. As in MT, the shared phrase is the main similarity. Ps 103^{LXX} shares ἡ ψυχή μου τὸν κύριον/"my soul the Lord" for נַפְשִׁי אֶת־יהוה/"my soul YHWH" (preceded by an imperative singular of εὐλογέω/"bless" for ברך/ "bless" rather than αἰνέω/"praise" for הלל/"praise" as in Ps 145^{LXX}) in Ps 103:1, 35^{LXX} and Ps 145:1^{LXX}, and ἐν ζωῇ μου ψαλῶ τῷ θεῷ μου ἕως ὑπάρχω/"in my life, I will make music to my God as long as I exist" (preceded by a future form of ᾄδω/"sing" in Ps 103:33^{LXX} but of αἰνέω/"praise" in Ps 145:2^{LXX}, both followed by ὁ κύριος as an object; ζωή/"life" is preceded by τῇ/"the" in Ps 103:33^{LXX} only) in Ps 103:33^{LXX} and Ps 145:2^{LXX}. There is no closing Hallelujah in either Psalm. They share κύριος/"Lord" for יהוה/"YHWH", θεός/"god" for אֱלֹהִים/ "god" (followed by μου/"my" for the suffix), οὐρανός/"heaven" for שָׁמַיִם/"heaven", πνεῦμα/"wind" for רוּחַ/"wind" (but also ἄνεμος/"wind"), γῆ/"earth" for אֶרֶץ/"earth", πᾶς/"all" for כֹּל/"all", δίδωμι/"give" for נתן/"give", αἰών/"eternity" for עוֹלָם/"eternity" (including εἰς τὸν αἰῶνα/"for the eternity" for לְעוֹלָם/"for eternity"), ἐπιστρέφω /"return" for שׁוּב/"return", ἄνθρωπος/"human" for אָדָם/ "human" (but also for אֱנוֹשׁ/"human"), ἐξέρχομαι/"go out" for יצא/"go out" (but also ἐξάγω/"lead out"), θεός/"god" for אֵל/"god", θάλασσα/"sea" for יָם/ "sea", οὐκ ἔστιν/"there is not" for אַיִן/"there is not", γῆ/"earth" for אֲדָמָה/ "ground", ζωή/"life" for חַיִּים/"life", ἁμαρτωλός/"sinner" for רָשָׁע/"wicked" (plural), and ὑπάρχω/"exist" for עוֹד /"continuance". לֶחֶם/"food" is translated as as ἄρτος/"bread" rather than τροφή /"food" (τροφή/"food" is shared but for אֹכֶל/ "food"). In addition to MT, ἕως/"as long as" and εἰμί/"be" are shared. As in MT, the two shared phrases are the main similarity, with the first one being shared

---

239 The shared ἕως ὑπάρχω/"as long as I exist" is noted by Bauks 2011, 1877 (referring to Kraus 2011, 1794), but it translates different Hebrew equivalents.

more fully with Ps 102^{LXX} than Ps 145^{LXX}. As in MT, Ps 145^{LXX} changes both εὐλογέω/"bless" and ᾄδω/"sing" to αἰνέω/"praise". This indicates that Ps 145^{LXX} refers to Ps 102–103^{LXX} rather than the other way round. Since unlike in MT both Ps 102^{LXX} and Ps 103^{LXX} are superscribed with τῷ Δαυιδ/"about David" but Ps 145^{LXX} is not, the more universal individual is stressed.

Psalm 144^{LXX}(=145^{MT}) and Ps 145^{LXX} share ἀνορθοῖ/"he raises up" with κύριος/"Lord" as subject and κατερραγμένους/"bowed down ones" as object, a collocation unique to Ps 144:14^{LXX} (καὶ ἀνορθοῖ πάντας τοὺς κατερραγμένους/ "and he raises up all the bowed down ones") and Ps 145:8^{LXX} (κύριος ἀνορθοῖ κατερραγμένους/"the Lord raises up bowed down ones"), though unlike in MT ἀνορθόω/"raise up" is used more often in LXX,[240] as is καταράσσω/"bow down" (though κατερραγμένους/"bowed down ones" is found only in these two Psalms and as the only participle of the verb).[241] The two Psalms also share θεός/"god" for אֱלֹהִים/"god" (followed by μου/"my" for the suffix), αἰών/ "eternity" for עוֹלָם/"eternity" (including εἰς τὸν αἰῶνα/"for the eternity" for לְעוֹלָם/"for eternity"), πᾶς/"all" for כֹּל/"all" (though also ἕκαστος/"each"), ἡμέρα/"day" for יוֹם/"day", αἰνέω/"praise" for הלל/"praise" (αἰνέσω/"I will praise"), κύριος/"Lord" for יהוה/"YHWH", οὐκ ἔστιν/"there is not" for אַיִן/ "there is not", γενεά/"generation" for דֹּר/"generation" (doubled, including with καί/"and"), υἱός/"son" for בֵּן/"son" and ἄνθρωπος/"human" for אָדָם/ "human" (genitive construction), δίδωμι/"give" for נתן/"give" (present participle), δίκαιος/"righteous" for צַדִּיק/"righteous", ὁδός/"path" for דֶּרֶךְ/"path", ἀλήθεια/"truth" for אֱמֶת/"truth", ποιέω/"make" for עשׂה/"make", φυλάσσω/"preserve" for שׁמר/"preserve" (φυλάσσει/"he will preserve"), ἀγαπάω/"love" for אהב/"love", and ἁμαρτωλός/"sinner" for רָשָׁע/"wicked" (plural).[242] In addition to MT, τροφή/"food" is shared but for אֹכֶל/"food" rather than לֶחֶם/"food". As in MT, a reference is likely, but the direction remains unclear.[243]

Intertextual links with Psalm 146–147^{LXX}(=147^{MT}) (see p. 218 on Ps 145^{LXX}), Psalm 148^{LXX} (see p. 162–163 on Ps 145^{LXX}), Psalm 149^{LXX} (see p. 121 on Ps 145^{LXX}), and Psalm 150^{LXX} (see p. 72 on Ps 145^{LXX}) are unlikely.

Isaiah 42:7^{LXX} only shares a single frequent word with Ps 145^{LXX}: τυφλός/ "blind" for עִוֵּר/"blind". פקח/"open" is translated with ἀνοίγω/"open" rather than the hapax legomenon σοφόω/"make wise", and δέω/"bind" for אסר/

---

240 Cf. Lust, Eynikel, and Hauspie 2003, s.v. ἀνορθόω: 16 times.
241 Cf. Lust, Eynikel, and Hauspie 2003, s.v. καταράσσω: 7 times.
242 חי/"life" is translated with ζῷον/"living being" rather than ζωή/"life". See fn. 82.
243 Gauthier 2014, 294, notes: "Ps 144(145):14 may be juxtaposed with Ps 145(146) partly for reasons of common vocabulary". Gauthier 2014, 315, speaks of a "Final Hallel collection (Ps 146–150)".

"bind" instead of πεδάω/"bind" (and ἐξάγω/"lead out" for אצי/"go out" instead of ἐξέρχομαι/"go out"). Isa 49:9^LXX shares no words with Ps 145:7–8^LXX as אסר/ "bind" is paraphrased with δεσμός/"bond" instead of πεδάω/"bind" (with Ps 145^LXX it also shares ἐξέρχομαι/"go out" for אצי/"go out", ὁδός/"path" for דרך/"path", and πᾶς/"all" for כל/"all"). Due to fewer lexical similarities references to Isa^LXX are even less likely than in MT; rather, shared topics are likely.

It is often argued that *1 Maccabees 2:63^LXX* quotes Ps 146:4[244] (rather than Ps 145:4^LXX even though 1 Mac is Greek),[245] leading to a date of Ps 146 and the Psalter[246] or the final redaction of the Psalter more generally[247] before 100 BCE.[248] 1 Mac 2:62–63^LXX reads: ⁶² καὶ ἀπὸ λόγων ἀνδρὸς <u>ἁμαρτωλοῦ μὴ</u> φοβηθῆτε ὅτι ἡ δόξα <u>αὐτοῦ εἰς</u> κόπρια καὶ <u>εἰς</u> σκώληκας ⁶³<u>σήμερον</u> ἐπαρθήσεται καὶ αὔριον <u>οὐ μὴ</u> εὑρεθῇ ὅτι <u>ἐπέστρεψεν εἰς</u> τὸν χοῦν <u>αὐτοῦ</u> καὶ ὁ <u>διαλογισμὸς αὐτοῦ ἀπολεῖται</u>/"⁶²And the words of a sinful man do not fear, because his splendour (is) to dirt and to worms, ⁶³today he will be exalted, and tomorrow he shall not be found, because he has returned to his dust, and his thought will perish." Thus, 1 Mac 2:62–63^LXX share the underlined words ἁμαρτωλός/"sinner" (here as an adjective "sinful"), μή/"not" and οὐ/"not", ἐπιστρέφω/"return", διαλογισμός/ "thought", and ἀπόλλυμι/"perish" (and αὐτός/"he" and εἰς/"in"). While the collocation of ἐπιστρέφω/"return", διαλογισμός/"thought", and ἀπόλλυμι/"perish" is unique to 1 Mac 2:63^LXX and Ps 145:4^LXX, none of the words are rare,[249] the forms and order of words show differences, and χοῦς/"dust" is used instead of γῆ/ "earth". Given that the topic of human mortality and returning to dust with similar shared words also features in other texts (e. g. Ps 103:29^LXX where χοῦς/"dirt" is collocated with ἐπιστρέφω/"return", Sir 10:9–11^LXX where σήμερον/"today", αὔριον/"tomorrow" and σκώληκες/"worms" are mentioned), there is not enough similarity with Ps 145:4^LXX to make a quote likely.

---

244 Cf. Duhm 1922, 475 (quote or reverse quote); Gunkel 1926, 613 (quote); Ballhorn 2004b, 305 (quote); Reindl 1981a, 118 (free quote).
245 As an exception, Gauthier 2014, 269, argues for an allusion to Ps 145:4^LXX.
246 Cf. Lange 1998, 116, esp. fn. 82 (reference); Zenger 2008g, 822 (allusion).
247 Cf. Dahmen 2000, 121 (reference); Jain 2014, 238 (reference, referring to Dahmen).
248 1 Mac is dated to around 100 BCE, cf. Engel 2016, 397. The assumed quote in Ps 146 also leads to emendations, see VI.1.7.
249 Contrary to MT, where מחשבתו/"thought" is a rare word used only in Ps 146:4 (Ps 145:4^LXX διαλογισμός/"thought") and Sir 3:24 (cf. Abegg and Parker [no year]a, loose translation with the hapax legomenon ὑπόλημψις/"speculation" in Sir 3:24^LXX). See fn. 173.

Results

For Ps 145^{LXX}, in almost all cases *unlikely references are even less likely* in LXX than in MT. This applies to Gen^{LXX} (as unlikely as in MT); Ex 15^{LXX}; Deu^{LXX}; Isa^{LXX}; and Ps 1^{LXX}. Ps 146 – 147^{LXX}(=147^{MT}); 148^{LXX} show no reference except for the common superscription; there is no reference at all to Ps 149^{LXX} and Ps 149^{LXX}, and neither to 1 Mac 2:63^{LXX}. At the same time, *likely references are as likely* as in MT. This applies to the references to Ex 20^{LXX} (including the indirect reference to Gen 1^{LXX}); Ps 102 – 103^{LXX}(=103 – 104^{MT}); 144^{LXX}(=145^{MT}).

VI.3.4 Content of Psalm 145^{LXX}

Who is called to praise in Psalm 145:1 – 2^{LXX}?
The addressees are as in MT, with the aspect of *lifelong praise* of the individual confirmed by the verbal translation of בְּעוֹדִי/"in my continuance" with ἕως ὑπάρχω/"as long as I exist". Unlike in MT, the calls to praise are *future forms*.[250]

Who is warned against in Psalm 145:3 – 4^{LXX}?
While there is no asyndeton with καί/"and" at the beginning of v.3b, as in MT ἐπί/"in" is repeated in v.3ab, and unlike in MT both "rulers" and "sons of men" are plural (LXX here spells out the collective aspect of בֶּן־אָדָם/"son of man").[251] Combined with v.4 which mixes singular (v.4a, probably going back to a literal translation of MT and referring to the humans in v.3b)[252] and plural forms (v.4b αὐτῶν/"their", referring back to v.3)[253] and gives reasons for the warning in v.3, it is still likely that *as in MT rulers and humans are equated*.[254] The dative relative pronoun in v.3b corresponds to לְ/"for" in MT,[255] and the

---

250 On the meaning of ψάλλω/"to sing praise" cf. Gauthier 2014, 260 – 262.
251 Cf. Kselman 1988, 588; Bauks 2011, 1878 referring to Bons 2011c, 1504 (exception in LXX, usually singular "son of man").
252 Against Bauks 2011, 1878 ("his breath" could refer to God in v.2); Zenger 2008g, 823 (subject of v.3a could be God): Since the two halves of v.4a are connected with καί/"and", the subject of both is the same, and God does not appear as a subject before v.10, it is unlikely that v.4a refers to God.
253 Cf. Bons 2009b, 894.
254 Against Zenger 2008g, 823 (LXX has two groups in view), but cf. Zenger 2008g, 812 (v.3^{MT} could be translated with two plural forms).
255 Cf. Reindl 1981a, 118.

total helplessness is stressed by πάντες/"all" in v.4b. Unlike in MT, v.4 uses *future forms.*

As in MT, the human rulers in vv.3–4 may be equated with ἁμαρτολοί/"sinners" in v.9, with the connection made stronger than in MT by ἀφανίζω/"destroy" in both v. 4 and v.9.

As in MT, ἄρχοντες/"rulers" may refer to rulers within Israel as well as those of other nations,[256] and πνεῦμα/"wind" is used for "breath".

What are human and godly actions in Psalm 145:5–9ᴸˣˣ?

Unlike in MT, the phrase ὁ θεὸς Ιακωβ/"the God of Jacob" is not unique to Ps 145:5ᴸˣˣ, but used especially in the Psalter in contexts of God's power and help for אֱלֹהֵי יַעֲקֹב/"God of Jacob". The nominal sentence with *beth essentiae* denoting the predicate עֶזְרוֹ/"his helper" in MT is confirmed in LXX where a genitive relative pronoun "his" is combined with βοηθός/"helper" as a predicate noun.[257] The aorist participle in v.6 refers to past creation.[258] Compared to MT, v.8ab are reversed in their order, with the restoration of broken ones following the freeing of bound ones, and the making wise of blind ones preceding the loving of righteous ones.[259] This line swap is not found in all LXX manuscripts,[260] the MT order is also found in 4QMessAp.[261] The hapax legomenon σοφόω/"make wise" as a translation of פקח/"open" regarding blind ones metaphorises blindness,[262] and this is stressed through the collocation with δίκαιοι/"righteous ones". κατερραγμένοι/"broken down ones" for כְּפוּפִים/"bowed down ones" stresses physical falling more than MT.[263] προσήλυτος/"stranger" refers to strangers generally as a standard translation of גֵּר/"stranger".[264] ἀναλαμβάνω/"lift up" for עוד/ "raise up" has the additional aspect of "to take up, to receive".[265] ἁμαρτωλός/

256 Cf. Lust, Eynikel, and Hauspie 2003, s.v. ἄρχων. This translation of נְדִיבִים/"noble ones" is typical for the LXX-Psalter, cf. Bauks 2011, 1877 referring to Brucker 2011f, 1630.
257 On predicate nouns cf. Smyth and Messing 1956, §910–911.
258 See p. 124 fn. 271.
259 Cf. Gauthier 2014, 287–290.
260 See Rahlfs 1979. 334. Cf. Bons 2009b, 894.
261 See VI.2.1.
262 Cf. Zenger 2008g, 823. On wisdom influence see VI.1.5.
263 Cf. Lust, Eynikel, and Hauspie 2003, s.v. καταράσσω.
264 Cf. Lust, Eynikel, and Hauspie 2003, s.v. προσήλυτος; Bons 2009b, 848, 895. It later designates someone who converted to Judaism, cf. Bauer, Aland, and Aland 1988, s.v. προσήλυτος.
265 Cf. Lust, Eynikel, and Hauspie 2003, s.v. ἀναλαμβάνω; Bons 2009b, 895.

"sinner" is a common translation for רָשָׁע/"wicked"[266] which as in Hebrew can be used as an adjective or a noun.[267]

What are kingship and Zion in Psalm 145:10^{LXX}?

Unlike in MT, Ps 145^{LXX} has a strong *future* aspect, with future forms in vv.2ab, 4ab, 9bc, and 10a. However, the reference to creation in v.6, present forms in vv.7c–9a, and the mention of long periods of time in v.10 make it likely that as in MT God's rule is not thought as an eschatological vision, rather as not just in the future but also the past and present.[268]

VI.3.5 Genre of Psalm 145^{LXX}

In Ps 145:8b, the hapax legomenon σοφόω/"make wise" metaphorises blindness.[269] This is sometimes seen as a hint towards wisdom influence on the LXX translation of the Psalter,[270] and hints towards a literary context.[271]

VI.3.6 Date of Psalm 145^{LXX}

The intertextual reference within LXX but outside the Psalter to *Ex 20^{LXX}* points towards a date of Ps 145^{LXX} *after the 3rd century BCE*,[272] in line with general considerations about a 2nd century BCE LXX-Psalter.[273] Thus, Ps 145^{LXX} is likely to have its time of origin after the 6th (because of MT), after the 3rd (because of

---

266 Cf. Hatch et al. 1998, s.v. ἁμαρτωλός.

267 Cf. Lust, Eynikel, and Hauspie 2003, s.v. ἁμαρτωλός; Gesenius 2013, s.v. רָשָׁע.

268 Also confirmed by the general meaning of ἐλπίς as "hope" rather than "expectation", cf. Bauks 2011, 1878 referring to Bons 2011c, 1506. Only Ps 145:10^{LXX} and Ps 9:37^{LXX}(=10:16^{MT}) have a future form for God's kingship, cf. Bauks 2011, 1879 referring to Bons 2011d, 1522 (aorists in Ps 46:9; 92:1; 95:10; 96:1; 98:1^{LXX}), but there is no intertextual reference, see fn. 231.

269 See p. 266, esp. fn. 262.

270 Cf. Gzella 2002,141–142; Zenger 2008g, 823 (interest in wisdom, Alexandria); Bauks 2011, 1878 (wisdom influence, referring to Gzella).

271 Cf. for the LXX-Psalter Gzella 2002, 33, 55.

272 Cf. Siegert 2001, 42 (Ex^{LXX} following Gen^{LXX}, both 3rd century BCE). However, manuscripts of Ex 20^{LXX} are not preserved from any time BCE, cf. Siegert 2001, 96 in combination with with Septuaginta-Unternehmen der Akademie der Wissenschaften zu Göttingen 2012.

273 See p. 16, esp. fn. 104.

Ex^{LXX}), *in the 2nd century BCE* (because of the LXX-Psalter). The use of σοφόω/ "make wise" may point to wisdom influence on the translator(s).[274]

VI.3.7 Unity of Psalm 145^{LXX}

Ps 145^{LXX} is one unit,[275] with no final Hallelujah in any Greek manuscript.[276] Regarding the superscription, some manuscripts miss out Αγγαιου καὶ Ζαχαριου/ "of Haggai and Zechariah" as in Ps 149–150^{LXX}.[277] This may indicate that the superscription is secondary,[278] though the opposite could also be the case.

VI.3.8 Overall Interpretation of Psalm 145^{LXX}

The Lord, the God of Jacob and Zion, is to be praised both by an individual (including in the *future*) with a group of listeners and by a group. The reasons for praise are God's *past* creation and help for powerless people (including in the *future*), *his giving of wisdom*, and his lasting kingship (including the *future*) in contrast to the mortality of human rulers. No specific time or place for praise are indicated. Both likely and unlikely intertextual references are as in MT.

---

274 See VI.3.5.
275 For the line swap in v.8ab see fn. 260.
276 The final Hallelujah is also missing in the Syriac version, cf. Elliger and Rudolph 1997, 1224.
277 See p. 17 fn. 109.
278 Cf. Zenger 2008g, 822–823.

VI.4 Comparison

Both DSS (11QPs[a] only; 4QPs[d] and 4QPs[e] do not contain Ps 146) and LXX are very *close* to MT, but DSS has an *additional passage referring to creation*, and LXX an explicit *future* aspect and a word related to wisdom.

DSS has a closing *Hallelujah* (the opening is not preserved) but LXX does not (a superscription at the beginning includes a transliterated Hallelujah). LXX manuscripts show variations of the frame.

Regarding *order*, Ps 146 is preceded by Ps 145 and followed by Ps 147 in MT and LXX (though Psalm 147[MT] is split), but not in DSS where the order is Ps 105 – 146 – 148. This weakens the likelihood of an original connection of Psalms 146 – 150.

Regarding *intertextuality*, DSS and LXX show no additional references and confirm the lack of references in MT or even weaken the likelihood of references in MT. In MT and LXX, a reference to or from Ps 145 as a neighbouring Psalm but not within the group of Psalms 146 – 150 weakens the likelihood of an original connection of Psalms 146 – 150.

VII Conclusion

Psalms 146–150 are originally separate texts. They were not originally written to end or frame the Psalter as a unit. This result is based on the analysis of differences to the Hebrew Masoretic Text in the Hebrew Dead Sea Scrolls and the Greek Septuagint as the oldest sources of Psalms 146–150, and on an intertextual analysis showing that Psalms 146–150 do not refer to one another or Psalms 1–2 at all and share almost no reference texts. Although Psalms 146–150 as a compilation form the end of the Masoretic Psalter, this is unlikely to have been their original place. Thus, the conclusion that Psalms 146–150 are originally separate texts is based on new text-critical and intertextual research which includes not only the Masoretic Text and Dead Sea Scrolls, but also the Septuagint.

Chapter I "Introduction to Psalms 146–150" first explains the view of the end of the Psalter in current research in Section I.1 "End of the Psalter": Psalms 146–150 are seen as one coherent group, sometimes called "Final Hallel", which forms the end of the Psalter. This view is based on Psalter Exegesis, i.e. the interpretation of Psalms in the context of the Hebrew Masoretic Psalter. In a diachronic approach, Psalter Exegesis seeks to supplement but not replace Psalms Exegesis, i.e. the interpretation of each individual Psalm. However, in the specific case of Psalms 146–150, Psalter Exegesis in current research often does partly replace Psalms Exegesis based on the argument that Psalms 146–150 are at least partly written for the context of the end of the Psalter and therefore must be read in this context only rather than as individual Psalms. This replacement has significant impact on the interpretation of Psalms 146–150, often leading to a stress on eschatology at the end of the Psalter. The argument of the original coherence of the end of the Psalter is based on three main reasons: the context of Psalms 146–150 in this order at the end of the Masoretic Psalter, the framing Hallelujahs of Psalms 146–150, and intertextual links between Psalms 146–150. However, all three of these reasons are highly problematic, as the two following sections of the introduction on the sources of Psalms 146–150 and their intertextual links demonstrate.

Section I.2 "Sources" introduces the oldest available sources for Psalms 146–150: the Hebrew Masoretic Text (MT), the Hebrew Dead Sea Scrolls (DSS), and the Greek Septuagint (LXX). In DSS, especially in the Qumran Psalms Scroll 11QPs^a, Psalms 146–150 are found in entirely different orders (such as Psalms 105–146–148–120) and with inconsistent framing Hallelujahs. In LXX, Psalm 147 is split into two Psalms, Psalm 151^{LXX} is found at the end, and there are different superscriptions instead of framing Hallelujahs. Both DSS and LXX also contain whole

DOI 10.1515/9783110536096-007

sentences not found in MT. Given these differences and their importance for the original connection of Psalms 146 – 150, and the unknown relation of MT and DSS for the Psalms, this section introduces a new text-critical approach in which the three different oldest text forms are not merged into one hypothetical original text, but interpreted separately and then compared to each other.

Section I.3 "Intertextuality" notes that so far commentators have mostly listed intertextual references for Psalms 146 – 150 without assessment. For a new comprehensive intertextual analysis of Psalms 146 – 150, this section provides general criteria for identifying diachronic intertextual references, especially the number, order, and frequency of the shared words, as well as procedures for analysing the direction of identified references with absolute or relative dates.

Section I.4 "Structure of this Study" formulates the hypothesis of a separate origin of each of Psalms 146 – 150 based on text-critical and intertextual observations. The investigation for testing the hypothesis includes a separate exegesis of each Psalm in each text form with a particular focus on intertextual references. For each Psalm in each source, following a translation from the Hebrew or Greek source and an outline, an analysis focussing on its form, including syntax, structure, and poetic devices, provides a framework for the interpretation of the content, and highlights overall features of the individual Psalm. The content is analysed taking into account both intertextual references and other similarities with texts and non-textual sources. The exegesis further includes an analysis of each Psalm's genre, date, and unity before an overall interpretation. For each Psalm, MT as the only complete text in Hebrew is analysed first, followed by the fragmentary Hebrew DSS before the Greek LXX. A comparison of the exegesis of each of the three text forms concludes each chapter. The five main chapters present the analysis of the individual Psalms 150, 149, 148, 147, and 146 in reverse order compared to MT for two reasons: Firstly, Psalm 150 as the final Psalm of the Masoretic Psalter is of special importance for the end of the Psalter, and attracts an especially large number of contradicting interpretations and intertextual associations. It is thus treated extensively including the critical analysis of numerous commentaries to serve as an example for the analysis of the other Psalms. Secondly, the reverse order emphasises the importance of reading Psalms 146 – 150 individually rather than in a progressing order. While any random order of the five Psalms would also emphasise this point, the reverse order has the pragmatic advantage of ensuring that the discussion of each Psalm may still be found easily without referring to the table of contents.

Chapter II "Psalm 150" in Section II.1 "Psalm 150^{MT}" demonstrates that contrary to some current scholarship, number symbolism is insignificant in Psalm 150, and no intertextual references can be substantiated at all. Regarding content, "his strong firmament" in Psalm 150:2 is a reason for praise, the list of instruments does not reflect music inside and beyond the temple or eschatological music, and "all the breath" in Psalm 150:6 refers to all humans. A cultic or literary setting and an absolute date (though there is a consensus for a postexilic date) cannot be made certain. Psalm 150 is one unit but the framing Hallelujahs are inconsistent in manuscripts. Overall, Psalm 150 invites universal praise.

Section II.2 "Psalm 150[DSS]" demonstrates that in 11QPs[a] Psalm 150 is preceded by the end of Psalm 149 but followed by another hymn. There is no opening Hallelujah. In MasPs[b], Psalm 150 is close to Psalm 147 but may have been followed by another text. The beginning and end are not preserved.

Section II.3 "Psalm 150[LXX]" shows that in Psalm 150[LXX] both an opening and a final Hallelujah are found. Number symbolism and intertextual references are even less probable than in MT. The firmament is God's place, the instruments vary. Genre and date remain uncertain. Psalm 150[LXX] is a unit but with variations in the framing Hallelujahs.

Section II.4 "Comparison" confirms the closeness of both DSS and LXX to MT. However, the framing Hallelujahs and the context of Psalm 150 differ. There is a complete lack of intertextual references in all text forms.

Chapter III "Psalm 149" in Section III.1 "Psalm 149[MT]" displays new results for Psalm 149: Contrary to some scholars, revenge is not restricted to the nation's rulers, despite the mention of a "written judgement" there are no intertextual references, the "faithful" are all of the people Israel rather than one specific group, there is no mention of resurrection, and the two-edged sword is an actual weapon. Psalm 149 eludes a precise allocation of hymnic setting and date (though there is a consensus for a postexilic date). Psalm 149 is a unit with an inconsistent Hallelujah-frame in versions. Given the lack of intertextual references, overall three possible interpretations of Psalm 149 remain alongside one another: the judgement is actual violence, or eschatological violence, or no violence at all but also praise.

Section III.2 "Psalm 149[DSS]" demonstrates that in 11QPs[a] Psalm 149 is followed by Psalm 150 but probably preceded by Psalm 143. The opening is not preserved, there is a final Hallelujah. A striking additional passage in Psalm 149:9[DSS] stresses Israel.

Section III.3 "Psalm 149[LXX]" shows that in Psalm 149[LXX] only an opening Hallelujah is found. Future forms in combination with semantic observations point towards an eschatological understanding of Psalm 149[LXX].

Section III.4 "Comparison" confirms the closeness of both DSS and LXX to MT, though there is a stress on Israel in DSS through the additional passage, and on the future in LXX. However, the framing Hallelujahs and the context of

Psalm 149 differ. There is a complete lack of intertextual references in all text forms.

Chapter IV "Psalm 148" in Section IV.1 "Psalm 148^{MT}" presents the novel results that for Psalm 148 number symbolism is insignificant, and no intertextual references can be substantiated. Despite similarities with Psalm 149, the lack of intertextual references makes an original connection or common authorship of Psalm 148 and Psalm 149 unlikely. Possible redactional connections between these two Psalms are conjectural. It is likely that Psalm 148 and Psalm 149 had different origins and were later placed next to each other because of their similarities. Psalm 148 further eludes a precise allocation of a hymnic setting and date (though there is a consensus for a postexilic date). It is a unit with an inconsistent Hallelujah-frame in versions. Overall, Psalm 148 expresses a universal idea of praise. However, the final reason for praise is Israel-specific.

Section IV.2 "Psalm 148^{DSS}" demonstrates that in 11QPs^a Psalm 148 follows Psalm 146 and probably precedes Psalm 120. There is no opening Hallelujah.

Section IV.3 "Psalm 148^{LXX}" shows that Psalm 148^{LXX} contains a superscription "Hallelujah; of Haggai and Zechariah", future forms, and an additional verse with a word-by-word reference to Psalm 32^{LXX}(=33^{MT}) leading to a stress on the universal aspect of creation.

Section IV.4 "Comparison" confirms the closeness of both DSS and LXX to MT, though there is a stress on universalism and future in LXX. However, the framing Hallelujahs and the context of Psalm 148 differ. There is a complete lack of intertextual references in MT and DSS. LXX, while mostly weakening the likelihood of references in MT, does refer to Psalm 32^{LXX}.

Chapter V "Psalm 147" in Section V.1 "Psalm 147^{MT}" demonstrates that Psalm 147 shows intertextual references to Deuteronomy 4, Isaiah 40, and Psalm 33, with references to Psalm 104 and Psalm 135 also being possible, but no references to Psalms 146, 148, 149, or 150. The references as well as the Psalm's content and late Hebrew language point towards a postexilic date, but its hymnic setting is unclear. Psalm 147 is one unit.

Section V.2 "Psalm 147^{DSS}" demonstrates that in 11QPs^a Psalm 147 is placed between Psalms 104 and 105, with its beginning and end not preserved. In 4QPs^d, Psalm 147 is placed between Psalms 106(?) and 104, with both an opening and a final Hallelujah. Contrary to some scholars, this section demonstrates that 4QPs^e does not contain Psalm 147. In MasPs^b, Psalm 147 is close to Psalm 150, with no Hallelujahs preserved.

Section V.3 "Psalm 146–147^{LXX}" shows that Psalm 147^{MT} equals two Psalms 146^{LXX}(=147:1–11^{MT}) and 147^{LXX}(=147:12–20^{MT}), both with the superscription "Hallelujah; of Haggai and Zechariah". Psalms $146-147^{LXX}$ show significant differences in their intertextuality both compared to MT and to each other: a reference to Psalm $103^{LXX}(=104^{MT})$ which can only be assumed in MT is clearly present through a word-by-word reference in an additional sentence in Psalm 146^{LXX}, but not Psalm 147^{LXX}, and a reference to Deuteronomy 4^{LXX} is found in Psalm 147^{LXX} only. Thus, universal creation is stressed in Psalm 146^{LXX}, Israel's uniqueness in Psalm 147^{LXX}. Both Psalms have future forms, but the future focus is on Israel in Psalm 146^{LXX} and on creation in Psalm 147^{LXX}.

Section V.4 "Comparison" shows that (apart from the split of Psalms $146-147^{LXX}$) both DSS and LXX are very close to MT. However, the framing Hallelujahs and the context of Psalm 147 differ. LXX adds a future perspective in both Psalms and shows substantial differences in its intertextual references. DSS and LXX also show two similarities against MT: a stronger reference to Psalm 104, and God as the grammatical subject of the final colon of Psalm 147.

Chapter VI "Psalm 146" in Section VI.1 "Psalm 146^{MT}" demonstrates that Psalm 146 contains intertextual references to Exodus 20:11 (and Genesis 1–2:4a indirectly), Psalms 103–104, and Psalm 145. There is no indication of a specific time or place for praise within Psalm 146, but the references as well as late Hebrew language point towards a postexilic date. The Psalm's genre and setting are unclear. It is a unit but with inconsistent Hallelujah-frames.

Section VI.2 "Psalm 146^{DSS}" demonstrates that in 11QPs^a Psalm 146 is followed by Psalm 148 and probably preceded by Psalm 105. There is an additional passage mentioning YHWH's creation and power. The beginning of Psalm 146 is not preserved, but there is a final Hallelujah. Contrary to some scholars, this section demonstrates that 4QPs^d and 4QPs^e do not contain Psalm 146.

Section VI.3 "Psalm 145^{LXX}" shows that in Psalm 145^{LXX} intertextual references as in MT, the verb "to make wise", and future forms are found.

Section VI.4 "Comparison" confirms the closeness of both DSS and LXX to MT. However, the framing Hallelujahs and the context of Psalm 146 differ. In both MT and LXX, there is a reference to or from Psalm 145, which weakens the likelihood of an original connection of Psalms 146–150 given that Psalm 145 is a neighbouring Psalm but not within the group of Psalms 146–150.

This analysis leads to the following results:

Regarding *sources*, the oldest available text forms of Psalms 146–150, the Hebrew Dead Sea Scrolls and the Greek Septuagint, show significant differences in the order, frame, and content of Psalms 146–150 when compared to the Hebrew Masoretic Text.

Firstly, regarding *order*, while Psalms 146–150 individually appear in all of the three oldest sources, MT is the only source where Psalms 146–150 are in this order, otherwise this is possible only for MasPs[b] which, however, is too fragmentary to confirm this order. 11QPs[a] and 4QPs[d] show different orders not only compared to MT but also compared to each other (Ps 104–147 in 11QPs[a], Ps 147–104 in 4QPs[d]). LXX splits up Ps 147 into Ps $146^{LXX}(=147{:}1-11^{MT})$ and Ps 147^{LXX} $(=147{:}12-20^{MT})$. Both 11QPs[a] and LXX do not have Ps 150 but forms of Ps 151 at the end.

Secondly, regarding the *frame*, MT is the only source where a Hallelujah-frame is present in all of Psalms 146–150. In DSS, many beginnings and endings are not preserved, but where they are preserved, the *opening* Hallelujah is missing twice in 11QPs[a] (Ps 148 and 150). In LXX, there are no *final* Hallelujahs at all except in Ps 150^{LXX}, and Ps $145-148^{LXX}(=146-148^{MT})$ are grouped together as four Psalms all with the superscription "Hallelujah; of Haggai and Zechariah" whereas Psalms $149-150^{LXX}$ share the superscription "Hallelujah". Additional sources such as variant Hebrew and Greek manuscripts and translations into other languages also show variations of the Hallelujah-frame.

Thirdly, regarding the *content*, the individual Psalms show few differences in all sources. However, compared to MT there are additional passages in both 11QPs[a] and LXX which stress the contrast of universal creation in some Psalms (Ps 146 in 11QPs[a]; Ps 146^{LXX}; Ps 148^{LXX}) with the uniqueness of Israel in others (Ps 149 in 11QPs[a]).

Overall, neither the order nor the frame which tie together the end of the Psalter in MT are present in the oldest factually preserved sources, while, with a split of Ps 147 in LXX, the individual Psalms *do* exist. Thus, the order and frame of Psalms 146–150 do not seem to be an integral part of the individual Psalms. In the debate about the development of different super- and subscriptions in MT, DSS, and LXX, this result mainly points to instability of these frames in antiquity, and the need for further comparisons of the three text forms for other Psalms. Psalms 146–150 also differ in their oldest sources through additions. For Psalms 146–150, the relation between MT, DSS, and LXX as the latter two depending on MT could not be proven. Psalms 146–150 in DSS do not presuppose the Masoretic Psalter, especially given that the end of MasPs[b] is not factually preserved. This result concurs with the possibility that Books IV and V of the later Masoretic Psalter were not stable until after the mid-first century CE. The deconstruction of a unit of Psalms 146–150 cannot be used as an argument for the dependance of 11QPs[a] on MT. While for Ps 146–150 the LXX text seems to be secondary to MT, this may not be true for the superscriptions, there are no LXX manuscripts for Ps $145-150^{LXX}$ from before the 4th century CE, and the date of these Psalms largely depends on the overall dating of the LXX-Psalter.

DSS and LXX show similarities against MT in Ps 147. This result generally implies that the separate parallel interpretation of factually existing text forms other than the Masoretic Text, especially the older Dead Sea Scrolls and the Septuagint, may be helpful for illuminating other biblical texts.

Regarding *intertextuality*, in MT Ps 148, 149, and 150 do not contain references at all. Ps 146 (with references to Ex 20:11 and indirectly Gen 1:1–2:4a, Ps 103–104, and Ps 145) and Ps 147 (with references to Deut 4, Isa 40, Ps 33, and possibly Ps 104 and Ps 135) have different reference texts with the single exception of one possible shared reference text, Ps 104. There are references to other Psalms in Ps 146–147, but contrary to assumptions about the end and frame of the Psalter *not* within the group Ps 146–150 (except for the framing Hallelujahs), or to Ps 1–2. Two arguments for an early date of the Masoretic Psalter need to be reassessed: Ps 146 does not quote 1 Mac 2:63^{LXX}, and there are no references to Ben Sira (only the other way round from Sir 51:12o to Ps 148:14).

DSS show little difference in their intertextuality as compared to MT, though this may be due to their fragmentary state, or lost reference texts. They do place Ps 104 next to Ps 147 in line with the intertextual reference in MT and LXX, and show a reference from 4QMessAp to the individual Ps 146. There is no indication of weaker intertextuality in DSS compared to MT. However, the fragmentary state of DSS often makes the comparison of intertextuality impossible.

In LXX, Ps 146–147^{LXX} share two reference texts with MT, but the split highlights different aspects (the universal creation Psalm Ps 103^{LXX}=104^{MT} in Ps 146^{LXX}, the election of Israel in Deut 4^{LXX} in Ps 147^{LXX}), and LXX shows differences in its intertextuality stressing the unity of the LXX-Psalter and at the same time leading to differences in the overall content of the specific Psalms (Ps 146^{LXX} has an additional creation passage exactly as in Ps 103^{LXX}, Ps 148^{LXX} an additional creation passage exactly as in Ps 32^{LXX}). LXX heavily weakens the likelihood of references in MT, and despite the two superscriptions shows no references within Ps 145–150^{LXX}. This result of a novel comparison of MT and LXX is especially noteworthy since generally the LXX translation of these Psalms is very close to MT.

Psalms 146–150 do not contain references to one another, and do not contain references to the same other texts with the one exception of Psalms 146 and 147 both referring to Ps 104 amongst other different texts. Thus, like the order and frame, intertextuality does not provide a basis for the case of an original connection of the "Final Hallel". In addition, DSS and especially LXX while generally being very close to MT show significant differences in their intertextuality. This result generally stresses the impact of reference texts or the lack of reference texts on the interpretation of biblical texts and implies that intertextual references may need to be assessed carefully in other biblical texts, including references in sources other than MT. In particular, LXX as an ancient witness has the potential of confirming or correcting arguments for the presence of intertextual references. Since different criteria for identifying intertextual references can lead to opposing results such as the original coherence of Psalms 146–150, a further discussion of such criteria is desirable, and the comprehensive lists and discussions provided here for Psalm 146–150 provide a basis for further research on diachronic intertextuality. The result of the intertextual analysis also stresses the need for interpretations of biblical texts based on the general semantics of words and on common general themes rather than intertextual references. Studies of the use of words and themes in different texts and times are desirable, and could further inform the interpretation of Psalms 146–150 as well as other biblical texts.

Regarding *content*, the overall interpretations of the individual Psalms show differences to one another, and to aspects stressed by an interpretation of Psalms 146–150 as one unit: In MT God's kingship appears in Ps 146 and 149 only, even though all of Psalms 146–150 are theocentric. With the possible exception of Ps 149, there is no eschatology at all in Psalms 146–150. Regarding the date of Psalms 146–150, only Psalms 146 and 147 prove to be postexilic, other dates are unknown (though there is a consensus for postexilic dates). DSS stress creation in Ps 146 but Israel in Ps 149. LXX has additions and future forms, with future forms appearing in all of Ps 145–149^{LXX} but not Ps 150^{LXX} contrary to the idea of a progression towards eschatology. Thus, for Psalms 146–150 Psalms Exegesis leads to very different results compared to Psalter Exegesis, and to a need to reassess eschatology as an argument for an early date of the Masoretic Psalter.

Overall, these results concerning the order, frame, and content of Psalms 146–150 in their oldest sources confirm the hypothesis of a separate origin of Psalms 146, 147, 148, 149, and 150. The end of the Masoretic Psalter is formed by a collocation of five originally separate Psalms. A comparison of the oldest preserved sources does not provide indications of a literary development of a series of Psalms at least partly written for the specific purpose of forming the end of the Psalter. Rather, the oldest factually preserved sources appear to place importance on Psalms 146–150 as individual texts. Thus, differences in content between Psalms 146–150 cannot be smoothed out by assuming the original coherence of this group. This result, based on text-critical and intertextual reasons rather than an interest in cult, is in agreement with scholarship arguing that compilers rather than authors must have brought about the later coherence of the collection of Psalms 146–150 in the Masoretic Psalter. Why these Psalms were compiled at the end of the Masoretic Psalter is a different question to whether the end of the Psalter is their original place. That the latter question can be negated generally implies that when asking about the *origins* of Psalms, a separate interpretation of individual Psalms is necessary before an interpretation in their context in the Masoretic Psalter, even if in the Masoretic Psalter the Psalms appear in groups. While Psalter Exegesis remains a valid addition to Psalms Exegesis, the end of the Psalter has to be interpreted based on Psalms Exegesis which cannot be replaced by Psalter Exegesis limited to the Masoretic Text.

VIII Abbreviations and Bibliography

VIII.1 Abbreviations

1 Esdr	1 Esdras[LXX] (Rahlfs: Esdrae I)
2 Esdr	2 Esdras[LXX] (Rahlfs: Esdrae II) = Ezra-Nehemiah[MT]
11QPs[a]	Qumran Psalms Scroll[a] (11Q5)
4QPs[d]	Qumran Psalms Scroll[d] (4Q86)
4QPs[e]	Qumran Psalms Scroll[e] (4Q87)
MasPs[b]	Masada Psalms[b] (Mas1f)
4QMessAp	Qumran Messianic Apocalypse (4Q521)
1QH[a]	Qumran Hodayot[a] (1QHa)
1QM	Qumran War Scroll (1Q33)
ANE	ancient Near East(ern)
DSS	Dead Sea Scrolls
fn.	footnote
HB	Hebrew Bible (as preserved in MT)
LBH	Late Biblical Hebrew
LXX	Septuagint
MT	Masoretic Text
NRSV	New Revised Standard Version
v./vv.	verse/verses

Biblical references with [MT] or without any addition refer to the Masoretic Text as edited in Elliger and Rudolph 1997, with [DSS] to the Dead Sea Scrolls text discussed in the respective paragraph, and with [LXX] to the Septuagint as edited in Rahlfs 1935. References to verses without any addition refer to the text analysed in the respective paragraph. The same English titles for biblical books are used for both MT and LXX to ease comparison (the Latin titles in Rahlfs' LXX edition can be found in the index of sources).

Abbreviations for biblical books (in the NRSV order) follow the NRSV edition Manser 2003, xiii. Abbreviations for deuterocanonical books (their order following Rahlfs' LXX edition) and abbreviations in the bibliography follow Schwertner, Siegfried M., ed. 2014. *IATG³ – Internationales Abkürzungsverzeichnis für Theologie und Grenzgebiete: Zeitschriften, Serien, Lexika, Quellenwerke mit bibliographischen Angaben.* 3., überarb. und erw. Aufl. Berlin: De Gruyter.

VIII.2 Bibliography

Abegg, Martin G., and Benjamin H. Parker. [no year]a. "Ben Sira Manuscript A I Recto, Image, Transcription by Martin Abegg, Translation by Benjamin H. Parker and Martin G. Abegg."

DOI 10.1515/9783110536096-008

Accessed February 01, 2016. http://bensira.org/navigator.php?
Manuscript=A&PageNum=1.

Abegg, Martin G., and Benjamin H. Parker. [no year]b. "Ben Sira Manuscript A III Verso,
Image, Transcription by Martin Abegg, Translation by Benjamin H. Parker and Martin G.
Abegg." Accessed February 01, 2016. http://bensira.org/navigator.php?
Manuscript=A&PageNum=6.

Abegg, Martin G., and Benjamin H. Parker. [no year]c. "Ben Sira Manuscript B IX Recto,
Image, Transcription by Martin Abegg, Translation by Benjamin H. Parker and Martin G.
Abegg." Accessed February 01, 2016. http://bensira.org/navigator.php?
Manuscript=B&PageNum=17.

Abegg, Martin G., and Benjamin H. Parker. [no year]d. "Ben Sira Manuscript B XXI Recto,
Image, Transcription by Martin Abegg, Translation by Benjamin H. Parker and Martin G.
Abegg." Accessed February 01, 2016. http://bensira.org/navigator.php?
Manuscript=B&PageNum=41.

Abegg, Martin G., James E. Bowley, Edward M. Cook, and Emanuel Tov. 2003. *The Dead Sea
Scrolls Concordance, Volume One, The Non-Biblical Texts from Qumran, Part One.*
Leiden: Brill.

Abegg, Martin G., James E. Bowley, Edward M. Cook, and Eugene Ulrich. 2010. *The Dead Sea
Scrolls Concordance, Volume Three, The Biblical Texts from the Judaean Desert, Part
One.* Leiden: Brill.

Ahn, So K. 2008. *I Salmi 146–150 come conclusione del Salterio: Estratto della tesi di
dottorato della facoltà biblica del PIB.* Roma: Pontificio Istituto Biblico.

Allen, Leslie C. 1983. *Psalms 101–150.* Word Biblical Commentary 21. Waco, TX: Word Books.

Allen, Leslie C. 2002. *Psalms 101–150, revised.* Word Biblical Commentary 21. [Nashville, TN]:
Nelson.

Anderson, Warren D. 1994. *Music and Musicians in Ancient Greece.* Ithaca, NY: Cornell
University Press.

Auffret, Pierre. 1995. *Merveilles à nos yeux: Etude structurelle de vingt psaumes dont celui de
1Ch 16,8–36.* Beihefte zur Zeitschrift für die alttestamentliche Wissenschaft 235. Berlin:
De Gruyter.

Auffret, Pierre. 2002. "Par le tambour et par la danse: Étude structurelle du Psaume 150."
ETR 77 (2): 257–261.

Baars, W. 1972. "Apocryphal Psalms." In *The Old Testament in Syriac according to the
Peshitta Version, Part IV, Fascicle 6, Canticles or Odes, Prayer of Manasseh, Apocryphal
Psalms, Psalms of Salomon, Tobit, 1 (3) Esdras,* edited by Leiden Peshitta Institute, i-x,
1–12. Leiden: Brill.

Ballhorn, Egbert. 2004a. "Die gefährliche Doxologie: Eine Theologie des Gotteslobs in den
Psalmen." *BiLi* 77: 11–19.

Ballhorn, Egbert. 2004b. *Zum Telos des Psalters: Der Textzusammenhang des Vierten und
Fünften Psalmenbuches (Ps 90–150).* Bonner biblische Beiträge 138. Berlin: Philo.

Barbiero, Gianni. 1999. *Das erste Psalmenbuch als Einheit: Eine synchrone Analyse von
Psalm 1–41.* Österreichische biblische Studien 16. Frankfurt am Main: Lang.

Barbiero, Gianni, and Marco Pavan. 2012. "Ps 44,15; 57,10; 108,4; 149,7: בלאמים or בל־אמים?"
ZAW 124 (4): 598–605.

Bartelmus, Rüdiger. 1995. "שָׁמַיִם." In *Theologisches Wörterbuch zum Alten Testament, VIII*, edited by Gerhard J. Botterweck and Heinz-Josef Fabry, 204–239. Stuttgart: Kohlhammer.

Barton, John. 2012. "Déjà lu: Intertextuality, Method or Theory?" In *Reading Job Intertextually*, edited by Katharine Dell and Will Kynes, 1–16. Library of Hebrew Bible/Old Testament Studies. New York: T&T Clark.

Bauer, Hans, and Pontus Leander. 1922. *Historische Grammatik der hebräischen Sprache des Alten Testamentes, Erster Band: Einleitung, Schriftlehre, Laut- und Formenlehre*. Halle: Niemeyer.

Bauer, Walter, Barbara Aland, and Kurt Aland. 1988. *Griechisch-deutsches Wörterbuch zu den Schriften des Neuen Testaments und der frühchristlichen Literatur*. With the assistance of V. Reichmann. 6., völlig neu bearbeitete Aufl. De Gruyter: Berlin.

Bauks, Michaela. 2011. "Ps 145[146]." In *Septuaginta Deutsch: Erläuterungen und Kommentare zum griechischen Alten Testament, Band II, Psalmen bis Daniel*, edited by Wolfgang Kraus and Martin Karrer, 1877–1879. Stuttgart: Deutsche Bibelgesellschaft.

Becker, Joachim. 1975. *Wege der Psalmenexegese*. Stuttgart: KBW.

Beentjes, Pancratius C. 1997. *The Book of Ben Sira in Hebrew: A text edition of all extant Hebrew manuscripts and a synopsis of all parallel Hebrew Ben Sira texts*. Supplements to Vetus Testamentum 68. Leiden: Brill.

Ben-Porat, Ziva. 1976. "The Poetics of Literary Allusion." *PTL* 1 (1): 105–128.

Ben-Zvi Institute. 2007. "Aleppo Codex Facsimile: Digital Photography and Website by Ardon Bar Hama." Accessed February 01, 2016. http://www.aleppocodex.org/newsite/index.html.

Berges, Ulrich. 2008. *Jesaja 40–48*. Herders theologischer Kommentar zum Alten Testament. Freiburg: Herder.

Bergman, J., Helmer Ringgren, and R. Mosis. 1973. "גָּדַל." In *Theologisches Wörterbuch zum Alten Testament, I*, edited by Gerhard J. Botterweck and Heinz-Josef Fabry, 927–956. Stuttgart: Kohlhammer.

Bergman, J., J. Krecher, and V. Hamp. 1973. "אֵשׁ." In *Theologisches Wörterbuch zum Alten Testament, I*, edited by Gerhard J. Botterweck and Heinz-Josef Fabry, 452–463. Stuttgart: Kohlhammer.

Berman, Joshua A. 2002. "The 'Sword of Mouths' (Jud. iii 16; Ps. cxlix 6; Prov. v 4): A Metaphor and Its Ancient Near Eastern Context." *Vetus Testamentum* 52 (3): 291–303.

Beyerle, Stefan. 2011. "גָּדַל." In *Theologisches Wörterbuch zu den Qumrantexten, Band I*, edited by Heinz-Josef Fabry and Ulrich Dahmen, 573–581. Stuttgart: Kohlhammer.

BibleWorks 9: Software for Biblical Exegesis and Research. 2013. Norfolk, VA.

Bickell, Gustav W. H. 1883. *Dichtungen der Hebräer: Zum erstenmale nach dem Versmaße des Urtextes übersetzt, Band III, Der Psalter*. Innsbruck: Wagner.

Bieberstein, Klaus. 2005. "Tempel, II. Geschichtlich, 4. Der Tempel von Jerusalem, a) Geschichte." In *Religion in Geschichte und Gegenwart, 8*, edited by Hans D. Betz, Don S. Browning, Bernd Janowski, and Eberhard Jüngel. 4. Aufl., 143–144. Tübingen: Mohr Siebeck.

Bieberstein, Klaus, and Hanswulf Bloedhorn. 1994. *Jerusalem: Grundzüge der Baugeschichte vom Chalkolithikum bis zur Frühzeit der osmanischen Herrschaft, Band 1*. Wiesbaden: Reichert.

Blachorsky, Joshua A. [2014]. "The Book of Ben Sira, Index of Passages." Accessed February 01, 2016. http://bensira.org/pdf/indexOfPassages/indexOfPassages.pdf.

Blass, Friedrich, Albert Debrunner, and Friedrich Rehkopf. 1979. *Grammatik des neutestamentlichen Griechisch*. 15. durchges. Aufl. Göttingen: Vandenhoeck & Ruprecht.

Bons, Eberhard. 2003. "Die Septuaginta-Version von Psalm 110 (Ps 109 LXX): Textgestalt, Aussagen, Auswirkungen." In *Heiligkeit und Herrschaft: Intertextuelle Studien zu Heiligkeitsvorstellungen und zu Psalm 110*, edited by Dieter Sänger, 122–145. Biblisch-Theologische Studien 55. Neukirchen-Vluyn: Neukirchener.

Bons, Eberhard. 2005. "Comment le psaume 32LXX parle-t-il de la création?" In *Interpreting translation: Studies on the LXX and Ezekiel in honour of Johan Lust*, edited by J. Lust, Florentino García Martínez, and M. Vervenne, 55–64. Leuven: Leuven University Press.

Bons, Eberhard. 2007. "Beobachtungen zur Übersetzung und Neubildung von Parallelismen im Septuaginta-Psalter." In *Parallelismus membrorum*, edited by Andreas Wagner, 117–130. Fribourg: Academic Press.

Bons, Eberhard. 2009a. "Psalmoi, Das Buch der Psalmen, Einleitung." In *Septuaginta Deutsch: Das griechische Alte Testament in deutscher Übersetzung*, edited by Wolfgang Kraus and Martin Karrer, 749–752. Stuttgart: Deutsche Bibelgesellschaft.

Bons, Eberhard. 2009b. "Psalmoi, Die Psalmen." In *Septuaginta Deutsch: Das griechische Alte Testament in deutscher Übersetzung*, edited by Wolfgang Kraus and Martin Karrer, 753–898. Stuttgart: Deutsche Bibelgesellschaft.

Bons, Eberhard. 2011a. "Psalm 151." In *Septuaginta Deutsch: Erläuterungen und Kommentare zum griechischen Alten Testament, Band II, Psalmen bis Daniel*, edited by Wolfgang Kraus and Martin Karrer, 1884–1885. Stuttgart: Deutsche Bibelgesellschaft.

Bons, Eberhard. 2011b. "Psalm 32[33]." In *Septuaginta Deutsch: Erläuterungen und Kommentare zum griechischen Alten Testament, Band II, Psalmen bis Daniel*, edited by Wolfgang Kraus and Martin Karrer, 1588–1590. Stuttgart: Deutsche Bibelgesellschaft.

Bons, Eberhard. 2011c. "Psalm 4." In *Septuaginta Deutsch: Erläuterungen und Kommentare zum griechischen Alten Testament, Band II, Psalmen bis Daniel*, edited by Wolfgang Kraus and Martin Karrer, 1504–1507. Stuttgart: Deutsche Bibelgesellschaft.

Bons, Eberhard. 2011d. "Psalm 9." In *Septuaginta Deutsch: Erläuterungen und Kommentare zum griechischen Alten Testament, Band II, Psalmen bis Daniel*, edited by Wolfgang Kraus and Martin Karrer, 1517–1523. Stuttgart: Deutsche Bibelgesellschaft.

Booij, Thijs. 2008. "Psalm 149,5: "They Shout with Joy on Their Couches"." *Biblica* 89 (1): 104–108.

Boring, M. E. 2009. "Numbers, Numbering." In *The New Interpreter's Dictionary of the Bible, Vol. 4*, edited by Katharine D. Sakenfeld, 294–299. Nashville, TN: Abingdon.

Bott, Travis. 2011. "הלל II." In *Theologisches Wörterbuch zu den Qumrantexten, Band I*, edited by Heinz-Josef Fabry and Ulrich Dahmen, 789–800. Stuttgart: Kohlhammer.

Braulik, Georg. 1986. *Deuteronomium 1–16,17*. Neue Echter Bibel: Kommentar zum Alten Testament Lfg. 15. Würzburg: Echter.

Braun, Joachim. 1994. "Biblische Musikinstrumente." In *Die Musik in Geschichte und Gegenwart, Sachteil, 1*, edited by Ludwig Finscher. 2., neubearb. Ausg., 1503–1537. Kassel: Bärenreiter.

Braun, Joachim. 1996. "Jüdische Musik, II. Altisrael." In *Die Musik in Geschichte und Gegenwart, Sachteil, 9*, edited by Ludwig Finscher. 2., neubearb. Ausg., 1520–1524. Kassel: Bärenreiter.

Braun, Joachim. 1999. *Die Musikkultur Altisraels/Palästinas: Studien zu archäologischen, schriftlichen und vergleichenden Quellen*. Orbis biblicus et orientalis 164. Freiburg, Schweiz: Universitätsverlag.

Braun, Joachim. 2009. "Musical Instruments." In *The New Interpreter's Dictionary of the Bible, Vol. 4*, edited by Katharine D. Sakenfeld, 175–183. Nashville, TN: Abingdon.

Briggs, Charles A. 1906. *A Critical and Exegetical Commentary on the Book of Psalms, Volume 2*. Reprint 1960. The international critical commentary on the Holy Scriptures of the Old and New Testaments. Edinburgh: Clark.

Brodersen, Alma. 2013. *Die Bedeutung der Schöpfungsaussagen für die Theologie von Psalm 147*. Biblisch-Theologische Studien 134. Neukirchen-Vluyn: Neukirchener Theologie.

Brooke, Alan E., Norman McLean, and Henry St. John Thackeray, eds. 1906–1940. *The Old Testament in Greek [Cambridge Septuagint]: According to the Text of Codex Vaticanus, Supplemented from Other Uncial Manuscripts, With a Critical Apparatus Containing the Variants of the Chief Ancient Authorities for the Text of the Septuagint*. 9 vols. Cambridge: Cambridge University Press.

Brooke, George J. 1998. "Shared Intertextual Interpretations in the Dead Sea Scrolls and the New Testament." In *Biblical perspectives: early use and interpretation of the Bible in light of the Dead Sea Scrolls: Proceedings of the first International Symposium of the Orion Center for the Study of the Dead Sea Scrolls and Associated Literature, 2–14 May, 1996*, edited by Michael E. Stone, 35–57. Studies on the Texts of the Desert of Judah 28. Leiden: Brill.

Brucker, Ralph. 2011a. "Psalm 146 [147,1–11]." In *Septuaginta Deutsch: Erläuterungen und Kommentare zum griechischen Alten Testament, Band II, Psalmen bis Daniel*, edited by Wolfgang Kraus and Martin Karrer, 1879–1881. Stuttgart: Deutsche Bibelgesellschaft.

Brucker, Ralph. 2011b. "Psalm 147 [147,12–20]." In *Septuaginta Deutsch: Erläuterungen und Kommentare zum griechischen Alten Testament, Band II, Psalmen bis Daniel*, edited by Wolfgang Kraus and Martin Karrer, 1881. Stuttgart: Deutsche Bibelgesellschaft.

Brucker, Ralph. 2011c. "Psalm 148." In *Septuaginta Deutsch: Erläuterungen und Kommentare zum griechischen Alten Testament, Band II, Psalmen bis Daniel*, edited by Wolfgang Kraus and Martin Karrer, 1881–1882. Stuttgart: Deutsche Bibelgesellschaft.

Brucker, Ralph. 2011d. "Psalm 149." In *Septuaginta Deutsch: Erläuterungen und Kommentare zum griechischen Alten Testament, Band II, Psalmen bis Daniel*, edited by Wolfgang Kraus and Martin Karrer, 1882–1883. Stuttgart: Deutsche Bibelgesellschaft.

Brucker, Ralph. 2011e. "Psalm 150." In *Septuaginta Deutsch: Erläuterungen und Kommentare zum griechischen Alten Testament, Band II, Psalmen bis Daniel*, edited by Wolfgang Kraus and Martin Karrer, 1883. Stuttgart: Deutsche Bibelgesellschaft.

Brucker, Ralph. 2011f. "Psalm 46[47]." In *Septuaginta Deutsch: Erläuterungen und Kommentare zum griechischen Alten Testament, Band II, Psalmen bis Daniel*, edited by Wolfgang Kraus and Martin Karrer, 1629–1631. Stuttgart: Deutsche Bibelgesellschaft.

Brueggemann, Walter. 1988. *Israel's praise: Doxology against idolatry and ideology*. Philadelphia: Fortress.

Brueggemann, Walter. 1991. "Bounded by obedience and praise: The Psalms as canon." *JSOT* 50: 63–92.

Brueggemann, Walter. 1993. "Response to James L. Mays, "The Question of Context"." In *The Shape and Shaping of the Psalter*, edited by J. C. McCann, 29–41. Journal for the Study of the Old Testament Supplement series 159. Sheffield: JSOT.

Brüning, Christian. 1998. ""Lobet den Herrn, ihr Seeungeheuer und all ihr Tiefen!" Seeungeheuer in der Bibel." *ZAW* 110 (2): 250–255.

Brütsch, Matthias. 2010. *Israels Psalmen in Qumran: Ein textarchäologischer Beitrag zur Entstehung des Psalters.* Beiträge zur Wissenschaft vom Alten und Neuen Testament 10. Folge 13 = 193. Stuttgart: Kohlhammer.

Bultmann, Christoph. 2007. "Deuteronomy." In *The Oxford Bible Commentary,* edited by John Barton and John Muddiman, 135–158. Oxford: Oxford University Press.

Burgh, Theodore W. 2009. "Music." In *The New Interpreter's Dictionary of the Bible, Vol. 4,* edited by Katharine D. Sakenfeld, 166–175. Nashville, TN: Abingdon.

Burnett, Joel S. 2011. "אֱלוֹהִים." In *Theologisches Wörterbuch zu den Qumrantexten, Band I,* edited by Heinz-Josef Fabry and Ulrich Dahmen, 178–190. Stuttgart: Kohlhammer.

Buttrick, George A., ed. 1955. *The Interpreter's Bible, Vol. IV, The Book of Psalms, The Book of Proverbs.* Nashville, TN: Abingdon.

Camponovo, Odo. 1984. *Königtum, Königsherrschaft und Reich Gottes in den frühjüdischen Schriften.* Freiburg, Schweiz: Universitätsverlag.

Carr, David M. 2012. "The Many Uses of Intertextuality in Biblical Studies." In *Congress volume: Helsinki, 2010,* edited by Martti Nissinen, 519–549. Supplements to Vetus Testamentum 148. Leiden: Brill.

Ceresko, Anthony R. 1986. "Psalm 149: Poetry, themes (Exodus and conquest), and social function." *Biblica* 67: 177–194.

Ceresko, Anthony R. 2006. "Endings and Beginnings: Alphabet Thinking and the Shaping of Psalms 106 and 150." *Catholic Biblical Quarterly* 68 (1): 32–46.

Cha, Kilnam. 2006. "Psalms 146–150: The Final Hallelujah Psalms as a Fivefold Doxology to the Hebrew Psalter: Ph.D. Thesis, Baylor University, Texas." Accessed February 01, 2016. http://search.proquest.com/docview/305357245?accountid=13042.

Cho, Sang Y. 2007. *Lesser deities in the Ugaritic texts and the Hebrew Bible: A comparative study of their nature and roles.* Deities and Angels of the Ancient World 2. Piscataway, NJ: Gorgias.

Christensen, Duane L. 2001. *Deuteronomy 1:1–21:9, revised.* 2nd ed. Word Biblical Commentary 6 A. Nashville, TN: Nelson.

Clements, R. E. 1993. "קטר." In *Theologisches Wörterbuch zum Alten Testament, VII,* edited by Gerhard J. Botterweck and Heinz-Josef Fabry, 10–18. Stuttgart: Kohlhammer.

Clines, David J. A. 2011a. *Job 38–42.* Word Biblical Commentary 18B. Nashville, TN: Nelson.

Clines, David J. A., ed. 1995. *The Dictionary of Classical Hebrew, Vol. II.* Sheffield: Sheffield Academic.

Clines, David J. A., ed. 1996. *The Dictionary of Classical Hebrew, Vol. III.* Sheffield: Sheffield Academic.

Clines, David J. A., ed. 1998. *The Dictionary of Classical Hebrew, Vol. IV.* Sheffield: Sheffield Academic.

Clines, David J. A., ed. 2001. *The Dictionary of Classical Hebrew, Vol. V.* Sheffield: Sheffield Academic.

Clines, David J. A., ed. 2007. *The Dictionary of Classical Hebrew, Vol. VI.* Sheffield: Sheffield Academic.

Clines, David J. A., ed. 2010. *The Dictionary of Classical Hebrew, Vol. VII.* Sheffield: Sheffield Academic.

Clines, David J. A., ed. 2011b. *The Dictionary of Classical Hebrew, Vol. VIII*. Sheffield: Sheffield Academic.

Coggins, R. 2007. "Isaiah." In *The Oxford Bible Commentary*, edited by John Barton and John Muddiman, 433–486. Oxford: Oxford University Press.

Cohen, A., and Ephraim Oratz. 1992. *The Psalms: Hebrew text & English translation with an introduction and commentary*. Rev. 2nd ed. Soncino Books of the Bible. London: Soncino Press.

Collins, Paul. 2008. *Assyrian Palace Sculptures: With Photographs by Lisa Baylis and Sandra Marshall*. London: British Museum.

Conrad, J. 1986. "נדב." In *Theologisches Wörterbuch zum Alten Testament, V*, edited by Gerhard J. Botterweck and Heinz-Josef Fabry, 237–245. Stuttgart: Kohlhammer.

Conybeare, F. C., and George St. Stock. 1995. *Grammar of Septuagint Greek: With Selected Readings, Vocabularies, and Updated Indexes*. Reprinted from the edition originally published by Ginn and Company, Boston, 1905. [Peabody, MA]: Hendrickson.

Cross, Frank M. 1973. "אֵל." In *Theologisches Wörterbuch zum Alten Testament, I*, edited by Gerhard J. Botterweck and Heinz-Josef Fabry. Stuttgart: Kohlhammer.

Crüsemann, Frank. 1969. *Studien zur Formgeschichte von Hymnus und Danklied in Israel*. Wissenschaftliche Monographien zum Alten und Neuen Testament 32. Neukirchen-Vluyn: Neukirchener.

Dafni, Evangelia G. 2006. "Psalm 150 according to the Septuagint: integrating translation and tradition criticism into modern Septuagint exegesis." *Verbum et Ecclesia* 27 (2): 431–454.

Dahmen, Ulrich. 2000. "Psalmentext und Psalmensammlung. Eine Auseinandersetzung mit P.W. Flint." In *Die Textfunde vom Toten Meer und der Text der hebräischen Bibel*, edited by Ulrich Dahmen, 109–126. Neukirchen-Vluyn: Neukirchener.

Dahmen, Ulrich. 2003. *Psalmen- und Psalter-Rezeption im Frühjudentum: Rekonstruktion, Textbestand, Struktur und Pragmatik der Psalmenrolle 11QPsᵃ aus Qumran*. Studies on the Texts of the Desert of Judah 49. Leiden: Brill.

Dahood, Mitchell J. 1970. *Psalms III, 101–150*. Anchor Bible 17,3. Garden City, NY: Doubleday.

Davies, G. I. 2007. "Introduction to the Pentateuch." In *The Oxford Bible Commentary*, edited by John Barton and John Muddiman, 12–38. Oxford: Oxford University Press.

Debel, Hans. 2008. ""The Lord Looks at the Heart" (1 Sam 16:7): 11QPsa 151 A-B as a "Variant Literary Edition" of Ps 151 LXX." *Revue de Qumrân* 23 (4): 459–473.

Debel, Hans. 2010. "Greek "Variant Literary Editions" to the Hebrew Bible?" *Journal for the Study of Judaism* 41 (2): 161–190.

Debel, Hans. 2011. "Rewritten Bible, Variant Literary Editions and the Original Text(s): Exploring the Implications of a Pluriform Outlook on the Scriptural Tradition." In *Changes in Scripture: Rewriting and Interpreting Authoritative Traditions in the Second Temple Period*, edited by Hanne von Weissenberg, Juha Pakkala, and Marko Marttila, 65–91. Beihefte zur Zeitschrift für die alttestamentliche Wissenschaft 419. Berlin: De Gruyter.

DeClaissé-Walford, Nancy L. 1997. *Reading from the beginning: The shaping of the Hebrew Psalter*. Macon, GA: Mercer University Press.

DeClaissé-Walford, Nancy L. 2009. "Wisdom in the Ancient Near East." In *The New Interpreter's Dictionary of the Bible, Vol. 5*, edited by Katharine D. Sakenfeld, 862–865. Nashville, TN: Abingdon.

DeClaissé-Walford, Nancy L. 2014. "The Meta-Narrative of the Psalter." In *The Oxford Handbook of the Psalms*, edited by William P. Brown, 363–376. Oxford: Oxford University Press.

Deißler, Alfons. 1955. *Psalm 119 (118) und seine Theologie: Ein Beitrag zur Erforschung der anthologischen Stilgattung im Alten Testament*. Münchener theologische Studien I, Historische Abteilung 11. München: Zink.

Dell, Katharine J. 2009. "Wisdom in the OT." In *The New Interpreter's Dictionary of the Bible, Vol. 5*, edited by Katharine D. Sakenfeld, 869–875. Nashville, TN: Abingdon.

Di Lella, Alexander A. 1966. *The Hebrew text of Sirach: A text-critical and historical study*. Studies in Classical Literature 1. The Hague: Mouton.

Dietrich, Manfried, Oswald Loretz, and Joaquín Sanmartín. 1995. *The Cuneiform alphabetic texts from Ugarit, Ras Ibn Hani and other places (KTU)*. 2nd enl. ed. Abhandlungen zur Literatur Alt-Syrien-Palästinas und Mesopotamiens 8. Münster: Ugarit.

Dimant, Devorah. 2012. "David's youth in the Qumran context (11QPsᵃ 28:3–12)." In *Prayer and Poetry in the Dead Sea Scrolls and Related Literature: Essays in Honor of Eileen Schuller on the Occasion of Her 65th Birthday*, edited by Jeremy Penner, 97–114. Studies on the Texts of the Desert of Judah 98. Leiden: Brill.

Dines, Jennifer. 2007. "Light from the Septuagint on the New Testament – or vice versa? 1 Genesis 1,16 and Colossians 1,16." In *Voces biblicae: Septuagint Greek and its significance for the New Testament*, edited by Jan Joosten and Peter J. Tomson, 17–34. Contributions to Biblical Exegesis and Theology 49. Leuven: Peeters.

Dogniez, Cécile. 2005. "L'intertextualité dans la LXX de Zacharie 9–14." In *Interpreting translation: Studies on the LXX and Ezekiel in honour of Johan Lust*, edited by J. Lust, Florentino García Martínez, and M. Vervenne, 81–96. Leuven: Leuven University Press.

Dotan, Aharon. 2001. *Biblia Hebraica Leningradensia: Prepared According to the Vocalization Accents and Masora of Aaron ben Moses ben Asher in the Leningrad Codex*. Peabody, MA: Hendrickson.

Duhm, Bernhard. 1922. *Die Psalmen*. 2., vermehrte und verbesserte Aufl. Kurzer Hand-Kommentar zum Alten Testament Abteilung 14. Tübingen.

Eaton, John. 2005. *The Psalms: A Historical and Spiritual Commentary with an Introduction and New Translation*. London: Continuum.

Edenburg, Cynthia. 2010. "Intertextuality, literary competence and the question of readership: Some preliminary observations." *JSOT* 35 (2): 131–148.

Elliger, Karl, and Wilhelm Rudolph, eds. 1997. *Biblia Hebraica Stuttgartensia [BHS]*. 5. verb. Aufl., verkleinerte Ausg. Stuttgart: Deutsche Bibelgesellschaft.

Emanuel, David. 2012. *From Bards to Biblical Exegetes: A Close Reading and Intertextual Analysis of Selected Exodus Psalms*. Eugene: Pickwick.

Engel, Helmut. 2016. "Die Bücher der Makkabäer." In *Einleitung in das Alte Testament*, edited by Erich Zenger and Christian Frevel. 9., aktualisierte Aufl., 389–406. Kohlhammer Studienbücher Theologie 1,1. Stuttgart: Kohlhammer.

Eshel, Esther, Hanan Eshel, Carol Newsom, Bilhan Nitzan, Eileen Schuller, and Ada Yardeni, eds. 1998. *Qumran Cave 4, VI, Poetical and Liturgical Texts*. Discoveries in the Judaean Desert 6. Oxford: Clarendon.

Fabry, Heinz-Josef. 1984. "לֵב." In *Theologisches Wörterbuch zum Alten Testament, IV*, edited by Gerhard J. Botterweck and Heinz-Josef Fabry, 414–451. Stuttgart: Kohlhammer.

Fabry, Heinz-Josef. 1986. "11QPsᵃ und die Kanonizität des Psalters." In *Freude an der Weisung des Herrn: Beiträge zur Theologie der Psalmen Festgabe zum 70. Geburtstag von Heinrich Gross*, edited by Heinrich Gross, Ernst Haag, and Frank-Lothar Hossfeld, 45–67. Stuttgarter Biblische Beiträge 13. Stuttgart: Katholisches Bibelwerk.

Fabry, Heinz-Josef. 1998. "Der Psalter in Qumran." In *Der Psalter in Judentum und Christentum*, edited by Erich Zenger, 137–163. Herders biblische Studien 18. Freiburg: Herder.

Fabry, Heinz-Josef. 2013. "יִשְׂרָאֵל." In *Theologisches Wörterbuch zu den Qumrantexten, Band II*, edited by Heinz-Josef Fabry and Ulrich Dahmen, 292–301. Stuttgart: Kohlhammer.

Fabry, Heinz-Josef, E. Blum, and Helmer Ringgren. 1993. "רַב." In *Theologisches Wörterbuch zum Alten Testament, VII*, edited by Gerhard J. Botterweck and Heinz-Josef Fabry, 294–320. Stuttgart: Kohlhammer.

Feuer, Avrohom C. 1985. *Tehillim: A New Translation with a Commentary Anthologized from Talmudic, Midrashic and Rabbinic Sources, Vol. 2*. Brooklyn, NY: Mesorah.

Filoramo, Giovanni. 1999. "Eschatologie, I. Religionswissenschaftlich." In *Religion in Geschichte und Gegenwart, 2*, edited by Hans D. Betz, Don S. Browning, Bernd Janowski, and Eberhard Jüngel. 4. Aufl., 1542–1546. Tübingen: Mohr Siebeck.

Fischer, Alexander A. 2009. *Der Text des Alten Testaments: Neubearbeitung der Einführung in die Biblia Hebraica von Ernst Würthwein*. Stuttgart: Deutsche Bibelgesellschaft.

Flint, Peter W. 1997. *The Dead Sea Psalms Scrolls and the Book of Psalms*. Leiden: Brill.

Flint, Peter W. 2000. "Variant Readings of the Dead Sea Psalms Scrolls against the Massoretic Text and the Septuagint Psalter." In *Der Septuaginta-Psalter und seine Tochterübersetzungen: Symposium in Göttingen 1997*, edited by Anneli Aejmelaeus and Udo Quast, 337–365. Mitteilungen des Septuaginta-Unternehmens (MSU) 24. Göttingen: Vandenhoeck & Ruprecht.

Flint, Peter W. 2013. "The Dead Sea Psalms Scrolls: Psalms Manuscripts, Editions, and the Oxford Hebrew Bible." In *Jewish and Christian Approaches to the Psalms: Conflict and Convergence*, edited by Susan E. Gillingham, 11–34. Oxford: Oxford University Press.

Flint, Peter W. 2014. "Unrolling the Dead Sea Psalms Scrolls." In *The Oxford Handbook of the Psalms*, edited by William P. Brown, 229–250. Oxford: Oxford University Press.

Foerster, Gideon. 2002. "Masada." In *Religion in Geschichte und Gegenwart, 5*, edited by Hans D. Betz, Don S. Browning, Bernd Janowski, and Eberhard Jüngel. 4. Aufl., 885–887. Tübingen: Mohr Siebeck.

Fox, Michael V. 2015. *Proverbs: An Eclectic Edition with Introduction and Textual Commentary*. The Hebrew Bible: A Critical Edition 1. Atlanta, GA: SBL Press.

Freedman, David N., and B. E. Willoughby. 1984. "מַלְאָךְ." In *Theologisches Wörterbuch zum Alten Testament, IV*, edited by Gerhard J. Botterweck and Heinz-Josef Fabry, 887–904. Stuttgart: Kohlhammer.

Freedman, David N., ed. 1998. *The Leningrad Codex: A Facsimile Edition*. Grand Rapids, MI: Eerdmans.

Frenschkowski, Marco. 2004. "Seligpreisungen." In *Religion in Geschichte und Gegenwart, 7*, edited by Hans D. Betz, Don S. Browning, Bernd Janowski, and Eberhard Jüngel. 4. Aufl., 1184–1186. Tübingen: Mohr Siebeck.

Frevel, Christian. 2016. *Geschichte Israels*. Kohlhammer Studienbücher Theologie 2. Stuttgart: Kohlhammer.

Fritz, Volkmar. 2002. "Tempel II, Alter Orient und Altes Testament." In *Theologische Realenzyklopädie, 23*, edited by Gerhard Müller, 46–54. Berlin: De Gruyter.

Füglister, Notker. 1999. "Ein garstig Lied – Psalm 149." In *Die eine Bibel – Gottes Wort an uns: Gesammelte Aufsätze*, edited by Notker Füglister, 30–49. Salzburger theologische Studien 10. Innsbruck: Tyrolia.

García Martínez, Florentino, and Eibert J. C. Tigchelaar. 1999. *The Dead Sea scrolls study edition*. Leiden: Brill.

Gauthier, Randall X. 2014. *Psalms 38 and 145 of the old Greek version*. Supplements to Vetus Testamentum 166. Leiden: Brill.

Gerstenberger, Erhard S. 1989. "עָנָה II." In *Theologisches Wörterbuch zum Alten Testament, VI*, edited by Gerhard J. Botterweck and Heinz-Josef Fabry, 247–270. Stuttgart: Kohlhammer.

Gerstenberger, Erhard S. 1994. "Der Psalter als Buch und als Sammlung." In *Neue Wege der Psalmenforschung*, edited by Klaus Seybold and Erich Zenger, 3–13. Herders biblische Studien 1. Freiburg: Herder.

Gerstenberger, Erhard S. 2001. *Psalms Part 2 and Lamentations*. Grand Rapids, MI: Eerdmans.

Gesenius, Wilhelm. 2013. *Hebräisches und Aramäisches Handwörterbuch über das Alte Testament*. 18. Aufl. Berlin: Springer.

Gesenius, Wilhelm, and E. Kautzsch. 1909. *Wilhelm Gesenius' Hebräische Grammatik*. 28. vielfach verb. und verm. Aufl. Leipzig: Vogel.

Giere, S. D. 2009. *A new glimpse of Day One: Intertextuality, history of interpretation, and Genesis 1.1–5*. Beihefte zur Zeitschrift für die neutestamentliche Wissenschaft und die Kunde der älteren Kirche 172. Berlin: De Gruyter.

Gillingham, Susan E. 1994. *The Poems and Psalms of the Hebrew Bible*. Oxford: Oxford University Press.

Gillingham, Susan E. 2008. "Studies of the Psalms: Retrospect and Prospect." *Expository Times* 119: 209–216.

Gillingham, Susan E. 2012. "Entering and Leaving the Psalter: Psalms 1 and 150 and the Two Polarities of Faith." In *Let us go up to Zion: Essays in Honour of H.G.M. Williamson on the Occasion of his Sixty-Fifth Birthday*, edited by Iain W. Provan and Mark J. Boda, 383–393. Supplements to Vetus Testamentum 153. Leiden: Brill.

Gillingham, Susan E. 2014. "The Levites and the Editorial Composition of the Psalms." In *The Oxford Handbook of the Psalms*, edited by William P. Brown, 201–213. Oxford: Oxford University Press.

Goldingay, John. 2008. *Psalms, Volume 3, Psalms 90–150*. Grand Rapids, MI: Baker Academic.

Görg, Manfred. 1993. "רָקִיעַ." In *Theologisches Wörterbuch zum Alten Testament, VII*, edited by Gerhard J. Botterweck and Heinz-Josef Fabry, 668–675. Stuttgart: Kohlhammer.

Görg, Manfred, and Gerhard J. Botterweck. 1984. "בְּוֹר." In *Theologisches Wörterbuch zum Alten Testament, IV*, edited by Gerhard J. Botterweck and Heinz-Josef Fabry, 210–216. Stuttgart: Kohlhammer.

Goshen-Gottstein, Moshe. 1962. "Biblical Manuscripts in the United States." *Textus* 2: 28–59.

Goshen-Gottstein, Moshe. 1966. "The Psalms Scroll (11QPsᵃ): A Problem of Canon and Text." *Textus* 5: 22–33.

Goshen-Gottstein, Moshe H. 1995. *The Hebrew University Bible, The Book of Isaiah*. The Hebrew University Bible Project. Jerusalem: Magnes.

Gosse, Bernard. 1994. "Le Psaume CXLIX et la réinterprétation post-exilique de la tradition prophétique." *Vetus Testamentum* 44 (2): 259–263.

Groß, Heinrich. 1986. *Ijob*. Neue Echter Bibel: Kommentar zum Alten Testament Lfg. 13. Würzburg: Echter.

Gunkel, Hermann. 1926. *Die Psalmen*. Göttinger Handkommentar zum Alten Testament II 2, 4. Aufl. Göttingen: Vandenhoeck & Ruprecht.

Gunkel, Hermann. 1933. *Einleitung in die Psalmen: Die Gattungen der religiösen Lyrik Israels, Zu Ende geführt von Joachim Begrich*. Göttingen: Vandenhoeck & Ruprecht.

Gunkel, Hermann. 1998. *Introduction to Psalms: The Genres of the Religious Lyric of Israel, Completed by Joachim Begrich, Translated by James D. Nogalski*. Edited by Joachim Begrich and James D. Nogalski. Macon, GA: Mercer University Press.

Gzella, Holger. 2002. *Lebenszeit und Ewigkeit: Studien zur Eschatologie und Anthropologie des Septuaginta-Psalters*. Bonner biblische Beiträge 134. Berlin: Philo.

Haag, Ernst. 1995. "Eschatologie II. Biblisch: 1. Altes Testament." In *Lexikon für Theologie und Kirche, 3*, edited by Konrad Baumgartner, Michael Buchberger, and Walter Kasper. 3., völlig neu bearb. Aufl., 866–868. Freiburg: Herder.

Haag, H. 1973. "בֶּן־אָדָם." In *Theologisches Wörterbuch zum Alten Testament, I*, edited by Gerhard J. Botterweck and Heinz-Josef Fabry, 682–689. Stuttgart: Kohlhammer.

Haag, H. 1984. "כָּתַב." In *Theologisches Wörterbuch zum Alten Testament, IV*, edited by Gerhard J. Botterweck and Heinz-Josef Fabry, 385–397. Stuttgart: Kohlhammer.

Hanhart, Robert. 2006. "Vorwort zur Neuausgabe, Introductory Remarks to the Revised Edition." In *Septuaginta: Id est Vetus Testamentum graece iuxta LXX interpretes*, edited by Alfred Rahlfs and Robert Hanhart. Ed. altera, IX–XII. Stuttgart: Deutsche Bibelgesellschaft.

Harl, Marguerite. 1994. ""Et il rassemblera les 'dispersions' d'Israël" Une note sur le pluriel de DIASPORA dans le Psaume 146 (147),2b." In *Le Psautier chez les Pères*, 281–290. Cahiers de Biblia Patristica 4. Strasbourg: Centre d'analyse et de documentation patristiques.

Hartenstein, Friedhelm. 2001. "Wolkendunkel und Himmelsfeste: Zur Genese und Kosmologie der Vorstellung des himmlischen Heiligtums JHWHs." In *Das biblische Weltbild und seine altorientalischen Kontexte*, edited by Bernd Janowski, Beate Ego, and Annette Krüger, 125–179. Tübingen: Mohr Siebeck.

Hartenstein, Friedhelm. 2003a. "Psalmen/Psalter, II. Altes Testament, 1. Sprache, Gattungen und Themen der Psalmen, a) Sprache." In *Religion in Geschichte und Gegenwart, 6*, edited by Hans D. Betz, Don S. Browning, Bernd Janowski, and Eberhard Jüngel. 4. Aufl., 1762–1763. Tübingen: Mohr Siebeck.

Hartenstein, Friedhelm. 2003b. "Psalmen/Psalter, II. Altes Testament, 1. Sprache, Gattungen und Themen der Psalmen, b) Gattungen." In *Religion in Geschichte und Gegenwart, 6*, edited by Hans D. Betz, Don S. Browning, Bernd Janowski, and Eberhard Jüngel. 4. Aufl., 1763–1766. Tübingen: Mohr Siebeck.

Hartenstein, Friedhelm. 2007. ""Wach auf, Harfe und Leier, ich will wecken das Morgenrot" (Psalm 57,9) – Musikinstrumente als Medien des Gotteskontakts im Alten Orient und im Alten Testament." In *Musik, Tanz und Gott: Tonspuren durch das Alte Testament*, edited by Michaela Geiger and Rainer Kessler, 101–127. Stuttgarter Bibelstudien 207. Stuttgart: Katholisches Bibelwerk.

Hartmann, Th. 1976. "רַב rab viel." In *Theologisches Handwörterbuch zum Alten Testament, II*, edited by Ernst Jenni, 715–726. Gütersloh: Kaiser.

Hatch, Edwin, Henry A. Redpath, Takamitsu Muraoka, Robert A. Kraft, and Emanuel Tov. 1998. *A concordance to the Septuagint and the other Greek versions of the Old Testament (including the Apocryphal books)*. 2nd ed. Grand Rapids, MI: Baker Books.

Hays, Richard B. 1989. *Echoes of scripture in the letters of Paul*. New Haven: Yale University Press.

Hendel, Ronald. 2008. "The Oxford Hebrew Bible: Prologue to a New Critical Edition." *Vetus Testamentum* 58: 324–351.

Hendel, Ronald. 2013. "The Oxford Hebrew Bible: Its Aims and a Response to Criticisms." *Hebrew Bible and Ancient Israel* 2: 63–99.

Herrmann, Klaus. 2004. "Zahl/Zahlensymbolik, IV. Judentum." In *Theologische Realenzyklopädie, 26*, edited by Gerhard Müller, 472–478. Berlin: De Gruyter.

Hillers, Delbert R. 1978. "A Study of Psalm 148." *CBQ* 40: 323–334.

Hornkohl, Aaron. 2013. "Biblical Hebrew: Periodization." In *Encyclopedia of Hebrew Language and Linguistics*, edited by Geofrey Khan. Leiden: Brill Online. Accessed February 01, 2016. http://referenceworks.brillonline.com/entries/encyclopedia-of-hebrew-language-and-linguistics/biblical-hebrew-periodization-EHLL_COM_00000390.

Hossfeld, Frank-Lothar. 2008a. "Psalm 103." In *Psalmen 101–150*, edited by Frank-Lothar Hossfeld and Erich Zenger, 52–64. Herders theologischer Kommentar zum Alten Testament. Freiburg: Herder.

Hossfeld, Frank-Lothar. 2008b. "Psalm 104." In *Psalmen 101–150*, edited by Frank-Lothar Hossfeld and Erich Zenger, 67–92. Herders theologischer Kommentar zum Alten Testament. Freiburg: Herder.

Hossfeld, Frank-Lothar. 2008c. "Psalm 145." In *Psalmen 101–150*, edited by Frank-Lothar Hossfeld and Erich Zenger, 789–807. Herders theologischer Kommentar zum Alten Testament. Freiburg: Herder.

Hossfeld, Frank-Lothar. 2015. "Synchronie und Diachronie – zur Konkurrenz zweier Methoden der Psalmenexegese im Blick auf das erste Psalmenbuch (Ps 1–41)." In *"Canterò in eterno le misericordie del Signore" (Sal 89,2): Studi in onore del prof. Gianni Barbiero in occasione del suo settantesimo compleanno*, edited by Gianni Barbiero, Stefan M. Attard, and Marco Pavan, 235–247. Analecta biblica. Studia 3. Roma: Gregorian & Biblical Press.

Hossfeld, Frank-Lothar, and Erich Zenger. 2011. *Psalms 3: A commentary on Psalms 101–150*. English translation by Linda M. Maloney, edited by Klaus Baltzer. With the assistance of L. M. Maloney and K. Baltzer. Hermeneia. Minneapolis, MN: Fortress Press.

Hossfeld, Frank-Lothar, and Erich Zenger, eds. 1993. *Die Psalmen I, Psalm 1–50*. Die neue Echter Bibel: Kommentar zum Alten Testament mit der Einheitsübersetzung Lfg. 29. Würzburg: Echter.

Hossfeld, Frank-Lothar, and Erich Zenger, eds. 2008. *Psalmen 101–150*. Herders theologischer Kommentar zum Alten Testament. Freiburg: Herder.

Hossfeld, Frank-Lothar, and Till M. Steiner. 2013. "Problems and Prospects in Psalter Studies." In *Jewish and Christian Approaches to the Psalms: Conflict and Convergence*, edited by Susan E. Gillingham, 240–258. Oxford: Oxford University Press.

Hossfeld, Frank-Lothar, E.-M. Kindl, and Heinz-Josef Fabry. 1989. "קָהָל." In *Theologisches Wörterbuch zum Alten Testament, VI,* edited by Gerhard J. Botterweck and Heinz-Josef Fabry, 1204–1222. Stuttgart: Kohlhammer.

Houston, Walter. 2007. "Exodus." In *The Oxford Bible Commentary,* edited by John Barton and John Muddiman, 67–91. Oxford: Oxford University Press.

Howard, David M. 1997. *The Structure of Psalms 93–100.* Biblical and Judaic Studies 5. Winona Lake, IN: Eisenbrauns.

Hübner, Ulrich. 2002. "Musik/Musikinstrumente, II. Geschichtlich, 2. Altes Testament." In *Religion in Geschichte und Gegenwart, 5,* edited by Hans D. Betz, Don S. Browning, Bernd Janowski, and Eberhard Jüngel. 4. Aufl., 1602–1604. Tübingen: Mohr Siebeck.

Human, Dirk J. 2011. ""Praise beyond Words". Psalm 150 as Grand Finale of the Crescendo in the Psalter." *HTS* 67 (1): 1–10.

Hupfeld, Hermann. 1871. *Die Psalmen: Übersetzt und ausgelegt, Vierter Band.* 2. Aufl. Gotha: Perthes.

Hurvitz, Avi. 2013. "Biblical Hebrew, Late." In *Encyclopedia of Hebrew Language and Linguistics,* edited by Geofrey Khan. Leiden: Brill Online. Accessed February 01, 2016. http://referenceworks.brillonline.com/entries/encyclopedia-of-hebrew-language-and-linguistics/biblical-hebrew-late-EHLL_COM_00000396.

Israel Antiquities Authority. 2012. "Leon Levy Dead Sea Scrolls Digital Library." Accessed February 01, 2016. http://www.deadseascrolls.org.il.

Israel Museum. 1995–2016. "The Digital Dead Sea Scrolls." Accessed February 01, 2016. http://dss.collections.imj.org.il.

Jain, Eva. 2014. *Psalmen oder Psalter? Materielle Rekonstruktion und inhaltliche Untersuchung der Psalmenhandschriften aus der Wüste Juda.* Studies on the Texts of the Desert of Judah 109. Leiden: Brill.

Janowski, Bernd. 2001. "Königtum Gottes im Alten Testament." In *Religion in Geschichte und Gegenwart, 4,* edited by Hans D. Betz, Don S. Browning, Bernd Janowski, and Eberhard Jüngel. 4. Aufl., 1591–1593. Tübingen: Mohr Siebeck.

Janowski, Bernd. 2003. "Psalmen/Psalter, II. Altes Testament, 3. Septuaginta-Psalter." In *Religion in Geschichte und Gegenwart, 6,* edited by Hans D. Betz, Don S. Browning, Bernd Janowski, and Eberhard Jüngel. 4. Aufl., 1774. Tübingen: Mohr Siebeck.

Janowski, Bernd. 2004. "Schöpfung, II. Altes Testament." In *Religion in Geschichte und Gegenwart, 7,* edited by Hans D. Betz, Don S. Browning, Bernd Janowski, and Eberhard Jüngel. 4. Aufl., 970–972. Tübingen: Mohr Siebeck.

Janowski, Bernd. 2012. "Psalm 1: Der Weg des Gerechten und der Weg des Frevlers." In *Psalmen,* edited by Friedhelm Hartenstein and Bernd Janowski, 7–54. Biblischer Kommentar Altes Testament 15/1. Neukirchen-Vluyn: Neukirchener.

Janowski, Bernd. 2013. *Konfliktgespräche mit Gott: Eine Anthropologie der Psalmen.* 4., durchges. und erw. Aufl. Neukirchen-Vluyn: Neukirchener Theologie.

Jastrow, Marcus. 1903. *A Dictionary of Targumim, Talmud and Midrashic Literature.* London: Luzac.

Jenni, Ernst. 1975. "גָּדוֹל gādōl groß." In *Theologisches Handwörterbuch zum Alten Testament, I,* edited by Ernst Jenni. 2., durchges. Aufl., 402–409. Gütersloh: Kaiser.

Jenni, Ernst. 1992. *Die hebräischen Präpositionen, Band 1, Die Präposition Beth.* Stuttgart: Kohlhammer.

Jewish Manuscript Preservation Society. 2013. "Friedberg Genizah Project." Accessed February 01, 2016. http://www.jewishmanuscripts.org.

Jobes, Karen H., and Moisés Silva. 2000. *Invitation to the Septuagint*. Grand Rapids, MI: Baker Academic.

Joosten, Jan. 2012. "The Impact of the Septuagint Pentateuch on the Greek Psalm." In *Collected studies on the Septuagint: From language to interpretation and beyond*, 147–156. Forschungen zum Alten Testament 83. Tübingen: Mohr Siebeck.

Joüon, Paul, and Takamitsu Muraoka. 2011. *A Grammar of Biblical Hebrew*. 3rd repr. of the 2nd ed., with corr. Subsidia Biblica 27. Roma: Gregorian & Biblical Press.

Kammerer, Stefan. 2002. "Musik/Musikinstrumente, II. Geschichtlich, 1. Bronzezeit bis Spätantike." In *Religion in Geschichte und Gegenwart, 5*, edited by Hans D. Betz, Don S. Browning, Bernd Janowski, and Eberhard Jüngel. 4. Aufl., 1600–1602. Tübingen: Mohr Siebeck.

Karasszon, Dezsö. 1992. "Bemerkungen zum Psalm 146." In *Goldene Äpfel in silbernen Schalen: Collected Communications to the XIIIth Congress of the International Organization for the Study of the Old Testament, Leuven 1989*, edited by Klaus-Dietrich Schunck and Matthias Augustin, 123–127. Beiträge zur Erforschung des Alten Testaments und des antiken Judentums 20. Frankfurt am Main: Lang.

Kaufman, S. A. [no year]. "The Comprehensive Aramaic Lexicon Project." Accessed February 01, 2016. http://cal1.cn.huc.edu.

Keck, Leander E., ed. 1996. *The First Book of Maccabees, The Second Book of Maccabees, Introduction to Hebrew Poetry, The Book of Job, The Book of Psalms*. New Interpreter's Bible 4. Nashville, TN: Abingdon.

Keel, Othmar. 1996. *Die Welt der altorientalischen Bildsymbolik und das Alte Testament: Am Beispiel der Psalmen*. 5. Aufl. Göttingen: Vandenhoeck & Ruprecht.

Keel, Othmar, and Timothy J. Hallett. 1978. *The Symbolism of the Biblical World: Ancient Near Eastern Iconography and the Book of Psalms*. London: SPCK.

Kellermann, D. 1973. "גּוּר." In *Theologisches Wörterbuch zum Alten Testament, I*, edited by Gerhard J. Botterweck and Heinz-Josef Fabry, 979–991. Stuttgart: Kohlhammer.

Kennicott, Benjamin, ed. 1780. *Vetus Testamentum Hebraicum; cum variis lectionibus: Tomus Secundus*. Oxford: Clarendon.

Kimḥi, David, Joshua. Baker, and Ernest W. Nicholson. 1973. *The commentary of Rabbi David Kimḥi on Psalms CXX-CL*. Cambridge: Cambridge University Press.

King, Philip J., and Lawrence E. Stager. 2001. *Life in Biblical Israel*. Louisville, KY: Westminster John Knox Press.

Kleer, Martin. 1996. *"Der liebliche Sänger der Psalmen Israels": Untersuchungen zu David als Dichter und Beter der Psalmen*. Bonner biblische Beiträge 108. Bodenheim: Philo.

Koch, Klaus. 1991. "Der Güter Gefährlichstes, die Sprache, dem Menschen gegeben… Überlegungen zu Gen 2,7." In *Spuren des hebräischen Denkens: Beiträge zur alttestamentlichen Theologie. Gesammelte Aufsätze, Band 1*, Klaus Koch, edited by Bernd Janowski and Martin Krause, 238–247. Neukirchen-Vluyn: Neukirchener.

Koch, Klaus. 1994. "Der Psalter und seine Redaktionsgeschichte." In *Neue Wege der Psalmenforschung*, edited by Klaus Seybold and Erich Zenger, 243–277. Herders biblische Studien 1. Freiburg: Herder.

Kolari, Eino. 1947. *Musikinstrumente und ihre Verwendung im Alten Testament: Eine lexikalische und kulturgeschichtliche Untersuchung.* Helsinki: Suomalaisen Kirjallisuuden Seuran [Finnish Literature Society].

Kornfeld, W., and Helmer Ringgren. 1989. "קדשׁ." In *Theologisches Wörterbuch zum Alten Testament, VI,* edited by Gerhard J. Botterweck and Heinz-Josef Fabry, 1179–1204. Stuttgart: Kohlhammer.

Kosmala, H. 1973. "גְּבַר." In *Theologisches Wörterbuch zum Alten Testament, I,* edited by Gerhard J. Botterweck and Heinz-Josef Fabry, 902–919. Stuttgart: Kohlhammer.

Kratz, Reinhard G. 1992. "Die Gnade des täglichen Brots: Späte Psalmen auf dem Weg zum Vaterunser." *ZThK* 89: 1–40.

Kratz, Reinhard G. 1996. "Die Tora Davids. Psalm 1 und die doxologische Fünfteilung des Psalters." *ZThK* 93: 1–34.

Kratz, Reinhard G. 2004. "Das Schᵉmaᶜ des Psalters: Die Botschaft vom Reich Gottes nach Psalm 145." In *Gott und Mensch im Dialog: Festschrift für Otto Kaiser zum 80. Geburtstag, II,* edited by Markus Witte, 623–638. Beihefte zur Zeitschrift für die alttestamentliche Wissenschaft 345/II. Berlin: De Gruyter.

Kratz, Reinhard G. 2012. ""Blessed be the Lord and Blessed be His Name Forever": Psalm 145 in the Hebrew Bible and in the Psalms Scroll 11Q5." In *Prayer and Poetry in the Dead Sea Scrolls and Related Literature: Essays in Honor of Eileen Schuller on the Occasion of Her 65th Birthday,* edited by Jeremy Penner, 229–243. Studies on the Texts of the Desert of Judah 98. Leiden: Brill.

Kratz, Reinhard G. 2013a. "Die Tradition, Einführung." In *Das Judentum im Zeitalter des Zweiten Tempels.* 2., durchges. u. überarb. Aufl., 123–125. Forschungen zum Alten Testament. Tübingen: Mohr Siebeck.

Kratz, Reinhard G. 2013b. "Innerbiblische Exegese und Redaktionsgeschichte im Lichte empirischer Evidenz." In *Das Judentum im Zeitalter des Zweiten Tempels.* 2., durchges. u. überarb. Aufl., 126–156. Forschungen zum Alten Testament 42. Tübingen: Mohr Siebeck.

Kraus, Hans-Joachim, ed. 1978. *Psalmen, 2. Teilband, Psalmen 60–150.* 5., grundlegend überarbeitete und veränderte Auflage. Biblischer Kommentar Altes Testament 15/2. Neukirchen-Vluyn: Neukirchener.

Kraus, Thomas J. 2011. "Psalm 103[104]." In *Septuaginta Deutsch: Erläuterungen und Kommentare zum griechischen Alten Testament, Band II, Psalmen bis Daniel,* edited by Wolfgang Kraus and Martin Karrer, 1791–1794. Stuttgart: Deutsche Bibelgesellschaft.

Kraus, Wolfgang, and Martin Karrer. 2009. "Einführung in den Gebrauch des Übersetzungsbandes." In *Septuaginta Deutsch: Das griechische Alte Testament in deutscher Übersetzung,* edited by Wolfgang Kraus and Martin Karrer, XVII–XXIII. Stuttgart: Deutsche Bibelgesellschaft.

Krüger, Annette. 2001. "Himmel – Erde – Unterwelt. Kosmologische Entwürfe in der poetischen Literatur Israels." In *Das biblische Weltbild und seine altorientalischen Kontexte,* edited by Bernd Janowski, Beate Ego, and Annette Krüger, 65–83. Tübingen: Mohr Siebeck.

Kselman, John S. 1988. "Psalm 146 in its context." *CBQ* 50 (4): 587–599.

Kuhl, Curt. 1930. *Die drei Männer im Feuer (Daniel Kapitel 3 und seine Zusätze): Ein Beitrag zur israelitisch-jüdischen Literaturgeschichte.* Gießen: Töpelmann.

Kühlewein, J. 1975. "גבר gbr überlegen sein." In *Theologisches Handwörterbuch zum Alten Testament, I*, edited by Ernst Jenni. 2., durchges. Aufl., 398–402. Gütersloh: Kaiser.

Kuntz, J. K. 1999. "Grounds for Praise: The Nature and Function of the Motive Clause in the Hymns of the Hebrew Psalter." In *Worship and the Hebrew bible: Essays in honour of John T. Willis*, edited by Matt P. Graham, 148–183. Journal for the Study of the Old Testament Supplement Series 284. Sheffield: Sheffield Academic.

Kynes, Will. 2012. *My Psalm Has Turned into Weeping: Job's Dialogue with the Psalms.* Beihefte zur Zeitschrift für die alttestamentliche Wissenschaft 437. Berlin: De Gruyter.

Lamberty-Zielinski, Hedwig. 1986. "נְשָׁמָה." In *Theologisches Wörterbuch zum Alten Testament, V*, edited by Gerhard J. Botterweck and Heinz-Josef Fabry, 669–673. Stuttgart: Kohlhammer.

Lange, Armin. 1998. "Die Endgestalt des protomasoretischen Psalters und die Toraweisheit: Zur Bedeutung der nichtessenischen Weisheitstexte aus Qumran für die Auslegung des protomasoretischen Psalters." In *Der Psalter in Judentum und Christentum*, edited by Erich Zenger, 101–136. Herders biblische Studien 18. Freiburg: Herder.

Lange, Armin. 2003. "Qumran." In *Religion in Geschichte und Gegenwart, 6*, edited by Hans D. Betz, Don S. Browning, Bernd Janowski, and Eberhard Jüngel. 4. Aufl., 1873–1896. Tübingen: Mohr Siebeck.

Lange, Armin. 2009. *Handbuch der Textfunde vom Toten Meer, Band 1: Die Handschriften biblischer Bücher von Qumran und den anderen Fundorten.* Tübingen: Mohr Siebeck.

Lawergren, Bo. 1998. "Distinctions among Canaanite, Philistine, and Israelite Lyres, and Their Global Lyrical." *Bulletin of the American Schools of Oriental Research* 309 (2): 41–68.

Lebedev, Victor V. 1998. "The Oldest Complete Codex of the Hebrew Bible." In *The Leningrad Codex: A Facsimile Edition*, edited by David N. Freedman, xxi–xxviii. Grand Rapids, MI: Eerdmans.

Leonard, J. M. 2008. "Identifying Inner-Biblical Allusions: Psalm 78 as a Test Case." *JBL* 127: 241–265.

Leuenberger, Martin. 2004. *Konzeptionen des Königtums Gottes im Psalter: Untersuchungen zu Komposition und Redaktion der theokratischen Bücher IV – V im Psalter.* Abhandlungen zur Theologie des Alten und Neuen Testaments 83. Zürich: Theologischer Verlag Zürich.

Leuenberger, Martin. 2005. "Aufbau und Pragmatik des 11QPsa-Psalters." *RdQ* 22: 165–209.

Leuenberger, Martin. 2010. ""… und ein zweischneidiges Schwert in ihrer Hand" (Ps 149,6): Beobachtungen zur theologiegeschichtlichen Verortung von Ps 149." In *The Composition of the Book of Psalms*, edited by Erich Zenger, 635–642. Bibliotheca Ephemeridum theologicarum Lovaniensium 238. Leuven: Peeters.

Levin, Christoph. 1993. "Das Gebetbuch der Gerechten: Literargeschichtliche Beobachtungen am Psalter." *ZThK* 90: 355–81.

Liddell, Henry G., and Robert Scott, eds. 1889. *An Intermediate Greek-English Lexicon ["Middle Liddell"].* Oxford: Clarendon. Online Edition. Accessed November 21, 2016. http://www.perseus.tufts.edu/hopper/text?doc=Perseus%3atext%3a1999.04.0058.

Liddell, Henry G., Robert Scott, and Henry S. Jones. 1996. *A Greek-English lexicon [LSJ].* 9th ed., rev. and augm. throughout, Oxford: Clarendon. Accessed November 21, 2016. Online Edition http://www.tlg.uci.edu/lsj/#eid=1&context=lsj.

Lipiński, E. 1986. "נקם." In *Theologisches Wörterbuch zum Alten Testament, V*, edited by Gerhard J. Botterweck and Heinz-Josef Fabry, 602–612. Stuttgart: Kohlhammer.

Lipiński, E. 1989. "עַם." In *Theologisches Wörterbuch zum Alten Testament, VI*, edited by Gerhard J. Botterweck and Heinz-Josef Fabry, 177–194. Stuttgart: Kohlhammer.

Loader, J. A. 1991. "God se hemelgewelf." In *Mens en omgewing*, edited by Vos, C. J. A and Julian Müller. 1ste uitg, 164–173. God, mens en wêreld 3. Halfway House: Orion.

Lohfink, Norbert. 1990. *Lobgesänge der Armen: Studien zum Magnifikat, den Hodajot von Qumran und einigen späten Psalmen.* Stuttgarter Bibelstudien 143. Stuttgart: Katholisches Bibelwerk.

Loretz, Oswald. 1979. *Die Psalmen: Beitrag der Ugarit-Texte zum Verständnis von Kolometrie und Textologie der Psalmen.* Alter Orient und Altes Testament 207. Kevelaer: Butzon & Bercker.

Loretz, Oswald. 2002. "Psalm 149 H. Gunkels Historismus – "kanonische" Auslegung des Psalters." In *Psalmstudien: Kolometrie, Strophik und Theologie ausgewählter Psalmen*, edited by Oswald Loretz, 351–380. Beihefte zur Zeitschrift für die alttestamentliche Wissenschaft 309. Berlin: De Gruyter.

Louw, Theo A. W. van der. 2007. *Transformations in the Septuagint: Towards an interaction of Septuagint studies and translation studies.* Contributions to Biblical Exegesis and Theology 47. Leuven: Peeters.

Lowth, Robert. 1753. *De sacra poesi Hebræorum: Prælectiones academicæ Oxonii habitæ a Roberto Lowth A. M. Collegii Novi Nuper Socio, Et Poeticæ Publico Praelectore.* Oxford: Clarendon.

Lust, Johan, Erik Eynikel, and Katrin Hauspie. 2003. *A Greek-English Lexicon of the Septuagint [LEH].* Revised Edition. Stuttgart: Deutsche Bibelgesellschaft.

Maas, Martha, and Jane M. Snyder. 1989. *Stringed instruments of ancient Greece.* New Haven: Yale University Press.

MacKenzie, Roderick A. F. 1970. "Ps 148,14bc: Conclusion or Title?" *Biblica* 51: 221–224.

Malchow, B. V. 1977. "God or King in Psalm 146." *BiTod* 89: 166–170.

Manser, Martin H., ed. 2003. *The Holy Bible, Containing the Old and New Testaments, New Revised Standard Version [NRSV], Anglicized Text, Cross-Reference Edition.* Oxford: Oxford University Press.

Marböck, Johannes. 2016. "Das Buch Jesus Sirach." In *Einleitung in das Alte Testament*, edited by Erich Zenger and Christian Frevel. 9., aktualisierte Aufl., 408–416. Kohlhammer Studienbücher Theologie 1,1. Stuttgart: Kohlhammer.

Martínez, Florentino G., Eibert J. C. Tegchelaar, and Adam S. van der Woude. 1998. *Qumran Cave 11, II, 11Q2–18, 11Q20–31.* Discoveries in the Judaean Desert 23. Oxford: Clarendon.

Mathys, H. P. 2000. "Psalm CL." *Vetus Testamentum* 50 (3): 329–344.

Mathys, Hans-Peter. 1994. *Dichter und Beter: Theologen aus spätalttestamentlicher Zeit.* Orbis biblicus et orientalis 132. Freiburg, Schweiz: Universitätsverlag.

McCann, J. C. 2014. "The Shape and Shaping of the Psalter: Psalms in Their Literary Context." In *The Oxford Handbook of the Psalms*, edited by William P. Brown, 350–362. Oxford: Oxford University Press.

McCann, J. C., ed. 1993. *The Shape and Shaping of the Psalter.* Journal for the Study of the Old Testament Supplement Series 159. Sheffield: JSOT.

Metzenthin, Christian. 2013. "כָּתַב." In *Theologisches Wörterbuch zu den Qumrantexten, Band II*, edited by Heinz-Josef Fabry and Ulrich Dahmen, 455–460. Stuttgart: Kohlhammer.

Metzger, M. 1970. "Himmlische und irdische Wohnstatt Jahwes." *Ugarit-Forschungen* 2: 139–158.

Meyer, Rudolf. 1992. *Hebräische Grammatik*. Berlin: De Gruyter.

Meyers, Carol L. 1991. "Of Drums and Damsels: Women's Performance in Ancient Israel." *Biblical Archaeologist* 51 (1): 16–27.

Michel, Diethelm. 1956. "Studien zu den sogenannten Thronbesteigungspsalmen." *VT* 6 (1): 40–68.

Millard, Matthias. 1994. *Die Komposition des Psalters: Ein formgeschichtlicher Ansatz*. Forschungen zum Alten Testament 9. Tübingen: Mohr.

Millard, Matthias. 1996. "Von der Psalmenexegese zur Psalterexegese. Anmerkungen zum Neuansatz von Frank-Lothar Hossfeld und Erich Zenger." *Biblical Interpretation* 4: 311–327.

Millard, Matthias. 2010. "Hallel." In: *Das wissenschaftliche Bibellexikon im Internet (Wibilex)*. Accessed February 01, 2016. https://www.bibelwissenschaft.de/stichwort/20353.

Miller, Geoffrey D. 2011. "Intertextuality in Old Testament Research." *Currents in Biblical Research* 9 (3): 283–309.

Miller, Patrick D. 1998. "The End of the Psalter: a Response To Erich Zenger." *JSOT* 80: 103–110.

Mitchell, David C. 1997. *The Message of the Psalter: An Eschatological Programme in the Book of Psalms*. Journal for the Study of the Old Testament Supplement Series 252. Sheffield: Sheffield Academic.

Mowinckel, Sigmund. 1957. *Real and apparent tricola in Hebrew psalm poetry*. Avhandlinger utgitt av det Norske videnskaps-akademi i Oslo. II. Hist.-filos. klasse 1957, no.2. Oslo: Aschehoug.

Mowinckel, Sigmund. 1962a. *The psalms in Israel's worship, Volume I: Translated by D. R. Ap-Thomas*. Oxford: Blackwell.

Mowinckel, Sigmund. 1962b. *The psalms in Israel's worship, Volume II: Translated by D. R. Ap-Thomas*. Oxford: Blackwell.

Müller, H.-P. 1976. "קדש qdš heilig." In *Theologisches Handwörterbuch zum Alten Testament, II*, edited by Ernst Jenni, 589–609. Gütersloh: Kaiser.

Müller, Hans-Peter. 1999. "Eschatologie, II. Altes Testament." In *Religion in Geschichte und Gegenwart, 2*, edited by Hans D. Betz, Don S. Browning, Bernd Janowski, and Eberhard Jüngel. 4. Aufl., 1546–1553. Tübingen: Mohr Siebeck.

Neef, Heinz-Dieter. 2011. "Daniel / Das Buch Daniel." In *Septuaginta Deutsch: Erläuterungen und Kommentare zum griechischen Alten Testament, Band II, Psalmen bis Daniel*, edited by Wolfgang Kraus and Martin Karrer, 3016–3051. Stuttgart: Deutsche Bibelgesellschaft.

Neumann, Friederike. 2016. *Schriftgelehrte Hymnen: Gestalt, Theologie und Intention der Psalmen 145 und 146–150*. Beihefte zur Zeitschrift für die alttestamentliche Wissenschaft 491. Berlin: De Gruyter.

Newsom, Carol. 1998. "Shirot ʿOlat HaShabbat." In *Qumran Cave 4, VI, Poetical and Liturgical Texts*, edited by Esther Eshel, Hanan Eshel, Carol Newsom, Bilhan Nitzan, Eileen Schuller, and Ada Yardeni, 173–401. Discoveries in the Judaean Desert 6. Oxford: Clarendon.

Ngunga, Abi T. 2013. *Messianism in the Old Greek of Isaiah: An Intertextual Analysis*. Forschungen zur Religion und Literatur des Alten und Neuen Testaments 245. Göttingen: Vandenhoeck & Ruprecht.

Niebuhr, Karl-Wilhelm. 1994. "Bezüge auf die Schrift in einigen "neueren" Qumran-Texten." *Mitteilungen und Beiträge, Forschungsstelle Judentum, Theol. Fakultät Leipzig* 8: 37–54.

Niehr, H. 1995. "צָפוֹן." In *Theologisches Wörterbuch zum Alten Testament, VIII*, edited by Gerhard J. Botterweck and Heinz-Josef Fabry, 715–719. Stuttgart: Kohlhammer.

Otto, Eckart. 1999. "Dekalog, I. Altes Testament." In *Religion in Geschichte und Gegenwart, 2*, edited by Hans D. Betz, Don S. Browning, Bernd Janowski, and Eberhard Jüngel. 4. Aufl., 625–628. Tübingen: Mohr Siebeck.

Ottosson, M. 1995. "תהֹ." In *Theologisches Wörterbuch zum Alten Testament, VIII*, edited by Gerhard J. Botterweck and Heinz-Josef Fabry, 725–728. Stuttgart: Kohlhammer.

Oxford Music Online. 2001–2014. "Grove Music Online." Accessed February 01, 2016. http://www.oxfordmusiconline.com.

Pardee, Dennis. 2003. "The Kirta Epic (1.102)." In *The Context of Scripture, Volume I, Canonical Compositions from the Biblical World*, edited by William W. Hallo and K. L. Younger, 333–343. Leiden: Brill.

Patterson, Richard D. 2007. "Singing the new song: an examination of Psalms 33, 96, 98, and 149." *Bibliotheca sacra* 164: 416–434.

Pietersma, Albert. 2001. "Exegesis and Liturgy in the Superscriptions of the Greek Psalter." In *X Congress of the International Organization for Septuagint and Cognate Studies, Oslo, 1998*, edited by Bernard A. Taylor, 99–138. Society of Biblical Literature Septuagint and Cognate Studies Series 51. Atlanta, GA: Society of Biblical Literature.

Pöhlmann, Egert. 1995. "Griechenland, A. Antike Musik." In *Die Musik in Geschichte und Gegenwart, Sachteil, 3*, edited by Ludwig Finscher. 2., neubearb. Ausg. Kassel;, 1626–1676. Kassel: Bärenreiter.

Prinsloo, W. S. 1992. "Structure and cohesion of Psalm 148." *Old Testament Essays* 5 (1): 46–63.

Prinsloo, Willem S. 1997. "Psalm 149: Praise Yahweh with Tambourine and Two-edged Sword." *ZAW* 109 (3): 395–407.

Puech, Émile. 1997. "Les manuscrits de la mer Morte et le Nouveau Testament." In *Qoumrân et les Manuscrits de la mer Morte: Un cinquantenaire*, edited by Ernest-Marie Laperrousaz, 253–313. Paris: Cerf.

Puech, Émile. 1998. *Qumrân grotte 4: Textes Hebreux (4Q521–4Q528, 4Q576–4Q579)*. Oxford: Clarendon.

Rad, Gerhard v. 1960. "Hiob XXXVIII und die altägyptische Weisheit." In *Wisdom in Israel and in the ancient Near East*, edited by H. H. Rowley, Martin Noth, and D. W. Thomas, 293–301. Supplements to Vetus Testamentum 3. Leiden: Brill.

Rad, Gerhard v. 1984. "Job XXXVIII and Ancient Egyptian Wisdom." In *The Problem of the Hexateuch and Other Essays: Translated by Trueman Dicken*, 281–291. London: SCM.

Rahlfs, Alfred, and Detlef Fraenkel. 2004. *Verzeichnis der griechischen Handschriften des Alten Testaments*. Septuaginta. Göttingen: Vandenhoeck & Ruprecht.

Rahlfs, Alfred, and Robert Hanhart, eds. 2006. *Septuaginta: Id est Vetus Testamentum graece iuxta LXX interpretes*. Ed. altera. Stuttgart: Deutsche Bibelgesellschaft.

Rahlfs, Alfred, ed. 1935. *Septuaginta: Id Est Vetus Testamentum Graece Iuxta LXX Interpretes*. Stuttgart: Württembergische Bibelanstalt.

Rahlfs, Alfred, ed. 1979. *Psalmi cum Odis*. 3., unveränderte. Aufl. Septuaginta 10. Göttingen: Vandenhoeck & Ruprecht.

Reif, Stefan C. 2000. *A Jewish Archive from Old Cairo: The History of Cambridge University's Genizah Collection.* Richmond: Curzon.

Reif, Stefan C. 2009. "Worship, Early Jewish." In *The New Interpreter's Dictionary of the Bible, Vol. 5,* edited by Katharine D. Sakenfeld, 903–910. Nashville, TN: Abingdon.

Reindl, Joseph. 1981a. "Gotteslob als "Weisheitslehre": Zur Auslegung von Psalm 146." In *Dein Wort beachten: Alttestamentliche Aufsätze,* edited by Joseph Reindl, 116–135. Leipzig: St. Benno.

Reindl, Joseph. 1981b. "Weisheitliche Bearbeitung von Psalmen." In *Congress volume: Vienna 1980,* edited by J. A. Emerton, 333–354. Vetus Testamentum Supplements 32. Leiden: Brill.

Reymond, Eric D. 2011. "גְּבַר." In *Theologisches Wörterbuch zu den Qumrantexten, Band I,* edited by Heinz-Josef Fabry and Ulrich Dahmen, 565–573. Stuttgart: Kohlhammer.

Riede, Peter. 2010. ""Doch du erhöhest wie einem Wildstier mein Horn": Zur Metaphorik in Psalm 92,11." In *Metaphors in the Psalms,* edited by Pierre van Hecke and Antje Labahn, 209–216. Bibliotheca Ephemeridum theologicarum Lovaniensium 231. Leuven: Peeters.

Riemann, Hugo. 1967. *Musik-Lexikon.* 12., völlig neubearb. Aufl. in 3 Bd., hrsg. von Wilibald Gurlitt. Mainz: Schott.

Ringgren, Helmer. 1973. "אֱלֹהִים." In *Theologisches Wörterbuch zum Alten Testament, I,* edited by Gerhard J. Botterweck and Heinz-Josef Fabry, 285–305. Stuttgart: Kohlhammer.

Ringgren, Helmer. 1977. "הלל I und II." In *Theologisches Wörterbuch zum Alten Testament, II,* edited by Gerhard J. Botterweck and Helmer Ringgren, 433–441. Stuttgart: Kohlhammer.

Ringgren, Helmer. 1982. "חָקַק." In *Theologisches Wörterbuch zum Alten Testament, III,* edited by Gerhard J. Botterweck and Helmer Ringgren, 149–157. Stuttgart: Kohlhammer.

Ringgren, Helmer. 1984. "בֹּל." In *Theologisches Wörterbuch zum Alten Testament, IV,* edited by Gerhard J. Botterweck and Heinz-Josef Fabry, 145–153. Stuttgart: Kohlhammer.

Ringgren, Helmer. 1989. "צָבָא." In *Theologisches Wörterbuch zum Alten Testament, VI,* edited by Gerhard J. Botterweck and Heinz-Josef Fabry, 871–876. Stuttgart: Kohlhammer.

Ringgren, Helmer. 1993a. "רוע." In *Theologisches Wörterbuch zum Alten Testament, VII,* edited by Gerhard J. Botterweck and Heinz-Josef Fabry, 434–438. Stuttgart: Kohlhammer.

Ringgren, Helmer. 1993b. "שׁוֹפָר." In *Theologisches Wörterbuch zum Alten Testament, VII,* edited by Gerhard J. Botterweck and Heinz-Josef Fabry, 1195–1196. Stuttgart: Kohlhammer.

Ringgren, Helmer, and Heinz-Josef Fabry. 1982. "חָסִיד." In *Theologisches Wörterbuch zum Alten Testament, III,* edited by Gerhard J. Botterweck and Helmer Ringgren, 83–88. Stuttgart: Kohlhammer.

Risse, Siegfried. 1995. *"Gut ist es, unserem Gott zu singen": Untersuchungen zu Psalm 147.* Münsteraner theologische Abhandlungen 37. Altenberge: Oros.

Risse, Siegfried. 1999a. "Warum ist es gut, unserem Gott zu singen? Zur Auslegungsgeschichte von Ps 147,1." *Pastoralblatt für die Diözesen Aachen, Berlin, Essen, Hildesheim, Köln, Osnabrück* 51 (8): 236–241.

Risse, Siegfried. 1999b. ""Wir sind die jungen Raben!": Zur Auslegungsgeschichte von Ps. 147:9b." *Biblical Interpretation* 7 (4): 368–388.

Roberts, J. J. M. 2009. "Temple, Jerusalem." In *The New Interpreter's Dictionary of the Bible, Vol. 5,* edited by Katharine D. Sakenfeld, 494–509. Nashville, TN: Abingdon.

Rodd, C. S. 2007. "Psalms." In *The Oxford Bible Commentary,* edited by John Barton and John Muddiman, 355–405. Oxford: Oxford University Press.

Römer, Thomas. 2015. *The Invention of God: Translated by Raymond Geuss*. Cambridge, MA: Harvard University Press.

Rösel, Martin. 2001. "Die Psalmüberschriften des Septuaginta-Psalters." In *Der Septuaginta-Psalter: Sprachliche und theologische Aspekte*, edited by Erich Zenger and Anneli Aejmelaeus, 125–148. Herders biblische Studien 32. Freiburg: Herder.

Ruppert, Lothar. 1986. "Aufforderung an die Schöpfung zum Lob Gottes. Zur Literar-, Form-, und Traditionskritik von Ps 148." In *Freude an der Weisung des Herrn: Beiträge zur Theologie der Psalmen Festgabe zum 70. Geburtstag von Heinrich Gross*, edited by Heinrich Gross, Ernst Haag, and Frank-Lothar Hossfeld, 275–296. Stuttgarter Biblische Beiträge 13. Stuttgart: Katholisches Bibelwerk.

Salvesen, Alison. 2003. "Psalm 151." In *Eerdmans commentary on the Bible*, edited by James D. G. Dunn and J. W. Rogerson, 862–864. Grand Rapids, MI: Eerdmans.

Sanders, James A. 1965. *The Psalms Scroll of Qumran Cave 11 (11QPsᵃ)*. Discoveries in the Judaean Desert 4. Oxford: Clarendon.

Sanders, James A. 1967. *The Dead Sea Psalms Scroll*. Ithaca, NY: Cornell University Press.

Sauer, G. 1975. "כל kōl Gesamtheit." In *Theologisches Handwörterbuch zum Alten Testament, I*, edited by Ernst Jenni. 2., durchges. Aufl., 828–830. Gütersloh: Kaiser.

Sautermeister, Jochen. 2000. "Psalm 149,6 und die Diskussion um das sogenannte waw adaequationis." *BN* 101: 64–80.

Sawyer, J. F., and Heinz-Josef Fabry. 1982. "ישע." In *Theologisches Wörterbuch zum Alten Testament, III*, edited by Gerhard J. Botterweck and Helmer Ringgren, 1035–1059. Stuttgart: Kohlhammer.

Scaiola, Donatella. 2010a. "La conclusione (Sal 146–150) e lo scopo del Salterio." *Rivista biblica* 58: 280–297.

Scaiola, Donatella. 2010b. "The End of the Psalter." In *The Composition of the Book of Psalms*, edited by Erich Zenger, 701–710. Bibliotheca Ephemeridum theologicarum Lovaniensium 238. Leuven: Peeters.

Schaper, Joachim. 1995. *Eschatology in the Greek Psalter*. Wissenschaftliche Untersuchungen zum Neuen Testament. 2. Reihe 76. Tübingen: Mohr Siebeck.

Schechter, S. 1896. "A Fragment of the Original Text of Ecclesiasticus." *Expositor* 19, 5th series (4): 1–15.

Schenker, Adrian. 2004. תורה נביאים וכתובים, *Biblia Hebraica quinta [BHQ] editione cum apparatu critico novis curis elaborato, Vol. 18, מגלות, Megilloth*. Stuttgart: Deutsche Bibelgesellschaft.

Schenker, Adrian. 2005. "Le Psautier à la lumière du Ps 151." In *Die Architektur der Wolken: Zyklisierung in der europäischen Lyrik des 19. Jahrhunderts*, edited by R. Fieguth and A. Martini, 21–27. Bern: Lang.

Schlenke, Barbara. 2011. "חֶסֶד." In *Theologisches Wörterbuch zu den Qumrantexten, Band I*, edited by Heinz-Josef Fabry and Ulrich Dahmen, 1025–1033. Stuttgart: Kohlhammer.

Schmid, Konrad. 2011a. "Ausgelegte Schrift als Schrift: Innerbiblische Schriftauslegung und die Frage nach der theologischen Qualität biblischer Texte." In *Schriftgelehrte Traditionsliteratur*, 269–284. Forschungen zum Alten Testament 77. Tübingen: Mohr Siebeck.

Schmid, Konrad. 2011b. "Schriftgelehrte Arbeit an der Schrift: Historische Überlegungen zum Vorgang innerbiblischer Exegese." In *Schriftgelehrte Traditionsliteratur*, 35–60. Forschungen zum Alten Testament 77. Tübingen: Mohr Siebeck.

Schmidt, Werner H. 1975. "אֵל ʾēl Gott." In *Theologisches Handwörterbuch zum Alten Testament, I,* edited by Ernst Jenni. 2., durchges. Aufl., 142–149. Gütersloh: Kaiser.

Schmidt, Werner H. 2011. *Alttestamentlicher Glaube.* 11., neubearb. u. erw. Aufl. Neukirchen-Vluyn: Neukirchener Theologie.

Schmutzer, Andrew J., and Randall X. Gauthier. 2009. "The identity of "horn" in Psalm 148:14a: An exegetical investigation in the MT and LXX versions." *Bulletin for Biblical Research* 19 (2): 161–183.

Schneider, Christiane. 2013a. "נְשָׁמָה." In *Theologisches Wörterbuch zu den Qumrantexten, Band II,* edited by Heinz-Josef Fabry and Ulrich Dahmen, 1050–1052. Stuttgart: Kohlhammer.

Schneider, Christiane. 2013b. "נְשָׁמָה." In *Theologisches Wörterbuch zu den Qumrantexten, Band II,* edited by Heinz-Josef Fabry and Ulrich Dahmen, 1050–1052. Stuttgart: Kohlhammer.

Schreiner, Josef. 1963. *Sion-Jerusalem, Jahwes Königssitz: Theologie der Heiligen Stadt im Alten Testament.* Studien zum Alten und Neuen Testament 7. München: Kösel.

Schuller, Eileen M., and Carol A. Newsom. 2012. *The Hodayot (Thanksgiving Psalms): A study edition of 1QHa.* Early Judaism and Its Literature 36. Atlanta: Society of Biblical Literature.

Schweizer, Harald. 1977. "Form und Inhalt: Ein Versuch, gegenwärtige methodische Differenzen durchsichtiger und damit überwindbar zu machen. Dargestellt anhand von Ps 150." *BN* 3: 35–47.

Sedlmeier, Franz. 1996. *Jerusalem – Jahwes Bau: Untersuchungen zu Komposition und Theologie von Psalm 147.* Forschung zur Bibel 79. Würzburg: Echter.

Seidel, Hans. 1981. "Ps. 150 und die Gottesdienstmusik in Altisrael." *Nederlands Theologisch Tijdschrift* 35: 89–100.

Seidel, Hans. 1989. *Musik in Altisrael: Untersuchungen zur Musikgeschichte und Musikpraxis Altisraels anhand biblischer und außerbiblischer Texte.* Beiträge zur Erforschung des Alten Testaments und des antiken Judentums 12. Frankfurt am Main: Lang.

Seidl, Theodor. 1999. "Exegese, IV. Biblisch, 1. Altes Testament." In *Religion in Geschichte und Gegenwart, 2,* edited by Hans D. Betz, Don S. Browning, Bernd Janowski, and Eberhard Jüngel. 4. Aufl., 1780–1783. Tübingen: Mohr Siebeck.

Seiler, Stefan. 2011a. "Psalm 104[105]." In *Septuaginta Deutsch: Erläuterungen und Kommentare zum griechischen Alten Testament, Band II, Psalmen bis Daniel,* edited by Wolfgang Kraus and Martin Karrer, 1794–1798. Stuttgart: Deutsche Bibelgesellschaft.

Seiler, Stefan. 2011b. "Psalm 113[144; 115]." In *Septuaginta Deutsch: Erläuterungen und Kommentare zum griechischen Alten Testament, Band II, Psalmen bis Daniel,* edited by Wolfgang Kraus and Martin Karrer, 1819–1822. Stuttgart: Deutsche Bibelgesellschaft.

Sendrey, Alfred. 1969. *Music in Ancient Israel.* London: Vision.

Septuaginta-Unternehmen der Akademie der Wissenschaften zu Göttingen. 2012. "Offizielles Verzeichnis der Rahlfs-Sigeln: Stand: Dezember 2012." Accessed February 01, 2016. http://rep.adw-goe.de/bitstream/handle/11858/00-001S-0000-0022-A30C-8/Rahlfs-Si geln_Stand_Dezember_2012.pdf?sequence=1.

Septuaginta-Unternehmen der Akademie der Wissenschaften zu Göttingen. 2013. "Kollation der Handschriften." Accessed February 01, 2016. http://adw-goe.de/forschung/for schungsprojekte-akademienprogramm/septuaginta-unternehmen/aufgabenbereiche/kolla tion.

Seybold, Klaus. 1984. "בְּ." In *Theologisches Wörterbuch zum Alten Testament, IV*, edited by Gerhard J. Botterweck and Heinz-Josef Fabry, 1–7. Stuttgart: Kohlhammer.

Seybold, Klaus. 1986. "נָבֵל." In *Theologisches Wörterbuch zum Alten Testament, V*, edited by Gerhard J. Botterweck and Heinz-Josef Fabry, 185–188. Stuttgart: Kohlhammer.

Seybold, Klaus. 1991. *Die Psalmen: Eine Einführung.* 2., durchges. Aufl. Urban-Taschenbücher 382. Stuttgart: Kohlhammer.

Seybold, Klaus. 1996. *Die Psalmen.* Handbuch zum Alten Testament I/15. Tübingen: Mohr.

Seybold, Klaus. 2001. "Akrostichie im Psalter." *Theologische Zeitschrift* 57 (2): 172–183.

Seybold, Klaus. 2003. *Poetik der Psalmen.* Poetologische Studien zum Alten Testament 1. Stuttgart: Kohlhammer.

Seybold, Klaus. 2007. "Anmerkungen zum Parallelismus membrorum in der hebräischen Poesie." In *Parallelismus membrorum*, edited by Andreas Wagner, 105–114. Fribourg: Academic Press.

Seybold, Klaus. 2010. "Textgenetische Hintergründe des 147. Psalms." In *Studien zu Psalmen und Propheten: Festschrift für Hubert Irsigler*, edited by Carmen Diller, Martin Mulzer, Kristinn Ólason, and Ralf Rothenbusch, 151–163. Herders biblische Studien 64. Freiburg: Herder.

Siegert, Folker. 2001. *Zwischen Hebräischer Bibel und Altem Testament: Eine Einführung in die Septuaginta.* Münsteraner judaistische Studien 9. Münster: Lit.

Simon, Maurice. 1983. *Rosh Hashanah: Translated into English with Notes, Glossary and Indices.* Hebrew-English Edition of the Babylonian Talmud. London: Soncino.

Skehan, Patrick W. 1973. "A Liturgical Complex in 11QPsa." *CBQ* 34: 195–205.

Skehan, Patrick W., Eugene Ulrich, and Peter W. Flint. 2000a. "4QPsᵈ." In *Qumrân Cave 4, XI, Psalms to Chronicles*, edited by Eugene Ulrich, Frank M. Cross, Joseph A. Fitzmyer, and Peter W. Flint, 63–71. Discoveries in the Judaean Desert 16. Oxford: Clarendon.

Skehan, Patrick W., Eugene Ulrich, and Peter W. Flint. 2000b. "4QPsᵉ." In *Qumrân Cave 4, XI, Psalms to Chronicles*, edited by Eugene Ulrich, Frank M. Cross, Joseph A. Fitzmyer, and Peter W. Flint, 73–84. Discoveries in the Judaean Desert 16. Oxford: Clarendon.

Skulj, Edo. 1998. "Musical Instruments in Psalm 150." In *The interpretation of the Bible: The international symposium in Slovenia*, edited by Jože Krašovec, 1117–1130. Journal for the Study of the Old Testament Supplement series 289. Sheffield: Sheffield Academic.

Slomovic, Elieser. 1979. "Toward an Understanding of the Formation of Historical Titles in the Book of Psalms." *ZAW* 91 (3): 350–380.

Smyth, Herbert W., and Gordon M. Messing. 1956. *Greek grammar.* Cambridge, MA: Harvard University Press.

Sollamo, Raija. 2006. "The creation of angels and natural phenomena intertwined in the Book of Jubilees (4QJuba)." In *Biblical traditions in transmission: Essays in honour of Michael A. Knibb*, edited by Charlotte Hempel, 273–290. Supplements to the Journal for the Study of Judaism 111. Leiden: Brill.

Sommer, Benjamin D. 1998. *A Prophet Reads Scripture: Allusion in Isaiah 40–66.* Contraversions. Stanford, CA: Stanford University Press.

Spieckermann, Hermann. 1989. *Heilsgegenwart: Eine Theologie der Psalmen.* Forschungen zur Religion und Literatur des Alten und Neuen Testaments 148. Göttingen: Vandenhoeck & Ruprecht.

Stadel, Christian. 2013. "כּוֹל." In *Theologisches Wörterbuch zu den Qumrantexten, Band II*, edited by Heinz-Josef Fabry and Ulrich Dahmen, 367–372. Stuttgart: Kohlhammer.

Steck, Odil H. 1999. *Exegese des Alten Testaments: Leitfaden der Methodik. Ein Arbeitsbuch für Proseminare Seminare und Vorlesungen.* 14., durchges. und erw. Aufl. Neukirchen-Vluyn: Neukirchener.

Steinberg, Julius. 2006. *Die Ketuvim: Ihr Aufbau und ihre Botschaft.* Bonner biblische Beiträge 152. Hamburg: Philo.

Steins, Georg. 2016. "Die Bücher der Chronik." In *Einleitung in das Alte Testament*, edited by Erich Zenger and Christian Frevel. 9., aktualisierte Aufl., 312–330. Kohlhammer Studienbücher Theologie 1,1. Stuttgart: Kohlhammer.

Stichel, Rainer. 2007. *Beiträge zur frühen Geschichte des Psalters und zur Wirkungsgeschichte der Psalmen.* Abhandlungen der Nordrhein-Westfälischen Akademie der Wissenschaften 116. Paderborn: Schöningh.

Strawn, Brent A., and Joel M. LeMon. 2007. ""Everything That Has Breath": Animal Praise in Psalm 150:6 in the Light of Ancient Near Eastern Iconography." In *Bilder als Quellen: Studies on ancient Near Eastern artefacts and the Bible inspired by the work of Othmar Keel*, edited by Susanne Bickel, 451–485. Orbis biblicus et orientalis Sonderband. Fribourg: Academic Press.

Talmon, Shemaryahu. 1966. "Pisqah Be'emṣaʿ Pasuq and 11QPsᵃ." *Textus* 5: 11–21.

Talmon, Shemaryahu. 1993. "Fragments of a Psalms Scroll from Masada, MPsᵇ (MASADA 1103–1742)." In *Minḥah le-Naḥum: Biblical and other studies presented to Nahum M. Sarna in honour of his 70th birthday*, edited by Marc Z. Brettler, Michael A. Fishbane, and Nahum M. Sarna, 318–327. Journal for the Study of the Old Testament Supplement Series 154. Sheffield: Sheffield Academic.

Talmon, Shemaryahu. 1999. "Hebrew Fragments from Masada." In *Masada VI, Yigael Yadin Excavations 1963–1965, Final Reports: Hebrew Fragments from Masada, The Ben Sira Scroll from Masada*, edited by Shemaryahu Talmon and Yigael Yadin, 1–149. The Masada Reports. Jerusalem: Israel Exploration Society.

Talmon, Shemaryahu, and Yigael Yadin, eds. 1999. *Masada VI, Yigael Yadin Excavations 1963–1965, Final Reports: Hebrew Fragments from Masada, The Ben Sira Scroll from Masada.* The Masada Reports. Jerusalem: Israel Exploration Society.

Tengström, S. 1993. "רוּחַ: I-VI." In *Theologisches Wörterbuch zum Alten Testament, VII*, edited by Gerhard J. Botterweck and Heinz-Josef Fabry, 385–418. Stuttgart: Kohlhammer.

Theocharous, Myrto. 2012. *Lexical dependence and intertextual allusion in the Septuagint of the twelve prophets: Studies in Hosea, Amos and Micah.* The Hebrew Bible and its versions 7. New York, NY: Clark.

Tomes, Roger. 2007. "Sing to the Lord a New Song." In *Psalms and prayers: Papers read at the Joint Meeting of the Society of Old Testament Study and Het Oudtestamentische Werkgezelschap in Nederland en België, Apeldoorn August 2006*, edited by Bob Becking and Eric Peels, 237–252. Oudtestamentische Studiën 55. Leiden: Brill.

Tournay, Raymond J. 1985. "Le Psaume 149 et la "Vengeance" des Pauvres de YHWH." *Revue biblique* 92: 349–358.

Tov, Emanuel. 2012. *Textual Criticism of the Hebrew Bible.* 3rd ed., rev. and expanded. Minneapolis: Fortress.

Tov, Emanuel. 2014. "New Editions of the Hebrew Scriptures: A Response." *Hebrew Bible and Ancient Israel* 3 (4): 375–383.

Tsumura, David T. 1988. "A 'Hyponymous' Word Pair: 'rṣ and thm(t) in Hebrew and Ugaritic." *Biblica* 69: 258–269.

Tucker, W. D. 2014. *Constructing and deconstructing power in Psalms 107–150*. Ancient Israel and Its Literature 19. Atlanta: Society of Biblical Literature.

Ulrich, Eugene. 1996. "Multiple Literary Editions: Reflections toward a Theory of the History of the Biblical Text." In *Current Research and Technological Developments on the Dead Sea Scrolls: Conference on the Texts from the Judean Desert, Jerusalem, 30 April, 1995*, edited by Donald W. Parry and Stephen D. Ricks, 78–105. Studies on the Texts of the Desert of Judah 20. Leiden: Brill.

Ulrich, Eugene. 1999. *The Dead Sea Scrolls and the Origins of the Bible*. Grand Rapids, MI: Eerdmans.

Ulrich, Eugene. 2000. "The Dead Sea Scrolls and Their Implications for an Edition of the Septuagint Psalter." In *Der Septuaginta-Psalter und seine Tochterübersetzungen: Symposium in Göttingen 1997*, edited by Anneli Aejmelaeus and Udo Quast, 323–336. Mitteilungen des Septuaginta-Unternehmens (MSU) 24. Göttingen: Vandenhoeck & Ruprecht.

Utzschneider, Helmut. 1989. *Künder oder Schreiber? Eine These zum Problem der "Schriftprophetie" auf Grund von Maleachi 1,6–2,9*. Beiträge zur Erforschung des Alten Testaments und des antiken Judentums 19. Frankfurt am Main: Lang.

van der Meer, Michael N. 2010. "The Question of the Literary Dependence of the Greek Isaiah upon the Greek Psalter Revisited." In *Die Septuaginta: Texte, Theologien, Einflüsse 2. Internationale Fachtagung veranstaltet von Septuaginta Deutsch (LXX.D), Wuppertal 23.-27.7.2008*, edited by Wolfgang Kraus, Martin Karrer, and Martin Meiser, 161–200. Wissenschaftliche Untersuchungen zum Neuen Testament 219. Tübingen: Mohr Siebeck.

van der Ploeg, Johannes P. M. 1974. *Psalmen, Deel 2, Psalm 76 t/m 150: Uit de grondtekst vertaald en uitgelegd*. Boeken van het Oude Testament 7,B,2. Roermond: Romen.

van der Vorm-Croughs, Mirjam. 2014. *The old Greek of Isaiah: An analysis of its pluses and minuses*. Society of Biblical Literature Septuagint and Cognate Studies 61. Atlanta, GA: SBL.

van der Woude, A. S. 1976. "עזז ʿzz stark sein." In *Theologisches Handwörterbuch zum Alten Testament, II*, edited by Ernst Jenni, 252–256. Gütersloh: Kaiser.

van Grol, Harm. 2011. "Three Hasidisms and Their Militant Ideologies: 1 and 2 Maccabees, Psalms 144 and 149." In *Between evidence and ideology: Essays on the history of ancient Israel read at the joint meeting of the Society for Old Testament Study and the Oud Testamentisch Werkgezelschap, Lincoln, July 2009*, edited by Bob Becking and Lester L. Grabbe, 93–115. Oudtestamentische Studiën 59. Leiden: Brill.

van Rooy, H. F. 1999. *Studies on the Syriac Apocryphal Psalms*. Journal of Semitic Studies Supplement 7. Oxford: Oxford University Press.

van Seters, John. 2006. *The Edited Bible: The Curious History of the "Editor" in Biblical Criticism*. Winona Lake, IN: Eisenbrauns.

Vanoni, Gottfried. 1991. "Zur Bedeutung der althebräischen Konjunktion w. Am Beispiel von Psalm 149, 6." In *Text, Methode und Grammatik: Wolfgang Richter zum 65. Geburtstag*, edited by Walter Gross, Hubert Irsigler, Wolfgang Richter, and Theodor Seidl, 561–576. St. Ottilien: EOS.

Vermès, Géza. 2011. *The Complete Dead Sea Scrolls in English*. 50th anniversary ed. London: Penguin.

Vincent, M. A. 1999. "The Shape of the Psalter: an Eschatological Dimension?" In *New heaven and new earth: Prophecy and the millennium. Essays in honour of Anthony*

Gelston, edited by A. Gelston, P. J. Harland, and Hayward, C. T. R., 61–82. Supplements to Vetus Testamentum 77. Leiden: Brill.

Vosberg, Lothar. 1975. *Studien zum Reden vom Schöpfer in den Psalmen.* Beiträge zur evangelischen Theologie 69. München: Kaiser.

Wagner, S. 1989. "עזז." In *Theologisches Wörterbuch zum Alten Testament, VI*, edited by Gerhard J. Botterweck and Heinz-Josef Fabry, 1–14. Stuttgart: Kohlhammer.

Watson, Rebecca S. 2005. *Chaos Uncreated: A Reassessment of the Theme of "Chaos" in the Hebrew Bible.* Beihefte zur Zeitschrift für die alttestamentliche Wissenschaft 341. Berlin: De Gruyter.

Watson, Wilfred G. E. 1984. *Classical Hebrew poetry: A guide to its techniques.* Journal for the Study of the Old Testament Supplement Series 26. Sheffield: JSOT Press.

Watts, James W. 2009. "Torah." In *The New Interpreter's Dictionary of the Bible, Vol. 5*, edited by Katharine D. Sakenfeld, 629–630. Nashville, TN: Abingdon.

Weber, Beat. 2003. *Werkbuch Psalmen II: Die Psalmen 73 bis 150.* Stuttgart: Kohlhammer.

Weber, Beat. 2009. "Ein neues Lied." *BN* 142: 39–46.

Weber, Beat. 2010. *Werkbuch Psalmen III: Theologie und Spiritualität des Psalters und seiner Psalmen.* Stuttgart: Kohlhammer.

Wegner, Max. 1963. *Griechenland.* Musikgeschichte in Bildern 2, Musik des Altertums, Lfg. 4. Leipzig: Deutscher Verlag für Musik.

Wegner, Paul D. 2006. *A Student's Guide to Textual Criticism of the Bible: Its History, Methods, and Results.* Downers Grove, IL: InterVarsity.

Weinfeld, M. 1984. "כָּבוֹד." In *Theologisches Wörterbuch zum Alten Testament, IV*, edited by Gerhard J. Botterweck and Heinz-Josef Fabry, 23–40. Stuttgart: Kohlhammer.

Weiser, Artur. 1966. *Die Psalmen: Übersetzt und erklärt.* 7. Aufl. Das Alte Testament Deutsch. Göttingen: Vandenhoeck & Ruprecht.

West, M. L. 1992. *Ancient Greek music.* Oxford: Clarendon.

Westermann, Claus. 1967. *Der Psalter.* Stuttgart: Calwer.

Westermann, Claus. 1968. *Das Loben Gottes in den Psalmen.* Göttingen: Vandenhoeck & Ruprecht.

Westermann, Claus. 1975. "הלל hll pi. loben." In *Theologisches Handwörterbuch zum Alten Testament, I*, edited by Ernst Jenni. 2., durchges. Aufl., 493–502. Gütersloh: Kaiser.

Westermann, Claus. 1980. *The Psalms: Structure, Content and Message, Translated by Ralph D. Gehrke.* Minneapolis: Augsburg.

Westermann, Claus. 1983. *Lob und Klage in den Psalmen.* 6. Auflage von Das Loben Gottes in den Psalmen. Göttingen: Vandenhoeck & Ruprecht.

Whybray, R. N. 1996. *Reading the Psalms as a book.* Journal for the Study of the Old Testament Supplement Series 222. Sheffield: Sheffield Academic.

Whybray, R. N. 2007. "Genesis." In *The Oxford Bible Commentary*, edited by John Barton and John Muddiman, 38–66. Oxford: Oxford University Press.

Willgren, David. 2016. *The Formation of the 'Book' of Psalms: Reconsidering the Transmission and Canonization of Psalmody in Light of Material Culture and the Poetics of Anthologies.* Forschungen zum Alten Testament, 2. Reihe 88. Tübingen: Mohr Siebeck.

Williams, Tyler F. 2001. "Towards a Date for the Old Greek Psalter." In *The Old Greek Psalter: Studies in Honour of Albert Pietersma*, edited by Robert J. V. Hiebert, Claude E. Cox, and Peter J. Gentry, 248–276. Journal for the Study of the Old Testament Supplement Series 332. Sheffield: Sheffield Academic.

Wilson, Gerald H. 1983. "The Qumran Psalms manuscripts and the consecutive arrangement of Psalms in the Hebrew Psalter." *CBQ* 45 (3): 377–388.

Wilson, Gerald H. 1985. *The Editing of the Hebrew Psalter.* Society of Biblical Literature Dissertation Series 76. Chico: Scholars.

Wilson, Gerald H. 1990. "A First Century C.E. Date for the Closing of the Hebrew Psalter?" In *Haim M.I. Gevaryahu: Memorial volume,* edited by Joshua J. Adler, 136–143. Jerusalem: World Jewish Bible Center.

Wilson, Gerald H. 1993. "Understanding the purposeful arrangement of psalms in the psalter: Pitfalls and promise." In *The Shape and Shaping of the Psalter,* edited by J. C. McCann, 42–51. Journal for the Study of the Old Testament Supplement Series 159. Sheffield: JSOT.

Witte, Markus. 2002. "Das neue Lied: Beobachtungen zum Zeitverständnis von Psalm 33." *ZAW* 114 (4): 522–541.

Witte, Markus. 2010. "III. Schriften (Ketubim), § 13 Der Psalter." In *Grundinformation Altes Testament: Eine Einführung in Literatur, Religion und Geschichte des Alten Testaments,* edited by Jan C. Gertz and Angelika Berlejung. 4. Aufl., 414–432. UTB 2745. Göttingen: Vandenhoeck & Ruprecht.

Witte, Markus. 2012. "The Psalter: Translation by Mark Biddle." In *T&T Clark Handbook of the Old Testament: An Introduction to the Literature, Religion and History of the Old Testament,* edited by Jan C. Gertz, Angelika Berlejung, Konrad Schmid, and Markus Witte, 527–549. London: T&T Clark.

Würthwein, Ernst. 1988. *Der Text des Alten Testaments: Eine Einführung in die Biblia Hebraica.* 5., neubearb. Aufl. Stuttgart: Deutsche Bibelgesellschaft.

Yarchin, William. 2015. "Were the Psalms Collections at Qumran True Psalters?" *Journal of Biblical Literature* 134 (4): 775–789.

Zenger, Erich. 1987. *Mit meinem Gott überspringe ich Mauern: Einführung in das Psalmenbuch.* Freiburg: Herder.

Zenger, Erich. 1993a. "Psalm 1: Wegweisung für die Gemeinde der Gerechten." In *Die Psalmen I, Psalm 1–50,* edited by Frank-Lothar Hossfeld and Erich Zenger, 45–49. Die neue Echter Bibel: Kommentar zum Alten Testament mit der Einheitsübersetzung Lfg. 29. Würzburg: Echter.

Zenger, Erich. 1993b. "Psalm 2." In *Die Psalmen I, Psalm 1–50,* edited by Frank-Lothar Hossfeld and Erich Zenger, 49–54. Die neue Echter Bibel: Kommentar zum Alten Testament mit der Einheitsübersetzung Lfg. 29. Würzburg: Echter.

Zenger, Erich. 1993c. "Psalm 33." In *Die Psalmen I, Psalm 1–50,* edited by Frank-Lothar Hossfeld and Erich Zenger, 205–210. Die neue Echter Bibel: Kommentar zum Alten Testament mit der Einheitsübersetzung Lfg. 29. Würzburg: Echter.

Zenger, Erich. 1997a. ""Daß alles Fleisch den Namen seiner Heiligung segne" (Ps 145,21). Die Komposition Ps 145–150 als Anstoß zu einer christlich-jüdischen Psalmenhermeneutik." *Biblische Zeitschrift* 41 (1): 1–27.

Zenger, Erich. 1997b. "Der jüdische Psalter – ein anti-imperiales Buch?" In *Religion und Gesellschaft: Studien zu ihrer Wechselbeziehung in den Kulturen des Antiken Vorderen Orients,* edited by Rainer Albertz, 95–108. Alter Orient und Altes Testament 248. Münster: Ugarit.

Zenger, Erich. 1997c. "Die Provokation des 149. Psalms. Von der Unverzichtbarkeit der kanonischen Psalmenauslegung." In *"Ihr Völker alle, klatscht in die Hände!": Festschrift für Erhard S. Gerstenberger zum 65. Geburtstag*, edited by Rainer Kessler, 181–194. Exegese in unserer Zeit 3. Münster: Lit.

Zenger, Erich. 1998a. "Der Psalter als Buch." In *Der Psalter in Judentum und Christentum*, edited by Erich Zenger, 1–59. Herders biblische Studien 18. Freiburg: Herder.

Zenger, Erich. 1998b. "The Composition and Theology of the Fifth Book of Psalms, Psalms 107–145." *JSOT* 23 (80): 77–102.

Zenger, Erich. 1999. "Der Psalter als Heiligtum." In *Gemeinde ohne Tempel. Community without Temple: Zur Substituierung und Transformation des Jerusalemer Tempels und seines Kults im Alten Testament, antiken Judentum und frühen Christentum*, edited by Beate Ego, Armin Lange, and Peter Pilhofer, 115–130. Wissenschaftliche Untersuchungen zum Neuen Testament 118. Tübingen: Mohr Siebeck.

Zenger, Erich. 2003. ""Durch den Mund eines Weisen werde das Loblied gesprochen" (Sir 15,10): Weisheitstheologie im Finale des Psalters Ps 146–150." In *Auf den Spuren der schriftgelehrten Weisen: Festschrift für Johannes Marböck anlässlich seiner Emeritierung*, edited by Irmtraud Fischer, 139–155. Beihefte zur Zeitschrift für die alttestamentliche Wissenschaft 331. Berlin: De Gruyter.

Zenger, Erich. 2008a. ""Aller Atem lobe JHWH!"." In *Was ist der Mensch, dass du seiner gedenkst? (Psalm 8,5): Aspekte einer theologischen Anthropologie. Festschrift für Bernd Janowski zum 65. Geburtstag*, edited by Michaela Bauks, 565–579. Neukirchen-Vluyn: Neukirchener.

Zenger, Erich. 2008b. "Das Buch der Psalmen." In *Einleitung in das Alte Testament*, edited by Erich Zenger. 7., durchges. und erw. Aufl., 348–370. Kohlhammer Studienbücher Theologie 1,1. Stuttgart: Kohlhammer.

Zenger, Erich. 2008c. "Exkurs: Die Komposition des sog. Kleinen Hallel bzw. Schluss-Hallel Ps 146–150." In *Psalmen 101–150*, edited by Frank-Lothar Hossfeld and Erich Zenger, 807–810. Herders theologischer Kommentar zum Alten Testament. Freiburg: Herder.

Zenger, Erich. 2008d. "Exkurs: Zur psalterredaktionellen Funktion der Halleluja-Rufe." In *Psalmen 101–150*, edited by Frank-Lothar Hossfeld and Erich Zenger, 64–67. Herders theologischer Kommentar zum Alten Testament. Freiburg: Herder.

Zenger, Erich. 2008e. "Psalm 119." In *Psalmen 101–150*, edited by Frank-Lothar Hossfeld and Erich Zenger, 337–391. Herders theologischer Kommentar zum Alten Testament. Freiburg: Herder.

Zenger, Erich. 2008f. "Psalm 135." In *Psalmen 101–150*, edited by Frank-Lothar Hossfeld and Erich Zenger, 659–672. Herders theologischer Kommentar zum Alten Testament. Freiburg: Herder.

Zenger, Erich. 2008g. "Psalm 146." In *Psalmen 101–150*, edited by Frank-Lothar Hossfeld and Erich Zenger, 811–823. Herders theologischer Kommentar zum Alten Testament. Freiburg: Herder.

Zenger, Erich. 2008h. "Psalm 147." In *Psalmen 101–150*, edited by Frank-Lothar Hossfeld and Erich Zenger, 824–837. Herders theologischer Kommentar zum Alten Testament. Freiburg: Herder.

Zenger, Erich. 2008i. "Psalm 148." In *Psalmen 101–150*, edited by Frank-Lothar Hossfeld and Erich Zenger, 838–853. Herders theologischer Kommentar zum Alten Testament. Freiburg: Herder.

Zenger, Erich. 2008j. "Psalm 149." In *Psalmen 101–150*, edited by Frank-Lothar Hossfeld and Erich Zenger, 854–871. Herders theologischer Kommentar zum Alten Testament. Freiburg: Herder.

Zenger, Erich. 2008k. "Psalm 150." In *Psalmen 101–150*, edited by Frank-Lothar Hossfeld and Erich Zenger, 871–885. Herders theologischer Kommentar zum Alten Testament. Freiburg: Herder.

Zenger, Erich. 2010a. "Einführung." In *The Composition of the Book of Psalms*, edited by Erich Zenger, 1–14. Bibliotheca Ephemeridum theologicarum Lovaniensium 238. Leuven: Peeters.

Zenger, Erich. 2010b. "Psalmenexegese und Psalterexegese: Eine Forschungsskizze." In *The Composition of the Book of Psalms*, edited by Erich Zenger, 17–65. Bibliotheca Ephemeridum theologicarum Lovaniensium 238. Leuven: Peeters.

Zenger, Erich. 2011 [1996]. *Psalmen: Auslegungen in zwei Bänden, Band I*. Aktualisierte Neuausgabe [Erstausgaben 1996]. Freiburg: Herder.

Zenger, Erich, and Frank-Lothar Hossfeld. 2016. "Das Buch der Psalmen." In *Einleitung in das Alte Testament*, edited by Erich Zenger and Christian Frevel. 9., aktualisierte Aufl., 431–453. Kohlhammer Studienbücher Theologie 1,1. Stuttgart: Kohlhammer.

Zięba, Zbigniew. 2009. "The poetic devices in Psalm 148." *The Polish journal of biblical research* 8 (1): 5–15.

Ziegert, Carsten, and Siegfried Kreuzer. 2012. "Septuaginta." In *Das wissenschaftliche Bibellexikon im Internet (Wibilex)*. Accessed February 01, 2016. http://www.bibelwissen schaft.de/stichwort/28417.

Ziegler, Joseph, ed. 1939. *Isaias*. Septuaginta 14. Göttingen: Vandenhoeck & Ruprecht.

Zimmerli, Walter. 1972. "Zwillingspsalmen." In *Wort, Lied und Gottesspruch, [Band 1]*, *Beiträge zur Septuaginta, Festschrift für Joseph Ziegler*, edited by Josef Schreiner, 105–113. Forschung zur Bibel 1. Würzburg: Echter.

Zobel, H.-J. 1982. "יִשְׂרָאֵל." In *Theologisches Wörterbuch zum Alten Testament, III*, edited by Gerhard J. Botterweck and Helmer Ringgren, 986–1012. Stuttgart: Kohlhammer.

Zobel, H.-J. 1995. "תָּקַע." In *Theologisches Wörterbuch zum Alten Testament, VIII*, edited by Gerhard J. Botterweck and Heinz-Josef Fabry, 753–757. Stuttgart: Kohlhammer.

Subject Index

Index of Sources

Hebrew Bible (Masoretic Text, MT)

Deuterocanonical Books